THE GREEK THEATER

THE GREEK THEATER

Leo Aylen

RUTHERFORD • MADISON • TEANECK
FAIRLEIGH DICKINSON UNIVERSITY PRESS
LONDON AND TORONTO: ASSOCIATED UNIVERSITY PRESSES

Associated University Presses
440 Forsgate Drive
Cranbury, NJ 08512

Associated University Presses Ltd
25 Sicilian Avenue
London WC1A 2QH, England

Associated University Presses
2133 Royal Windsor Drive
Unit 1
Mississauga, Ontario
Canada L5J 1K5

Library of Congress Cataloging in Publication Data

Aylen, Leo, 1935–
  The Greek theater.

  Bibliography: p.
  Includes index.
  1. Theater—Greece. 2. Greek drama—History and
criticism. I. Title
PA3201.A95 1985   882'.01'09   82-49313
ISBN 0-8386-3184-3

Printed in the United States of America

CONTENTS

PREFACE

The viewpoint of this book is that of a theater director contemplating the production of a Greek play. It is written for drama students, for performers, and for anyone interested in the theater. Because there are not too many performance professionals who have been trained in the Classics, and so a viewpoint such as this on the Greek plays is relatively rare, I hope that the book may be of interest to classicists also.

I have translated all quotations from critical works unless a translation has already been made. I have translated all quotations from the plays. I have rendered the spoken dialogue verse either into English blank verse, or, more often, into a four-stressed line. I have translated the sung lyrics isometrically, keeping the complicated metrical schemes of the originals. They would, in other words, be able to be set to the same musical note values as those of the fifth-century dramatists.

Two special problems arise in conjunction with translating Aristophanes: the names of his characters, and his bawdry. Many of Aristophanes' names contain a character description. The translator must produce a name that will sound plausible as a modern English or American name, while containing the same elements of character description as the original Greek. Final decision on such complicated connotation is bound up with decision on the tone of a particular production. The name of the leading character in *The Birds* is perhaps the most complex. *Pisthetairos* is made from *hetairos*, "comrade" and *pisth-*, which has to do with trust, trustworthiness. When commissioned to translate *The Birds* for the BBC. I translated *Pisthetairos* as Trustworth, and his fellow comic as Hopegood, two plausible British names. Having reexamined Ben Jonson's names in the course of writing this book, I thought of a twentieth-century version of Jonson, and translated *Pisthetairos* as Mr. Utrustmeebuddy. Theater professionals with whom I have discussed the problem delight in Mr. Utrustmeebuddy which conveys both the fake trustworthiness and the flamboyance of the character. Scholars find such a translation too highly colored, away from actual theatrical production. In this book, therefore, I have made an exception to my general rule of translating as for theatrical production, and used deliberately colorless versions of Aristophanes' character names. I discuss the range of possibilities briefly in Appendix 2.

Aristophanes' humor is based on sex and scatology. There appears to be no limit to what he showed on stage or what he made his characters say. Correct translation of Aristophanes into modern English must involve the use of "four-letter words." To those who have grown up with the bawdry, nudity, eroticism, and "four-letter words" of the modern American and British theater, there is nothing very shocking about such translation of Aristophanes, and, indeed, to such people, now probably a majority among theatergoers, the substitution of latinate euphemism for Anglo-Saxon directness would seem actually tasteless. After careful discussion, it has been decided to follow the example of the outstanding Aristophanes scholar, Sir Kenneth Dover, and make use of the "four-letter words" as he does. See Sir Kenneth Dover, *Aristophanic Comedy* (London: Batsford, 1972). To those who dislike such explicitness I can only plead that, given the sexual explicitness and abundant use of "four-letter words" in modern American movies, any other course would be a mistranslation of Aristophanes into modern English. I return to this in Appendix 2.

Except where noted, all references to the plays are to the line numbers of the Oxford Classical Text. Other editions differ slightly in their line numberings. See Scriptorum classicorum biblioteca Oxoniensis (Oxford: Clarendon Press) under the name of the relevant playwright.

The Budé bilingual edition has a few notes and facing prose translation into French. It has a steadily high standard of scholarship, and offers the only modern translation of Seneca's plays. See Collection des Universités de France, publiée sous le patronage de l'Association Guillaume Budé (Paris: Société d'Édition "Les Belles Lettres") under the name of the relevant playwright.

As far as I know there is only one book that provides English translations of all the tragedies (except for *The Searching Satyrs)* into verse and prints the line numbers of the original Greek: David Grene and Richmond Lattimore, eds., *The Complete Greek Tragedies,* 9 vols. (Chicago: University of Chicago Press, 1953–59). Only in this version, and the Loeb editions discussed in the next paragraph, will it be possible for the Greek-less reader to follow the line references more or less accurately.

The bilingual Loeb Classical Library, with facing English translation, varies enormously in the standard of its different volumes. On the one hand, there is the impeccable scholarship of *Select Papyri III,* which includes *The Searching Satyrs,* edited with prose translation by D. L. Page, or the recent fragments of Aeschylus, attached as an appendix to the revised second volume of Aeschylus and edited and translated by H. Lloyd-Jones with equal meticulousness. (*Select Papyri III* was published in 1962, the revised *Aeschylus* in 1963). On the other hand there are the limp and inaccurate verse translations of both Sophocles and Euripides. The Loeb Classical Library, however, does provide a more or less complete set of texts in English of some sort; even Herodas is available, and it supplies an outstanding version of a Greek playwright into English. The Loeb volumes will be found in catalogs under the classical author required. They have all been simultaneously published in London and the United States. The London publisher is William Heinemann; the American publisher changed from G. P. Putnam's Sons to the Harvard University Press. Catalogs will include the words "Loeb Classical Library."

The two outstanding complete renderings of authors are both Victorian and therefore dated. But they are still necessary works to consult. They are as far opposed to each other as could be. On the one hand there is Jebb's *Sophocles*, a scholarly edition with copious notes and pedantically accurate translation, enormously helpful for elucidating meanings, hardly the book to read in the theater. On the other hand there is Rogers's *Aristophanes*, a rendering into Gilbertian verse. With only a few of Rogers' notes—and it is the translation, not the notes which is important—this is printed in the Loeb edition. Of all the translators Rogers is still the only man to have created an English version with real style. We cannot use it now, because he bowdlerizes. In addition his verse is dated. But it is full of pace and liveliness. See *Sophocles, the Plays and Fragments*, ed. and trans., R. C. Jebb (Cambridge: Cambridge University Press, 1883–1907), and *Aristophanes*, trans. Benjamin Bickley Rogers, Loeb Classical Library (London: William Heineman; New York: G. P. Putnam's Sons, 1924).

There are some excellent versions of Aristophanes into English made since the Second World War, mostly published as separate volumes containing one play, sometimes in a volume containing three plays together. No translator, to my knowledge, during this period, has translated all of Aristophanes. The Greek-less reader should perhaps make a point of comparing different versions.

There are Penguin translations of Menander, Terence, and some Plautus. *Menander, Plays and Fragments*, trans Philip Vellacott (Harmondsworth: Penguin Books, 1973); *Plautus, "The Rope" and Other Plays*, (1964) and *"The Pot of Gold" and Other Plays* (1965), both volumes trans. E. F. Watling; and *Terence, "The Brothers" and Other Plays*, trans. Betty Radice (1976), all these being published at Harmondsworth by Penguin Books.

In my references to fragments, I have considered convenience rather than consistency. The complete editions of fragments, under types of poetry—tragedy, comedy, lyric—were made during the nineteenth century, and have not been revised in toto. Since then, many new fragments have been discovered, especially in papyrus. Most numberings of the fragments base themselves on the nineteenth-century collections, and therefore will not be very different from collection to collection. For Aeschylus, I have referred to the numberings in the Loeb Aeschylus. See Aeschylus, with an English Translation by Herbert Weir Smyth, The Appendix containing the more considerable fragments published since 1930 and a new text of Fr. 50, ed. Hugh Lloyd-Jones, Loeb Classical Library (London: William Heinemann Ltd; Cambridge: Harvard University Press, 1963), and see p. 374 especially for Lloyd-Jones's authority for his numbering of the new fragments. For Sophocles, I refer to Jebb–Headlam–Pearson. See *The Fragments of Sophocles*, ed. with additional notes from the papers of Sir R. C. Jebb and Dr. W. G. Headlam by A. C. Pearson (Cambridge: Cambridge University Press, 1917). For Euripides, I refer to Nauck: *Tragicorum Graecorum Fragmenta*, ed. Augustus Nauck, with supplement containing new fragments ed. Bruno Snell (Hildesheim: Georg Olms

Verlagsbuchhandlung, 1964). For the comic poets I refer to Kock: *Comicorum Atticorum Fragmenta*, ed. Theodor Kock (Leipzig: Teubner, 1880). For non-theatrical lyric poetry, I refer to Bergk: *Poetae Lyricae Graeci*, ed. Theodor Bergk (Leipzig: Teubner, 1866). For the Pre-Socratics such as Heracleitus, I refer to Diels and Kranz: *Die Fragmente der Vorsocratiker*, ed. Hermann Diels, 11th ed. rev. Walther Kranz (Zürich and Berlin: Weidmannsche Verlagsbuch-handlung, 1964). I have not cluttered the text with further reference to these sometimes very weighty tomes, merely giving references to a simple fragment number.

There are ancient lives of the fifth-century poets, probably written by the scholars of Alexandria. I have not come across translations of them into English. I refer to them simply as *Life of Sophocles* and so forth. There is also useful biographical material in the ancient synopses of some of the plays.

In my spelling of classical names and terms I have tried to follow current practice, in which there is neither logic nor consistency. The more familiar a name or term, the more likely the Greek is to be latinized. Anomalies abound. Most usually, for example, one sees the word *strophē*, ending in a long eta, spelt with one *e* in English; the word *trochee*, ending in the same long eta, seems to be more often spelt with double *e*. I have put the macron over the letter to indicate eta or omega only when its absence would affect the word's pronunciation. I have included appendices with definitions of all the technical Greek terms used.

The central thesis of this book—on the choreographic code of the Greek plays—relies on my work with the plays rather than on the work of previous scholars. But I am immensely grateful for having been able to discuss this thesis, as it was being formed, with that great scholar, Professor T. B. L. Webster. I feel much more confident in publishing, having had the stamp of his approval and the guidance of his learning, although, alas, he died without being able to see the finished book.

I am also grateful to John G. Griffith. Apart from various words of encouragement at different times about my work in the Classics, ever since he was my examiner in Honour Moderations at Oxford, he was my host at the Oxford Classical Society when I read a paper sketching the thesis from which this book has developed. His support and encouragement then greatly helped me to develop my ideas fully.

I am indebted to a book that does not appear in the bibliography and has not been published in the form in which I read it. I was asked by a publisher to write a reader's report on a manuscript submitted by Alex Gross. I felt obliged both to praise and to condemn strongly. The publishers decided to pay more attention to my condemnations than to my praise and did not publish his manuscript. Where Gross's work was excellent was in drawing attention to the riot and revel of Greek drama, and to those aspects of Aeschylus and Sophocles that more prudish ages than our own have tucked away from view.

Dr. Peter Arnott read an early draft of this manuscript. I am grateful for conversations with him. One of these was televised by CBS TV, and I hope that the liveliness of the conversation, on record for all to see, is the most vivid way in which I can acknowledge my thanks for contact with his lively mind.

I thank Dr. Robert White, Hunter College of the City University of New York, and also Dr. Michael Anderson, University of Bristol, England, for reading the manuscript and for making many valuable suggestions, which I have tried to incorporate. I am also grateful to a publisher's reader who wrote about the manuscript with bitterness and spite, but who also made some useful suggestions, which I have tried to incorporate. He prefers to remain anonymous.

I acknowledge my debt to the casts, choreographers, dancers, and musicians in a number of productions of the Greek plays that I have had the good fortune to direct, not least to my singer, composer, dancer, and choreographer wife, Annette Battam, who has had from time to time to translate my gropings into theatrical reality within the exigencies of the commercial theater.

In another way I am grateful to Dr. Jonathan Miller, for many stimulating discussions and arguments while we made our two television films of Plato dialogues—*The Drinking Party* and *The Death of Socrates*. The relative ease with which Plato turns into television drama helps to clarify the difference between the drama of fifth-century Athens and almost all other western dramatic writing, including the later Greek.

All of these people will, I am sure, understand if I give top billing in my thanks to the man who has probably done most to spread awareness of Greek theater throughout America and Britain in this generation. I had the great privilege of working under him while he was professor of Greek at Bristol University. I had the laughter-spilling task of directing him as Socrates for a student production of *The Clouds* in Greek. H. D. F. Kitto, master of socratic irony, you have graced the theater with humor as well as wisdom, and every one of us who is at all interested in ancient Greece will have read something by you. I cannot possibly say how much my own awareness of the Greek poets has been enriched by your guidance. I had hoped to end this preface with a personal dedication to you. But since you have died before my manuscript reached the printers, I must dedicate instead—

in memoriam H. D. F. K.

κατεύχομαι ἐν καθαρῷ βῆναι...

The translations from the *Oedipus at Colonus* on p. 339 and the *Electra* on p. 191 are reproduced by permission of Sidgwick & Jackson from a collection of my poems and translations: Leo Aylen, *I, Odysseus* (London: Sidgwick & Jackson, 1971). Other passages, translated on pp. 188 and 290, are reproduced by permission of Methuen & Co: Leo Aylen, *Greek Tragedy and the Modern World* (London: Methuen, 1964).

THE GREEK THEATER

1

THE EMPTY SPACE

The ancient theater is not an empty space. It is a space full of spirits that dare us to approach and touch them. The center of the theater of Dionysus at Athens was an altar on which incense smouldered to the lord of the theater, who was also lord of life.

The origins of the theater are forms of worship—active, vigorous celebrations of living gods.

During the last three and a half centuries the theater of Western Europe has been growing away from its origins. Now the theater is mostly dead. Now the space is indeed empty.

"We do not know how to celebrate, because we do not know what to celebrate." So writes Peter Brook, one of the greatest living theater directors, in a book from whose title this section starts.[1] It is a book that frankly acknowledges the theater has lost its way. Our sense of an empty space is all the stronger because it is being described by a man who has tried harder than most to fill it with life.

Every theatrical tradition that we know has started as an aspect of worship. The near contemporary playwright with the most influence today is Berthold Brecht. His reinvigoration of our theater is directly connected with his adherence to what he would call the only true religion of the twentieth century— Marxism. One of the proper tests for Marxism as a religion will be its ability to create a theatrical tradition—a test whose result will be seen in the next generation.

The empty space.

Our theater is dead, our space is empty, because our culture is lost and sick. The only way our theater will live again is if our culture can find a way to worship its gods. That cure for sickness, and that search, present too vast an undertaking for the theater on its own. But, as we look at the past, we can see that ages of great spiritual energy have also been ages of great theater. Even if a reborn theater cannot cause, on its own, a reborn society, yet part of what we mean by a reborn society may very well be a reborn theater.

Our space is empty. We grope around in the emptiness. But at least we know that we are only groping. While we wait for our society, at the moment a slave

15

to its technology, to free itself through more advanced technology, or alternatively, while we work in other places than in the theater toward a new freedom and a new society, it may well be worth spending a little time on considering how great theater and a free society have in the past combined to enrich each other in a process of mutual growth.

In our quest for a living theater, do we need to go further back than Shakespeare? Ask English speakers who is the greatest poet, the greatest man of the theater, and they will say, "Shakespeare." Ask any African, and he will probably agree. Is there anyone in the world with any awareness of the theater who would deny Shakespeare's supreme status? I doubt it. It is not the purpose of this book to praise the Greeks at the expense of Shakespeare. Far from it. But we are now reaching the happy state when the modern theater can be said to understand Shakespeare, when it is possible to see productions that really do present Shakespeare's intentions. Would we have said the same of the productions of forty years ago, let alone a hundred? How recently, for example, has it become the custom to present Shakespeare's plays without cuts?

Our deepened relationship with Shakespeare depends on a complex variety of situations appropriate to our society as they were not to a previous generation. To name them all would be a book in itself. I name a few, summarily, and at random. It would be wrong, first of all, to ignore the fact that Shakespeare's politics—of princes and princely factions—are once again part of twentieth-century politics in Africa and the Middle East. Zulus educated in English literature enrich their understanding of their great leader Shaka by comparing his wars with the wars described in *Macbeth* and enrich their—and our—understanding of Shakespeare with their knowledge of and attachment to Shaka. Ugandans have seen the story of *Macbeth* come out of the theater and maul their own lives. Second, and in complete contrast, we are now in a position to see Shakespeare in his proper place in the history of the British theater—as the end of the rich medieval tradition whose greatest expression was the mystery cycles. It was not so long ago that E. Martin Browne was responsible for the first production of a mystery cycle in four hundred years. Thirdly, and again in contrast, we can see that in Britain, and to a lesser extent in the United States, there is now a strong tradition of collaboration between scholars and men of the theater, above all exemplified in the work of the Royal Shakespeare Company. How recently used it to be said that academic study was hostile to theatricality. And so on. Our relationship with Shakespeare grows steadily richer, in a multiplicity of ways.

We have not reached this closeness with the Greek dramatists. Although every modern society, consciously or unconsciously, refers its customs to those of ancient Athens, although practically every political, social, or psychological concept we use derives from concepts created by Greek thinkers in ancient Athens, and although every generation of Western poets, thinkers, and artists for several hundred years has acknowledged its debt to the Greeks, the unique achievement of the Greek theater has never been a central point of reference in our culture. The sculptors of the Renaissance drew on the art of Greece; the architects of the seventeenth and eighteenth centuries drew on the buildings of Greece; the scientists and philosophers from the Middle Ages to the present day have drawn on the thought of Greece. Perhaps it is for our own time to achieve its renaissance through the theater of Greece.

I should like to think of this book as the start of a new tradition of collaboration between scholarship and the theater with respect to the Greek plays comparable to that which already exists with respect to Shakespeare. A working theater director today will, if about to put on a Shakespeare play, consult the books about Shakespeare. A working theater director about to put on a Greek play will be likely to say, "Of course we cannot recapture the conditions in which Sophocles staged his *Antigone*," and then he will try and present the play independently of the scholarly knowledge about it. Modern productions of Greek plays bear less resemblance to their original than the *Romeo and Juliet* of Vincent Crummles and his ilk.[2] Nowadays we laugh at Victorian versions of Shakespeare, but Mr. Crummles thought he was making Shakespeare more theatrical. We can now see that a real attempt to present Shakespeare's true intention is far, far more theatrical than any travesty. My hope is that this book will help—just a little—some working theater director to see that an equivalent attempt truly to present Sophocles' intention will be far, far more theatrical than the current travesties. I doubt if Mr. Crummles's *Romeo* was boring. But how many productions of Greek plays have we attended out of duty, knowing in our heart of hearts that we were bored. And to make Sophocles boring is a travesty even worse than to do what Nahum Tate did and give *King Lear* a happy ending.

The empty space. Let us give that phrase another connotation. The empty space of a rehearsal room. A director and his cast. The text of a fifth-century Greek play. How can we, in our different society, with our very different preconceptions, present to a modern audience the intention of Aeschylus?

Impossible? Perhaps. But surely worth a try. In one way we know so little. But in another we know so much. The work of scholars and archaeologists has reconstructed the Greek theater. There is more agreement on the stage of Sophocles than there is on the stage of Shakespeare. There are many pictures. No other theatrical tradition has left anything like the number of pictures that we possess of Greek theatrical performances until the photography of the present day. We know more or less exactly how the roles were allocated to the actors. We can pick up a text and see exactly what parts of the play were spoken, what parts were chanted, and what parts were the danced songs. We can read the text of the songs and see the exact rhythmic notation in quarter notes and eighth notes of every song. With all this knowledge, is it right to say, "Of course we cannot recapture the conditions of the Greek theater." Perhaps we have not tried hard enough. Mr. Crummles would have said, "Of course we cannot recapture the conditions of Shakespeare's theater."

The empty space. A director and cast in a rehearsal room. A director and cast trying to enter as fully as possible into the theatrical intentions of four masters of the theater. This image reveals the book's premise. A scholar in his study or lecture room may say, "We do not know whether Aeschylus used a crane in this scene." A theater director, putting on the play in which this scene occurs, will read the same evidence that the scholar has read, but he will then have to make up his mind. Basing the decision on what is known about the other uses of the crane and on his understanding of the rest of the play—and the rest of Aeschylus' work—he will have to make up his mind, and say, "Yes, we use the crane," or "No, we do not use the crane." For the theater director to remain undecided, or to fudge his indecision, is worse than to decide wrongly. We who work in the theater must remember the first group of souls in Dante's hell—the ones who couldn't make up their minds (3.22–51). True, they are near the gate. But how contemptuously Virgil dismisses them: "Let us not talk of them, but look, and pass" (51).

Director and cast in a rehearsal room. The premise of this book is that its conclusions must be tested in performance. Let us take an example from comedy. Aristophanes constructed his plays very cleverly to get laughs. We must try and work out how he would have got his laughs. There is a famous passage in the *parabasis*[3] of *The Clouds* where the chorus leader describes to the audience Aristophanes' comedy. "We're nice and clean," he says. "No one wears a phallus, thick and red; no one dances the vulgar *kordax;* no one shouts, 'Ow! Ow!" Nor does this poet exhibit his plays twice" (537–46). Later in the play there will be many shouts of "Ow! Ow!" (1321 ff.). And this *parabasis* was indeed written for the second production of the *Clouds*. In spite of the fact that the action of the play obviously contradicts the words of the chorus leader in two instances, scholars have used this passage as the basis for many arguments as to the relative cleanness of Aristophanes' comedy, and have even used it to dispute his employment of the phallus, which we can see on contemporary pictures. Surely, there is only one way to produce this speech for laughs: make each of the things happen that the speaker says do not happen. I do not believe that any comedian since the world began has ever claimed to be cleaner than his rivals and meant it. Saying one thing while doing the opposite is a standard, successful way of getting laughs.

Each to his own empty space. I write this book from the viewpoint of the rehearsal room, because that is my viewpoint. My professional life is spent, and has been spent, not as a scholar in a university, but in writing and directing films for television, or in the theater, or in performing my poetry in theaters round the world. From time to time I have been involved in making television entertainment out of Homer, or Plato, or even, on a small scale, Sophocles. Apart from these brief ventures, the four Athenian dramatists have been a constant inspiration and help in work that apparently has nothing whatsoever to do with ancient Greece. This book is my attempt to explain their mastery—for myself, and for those who choose to come with me. It is written with as much scholarship as I can muster, and with deep awareness of the many scholars who have cleared our empty space of artificial ghosts and prepared the diagrams from which we can work. But it is also written in the belief that the Greek theater contains a mystery: one we can enter—to what degree we do not yet know—but one we can enter only by performing, by attempting to re-create, from what they have left us, the four poets' theatrical totality.

Three general points about the Greek theater need to be made at the start. The first one is historical. It is no exaggeration to say that the study of the theater of antiquity is the study of what went on in the theater of Dionysus at Athens. If we pick up books called histories of the Greek and Roman theater, or histories of the ancient theater, we shall read a story of theatrical perform-ances from 700 B.C. or even earlier to A.D. 800. But everything we need to learn about the theater of antiquity can be learnt by studying the four Athenian poets of the fifth century. The story of the ancient theater is the story of a strange, colorful, shape-changing, ultimately unknowable creature, tended by these four poets until it had demonstrated postures of rampant beauty, which then died when they died, and was stuffed to look more or less like the living creature. A clockwork engine was put inside it, and it was moved around for hundreds of years by people who never thought that it had ever been more than a clockwork toy. The study of the ancient theater is the study of a hundred years of miraculous life and about twelve hundred years of mechanical simula-tion. An easy example of this is provided by the so-called Roman theater, on the history of which many books have been written. Strictly speaking, there is no Roman theater whatsoever. There are plays in Latin, but they are no more Roman plays than an American adaptation of Cocteau or Anouilh today could be described as an American play. During the twelve hundred years which the theater of antiquity continued its mechanical, dead existence, nothing was discovered upon which the modern Western theater has not improved. During the fifth century at Athens a mystery was created that we are only just begin-ning to understand.

The second general point is about this mystery itself. The center of the theater of Dionysus was an altar around which men danced. The center of Athenian drama was an interconnection of dance and worship so absolute that the two were indistinguishable. In one of the dances in the *Oedipus the King* (863–910, especially 895–910), the chorus sing, "If the fabric of my religion is no longer valid, what is the point of me dancing?"[4] The center of the mystery that is the Athenian theater lies in the dance.

I spoke earlier about the fruitful collaboration between theater directors and scholars in Shakespeare, and I implied that there could be the same kind of fruitful collaboration with the Greek theater. I was of course wrong. No con-temporary theater director of those who would wish to direct Greek plays is competent to do so. For none are dancers. What is one of the most notable things remembered about Aeschylus' senior contemporary Phrynichus? That he invented "as many dances as there are waves in the sea."[5] What was the first public achievement of Sophocles? To be picked from all his contemporaries at the age of fifteen to perform, naked, the dance in celebration of the lifesaving Athenian victory at Salamis.[6] No one can fully understand the mind of Sophocles, master choreographer, unless he is himself a dancer, just as no one can understand what it is to run in the Olympics from merely watching the 1,500 meters on television. How ludicrous we would find a production of *West Side Story* that presented the sung dances as free verse speech, broken up between different members of the chorus. To present the sung dances of the *Oedipus the King* or *Bacchants* in such a way is even more ludicrous, since the meaning of the sung dances of Sophocles is infinitely more central to the meaning of his plays. Even Plato, unsympathetic though he was to the fifth-century poets, used the word *achoreutos*—which means "without dance training"—to mean "uneducated."[7] The stigma of achoreutian incompetence that I have put on the theater directors must also be put on me. I too, like most Western twentieth-century men, lack dance training. Even the lucky few—those capable of holding down a job in the chorus of a Broadway musical—are still not ready to work at a Sophocles play. For the dance of Sophocles was dance as a part of worship, dance as worship itself. Zulu Christians dance in the Mass as naturally as they sing in the Mass. (So does most of Africa; my only experience is with the Zulus.) But their dance is formless—a generalized expression of rejoicing. Nevertheless, a company of, for example, Zulus, still in touch with pre-Christian worship, still naturally performing the war dances of their great-grandfathers, still with a sense of ceremonial alive enough to adapt to different forms of worship, would, I am sure, teach us a great deal about the *Oresteia*, if they transposed its story into their own history. The Balinese temple dances are an act of worship, and are both thoroughly formalized and thoroughly mimetic. Perhaps our full understanding of Sophocles will come under the guidance of a Balinese who has learned classics. The Balinese ceremonial is, admittedly, so highly structured in all its details that it may be harder to use it as an imaginative jumping-off point than the less specific African energy. At any rate it should be clear that there are several cultures in the world today in which worship and dance are still interconnected. It is from the people of these cultures that we will learn about fifth-century drama as living ritual. But until the Zulu and Balinese scholars arrive to talk with authority about ancient Greece, it is my hope that this book may serve for a little while as notes along the way.

The third general point to bear in mind about the Athenian theater of the fifth century is that it was a totality of experience, in which religion, poetry, and theatricality were inseparable: every play was an act of moral and political commitment; every play was an act of worship, and it was through this that every aspect of theater was held in balance with all the others. Words, music, dance, and spectacle, whether in tragedy or comedy, combine to form a total rhythm that can be analyzed only in terms of itself. Nietzsche and Wagner developed the concept of the *Gesamtkunstwerk* as commentary to Wagner's music drama. All the arts, working together in a totality. The concept is very relevant to the drama of the fifth century. It is not relevant to Wagner, where, whatever theories were advanced, the other arts remained thoroughly subservient to the music. Music is, outstandingly, the art with which to express intensity of emotion. If the emotion is to be defined with precision, or if one emotion is to be related to another, words are necessary. Still more are they necessary if emotion is to be related to intellectual problem solving or political action. The fifth-century poets were inherently better able to create such a *Gesamtkunstwerk* with words dominant, because of the nature of Greek poetry and its radical difference from the poetry of any modern language.

We need to hold fully in our imaginations all the time that Greek poetry and music were one. Except for the iambic trimeter—the meter of the dialogue verse in the plays—all archaic Greek poetry was sung in one way or another.[8] Furthermore, once a Greek poet had written a line of a lyric, he had automatically composed its musical rhythm in exact notation. This will be discussed in more detail later in Chapter 4, "Music." Here it may best be understood in reverse. If we consider the English blank verse line, we realize that in English poetry, as in the poetry of all other modern Western languages, rhythm depends on meaning. We cannot write out a rhythmical notation by writing out a line of verse. The first line of *The Faerie Queene* seems to be about the nearest that a line of English verse comes to dictating its own rhythm:

A Gentle Knight was pricking on the plaine,

But even in this straightforward example there are ambiguities: "pricking" is not really the same length as "on the", for instance. When, however, we consider a line like the first of the last paragraph in *Lycidas*, we are forced to realize fully the ambiguity of English rhythm:

Weep no more, woeful shepherds, weep no more.

Here it is obvious that there are many more possibilities, and that my version is even more obviously one setting, one interpretation, an arbitrary choice on my part.[9] Furthermore, unlike the Spenser line, this one contains no bar lines. To insert them would even more obviously be to interpret, rather than merely transcribe, Milton's rhythm. If the attempt to write the exact rhythm of one line of English verse can present so many ambiguities, it is obvious that the music of English song is always an interpretation of the words, in a way that the music of ancient Greek song was not.

To say that we possess the rhythmic notation in quarter notes and eighth notes of every song in the Greek plays is in no way new. Scholars have always known that. It has not, however, penetrated to the theater. If it had, it would be realized that it was ludicrous to say that we know nothing of Sophocles' music. For surely, a musician who looks at the score of a song, without melody but with exact note values, knows a very great deal about that song. In other words, a musician can, if he wishes, learn a considerable amount about Sophocles' music, simply by reading Sophocles' script. I am going to go further. It has always been known what parts of a Greek play were dances—the sung lyrics. The musical rhythm of these dances has always been known, because it is the rhythm of the songs. Pictures and written descriptions are available to indicate to us the variety and virtuosity of ancient Greek dance. Furthermore, the nature of the system provides us with a code for the choreography. This code we can crack, simply by reading the system.[10] This cracking of the choreographic code has not been done before, so far as I know, and so this thesis—and its ramifications through the rest of the book—is, in scholarly terms, something new. To those scholars who think that such a thesis should first have been proposed in a specialist publication I can only apologize. The nature of the thesis is such that there is only one way to argue it. Let us meet—in an empty space, with all the time in the world. Let us have with us a choreographer—or several choreographers—and a group of dancers. Let us then go through every song, every system, in the entire corpus of Greek drama, with one proviso only—that we must end up with a choreography, that we cannot just leave the song unstaged. We will then find that the choreography of Aeschylus and Sophocles does impose itself on us, that once we actually start to block these dances, certain images will be created, and these images will provide the center of what these miniature examples of *Gesamtkunstwerk* are all about.

Aeschylus and Sophocles as choreographers: this fact about them may be almost as important for our insights into their minds as the fact that they are poets. Certainly it is the case that once we start to read the lyrics of Greek drama, not only as poems but also as scenarios for dance, once we really acknowledge the centrality of the musical parts of fifth-century drama, then we are led into a new understanding of the drama's form, of the unique life that was fifth-century drama as opposed to the clockwork simulation that was the drama of later centuries.

There is another way through which to look at this concept of *Gesamtkunstwerk* in general. We read fairly frequently in the work of literary critics the terms *actors' theater, writers' theater, directors' theater.* Critics have, on the whole, been inclined to distinguish between writers' theater and "performers' theater"—whether actors' or directors'—and to praise the former while denigrating the latter. Today, when the most important person is usually the director—the person who puts the various elements, of actor's performance, words, music, and picture, together, whether in the theater or on film—it is more useful to think of the Greek dramatists as directors, or rather director-choreographers, who were also poets, rather than as writers like the writers of today, separate from the theater and the people of the theater.

We shall see that, at the end of the fifth century, directors' theater was giving way to actors' theater, and that the dead theater of later antiquity was certainly an actors' theater. May I define the difference between these two theaters with a hypothetical example. Suppose that a singer complains about a word in a song lyric. At this point in the song a climactic high note is required. The word contains an awkward vowel sound or too many consonants. In actors' theater the singer wants the high note to show off his performance; the words, the point of the song at this particular moment in the play, can be forgotten; the important thing—so the singer argues—is that the moment should be "good theater." In writers' theater the writer has the power to insist that the point of the song is more important than the singer's narrow definition of "good theater." In directors' theater the director—with the power to enforce the decision—will consider what most helps the central point of the play: that the word should be changed so that the vocal climax will be as effective as possible, or that the vocal climax should be lessened so that the word can be heard. If the director happens to be the writer as well, he must still take this kind of decision. As we consider the theatrical command of the fifth-century poets, it is better to think of them as total men of the theater—director-choreographers—balancing words, music, choreography, actors' individualities, and scenic effects as aspects of a totality rather than as poets who then decorated their words with musical and theatrical embellishments. They were, after all, competing for a prize in a popular theater before an audience of fourteen thousand or more. They needed to make their plays into total theatrical successes.

The empty space. Ourselves, in a rehearsal room. We start to consider the mystery that is fifth-century drama. But of course our own mental space is not empty. It is littered with the remains of out-of-date scholarship and criticism, and with odd memories of inadequate modern productions. However much we may know about the Greek theater intellectually, it is as well to remind ourselves constantly of the way in which we have been conditioned to imagine it.

Many people today—perhaps the majority—if asked what is the nature of Greek tragedy, will include in their answer reference to the "tragic hero." This concept is utterly irrelevant to any of the extant Greek tragedies. It enters discussion solely as a result of the misunderstandings of scholars and critics of an earlier generation. There are no doubt numbers of people who have read Aristotle's *Poetics* only in English who will refer to the concept of the tragic hero. Aristotle never mentions such a being. Bywater, who made the standard English translation, introduced the words *the hero* into his version of the discussion of changes of fortune (7. 1451A. 11–15), and into the discussion of the kinds of people to whom these changes of fortune should happen (13. 1452B. 34 ff.). Bywater turns Aristotle's plural reference to "good men" and "bad men" into a singular. To Bywater, Tragedy had to be about heroes, and so he thought that Aristotle was talking about heroes. There are no tragic heroes in any Greek tragedy, and if we try to analyze any of the great plays in these terms we shall be forced into ridiculous contortions: the *Antigone* will "break in half"; we shall not be able to decide who is to have the title of hero in *The Bacchants;* worst of all, we may find ourselves calling the *Oresteia* or *Oedipus at Colonus* "not quite tragedy." In one or two plays, perhaps only the *Prometheus Bound* and *Oedipus the King,* will we find a character bearing some coincidental relationship to the stereotype of the tragic hero as understood from the plays of seventeenth-century France and the critical discussions accompanying them. That is all. In discussion of the Greek plays, the concept of the hero is incorrect and misleading. There is no longer any need to argue this seriously. The only plays that Bywater saw were those of the bourgeois theater of his day. We, with our far wider range of theatrical experience, can see that plays do not need heroes. The medieval mystery cycles; the Ramayana; a modern musical such as *Chicago;* numberless plays of the avant-garde "fringe."—it is obvious to us that there are other ways of constructing plays than building them round heroes. Why waste time trying to apply a concept developed centuries later to plays written without the concept, and no worse for that.[11]

The notion of the tragic hero, however misleadingly applied to fifth-century drama, has left an accompanying false impression of the Greek tragedies as "heroic"—works of the same "high seriousness," to use Matthew Arnold's term, as the plays of Racine or the operas of Wagner; something solemn and statuesque. Broken chamber pots—statuesque? Fifty men raping fifty girls—statuesque? Erotic dancing—statuesque? Men transformed into birds—statuesque? The notions of high seriousness and heroic drama, so applicable to the plays of Racine or the operas of Wagner, have no relevance to the riot and rampage of Aeschylus, Sophocles, and Euripides. To those who, unfamiliar with the actual plays and fragments, still find this notion surprising, I cannot put a note referring them to a few pages in a later part of the book. I can only ask them to read on. The riot and rampage—the carnival liveliness—of fifth-century drama is all-pervasive.

The notion of Greek tragedy as statuesque derives from an obvious mistake. At one time it was thought that fifth-century actors wore blocked up shoes and elevated masks to increase their height. It is difficult to understand how this was believed—given the clear pictures of actors in the fifth century dangling on their fingers an exactly natural mask, and wearing footwear that resembled socks. But there are a surprising number of general books on the theater that still contain this incorrect information with its thoroughly misleading implications. This will be discussed fully in Chapter 4, "Masks and Costumes."

But of course the main mistake has been to treat the actors, not the chorus, as central. And the majority of both average theatergoers and average people in the theater is still inclined to say that Greek choruses mean speeches in free verse. The shade of Sophocles must twist and writhe in embarrassment at the unshaped mouthings that purport to represent his taut lyrics, written in stricter verse forms than anything in western literature. But worse than the insult to his poetic craft is the insult to his theatricality. How could directors, who call themselves educated, make his chorus songs so boring!

The empty space. Let us clear our heads of the clutter from the dead Western bourgeois theater. Let us clear our heads of the clutter of past mistakes by scholars and critics—mistakes that the scholars and critics have now discarded—and let us approach these four masters of theatricality with our normal theatrical instincts alert. We are now aware of how many stage directions Shakespeare has written into his poetry. Let us be alert for the similar stage directions in the poetry of Aeschylus and Aristophanes.

Of course it is easier for us than it was for preceding Western generations. To our parents the theater was merely bourgeois comedy, an evening's entertainment, naturalistic representation of trivial people, occupying the attention at one level only, of no significance. To us, it is what? A multiplicity. Probably the strongest agent in changing our awareness of theatrical story is the TV commercial. To us who are used to its speed, how slow old movies seem. The TV commercial, telling its story as fast as possible, using any means that suggest themselves, is perhaps the best model of theatrical experience available today. How sad that such virtuosity of direction, photography, editing, music, dance, and spectacle should be used merely to sell Martini or toilet tissue.

At least we are aware that, since the majority of our drama is absorbed from the two-dimensional screen in our living-rooms, the theater, if it is to have any place in our culture, must be an experience whose meaning lies in the bringing together of a crowd of people to share in something that they could not share in without so coming together. I do not need to go to a theater to see the story of a couple with marital troubles; such a story can be shown to me with far greater subtlety in the close-ups of the TV screen. We talk—and it has almost become a cliché—of the need for theater to be "a rite." Luckily I do not have to define what I mean by this. For if we wish our theater to be a rite, then we must surely be able to learn from the rite that was the Athenian theater.

The nearest that the majority of Westerners come to the heightened theatrical experience to which we are referring when we talk of "theater as rite" is in a rock concert. There have been times in the last twenty years when a great number of people have felt that rock music was leading them into new insight, a new religious experience. Probably this feeling was more widespread in the late 1960s than it is today, though, as I write, a new rock star may be about to sweep America and Britain off into ecstasy again. But whether this happens or not, we have seen that rock music cannot lead in that sense to new insight, new religious experience, a new society. I do not imagine, for example, that many politicians—if any at all—feel the need to follow their teenage sons and daughters to rock concerts, as they might have done for a few years in the late 1960s.

Rock music at its best is like Wagner—enormously effective at driving an emotion to extremes of intensity, but unspecific, unconcerned with relating one emotion to another, or emotions to thought and political action.

Where we are most clearly at an advantage over our parents in our relationship to fifth-century theater is in comedy. For nearly the whole of Western history, the type of our comedy has been the restrained naturalism of Menander. Now all that has changed. How it started, we need not say. Perhaps with the surrealists in the 1920s. Perhaps with "The Goon Show," the British radio comedy show of the 1950s and 60s. Perhaps with Olsen and Johnson of "Hellzapoppin," the American radio comics of the 1930s and 40s whom the Goons took as a model. Perhaps with the Marx Brothers. Now it hardly matters. Rowan and Martin's "Laugh-in," "Monty Python's Flying Circus"—the new humor has flooded everywhere. Surrealism, fantasy, a sense of "anything goes," often mixed with political satire, this is the kind of humor to which we are now used. And of course, the four-letter words. Not yet on television, but certainly in the new comedy theaters of both America and Britain. Laughing in this sort of way, we are not far from the laughter of Aristophanes.

I have said that there is no point in going to the theater to see naturalistic plays. Now clearly enough, people in that small proportion of the population who are theatergoers do go to see naturalistic plays. Theatergoers are conservative; playwrights may well be better off financially if they write plays that can be transferred easily to television. But naturalism is no longer regarded as necessary. At one time it was thought to be the best—or indeed the only—way to write for the theater. At one time all plays had for their set three walls of a room. Now it is obvious that naturalism is a convention, like any other convention. Our theater has an open stage, or no stage at all. Very few plays have completely naturalistic settings. I have written elsewhere of how naturalism in the theater went with a philosophy that we now see to be relevant only to a world view based on nineteenth-century physics and therefore inadequate to the ever expanding vistas of late twentieth-century science.[12] The case made in that earlier book can rest. I should imagine that few would wish to argue it now. The glimpsed possibilities of our world view, symbolized by the ever more bewildering paradoxes of particle physics, the models of computer science, or the paradoxes of astronomy such as black holes patently demand a more flexible philosophy than mid-twentieth-century empiricism, a more flexible theater than the three-walled set and the so-called well-made play. It may now be difficult to define the state of contemporary theater, but, at least in the experimental avant-garde, there is a willingness to forget definitions, to consider anything as theater that works in the theater. From this point of view we are much more easily able to approach the theater of Dionysus than our parents were.

Critics who approached fifth-century drama with an experience of the theater confined to well-made plays committed horrifying mistakes about the rhythm of Aeschylus and Sophocles. Talk of theatrical or dramatic rhythm is difficult. The conversation quickly dissipates in vague generalities. Such rhythm, however, is a very concrete thing in a film cutting room—frames of celluloid in fact, running through the gate at twenty-four or twenty-five frames a second.[13] I have said that naturalism is a convention like any other convention. Once one has cut a documentary film, one sees how much convention is involved. Of course it is possible to cut a film like the well-made plays of an earlier generation. But what a stilted film it makes. In the early days of film editing it was thought that if we are to show a man going from the White House to the Empire State Building, we must show something of how he travels from one place to another. Now we know that this is not only unnecessary, but also misleading. For by showing the journey we are giving it significance in the audience's mind. If the journey is utterly unimportant, then our naturalism will misinform the audience.[14] Film montage can bind all sorts of disparate entities, provided that the rhythm of the montage is right. We can show a man's character by a montage of his different activities. But if we spend too long on one activity, our audience will lose the sense of the montage. We can unite cannibals in Papua, commissars in the Kremlin, mine workers in South Wales and socialites in Los Angeles, if we make a montage in which all these people, each utterly different from the rest, are shown in their brief scenes eating. The right visual connection between shot and shot, combined with the right length of time for which the shot is held, can create a montage that feels right, that has good rhythm. Even utterly disconnected shots can be connected by cutting to music. The rhythm of the cutting will make the audience feel a connection, even if none is visible. This all-embracing rhythm, which any film editor learns as the basis of his craft, is the center of dramatic form. Naturalistic plot making is one very confined, highly artificial subspecies of the form. It is far easier to approach the rhythm of fifth-century drama from a film cutting room than from a well-made play.

Director and cast sit in the empty space of the rehearsal room, waiting to approach the mystery of a fifth-century play. A sense of the deadness of Western theater now. A sense of the power of the fifth century. Can we penetrate the mystery? Our sense of humor will help us; the way in which we laugh is much nearer to Aristophanes' laughter. Our sense of dramatic rhythm, trained in the television cutting rooms, is far more able to cope with the *Gesamtkunstwerk* rhythm of the Greeks. And even if we are not dancers, yet we are probably much more aware than our parents were of the need for dance training, dance expression, the need to learn body language. The work of scholarship over the last hundred years has presented us with clear diagrams, clear parameters within which to work. Scholarship, for the most part, tells us, "It must have been either this . . . or that." A theater director must choose between them and decide for this rather than that. This book has tried to write itself from the viewpoint of the director in process of choosing.

An exercise I have found helpful in various drama workshops I have conducted on the Greek theater: we close our eyes and see in our imagination the statues of ancient Greece: clean, white marble—suitable image of the cool rationality for which the ancient Greeks are famous. Pause. The Greeks painted their statues in bright colours. The Parthenon, now an open ruin, was, as all other temples were, a closed-in shrine of small spaces, full of gold and darkness. Ancient Greece was not Palladian architecture. Its culture had much more of what we would now call an oriental flavor.

There does exist a culture through which we can approach fifth-century Athens: the Hindu. The Hindus are the only Indo-European race to have retained their original polytheism. A Hindu culture, especially in a place like Bali, relatively untouched by other cultures, offers the nearest parallel to the Athens of Sophocles. Life is god-centered; the gods are involved in all human activities. They are a colorful pantheon; there is no theology, only stories. Nor is there a fixed number; new gods may be added. The ceremonies are varied and colorful; the statues glitter with gold. If we are to imagine ancient Greek music, dance, and drama, we must start from Bali. A Hindu musician talks of the characters of the different ragas, his musical modes. Such talk is very similar to the remarks of Greeks like Plato on the character of the varying Greek modes. Balinese life—and certainly drama—is dance-oriented. Dance has importance, and it is interconnected with their worship: for them, worship without dance would not be proper worship. Their dance is immensely complicated; it is a language to be learned, and in which to communicate. Every part of the body is used in the dance; the dance of the hands is very important. All these things are equally true of the Greeks, even down to the fact that they had a special work—*cheironomia*—to describe hand-dancing. In one further aspect, Hindu and Greek culture are at one: both center on the erotic. The festivals of Dionysus were as flamboyant a celebration of sexuality as anything in Hindu religious art; and, just as in Hinduism, sexual celebration is indistinguishable from religious celebration.

This book has been written from the following beliefs: first, that our theater is sick and confused, because our society is sick and confused, and that one of the ways in which we might bring health to our society is to bring health to our theater; second, that a real attempt to perform the plays of the four Athenian poets as nearly as possible as they performed them would open our theatrical imaginations even more widely than truthful performance of Shakespeare has done—for Shakespeare, even in the hands of Vincent Crummles, has never been fully lost to us; and third, that we are in a better position to attempt such performance than previous generations. But even with our minds charmed and empowered by the magic of Bali, it will be a difficult task, indeed one that will often seem impossible. Nietzsche did not get much right; but this he did get right:

Fast jede Zeit und Bildungsstufe hat einmal sich mit tiefem Missmuthe von den Griechen zu befreien gesucht, weil Angesichts derselben alles Selbstgeleistete, scheinbar völlig Originelle, und recht aufrichtig Bewunderte plötzlich Farbe und Leben zu verlieren schien und zur misslungenen Copie, ja zur Caricatur zusammenschrumpfte.[15]

Notes

1. Peter Brook, *The Empty Space* (London: Macgibbon and Kee, 1968), p. 47.
2. Charles Dickens, *Nicholas Nickleby*, chaps. 23, 24, 29, 30, and the delightful realization of the Crummles *Romeo* in the Royal Shakespeare Company's 1980 production, now on film.
3. For the meaning of terms used, see Appendix 3.
4. I return to this point in Chapter 5 and again in Chapter 10.
5. Plutarch *Table Talk* 8.9.732E.
6. *Life of Sophocles* 3.
7. Plato *Laws* 2.654A.
8. For notes on Greek meters, see Appendix 4.
9. However we stress the line, the first "Weep no more" will not be exactly the same length as the second "Weep no more." It would be equally possible, and equally compatible with Milton's intention, to make the first longer than the second. It is a most graphic example of the way in which the rhythm of English poetry is inseparable from its meaning.
10. See Chapter 5, "The System."
11. For a full discussion, see H. D. F. Kitto, *Form and Meaning in Drama* (London: Methuen, 1956); John Jones, *On Aristotle and Greek Tragedy* (London: Chatto & Windus, 1962); Leo Aylen, *Greek Tragedy and the Modern World* (London: Methuen, 1964), passim, and summarized pp. 155–57.
12. Leo Aylen, *Greek Tragedy and the Modern World* (London: Methuen, 1964), especially pp. 169–228.
13. Movie film runs through the gate at twenty-four frames a second; television film in most of the world at twenty-five, for technical reasons we need not go into here. (The American television system involves further complications: the film runs through the gate at twenty-four frames a second, but certain frames have to be repeated.) The difference is invisible to the human eye.
14. Intentional misleading of the audience in this way occurs constantly in Alfred Hitchcock's films. His control of film rhythm is masterly.
15. "Nearly every age and stage of culture has at some time or other sought with deep displeasure to free itself from the Greeks, because in their presence, everything self-achieved, sincerely admired and apparently original, seemed all of a sudden to lose life and colour and shrink to an abortive copy, even to caricature." Friedrich Nietzsche, *The Birth of Tragedy*, trans. W. A. Haussmann (London: J. N. Foulis, 1909), p. 113.

2

HISTORICAL SUMMARY

The history of the Greek theater is, as I have said, the history of a hundred years or so of life, twelve hundred years of imitation. To study the life and how it died is the center of all study of the Greek theater. But it may be as well to precede this with a summary of the main events that affected the development of the theater, as a background to the plays we possess.[1]

In 534 B.C., the Athenian tyrant Pisistratus founded the festival of the City *Dionysia*, whose main purpose was the presentation of plays and dithyrambs as a sacred competition.[2] During the preceding century a form of dance drama had been developed to considerable subtlety, mainly in the Dorian parts of Greece. During the thirty years in which Pisistratus had been in power, an Athenian poet-choreographer called Thespis had developed this dance drama in the countryside of Attica, and he had then introduced spoken prologues and interludes between dances and thereby extended the possibilities of storytelling in this new art form, which had clearly become very popular by the time it was made the center of the new festival in 534.

Two years after Pisistratus died in 527, Aeschylus was born. His childhood was spent in Athens ruled by the tyrant's sons, Hipparchus and Hippias, who continued their father's keen patronage of the arts. Hipparchus was assassinated in 514, however, for a personal grudge, and Hippias reacted by changing what had been a benevolent rule to something much more savage. He was expelled in 510, and an upper- to upper-middle-class democracy was installed in Athens. The tyrants had patronized the arts; with the sense of freedom aroused by the institution of democracy, the arts developed even further. This mood of effervescence helped Athens to confront the Persian invasion. In 490 the middle-class Athenians—among them Aeschylus—enlisting as heavy-armed part-time infantry, as was the custom in all Greek cities (except Sparta, whose army was full-time) confronted on their own the vast Persian army at Marathon and made it flee. It was a victory to change the course of history. Encouraged by this, the Athenians, under their new leader Themistocles, led an alliance of Greek cities against the second Persian invasion in 480. Themistocles had insisted that Athens build ships, and it was this new navy that defeated the Persians. Aeschylus also fought as a hoplite at Salamis, the naval battle, and so proud was he of his military experience that his epitaph makes mention of this only, not mentioning his poetry at all. By this time, however, he had won his first victory in the dramatic festival of 484 and was a friend of Themistocles, who was now the leader of a radical movement to extend political power more widely through the classes. Although the war with Persia continued, Themistocles was keener to protect Athens from her former Greek ally, Sparta. Two parties developed, and Themistocles was forced to leave Athens and go into exile. In a major attempt to save him, the two most important poets of Athens, Aeschylus and his older contemporary Phrynichus, had put on plays dealing with the defeat of Persia: in 476, Phrynichus' *The Phoenician Women*, and in 472, Aeschylus' *The Persians*, the earliest extant Greek play. *The Persians* requires two actors for its performance. Aeschylus had introduced a second actor besides himself, and this became the usual practice for some years.

After the exile of Themistocles, Aeschylus does not seem to have been so closely involved with politics. He made more than one visit to Sicily, where there was a flourishing theater patronized by the tyrants of Syracuse and Gela. We do not hear of any Sicilian tragic poets, but there are many fragments from the work of Epicharmus, a comic poet who flourished there at this time. From what we can gather, his work shows great diversity; the fragments refer frequently to food, and there are comic lists. His plays were often mythological burlesques. He probably had a chorus, though there are no fragments in lyric meters, and therefore the chorus may never have sung and danced in systems but only chanted. Nor does his comedy appear to have had any of the political reference that was central to Athenian Old Comedy. It is argued as to whether Epicharmus was writing successfully before or after the introduction of competitions for comedy in Athens. This took place in 486, when the first victor was Chionides, about whom virtually nothing is known.

Sophocles was born in 495. His first public appearance as a boy of fifteen, in 480, was to lead victory celebrations after Salamis with a nude dance to his own lyre accompaniment. His first victory in the tragic competitions was in 468. Although he was clearly an excellent dancer and appeared as Nausicaa in one of his early plays, he soon gave up acting because of a "small voice."[3] Relatively early in his career Sophocles managed to raise the number of actors from two to three, an innovation that Aeschylus was soon to make use of also.

Sophocles was a friend of Pericles, an aristocrat who as a young man took up the leadership of the radical party vacated by Themistocles. The spokesman of this class was Aeschylus, although there is no evidence that he was a friend of Pericles himself. The climax of the radical program was a series of reforms introduced by Pericles and Ephialtes in 462, which deprived the *Areopagus*, up till then a political upper house, of all powers except that of being the supreme court of law. Aeschylus' *The Suppliants*, probably produced in 463, is very much concerned with democracy, but the climax of his work, the *Oresteia*, refers directly to these reforms brought in four years before its production in 458.

By this time Athens had become very rich. After the defeat of the Persian invasion, a league of maritime Greek states had been formed under the leadership of Athens to free the subdued Greek cities of Asia Minor. This campaign had been successful and, at the same time, had become more and more an exclusively Athenian venture. The allies had preferred to pay tribute money rather than themselves fight in their own ships. Four years after the *Oresteia*, in 454, the league's treasury was moved from the island of Delos to Athens, ostensibly for safer keeping; its removal is usually taken as a symbol of the change from a league of freely associating cities to an Athenian empire compelled to pay tribute, which Pericles would partly use to build temples to the gods in Athens.

Athens became also the intellectual capital of the Greek-speaking world. The thinkers, philosophers, and scientists from Ionia came to Athens. It seems likely that Aeschylus met Anaxagoras, who was in Athens at this time. Certainly some of his ideas are related to ideas expressed in the writing of all three tragic poets. But it was Euripides, born in the year of Salamis, who was most influenced by the new attitudes of thought that derived from the presence of these newcomers.

After the *Oresteia*, Aeschylus returned to Sicily and produced his *Prometheus Bound* in Gela, which had recently expelled its tyrants and instituted a democracy. Soon after that he died. After his death it seems to have ceased to be usual practice for a poet to act the principal role in his play. Now even the leading part was given to an actor after the custom introduced by Sophocles. The importance of the actor was officially recognized when a competition for leading actors was made part of the City Dionysia in 449.

Euripides had been selected to enter the competition for the first time in 455 and won his first victory in 441. Sophocles presented the *Ajax* in the mid 440s, and the *Antigone* probably in 440. As a result of this play he was elected one of the generals under the supreme command of Pericles for the war against Samos, one of the most powerful of Athenian "allies," which had revolted and had to be subdued. The office of general was political as well as military, and it may be that Sophocles was elected into the most important office of state more as an "ideas man," rather as Milton was co-opted into Cromwell's government. But it is important when we consider Sophocles' work to realize that he had first-hand experience of command and, by his friendship with Pericles, was in close touch with all important decisions taken during the period of Athens's supremacy.

In 446, the probable year of Aristophanes' birth, a thirty-year peace between Athens and Sparta was signed. It was not to be kept longer than fourteen years, and it was during this short period of peace, interrupted anyhow by the Samian War, that most of the great temples in Athens were built. Pericles was responsible also for rebuilding the theater, and probably for introducing stone seats. He also built the Odeion, which was completed in 443, where the *proagōn*, described in Chapter 3, would be held. To this period belongs Euripides' *Alcestis*.

It is right to notice that the achievements of fifth-century Athens coincided with a period of almost continuous fighting—with Persia, Sparta, and her own rebellious so-called allies. But the war that started in 432 was more serious. It was Pericles' policy to rely mainly on his fleet, while insisting that the Athenians abandon their farms and crowd within the city fortifications. Pericles' policy had he remained to guide it would very likely have proved completely successful. But he died in 429. With their fleet able to import corn, the Athenians could afford to let the invading Spartan armies ravage their land. But plague broke out in the cramped conditions within the fortifications, and although the first Peloponnesian War left Athens rather more powerful than before, there was a great war-weariness by the time peace was made in 421.

To this period belong *The Women of Trachis* and *Oedipus the King* of Sophocles, the latter seared by the facts of the plague. We have also a number of Euripides' plays: the *Medea, Children of Heracles, Hippolytus, Hecuba,* and perhaps *Cyclops, Heracles,* and *The Suppliant Women.* We also possess some of the early successes of Aristophanes, whose first production was in 427, and who was victorious with *The Acharnians* at the *Lenaia,* described in Chapter 3, in 425, with the *Knights,* also at the *Lenaia,* in 424. *The Clouds* came third in 423, *The Wasps* was presented in 422, and was either first or second, and *The Peace* came second at the *Dionysia* in 421. For a comic poet, a victory at the *Lenaia* seems to have been just as satisfying as one at the *Dionysia.* But for tragic poets a *Lenaia* victory was less prestigious, although both Sophocles and Euripides entered tragedies there. The competitions both for comic poets and comic actors at the *Lenaia* had been instituted in either 442 or 440. The competitions for tragic poets and tragic actors came a few years later.

Throughout the Peloponnesian War the fleet's importance meant that the lowest classes, who provided the rowers, began to realize their power in the state. After the death of Pericles a series of popular demagogues gained control of Athenian policy, relying for their influence on the lower classes, to whom the war was on the whole beneficial. For they had no land to be ravaged, and the constant need for the fleet kept them employed and paid. The first of these warmongering demagogues was Cleon, who became the most powerful man in Athens. It is indeed doubtful whether peace would have been signed in 421 if he had not been killed the year before. Both Euripides and Aristophanes devoted their main political energies to opposing the war. Aristophanes' second production, *The Babylonians,* when he was still under twenty, had been an attack on the way that Athens treated her subject allies, and a personal attack on Cleon. For this Cleon indicted him on a charge of impiety. No doubt the political motivation was obvious. Aristophanes does not seem to have been abashed. After the daring pacifism of *The Acharnians,* he attacked Cleon again in *The Knights.* With a first prize two years running for these plays, Aristophanes was now too popular; Cleon could not touch him. Euripides was also prosecuted by Cleon for impiety, presumably for the same political motive.[4] By this time he had already presented two of his most savage antiwar plays, the *Hecuba* and *Suppliant Women.*

At the age of ninety-three, old Cratinus had beaten Aristophanes' *Clouds* into third place. His working life must have spanned almost the entire life of Old Comedy since it was first officially recognized in 486. The few fragments show that his work was recognizably of the same genre: there is surrealist fantasy, political satire, and mythological burlesque. Nothing that survives shows anything approaching the sheer intensity of lyric poetry that we find in Aristophanes' greatest songs, but this may be merely the chance of papyrus finds.

There is an important fragment (307) of Cratinus that connects Aristophanes and Euripides as the up-to-date bright fellows:

> Hey, the theater gossip's going, get you, what a wise one!
> What a supersubtle whizzing wit, what Euripidaristophanizing.

It is usually said by scholars that Aristophanes hated Euripides. For this there is no real evidence. In *The Frogs* Euripides is mocked. So is Aeschylus. In Aristophanes' *Acharnians* Euripides appears as a character in an amusing scene, where his role is that of the kitchen-sink dramatist. The *agōn* is a beautiful parody of Euripides' nonextant *Telephus*, with Dikaiopolis (Just City)[5] defending his life by threatening to kill his hostage, the charcoal basket (331 ff.). *The Women at the Thesmophoria* is entirely devoted to Euripides. The women decide to revenge themselves on him for the unkind things he has said about them. But Euripides was known to be very sympathetic to the cause of women and wrote many beautiful passages that show great sensitivity to their situation. We think for instance of Medea's speech on the lot of women (*Medea*, 230 ff.) and especially her remark that she would rather face enemy spears three times than bear a child once (250–51). *The Women at the Thesmophoria* contains scenes in which the character Euripides appears as hero of parodies of his recent successful plays. One of the things that the play deals with is the nature of poetic, theater reality. Euripides is presented as the type of the poet. Nothing could be more complimentary. Even in *The Frogs* there is a delight in Euripides' poetry as it is mocked. Aristophanes and Euripides must have met frequently at the festivals. At the very least, the younger comic admired the older tragic poet, who shared his sympathy for women and hatred of war. Certainly they must have had many conversations together over matters theatrical.

Because Socrates is caricatured as the central character in *The Clouds*, unimaginative scholars have suggested that Aristophanes hated him too. There is a tradition that Socrates stood up in the audience to be recognized at the first performance of *The Clouds*.[6] More important is the evidence of Plato's *Symposium* or *Drinking Party*, written in the 380s, some time after Socrates' death, describing a party in 417 given by the young tragic poet Agathon to celebrate his first prize. Here Socrates and Aristophanes are shown as good friends, still arguing about tragedy and comedy through a haze of alcohol and sleep after the other guests have collapsed (223C–D).

I have gone into such detail about this point because it is important to grasp that Athens at this time was a tightly knit community where the poets, artists, and thinkers all knew each other well. Much of Aristophanes' satire appears to us more savage than it really is. It is, as it were, satire within the family. Members of a family may abuse each other with great violence but the abuse means something different from abuse of or by outsiders. It is often said that a modern production of Aristophanes can work only within a university, for a modern university, with its strong sense of community, its savage in-fighting, and its possession of time for discussion or conversation, is the nearest our society can come to the life of fifth-century Athens, where the middle classes lived off the proceeds of their farms but left them to be run by slaves, while they themselves spent their time in bodily, mental, and spiritual exercises.

Euripides and Aristophanes also shared acquaintance if not friendship with the poet-musician Timotheos, who was responsible for developing a new musical style characterized by its mixture of many tempi, its independence of the system, and, as a result, its increasing dominance over the words. Both Euripides and Aristophanes developed his innovations with obvious delight. But we can see in some of Euripides' work in the last ten years of his life a looseness of poetry incompatible with the *Gesamtkunstwerk*, where every syllable and gesture has point. The new music was one of the developments that would kill fifth-century drama.

Five years of peace had encouraged Athenian aggressive imperialism. First they attacked the small Dorian island of Melos, which had never been a member of either the Athenian or the Spartan bloc. When Melos finally fell the Athenians voted to put all the men to death. This act of brutality was quickly followed by a decision to send an expedition to Sicily. Ostensibly to help a Sicilian ally, it was in effect an attempted invasion of Syracuse, the most powerful city of the island, and an act of unmitigated aggression. The inspiration behind the expedition was the brilliant and unstable relative of Pericles, Alcibiades. He was made one of the generals, another being the cautious Nikias, much against his will. Just before the expedition sailed a scandal struck Athens. It was the custom to have outside one's house a herm—a statue of a fertility spirit or household god, to which incense was burned and prayers offered. As fertility spirits, the statues had erect penises. One May morning, it was discovered that a great number of statues had been mutilated. This sacrilege was regarded as an extremely ill omen. The enormous expedition was allowed to sail after a while, but when it was on its way to Sicily, Alcibiades was recalled to face trial, as he had been implicated in the sacrilege. He chose instead to escape to Sparta, where he gave two pieces of advice to the Spartans that were very largely responsible for Athens's eventual defeat: they should build a fort on Athenian soil, from which they could ravage the land continually; and they should send a Spartan general to Syracuse to take command. As a result, the Athenians in Sicily, under the incompetent command of Nikias, suffered a total defeat two years later, losing all of their ships and all of their men.

In 415, just before the expedition sailed, Euripides presented one of his few trilogies, of which we possess the third play, *The Trojan Women*, possibly the greatest antiwar poem ever written. It was voted second, clearly not being to the mood of the time. The next year Aristophanes presented *The Birds*. Although this is apparently pure fantasy, there are quite recognizable allusions to Athenian aggression and to sacrilege. The central character, a typical brash Athenian, is presented with brilliant ambivalence: he is a lovable rogue. But the play won only second prize, though many people now think that it is Aristophanes' best.

Almost certainly, that year also saw the *Iphigeneia in Tauris*, the first of a series of plays by Euripides that have a feeling of fantasy about them. About this time Agathon presented his *Antheus*, the first tragedy with an invented plot. The *Iphigeneia in Tauris* is the earliest play where it is possible to analyze its structure in terms of the interrelation of characters, which we call "plot," without losing too much of what the play is about. Two years later, in 412, Euripides presented the *Ion* and *Helen*, which are even more plays of plot, beginnings of the modern theater. They are no longer rites, but pieces that can exist in a secularized theater as fantasy. Although the *Philoctetes* of Sophocles is not a play of this nature, its structure bears some relation to this new theater of plot. Sophocles, now well over eighty, was not above learning from his younger contemporaries.

Aristophanes' plays during the last ten years of the war are more intensely and more obviously rites, activities of worship. These three—the *Lysistrata* in 411, *Women at the Thesmophoria* in 410, and *Frogs* in 405—are also his most perfect plays formally. In the latter two there is a deep exploration of the nature of theatrical reality. Pun and parody, always central to his humor, acquire in and through these masterpieces the status of a world view. It is central to our understanding of Athenian culture that we should realize that these wild fantasy-farces are also major religious poems.

After the Sicilian disaster in 413, Athens never fully recovered. The Spartan side now had a navy and were able to encourage Athenian subject states to revolt. The Athenians appointed ten commissioners to oversee public affairs, one of whom was Sophocles. At his age his job must have been largely to boost morale. In 411 there was a coup d'etat by a group of oligarchs, members of the upper classes. But the rule of the Four Hundred, so-called from the number of the conspirators, lasted only a few months. A new constitution was created, giving franchise to the Five Thousand, the men of some property, and Alcibiades was recalled to treat with Persia and prevent her coming into the war on the Spartan side. A year later Alcibiades defeated and destroyed the Peloponnesian navy at Cyzicus, and full democracy was restored. In the summer of 407 Alcibiades returned to Athens and was voted command of the war. With an escort of soldiers he made sure that the annual festival procession from Athens to Eleusis could take place that September. Since the Spartans had occupied the fort of Decelea, this had been impossible. But in the spring of 406, the Athenian fleet suffered a minor defeat at Notion at the hands of the new, brilliant Spartan admiral, Lysander. Alcibiades, though not present, was voted out of office, left Athens for his castle on the Hellespont, and took no further part in the war.

Having presented the *Orestes,* a piece of mad, baroque savagery and one of the most brilliant explorations of the many levels of theatrical reality, Euripides left Athens, disappointed at the lack of success that he had met with in his life. At the court of the king of Macedon, he wrote and probably produced *The Bacchants,* and then died early in 406. Sophocles, hearing the news at the beginning of the City *Dionysia* as he was going into the *proagōn* to announce his play, brought on his performers in black, without wreaths. *The Bacchants, Iphigeneia at Aulis,* and the lost *Alcmaeon at Corinth* were produced posthumously and won first prize.

Athens had won another naval victory, at Arginusae in 406. But many seamen were lost in a storm that followed the battle. In anger at the loss of these men, the Assembly accused the generals in charge of failing to pick them up. Eight generals were condemned to death and six executed, two having prudently sailed away. The Spartans again advanced peace terms on the basis of the status quo, and offered to evacuate Decelea—the same terms as they had proposed after the battle of Cyzicus, four years before. Again the peace was rejected, this time at the instigation of the demagogue Cleophon.

For this desperate situation the ninety-year-old Sophocles wrote his *Oedipus at Colonus* but died before he could see it produced. With both tragic poets dead, Aristophanes wrote his *Frogs* as a plea for unity in Athens and peace with Sparta. It was produced in 405 at the *Lenaia* and won first prize to great acclaim. But peace was not made, and in the summer the Athenian navy, stupidly commanded, was destroyed by Lysander at Aegospotami. The war was over, although Lysander delayed some months before sailing to Athens, destroying the fortifications and imposing an oligarchic government—the Thirty.

Athens was bankrupt, and many were very hungry, since the economy had relied on importing corn. The Spartan-supported oligarchy lasted less than two years, but it is not an exaggeration to say that the spirit of Athens was broken. The restored democracy put men to death as acts of political reprisal, among whom the most notoriously innocent victim was Socrates, forced to drink hemlock in 399. Reference was made to *The Clouds* at his trial,[7] and this, on top of the defeat of Athens, may well have broken Aristophanes' heart. His next play was not presented until 393, and it is like a shadow of his earlier work. There were no longer funds for a proper comic chorus. There are none of the complex dances of the earlier plays. But there is also a lack of political intensity; how could there be the satire of a play like *The Knights* in a society that had put Socrates to death?

Quite suddenly also, perhaps within a generation, there was a major change in religious attitude. The last two plays of Aristophanes are unique in containing neither prayer, hymn, nor dance invocation of the gods, nor celebration of a rite. Gold had been melted off the statues of the gods to pay for the war, and still Athens had lost. The ceremonials of the city's worship no longer seemed to relate to religious experience. A split developed between the intellectuals, of whom Plato was typical, and the ordinary people, the latter developing more incoherent magical superstitions, the former, as discussed in Chapter 10, adopting an attitude somewhat the equivalent of Protestantism. Rites and ceremonies no longer seemed to have any real function in life. Philosophy was more important than poetry. The major function of the theater was to provide sensational entertainment and display opportunities for the actors, who now became much more important than the poets.[8]

The squabbling politics of the Greek city states continued for most of the fourth century. But the kingdom of Macedonia was becoming the most important power. In 338 Athens and Thebes were defeated at Chaeronea by Philip of Macedon, and from then on Athens would never be fully in control of its political identity. About this time Lycurgus rebuilt the theater and encouraged the revivals of fifth-century plays. It was the beginning of the process that dignified and ossified tragedy into grand opera. Soon after appeared the first examples of what is known as New Comedy, which was to last as the standard comedy for centuries and influence the modern theater at every turn. The only examples we possess in Greek are by Menander, one of the first—if not the first—writer of this genre, a kind of play making derived from plays like Euripides' *Iphigeneia in Tauris*, and now based upon an endlessly repeatable formula. They are plays of ordinary life whose success depends on the skilful manipulation of coincidence to form a plot that keeps the audience guessing. They involve no issues of importance, and the humor consists merely of amusing situations or witty remarks; there is nothing of the total laughter of an Aristophanes play.

Plays were now written to be toured, and the festival of Dionysus became relatively much less important. New Comedy could be played all over the new empire established by the conquests of Philip's son, Alexander, and a little later even in the Western empire, governed by Rome but culturally dominated by Greek thought, Greek writers, and Greek theater. Menander was born in 343 and wrote about a hundred plays in his relatively short life, of which we possess one complete, early example, three nearly complete plays, three plays of which about half the text remains, and a number of sizable fragments. We have twenty-six adaptations of New Comedy into Latin: twenty by Plautus, who lived about a century after Menander, and six by Terence, a freed Carthaginian slave brought up in Rome in the generation following. Plautus probably started life as an actor; Terence was a favourite of the leading intellectuals in Rome in the middle of the second century B.C., though he was not outstandingly successful and left Rome at the age of twenty-five never to return.

Plautus and his contemporaries were able to watch the Greek theatrical performances in Sicily and the south of Italy, where drama seems to have flourished consistently since the fifth century, though we hear little of any writers of note. Perhaps most interesting is the first writer of prose sketches,

Sophron of Syracuse, none of whose work survives.[9] It certainly, however, influenced Theocritus, who was born in Syracuse but spent most of his life in Alexandria, the city founded by Alexander at the mouth of the Nile, which was rapidly to become the most important cultural capital as the center of the Ptolemies' Egyptian empire. But although Theocritus has an ear for dialogue and character, none of his dramatic poems were meant to be acted. And although Alexandria in the third century had a flourishing community of poets, there seem to have been no plays of distinction. Webster has noted that we know the names of sixty tragic poets between the third and the end of the first centuries B.C., but not a line of their work survives.[10] The only dramatic writing of this period surviving in Greek are the seven sketches of Herodas, who spent some of his life in Alexandria, although he does not seem to have been born there.

It is a strange story. Performances of tragedy and comedy seem to have continued under the Roman Empire, and new plays were being presented in Athens in the reign of Hadrian, at the end of the first century A.D. Tragedy consisted of a relatively small series of stock plots into which minor variations were introduced, no doubt to suit the voice or temperament of the actor-manager of the particular tour. The chorus had been relegated to unimportance by the time of Lycurgus, though choruses were occasionally employed throughout later antiquity as decorative additional entertainment. From the reign of Nero we possess nine tragedies by Seneca, all of them variations of Greek originals. But high-born Romans did not write for the degrading theater; these plays are written for reading aloud in a salon, not for acting. Almost certainly they received their first stage presentation during the Renaissance.

The major dramatic art form of the Roman Empire[11] was the pantomime, invented in 22 B.C. by two freed slaves, Bathyllus of Alexandria and Pylades of Cilicia. A solo dancer performed a dance mime while a chorus at the side sang an accompanying story. It was enormously successful, and the great pantomimists became people of importance, the most notable of all being Theodora, who caused a furore by her marriage to the emperor Justinian in the sixth century A.D. At no stage was the profession of pantomimist respectable, as the profession of tragic actor in Athens in the fifth and fourth centuries had been.

Since these are the facts, any history of the theater of antiquity is bound to spend far longer on fifth-century Athens than on all the rest of antiquity put together. For a study such as this, which concentrates on those plays that we possess in a state to make it reasonable to ask how they can be produced in the theater, the balance is even more one-sided. We possess seven plays of Aeschylus, seven of Sophocles, eighteen of Euripides, and eleven of Aristophanes. We possess an anonymous tragedy, almost certainly of the early fourth century, attributed to Euripides, the *Rhesus.* Of Menander we have one play, three nearly complete plays, and three half-plays, and we possess twenty-six Latin adaptations of Greek New Comedies, twenty by Plautus and six by Terence. There are the seven versions of tragedy by Seneca not intended for performance, and the *Octavia* by pseudo-Seneca, a play made on the same lines as his, but with a plot based on recent events in the reign of Nero. With the exception of the sketches of Herodas and what else we can glean about the popular, mainly nonverbal theater, that is all.

How willingly would one barter the corpus of New Comedy for the last play of the *Oresteia.* Interesting though some of the details of Menander, Plautus, or Terence are, there is in general little for the modern theater to learn from them. Such inspiration as they have to offer has already been absorbed. *The Comedy of Errors* is an adaptation of *The Brothers Menaechmus,* by Plautus, which improves on its original. Molière is the greatest writer of New Comedy, and the best way to study details of the variations on a stock formula that is the essence of New Comedy would be to consider the way in which the formula has survived changes of language and culture throughout the centuries from the Greeks of the fourth century B.C. and their adapters to the playwrights of the Renaissance in several countries, whose tradition continues unbroken in the work of such writers as Oscar Wilde and Georges Feydeau, to the way in which the formula is still maintained in television serials of today. In a short study of the Greek theater such as this, the trivia of New Comedy must be only a postscript. To us now, searching for a new raison d'être for our theater, it is important to understand that, for its time, the theater of fifth-century Athens was everything that theater can ever be, and that in the study of forty-three plays by four poets we can discover everything about how theater lives and dies, and possibly even how theater may live again.

Notes

1. See Appendix 1 for a chronological table with dates.
2. See Appendix 3 for meanings of terms used.
3. *Life of Sophocles* 4.
4. Satyrus *Life of Euripides* 39 X.
5. For the translation of Aristophanes' character names, see Appendix 2.
6. The story is told by Aelian in his *History* 2.13. Webster assumes that Socrates stood up to show what a good likeness the stage representation was. See T. B. L. Webster, *Greek Theatre Production,* 2d ed. (London: Methuen, 1970). Dover assumes the opposite, that Socrates' action was to imply, "Do I look like the sort of man who's playing the fool on stage?" See Aristophanes, *The Clouds,* ed. Sir Kenneth Dover (Oxford: Clarendon Press, 1968). However we interpret the action, it must surely have been a good-humored one.
7. Plato *Apology* 18.D.2.
8. In 341 it was decreed that each actor must perform for all three poets, in one play by each of them. This obviously indicates that to have the winning actor was by then considered an impossibly unfair advantage for any poet, and it therefore demonstrates the major importance of the actors.
9. The usual word for these sketches is "mime," which is merely a transliteration of the Greek word. It is, unfortunately, confusing, because these "mimes" were not mimes in the modern sense at all, but short sketches in dialogue. For further discussion, see Chapter 12.
10. T. B. L. Webster, *Art and Literature in Fourth Century Athens* (London: Athlone Press, 1956), p. 114.
11. In a study such as this it is important to remember that the so-called Roman Empire was in all senses except politically a Greek empire. Apart from Rome itself, every important city was Greek-speaking, not Latin-speaking. More or less every development in thought and art came about through Greek speakers, not Latin speakers, although the former were by no means all Greek by race.

3

FESTIVAL DRAMA

The Festivals of Dionysus

One is the Lord of Death, and Dionysus of the raving maenads.
(Heracleitus, frag. 15)

The Greek plays of the fifth century were very directly and obviously part of a rite, acts of worship offered to a mysterious spirit power. The conventional prettified pictures of the Olympian gods, developed during the Hellenistic period, when the gods had ceased to be objects of real worship, and spread through Western culture by artists of the later Renaissance, have nothing to do with the conceptions of the archaic Greeks. But the picture of Dionysus was trivialized the most. At the center of the Athenian drama is a being of terrifying power, known by more than one name, and apparently with several contradictory characteristics.

We cannot trace the beginnings of the worship. It used to be thought that he was not originally a Greek god, but recently discovered evidence has shown this to be wrong.[1] Dionysus was worshiped in Mycenean times. It has been suggested, however, that the name Bacchus may have been Lydian, and that the Dionysiac worship may have been reinvigorated at intervals in early Greek history by Eastern influences.[2] Another name, Iankos, was probably the original Attic name. By the fifth century, was it simply a matter of one god with three different names? We cannot be sure. At any rate it helps to remind us not to press Greek religious experience into too rigid definitions.

Dionysus was the lord of fertility and growth, and also lord of the lightning.[3] He was particularly god of the dance and was celebrated in a dance of women on the mountains in midwinter every alternate year. This dance, in which the women became possessed, culminated in an act of eating raw flesh, which had probably once been an act of ritual cannibalism.[4] Since the activity of becoming drunk on wine could be a way to new insights, new senses of communion, Dionysus was also to be found in wine and drunkenness.

What has been less discussed, however, is the connection between Dionysus and Hades, the lord of death. Throughout this century scholars have argued over two theories for the origin of tragedy: that it was always Dionysiac, or that it arose in connection with ceremonies for the dead. It now seems clear that this was a false opposition. As we shall see, Dionysus and the dead were always intimately connected. The fragment of Heracleitus quoted above is central in our approach to Dionysus.

When we consider the festivals of Dionysus at Athens, we notice that they are all winter festivals. The various small towns and villages celebrated their own Rural *Dionysia* during December. The *Lenaia*, which was probably the city of Athens's Rural *Dionysia*, was celebrated in January. The *Anthesteria* was celebrated in February. Even the City *Dionysia*, which was deliberately founded by Pisistratus specifically as an occasion to present plays, was in March. Even in Greece this is not the ideal time of year to sit for an entire day on cold stone or draughty wooden steps. We would expect it to have been at least a month later. It would seem that it was necessary that Dionysus should be worshiped in the dead time of year, not at a period of fertility like spring or vintage, as we might expect. A god of fertility, worshiped in the dead time of the year. The same spirit—lord of death, and lord of life and the dance. This mystery, which we cannot define further, is central to our understanding of the drama his worship evoked.[5]

The *Anthesteria* lasted three days, each one being deemed to start at sunset. The first day was called the *Pithoigia*, the blessing of the new wine. Jars containing the wine from the autumn before were opened; a libation[6] was poured to Dionysus, and then the wine was drunk. By this action taboo was removed from food and drink so that the people could enjoy them. The second day, called the *Choes* or pitcher-feast, was a day of general drinking. The main event was a ceremonial drinking match inaugurated by the King Archon to the sound of a trumpet. Tradition derived this custom from Orestes' arrival in Athens, as shown in Aeschylus' *Eumenides*. In order to avoid polluting the Athenians, Orestes had to drink out of a separate cup from that of his hosts. In order to avoid embarrassing Orestes, his hosts all drank from separate cups themselves. In the afternoon the figure of Dionysus was escorted in procession in a car shaped like a ship on wheels to a special sanctuary in the precinct of Dionysus *en Limnais*, in the Bogside.[7] During the procession there was ritual mockery of prominent individuals. At sunset, when the third day of the festival had begun, there was the Sacred Marriage between the wife of the King Archon and Dionysus. The *Chutroi*, the day of pots, was a more solemn day, a feast of All Souls, so to speak, when the dead were supposed to walk abroad, and houses were smeared with pitch as a precaution against them. The day took its name from the pots in which a kind of porridge was offered to Dionysus and Hermes Chthonios—Hermes, escort of souls to the underworld.[8] Prayers were said for the dead, especially those drowned in Deucalion's flood. The revels, however, continued on the *Chutroi*,[9] and it is certainly hard to imagine the Greeks, or any race for that matter, suddenly sobering up at sunset after a day of drinking. All aspects of the festival are inextricably linked, though scholars have on the whole tried to separate them. Their own culture, far removed from a living rite such as this, has prevented them from seeing that no living rite is likely to conform to neat, logical categories.

The *Anthesteria*, then, was a time of carnival, festivity, and drunkenness; it was also a celebration of the dead; and it was connected with an event in the distant past when, at Athens and through Athens, Orestes had somehow been purged of guilt. All three of these elements are extremely relevant to the drama, and their existence alongside each other in the oldest festival of Dionysus helps to show us the enormously complicated nature of the god.

The most important image for us as we consider the *Anthesteria* is *The Frogs* of Aristophanes, and in particular the frog chorus, whose opening stanza runs as follows:

> *Chorus of Frogs.*
> Brekekekex koahx koahx.
> Brekekekex koahx koahx.
> We are the pond-bogside kids.
> So blow that horn. We've arrived
> Hymn-singing. How d'you like this tune? Some rhythm!
> Koahx koahx.
> Once—oh what a beat we had.
> We sang for the Lord of Life
> Bogside Dionysus' shrine,
> Smashed as a blessed pitcher
> Pouring the blessed liquor,
> We'd rave to the shrine, and we were . . alive . . people.
> Brekekekex koahx koahx.
>
> (209–20)[10]

Dionysus is on his way to Hades, rowing across an unnamed lake. In the normal stories this would be the lake of Acheron, but Aristophanes is careful not to name it here. Dionysus is shown in what must have been a boat on wheels, like the ship-car of the *Anthesteria*. Around him appear the chorus of frogs, who sing that they are the ghosts of the worshipers of Dionysus *en Limnais*. This name of the shrine, 'in the Bogside,' must have referred to a bog that had at one time been there and had no doubt long since been drained. Pun is a way of thought with Aristophanes, as may be seen in Chapter 7. The name of the shrine, which had long since lost its significance, conjured up for him a shape, which would be both funny and mysterious, in which his ghosts could be shown. We are tempted to say, because both Dionysus and the ghosts of his worshipers are presented as caricature, that this sequence is a caricature of the *Anthesteria*. It would be more correct to imagine it as a gargoyle, an image both lyrical and grotesque, as much a part of Dionysiac worship as the gargoyles of a medieval church were part of medieval Christian worship. Aristophanes' image is far larger than any explanations of it that we may offer. We can, however, note that the play, of all those of the fifth century the most concerned with the nature of theatrical experience, presents for one of its climaxes a reminder of that most complex worship of that most complex god, as center and source of all theatrical experience.

The details of the Rural *Dionysia* no doubt varied from place to place. But the central feature of the festival was a procession in which the phallus was carried. Our best impression is again gained from Aristophanes. In *The Acharnians*, Dikaiopolis—Just-City—has concluded a private peace treaty and holds a Rural *Dionysia* all to himself in celebration. His procession is on a small scale because the only people able to take part are himself, his wife, his daughter, and his slave. But the elements of his procession clearly refer to the main elements of the normal festival. First went a girl carrying a basket in which was a consecrated loaf. Part of the ceremonial was to pour over this loaf a kind of thick soup. Behind the basket-girl came the phallus, the image of fertility. Just-City brings up the rear of his procession, presumably standing for both the conductor of the ceremony and the attendant group of revelers. He shouts abuse at his daughter as the revelers would at prominent citizens. The procession culminates in the phallic hymn to Phales, a god whose name derives from the phallus, a rustic version of Dionysus. This hymn, with its combination of lyric intensity, fooling, and eroticism, sums up very well the spirit of a Dionysiac festival.

Just-City. Pleace and blessing. Peace and blessing.

Come virgin with the basket, lead us forth.
Come Xanthias, hold the phallus-pole erect.

Set down the basket, daughter. Let us begin.

Daughter. Hand me the ladle, mother, so that I
May pour the soup over the holy loaf.

Just-City. All shall be well. Lord Dionysus, grant
That this procession be a joy to thee.
And bless this village festival of thine
We celebrate within the family
Free of the war. And grant that my peace treaty
May seem as fine for all the thirty years.

Beautiful daughter, see you bear the basket
Beautifully.
      Look carving knives!
              How blest
Shall be the man who weds you an' gives you kittens
Fair as yourself—when farting at the sunrise.

Proceed.
      Beware. Such crowds! Watch out for tricks.
Someone might nibble your little golden bits.

Xanthias, walk behind the basket-bearer.

Both of you, raise the phallus-pole erect.
I'll follow you, singing the phallic hymn.
Wife, you can watch us from the roof.
                                        Proceed.

(He sings)
Phallique, good friend of Bankios,
Filling the night with parties,
Making love to all the wives
And all the little sweeties,
Join me at my country seat
Home from six years' fighting.
No generals. No fuss. It's all for us—
Peace in a private Blighty.

Phallique, Phallique, it's so much fun
To catch a woodcutter's daughter
Sneaking logs from a highland forest,
Fling my arms around her,
Spread her out on the mountainside
And crack her little walnut.
Phallique, Phallique, have a drink on me,
Have a drink for Hangover Morning.
Down in one gulp from a tankard of peace
As I fasten my shield to the chimney-piece.

                                        (241–79)[11]

The *Lenaia*'s name is most probably derived from a word that means "maenads"[12] and therefore probably centered on an ecstatic dance of women with thyrsi and torches, to the music of *auloi* and *tympana*. It has therefore no doubt connections with the winter dance of the women referred to above. It also featured a phallic procession and abuse of well-known figures. Dramatic competitions at the *Lenaia* were introduced, probably in 442. For the tragic poets the *Lenaia* was a less important competition. For the comic poets, however, victory at the *Lenaia* seems to have been as good as victory at the *Dionysia*. Tragic poets had merely to enter two tragedies instead of the four plays, one being a satyr play, necessary for the City *Dionysia*.

As we should expect with a festival deliberately founded rather than growing unconsciously, the City *Dionysia* is much more straightforward. There is very little argument now as to the course of events during the week of celebrations.[13] The god celebrated was Dionysus of Eleutherai, not *en Limnais*. As Catholics make a distinction when celebrating the Blessed Virgin under varying subtitles, so did the Greeks in celebrating Dionysus. There is a slightly different feel about the way in which the saint or god is thought of on the different occasions.

The festival started with a procession in which the old statue of Dionysus was taken from its temple by the theater into the Agora. There dances were held in front of the statues of the twelve gods, and from there the procession moved out of the city to the village of Eleutherai. After dark the procession returned by torchlight to the precinct of Dionysus. It seems to have been of the same nature as that of the Rural *Dionysia,* only of course much more splendid. It was probably headed by the girl carrying the basket with the sacred loaf; it certainly included the phallus. An important role was played by the ephebes, the young men of military age, who escorted a bull for sacrifice. Also taking part were the metics, the resident aliens of Athens, wearing ceremonial robes of scarlet. The participants in the dramatic contests were also in the procession. The *choregoi* vied with each other in the splendor of their own robes as well as of those in which they had dressed their actors and chorus. The climax of the procession was the sacrifice of the bull to Dionysus in the precinct, perhaps in the theater itself. The statue of Dionysus remained in the theater throughout the performances. Also included in the festival celebrations was a *kōmos*—a revel—something much less organized than the procession. Most probably this happened at the end of the festival week. Alternatively, it may have taken place in the evening of the day of the procession.

The rest of the festival took five days. On each day a comedy was performed in the evening.[14] The rest of the time was filled on three days by the four plays submitted by the selected three tragic poets. The other two days saw the dithyrambic competition—five boys' choruses on one day, five men's choruses on the other. The dithyrambic competitions were tribal. Each tribe selected two *choregoi,* one for boys and one for men. The *choregos* then selected his poet and *aulos*-player, who did not, however, have to be members of the tribe. Indeed it is interesting that many of the successful dithyrambic poets during the fifth century were not Athenians. The dithyramb, originally a riotous dramatic dance, was now a much more stately performance. It was sung by a chorus of fifty, with relatively little movement. Since each chorus was selected from within one tribe, it is likely that they were much more amateur than the choruses for the drama. The competition was more musical than dramatic, though clearly it would be important that the groupings and costumes should be beautiful. At some point in the proceedings, selection was made so that each tribe sent in only either a man's or a boy's chorus, but not both.

It was the rule that the tragic poets should enter four plays, one of which had to be a satyr play: this was usually, though not necessarily the fourth to be shown. Poets who wished to compete sent their plays in to the archon in charge of the festival, who decided which poet should be "granted a chorus." *Choregoi* were selected from among the wealthy citizens. The duty was one of the public offices that it was necessary for the rich to perform when selected, unless they could point to someone richer than themselves.[15] The *choregos* acted as producer, being responsible for hiring the chorus, the *aulos*-player, the mute extras, and the trainer for the chorus if the poet either required an assistant or, as happened later, relinquished this work to a specialist. The *choregos* also paid for the costumes and the masks, the training of the chorus, and their accommodation under one roof while they were being trained.[16] Once it was no longer the custom for the poet himself to act, the actors were chosen by the state—that is, by the archon in charge of the festival. This no doubt was settled about 449, at the time of the first competition for actors. Presumably then the three principal actors were allotted to the three poets by lot. Probably each principal actor chose his own second and third actors.

A few days before the festival, the *proagōn* took place in the Odeion, next to the theater.[17] The competing poets appeared with their *choregoi,* and with the actors wearing wreaths and in their robes, but unmasked. The poet described the plays he was about to present and gave a short outline of the stories.

During the festival the proceedings started each day at dawn. Throughout the heyday of Athens's power it was a major opportunity for demonstrating the glory of Athens to the world, and it was customary to display the tribute from the allies in the theater. Before the plays the orphan children of men who had fallen in battle for Athens paraded in the theater fully armed to mark their year of reaching military age. At some stage in the festival honors would be given to distinguished citizens and foreigners. There was a public holiday for the complete duration of the festival, and no one could engage in legal proceedings. Even prisoners were released on bail to attend the performances. After the festival a special assembly was held to debate its conduct, and to allow any complaints to be aired.

Considerable care was taken over the selection of the judges. First, the Council chose a list of names from each of the ten tribes. At this stage it was clearly possible for the *choregoi* to bring pressure that certain people should be chosen. But then each tribe's set of names was placed in a sealed urn bearing the tribe's name, and it was an offence punishable by death to tamper with the urns. At the beginning of the competition, the ten urns were placed in the theater, and the archon drew one name from each. The ten people whose names were drawn swore to give an impartial verdict, though no doubt they were influenced sometimes by popular applause and no doubt there were sometimes attempts at bribery. At the end of the competition, each judge wrote his order of merit on a tablet, which was placed with the others in an urn. Five tablets were then drawn from the urn at random, and it was these that gave the decision. The winners were then crowned in the theater, and the final task of the *choregos* was to provide the victory party. Though the poets selected to compete were paid, there is no evidence that the winner received any extra money.[18] The victorious leading actor, however, was automatically selected for the next year's competition.

The greatest instances of civic enthusiasm in the modern world pale before the religious and civic enthusiasm of the Athenians. The price of a theater ticket was two obols. An average laborer's daily wage was three obols, which meant that a theater ticket was a considerable expense, though late in the fifth century a fund seems to have been provided so that the poorest people could enter free.[19] Demosthenes says that the Athenians spent much more on festivals than they ever spent on naval expeditions.[20] Rich citizens were quite frequently known to volunteer for services such as *choregia.* And some *choregoi* spent their entire estate on the festival.[21] Demosthenes' speech, *Against Meidias,* accusing him of interfering with his performance of *choregia,*is an invaluable piece of evidence. It shows us the grandeur of the occasion and the expense incurred by the *choregos.* It shows us, above all, the sacredness of the festival. Even *choreutai* are exempt from military service (13). They too are ministers of the god. Demosthenes, however, goes even further than that. Meidias has attempted to destroy the costumes Demosthenes has had made and the gold crowns that he and his colleagues will wear in the procession. This Demosthenes calls sacrilege, since the costume is sacred raiment. Here we may feel that Demosthenes is stretching the law as far as he can. But he is able to quote instances where the Athenians had voted the death penalty for someone who had struck his personal enemy in the theater (180) or had ejected someone from his seat (178). Of such importance was it that the auditorium should not be disturbed and that the sacred competition should proceed at all times with decorum.

An extremely hard-fought competition, success in which guaranteed the winner enormous prestige; ostentatious display of Athens to the world; a week's carnival; ecstatic worship of the lord of life and death, the power behind nature, at the moment in the year when nature seems dead; these are some of the implications of the festivals of Dionysus. These elements helped to shape the plays that we possess and should be borne in mind as we consider how to stage them. But the most essential element of the festival, and the one hardest for us to bear in mind, is the multifaceted personality of the god Dionysus, for whom both festival and plays were made. If the worship of Dionysus is ecstatic dancing through which the dancer becomes possessed by the god, and if at the same time the god's festival consists of plays, then the justification for these plays is that somehow through them we in the audience also may become possessed by the god—initiates.

A glimpse of what this meant to the Athenians is provided by a joke in *The Frogs* (140–41, 270) that carries enormous reverberations of meaning. Dionysus is about to go down to Hades. He is told by Heracles that he will have to pay his fare to Charon, the ferryman. This will be two obols. Now the fare in traditional mythology for a corpse was one obol only; the point of the joke is that two obols is the price of a theater ticket. The reference to the two obols is repeated when Dionysus finally hands over his fare, having crossed into Hades (270). We must not be allowed to miss Aristophanes' point. We might say in a sense that it is a return fare; Dionysus is in Hades alive. He is like the second chorus of the play, who will soon appear: the initiates in the mysteries, the people who are alive among the dead. The act of paying one's two obols is in a sense a kind of initiation by which we enter the kingdom of the dead and still live. The earlier conversation with Heracles continues by Dionysus asking how the two obols got down to Hades, and Heracles saying that Theseus took them down (143). Theseus was the particular hero of Athens, who was supposed to have descended to Hades alive and returned. The line almost implies: it was Athens who took the two obols down, Athens who introduced theater tickets to Hades. The joke reverberates further: we Athenians, by virtue of our privilege as Athenians, as members of the audience of the theater of Dionysus, can for only two obols enter the world of death, and, like Theseus, come back to life again, since we are initiates. This is the strongest possible definition of the theatrical experience, that it is an actual initiation.

The Beginnings of Greek Drama

The origins of all drama lie in worship, a fact patently obvious from study of the Greek plays, or modern Western drama, derived as it is from the miracle cycles and ultimately from the Mass. Western drama, however, whether in Spain, France, or England, reached its apogee of creativity outside the church building. The drama of Dionysus stayed for longer within the confines of the worship of Dionysus. Its greatest period of creativity took place when the drama still happened, as it were, inside the church building. This is the uniqueness of Greek drama: we possess forty-three plays of the greatest possible diversity that belong to the period when the drama was obviously a part of worship.

Another kind of study than this would require to spend much longer on the other Mediterranean races that clearly possessed some kind of dramatic ritual. But we are concerned with the kind of questions that can be explored in conditions of performance, and none of these races' drama survives in enough quantity for us to ask meaningful questions. Without a doubt Canaanites, Hittites, and Egyptians possessed some sort of dramatic ritual long before the Greeks. Elements of an obvious fertility ritual appear in several texts. One such is the Canaanite *Poem of Dawn and Sunset.*[22] After certain ceremonial actions—lopping the vine, cooking a kid in milk, and bringing on the statues of the goddesses Asherat and the virgin Anat—a hymn is sung. Then the supreme god, El, represented as an old man, comes on to fetch water for cooking. He is seen by two girls, who are excited by his liveliness. El puts down his stick and staff, no doubt the symbols of his old age. Shooting an arrow into the air, he kills a bird, which he buries. He then attempts to seduce the girls. They are not quite sure if he is courting or adopting them and call him "Father" and "Husband" alternately. An erotic scene follows in which he lies with them both, making them pregnant with Dawn and Sunset. Later the women describe their encounter with El to their husband, and later still the children are born. They are miraculous babies and have to be suckled by the goddesses, since they have enormous appetites. Small fragment though this is, there seems no doubt of three things: that this piece involved some community ceremony; that the story is an attempt to explain the way things are; and that its presentation is boisterous and even farcical.

It is possible that dramatic rituals were being celebrated in Egypt as long ago as 4000 B.C., and they were certainly taking place in 3200 B.C. The most famous of these is the so-called Abydos Passion Play, or the Osiris Passion Play. This is a reenactment of the story of the god Osiris, his death and dismemberment, and the reassembling of his limbs by Isis, his wife and sister, and Horus, his son. There is argument about the interpretation of the hieroglyphics, but it seems reasonably certain that there were short speeches in character, and some audience participation in the reenactment of mock battles.[23]

Granted the obvious indebtedness of Greek sculpture to Egyptian sculpture, it is almost inconceivable that Egyptian drama had no influence on Greek drama. Herodotus in his *Histories* describes two semidramatic ceremonials that he saw during his visit to Egypt soon after 460 B.C. At Papremis the priests of the temple arm themselves with clubs on a certain day at sunset and stand guard outside the temple. Opposite them stand more than a thousand men, also with clubs. On the day before the festival the image of the god has been taken away in a small wooden shrine covered with plates of gold. Now, this is put on a four-wheeled car and dragged back to its temple while the two opposing sides fight with their clubs, the priests helping the image back into the temple, the others opposing it. Herodotus thought that some people even died, though the Egyptians insisted that no one was killed (2.63). Herodotus also describes processions to Dionysus (2.48) exactly the same as in Greece except that the Egyptians do not carry the phallus but pull large images of the god about with strings; nor do they have choruses dancing. Herodotus very confidently derives the Dionysiac ceremonials entirely from Egypt (2.49). This is of course false. Herodotus exaggerates the cultural importance of Egypt with the same inverted snobbery that made Englishmen of the last hundred years attribute everything civilized to Frenchmen or Italians. Greek drama cannot directly owe its origin to an Egyptian influence, since there is no evidence that the dancing chorus, the essential element of Greek drama, was found except among Greeks. But given the richness of Egyptian civilization, it is quite likely that some elements of Egyptian performances may have been transported to Greece, or even directly copied.

Semidramatic rituals such as Herodotus describes are common to many primitive cultures. Certainly most of the Mediterranean races show something similar. What is special to the Greeks is the extent to which their early rituals involved dance. Furthermore, from very early times, the Greeks possessed a mythology far more vividly characterized than that of most other races. Whether these two things depend on one another we cannot say. All that we can say is that from very early times the Greeks had at their command a considerable number of mimetic dances with which to celebrate seedtime, harvest, or weddings, and that also from early times the dancing seemed to develop as a way of telling stories. A beautiful description of some of these early dances is found in the story of the making of Achilles' shield. The poet's imagination runs away with him, and he describes not so much a piece of metalwork as the scenes that the metalwork represented.[24]

As we consider the development of these dances into the diversity of fifth-century drama, it is fundamental to remember the nature of Dionysus as both god of fertility and god of the dead. We now have enough evidence to trace the story in adequate detail, and our evidence agrees with the account given by Aristotle in the *Poetics*. (4. 1449A.9). Drama developed from improvisations between a chorus and its leader. The origin of tragedy was the dithyramb, that of comedy the phallic song. At first it was a satyric thing with short plots and dialogue that got laughs. The basic meter was the tetrameter because it was full of dancing. When speech was introduced, so was the iambic, which is the meter appropriate to speech. Tragedy then became more dignified.[25] Aristotle also alludes to a tradition that credits the Dorians with having discovered both tragedy and comedy.[26]

With the benefit of recent archaeological evidence, we can now expand this story somewhat. The cult of Dionysus is as old as Greek history, dating back to Mycenean and Minoan times. But at intervals the cult experienced revivals, and these revivals went with developments in the worship. The special forms of Dionysiac worship involved dances of girls as maenads, and men in grotesquely padded costumes. These dances of fat men have an obvious fertility significance. There is, further, a very close connection between the fat men and the mythical creatures called satyrs, spirits of the woods, half man and half beast, always associated with the worship of Dionysus. The animal elements in these creatures seem to have been mostly goat, though in some early pictures there are horse elements also.[27] We may assume that men would dress in the padded costume when representing satyrs. Artists, however, developed a tradition of showing satyrs as creatures half man and half beast, principally goat. Later, as the dances became more and more representational drama rather than pure ceremonial, a satyr costume, similar to the artists' imaginings of a satyr, was employed for the performance.

The connection of Dionysus and his fat men or satyrs with the cult of the dead also seems to derive from earliest times.[28] It is possible to find the beginnings of drama in the alternations between leader and chorus that made up the normal lament for a dead man, as, for example, at the funeral of Patroclus, when Achilles led the lament.[29] That this ceremony had an effect on the final form of Greek tragedy cannot be doubted, simply from the emphasis on death in tragedy, and the number of actual laments.

Aristotle says that tragedy originated with the dithyramb. The first mention of this comes in a two-line fragment of Archilochos, the Greek lyric poet of Paros, who flourished in the first half of the seventh century B.C.

> Dionysiac dithyrambs—I lead 'em fine,
> When my wits have been thunderstruck with wine.
>
> (Frag. 77)

A new inscriptional life of Archilochos has recently been discovered.[30] From it we learn that Archilochos tried to introduce a fertility cult of Dionysus into Paros. The men of Paros opposed him and went sterile. When they consulted the Delphic oracle about this they were told to honor Archilochos and presumably to introduce his cult. The inscription ends with a very fragmented poem of Archilochos that mentions Dionysus, unripe grapes, honeysweet figs, and a fertility spirit called Oipholios.

At the end of the seventh century we hear of a poet in Corinth called Arion who developed the dithyramb considerably. He seems to have introduced the satyr mask and costume of shaggy loincloth with phallus and tail as a result of which the dances became known as *tragikoi choroi*—goat dances. The dances of fat men, however, continued also.

It may have been Arion who contributed the most important element of all to the dithyramb, and indeed to Greek drama as a whole, the system of matching *strophē* and *antistrophē* discussed in detail in Chapter 5. By the time of Stesichoros, who lived sometime between 640 and 560 B.C., this technique was well developed. Stesichoros wrote a lyric version of the *Oresteia* in two parts of perhaps 1,000 lines each. Unfortunately, very little of it survives. This considerable work was not a dithyramb, since it was accompanied by the lyre, not the *aulos*. It is usually thought that the strophic system was originally conceived for the dithyramb, since it is in the drama that grew out of the dithyramb where it reaches its greatest heights of subtlety. But it came to dominate every form of public sung and danced poetry. In contrast, the hymns of Pindar are often monostrophic: a stanza's pattern is repeated a number of times, something that occurs only very rarely in the drama, and usually only in the context of a hymn, as in the hymn of the initiates to Dionysus in *The Frogs* (399–416). The hymns of Pindar probably involved relatively little movement. It was mainly a matter of repeating a tune to different words. The essence of the system as used in drama, or in the predramatic dances, is that both tune and movement pattern are repeated to different words. This is the root and center of Greek drama. We do not know how it began. But symmetrical movement, first to one side and then to another, seems basic to human beings. We have only to look at children's games. It is also obvious that it could easily hold a ritual significance.

If it was Arion who developed the system, Aristotle's allusion to the Dorians having originated tragedy makes obvious sense. Even in the fifth century the Athenian poets wrote Dorian vowel sounds into the parts of the drama that were sung, just as English pop singers of today mostly sing with a kind of American accent, because Dorian Greek and American English have vowel sounds that are better for singing. The early developments about which we hear are all from the Dorian parts of Greece. There is, for example, the story told by Herodotus in his *Histories* of how Cleisthenes, tyrant of Sicyon in the first third of the sixth century, took the dances that had been held in honor of

Adrastus, and "gave them back" to Dionysus (5.67). We should assume that at this time dramatic dances performed by fat men or satyrs in honor of the dead or Dionysus, or both, were relatively common in several cities of Greece.

A little later, in the middle of the sixth century, an Athenian dancer-poet called Thespis, touring the country with dramatic dances similar to those of Arion, introduced episodes in spoken verse into his performances, spoken from a temporary stage, probably a wagon. The iambic verse form had become familiar to Athenian poets in the previous generation; the poet-lawgiver Solon, who had shaped the constitution of Athens, had written extensively in this meter. His poetry, concerned with moral and political behavior, may well have influenced the new drama, which would also share his moral and political concern.[31]

There is a tradition that Thespis introduced the use of a mask, which I find unlikely. For if there were no masks until Thespis, why did the chorus wear masks? Traditions also have it that Thespis painted his face with white lead, and that he and his fellow performers smeared their faces with wine leaves. As far as we can see from the vase paintings, satyrs tend to have red faces and maenads white faces. It would seem more likely that the custom of dancing masked or with a face smeared with paint is very old indeed. The object of the dance is to lose one's individual personality in the group ecstasy. Alternatively, the mask may have been introduced at the moment when the dances of the maenads started to be performed by men dressed as women, instead of by girls, a change that seems to have come about during the eighth and seventh centuries. Certainly it would seem likely that the satyr costume introduced by Arion must have included a mask, since satyrs are always shown with animal ears. Thespis, however, would have needed to show the different characters of his story. And so for the first time his mask would need to be a character mask. In this sense, he may well be the inventor of such masks.

If we have properly cleared our imaginations of neoclassicist white marble, and keep instead before our eyes such pictures of Greek ceremonial as the phallic procession of *The Acharnians* already referred to, there is no especial difficulty about this story. For nearly a hundred years scholars have, however, argued about it at great length. These arguments have contributed to the clutter of misconceptions with which our unthinking imaginations cannot help approaching Greek drama. First, there have been the various theories that derive Greek tragedy from the death of the year-god, something like the Osiris drama. Alternatively it has been suggested that it began with the cult of dead heroes. As they stand these theories have long been discarded, since they center on the sufferings of a hero, and there are no heroes in the extant Greek tragedies—understandably enough since the form began as a group dance. But provided that there is no attempt to derive tragedy from anything other than the central chorus dance, we can say that there may well be elements in it of the basic fertility theme, the death and rebirth of the year. There are certainly elements connected with the actual lament for the dead. And these two elements are reasonably expected in a rite that celebrates Dionysus, god of fertility and death.

Second, there has been considerable argument over Aristotle's remark, mentioned earlier, that tragedy developed out of the satyric. The argument takes various forms, but it is based on an attitude of mind that conceives anything called "satyric" as funny and grotesque; anything called "tragedy" as noble and solemn. It is worth quoting two passages from Pickard-Cambridge: "It is extraordinarily difficult to suppose that the noble seriousness of tragedy can have grown so rapidly, or even at all, out of the ribald satyr drama."[32] While discussing the choruses to honor Adrastus in Sicyon, he writes: "It is almost inconceivable that these tragic choruses, having reference to the sufferings of the hero, should have been performed by ithyphallic demons with the limbs of goats."[33] Such statements reveal the limitations of the culture within which Pickard-Cambridge wrote. The ithyphallic demons dance as appropriately for the hero's sufferings as the demons of the Middle Ages cling grotesquely to the capitals of cathedrals. Furthermore, as we consider the tragedy of the fifth century, we shall see that, although it is extremely serious, there are several scenes to be played for laughs. I have alluded before to those scholars and critics who have confused the drama of Aeschylus with the Tragedy of the Renaissance, because, by writing away from the theater, they have ignored his theatricality: his humor, his stage effects, and, above all, his dance.

Books on the origins of Greek drama almost invariably spend considerably more time on the origins of tragedy than on those of comedy, partly because more emotion has been involved in discussions of tragedy than of comedy. Aristotle derives comedy from the phallic songs. It is generally agreed that the name implies that it grew out of the kōmos, the revel. The details of how this developed are hard to discover, but the general outline is clear. Comedy, like tragedy, grew out of a choral performance. The participants were masked and in costume, often dressed as animals of various sorts. The surviving pictures show a great variety: birds, fish, knights on horseback, giants on stilts, ugly women, men wrapped in cloaks, as well as fat men and satyrs. It seems that this performance may have been more in the nature of a dance along a street, rather than a dance in one place. Aristophanes' plays contain three sequences that are clearly traditional: parodos, agōn, and parabasis. From the way in which these are used we can detect roughly the original form: in the parodos the chorus dance in, or dance along the street. They then meet either an individual or another chorus. The result is the agōn, the contest. When one or the other has won, the chorus turn to the audience, probably dancing more or less on the spot, for some direct words to them; this turning aside being the parabasis. Essential to the performance is the mockery of prominent individuals; originally no doubt an imprecation against evil spirits. The entire performance was chanted to aulos accompaniment, and the dancing was of the basic sort that accompanies tetrameters: iambic, trochaic, or anapestic.[34] All the other elements of Old Comedy could have developed parallel with the development of tragedy, so that iambic scenes and lyric dances were added before, after, and eventually even in the middle of the traditional elements derived from the *kōmos*.[35]

It will be apparent from this short discussion that the evidence at our disposal presents a clearer story than the scholars' interpretations. Almost all the difficulties that have been created have arisen through theorists who have attempted to derive their idea of Tragedy from the dance of Archilochos. This is perhaps a point to emphasize that when I say "tragedy" without a capital "T" I mean simply a play entered for the tragic competition in the festivals of Dionysus at Athens, that when I say "comedy" I mean simply a play entered for the comic competitions, and when I say "satyric" I do not wish to imply anything more than that satyrs were involved in the performance. We should not expect to be able to encompass the secret of the three types of fifth-century drama with our definitions. All that we can hope to do is to imagine a little more clearly the plays in the context of the festival of which they were part: a carnival, a display of the city to the world, and a religious rite. These three elements clearly relate to elements in the development of tragedy from the original dithyramb: that it was a riotous dance; that it acquired political significance at Sicyon to such an extent that a new tyrant must change its outlet, and it acquired further political intensity by adopting the meter of Solon's political philosophy; above all, that it was first and foremost a rite of worship, a way to become in touch with the god. At this stage it is worth pursuing each of these three aspects a little further in detail.

Drama for Carnival Week

The climax of Aeschylus' *Suppliants* is a wild dance of attempted rape, probably involving a hundred dancers.[36] Greek drama of the fifth century gives opportunity for every sort of colorful stage effect and appeals to all the primitive emotions. Such effects and such emotionalism detract from the deep seriousness of the poets' commitments and the audience's involvement in no way whatsoever, any more than the joyous theatrical flamboyance of the miracle cycles interferes with the driving purpose of showing God's will for man. From Aristotle to T. S. Eliot there have been learned and refined men who have aligned good taste with a lack of flamboyance and encouraged us to prefer what is ponderous and uncolorful for its supposed greater seriousness. This alignment has nothing whatsoever to do with the work of most of the great poets, and certainly nothing whatsoever to do with the Greeks. But the effects of pseudoscholarship are so strong at this moment that it is necessary to spend a little time emphasizing the carnival aspect of the festivals of Dionysus and the way in which this affected the composition of the plays.

Aristotle wrote in the passage discussed above that tragedy evolved from the satyric, and from diction that got laughs. This immediately follows his remarks about Aeschylus' and Sophocles' contribution to tragedy—increasing the number of actors. It is therefore possible that Aristotle's reference to the way tragedy evolved out of the satyric may refer to developments in tragedy since the death of Sophocles. That is the natural way to take his sentences. At any rate, study of the existing plays confirms that tragedy was very closely connected with the satyric for most of the fifth century.

Pratinas, a poet about whom we know almost nothing, was a man clearly devoted to satyr plays. He appears to have been responsible for the rule that each tragic poet must include in his entry one play with the genuine "tragic" chorus, that is, a goat chorus of satyrs. In the muddled condition of our critical concepts at the moment, it is important that we should not theorize from this that tragedy had become too dignified and that the audience wanted some farce, because there is no evidence that tragedy had become too dignified, and it is wrong to define satyr plays as farces. It is perfectly sufficient to say that Pratinas' move was passed because the Greeks in 509 wanted the festival to contain the original and central element of their drama—the chorus of fertility spirits in goatskin. The presence of this reminder of the origins of their drama colors all the great drama of the fifth century and affects the whole of Greek thought. Ion of Chios declared that virtue, like the four plays of the tragic poets, requires a satyric element.[37]

The body of critical opinion, which has tried to solemnify the work of Aeschylus and his colleagues into tedious monotone, would perhaps agree with the preceding paragraph but say that the point of the satyr play was to drain the dross of revelry from the festival offering and keep it separate. Such a position could be maintained only by ignoring Aeschylus' *Suppliants*.[38] Recent papyrus discoveries have helped to break this attitude further. We are now in a position to reconstruct the outline of Aeschylus' trilogy on the story of Perseus. The three plays are *The Net-Haulers*, *Phorcides*, and *Polydectes*. The story is that King Acrisius was warned that if his daughter Danae bore a son, the son would kill him. Consequently he immured her, but she was visited by Zeus in a shower of golden rain. When Acrisius discovered that Danae had given birth, he put her out to sea in a chest. She was, however, washed up on the shore of another country. She was looked after by the king of that country, Polydectes, who fell in love with her. In order to pursue his plan of marrying her, he sent her son Perseus, now grown-up, to fetch the head of Medusa the Gorgon, in the hopes that Perseus would be turned to stone by the Gorgon's glance. With the help of Athene, however, Perseus succeeded in cutting off Medusa's head. On his return, Polydectes looked at the head of the Gorgon and was turned to stone. The first play must have presented the arrival of Danae and the infant Perseus on shore in the chest; the second, the slaying of the Gorgon. The daughters of Phorcis are the Graiae, the old hags who are sisters and guardians of the Gorgons, three sisters who were born old women and possessed between them one eye and one tooth. The third play, presumably, presented the confrontation between Perseus and Polydectes and possibly the accidental killing of Acrisius. We possess nothing of the second or third play, and therefore we cannot be too sure of the events depicted. But Aristotle mentions the *Phorcides* and *Prometheus* as a special genre of tragedy together with those plays set in Hades. This and what we know of the story certainly suggest a strong element of the grotesque. But, much more important, we now possess two fragments of *The Net-Haulers,* which show that the chest with Danae inside was hauled up out of the sea on stage by a chorus of satyrs. A later fragment shows that an attempt is made to seduce or even rape Danae, probably by Silenus, the father of the satyrs.[39] Beauty chased by satyr lust is a common theme in satyr plays. What is unusual is that this is the first play in Aeschylus' group.[40] Confronted with this we cannot say that the satyric element was kept separate from the tragedies. Considering the nature of the festival, and the way in which tragedy had evolved, there is no reason why we should try to separate them.[41]

I have refused to define *satyric* because that is precisely something we cannot do. The satyrs answered to an aspect of the common Greek religious experience. They were part of the data of being alive at the time. The nearest analogy would seem to be the medieval gargoyle. The medieval Christian might say that gargoyles were necessary as part of his worldview because the nature of the world is such that it frequently appears to be a vast practical joke. Or he might say that the gargoyle was necessary because laughter is one of the most intimate means of human relationship, and unless we can laugh at or with the power or powers that rule the world we cannot relate fully to them. But such statements are only attempts to confine a living element of a once living religion within dead analysis. We should certainly notice that the satyrs are in a sense our lower instincts, carried to excess. They are lustful, lazy, greedy, and cowardly. They are the beast in us—wild, beautiful dancers, uncontrolled. Their father, however, is Silenus, a fat, drunken, lecherous old man. Even today, in our sophisticated society, we sometimes meet men or women who have let themselves go completely to seed. Fat, incompetently lecherous, drunken and debauched—there is something marvelous about them. Their total pursuit of pleasure mocks our desires. We think also of the unique portrayal of this character in Falstaff. Fat rogue as he is, there is something godlike about him. He is of the earth.

As we contemplate the drama of the fifth century, we must never forget the satyrs, since it is their dance that is at the center of the drama. The satyric element involves four things that are also obvious elements in any large popular carnival: drunkenness, sexuality, laughter, and marvelous happenings. These we would expect at a festival in Greece. Elements of these we can find in the extant plays. We must also remember that the only complete plays of Aeschylus and Sophocles we possess are the selection made by the decorous Byzantine schoolmasters for their pupils to study. In the extant plays there is enough of the satyric. But it is likely that the plays not selected would have been more rambunctious and bawdy. This impression is confirmed when we look at some of the fragments.

Although it is not his most important attribute, Dionysus was the god of wine. Drunkenness was regarded as a state of "being high," a state of desirable release, to be cultivated, not something to be condemned, as it is in a Puritan culture. Aristotle wrote a treatise on drunkenness.[42] Chamaeleon said that Aeschylus wrote his tragedies when drunk, and we learn elsewhere in Athenaeus of the delight with which Aeschylus showed men on stage drunk, although Athenaeus also says that Aeschylus was the first to do this—in the *Cabiri.*[43] This was a play about the first stop of the Argonauts on their voyage, at Lemnos, seat of worship of the Cabiri, the ancient earth gods, who were apparently the chorus. The Argonauts were provided with lavish hospitality and abundance of wine, and the result was some sort of drunken scene. But the presence of the old gods on stage suggests something much more mysterious than a mere drunken orgy. The play is surely more likely to have shown a mystical high on wine, which a later age, more restricted by decorum, would have hardly understood. But Aeschylus also wrote *The Bone-Gatherers,* which has always worried scholars devoted to an idea of an Aeschylus who wrote like Corneille. Athenaeus describes how Aeschylus makes his ancient Greeks so drunk that they break chamber pots over each other's heads, and quotes the following speech from the play:

> Here is the man who made me a laughing stock
> Hurling that foul malodorous chamber pot
> Unerringly at me. On my head it struck,
> Shattered and shipwrecked into little pieces
> Breathing a perfume not of frankincense.

(1. 17C)

Here it seems that the sequence has no more significance than Aeschylus' theatrical delight in a drunk scene. The obvious excessiveness of these two scenes from plays that do not survive should make us look again at the sequence in the *Alcestis* when Heracles staggers out of the guest chamber, where he has been feasting while the household mourns Alcestis' death. (773 ff.). The theatricality of the play will be strengthened if this scene is played very broad—grotesque farce, in contrast to the sadness of what has gone before and what will follow. The dialogue suggests that Heracles is behaving excessively. The speech of the servant preceding his entrance (747–72) describes in no uncertain terms the amount he has drunk. And Heracles himself appears to be attempting to seduce the servant (790–91). Once we realize that scenes such as these are natural to fifth-century drama, we can allow the scene to find its natural theatrical level, which will be grotesque drunken farce, a scene well in keeping with one of the standard images of Heracles, such as is shown in *The Frogs* (38–165, 460–673). One of the excitements of this beautiful play is that it is this drunken, lecherous, slightly grotesque muscleman who brings back the silent Alcestis from the dead, his crude vitality balancing her sad self-sacrifice of total, humble devotion.

It would be surprising if a drama such as that of the fifth century did not deal with sex. Athenaeus refers to the fact that some have called tragedy "pederasty" since the erotic is so prominent a theme. Sophocles, described as a man "devoted to enjoyment" who pointed to his self-control only as an old man when his powers were failing, was particularly fond of young boys, while Euripides was fonder of women and adultery.[44] The plays Athenaeus cites as particularly erotic are the *Niobe* of Sophocles, involving the beautiful children of Niobe, and *The Myrmidons* of Aeschylus, in which the love of Achilles and Patroclus is presented as definitely sexual. No fragment longer than a line survives from the *Niobe*, but Athenaeus quotes two lines from Achilles' address to the corpse of Patroclus in *The Myrmidons:*

> You've scorned the holy ceremony of our thighs,
> So ungrateful for all my many kisses.[45]

We should also take note of the apparent outline of Sophocles' play, *The Lemnian Women.* There is very little to go on, but there seems no doubt as to the main events that must have been portrayed. The play concerns the arrival of the ship *Argo* at Lemnos. Aphrodite had punished the women of Lemnos for neglecting her worship and had made them offensive to their husbands, who had then neglected them and brought over girls from Thrace. In revenge the women had killed their husbands. Now they met the *Argo* in full armor and prevented the Argonauts from landing except on the promise that they would have sexual intercourse with them.[46] We must not press our scanty knowledge too far, but it is interesting to speculate as to what Sophocles' choreographic talent would have made of the dance of the girls in armor, and the battle. The conclusion of the play can hardly have failed to give his talents for erotic imagery full scope.

It would be surprising indeed if a people as interested in the erotic as the Athenians produced a drama free of erotic elements. Apart from fragments, there are several extant plays that emphasize the erotic. There is the powerful imagery of the dance to Love in the *Antigone* (781–801).[47] There is Sophocles' *Women of Trachis,* and Euripides' *Medea* and *Hippolytus,* three plays whose central theme is erotic passion, whose language is full of sexual imagery, and whose scenes reveal great insights into sexual psychology. As we might expect, however, it is in the dances of the chorus that erotic imagery has greatest freedom. This has allowed critics who have ignored the dance to underestimate the power of this imagery. It would be difficult to escape from the sexual power of the *Antigone* chorus properly danced. It is certainly impossible to ignore the flagrant eroticism of Aeschylus' *Suppliants,* girls ripe as summer fruit (998), or the assault on our sexual imaginations of the rape scene (825 ff).

If the Greek plays are studied without reference to theatrical performance, there is a tendency to play down both the amount of theatrical effects they require, and the flamboyant imaginations of the poets who created them. If a carnival audience is to be kept in very uncomfortable seats from dawn till dusk, it needs marvels to keep its mind from straying. There are plenty of such marvels in the extant plays: Medea's departure in a flying chariot of the Sun (1317–1414); the thunder and lightning with which the manifestation of Diony- sus is accompanied in the so-called palace miracle in the *Bacchants* (576–603);[48] and the end of the *Prometheus Bound.*[49] These are not only exciting stage effects. They are theatrical marvels presented as an image of the fact that the real world is full of marvels, to an audience that believed in the likelihood of a marvel happening to them. The world of the Greek plays is not a world of statuesque white marble, but of gold and glitter, men and spirits whirling in a dance.

This impression can be helped by considering a few more fragments. With *The Persians* in 472 Aeschylus presented the *Phineus* as second play. That year he presented four separate plays, not a connected tetralogy. Of the *Phineus* a synopsis survives. The Argonauts arrive at the home of Phineus, the blind prophet. His blindness was no doubt part of some divine punishment, and in addition the gods sent against him the Harpies, winged female creatures who swooped down and snatched his food away before he could eat it, and left what food they did not take smelling so foul that it was uneatable. The Argonauts asked Phineus for advice about their voyage. This he refused to give until they had driven the Harpies away. Accordingly, the Argonauts laid out a banquet as bait. When the Harpies swooped down to eat it, the sons of the North Wind, Zetes and Calais, drew their swords and chased them through the air. Given that Aeschylus could make use of a vast double chorus in *The Suppliants,* it is possible that the final confrontation of the *Phineus* is also between two cho- ruses, of Argonauts and Harpies, in a violent dance involving use of the *mēchanē.* Alternatively, since the synopsis mentions Zetes and Calais, we may assume a dance involving merely them and a leading Harpy, making use of the *mēchanē.* Whatever the details, there seems indubitably to have been a violent theatrical denouement.

There seems little doubt that Sophocles presented in his *Tereus* the trans- formation of Tereus into a hoopoe as the culmination of his story of rape and cannibalism. The play is caricatured in Aristophanes' *Birds,* when the two comics meet the Hoopoe for the first time (92–106). They are confronted with a bedraggled, mock-heroic figure, with a triple crest but only a few feathers—a bird in moult. His beak is ridiculous. It is specifically said that this is what Sophocles did (100–101). Naturally, Aristophanes creates the bedragglement; we need not assume that Sophocles made a tawdry effect. But there can be no doubt that Sophocles showed a man-hoopoe on stage, a man with a birdmask, beaked. And therefore Sophocles took delight in miraculous transformations, as we should expect from any master of the theater such as he was. Sophocles enjoyed magic, as we see from the short fragments of *The Root-Cutters,* a play about Medea and her spells. Fragment 534, probably a messenger speech, presents a very strong atmosphere with its vivid description of Medea hiding in her basket the roots she has been cutting with her bronze sickle, "naked, and shrieking girlish cries."[50]

The comedy of Aristophanes is not called comedy because it contains laughs, and though its form is a kind of rhythm of laughter,[51] yet laughter is not its whole purpose. For part of its purpose is worship, and at the center of all the fifth-century plays there are hymns to the gods where laughter has no place. Comedy is so called because it is derived from the *kōmos*. If we do not define comedy in terms of laughter, then there is no reason to exclude laughter from the tragedies. The tragic poets were not writing Tragedy as understood by the Renaissance.

That the tone of several of Euripides' plays is, in the modern sense of the word, comic, few would deny. In works of criticism it is customary to refer to Euripides' tragicomedies, meaning plays such as the *Helen, Ion* or *Iphigeneia in Tauris*. This is allowable, for example, in a discussion of how Euripides developed a new kind of play form that paved the way for New Comedy a hundred years later. But we must not allow ourselves to forget that to the fifth century they were tragedies like all the other tragedies, plays accepted and applauded as entries for the tragic competition.[52]

With the exception of these plays by Euripides and the *Prometheus Bound* and the *Antigone*, all of which will be discussed further, the scene in a tragedy most obviously to be played for laughs is the arming of Iolaus in Euripides' *Children of Heracles* (720–47). Iolaus is the old companion of Heracles, who boasts of how they went fighting together, and who, now that Heracles is gone, is the guardian of his children. With the children he is forced to take refuge at the Athenian altars, and the arrival of the chorus of old men of Marathon, and then of the king of Athens, just saves him and the children from being dragged off by the servants of Eurystheus, king of Thebes and enemy of Heracles. In the negotiations as to whether Athens will offer them protection, and with the later discovery that a child of Heracles must offer up his life to save Athens in the fight with Thebes, Iolaus is weak, slightly pompous, but of noble intentions, since he tries to offer himself, unsuitable though he is, for the sacrifice. At this point it is announced that Heracles' son Hyllus has arrived to help in the battle, and Iolaus announces that he too will go and fight. The servant who has brought the news of Hyllus ridicules this intention. This sequence is obviously to be played for laughs (680 ff.). For example:

> *Servant.* If your hand can't hold, your eyes won't wound.
> *Iolaus.* What! I'm so strong, I'll go right through the shield.
> *Servant.* Go? You'll first fall flat on your face.
>
> (684–86)

Iolaus has no armor, but he sends the servant into the temple to bring out a suit of captured, dedicated armor that he has seen hanging there. From the words of the servant (720–25), we gather that the arming is an awkward business. Iolaus does not have time to get it all on and will therefore exit awkwardly clutching bits and pieces. The servant continues to talk to him with the patronizing humor of the young and fit to the old and infirm that he showed in the passage quoted earlier. The effect of line 729 is "You need a nanny as you go to war." Worse still, even though he is not yet wearing the full weight of his armor, even though he is walking very slowly, Iolaus keeps stumbling (730–35). There is pathos mixed with the humor, but it is a scene that must get laughs. It is a beautiful preparation for what we will hear later as the messenger describes what happened in the battle (799 ff.). A miracle happened, and Iolaus, praying for strength, was given it for the day. It is through the pathetic old man, at whom we have just laughed, that the gods have given victory in battle to the Athenians. Iolaus does not appear again onstage. We are left with the memory of his ridiculous exit and the story of his success.

It is very much part of Euripides' nature to show grotesque and slightly ridiculous people as the ones in touch with the gods. There is a parallel to the Iolaus scene near the beginning of *The Bacchants*. The beautiful *parodos* has just ended with climactic leapings, as the undulating bodies of the maenads, crying in ecstasy, gallop like foals by their mothers, flinging out their limbs and bounding in the power of the god's possession (135–69, especially 165–69).[53] The dance ends, and on comes blind Teiresias, dressed with the bacchants' fawn-skin, garlanded with ivy and brandishing a thyrsus (170). Cadmus comes out to meet him, dressed in the same incongrous way (178). The dialogue clearly implies that Cadmus, at any rate, is trying out a few dance steps. This tentative activity and the incongruous costume cannot but be funny after the musical climax and excited dancing of the *parodos*. Part of the genius of Euripides is to use our laughter in the audience as part of the rhythm of his play. "Yes," say the later events of *The Bacchants* or *Children of Heracles*, "You laugh at these silly old men. But they are nearer the gods than you. Watch out." It is a use of laughter not to detach the audience from the action but to involve them more closely in it.

The basis of the Greek plays is that they were items in a carnival in which poets, actors, chorus, and audience all took part, just as they all took part in the procession with which the carnival opened. Audience involvement is a phrase much used today in the theater, and many devices have been employed to attempt to bring the audience into the action, most of them merely creating extra self-consciousness. The audience involvement of the Greek theater was due to the awareness of all those present in the theater that they were taking part in a real rite of worship. The effect of this is a different quality in the laughter. This is something very nearly indefinable, something to be perceived only in the totality of all the extant plays taken together. Effects such as the use of audience laughter by Euripides, as discussed above, are a small part of this. So is the fact that Aristophanes' satire is, as it were, within the family. Aristophanes went to parties with Socrates, and they got drunk together. It is a basic fact of human experience that it is a well-knit family or working team that shouts the loudest mutual abuse. A less well-knit family does not dare. Athens in the fifth century was a society remarkably at one; at one with its spirits, at one with its desires, at one in its exuberant pursuit of excellence. And in the center of all this was the rite of Dionysus, and its theater. Just as today we find that it is in a group of Irish Catholics, with dogma bred into their very marrow, that we will hear the most ribald jokes of apparent blasphemy, so in the fifth century the rite of Dionysus gave the Athenians almost total freedom. This allows the tragic poets to get laughs without diminishing the seriousness of their tragedies. This is at the center of Aristophanes' extreme laughter; Aristophanes' themes are as serious as those of the tragedies.

A close-knit family joining together in the family rite, with the freedom that this gives to shout abuse at each other and to guffaw at what they all know they take with the uttermost seriousness. Poets, actors, and audience joined in one activity. These are generalizations. How can they be tested in the context of the plays themselves? One way perhaps is to see how Aristophanes involves the audience in the action of his plays, since Aristophanes had more chance than the tragedians to create an obvious involvement. Another, perhaps, is to think of the relationship of the poets to each other.

Aristophanes' use of the audience is manifold and subtle. Perhaps the most dramatic moment of all is when the character of Dionysus in *The Frogs* runs in terror for protection to the priest of Dionysus, sitting in the front row of the theater (297 ff.). It is an enormously funny moment. It is also an enormously complex theatrical image, forcing us to ask many questions at once as to the nature of theatrical reality. It is also a joke that has no meaning unless Dionysus is a real spirit and the worship of Dionysus is real worship. Another moment is the erotic climax of the *Peace*, too complex except to be discussed in greater detail, as is done in Chapter 7. For Aristophanes, audience reaction is something to be orchestrated and made part of his rhythm. In *The Knights* there is a moment of audience involvement that is deliberately broken. Demosthenes, determined to oust Cleon, here represented as a slave of Demos (Man-in-the-Street), has found someone really from the dregs, lowest of the low, the sausage seller. He now has to urge the sausage-seller to action, to compete against Cleon. He takes him and points the audience out. Look, he says, you will rule them. "You'll prune the generals, and stamp on the Council." (166). In the next line he alludes to the custom of giving free meals to distinguished citizens in the council chamber. "And in the Council Chamber," he says, and the audience expects him to say, "You'll dine at the public expense," but he finishes abruptly, "You'll fuck." The unexpected end gets its laugh, and the involvement is broken. But a little later, after the arrival of the chorus of Knights, the young aristocrats, who have decided to join up with the sausage-seller against Cleon, the argument is joined in earnest. Cleon starts to denounce the sausage-seller to the council officials sitting in their privilege seats in the front row of the theater (300 ff.). As the *agōn* develops, with the chorus of knights backing the sausage-seller, the audience is dragged into the action on Cleon's side. At that time,

Cleon was by far the most powerful man in Athens, and, as he had just won a notable victory in the war with Sparta, most of the audience would be on his side. *The Knights* is perhaps the hardest of Aristophanes' plays to produce now. The play is lopsided without the presence of Cleon sitting in the audience and the most powerful man there. But given his presence, and given the way in which Aristophanes manipulates the audience's sympathy, it is a piece of brilliant construction and very funny. The manifold ambivalence of the play in its original setting is increased if we accept the story that Aristophanes himself played the character of Cleon.[54]

Aristophanes satirizes Cleon by playing him. Cleon is in the audience, having prosecuted Aristophanes two years ago. Aristophanes wins first prize. Of such is the texture of this family laughter that is the carnival of the Dionysiac festivals. One small instance of how this rubbed off on the poets is the way in which they all parodied each other. There is no need to spend time here on Aristophanes' parodies of Aeschylus and Euripides. Apart from many other instances, there is the second half of *The Frogs*, entirely devoted to parody of the two poets. Aristophanes does not parody Sophocles so much, and the man-hoopoe already alluded to is the most vivid. Sophocles may well have been parodied less, not out of a false respect, since to parody is to show admiration, but because Sophocles is a poet like Pope, a craftsman who realizes all the implications of what he writes as he makes his poem, and so leaves far fewer implications for the parodist to develop. Euripides parodies Aeschylus. *The Phoenician Women* contains parody of *The Seven against Thebes*, which seems to have been revived at this time. Certainly there is little sense in Eteocles' remark (*Phoenician Women*, 751-52) that it would take too long to describe each invading champion while the enemy are at the gates, unless he is having a dig at Aeschylus for the unrealistic way in which he devotes long speeches to full descriptions of each invading champion and his opponent (*Seven against Thebes*, 375-685). Euripides also has a dig at Aeschylus' recognition scene between Orestes and Electra in *The Libation-Bearers* (164-234). In the *Electra*, the tutor describes the various tokens that "show" that it is Electra's brother who has arrived (520-44). Electra ridicules him. How could man's hair and girl's be alike; how could her footprint be the same size as her brother's; above all, how on earth could they expect Orestes to return wearing the recognizable clothes he had worn when he left, since he left as a tiny baby? These are the three recognition tokens Aeschylus uses, and the dig at the older poet is clear.

What is more surprising is that Euripides also parodies Aristophanes. That a tragic poet should parody a comic one may again conflict with too narrow an idea of both tragedy and comedy; it certainly helps to indicate the mutual respect in which Euripides and Aristophanes held each other and the closeness with which poet worked with poet. The passage parodied is from *The Birds* (209ff.), where the hoopoe calls the nightingale. Euripides alludes to this delicately in the *Helen*, produced two years later. He starts a chorus with an invocation to the nightingale (1107 ff.), and then includes a direct allusion

(1111–12) with two lines unusually set to anapest chant in the middle of a sung lyric. The reason for this musical anomaly is that the passage in *The Birds* is an anapest chant, not a song. The two lines contain three words exactly the same as in two lines of *The Birds* passage (213–14). One of the words, which means "trilling," is an unusual one. In the *Ion*, produced at the same festival, Euripides continues his allusions to *The Birds*. The hoopoe follows his call to the nightingale with a very elaborate song, a free monody calling the various species of birds to him (227–59). In the *Ion*, Ion is given an equally elaborate monody, while he cleans out the temple and chases away the birds that start swarming in and fouling the place (158–83).

Those who wish to foist on us their idea of a solemn tragedy without color or laughter are likely to regard Sophocles as the epitomy of this art form. Aeschylus has perhaps some primitive elements left in him, and Euripides begins to show traces of decadence. But Sophocles is "pure marble," to use a phrase of Blaiklock's.[55] Since such pure marble is a fiction throughout the fifth century, it is as well to close this section with a quotation from *The Banqueters* of Sophocles, preserved by Athenaeus. In this, Sophocles parodies the speech from Aeschylus' *Bone-Gatherers* already quoted. The first line and a half are direct quotation. The tone is obviously mock-heroic, and the humor is somewhat schoolboy. It does not conflict with the character of Sophocles as we know it from the various anecdotes associated with his life. Nor does it make him less of the company of the great poets, because he, like so many of the great poets, had a fondness for so-called bad jokes. This also is part of the Dionysus carnival.

> But he in anger hurled unerringly
> The foul malodorous chamber pot. Upon
> My head the vessel shattered, and its breath
> Was hardly frankincense. I shuddered at
> A smell not too delightful.[56]

Plays for the Citizens Assembled

Few people today, reading for the first time the *Oresteia*, *Oedipus at Colonus* or *The Frogs*, would immediately feel that they were political gestures. As we examine them in detail, we begin to realize that these three plays, apparently so timeless, relate very closely to events contemporary with their first production. The plays themselves are political actions, designed to influence the Athenian people in a particular way. Examination of the background reveals detailed reference to contemporary events in many plays. But in almost all of them there is a feeling conveyed: after the play, we as a community must do such and such.

As we discuss the political commitment of the fifth-century plays, we must remember that the words *political commitment* in intellectual circles today in most countries of the world have lost their meaning, since writers are described as "committed" only if they are committed to left-wing ideology. It is essential to remember that in Athens there were no political parties. Any Athenian citizen could speak in the Assembly. If he could capture the attention of the citizens, and persuade them, his motion was passed. The elected officers were constantly accountable to the Assembly, which was very different from a Parliament or Congress full of career politicians frightened to rock the party boat. Any member of the audience in the theater knew that after the festival was over he could put a motion immediately before the Assembly.

Sometimes the poet uses his play as direct incitement to political action. Aristophanes hated the Peloponnesian War before the majority of the Athenians hated it. To present *The Acharnians* when he did was a direct political action. The central character, Dikaiopolis—Just-City—makes a private peace with Sparta, and most of the play will consist of his flaunting the joys and luxuries of peace in mockery of the generals and warmongers. But first he must confront the chorus of old soldiers (496ff.). The scene has been prepared as a parody of Euripides' *Telephus*. Just-City has been to call on Euripides for pieces of his poetry, represented here by "kitchen-sink" props. We are prepared for pun, parody, and farce. But at this moment Aristophanes surprises us with a minor coup. Instead of merely addressing the chorus, Just-City turns directly to the audience, and the first part of his speech is straight, without one laugh. It is as if the audience in the theater has been turned into the audience in the Assembly, most of whom would still be voting for war. In the course of the speech Just-City identifies himself with Aristophanes (502–6) and refers to the way in which Cleon had attacked him for harming the city while visitors were present, that is, during the City *Dionysia* on the occasion of the performance of *The Babylonians* the previous year. Now, says Just-City/Aristophanes, it is the *Lenaia;* we are on our own, without the foreigners. Now, the implication is: let us have some real discussion. It is a moment of direct political confrontation. Naturally, the speech turns back into farce soon; a comic must get laughs. But the unexpected directness must be remembered as a moment of frisson. *The Acharnians* won first prize. But peace was not made. The play, however, may have started to open people's eyes to the possibility of peace. In all history few poets can ever have expected to have much direct influence on immediate political action. But in certain cultures, of which fifth-century Athens is perhaps the most notable example of all, they act as if they could. We may call it their illusion. But it is this illusion that keeps society constantly preoccupied with thinking of ways to improve, and such a fervid striving after ever greater excellence is the mark of the highest civilizations. To bridge the gap between dreams and politics is the task of poets. In this respect a great society depends upon the possession of great poets.

It is perhaps a defining characteristic of the greatest poets of all to love passionately many different things and people that to others might seem incompatible. Lesser minds confuse the far-reaching commitment of Homer, Chaucer, or Shakespeare to the world in its diversity, with a lack of specific commitment to anyone or anything in particular. It is the task of the poet to give life to whatever he touches; it is especially the task of the dramatic poet to give life to opposing sides of an argument. In important matters of politics it is unusual for all right to be on one side. It is the job of a politically committed poet to clarify the nature of the political choice by presenting both choices as vividly as possible. This may be more important than presenting his own solution with the maximum forcefulness. For poetry can work only by creating heightened awareness within which each man can make his own decisions more clearly.

All four Athenian poets are careful always to make a distinction between the rightness and wrongness of an action, and the attractiveness of the character performing it. This is a necessary balance between the need of the poet to create a world with all the impartial vitality of life itself, and the need of the committed citizen of vision to help his state to a better condition. This distinction applies much more generally than just in matters of politics. We have already noted in the last section the way in which Euripides takes delight in making figures whose action he commends look ridiculous personally. We shall find the converse later, in Chapter 7, in our examination of Sophocles' Ajax, and Aristophanes' Pisthetairos (Persuader) in *The Birds*.[57] Both are villains. Ajax is childish, lachrymose, jealous, and revengeful, a bad man to command troops. But he is loved by his followers and by his neglected wife, and by all around him; and Sophocles gives him about the finest dialogue verse he ever wrote. Pisthetairos stands for what Aristophanes hates, the aggressive and blasphemous warmonger. But he is an attractive rogue, who gets everything that he wants and ends in triumph, banquets, and heavenly sex. Creon in the *Antigone* is by no means a villain. Yet what he does is monstrous, as we shall see in Chapter 8. Above all perhaps, *The Frogs*, also discussed in Chapter 8, asks us to make up our minds independently of the attractiveness of the characters who present the argument. The Greek poets are realists, knowing full well that the right cause is, as likely as not, presented by the wrong people, and that being right does not make a man attractive.

It is important to remember that the Greek poets were in a very real sense teachers. "Children have teachers; grown-ups the poets" says Aristophanes in *The Frogs* (1054–55). Although in *The Frogs* he is much more subtly ambivalent than to present poetry as just moral exhortation, the play achieved what was then a unique success for a comedy of being voted a second production because of the straight politico-moral exhortation of the *parabasis;* a request in the first speech (686–705) to reenfranchise those who had been deprived of citizenship because of their conduct at the battle of Arginusae; in the second speech (718–37) a request to make use of the upper classes in the state. Homer was used as

Christian Protestants have used the Bible, as a store of vivid examples of conduct. The dramatic poets, tragic and comic, carry on this tradition. The word for "teach" is the same as the word for "put on plays"—*didaskō*.

The stories of tragedy are stories from history. Archaeology has established anyhow that there was a Trojan War, and if we needed further confirmation, the first book of Thucydides clearly shows that educated Greeks accepted the epic cycles as history.[58] The fifth century did not care about historical accuracy as much as we do; the poets took considerable liberties with the details of their material and the characters involved in the events presented. But this was true whether the event was far in the past or within living memory. Aeschylus distorts the actual course of events in *The Persians* in order to make sharper the point of the play.[59] Events from the past are presented in terms of the present. Aeschylus' *Suppliants* and Euripides' *Children of Heracles* and *Suppliant Women* are all concerned with the question of a state going to war to protect innocent victims. In each play the decision is presented to the king of the state in question, since historically it is he who would have taken the decision. But in each play also the decision is referred to an anachronistic assembly of the people, since the concern of Aeschylus and Euripides is that this question should be debated now, in terms of the Athenian assembly, with whom rests sovereignty now. Events from the past are chosen that will mirror present problems. Events from the very recent past were chosen, at any rate by Aeschylus and Phrynichus, as we saw in Chapter 2. We can see that the Persian invasion of Greece in 480 was a suitable subject for Aeschylus to turn into a play eight years later, because the deliverance of Greece from the Persians was an event in which all Greece felt very clearly the hand of the gods.[60] By the time of Aristotle it is clear that the Greeks had lost the idea that tragedy was a matter of events in history. It is possible that throughout the fifth century the notion that part of tragedy's function was to explore history gradually weakened. We do not hear of recent history being treated by Sophocles or Euripides. This may have been partly a question of temperament. Such evidence as there is suggests also that, of the four poets, it was Aeschylus who was the most actively involved in particular political campaigns.

The most direct connection between a political event and a production of a tragedy is Phrynichus' presentation of his nonextant play, *The Capture of Miletus*, in 492, a year after the town had been captured by the Persians. Phrynichus was a friend of Themistocles, whose main preoccupation at this time was to alert the Athenians to the need for arming against the risk of Persian invasion and protecting potential allies in Ionia. The immediacy of the sufferings of Miletus was too much for the Athenian audience: they fined Phrynichus the enormous sum of 1,000 drachmae, and passed a law forbidding any further productions of the play.[61] Both Phrynichus' *Phoenician Women*, produced in 476 with Themistocles as *choregos*, and Aeschylus' *Persians*, produced in 472, were direct attemps to focus support for Themistocles, leader of the radicals who were opposed to Sparta, now hostile to the Athenian leadership of Greece. The more aristocratic faction, led by Cimon, the principal liberator of Ionia from Persia, was pro-Spartan. This faction gained the ascendancy and succeeded in exiling Themistocles soon after *The Persians*. The focus of the radicals' actions became an alliance with Argos against Sparta, and, at home, the abolition of the power of the *Areopagus*. Aeschylus continued his support of these radical aims. The *Suppliants* tetralogy, almost certainly produced in 463, conveys an approval of Argos. The character of King Pelasgus is entirely admirable. But in addition, his action is that of a democrat who acts with chivalry. It is an indication of Aeschylus' political message: the middle classes must run the country; but they must act with a code of honor as strict as the old aristocratic code.

In the *Oresteia* Agamemnon is made king of Argos, though Homer makes him king of Mycenae. In 458 alliance with Argos was still important to the radicals. But the *Oresteia*'s most notable reference to contemporary events is to the abolition of the political powers of the *Areopagus* four years before. It had been left as supreme court only. In the *Eumenides* Aeschylus presents the founding of the *Areopagus* as supreme court by Athene, patron goddess of Athens, to try the case of Orestes that had left its mark on the form of ceremonial at the *Anthesteria*, a case in which a god, Apollo, is advocate, a crowd of powers whom men dare not name are prosecution, and Athene herself gives casting vote as president of the Athenian jury. There is only one way to take this stage image: Aeschylus is dignifying the juridical functions of the *Areopagus* as much as he can, and therefore approving the reforms. But the *Eumenides* also contains the passionate pleas and savage warnings on behalf of moderation, sung by the Furies and reiterated by the reasoned speech of Athene. (490–565, 681–706). Ephialtes, Pericles' colleague as introducer of the *Areopagus* reforms, had been murdered in 461. The second half of the *Eumenides* reverberates with Aeschylus' call for moderation and unity, the need for restraint and for avoiding the extremes of revolution, and above all the need for democracy to have the fear of hell. Of all the great poems ever written, the *Oresteia* is perhaps the most socially optimistic. The *Commedia* is a vision of heaven, with which earthly politics are all too obviously discordant; *Piers Plowman* ends not with the triumph of Christ but with the corruption of contemporary politics; Shakespeare's statement ends with lonely Edgar and the broken wand of Prospero. The *Oresteia* says, "Now we have achieved some freedom. Possibly, just possibly, we could keep this, if we are very, very careful."[62]

General against Samos, friend of Pericles and therefore intimately connected with both his rise to power and the period when he effectively ruled Athens, and finally a member of the body elected to supervise the affairs of Athens for the last ten years of the war, Sophocles must have been close to all the important political decisions taken in Athens for over forty years. The effect of this on his work is the thoroughly unsurprising result that he was preoccupied with what makes a good leader, what is involved in political decision taking. This preoccupation is noticeable in five out of the seven extant plays. In the *Ajax* we are presented with the contrast between Ajax' irresponsibility and the sound sense of Odysseus, and the way in which Odysseus takes command of his nominal superiors, Menelaus and even Agamemnon, by virtue of his better grasp of what is really important. The *Antigone* examines in detail the character of a man not up to supreme command, contrasting the inadequacies of Creon with the instinct for leadership of his son Haemon. *Oedipus the King*, though less preoccupied with this issue, nevertheless presents the contrast of Oedipus and Creon, who, incidentally, is an utterly different character in this play from Creon in the *Antigone*. We are left with the impression at the end of the *Oedipus the King* that Thebes will now be governed better under Creon than under Oedipus, though of course with fewer flashy successes. I cannot help connecting this play—showing as it does the man holding power acting with paranoid irresponsibility[63]—with the fact that it was written during the one period of Sophocles' maturity when he was not in touch with the important decision maker in Athens, Cleon, the impulsive and unstable current hero of the Athenians. The *Philoctetes* is about political expediency. Odysseus, here the type of the unscrupulous politician, makes Neoptolemus decide to cheat Philoctetes for the benefit of Greece's military success. Neoptolemus comes to decide that he cannot do this.

Sophocles, however, has no hesitation in linking a commander's wisdom very closely to his contact with the numinous. Odysseus of the *Ajax* is sensible not to wish to insult Ajax' dead body and by this shows his fitness for high command. Behind his sensible reasoning is his awe of the wrath of the gods. For to insult the dead is to insult the gods. All of this is summed up in one speech (1332–45). The inadequacy of Creon in the *Antigone* is exposed because he does precisely that: insults the gods by insulting the dead. The good sense of Creon in the *Oedipus the King* is demonstrated by the fact that he will not decide on his own what to do with the polluted Oedipus. He will wait for the answer of the oracle (1442–43). At the end of his life Sophocles presented his image of the ideal ruler in the Theseus of the *Oedipus at Colonus:* a king completely in command of his people, but who acts for the benefit of his people, taking them into account (631–37); a leader with charisma and sound judgment; but first and foremost a priest-king who leads his people in sacrifice before he leads them in battle. (888–89). Sophocles himself was priest as well as general.

Euripides seems to have been much less involved in direct political action than either of his predecessors. Throughout his plays, however, runs a vivid and constant compassion for the oppressed: for the weak, for the old, for women, and above all for the victims of war. It is significant that, apart from the satyrs of the *Cyclops* and the apparently mixed chorus of the *Alcestis*, there are only two male choruses in all his extant plays, in the *Heracles* and *Children of Heracles*. And in both of these they are old men, frustrated at their weakness.

The Children of Heracles was presented near the beginning of the Peloponnesian War and is about whether there can be a just war. It is significant that it is set on Athenian soil, and that the chorus are old men of Marathon. The implication of the play is that there can be a just war, if it is to protect the weak, and that cities, as individuals, do have this duty.[64] In this play Euripides, like Sophocles, stresses the importance of the right ritual actions as a guarantee of right political decisions (333–52). The rest of his work no longer asks whether war can be justified but concentrates on presenting the degradation that war brings. The directly antiwar plays are the *Hecuba, Suppliant Women,* and *Trojan Women.* But there is a passionate sense of war's degradation in the *Andromache, Electra, Orestes,* and *Iphigeneia at Aulis* as well. His most passionate sustained diatribe against war is *The Trojan Women.* No one can impugn his political courage. This play was presented in the spring of 415, as the Athenians were preparing to invade Sicily. In spite of its great passion, it only came second.

Aristophanes shared Euripides' concern for the better treatment of women and was perhaps an even more passionate opponent of the war than Euripides. Peace is the obviously central theme of the *Acharnians, Peace,* and *Lysistrata.* But the question of peace and war also dominates *The Birds* and *The Frogs.*[65] Aristophanes' support of women seems partly to derive from his hatred of war. War seems to be all that men can do; therefore, since through this they have made such a mess of things, let the more sensible women take over. This is the theme of the *Lysistrata,* and *The Women at the Assembly. The Women at the Thesmophoria* too, though less directly concerned with daily politics, makes the audience ask itself about whether women do get a fair deal.

The Frogs, Aristophanes' most subtly ambivalent play, ends quite directly with the chorus chanting in the sacred dactylic chant, "Get rid of Cleophon." Cleophon was the last of the three demagogues on whom Aristophanes vented his satire, the other two being Cleon and Hyperbolus. All three stood for the same thing—flatter the lowest classes, the men who rowed in the fleet, and with their help continue the war; for the lowest classes stood to gain by war. All three therefore are characterized by the fact that they owe their influence to the power of the mob, and all three are warmongers. Cleophon's vote to continue the war, after the battle of Arginusae, destroyed Athens. Aristophanes sees this precisely, and dismisses him with cold fury. His references to Hyperbolus, who was less important, are brief and rude (*Peace* 681–92, 921). Some critics think that Aristophanes shows an almost malevolent hatred of Cleon, who had, after all, prosecuted him. Certainly he must have hated his warmongering policies. Certainly the language he applies to Cleon is violent. But politicians expect to be caricatured with violence, and I have tried to stress the fundamental unity of Athens that gave opportunity for greater apparent disagreement within the family. *The Knights* presents the discomfiture of Cleon, but by a rogue even worse than himself. And the play is farce; there is not really much to which a successful politician could take exception. Cleon must have been a remarkably intelligent man; he knew that he had been very lucky and was receiving credit for the victory of Pylos, which was entirely due to the generalship of Demosthenes. He also knew that he was at that moment untouchable, because of the success of his policy. It is customary to say that in *The Knights* Aristophanes is taking revenge on Cleon for his prosecution of him after the *Babylonians.* It is difficult to be sure without producing the play; and production is almost impossible since the play depends so much on being about the most important man in the state. I am more inclined to think that Aristophanes' laughter is still on top. Aristophanes had been acquitted of the charge laid by Cleon. *The Knights* is savage farce, but very much farce. If it was to anyone else but the top politician, Demosthenes' pep talk to the sausage seller would be fairly savage:

> Open his mouth with your butcher's hook
> Screw your tool in his tongue.
> Pull him inside out
> Stretch all of his holes,
> Till we get a good look
> At his ass full of boils.

(375–80)

Applied to Cleon, this is less savage because it is funnier. Boils on the ass are not very funny. Boils on a politician's ass are funny, because a politician is a man par excellence who overvalues his own dignity.

Aristophanes has almost infinite variety in the kind of laugh he creates. Each individual that he mocks obtains his own kind of mockery, always distinct. Only in three instances, I think, is Aristophanes indiscriminate. First, all generals are always figures of fun; he makes no difference between Demosthenes and Nikias in *The Knights,* though Nikias was a bad general, and Demosthenes a good one. Aristophanes' tolerance does not extend to generals, and he attacks them as savagely as he can, for what could be worse for a general than to be laughed at as silly? Second, all purveyors of oracles are dishonest, bamboozlers of simple folk.[66] Third, Aristophanes is really savage over the sycophants, the professional informers who prosecuted people and then appropriated their property.[67] With these men his real hatred shows through his medium of farce.

Books on Aristophanes almost invariably divide into those that consider him primarily as a man with political ideas—a satirist—and those that consider him primarily as a comic—a man of the theater concerned to get laughs. This seems to me a false dichotomy. His plays are constructed in terms of a rhythm of laughter, where paradox piles on paradox, pun on pun, and do not make sense except through their laughter. He is a poet of laughter, because that is his job. But laughter rooted in real human problems is deeper laughter. Fantasy, particularly, needs to be rooted in human and social reality. His political concern gives depth to his laughter. Conversely we should notice that if something has made us laugh excessively, we shall remember it for a long time. Aristophanes' extreme farcical moments will be remembered. But as we do remember them, we start to realize the serious implications behind the laughter.

With this qualification—that the idea depends on the laughter—we can say that every Aristophanes play contains a serious idea affecting the conduct of the state. *The Acharnians* is about peace and war. *The Knights* is about winning power in the Assembly, about the way in which the sovereign people of Athens have to be bribed and cajoled into supporting a policy or a politician, with the implication that this will almost certainly cause the worst politician to obtain influence, the worst policy to be adopted. *The Wasps* is the reverse of this. It is about the people, who think that they are sovereign, and tells them that they are really no better than slaves, since they have to line up for what is in effect dole money. They think that they are sovereign judges, as they sit on the jury. But really they are dependent on drawing their pay. *The Wasps,* like *The Knights,* asks basic questions about the foundations of Athenian democracy. *The Peace* is less intense, more a celebration of the peace now almost concluded than a debate about its merits. *The Birds* is about colonizing man, adventurous, blasphemous, arrogant, the typical Athenian. The *Lysistrata* is about peace, and about revolution, a play produced a few months before the oligarchic coup d'etat, only too topical. It, like *The Women at the Thesmophoria*, asks about the status of women in society, as does the later *Women at the Assembly. The Frogs* is about peace, and unity in the state, and the dependence of a civilized state on the possession of good poets. The *Wealth* is about the redistribution of wealth.

New Comedy has no political involvement and is extremely limited in its laughter. The comedy of Aristophanes is unlimited in both directions. Possibly the two are connected. It may well be that it is always the artists who are inspired with a purpose apparently outside their art who expand the art itself. It is surely incontrovertible that the rich theatrical abundance of the fifth-century plays, at which I have attempted to hint in the previous section, has a very close connection with the equally strong political commitment of the one comic and three tragic poets whose work survives. Concerned as they are with extending the range of their craft, they are above all concerned with a better society. Aristophanes in this is as committed as the tragic poets, and the political depths of his laughter are as sure a sign as any of the total commitment of Athenian society to continual political enquiry. "In diesem Sinne hat Aristophanes wie Socrates gewirkt und das Gedächtniss seines Namens für alle Zeiten gesichert." So Gerlach ends his book on Aristophanes and Socrates.[68] Aristophanes had as strong a political vision as Socrates. Socrates, like Aristophanes, pushed society toward that vision by ridicule. Laughter and political commitment mix in the rite of Dionysus, from which both derive their nature.

Drama for the God of the Theater

Every extant fifth-century play contains either a hymn, prayer, or thanksgiving to the gods, or a ritual act such as a funeral procession. Some, of course, contain more than one such instance of worship.[69] The theater was at the center of Athenian culture because it had come to be the center of Athenian worship, providing the most vivid means yet discovered of meeting the spirit powers, finding out how they worked, and living accordingly.

Modern Western culture, which so often finds god-centered piety incompatible with rationality, needs constant reminders for its imagination to grasp the god-centeredness of the Athenians. It is worth noticing how often Socrates is described at prayer, how important to him, type for all time of the rational Athenian, were acts of piety such as prayer and sacrifices, and how much attention he paid to oracles and dreams. A vivid example is provided at the memorable party described by Xenophon, whose erotic cabaret, described in Chapter 12, so delighted Socrates. After dinner, while the tables were being cleared away, the guests poured libations and sang the paean (*Symposium*, 2.1). It is difficult to conceive a stag party of modern businessmen, intellectuals, and trend-setters, out to see a strip show, concluding dinner by saying grace and singing a hymn.

Even in the fourth century, when the connection between theater and worship had been loosened, Demosthenes can claim, as we saw earlier, that even unworn costume, destined for display at the festival, is sacred. During the fourth century actors were used frequently as ambassadors, because the actor's person was always immune throughout the Greek world; for the actor was minister of the god. How much stronger must have been the sense during the fifth century that the poets were special ministers of Dionysus.

Almost certainly Aeschylus, Sophocles, and Aristophanes were initiates into the Eleusinian mysteries. We know that Aeschylus was prosecuted on a charge of revealing what went on in the mysteries.[70] It is inconceivable that Aristophanes could have written *The Frogs*, with its chorus of initiates, unless he too was an initiate. About Sophocles we do not know, but since initiation was an honor for privileged people in the state, there could hardly have been anyone deemed more suitable than the most successful tragic poet. One fragment suggests very strongly that he too was an initiate.

> Triple blessings on those men
> Who've gazed upon the rites, and then depart
> Down into death. That place for them alone
> Is life; for all the others total evil.

(Frag. 753)

We know very little about the Eleusinian mysteries because of the very strict rule of secrecy. But their main function was to provide a series of ritual actions as a result of which the soul of the initiate would live after death. If Sophocles did believe, as seems likely, that his soul would continue to live, then this helps to explain the clear-eyed acceptance of the fact of death that is one of the great strengths of fifth-century tragedy, and especially so in the poetry of Sophocles. But is is necessary to emphasize that the hope of life after death plays no conspicuous part in any of the extant tragedies. Whatever one's belief about immortality, there is no denying the fact of death—monstrous, ever-present, the one utterly inevitable.

At some time during the 420s, no doubt as a result of the plague, the cult of the healer god Asclepius was introduced to Athens. Involved in this cult was a sacred snake. Sophocles was appointed a priest of the cult and looked after the sacred snake.[71] It is important that we remember Sophocles, the poet par excellence of Athenian clear thinking, as priest of a chthonic cult. For the modern rationalists who find this difficult to understand or accept, a rejoinder by Gabriel Germain in his perceptive book on Sophocles is appropriate: "Allons-nous, à cause de cet animal, classer Sophocle parmi les superstitieux et les attardés? L'Inde nous répondrait: mieux vaut voir Dieu dans un reptile que de rester aveugle à sa présence."[72]

To understand the religion of the fifth-century Athenians is the first prerequisite for understanding the drama. To get inside another age's religious beliefs is perhaps the hardest imaginative activity of all. Religious belief par excellence cannot be reduced into neat, detachable statements. The religion of the fifth-century tragedies can be studied only in the totality of all the plays together. Since that has been my main preoccupation in another study, it is necessary to refer to that for a more detailed examination.[73] Professor Kitto's criticism of Greek tragedy is now widely and justly famed.[74] Central to his assessment of the form of Greek tragedy is his insistence that all the plays are plays about the ways of the gods, that it is this theological preoccupation which gives them their form, and that therefore every reference to the gods must be studied very closely and treated as if the poets meant exactly what they said. It is no denigration of Kitto to say that in a sense he was pointing out the obvious, because critical thinking about the Greek tragedies had reached such a tangle of learned contortions that to point out the obvious was no mean feat of scholarship. Kitto had to argue, with all the force of his scholarship, wise understanding, and humor, a case that, once having been argued, we can see to be so obvious as to require no argument. His thesis after all is the straightforward one that these great poets meant what they said—exactly. In the course of his argument, needless to say, he uncovered very many insights as to the nature of these poets' theology. In my brief summary here I am indebted to his understanding, as anyone who writes on this subject will be for a long time to come.

A useful way by which to approach understanding of the religion of the fifth century is through a common illogicality, often encountered in arguments about religion. How can there be a God, it is often asked, if He allows such horrors to happen in the world. The train of thought is patently fallacious. The question of God's existence is totally separate from questions about His nature. The fallacy arises because, obviously, we would like to believe that God is a nice fellow like ourselves. Because of the horrors we encounter in life, we conclude pretty rapidly that God is not a nice fellow like ourselves. The important questions about the existence and nature of God must surely be asked only in connection with the facts of intolerable human suffering. In the fact of such suffering there are not many possible conclusions to be drawn. We can say that the world came about entirely by chance, and therefore that human suffering occurs by chance. We can say that the universe is a battle of warring powers, and that in this battle it is only too likely that the innocent will be hurt. The only other course is to accept the paradox that is central to both Judaism and Christianity that a good God ordains man to suffer, and that each individual for himself must accept, even welcome, his own suffering, because man's raison d'être is to choose heaven or hell, and the activity of choosing heaven is connected with welcoming one's own suffering.

This oversimplified preliminary is necessary because there have been a number of books written that seek to show how the Greek tragic poets could not have accepted a world view that made the gods inflict such suffering on human beings. These books are the hangover of the comfortable thoughts of comfortable middle-class thinkers in the peace of the nineteenth century. They are not worth treating seriously in the savagery of the twentieth century, when hardly a day goes by without bringing us up against the intolerable sufferings of human beings. The religion of the Greek tragedies is certainly intolerable, but not as intolerable as Christianity with its doctrine of the possibility of suffering for all eternity. All religions worthy of serious consideration—whether theist or atheist—are intolerable. Life is intolerable. However cushioned our own life may be, we face the prospect of death, which is just as intolerable for someone crumbling under the weakness of old age as it is for someone suddenly cut off in the bloom of youth. The intolerable is where we start.

A central notion to the understanding of archaic Greek religion is that of Dikē, a rhythm of nature and moral action in harmony. If an action is performed that breaks this harmony, then reactions will follow, until equilibrium is restored. The action may be something like Agamemnon killing his own daughter Iphigeneia as a sacrifice for the voyage to Troy, an action that prompts the obvious revenge of Clytemnestra, who kills Agamemnon. Or it may be the neglect of one of the spirit powers: Hippolytus offending Aphrodite by paying excessive respect to Artemis. As a result, he is smashed by Aphrodite. Or it may be vaguer and more intangible. Creon in the Antigone orders that a corpse should be left unburied. This also is an offense against the way things are or should be. Destruction automatically follows.

With the notion of Dikē goes the notion of Sophrosynē. The nearest approach to understanding this concept is through the Jewish idea that "the fear of the Lord is the beginning of wisdom." The man who is sōphrōn understands how Dikē applies to him, understands the kinds of actions that he might take that would cause Dikē to react and smash him, and so avoids taking them.

With one or two notable semiexceptions to be discussed in Chapter 6—all of them late in the fifth century—the form of all Greek tragedies is the presentation of an action that breaks the harmony of Dikē, and the reactions that result.

Once a man has performed such an action he will be caught up in the process of *Atē*, destruction that brings with it delusion. Because many of the plays present this initial action obliquely, a thoroughly erroneous doctrine has been propagated by some scholars that "the Greek heroes are pawns of Destiny."[75] Agamemnon's moment of choice is presented with great clarity in the *Oresteia*, but during the first great dance.[76] When Agamemnon appears onstage (810 ff.), he is depicted as a man who no longer has freedom of action, because he is now well and truly in the grip of *Atē*.

Those critics who wish to affirm that Greek tragedy shows men in the grip of a remorseless fate usually center their argument on Oedipus. Now, it is perfectly true that in the *Oedipus at Colonus* Sophocles presents the sufferings of Oedipus as unavoidable, because his interest in this play is to show how Oedipus has been turned into the chthonic power that he is now becoming. In the same way the decision of Agamemnon in Sophocles' *Electra* is also presented as unavoidable, because Sophocles, unlike Aeschylus, merely wishes to focus attention on the action of Clytemnestra in killing her husband and committing adultery with Aegisthus, which action has reacted by making Electra into a person who will kill her mother. In the *Oedipus the King* we are shown quite clearly Oedipus' moment of choice. Oedipus went to the oracle to find out who his parents were and was told that he would kill his father and sleep with his mother. In reaction to this, he ran away—a free action.

> As soon as I heard this I hurried from Corinth,
> Followed the stars, escaped to a place
> Where I could never see the shame
> Of my foul oracles fulfilled.
>
> (794–97)

As a result of this—disaster. Throughout the events actually shown on the stage, Oedipus is not free. He is being swept along by *Atē*. But there is no doubt that he could have acted otherwise.

We feel the situation of Oedipus so acutely because the action he took seems so much the right and proper thing to do. It was not, however, a sensible thing to do. There had been doubts about his parentage, and throughout the play we see Oedipus acting impulsively, not sensibly, not in the way a good leader should act. The concept of *Dikē* and its companion concept, *Sophrosynē*, are by no means purely moral ones as we today define moral. *Dikē* is a principle of action and reaction throughout the natural order; *Sophrosynē* is the understanding of this principle. The two concepts can most usefully enlarge the vocabulary of twentieth-century moral discourse. For nowadays we are being asked to evaluate actions such as that of a train-driver who gets drunk and as a result kills a hundred people. We do not excuse such an action by saying that he did not know what he was doing. The philosophy of Greek tragedy recognizes that there are many occasions in life where good intentions are not enough, though of course the power of the *Oedipus the King* to move our emotions derives very much from the fact that we sympathize so much with Oedipus' impulse.

The greatness of Sophocles as a poet is the clarity with which he understands how these things happen and the clear-eyed way in which he looks straight at the innocent suffering that results. All his surviving work presents such a balanced wisdom that it is difficult for anyone to understand without not only long study but also a full experience of life. The first play of his that we possess was, after all, written when Sophocles was about fifty. Euripides is much less balanced, and it is easier to get quick, strong impressions of his attitude to *Dikē*, because his generation was beginning to doubt the validity of such formulations.

The action of the *Hippolytus* is the insult that Hippolytus pays Aphrodite by deliberately ignoring her. In the prologue Aphrodite appears and says that she will destroy Hippolytus for not respecting her. She does not mind him honoring Artemis, goddess of chastity, but she requires some honor too. Hippolytus' servant offers a wreath to the statue of Aphrodite, praying the goddess to forgive his master for honoring only Artemis. "Gods should be wiser than mortals," he says (120). But that is not the way gods work. Their nature is such that they must react to insult, automatically destroying the man who insults them just as electricity destroys the man who cuts a live wire. Hippolytus is destroyed. Artemis appears at the end of the play to make it clear that he has indeed been destroyed by Aphrodite, and that she could not prevent it (1328–30). She will, however, destroy one of Aphrodite's followers as recompense. The master plan for Hippolytus' destruction is Aphrodite's. But his actual death is caused because his father Theseus cursed him, in ignorance of the truth. Theseus had been granted by Poseidon that three curses he uttered would come true. The curse is efficacious, whether used rightly or wrongly. Gods' actions are irrevocable, and gods cannot weep (1396).

The action of *The Bacchants* is the rejection of Dionysus and his worship, first by the people of Thebes, and then specifically by King Pentheus. The general rejection brings about Dionysus' first reaction, which sends the women of Thebes raving in hysteria. Pentheus is given the chance of allowing Dionysus to calm this hysteria and bring the bacchants back to their right mind. Pentheus refuses (787 ff., especially 809–10) and so is destroyed by Dionysus, who uses Pentheus' raving mother as his instrument. Dionysus appears at the end to send into exile not only her, but also her father Cadmus, although Cadmus had tried to worship Dionysus. Then follow five lines of dialogue, vital for the understanding of fifth-century religion:

Cadmus. Dionysus, we implore you, we have sinned.
Dionysus. Too late you knew our nature, not when you should.
Cadmus. We know this, but . . . you press upon us hard.

Dionysus. Yes, for by you I was outraged . . . a god.
Cadmus. Gods should not be like mortals in their anger.
Dionysus. My father Zeus approved this long ago.

                                                                        (1344–49)

Cadmus, like Hippolytus' servant, expresses a feeling that gods should be above striking back like this. Dionysus does not deign to answer such a ridiculous statement. Gods must be respected, or they will strike. And the blow will be of such force that other, innocent people are likely to be hurt.

A short summary such as this has inevitably had to be simplistic. Some qualifications need to be made. First, the doctrine of *Dikē* is a summary culled from the plays. There was no neat formulation of this doctrine for Sophocles to learn in childhood. I have used the term *theology,* but there was no theology in the Christian sense, no body of dogma, no set of beliefs to which one assented or dissented. As I have already said in Chapter 2 and will say again in Chapter 10, the breakdown in culture that took place relatively quickly after the end of the Peloponnesian War and made it impossible ever to write plays like those of the fifth century again, was bound up with a change in attitude to the Olympian gods, a sense that their ritual was no longer central to life but was a decoration, unnecessary for the wise man. Discussion of this question, and in particular of the way in which Euripides stands between the different attitudes of the two generations, often poses such questions as "Did Euripides believe in Dionysus?" Now that would seem to us to be a central question for religion. But it would have been a senseless question to Euripides. The gods were inseparable from their worship, until Plato started to define them. We can see this best, as so often, by an oblique example. Even Plato did not fully possess the category of truth and falsity. His argument against the poets rests on his confusion of the category true/false with that of fact/fiction.[77] Even more so, Euripides, a generation earlier, did not have the philosophical equipment to ask, "Is it true that Dionysus exists?" For the fifth-century Greek, Dionysus is "that to which I pray in the theater, the experience I have when I drink wine or go ecstatic dancing, the being represented in the statue I can see and touch."

For this culture any power is a *theos.* Philoctetes' bow is a *theos* (*Philoctetes,* 657). Human beings would soon be worshiped as *theoi,* because they appeared to wield more power than the Olympians.[78] The numinous is immanent everywhere. We become aware of it through its power. This is something almost impossible for a modern Westerner to understand though an Indian would find much less difficulty. It is helpful as we consider the so-called atheism attributed to Euripides and Socrates in the plays of Aristophanes. For during Aristophanes' lifetime, incoherently, without the categories, the questions were being asked, "Is god. . . ?" "Is Dionysus. . . ?" Aristophanes makes a similar joke about both Socrates and Euripides. In *The Clouds* Socrates is made to say that he does not deal with the gods (247–48), that he treats them as nothing (423) and explains phenomena without them (369 ff.). He is even made to say that Zeus "is not" (367). But he treats the clouds exactly as if they were traditional gods of the Olympian pantheon, to be invoked as one would invoke Zeus or Dionysus:

Socrates. Peace and blessing old man. Listen, listen to the prayer.

Oh lord the king, immeasurable Air, who holdest the earth
                                                    suspended,
Oh shining Space, oh divine lady Clouds,
                        who wield the thunder and lightning,
Draw near, appear, hover in the air, ladies,
                        over your disciple.

Twister. Hey wait! Hey wait! Give us time to wrap up.
                Rain, hold your splish-splitter-splat.
To think of leaving home—what a twit—
                without my waterproof hat.

Socrates. Draw near oh clouds, manifest yourselves,
                honoured ones, to this . . . er . . . human?
From wherever you're resting—
                the steep holy slopes of snow-covered Olympus,
Whether you're leading the holy dance
                for the nymphs in the gardens of the ocean,
Whether you're dipping your golden basins
                in the Nile's river basin,
Staying by the lake of Meiotis,
                or the snow-capped summit of Mimas,
Oh hear us, accept our sacrifice,
                look favourably down on our rite.

(263–74)[79]

The further joke of the play is that the clouds turn out to be spirits, behaving very much like a comic poet's version of Dionysus in *The Bacchants.* The further joke is that Socrates was conspicuous for his piety. In the same way, Euripides in *The Frogs* is asked to invoke the gods with incense before starting to compete in the poetry contest. He says that he has other gods to whom he will pray, and invokes "Air, and the twists of the tongue, and wit, and critical nostrils" (888 ff.). To Aristophanes, as to a Hindu, there is no great difficulty in accepting a few new gods. To Aristophanes, the joke is that they are such dull ones.[80]

A second qualification to this summary of the theology implied in the Greek plays must be mentioned. Acceptance of the gods did not imply that one could not mock them. In the same way the medieval Christians laughed at a number of the saints, though of course not all. Some of the Greek gods also were never mocked. There is no instance of Athene being ridiculed, and not many of Zeus, though Zeus is made to look ridiculous more than once in the *Iliad*. But the tradition of laughter at the gods goes with the acceptance of them as actual beings, able to order the course of events. It is partly perhaps that the Greeks saw the humorous side of the functions of the various gods. Ares, god of war, acquires the characteristics of a braggart soldier, and so it is peculiarly funny to show him helplessly trapped in bed with Aphrodite.[81] Drunkenness involves us in ridiculous positions; so does sex. The god of wine, therefore, and the goddess of sex are frequently made to look ridiculous. Ritual too, very easily lends itself to parody, though this may require a slightly more sophisticated sense of humor. We find several such parodies in both Aristophanes and Euripides.

Both Aristophanes and Euripides make use of parody, especially religious parody, to create a kind of multiple theatrical texture in their work. Euripides takes delight in the fake procession of the *Iphigeneia in Tauris*, as Iphigeneia pretends to lead Orestes and Pylades to purification (1222ff.), or the very similar fake funeral in the *Helen*, when Menelaus conducts what are supposed to be his own rites (1390ff.). A much more complex sequence occurs in the *Orestes* (1225ff.). Here, Orestes, Electra, and Pylades pray to Agamemnon to aid their enterprise, in this play merely a treacherous murder. Their prayer is a parody of the great *kommos* in Aeschylus' *Libration-Bearers* (306–478). Much of the *Orestes* is comedy, and the comedy comes through parody. The question is, How much? If the whole play is mainly for laughs, then this moment of direct parody of an intense religious ceremony will turn our laughter sour by reminding us that what we are laughing at is the story and morality of the *Oresteia*, Athens' greatest drama. If, as I myself feel, the central mood, though full of laughter, is more that of bitterness, then this moment of direct parody, this theatrical reminder of Aeschylus' work, will relieve our bitterness temporarily with a wry smile.[82]

Similarly we find in Aristophanes moments of deep devotion. All his fifth-century plays contain hymns: dances to the gods to be taken straight. Even the apparently blasphemous birds sing to the Muse of the forest (737ff.). But equally Aristophanes seems to display unlimited license in mockery of the gods; Philocleon (Friend-of-Cleon) brandishes what is apparently the G-string of the sacred image of Hestia, the household goddess; (*Wasps* 844); Pisthetairos (Persuader) thrusts his phallus at Iris, messenger of the gods (*Birds* 1256); and above all, in *The Frogs*, Dionysus himself, lord of the theater, is beaten. That Dionysus could be mocked as he is in *The Frogs* provides a central image on which our minds can fasten in our attempt to understand Greek drama. In this, as in many other ways, *The Frogs* is one of the most important plays to study in detail. Hestia's G-string is more important than it would appear: what is being mocked at this point is a household icon; and we know from the incident of the herms that the Athenians were extremely sensitive over their household icons.[83]

In religious as in political talk, Aristophanes moves from absolutely straight dialogue or song to total foolery. The great peace-making speech of Lysistrata (Disband-the-Army) starts with a passionate declaration of the unity of all

Greeks, spoken in utter seriousness (1112ff.). It turns into a farce in which overseas possessions become sexual organs. An excellent example of the way in which Aristophanes plays with religious emotions is in *The Women at the Thesmophoria*. In the middle of the play, Mnesilochus, dressed as a woman in order to attend the women's rite, which no man is allowed to attend, has been discovered by the effeminate Cleisthenes, allowed in as a kind of honorary woman himself. Mnesilochus' clothes are pulled off for a scene of crude farce. Mnesilochus pushes his phallus round to the back, and then, as Cleisthenes runs round to his back, Mnesilochus pushes it round to the front again (636ff.). Mnesilochus is seized, and the chorus of women start to search in case there are other men concealed where they should not be. A dance then follows to a song whose words would be totally appropriate to tragedy: the gods are not blind; doom will strike the transgressor (668–85). This is the kind of hymn that women might sing at the Thesmophoria; it must be taken straight. This is the *strophē*. At the end of it, Mnesilochus snatches a woman's baby from her arms. He takes refuge at the altar holding the baby as a hostage. *The antistrophē* (707–25) then follows. Both *strophē* and *antistrophē* clearly imply a dance that circles the altar. But in the *antistrophē* Mnesilochus is at the altar and from there sings one or two interspersed lines. The feeling is now dramatic rather than ritual. But the mood is like tragedy. We in the audience cannot quite understand what is happening, as the tension in the dance builds, and then, after the dance ends, the women run to get sticks to burn Mnesilochus out. He in turn prepares to kill the baby and starts taking off its clothes. As we catch our breath, we are suddenly surprised. The "baby" turns out to be a wineskin. We have been caught up in the atmosphere of worship provoked by the *strophē*, we have then been involved in what seems to be a situation of strong drama, while feeling all the time that this is wrong, since we are surely in a comedy. Then, as our nerves are fully stretched, the tension is dissolved in a burst of laughter, and the scene continues as a parody (655–732). But that is not all. The Thesmophoria is a fast, with all wine forbidden by religious taboo. The woman who sneaked in the wine was breaking the rule of the rite. Inside our laughter there is a frisson created by the ultimate seriousness of the ritual. It is an example such as this, perhaps even more than the obvious devotional elements present in all the tragedies and comedies, that emphasizes the total dependence of the Greek theater in all its richness on the worship of which theater was part.

I have drawn attention to the way Aristophanes ranges from the complete foolery of, for example, the crow-priest's sacrifice in *The Birds* (851–902) to the complete devotional sincerity of the hymns such as those in the *parabasis* of *The Knights* (551–64, 581–94). It might be asked how one is to recognize what is devotional sincerity and what is mockery. Our best guide to devotional seriousness is the lyrical intensity of the verse. Socrates' invocation of the clouds, for instance, already referred to, acquires a religious intensity through the strongly visual imagery and the resulting lyrical intensity. The poet's lyricism deepens the religious intensity of the hymns in *The Knights,* just as the sense of the numinous evoked by the women's festival gives depth and complexity to the poetry in the example quoted from *The Women at the Thesmophoria.* To the Greeks, who had no theology, only poems about the gods, religion and poetry were in a very real sense one. There have been many critics of Aeschylus who have concentrated on the depth of his religious thought to such an extent that they appear ignorant that he is a poet. Conversely, there have been other critics who have insisted that he is primarily a poet but have implied in this that he did not think deeply about the gods. "Esaltare il teologo, il filosofo, il pensatore religioso, spesso vuol dire rimpicciolire e fraintendere la sua poesia." So writes Perrotta.[84] If we do not accept this to be a false distinction, then we shall not penetrate very far into the mystery of fifth-century drama, where religion and poetry are in a very real sense one, where theater is part of worship, and where the poets are ministers of the gods, but ministers by special virtue of their craft as poets.

Notes

1. Sir Arthur Pickard-Cambridge, *Dithyramb, Tragedy and Comedy,* 2d ed. rev. T. B. L. Webster (Oxford: Clarendon Press, 1962), pp. 8–9.
2. Cf. Euripides, *Bacchae,*ed. E. R. Dodds (Oxford: Clarendon Press, 1960), pp. xx–xxv. Dodds, however, accepts that Dionysus was not originally Greek.
3. Euripides *Bacchants* 576ff.
4. Dodds, Introduction to the *Bacchae,* pp. xvi–xx.
5. It is important to notice a remark of Pausanias (*Periegeta* 6.25), that only in Elis is there worship of Hades. Elsewhere the god of death received his due in the worship of Dionysus.

If a poet-critic may be allowed to refer to his poetry as amplification of his criticism, I have used the character of Dionysus the destroyer-lifegiver in my science fiction poem-play *Red Alert: this is a god warning* (London: Sidgwick & Jackson, 1981). Working such a figure of Greek mythology into a modern fiction made me realize that—far from his lordship of death being incompatible with his life-enhancing energies—it is precisely because he is lord of death that the combination of his life-enhancing energies makes sense in terms of his total character.

6. See Appendix 3 for meanings of terms used.
7. See Chapter 8. See also Sir Arthur Pickard-Cambridge, *The Dramatic Festivals of Athens,* 2d ed. rev. John Gould and D. M. Lewis (Oxford: Clarendon Press, 1968), pp. 19–25, for a discussion of the location of this shrine. I have used this translation of *en Limnais* deliberately since I cannot believe that the bog still existed in Aristophanes' day. Names continue long after they are no longer appropriate (in the London street called London Wall, the wall has long ago disappeared). The location of the shrine is obviously important when we consider the tone of the frog chorus (*Frogs* 208–69).
8. See Pickard-Cambridge, *The Dramatic Festivals of Athens,* pp. 1–25, where all the texts bearing on the *Anthesteria* are printed. However Pickard-Cambridge could not fully grasp the nature of the festival, because he could not understand how a day of drunken revelry could be combined with an All Souls' Day, and thought that they were perhaps originally two separate festivals. Our generation need see nothing unnatural in the association. It occurs in Latin America today, and was, for example, well demonstrated in Marcel Camus's film, *Orphée Nègre.* It is illogical but natural to laugh and booze at funerals. Pickard-Cambridge wanted to change the text that refers to the offering of porridge to Dionysus and Hermes (Scholiast to Aristophanes *The Acharnians* 1076–77). Cf. Pickard-Cambridge, *The Dramatic Festivals of Athens,* p. 3, passage 5, and p. 13 n.3. His only reason for this emendation was his belief, now seen to be unjustifiable, that the two elements of the festival had to be separate.
9. See Aristophanes *Frogs* 217–19.

10. See Chapter 8 for a complete translation and further discussion of this sequence.

11. The phallic song, 263–79, is astrophic. "Blighty," the British First World War slang word for "Home from the Front," is such a perfect translation of the Greek that I have used it in spite of the fact that the word is dated.

12. See Pickard-Cambridge, *The Dramatic Festivals of Athens*, pp. 29–34, for a discussion of this derivation. He prints all the texts on the *Lenaia*, pp. 25–29.

13. See Pickard-Cambridge, *The Dramatic Festivals of Athens*, pp. 57–125, for a detailed discussion.

14. See Aristophanes *Birds* 786–89.

15. A rich man nominated for any public service such as *choregia* could nominate someone else and challenge him either to perform the service or to exchange estates. This brilliantly straightforward device ensured that the services were indeed performed by the richest citizens.

16. No doubt they normally stayed in his own house. In case this should lead to a *choregos* taking advantage of minors, no one was allowed to be *choregos* for a boys' chorus until he was over forty. See Pickard-Cambridge *The Dramatic Festivals of Athens*, p. 75 and n. 4.

17. The *proagōn* may have been instituted no earlier than the building of the Odeion in 443 B.C. There is no evidence for the ceremony before that date.

18. See Aristophanes *Frogs* 367. Hesychius under *misthos* also refers to the payment of comic poets. There is no specific reference to the payment of tragic poets. But they can hardly have failed to receive the same treatment.

19. Pickard-Cambridge, *The Dramatic Festivals of Athens*, pp. 266–68.

20. *Philippics* 1.35.

21. Demosthenes *Against Meidias* 61.

22. See Theodor Gaster, *Thespis. Ritual, Myth and Drama in the Ancient Near East* (New York: Henry Schuman, 1950), pp. 225–56.

23. See George Freedley and John A. Reeves, *A History of the Theatre* (New York: Crown Publishers, 1941), pp. 5–7.

24. Homer *Iliad* 18. 473–608.

25. As a summary this makes perfectly good sense. If we require to consider Aristotle's evidence in detail, we must ask at what date he considered that tragedy became dignified. Between his reference to the origins and his remarks about the satyric and dignity he interposes that Aeschylus added a second actor, and Sophocles a third. The normal sense of this would be that tragedy became dignified after the time of Sophocles, which agrees with my general contention in this book. We probably should not press Aristotle too close, however. The *Poetics* is a set of lecture notes. Aristotle is making several points, not presenting a finished paragraph.

26. Aristotle *Poetics* 3.1448A.29ff.

27. As we look at the various pictures of satyrs, it is difficult to talk with confidence of goat-satyrs and horse-satyrs as different beings, since we are concerned with figures who are after all mostly human in form. I therefore accept that such differences as the pictures show are minor variations in what is basically one form. But there has been considerable scholarly argument about this. Webster concludes that there is an identity between fat men and satyrs, and that the smooth horse elements—as opposed to shaggy goat elements—in some satyrs' costumes do not indicate any real difference of type. (Sir Arthur Pickard-Cambridge, *Dithyramb, Tragedy and Comedy*, 2d ed. rev. T. B. L. Webster (Oxford: Clarendon Press, 1962), pp. 113–16.

28. The evidence for this is summarized by Webster in Pickard-Cambridge, *Dithyramb, Tragedy and Comedy*, pp. 103–4.

29. Homer *Iliad* 23.12.

30. Webster summarizes what can be deciphered in Pickard-Cambridge, *Dithyramb, Tragedy and Comedy*, p. 10. See also T. B. L. Webster, *Greek Art and Literature, 700–500 B.C.* (Melbourne: University of Otago Press; London: Methuen, 1959), p. 47 n.15, p. 49 nn.26 and 27.

31. Gerald Else, in *The Origin and Early Form of Greek Tragedy* is concerned to argue that Solon was the only significant inspirer of Greek tragedy, and that all that had gone before is irrelevant. His book is hopelessly one-sided. He pays no attention to the early dances because he appears unaware of the importance of the chorus in fifth-century drama. But his book has had the useful result of reminding us of Solon. It is important, for example, that there is no evidence for political concern in Epicharmus' comedies. One of the strengths of Athenian tragedy and comedy is its development in conjunction with the rise of the Athenian democracy and the accompanying deep thought on political matters that characterizes the Athenians from Solon to Socrates.

32. Pickard-Cambridge, *Dithyramb, Tragedy and Comedy*, pp. 92–93.

33. Ibid., p. 102.

34. See Appendix 4 for notes on meters.

We should assume that the original *kōmos* did not involve any lyric systems, and that the alternation of lyric stanza and chanted speech in tetrameters characteristic of an Aristophanes *parabasis*, and known as an epirrhematic syzygy, developed later, when comedy, like tragedy, was performed at the festival, and so the form of tragedy helped to influence the form of comedy.

35. Pickard-Cambridge, *Dithyramb, Tragedy and Comedy*, pp. 132–87, spends much space discussing the question as to whether Attic comedy was derived from Dorian sources. That there were some sort of comic performances elsewhere than at Athens seems likely, and that the Athenian poets took what they could from where they could is also likely. But there is virtually no evidence that establishes Dorian comedy as being earlier than Attic. We cannot even be sure whether Epicharmus was earlier than Chionides, or vice versa, whether either effectively influenced the other, or whether comedy developed more or less independently in Athens and Sicily.

36. See Chapter 7, "Aeschylus".

37. Plutarch *Pericles* 5.154E.

38. Until relatively recently it was fashionable to do precisely this. Criticism of this play provides an awful warning for scholars. Because traditions of scholarship had failed to realize that the chorus in fifth-century tragedy is always central, with only a very few, late exceptions, it was almost universally decided that *The Suppliants*—because of its huge amounts of chorus lyrics—was a very early play, possibly written about 490 B.C., twenty years before *The Persians*. Then a fragment was discovered showing that the four plays of which it was the first won the prize, with Sophocles second, and therefore must have been presented later than 468, the date of Sophocles' first competition. The evidence for this is now generally accepted as incontrovertible. See H. D. F. Kitto, *Greek Tragedy*, 3d ed. (London: Methuen, 1961), pp. 1–2, for a summary of the evidence. Kitto himself, however, remains a little dubious.

Once we know that *The Suppliants* was probably written only five years before the *Oresteia*, we are forced to take it as seriously as the *Oresteia*, since it is an expression of Aeschylus' full poetic, religious, and theatrical maturity.

39. Aeschylus, frags. 274, 275.

40. A scholar who prefers to remain anonymous argues that we have no evidence that *The Net-Haulers* was the first play of the group. No; except that it presented the beginning of the story, and Aeschylus, being a straightforward man of the theater, not a scholar, when telling his stories probably began at the beginning.

41. It is interesting to notice the suggestion in the Loeb edition of Aeschylus that the *Phorcides* may be a satyr drama. *Aeschylus, with an English Translation by Herbert Weir Smyth*, the Appendix edited by Hugh Lloyd-Jones (London: William Heinemann; Cambridge: Harvard University Press, 1963), p. 470. No other example is known of a poet submitting two satyr plays. But if the reason for the satyr plays is as I have suggested, there would be nothing against this. Whether or not it is a satyr play, we must admit that the element of grotesque permeates the whole trilogy.

42. Athenaeus *Deipnosophists* 2.44D.

43. Ibid. 1.22A, 1.17C, 10.428F.

44. *Deipnosophists* 13.601A, 12.510B, 13.603E–604F.

45. *Deipnosophists* 13.602E.

46. Scholiast to Apollonius Rhodius *Argonautica* 1.769.

47. See Chapter 8.

48. See Chapter 4, "Setting."

49. See Chapter 8.

50. Herwerden could not bear the idea of Medea being naked and wanted to emend the word. To such lengths will prejudice go. See Sophocles, *The Fragments of Sophocles*, edited with additional notes from the papers of Sir R. C. Jebb and Dr. W. G. Headlam by A. C. Pearson (Cambridge: Cambridge University Press, 1917) p. 175.

51. See Chapter 6, "The Form of Aristophanes' Comedies."

52. We know from *The Women at the Thesmophoria* that the *Helen* was a popular play, as was the nonextant *Andromeda*, whose tone seems to have been similar to the *Helen's*.

53. For the maenad dance movement, see Chapter 5, "The Variety of Greek Dance."

54. Scholiast to *Knights* 230ff.

55. E. M. Blaiklock, *The Male Characters of Euripides* (Wellington: New Zealand University Press, 1952), p. xi.

56. Frag. 565. Athenaeus *Deipnosophists* 1.17D.

57. For translation of Aristophanes' character names, see Appendix 2.
58. Thucydides *Histories* 1.3,9,10. It is astonishing that this seems to have escaped the attention of some notable scholars. Professor Dodds, for example, starts his excellent introduction to *The Bacchants:* "Unlike most Greek tragedies the *Bacchae* is a play about an historical event—the introduction into Hellas of a new religion." How can he maintain that the rest of Greek tragedy is not historical, when Thucydides discusses the details of Agamemnon's armaments, and Schliemann has shown that Troy was sacked?
59. See H. D. F. Kitto, *Greek Tragedy*, pp. 33–45, for a discussion of the details of these changes.
60. See Leo Aylen, *Greek Tragedy and the Modern World* (London: Methuen, 1964), pp. 46–49 for a discussion of *The Persians*, and pp. 30–33 for a fuller discussion of the factual nature of Greek tragedy.
61. Herodotus *Histories* 6.21.
62. This is a summary acount of Aeschylus' political involvement. For the details, see Anthony J. Podlecki, *The Political Background of Aeschylean Tragedy* (Ann Arbor: University of Michigan Press, 1966), whose argument I have followed closely.
63. E.g., Oedipus' wild accusations against Creon, *Oedipus the King* 378, 532ff.
64. The details of the political background of this play are important, but complex. The play is not one of Euripides' best, and it has been suggested that it was written in a hurry. See Ralph Gladstone's Introduction to the play in David Grene and Richmond Lattimore, eds., *The Complete Greek Tragedies, Euripides I* (Chicago: University of Chicago Press, 1953–59). For an excellent full discussion of this play and *The Suppliant Women* see G. Zuntz, *The Political Plays of Euripides* (Manchester: Manchester University Press, 1955).
65. See Chapters 7 and 8 respectively.
66. E.g., *Birds* 959–91.
67. E.g., *Birds* 410–69.
68. Franz D. Gerlach, *Aristophanes und Socrates* (Basel: Commissionsverlag der Chr. Meyrischen Buchhandlung; W. Meck, jr., 1876). "In this sense Aristophanes has acted like Socrates, and preserved the memory of his name for all time."
69. This is not true of *The Women at the Assembly* and *Wealth*, Aristophanes' two fourth-century plays. With only these two plays surviving, we cannot generalize with too great confidence. But the lack of hymns seems to demonstrate how quickly the change of religious attitude, which we find in the work of Plato, writing at the same time, is reflected in the drama.
70. See Aristotle *Ethics* 3.1. 1111A 9–11, Aelian *History* 5.19, Clement of Alexandria *Miscellanies* 2.387. Croiset discusses this briefly. Maurice Croiset, *Histoire de la Littérature Grecque* (Paris: E. de Bocard, 1928), 3:178–79.
71. Plutarch *Numa* 3; *Etymologicum Magnum* under *Dexion*.
72. Gabriel Germain, *Sophocle* (Paris: Éditions du Seuil, 1969), p. 27. "Because of this animal, are we to class Sophocles with the backward and the superstitious? The Indian would answer us: better to see God in a reptile than to remain blind to his presence."
73. Aylen, *Greek Tragedy and the Modern World.*
74. H. D. F. Kitto, *Greek Tragedy* (London: Methuen, 1961), and *Form and Meaning in Drama*, (London: Methuen, 1956).
75. E. R. Dodds, *The Greeks and the Irrational* (Berkeley and Los Angeles: University of California Press, 1951), p. 7 and passim. Dodds clearly establishes this doctrine to be erroneous. He shows that the notion of overriding Destiny is Hellenistic, and therefore was not part of the thinking of the fifth century. It is therefore misleading and quite irrelevant to apply it to the tragedies. Doctrines about determinism in Greek tragedy are mainly due to concentration on the misleadingly termed heroes, instead of on the dance of the chorus. The events portrayed were in a sense inevitable, because they were events that had already happened in history. The whole matter is discussed in greater detail in Aylen, *Greek Tragedy and the Modern World*, passim.
76. His dilemma during the fourth system, 192–217; his action, 218. See Chapter 7.
77. *Republic* 2.377.
78. The earliest evidence of such worship among Greeks involved Lysander, the Spartan admiral who defeated Athens. See Plutarch *Lysander* 18.2, who derives this information from Douris. Plutarch also includes a four-line paean to Lysander.
79. The whole sequence is changed in anapest tetrameters catalectic. See Chapter 7 for further discussion of this passage.

80. There is an interesting ambiguity about the staging of this moment in *The Frogs*. In 888 Dionysus offers the censer to Euripides, who answers with the word, *kalōs*, which can mean either "good" (the English word used semi-adverbially, to apply to the totality of Dionysus' action) or "no thank you!" Most commentators take it as the latter. See for example Benjamin Bickley Rogers, *Aristophanes* (London: William Heinemann; Cambridge: Harvard University Press, 1924), 2:376–77; or W. W. Merry, *Aristophanes: "The Frogs," with Introduction and Notes* (Oxford: Clarendon Press, 1884), Notes, p. 45. But it is much funnier if we take it as the former meaning. Then Euripides will take the censer, and perform his prayer to his new gods while swinging the censer appropriate to the worship of the old ones.

81. Homer *Odyssey* 8.266ff.

82. For a fuller discussion, see Chapter 7.

83. There is some controversy as to whether Aristophanes felt any limits to possible mockery of the gods or of ritual. Arnott, for instance, argues that sacrifices could not be shown onstage. But apart from taboos, an actual sacrifice of a lamb would be difficult to stage. See Peter Arnott, *Greek Scenic Conventions in the Fifth Century B.C.* (Oxford: Clarendon Press, 1962), pp. 53–56.

84. Gennaro Perrotta, *I Tragici Greci*, (Firenze: Casa Editrice G. D'Anna, 1931), p. 18. "Exalting the theologian, the philosopher, the religious thinker, often means diminishing and misunderstanding his poetry."

4

PRODUCTION

Setting

It now seems likely that when the City *Dionysia* was founded and the dramatic competitions began, the plays were performed in front of the old temple of Dionysus at the bottom of the Acropolis hill. The chorus danced on the flat, and the audience stood round watching them, while the poet performed his linking speeches on the temple steps. As the plays became more popular, it became obviously much more difficult for the audience to see. The slope of the Acropolis was so near. It must have seemed only common sense to perform in such a way that the audience could stand on the slopes of the hill. This meant that the facade of the temple could no longer be used. Instead a *skēnē*[1] was put up to provide a backdrop for the action and a dressing room for the performers. This took place at some point early in the fifth century. The next natural step would have been to provide wooden benches for the spectators. This we learn happened. We also learn that on one occasion this seating collapsed.[2] Probably as a result of this, a more permanent structure was then created, more or less in the shape we associate with Greek theaters. Apart from any stone used to bind the slope of the auditorium or to act as foundation for the *orchestra,* all construction was in wood, and so no trace survives. It was Pericles, about the time when he built the Odeion, who created a more permanent theater. He moved the site slightly, so that he could use a steeper part of the slope, and he constructed stone walls to prevent subsidence. He may or may not have provided the stone seats.

Since the word *skēnē* means "tent," it would seem likely that in the early stages of the festival, the *skēnē* was indeed a tent. But the vast majority of Greek plays take place outside a temple or palace. This convention seems most likely to have been established if, as soon as the playing area was moved from in front of the temple of Dionysus, the *skēnē* was built as a replica of the temple. Its name could, after all, have acquired its theater connotation during the earlier period when Thespis was touring the countryside. Alternatively, the first *skēnē* may have been mainly painted canvas, and partly acquired its name from being made of canvas. Whatever the exact circumstances, by the time of

Aeschylus it seems that the *skēnē* was a permanent temple-like building of wood, solid enough to support considerable machinery. A building made of wood no doubt required relatively constant modification: particular pieces of construction for particular plays, and new inventions to make effects easier. It is sensible to assume that the *skēnē* gradually became more and more elaborate through the fifth century, with frequent rebuildings. There is no evidence that the Periclean reconstruction of the auditorium affected the *skēnē*.[3]

About 330 B.C. the orator Lycurgus ordered a complete rebuilding of the theater in stone. The work may have taken some time to complete, but it seems plausible to consider all the changes as belonging to one plan.[4] The *skēnē* was now built in stone, and the stage raised high above the *orchestra*, since the chorus was no longer part of the play, and therefore there was no need for communication between chorus and actors. Tragedy was now able to rigidify into the statuesque conventionalism that would characterize it for the rest of antiquity. After the high stage came the mask with the *onkos*—the elevated forehead, which gave the actor greater height—and the built-up boots, which added height to his lower half. Then, to compensate for the elongation of the actor's figure, his costume was padded out at shoulders and waist. Standing, or strutting slowly on the raised stage, the stars of the time sang their tailor-made versions of Medea or Oedipus, and the audience attended for convention and snobbery. In Roman times the *orchestra* was adapted so that it could be used for gladiatorial shows or flooded for sea fights.[5]

At the time of Periclean reconstruction, the *orchestra* was a circle sixty feet in diameter.[6] We may assume that the earlier theater, in which Aeschylus put on his plays, had roughly similar dimensions. In the center of the *orchestra* was an altar, on which sacrifice was made to Dionysus at the beginning of each day of the festival. On the base of the altar stood the *aulos*-player during all the time that the chorus was in the *orchestra*. The *coryphaeus* may also have used it as a raised level from which to address the chorus. But it seems that its function was more ritual than dramatic.[7] There is no suggestion that the *aulos*-player was ever mixed up in the action.

I myself believe that the *skēnē* was always a wooden temple facade with a main door. In place of an actual temple was a shallow room, used for dressing and storing props, in which the machinery was operated. When Lycurgus built the *skēnē* in stone, the facade was naturally made more splendid. This stone facade allowed no naturalism of setting, being completely inflexible. Even during the fifth century there can have been no time for major scene changes during the festival day.[8] If the custom originally had been to perform in front of the temple, then the audience would easily accept that facade to represent not only a temple, but also a palace or house or even a cave. Provided the dialogue makes it clear where the action takes place, the audience need have no difficulty in relating the imagined to the actual setting.

Later in the fifth century it seems probable that the *skēnē* was extended at each side, and therefore that there were extra doors, one on each side. There is argument about this, because the extant plays do not show much use being made of these extra doors. Our sense of the Greek love of symmetry makes us refuse to believe in a *skēnē* that had merely one side door. But there is no extant play that requires more than one extra entrance. There are, however, a number that do seem to require one extra entrance. The earliest is *The Libation-Bearers.* (734, 781, 838) The nurse comes out of the house and goes off to fetch Aegisthus. It is perhaps possible that she goes down one of the *parodoi*, and therefore that he returns up it, in other words that the nurse and Aegisthus are played by the same actor, and that there was somewhere at the bottom of the *parodos* for him to change his mask. However, several plays of Aristophanes certainly seem to demand a side entrance. I cannot believe, for example, in *The Clouds* that the same entrance represents the house of Strepsiades (Twister)[9] and the think-tank. Twister makes such a point of going to the think-tank, and coming home. If there was no differentiation of place, the audience would be muddled. Furthermore, there are points about the entrance to the think-tank that suggest very strongly that it should not be the entrance also to Twister's home.[10] I therefore conclude, though not on incontrovertible evidence, that there were side buildings with side entrances from quite early on in the fifth century, but that for some reason they were not used very often.

Aristotle says that Sophocles invented scene painting.[11] Needless to say, this statement has caused much controversy. At some stage in the history of the Greek theater, *periaktoi* were introduced—prism-shaped blocks that could be revolved to show a different face to the audience, and therefore create a different scene. These could have been set into the *skēnē* facade, one on each side of the main entrance. If the block was triangular, then it would offer three possibilities of scene, one for each of its three sides. For a temple there could be a colonnade; for a house the panel would perhaps be plain; and there could be pictures of trees and plants to represent an exterior. If we look at the vase paintings, we see how the Greeks depicted background, with some detail, but not with complete naturalism. I see no good reason to doubt Aristotle, and therefore conclude that Sophocles introduced *periaktoi*, probably early in his career at the time when he introduced the third actor. It is unlikely that the *periaktoi* ever provided more than a choice of conventional representations. If it had become customary to provide a genuine set, then the later theater would never have tolerated the stone building that created a totally inflexible facade.

The actors mainly performed on a shallow stage raised from the *orchestra* by a few steps, and corresponding to the terrace in front of a temple. The plays suggest that while actors and chorus could touch each other, as in the *Iphigeneia in Tauris*, (1056–78) when Iphigeneia walks among the chorus touching a *choreutes'* cheek and clasping another's knees, there is mostly a sense of space between them. The *parodos* of the *Oedipus at Colonus* (117ff.) definitely suggests that the chorus are in an area distinct from that occupied by Oedipus and Antigone.

The *skēnē* building had a flat roof, accessible from inside. The *Agamemnon*

opens with the watchman on the roof. Here gods might appear to speak prologues or epilogues.[12] There is no reason however to suppose that gods would
only appear on the roof, and, for example, Apollo clearly performs on the same
level as everyone else both at the beginning of the *Eumenides* and during the
trial (64ff., 179ff., 576ff.).

Between the auditorium and the actors' terrace were the *parodoi*, wide paths
abutting onto the *orchestra* along which the chorus normally made their entrance and exit, which gave the name *parodos* also to the entrance song of the
chorus. It is likely that there was a wall on the *skēnē* side of each *parodos*,
behind which an actor could go without being seen, in order to make an
entrance up a *parodos*. During such an entrance the actor would be in view for
quite a time from a large part of the auditorium. There are frequent instances
when the arrival of a character is announced several lines before he is properly
onstage. The anapest march, which always begins the *parodos* song in the
earliest plays, was clearly designed so that the chorus could start singing while
they proceeded up the last part of the *parodos*. The chorus could also, on
occasion, enter from the *skēnē*. The two semichoruses of *The Trojan Women*
certainly do. (153ff., 176ff.) I believe that the two choruses of *The Frogs*, the
frogs themselves and the initiates, must have entered from around the *skēnē*
building.[13] There is no reason why there should not have been a gap between
the back wall of the *parodos* and the actors' terrace, providing an alternative
entrance, masked by the back wall of the *parodos*.[14]

The two main pieces of stage equipment were the *mēchanē* and the *ekkyklema*. The *mēchanē* was a crane that could lift more than one man over the
top of the skēnē building and lower him on to the terrace.[15] Clearly, a man on
his own would need a complicated harness for safety. It would be possible to
lift someone in harness into the air, but it would be difficult and very ugly for
him to get out of his harness on the ground. If anything other than an appearance in the air was required, the crane carried some sort of vehicle in or on
which the actor sat. This made mounting and dismounting possible in view of
the audience. The greatest weight it was required to carry, as shown by the
extant plays, seems to have been for Medea's exit (*Medea*, 1317ff.), where she
appears in a flying chariot of the sun with the bodies of her dead children.[16] The
most complicated movements required occur in the *Peace*. Trygaeus (Vintage),
sitting on his dung beetle, is flown up to heaven. He chants eighteen lines of
anapest dimeters[17] during which time he is swung around violently enough to
convey a sense of space travel, (154–72) and then lowered back to the terrace
from which he had started (173–79). If one is to convey the sense of a journey
through space while ending where one started, it would seem that a certain
amount of lateral movement is necessary, though perhaps the cavortings of the
dung beetle were enough both for this and to motivate Trygaeus' cry to the
crane operator that if the movement goes on he will be feeding his dung beetle
(176).

The main purpose of the *ekkyklema* was to show interiors. The simplest reconstruction of it so far proposed makes it a semicircular floor on wheels attached to part of the *skēnē* wall next to the main doorway, which part of the wall was hinged. This hinged wall would then be opened outward like a door until it was flush with the next part of the *skēnē* wall, exactly like an open door, while the attached semicircular floor had been revolved through 180 degrees until it was completely outside the *skēnē*, forming a small, slightly raised area, with the straight side of the semicircle against the *skēnē* wall. It was thus a convenient conventional means for displaying a tableau of what would in real life take place inside the building. In the *Eumenides* a considerable amount of action takes place inside the temple of Delphi (64ff.). Apollo speaks to Orestes in the midst of the sleeping Furies, and then, later, the ghost of Clytemnestra appears to wake the Furies and order them to pursue Orestes after his escape. A number of the chorus, though not perhaps all, would need to have been revealed on the *ekkyklema*. With Apollo, Orestes, and the sacred *omphalos* stone, this *ekkyklema* would have to take twenty men without crowding. Like the *mēchanē*, this machine was devised for tragedy but was of course, seized on with delight by the comic poets as a chance for parody.[18]

It appears that there was a stage altar in addition to the central altar in the *orchestra.*It is difficult to see exactly where it could have stood: if it was central it would have masked the main entrance, which must have been central; but any other position appears wrong given the symmetry of the whole theater. But its existence seems established.[19] In the numerous scenes that involve a tomb, the tomb was represented by an altar. For, in *The Women at the Thesmophoria*, there is a scene parodying Euripides' *Helen*. Mnesilochus says that he is sitting on Proteus' tomb. His female guard tells him to go to hell for daring to say that an altar is a tomb (887–88). There is no point in the joke unless this use of an altar to depict a tomb is a regular convention. I myself doubt, however, whether this altar was a permanent feature. More probably there were several different altar-type structures that could be used as required. For much of Aeschylus' *Suppliants* his chorus of fifty cling to the altar. Could this have been the same size as something on which one man can sit? There seems no reason why we should not suppose several altars, out of which the poet-director would choose the most suitable, but one of which would always be used.

It appears also that it was customary to have images of the gods on the terrace, probably on each side of the main entrance. Sometimes these are very much part of the main action. Hippolytus puts a wreath on the statue of Artemis (73ff.), and, in an attempt to redress the balance, his servant prays to the statue of Aphrodite standing opposite (114–120). A more central use even than this is found at the end of *The Clouds*, which will be discussed in detail in Chapter 7.

We notice references in the theater writers of later antiquity, like Pollux and Vitruvius, to various pieces of theatrical machinery such as thunder machines and lightning machines. It may well be that these are only late devices, belonging to the Hellenistic and Roman theater. Most modern writers assume that the stage machinery gradually became more complicated, and that gradually more devices were invented. I am not sure that this should be accepted. Once the *skēnē* was stone, with a highly ornamented facade, there would have been far less flexibility of staging than there was with the fifth-century wooden *skēnē*. And the plays had become so limited in their theatrical scope: New Comedy is content with houses and doors; Aristophanes demands flying dung beetles and ships on wheels. It would not surprise me, therefore, if one day it was proved that virtually all the machinery for stage effects about which we read belongs to the flexible and fertile fifth century rather than to the tame and conventional later period.

Discussion of the staging of these plays will ultimately rest on the writer's own predilections for or against stage machinery. Arnott's book, *Greek Scenic Conventions,* tends to argue for minimum physical machinery, to argue that nearly everything was left to the audience's imagination. This is probably because Arnott presents the Greek plays with brilliant success to a modern audience as marionette shows, making no use of set. In other words, his own lifetime's practice of presenting the plays with minimum theatrical effect cannot but have influenced his ideas about the amount of theatrical effect the fifth-century poets employed. But I do not think that they were anything like as austere in staging as he makes them out. Aeschylus, Euripides, and Aristophanes, and Sophocles to a lesser extent, give off a delight in sheer theatricality—pageantry, processions, numbers of extras, and color. I would expect them to take equal delight in whatever their carpenter could give them in terms of stage machinery. This delight has very little to do with naturalism; it is not the desire to imitate life that calls up these effects, though no doubt it can sometimes be a desire to make the thing real that inspires the theatricality. We notice this with many of the effects of staging in the English miracle plays, such as the building of Noah's Ark; Noah actually drives in nails, but the laying of the pitch has somehow "already been done"; for hammering nails onstage is good theater; caulking and pouring pitch on a boat is messy and takes a considerable time.[20]

Two examples will serve for each potential director of the Greek plays to pose the question to himself. In *The Persians,* the ghost of Darius is invoked and finally appears from his tomb (681). The stage direction in Weir Smyth's Loeb edition reads: *"The ghost of Darius rises from his tomb."* There is, however, no evidence for trapdoors in the Greek theater, though certain scholars, notably Anti, have tried to make out a case for them.[21] Could the audience of 472 B.C. have accepted Darius simply walking on through the main entrance in broad daylight? I myself do not believe this. Therefore there must have been some altar-tomb construction capable of concealing an actor. The choice is clear: an entrance lacking all verisimilitude, or a special piece of stage carpentry. Neither answer can be proved right. Whichever answer we give, we shall support with reference to the rest of the corpus. But this support will merely reveal our innate inclination to favor either machinery or no machinery.

The second example is the much argued-over "palace miracle" in *The Bac-chants* (576ff.). Reference is made to thunder and lightning, the palace totter-ing, and fire on the tomb of Semele. Here again it is possible to say that nothing whatsoever happened, and that the effect was created purely by the words sung and the dance of the chorus. This seems to me a little tame. I do not believe that it would be necessary to do anything to the palace building. The shaking could very easily be conveyed in the dance of the chorus, providing that something happened really to take the audience by surprise. What is necessary is a deafen-ing sound and, if possible, flashing light. Plato's attack on the poets in *The Republic* contains a recipe for a theater purged of all sensationalism (3.392C–398).[22] One of the effects he outlaws is thunder. We read in Pollux of the *keraunoskopeion* and *bronteion*, the former a "high *periaktos*", the latter a sack of stones under the stage.[23] A *periaktos* as described above, with sides made of shiny metal, revolved very fast, would catch the bright Greek sun and make quite strong flashes. And a rolling mass of stones together can make a thunder-ous noise. If in addition they had managed to devise some kind of resonator into which the actor playing Dionysus could shout his great offstage cries, an awe-inspiring effect could be created by very simple means. In a mountainous country an echoing voice and the sound of stones rolling would be easily suggested by experience in the hills. Macedonia, where *The Bacchants* was written, is especially mountainous. Our decision as to what happened must rest on our own emotional response as to what ought to happen. Exploration of the existing evidence will take us only so far. Finally to understand what took place in the theater of Dionysus requires an imaginative entry into the actual minds of the great poets who wrote for it.

Actors

In the early part of the fifth century, the standard team for tragic competi-tions was the poet, a second actor, the *aulos*-player and twelve members of the chorus, with as many extras as the poet wanted and was able to persuade the *choregos* to pay for. Soon after Sophocles started competing, he was able to get the regulations changed, so that three actors were allowed. Some time later the chorus was increased to fifteen. It is natural to ask why the poets and their audience remained content with three men playing between them all the roles, male and female, in a tragedy. One reason would seem to be financial. The actors were paid not by the *choregos* but by the state. A poet with flamboyant taste like Aeschylus, who had a reputation for winning the competition, would be able to persuade his ambitious *choregos* to spend money on extras, and even on the vast number of dancers required by the *Suppliants* tetralogy. But there was no doubt a fixed sum allotted by the state to be spent on the actors, and it would have been much harder to alter such a regulation.

Second, as with the setting, the Athenian audience did not require naturalistic representation. The performance was a dance drama to which spoken prologue and episodes had been added. Actors and dancers were part of a ritual reenactment of a story whose evocative power was already well known to the audience. A different technique would be required from that of the naturalistic theater, though as time went on and actors vied with each other to win the acting prize, their ability to be different people on stage no doubt developed with great precision and subtlety.

Third, it is necessary to remind ourselves that the Greek actors were, like the poets, highly regarded members of the community, performing masked as ministers of the god. The medieval audience who saw the early liturgical drama in the churches would not have asked why all the characters were represented by monks. Monks were the people who did the representing.

Fourth, a good actor, in a mask that covers the whole of his face and the top of his head, acting mainly with his body and voice in a style that will carry to an audience of fifteen thousand, some of whom are three hundred feet away from him, will of course be able to change the way he presents himself enormously, though the very fact of the actors' competition would mean that the leading actor would always take care that everyone would know which roles he was performing.

Apart from knowing that there were competitions for the comic actors, we know nothing about them. The existing plays of Aristophanes mostly require four actors and could not be performed with three; they also include numerous small bits of dialogue that must have been given to extras. There is no evidence at any time of one man acting in both comedy and tragedy, and it is natural to imagine that the training of a comic actor was less rigid than that of a tragic actor. Similarly, he cannot have enjoyed the status of a tragic actor. Accordingly he may have been paid less, and so the festival fund may have been adequate to allow for four comic actors.

Given that there are certain scenes in Aristophanes where four actors appear, we know that four actors took part.[24] What we do not know is whether the fourth actor was confined to the minimum needed, or whether the parts were more evenly distributed.[25] So many of the parts in Aristophanes, however, are quick sketches, funny turns that last only a few minutes onstage, that it would not matter too much to which actor we allocated them. There is an interesting problem in *The Frogs*, which is best discussed in Chapter 8.

The *Oedipus at Colonus* can only be performed by four actors. Scholars have contorted themselves to show that three could manage it, but all solutions involve splitting the role of Theseus between more than one actor.[26] This seems ridiculous. The *Oedipus at Colonus* is an exception to prove the rule, and also to clarify for us neatly the meaning of the regulations. For the *Oedipus at Colonus* was written as Sophocles was dying and was produced posthumously, possibly not even in the competition. Sophocles had been the outstanding tragic poet, dominating the festivals for forty years and winning almost every alternate year. He was a priest of Asclepius and a *proboulos*, a member of the special council to supervise the war. It is not difficult to see why an exception might be made for him. Certainly, there must have been many people ready to vote some extra money for the production of the *Oedipus at Colonus;* might there not even have been an actor ready to take that role for no pay?

We can detect, I believe, several plays in which the poets made very deliberate use of the three-actor convention. In particular it is interesting in the three earliest plays of Sophocles, where the leading actor plays more than one role. In the *Ajax* he plays Ajax and Teucer, two brothers, both headstrong and angry. But while Ajax has nobility, Teucer has only meanness. The play is not about Ajax, because Sophocles did not make plays like that. It is about the action of Ajax, and Teucer as part of that action, showing up the action of Ajax in a necessarily worse light once Ajax has gone. In the *Antigone* the second actor has the vast and varied part of Creon, onstage nearly the whole time. The leading actor plays Antigone, Teiresias, and the messenger. The play is about an action of Creon that brings the reaction of heaven. The reaction comes in the action of Antigone, the arrival of Teiresias to tell Creon he is wrong, and the messenger, who tells of Creon's final disaster, in the death first of his son, and then of his wife.[27] *The Women of Trachis* is about how love destroys both Deianeira and her husband, Heracles. The leading actor plays first the weak and helpless woman, and then the tough warrior, now wracked with the poison from which he is dying. Both people are in a sense one victim of one action. The convention helps Sophocles to point his meaning.

Euripides' plays have a looser structure than those of Sophocles, and so it is less easy to allocate the roles with any confidence. In the *Medea* there is a possibility of symbolic linking such as Sophocles seems to have practiced. The leading actor must play Medea. The second actor could then play Jason, Creon, the tutor, and Aegeus, people she dominates and dupes. This would leave only the messenger and the nurse for the third actor. But since the messenger speech is perhaps the finest in the play, no third actor would be unhappy with that allocation. A similar arrangement may apply to the *Hippolytus.* The leading actor could play Hippolytus and the messenger who announces his death. Then the second will play Aphrodite and her instruments of vengeance: the nurse and Theseus. The third actor will then play the servant, Phaedra, and Artemis. A similar pattern could be found in *The Bacchants.* The leading actor could play Dionysus and the one man who understands him, Teiresias. The second actor would then play Pentheus and Agave, the two main opponents of the god.

Such symbolic linking of roles can help to emphasize the form of the plays while at the same time providing opportunities for the actors to act characters very different from one another. There can be no doubt at all that the leading actor in *The Women of Trachis* played both Deianeira and Heracles. There can be no doubt that, once we realize this, the form of the play makes sense. The play does not break in half, but many critics writing from the point of view of the naturalistic theater have thought that it did.

One of the boldest uses of the convention occurs in the *Oresteia*. At the moment of most acute personal crisis in the entire trilogy, Orestes is finally confronted by his mother, face-to-face, knowing that he has to kill her. Naturally he loses his nerve. He turns to his friend Pylades and asks what he is to do. Pylades is played by a mute. But at this moment he says three lines (900–903). These are central to the entire trilogy: what would become of Apollo's prophecy; choose any enemies rather than the gods. Aeschylus brings off a coup de theatre, because the audience are not expecting the mute to speak, and it is as if the god himself had spoken.[28]

There seems, as I have said, to have been almost unlimited freedom as to the number of extras allowed. Sophocles was more modest in his demands than the other three poets. Creon in the *Antigone* has extra guards to attend him. Lichas in the *Women of Trachis* leads a crowd of Heracles' captives (225). The opening of *Oedipus the King* shows a crowd of extras thronging Oedipus' palace steps to beg him to do something to remove the plague from the city, Creon in the *Oedipus at Colonus* has attendant soldiers. The other poets are much more lavish. Aeschylus gives attendants to Xerxes in the *Persians*, but in *The Suppliants* he has a chorus of fifty Danaids, a chorus of fifty Egyptian suitors, a chorus presumably of fifty attendants, one for each Danaid, and, at the moment when the rape of the girls is prevented, King Pelasgus enters with a bodyguard large enough to look capable of stopping the fifty Egyptians (911). In the *Oresteia* Agamemnon enters in a chariot with attendant guards. Aegisthus appears at the end of the *Agamemnon* with enough guards to dominate the chorus (1578 ff.), while in the *Eumenides* there are the Athenian jurors who try Orestes, and there is the procession with which the trilogy ends. Euripides makes even more lavish use of extras. Nine of his plays have funeral processions; *The Suppliant Women* and *Phoenician Women* have two each. There is a second chorus in the *Hippolytus*, a chorus of huntsmen who attend Hippolytus. They go into the house at line 112. At line 120 the main chorus, women attending Phaedra, start their dance. It would seem impossible for the first chorus to make the relatively complicated costume change in time. It would be natural if they came on at the end of the play attending the dying Hippolytus (1342). We must therefore assume that they are a genuine second chorus. The short song they sing (61–72) is musically uncomplicated. It does not involve a system dance. At the beginning of the *Ion* there is a gathering of worshipers. The *Trojan Women, Electra, Iphigeneia at Aulis* all have entrances in chariots of some sort. It does not seem necessary to assume two choruses in *The Frogs*. Having played the frogs, the chorus would have time to change in the dressing room before reappearing as the initiates.[30] In the *Lysistrata* there may have been more than twenty-four *choreutae*. For most of the play there are two choruses, one of men, one of women. But it is possible that these were two semichoruses of twelve each. At line 1043 they unite to form one chorus. At 1247 there is a song and dance by a Spartan chorus, answered a few lines later by the Athenian chorus. This would suggest that the Spartan embassy arrives (1072) with a train of attendants who are in fact dancers, and that, having arrived as a band of extras, they later reveal themselves as a second chorus. There would therefore be presumably twenty-four of them. It is unnecessary to specify the details of the extras in Aristophanes' plays, since there are so many of them. As I said earlier, there was less hesitation in giving small amounts of dialogue to extras in comedy than in tragedy.

Children were frequently employed as extras, and I see no reason why they should not have occasionally been required to speak. The amount of dialogue given to a child is never more than a line or two, and it would not have been difficult to train an intelligent child that far. What is more controversial is the question of women extras. Wilamowitz suggested that naked girls appeared as extras quite frequently in the Aristophanes plays.[31] His list includes the two girls whose breasts Dikaiopolis (Just-City) fondles in the finale of *The Acharnians* (1190 ff.), the girl *aulos*-player with whom Philocleon (Friend-of-Cleon) plays at the party in *The Wasps* (1326ff.). Theoria in the *Peace,* (706ff.) the nightingale girl *aulos*-player who accompanies the *parabasis* of *The Birds* (667ff.) and Majesty, the girl friend of Zeus, given to Pisthetairos (Persuader) in the finale (1720ff.), the spirit of reconciliation in the *Lysistrata* (1114 ff.), the stripper by whom the Scythian guard is outwitted in the finale of *The Women at the Thesmophoria* (1175 ff.). Pickard-Cambridge suggests also the spirits of peace at the end of *The Knights,* (1389ff.), and the Muse of Euripides mocked by Aeschylus in the competition of *The Frogs* (1306 ff.). If these parts were all played by women, then we should surely include also the two Megarian girls in the *Acharnians* (729 ff.), since the point of the scene depends on the exhibition of female private parts.

An age as sexually unabashed as fifth-century Athens may well have enjoyed the sight of beautiful naked girls, provided that they were of an inferior status, and therefore possible objects of sexual exploitation, as the cabaret performers were.[32] In all the instances quoted, the characters depicted are prostitutes, except for the two Megarian girls, who are preparing to be prostitutes rather than starve. I myself see no reason for either the nightingale or the Muse of Euripides to be completely naked, though they are certainly so scantily clad as to offer erotic provocation. The spirits of Peace in *The Knights,* Theoria in the *Peace,* and Majesty in *The Birds* present sexual delight as an image of the feasting that is peace and victory. They are like temple prostitutes, offering their sex as something sacred. Nudity is abundantly right. The dialogue makes it absolutely clear that Theoria, Friend-of-Cleon's girl, and the two Megarian girls are stark naked, since there are references both blatant and punning to their visible private parts. The action indicates that the stripper in *The Women at the Thesmophoria* is completely nude for a moment. The rest are either nude or as near nude as makes no difference. As we decide whether these naked girls were in fact naked girls, or men dressed as naked girls down to the specifics of pubic hair or plucked pubic hair (*Peace,* 868) we can only rely on our sense of what would be more seemly. For my own part I feel sure that the flagrant eroticism of the sequence in the *Peace* would be more tasteful with a beautiful naked girl than with a man displaying female private parts, particularly given the custom of offering a girl of slave or semislave status to a guest at a party much as one would offer a drink.[33] It is an important question for us to decide as we face up to understanding the obvious eroticism of Aristophanes, since the present generation is the first for a long time that can begin to do this.

It does not take much imagination to realize the demands made by the great roles of both tragedy and comedy on the actors' physique and emotions. The title role in Sophocles' *Electra* is perhaps the greatest single character role in all the plays. But it does not require much singing. Electra's solos are nearly all anapest chant. The leading actor in the *Antigone* has to follow Antigone's long *kommos* (806–83), which demands considerable singing ability, with a change into the role of the old prophet Teiresias. In the later plays of Euripides, the leading actors are, of course, required to sing much more.[34] It is interesting to notice that the Indians divided music into three octaves: the chest, the throat, and the head octave. This implies that the entire range of the voice was used, and that men used falsetto as a normal part of their vocal equipment. It is likely that the Greeks did the same, and it is difficult to imagine one actor conveying both Deianeira and Heracles without extensive use of falsetto. It is interesting to speculate as to whether Antigone's *kommos* was sung falsetto; the most virtuoso aria of all Greek drama, that of the Phrygian slave in the *Orestes*, must have been falsetto, for the slave is a eunuch (1369–1502).[35]

The audience was extremely sensitive to the nuances of an actor's diction. The best example of this is the story of the tragic actor Hegelochos, who became a stock joke for mispronouncing an apostrophe.[36] The mistake he made must have been infinitesimal; it is almost impossible for us to conceive such aural subtlety. But clearly, the Greek actor, in his full mask, needed a virtuosity of vocal technique beyond that of the modern actor.

As we come to consider the dances, we realize the variety and vitality of the mime available to the poets. The actors too must have made use of mime, perhaps particularly in comedy. A good example is the scene in *The Clouds* between Strepsiades (Twister) and the student in the think-tank (133–220). The student must surely mime while he describes how Socrates measures flea jumps, demonstrates that the gnat's hum is a fart, and uses a spit to filch a cloak, in this case Twister's. It is a vivid cameo part, depending for its success almost entirely on the physicality of these actions.

I have chosen both these examples because, although they demonstrate the demands made on an actor's skill, what is required is a certain sort of virtuosity rather than naturalistic character portrayal. On occasions, extreme subtlety of character drawing is required. But in the case of the flea-miming student, the role requires hardly any character portrayal at all, and more than minimal attention to character would detract from the fun of the miming. This is something that permeates all fifth-century drama. The Athenian poets did not start with character drawing; they started with a dance for the god. The portrayal of character was added as an accessory, sometimes a very important one, but always an accessory to the central purpose of the work, which must be analyzed dramatically in other terms than the pure interaction of character, and analyzed theatrically in such a way that we realize the climaxes do not always involve the principal actors climactically. By the time that the leading actor was the most important element in the play, Athenian drama had become a dead formula.

Masks and Costumes

As we might expect, the costume for most of the characters in the tragedies and satyr plays was based on normal Athenian costume. The main garments are the *chiton* and the *himation*. The *chiton* is a tunic made from one square piece of cloth, and the *himation* is also a square piece of cloth, draped over it. The needs of the dramatic performances caused sleeves to be added to this basic costume. Most probably they were first added to the costume of the *aulos*-player. A musician's fingers must be kept warm, and to play at the *Lenaia* in January must have been often quite an ordeal; even at the *Dionysia* in March a warm day was by no means certain. The vases indicate anyhow that the *aulos*-player wore the most elaborate and splendid costume of all the performers. This splendor may well have dated more or less from the beginnings of the festival. In the early fifth century, there was a great interest in plays about the East, and the sleeved tunic seems to have been used for oriental characters, and then gradually to have become the standard costume for all actors in tragedy. Clearly, it would be useful to have a costume that covered neck and arms if men were to act women, since these parts of the body look so different. Women in real life and on the stage wore long *chitons*, with the exception of maenads, whose *chitons* are knee-length.

The satyr chorus were naked except for a hairy loincloth to which was attached an erect penis, natural size, and a tail. Their mask was more or less human, but with animal ears. It was painted red. Silenus, the father of the satyrs, wore a hairy body stocking and had a bearded mask with animal ears. He does not seem to have been padded. The human characters in satyr plays seem to have been dressed normally.

Quick changes are of course easier when there is a mask. The modern actor is handicapped because he cannot take clothes off by pulling them over his head without disturbing his hair style. The Greek mask covered the top of the head, and so an actor did not need to worry about his hair. We may therefore assume that the leading actor of *The Women of Trachis* would change completely between Deianeira and Heracles, wearing a long *chiton* for the former, and a shorter one for the latter. But no doubt maximum use was made of additional items of costume such as the lion-skin, which automatically indicated Heracles, and which could so easily be slung across the shoulders and, with a change of mask, automatically indicate a change of character.

Both satyrs and maenads were barefoot. Some other choruses must have appeared barefoot too, those of slave women, for instance. Similarly, when appropriate, actors would be barefoot. There seem to be two kinds of foot-wear. Both were almost like socks, with minimal soles. Both types came up to the top of the calf. One was open from instep to shin, with crisscross lacing, a kind of boot-moccasin. The other was exactly like a sock and could be worn on either foot. It was called *kothornos*, and was typically the footwear of women and also of Dionysus himself. Theramenes, a politician who managed to trim his politics to the party in power during the revolutions in Athens during the last decade of the fifth century, was nicknamed "Kothornos" because he was a boot that could be worn by either foot.[37] Either type of boot could have its top cuffed, or ornamented, or both.[38]

The masks were naturalistic representations, without distortions. The mouths are usually slightly open, in the best compromise between open and closed. They were probably made of stiffened linen, and were very light, since they could be dangled on the fingers. They had hair that would cover the wearer's hair. Presumably this went over the band that attached the mask to the head. Satyrs' masks were painted red, and most female masks are painted white in the vase pictures, so presumably this was the usual practice in the theater also. Athenian women went about much less than their men. They would therefore have been less sunburned.

I have suggested earlier that it is most likely that the use of the mask dates back to very early times, and that its first significance is exactly the same as that of the face-painting we find in many primitive tribes who either mask or paint their faces as a gesture of identity-surrender in the mystical experience of the ritual dance. Unless we place the donning of the mask very early in the de-velopment of the dance drama, it is difficult to see why the chorus should have been masked.

The satyr *choreutae* on the famous Pronomos vase of about 400 B.C.[39] do not all have exactly the same loincloth. It is harder to be sure if their masks are all identical. There is no reason to suppose that all members of a chorus should be dressed and masked exactly the same, although it was no doubt unusual to make more than the minimal differentiation shown in the Pronomos vase un-less the situation called for it.

At first, no doubt, there was no great attempt to differentiate character by the actor's mask either. But during the fifth century the art of mask making must have advanced along with that of sculpture and vase painting. By the time of Aristophanes we know that it was customary to make portrait masks for the real-life characters depicted. Aristophanes apologizes in *The Knights* (230–33) for not giving the character of Cleon a recognizable mask. We may presume therefore that all the other recognizable characters in Aristophanes' plays did have portrait masks. Accordingly, every extant fifth-century play by Aristophanes contains at least one portrait mask, and most, more than one.[40]

There are some allusions to an obvious change of mask within the portrayal of one character. In *The Clouds* Pheidippides (Horsey) is someone addicted to chariot racing, an outdoor type. When his father persuades him to enter the think-tank, he comes out pallid, and his father hails the beauty of his changed, pasty-faced sophistical complexion (1171). The joke in this case is stronger if the change in complexion is so exaggerated that the audience notices it before the dialogue points it out. Clearly, there must have been some mask changes in tragedy also, as when Oedipus emerges blind and bleeding (*Oedipus the King,* 1307 ff.) or Polymestor crawls out in the same condition (*Hecuba,* 1056 ff.). Visible blood on the face is necessary in both these cases. There are other occasions where a change of mask might have helped the portrayal of a character. I myself feel that in that kind of instance the mask was not changed, and therefore I confine the number of mask changes to a very bare minimum.

Once, however, we grant that nearly every Old Comedy play displayed some portrait masks, and that some characters changed their masks, we must admit almost unlimited freedom to the mask maker, at any rate of the later fifth century. Writers such as Pollux[41] list types of masks, but these stock masks apply to the stock characters of New Comedy, and no doubt especially to a touring company, which would have to take with it enough masks to represent all the characters portrayed. This has nothing to do with the theater of Aristophanes.

The details of the Old Comedy costume, whether of actors or chorus, seem also to have allowed almost unlimited variety. There was certainly no necessity for the chorus all to be dressed alike, though no doubt they were not always as gaudily individual both in mask and costume as in the chorus of birds, who enter one by one as different species of bird (260 ff.). From the feminine fripperies of Agathon (*The Women at the Thesmophoria* 96 ff.) to the grotesque armor of Lamachus shattered by his disastrous battle (*The Acharnians,* 1190 ff.), from the scanty rags of the shivering poet who visits Cloudcuckooland (*The Birds,* 903 ff.) to the ludicrous oriental splendor of the gibbering Persian ambassador obstructing the process of Just-City's peace (*The Acharnians,* 100 ff.), every variation of rich and poor, beautiful and grotesque, exotic and ordinary is waved in our faces.

The traditional basic comic costume consisted of a short *chiton* that did not cover the loins. It was padded so that both belly and buttocks were grotesquely enlarged. Underneath the *chiton* the actor wore tights, to which was attached a vast phallus made of leather, sometimes erect and sometimes not. There is also a similar costume, which consisted of a flesh-colored body stocking, also grotesquely padded in belly and buttocks, to which the phallus was attached. With both these costumes sleeves are normal. Comic choruses do not seem to have worn the phallus, and there are no obvious references to its being worn in the extant plays. The chorus of old men in the *Lysistrata* would be an obvious choice. But it seems very unlikely that they did, or we feel that the old women's chorus would make a joke about it. For the old men comment rudely about the women showing their cunts when they do the hick kick (824). Presumably a chorus of old men would wear a longer *chiton*, more like the costume of everyday life.

In the *parabasis* of *The Clouds* (537ff.), when Aristophanes does his act of fake innocence discussed in Chapter 1, the first vulgarity he disclaims is the phallus. Presumably, by this time some of the more sophisticated members of the audience were claiming to have grown out of what was very much part of the primitive fertility ritual. It seems likely therefore that not all Aristophanes' actors would have worn one. It is also apparent from the vase pictures that there was considerable variety in the type of phallus, and therefore it would seem probable that a poet of Aristophanes' inventiveness would get the maximum amusement out of creating a phallus to suit the character who wore it. Clearly, that of Persuader in *The Birds* is large and erect, from his language as he attempts to rape Iris, the messenger of the gods. "Call me old? I've got a hard on like a battleship" (1256). In one of Aristophanes' most creative phallus jokes, we get a good picture of Friend-of-Cleon's quite different phallus. Friend-of-Cleon has left the party, dragging off the naked or nearly naked *aulos*-girl, who, like some cabaret artists in all periods of history, is deemed available sexual material for the guests. Friend-of-Cleon climbs the steps of the terrace.

Friend-of-Cleon.
Come up here, my little golden grasshopper. Put out your hand. Catch on
  to this rope.
Hold on.
Look out. The rope's rotten.
Never mind. Rubbing it does it no harm.

(*Wasps*, 1342–44)[42]

During the fourth century both phallus and padding disappeared from the comic costume, and, by the time of Menander at the end of the century, comic costume was more or less the same as the ordinary daily costume of the Athenians. Then it became the turn of the tragic costume to become very different from that of real life. The robes grew more formal; the shoes acquired the notorious blocked-up soles; the mask was elongated upwards, and body padding was added to fill out what would otherwise have been an overelongated figure. Costume fitted the plays: ordinary for the ordinariness of New Comedy; grotesquely statuesque for the pompous solemnity of the grand opera into which tragedy had rigidified. In the fifth century the tragic costume was not too far from the costume of real life, as a reminder that the tragedies were very much about real life, while, if the costume of Old Comedy hammers at us the word fertility, certainly fertility in more senses than the sexual is a mark of the wild imaginings of Aristophanes.

Music

It has been customary for scholarly writing on the subject of Greek music to give the impression that we know very little about it. It is certainly the case that practically every modern production of the Greek plays reveals complete ignorance of the musical requirements. But careful consideration shows us that we know a very great deal about the music of the Greek plays, in a sense much more than we know about the details of the music in Shakespeare's plays, certainly of the way in which Shakespeare used music to build the total rhythm of his drama.

It is said that we do not know very much about ancient Greek music because we do not know very much about their melodies. It would be truer to say that there is a well-defined limit both to our knowledge and to our ignorance. I will return to this later. It is necessary to start this discussion by summarizing what we do know.

We know with the utmost precision down to the last note exactly what was spoken, what was sung, and what was chanted in every Greek play.[43] Furthermore, we know to the last note the exact rhythmic notation of every song. We know the emotional connotations of the main tempi, using tempo in the way a jazz musician uses it, in which a particular tempo implies a particular rhythm. We have a fair guide to the tempo in the sense of metronome marking. Most musicians would unhesitatingly say the rhythm of a piece of music is the most important element of its form. Most musicians would agree that to possess the complete score in rhythmic notation is a long way toward possessing the complete score.

The only parts of tragedy or comedy that were spoken are the passages in iambic trimeters, the meter of dialogue verse, which it used to be natural to translate into English blank verse, and for which in modern English verse there is no obvious equivalent.[44] An actor wishing to make dramatic sense of the great speeches of tragedy, particularly in a vast auditorium, will need to use the full range of pitch in his spoken voice. It is possible that sometimes an even more musical delivery was used. The one formal device used frequently in the spoken parts of tragedy in particular is stichomythia, where each actor speaks exactly one line and is answered by one line. But I do not myself believe that the dialogue verse was ever intoned. For, first, the poets had at their disposal a variety of chants whenever they wanted that kind of effect. Second, the dialogue verse, particularly of Sophocles, is always so exquisitely constructed that the word containing the action, the gesture, of the line, is always in exactly the right place; it is so much *gestiches Sprach*—speech as gesture—to use Brecht's phrase. If the dialogue verse is so packed with pace and action, then a too musical delivery would hamper its effect.

Parakataloge is the term applied to all sequences in between speech and song. I assume that it mostly implied a chant with many syllables on one note, or a very primitive tune of only a very few notes. But it seems that it may well have covered the entire range between speech and song, from something very near speech but against a musical accompaniment, to something almost song. On occasions its use seems very like recitative in some opera; often it is like liturgical chant; sometimes it seems to be a kind of colored and heightened declamation.

It is used for nearly every employment of anapests. In some plays of Aeschylus the *parodos* starts with a long march around the *orchestra* while the chorus chants anapests, nearly all dimeters.[45] This may well have been the standard opening of the early tragedies. Anapest dimeters are frequently used for short linking sequences during dialogue scenes, as when the chorus announces the arrival of a new character. They are also frequently employed in the middle of sung lyrics. Sometimes, in a duet between actor and chorus, the actor is mainly given anapests, while the chorus sings the lyrics. This was no doubt because great actors were not always great singers. Electra in Sophocles' play of that name has very little actual lyric to sing. But we notice, for example, in the *parodos* of the *Electra* that after the opening anapests chanted by Electra solo (86–120), the anapests with which she answers each chorus stanza are in Dorian dialect, which must mean that they were sung, though obviously to a simpler tune than a passage in a lyric meter (121–250). We notice that, very gradually during this *parodos*, Electra is given more and more lyric meter in comparison with anapest. Clearly, her part builds in melodic interest to the *epode* (233–50), which is a fully developed lyric, giving Electra the opportunity to dominate the chorus in her music and dance. In the *parodos* of the *Antigone* (100–162) lyrics and sung anapests alternate. Here it seems merely that Sophocles is using this technique for a change of texture: the anapest sections are obviously appropriate to the marching of the enemy and the vengeance of God, which they present.

All of the three original sequences of comedy—*parodos*, *agōn*, and *parabasis*—are chanted (except of course for the sung lyrics). They are in tetrameters, either anapest, iambic, or trochaic. These imply a characteristic movement: anapests a march, iambics a stylized walk, and trochees a run. The chorus of knights gallop on chanting trochees (*Knights*, 247ff.), while the old men of *The Wasps* enter to laborious iambics (230ff.). Anapest tetrameters convey a certain solemnity. They are the standard chant for the first speech of the *parabasis*, to such an extent that the bird chorus can say, "Let's begin the anapests." (684). In the *agōn* of *The Clouds*, Just Logic chants his speech in anapests, the rhythm of nobility (961ff.), while Unjust Logic makes his answer in the meaner iambics (1036ff.).

When a passage in tetrameters reaches a climax, it frequently changes to dimeters, which clearly has the effect of speeding it up. A passage of these dimeters in comedy was called a *pnigos*—a choke—because it was customary for the actor to deliver it in one breath. Whatever movement was being performed during the tetrameters would no doubt now be performed in double time, thus rounding the sequence off and raising applause.

Of the three "long line" meters, we find only trochaic tetrameters in tragedy. They were apparently common in the earliest tragedy.[46] They are used in *The Persians* in passages that are rather specially important, to give a kind of emphasis (155–75, 215–48, 703–58). Sophocles does not use them in the extant plays. Euripides uses them to speed up the action, sometimes to give almost the feeling of Aristophanic breathlessness. The earliest play of his in which they appear is the *Heracles,* where the dance of Madness over the roof of Heracles' home is in trochaic tetrameters (855–73).[47]

Nearest to liturgical chant are dactylic hexameters, the meter of the Homeric epics, the meter of oracles and sacred utterances in general. These are used by all the poets, always for some sacred utterance, or in Aristophanes sometimes for a parody of such an utterance. There is one example of a lament chanted in elegiac couplets (*Andromache,* 103–16), but this seems to have been very unusual.

All ancient Greek lyrics were sung, and none were ever written except to be sung, since what the grammarians refer to as lyric meters are patterns that dictate exactly the rhythm of the song. If we are talking prosody we say that Greek poetry was scanned by quantity in longs and shorts, as opposed to the accentual scanning of verse in modern languages. It would be much simpler and equally correct to say that Greek poetry was composed in a pattern of quarter notes and eighth notes, and that, because the note value of every syllable positioned in a lyric line was fixed, rhythmic composition consisted only in arranging syllables and syllable patterns until a pleasing and appropriate stanza was reached.

Once spoken verse had been invented, relatively late in Greek literary history, the composition of verse developed more flexibility. The iambic trimeter is constructed rhythmically half-way between the system of Greek lyric and the indeterminate scansion of the English blank verse line whose rhythm is part scansion and part meaning, that is to say, pace. The iambic trimeter, particularly in comedy, allows, for instance, anapests for iambics at certain points of the line. This indeterminacy of note values could not be allowed in lyrics. All lyrics are composed in quarter notes and eighth notes only; there is practically

no substitution even of two eighth notes for a quarter note, and ♩ always = ♩ throughout a stanza. Furthermore, by reading a lyric stanza we can immediately read off the note values, since which syllables are worth a quarter note and which an eighth note is governed by rigid rules.[48]

The sung lyrics in the plays are composed almost entirely in systems: pairs of matching stanzas called *strophē* and *antistrophē.* Since *strophē* and *antistrophē* were set to the same tune,[49] we can easily detect the musical phrase endings of this tune by seeing in the text the points where the sense comes to a stop in both *strophē* and *antistrophē.* Clearly, these were the main breath pauses, the subsidiary climaxes. We usually find at least one in the middle of each system. We can go further. By analyzing from the text possible short breath pauses and considering the amount of time between each, we can arrive at a fair estimation of the tempo of the song. When we combine this analysis with the mood of the words, we can be confident that we are not far from the original.[50]

Greek lyrics were composed by fitting together certain patterns of note values into larger groupings. Some of these basic patterns have a very clear emotional ·connotation. The dochmiac [♪♩ ♩ ♪♩] always ex-cited, whether through fear, sorrow, or joy. The anacreontic [♪♪♩ ♪♩ ♪♩♩] suggests its original use—the rhythm of drinking songs. The ionic a minore [♪♪♩ ♩] and the ionic a majore [♩ ♩ ♪♪] are both slow three-time tempi. They are used for the dances of the maenads and the languid dances of the Orient. To the Greeks these were clearly very similar tempi. To a modern musician, working in terms of beats in a bar, [♪ ♪ ♩ ♩] is identical to [♩ ♩ ♪ ♪] But to a modern musician [♪♪♩ ♩ | ∕ | ♩ ♩ ♪♪] is also identical to [♩ ♪ ♪ ♩], another three-in-a-bar tempo, different only in that the eighth notes are on the second beat instead of the first or third. To the Greeks, [♩ ♪ ♪ ♩] was a totally different tempo—the choriambus, a much more excited music. This example shows how the various so-called meters were not only patterns of notes, but patterns of notes implying a style of performance. There are possible modern comparisons: waltz tempo, for example, means fast three-time, with a heavy accent on the first beat of the bar. A jazz waltz is also in fast three-time, but with a heavy accent elsewhere than on the first beat, as in "Something's Coming" from *West Side Story*, where the accent is on the second half of the second beat.

As we might expect, there are a number of meters that are not very specific as to mood. There are, for example, a great number of choruses that use some kind of an iambic or trochaic pattern; there is the more stately dactylo-epitrite, consisting of varying numbers of dactyls [♩ ♪ ♪] followed by varying numbers of epitrites [♩ ♪♩ ♪] Given that it is a more stately tempo, its use is very varied.

The choruses were sung by the whole chorus in unison as they danced, accompanied by the *aulos*-player, who was also the conductor. What is very difficult for us to grasp is that their enormously complex dance was kept in time without percussion, by one wind instrument on its own.

The *aulos* was a wind instrument with a double reed, somewhat like a primi-

tive oboe, and presumably therefore resembling the medieval shawm. However, considering that it was the only instrument used to accompany a large
chorus, in a vast auditorium, it must have had the penetration at least of a
cornetto. Pictures of an *aulos*-player often show him with two *auloi* in his
mouth. As in the Middle Ages,[51] this was to give him more notes to play, not so
that he could play a drone. It would seem that by the fifth century the *aulos*-
player would have had about fifteen or sixteen notes at his command. This
would be quite adequate, provided that he carried a different pair of *auloi* for
each mode required in the course of the play.

Solos were accompanied by a lyre, played behind the *skēnē*,[52] as were the
early chorus dance dramas of Stesichoros. There is evidence that *aulos* and lyre
could be played together. One reference is in a comic poet, but, although it is
from a play, it may not refer to such a duet on stage.[53] The other reference is to a
cabaret performance.[54] Must this not have involved some primitive harmony?
Given the relatively crude state of both instruments, it is very hard to believe
that they could have played the same notes. For what is easy on the lyre would
not necessarily be easy on the *aulos* and vice versa. Further, when Aristophanes
parodies the lyrics of Euripides in *The Frogs* accompanied by a lyre, he makes
up a word for the strumming that would be the normal first sound anyone
makes on such an instrument—*tophlattothrat* (1286ff.). How can one strum a
stringed instrument euphoniously without creating harmony, however primi-
tively? Furthermore, there is a suggestion that the note accompanying a piece of
chanted *parakataloge* was higher than the note sung. All these small pieces of
evidence, however, are set aside by the historians of music, who say that there
was no harmony before the Middle Ages.

Later in *The Frogs*, when Aeschylus sings a mock Euripides lyric, he refuses
to use the lyre to accompany himself, deeming such rubbish worthy only of the
castanets that are played by Euripides' Muse (1309–63). Castanets, made out of
shells or pottery, were sometimes used, but only rarely. It is surprising that the
tympanon, the small kettledrum used in the worship of Dionysus, never seems
to have been used in tragedy.

In *The Frogs* a rare stage direction is preserved that says there was an instrumental introduction to the song immediately following (1263). It would seem
likely that when the *parodos* of a play starts straight off with a sung lyric, which
could only be performed with the chorus all in their positions in the *orchestra*,
there must have been an instrumental solo to cover the end of their march up
the *parodoi* into the *orchestra*. We need suppose no more than that the *aulos*-
player played the tune of the song about to be sung. There is no evidence to
suggest that Greek music had any real independence of the words with which it
was inextricably linked.

The ancient Greek modes seem to have been very much the same as the ragas
of Indian music. Each mode carried a different emotional association depending on the relationship between the adjacent tones, semitones and quarter
tones, which made up the gamut of that particular mode. Musical color, which

in modern Western music is supplied by harmony and orchestration, was there-
fore supplied in Greek music, as it is in Indian, entirely by the choice of mode.
The Greek musician had many different modes from which to choose. Each
named variety had three subvariants: diatonic, chromatic, and enharmonic.[55]
Certain modes had very obvious emotional connotations, above all the martial
Dorian mode. Aristoxenus regards the martial Dorian and the emotional Mixo-
Lydian as the two modes most suitable for tragedy. He also says that Sophocles
was the first to introduce into tragedy the Phrygian mode, which was appropriate to dithyramb.[56] By the time of Sophocles the dithyramb was a stately
performance, and dactylo-epitrite was a favorite meter. We may perhaps assume, then, that the occurrence of dactylo-epitrites suggest the possibility of
the Phrygian mode. For Plato, only the Dorian and Phrygian modes were
suitable. He wishes to ban the Mixo-Lydian and Syntono-Lydian as suitable
for laments, and the Ionian and Lydian as suitable for drinking parties (*Republic*, 3.398E–399A). If we are thinking of the emotional significance of the
modes, we should perhaps compare the way that a Western audience reacts to
orchestration: anyone will find the trumpet stirring: clearly, more or less any
Greek could react in the same way to the Dorian mode. But the greater subtleties of orchestration cannot be analyzed except by a trained musician. Similarly, no doubt, only a trained musician could appreciate the choice of one
mode rather than another when the modes had less obvious connotations.[57]

The emotional connotations of a raga are not inherent in the relationships of
the notes in its gamut, so much as developed over a period of time through the
music played in that raga. Even if we are sure of the note relationships within,
for instance, the Dorian mode, we cannot reproduce the emotional connotations of the original simply by composing notes belonging to the original.
Modern Western ears are probably irretrievably too coarsened for hearing color
though modal intervals, just as they are immensely sharpened for hearing
harmony. In this sense we can never reproduce the music of Sophocles. But if
an Indian composer were to set a Sophocles chorus to the raga appropriate to
the mood of the piece, making use of the exact rhythm score that Sophocles has
left and using only a unison tune accompanied in unison by a rough reed
instrument, then for his audience he would have got very near indeed to the
music of Sophocles.

Discussion of the music in the Greek plays, just as discussion of all the other
aspects of their production and staging, should make us realize that we know
the general principles in very adequate detail. The right designers and the right
composers, after proper study of all the available material, could come up with
a very fair reconstruction of what happened in the theater of Dionysus during
the fifth century. What is lacking is our emotional relationship with the details.
We cannot recapture so easily Sophocles' emotions on hearing the Mixo-Lydian
mode, or on holding a phallus in his hand. Our reconstructions might feel
dead. But it is not as if we were attempting such a reconstruction without any
assistance to our emotions. We are working through the words of four very

great poets indeed. The production implications of their words provide us with a web of emotional connotations into which we can fit visual details of costume or staging and aural details of music. Necessary as the great works of scholarship on the texts and monuments to do with the Greek theater have been, they are still not enough. Finally, the reconstruction of the staging of the plays of the fifth century is, more than a work of scholarly research, an effort of poetic imagination.

Notes

1. See Appendix 3 for meanings of terms used.

2. See Sir Arthur Pickard-Cambridge, *The Theatre of Dionysus in Athens* (Oxford: Clarendon Press, 1946), pp. 11–12, for texts bearing on this incident.

3. For detailed argument about the development of the theater building see Pickard-Cambridge, *The Theatre of Dionysus in Athens.* For further discussion of both building and the mise en scène of the plays, see T. B. L. Webster, *Greek Theatre Production* (London: Methuen, 1970), Peter Arnott, *Greek Scenic Conventions in the Fifth Century B.C.*(Oxford: Clarendon Press, 1962), and, with respect to Euripides, Nicholas C. Hourmouziades, *Production and Imagination in Euripides* (Athens: Greek Society for Humanistic Studies, 1965).

4. See Pickard-Cambridge, *The Theatre of Dionysus in Athens*, pp. 134–74, for detailed discussion.

5. Later changes in the theater are described by Pickard-Cambridge, *The Theatre of Dionysus in Athens*, pp. 175ff.

6. Webster remarks in *Greek Theatre Production*, p. 4, that in Drury Lane Theatre the distance from the stage to the front of the dress circle is forty-eight feet, as compared with the sixty feet across the *orchestra* from the actors' terrace to the front row of the audience. He estimates the distance from the actors' terrace to the back of the Periclean auditorium as being about three hundred feet.

7. See Chapter 7, where I suggest a use for it in the *Oresteia*, and Chapter 8.

8. The performances altogether cannot have lasted more than twelve hours. A reasonable rough allocation of time would then allow two hours for a tragedy or comedy, one and a half for a satyr play, half an hour for the opening proceedings, and half an hour between each play.

9. For translation of Aristophanes' character names see Appendix 2.

10. See Chapter 7.

11. *Poetics* 4.1449A.18.

12. There is no need in any of the extant plays to assume a separate *theologeion*—god-balcony— above the flat roof as described. Certainly at the end of the *Orestes*, Orestes is on the roof about to murder Hermione when Apollo appears above to stop him. But Apollo is on the *mēchanē*. (*Orestes*, 1625).

13. See Chapter 8.

14. This possibility provides an extra question in the argument about side entrances. A side entrance is certainly required in *The Clouds* to represent a house—Twister's—separate from the think-tank. Aegisthus, however, in *The Libation-Bearers* could perhaps have entered from around the side of the *skēnē*.

15. Arnott conceives it as a counterbalanced jib, partly because Antiphanes the comic poet describes it as "like a finger." See Antiphanes, frag. 191, Arnott, *Greek Scenic Conventions in the Fifth Century B.C.*, p. 73.

16. See Chapter 8 for my discussion of the chorus entry in the *Prometheus Bound*, which I do not believe took place on the *mēchanē*.

17. See Appendix 4 for notes on Greek meters.

18. For example, see *The Women at the Thesmophoria* 95–265. Agathon, the camp tragic poet, has to be wheeled out for his scene. Part of the joke is tragedy's dependence on stage devices, a frequent dig of the comic poets.

19. Arnott, *Greek Scenic Conventions in the Fifth Century* B.C., pp. 43–65, argues at length that this altar was a permanent feature of the actors' terrace, and that it served to represent any altars or tombs required by the drama.

20. *Wakefield Cycle, Noah,* 279–82.

21. Carlo Anti, *Teatri Greci Arcaici da Minosse a Pericle* (Padova: Monografie di Archeologia, no. 1, 1947), pp. 92–108 and passim. Arnott, *Greek Scenic Conventions in the Fifth Century* B.C., unfortunately does not deal with this problem.

22. See Chapter 10.

23. Pollux, *Onomastikon,* 4.130.

24. E.g., *Lysistrata* 77–244.

25. Pickard-Cambridge analyzes the distribution of parts in all the Aristophanes plays. See Sir Arthur Pickard-Cambridge, *The Dramatic Festivals of Athens* 2d. ed. rev. John Gould and D. M. Lewis (Oxford: Clarendon Press, 1968), pp. 149–53. He bases his distribution on the principle of allotting as little as possible to the fourth actor. We have simply no means of saying whether this is sound.

26. Pickard-Cambridge, *The Dramatic Festivals of Athens,* pp. 142–44, suggests a distribution of parts that involves the great role of Theseus being split between all three actors, and summarizes the other theories, all of which involve splitting the role of Theseus and should therefore be dismissed.

27. See Chapter 8.

28. Pickard-Cambridge, *The Dramatic Festivals of Athens,* p. 140, is anxious to avoid this. He suggests that the third actor plays the servant who announces Aegisthus' death, does a quick change, and then reappears as Pylades. Pickard-Cambridge gives him from 886 to 899 to do his change. I see no reason for the servant to leave as soon as he has spoken. Nor is there good reason for Pylades to come on after Orestes as Pickard-Cambridge suggests. If the servant were to leave at all, the natural place would be at 891, which is the moment of Orestes' and Pylades' entrance. The servant must stay on. Pylades is a mute who speaks.

29. See Chapter 7.

30. See Chapter 8, where this is discussed further.

31. Aristophanes, *Lysistrate,* ed. Ulrich von Wilamowitz-Moellendorf (Berlin: Weidmannsche Verlagsbuchhandlung, 1927), pp. 186–87.

32. See Chapter 12.

33. See Chapter 7, for a further discussion of *The Peace.*

34. See Chapter 5.

35. See Chapter 7.

36. The line in question is from Euripides' *Orestes,* 279. It ends *galēn' horō,* meaning "I see calm weather." He apparently pronounced this as *galēn horō,* which means "I see a weasel." We know that Hegelochos became a stock joke from the way in which he is referred to in Aristophanes, *Frogs,* 304. See also the scholiast on that line. It is very difficult for us to conceive what the difference in pronunciation could possibly be. It certainly must have been very slight. There is a different accent on the second syllable, and this signifies that a different tone was used. We now, however, know nothing of the tonal system of ancient Greek, and since no modern western language is tonal, it has been difficult to give proper consideration to that aspect of the ancient Greek language. It can only be approached via our understanding of modern tonal languages— languages in which the pitch at which a word is spoken determines its meaning just as much as the pattern of vowels and consonants. Thai—and, I believe, Chinese—has a relatively straightforward tonal pattern: five tones—high, medium, low, falling, rising. Zulu, and certain other African languages, such as Yoruba, are much more complicated. Zulu has at least twelve different tones. For certain Zulu verbs the pitch difference between second and third person singular is almost impossible for an adult westerner ever to learn to distinguish out of context. Even in the age of tape recorders it is very easy for a westerner attempting Zulu to get his tones wrong and commit some grotesque faux pas which will be greeted with howls of laughter. Part of our inability to understand fifth-century drama is due to our aural insensibility. There is plenty of work on ancient Greek waiting to be done by Zulu-speaking scholars.

37. Xenophon *Hellenica* 2.3.30–31; Pollux *Onomastikon* 8.90–91.

38. The word *kothornos* came to be applied so especially to stage footwear that, when shoes with blocked-up soles were introduced, the word *kothornos* was applied to them. Because *kothornos*

was used for the socklike boot of the fifth century, later writers imagined that the boots with blocked-up soles had also been in use during the fifth century, thus causing the widely held misunderstanding about these blocked-up boots.

39. Reproduced, e.g., in Pickard-Cambridge, *The Dramatic Festivals of Athens*, fig. 49.

40. Only *The Peace* has less obvious demands for personal caricature masks. But even in this play there are the sons of Lamachus and Cleonymus. The humor surely requires them to be presented in the kind of caricature that will identify them with their well-known fathers.

41. Pollux *Onomastikon* 4.143–54.

42. There have been attempts to show that Aristophanes eschewed the phallus altogether in his plays, which seem absurd in view of a passage such as the above. Beare conducted an argument with Webster in the pages of the *Classical Quarterly*, Beare attempting to deny its use, Webster arguing that it was used. See W. Beare, "The Costume of the Actors in Aristophanic Comedy," *Classical Quarterly (CQ)*, n.s., 4 (1954): 64–75; T. B. L. Webster, "The Costume of the Actors in Aristophanic Comedy," *CQ*, n.s., 5 (1955): 94–95; W. Beare, "Aristophanic Costume Again," *CQ*, n.s., 7 (1957): 184–85; T. B. L. Webster, "A Reply on Aristophanic Costume," *CQ*, n.s., 7 (1957): 185; and W. Beare, "Aristophanic Costume: A Last Word," *CQ*, n.s., 9 (1959): 126–27. Beare's main argument is that not all the characters could possibly wear the phallus. Naturally. Many are women. Beare feels distaste for the idea, for instance, of Aeschylus in *The Frogs* wearing a phallus. This may do no more than reveal his prejudices. If the household icons of the Athenians were sculpted with erect penises, then surely they would not wish to deny this emblem of power to their great, powerful poet.

43. A pedant might wish to argue that there are a few lines of iambic trimeters in the middle of sung passages, about which we cannot be absolutely sure as to whether they are spoken or chanted; and there are a few sequences of anapests in the middle of sung passages of which we cannot be absolutely sure as to whether they were chanted or sung. My own feeling, however, is that *parakataloge*—like our recitative—covered the complete range between speech and song, from what was more or less speech with certain notes pitched, spoken to an accompaniment, to what was virtually a sung tune. So that, even if we cannot say instantly of these minimal borderline cases whether they are speech or chant, chant or song, we can, at any rate, say that they are all *parakataloge*.

44. See Appendix 2 for principles of translation.

45. E.g., *Persians* 1–64; *Suppliants* 1–39; *Agamemnon* 40–103.

46. Aristotle *Poetics* 4.1449A.21.

47. See Chapter 6, "Form as Dance."

48. For a slight modification of this statement, see Chapter 5, "The Variety of Greek Dance," and Appendix 4 under *dochmiac* and *dactyl.*

49. Scholars will dispute anything, and this has been disputed. But if they were not so set, what on earth was the point of the poets torturing themselves and their language to create the enormous difficulties of the system? If the system has the musical, choreographic, and dramatic point that it seems to have, then it is an artistic invention of the highest order. If it was merely an exercise in prosodical complexity, then it was a pointless waste of all but a grammarian's time. Aeschylus and Sophocles were practical and practicing theater directors and musicians. They must not be treated as pedants. Such an attitude as I have scorned receives short shrift also in Dale's masterly book: A. M. Dale, *The Lyric Metres of Greek Drama* (London: Cambridge University Press, 1968). This is the outstanding work on meter largely because all her discussions of meter have a constant underlying reference to music.

50. Such an analysis, amongst much else, is given, chorus by chorus, in Webster's discussion of chorus dances: T. B. L. Webster, *The Greek Chorus* (London: Methuen, 1970).

51. For example, a gargoyle in Thaxted Church, Essex, England, shows an instrumentalist with two pipes in his mouth.

52. The Furies call their song *aphorminkton*—sung without the lyre (*Eumenides* 332–33). This suggests that some choruses could be accompanied by the lyre. But this can hardly have happened in drama, since a lyre player within the *skēnē* would have been too far away from a chorus dancing at the front of the *orchestra*.

53. See Athenaeus *Deipnosophists* 14.618B, who quotes Antiphanes.

54. Xenophon *Symposium* 3.1.

55. I use the first two words not in their modern sense. The Dorian mode, for example, has the following pattern of intervals:

diatonic: semitone, tone, tone, tone, semitone, tone, tone.
chromatic: semitone, semitone, minor third, tone, semitone, semitone, minor third.
enharmonic: quarter tone, quarter tone, major third, tone, quarter tone, quarter tone, tone.

56. Quoted in *Life of Sophocles* 23.

57. The principal texts that describe the emotional connotations of the Greek modes are Plato *Republic* 3. 398E, Aristotle *Politics* 5 (8) 5.1340A.38ff., 5 (8) 7.1342B.20ff., and 6 (4) 3.1290A.20ff.; Aristoxenus *Harmonics* 2.37.

5

DANCE DRAMA

The Variety of Greek Dance

The word *achoreutos* means "without dance training." Even Plato, whose attitude to education as to life was extremely puritanical, says that to be *achoreutos* is to be *apaideutos*, "uneducated." (*Laws* 2.654A). The dance was central to Athenian culture in a way that a Balinese would understand precisely but we find hard to imagine.

The central chorus, which sums up the *Oedipus the King* also sums up the crucial balance that is the *Gesamtkunstwerk* of fifth-century drama. "If the wrong-doer is unpunished, what is the point of dancing?" (863–910). The justification for the dance is that it is an activity of worship. Again the Balinese can understand. The Westerner finds such an inextricable connection hard.

It is the art of dancing in a chorus that was especially connected with worship. In later antiquity the art of solo dance developed great virtuosity, and Lucian considered that dance started as an art on its own only when it severed its connection with the theater.[1] But by then it had long since ceased to be central to the culture of the people or to have any real significance in their lives.

In the plays of the last decade of the Peloponnesian War we can detect the beginnings of the religious change I have referred to before that culminated in the religion of Plato, for whom the worship of the Olympian gods was only important as a kind of emotional entertainment for those people—the majority—who were not intelligent enough to understand philosophy. With this change in religious belief we can see a change in attitude to the chorus dance. The two go hand in hand. The chorus of the *Oedipus the King* is right. If oracles are no longer valid, if the old forms of worship no longer work, then what is the point of the dance in chorus? Let a few professionals dance if they wish. Dance has nothing to do with me.

Dance, then, is not just an element in the staging of the fifth-century plays like costumes or music. It is a central flavor of the culture, as perhaps it is still in Bali. Until we appreciate this, we cannot approach the work of Aeschylus and Sophocles. To make the chorus of a fifth-century play stand and recite free

114

verse is much more ludicrous even than making the chorus of a modern musical do so.

The choruses of fifth-century drama include some very great lyric poems. But when they were performed, they were received as *Gesamtkuntswerk*—song, dance, groupings, color, and spectacle together. We always misunderstand them if we criticize them as if they were poems to be read on the page. It is common to read literary criticism that refers to the "conventional statements" of the chorus. Even conventional statements, properly placed in context and beautifully sung and danced, acquire deep meaning as *Gesamtkunstwerk*. "Amen" could be said to be a conventional statement. But there are some very beautiful Amens in the work of some of the Renaissance composers. In Germain's normally perceptive book on Sophocles, there is a passage that refers to the chorus of the *Antigone* and reveals the misconception of the chorus that comes from treating it merely as a literary poem: "Les lois du lyrisme veulent qu'il s'exprime par rappels de grands myths ou par sentences de sagesse plutôt que par effusions humaines. Du moins le ton parle-t-il. C'est la chaleur dans la voix qui a manqué aux vieillards d'*Antigone*."[2] The thought of fifteen men singing "effusions humaines" while leaping or kicking their legs in the air is ludicrous. Even in Christian liturgy it is noticeable that it is not the poems of most intense personal devotion that make the best hymns but the ones whose emotion can be expressed by a crowd of people singing all together. Because the Greek worship was also danced, and watched by a crowd of spectators, the emotion needed to be generalized. Anything else would have been inappropriate.

A further consequence of the fact that the choruses were total *Gesamtkunstwerk*—all the arts working in harmony—was that they provided an emotional medium for everyone in the audience. We know now, from psychologists' tests as well as from common sense, that each person perceives in a slightly different way. Some dream in color, some in monochrome. Some are incapable of abstract thought; some are incapable of visualizing even a person's face at the other end of a telephone. Some people's musical sense is extremely acute, and their sense of language is limited. Not everyone is a philosopher. But the Greek choruses could be appreciated as sung poems, and there is plenty in the poetry to occupy one's attention. They could also be appreciated as almost abstract patterns of color—moving pictures—or as tunes, or as complicated dance routines. From the man who was primarily interested in political problems to the man who was concerned with the new dance steps, there was a means whereby the choruses provided a dramatic vehicle for each one's emotional experience. "Die rätselhafte Einheit von Wort, Gedanke, Rhythmus, Gebärde, Tanz, Gesang, Instrumentalklang, sie ist der Mutterschoss der Tragödie." So writes Kranz.[3] It is this unity that we must never forget. To understand and recreate this, it is with the unity of word and dance that we must start. For in the details of the system we can see the *Gesamtkunstwerk* in operation phrase by phrase. The dance is therefore not only by far the most important element of production, by far the hardest for the modern West to understand, and therefore the element that needs most study, but it is also the element that, studied in detail, reveals most of the mind of fifth-century men of the theater once we start considering them as men of the theater and not as writers only.

It was notable in antiquity that Athenians were keen dancers,[4] just as it is still notable today that the Greeks are much keener dancers than most other European races. Old people dance in Greece today; I have often seen old men dancing with both skill and abandon. Similarly, Athenaeus comments on how, in Athens especially, old men continued to dance.[15] The skill of the chorus work in drama was based on the fact that everyone danced, and therefore members of the audience, as practitioners themselves, would appreciate good and bad dancing.

Supposing that someone was writing about the dance of the mid–twentieth century in two thousand years time and had only a few references in scattered books upon which to base his study, he might have acquired some knowledge of certain dance movements: for instance, the strathspey, jiving, the waltz, and the Susie Cues. Although these could all be described as types of dance, as words they are not of the same class. The strathspey is a type of step and a musical tempo, but there is no dance called "the strathspey," since every strathspey dance will have a special form and a special title. Jiving covers quite a wide range of activity and musical tempo. The waltz can be any one of three things: a movement, a musical rhythm, and a specific dance; while the Susie Cues is a type of step commonly used in many different varieties of modern musical comedy dance. As we read the ancient authors about the various types of dance, we must qualify our knowledge by realizing that we cannot be quite sure to what class of dance movement the authors are referring, to something like the waltz or to something like Susie Cues. But with this qualification there are a number of references that give us a colorful impression of the variety of ancient Greek dance.

First, there are the three dances appropriate to the three types of drama. The tragic dance is the *emmeleia*. Most of the references to it, unfortunately, belong to a time when tragedy had become statuesque and dignified. Presumably the *emmeleia* sobered up to match. But there is one vivid presentation of old-fashioned tragic dancing. The finale of *The Wasps* (1474–end) presents old Friend-of-Cleon, drunk at the party, challenging anyone to compete with him in old-time tragic dancing. The "dances with which Thespis competed" are mentioned (1479). This is an exaggeration since Thespis would have been dead eighty years. Later, Phrynichus is mentioned (1490) and this is much more reasonable, since he would have died not more than thirty years before Aristophanes was born, and there would still be men of Sophocles' generation alive who had seen Phrynichus, a man who claimed to have invented as many steps as the waves in a winter sea.[6] Friend-of-Cleon does refer obliquely to the dance as an *emmeleia,* since, having already done some dancing, he says that he will destroy his modern competitors with an *"emmeleia* of the fist" (1503). The movements he performs are very varied. First he twists his ribs. Then he does the "Phrynichus crouch," like a cock, followed by the high kick and some sort of twirling about. The climax of the old-timer (1516ff.) appears to be wild high-kicking. There is reference to spinning like a top, but this is perhaps what the moderns do. About the time of the first production of *The Wasps* the pirouette was introduced as a dance movement. A high-kicking war dance would be a very natural basis for the central dance of tragedy, especially during the warlike mood of the Persian invasions.

The *kordax* was apparently a solo dance, and used only in comedy. It is described as a comic dance with lewd movements of the buttocks.[7] All references to the *kordax* treat it as a lascivious and vulgar dance, associated with drunkenness and loose behavior.

The *sikinnis* was especially the dance of the satyrs. Athenaeus describes it as the fastest dance.[8] "It has no emotional content and so it gets a move on." It seems to have involved many leaps, and it is reasonable to assume that the satyr depicted on the Pronomos vase is performing a movement out of the *sikinnis:* right hand on hip; left hand stretched out straight, thumb horizontal and fingers erect.[9] I think he has just left the ground in a leap; his right foot is pointing down; his left leg is raised with thigh parallel to the ground and left toes pointing.

It is worth consulting the lists of dances given in Pollux, and comparing them with those described in Athenaeus.[10] Of course some movements may be later than the fifth century, but Athenaeus intersperses his discussion with quotations from fifth-century poets, so the list need not be badly wrong. Pollux gives the following tragic dances: hand upturned; basket; hand downturned; receiving the wood, which was probably baton-passing; double; pincers; somersault; passing four, which seems to have been a movement where a dancer moved from the last rank of five to the front. This list is reasonably clear. Even if we cannot immediately put a movement to "basket," it conjures up several vivid possibilities. Athenaeus' list includes comic as well as tragic dances: swordthrust; a dance that involves kicking the buttocks with one heel after another; two kinds of owl dance, which is interpreted as a stooping and gazing movement with one hand shading the brow, a dance mentioned in Aeschylus' *Envoys;* pounding the mortar; pouring out the barley; canceling debts, whatever movement that implied; spinning top; a dance involving some kind of movement with the elbow; he also mentions Pollux' hand upturned and downturned, the basket, baton-passing, and pincers, and goes into some detail with the *kallabides.* This involved some kind of hootchy-kootchy hip movement. Photius the lexicographer defines it as "striding indecorously and pulling through one's hips with one's hands." There is a more vivid description quoted by Athenaeus from Eupolis' *Flatterers.*

He dances the kallabides
Shitting sesame seeds.[11]

Athenaeus' discussion mentions many other dances and types of dance, but the ones I have referred to provide the strongest visual images of actual movement.

Two things perhaps stand out as we consider such lists. First, many of the dances appear to involve only the upper part of the body. There was a special word for hand-dancing—*cheironomia*—and movements of the hands had great importance, just as they do in Indian dancing. Second, we notice the high mimetic quality of many of the dances. Some of this mime clearly involved a conventional dance language such as we find in Indian dancing. Otherwise it is difficult to see how to perform the "canceling debts" dance. But clearly also there is a delight in the more basic mime, the sheer imitation of nature. Athenaeus spends some time discussing *morphasmos,* which involved representing many different people or creatures in succession. This, as we might imagine, could be comic. But it is an indication of the Greek delight in mime, as developed as their delight in song or poetry. We should not expect the dance of the Greek chorus to be any less expressive than the verse.

It has now been established that certain dance movements persisted in Greek culture from the earliest times. Furthermore, the meticulous work of Professor Webster especially has established that we are justified in connecting particular dance movements with particular meters used in the lyrics. The importance of this work can hardly be overestimated for our understanding of Greek drama.[12] Not only do all Greek lyrics contain a built-in rhythm score; they also contain choreographic instruction in the meters they use.

The meter with the clearest and most immediate choreographic instruction is the dochmiac. It appears to have developed in and for tragedy, unlike the majority of rhythmic patterns, which were developed in the dance long before the tragic festival was instituted. It is very likely that the dochmiac was invented by Aeschylus. It is unlike other meters, in that it is used both with other patterns in lyrics and also on its own for short, wild interjections. It is also noticeable that it is frequently the main meter for solo laments, especially in plays where it is likely that the poet could not call on too great a solo singer, such as the lament of Creon in the *Antigone,* which is nearly all dochmiacs. Since Creon is taken by the second actor, it is reasonable to guess that Sophocles would not have written anything too complicated musically, since at that period he would have been unlikely to find two great solo singers in his team of three actors. I think we can say without any doubt that what defined the dochmiac was a particular violent movement, almost certainly involving a kick. Unusually for a lyric meter, there are many variations in the note values. Its basic pattern is: ♩♪ ♩ ♩ ♪♩ | A combination of three and five; obvious syncopation. But there are a very great number of variations, some of which seem very unlikely:

The only possible reason for this great variety is that the movement was so vigorous and characteristic that it imposed itself totally on the note values of the words. This would also explain why it was easier to sing: the movement was so vigorous that it did not allow too much singing. This and the synocopation of the primary version insist that there must have been at least one kick.

Another instruction for kicks is the cretic: ♩ ♪ ♩ Five-time; obviously related to the dochmiac, and often used in connection with it. It is particularly associated with places where speed of movement is important. It was perhaps very much associated with the *sikinnis*. Though, of course, we have so little left of the satyr plays with which to test the ideas of the satyr dance, we notice that in the *Cyclops* both the excited astrophic songs of the chorus surrounding the actual blinding of the Cyclops contain many cretics (608–23, 656–62).[13]

The slow three-time of the ionic meters already discussed, and of their many variants, is especially linked to sinuous movement with back-bends, as we see from the vase pictures to be characteristic of the maenads' dances. Dactyls always imply a very stately movement, though clearly the frequent dactylo-epitrites of the later plays allow much more variety of movement than the opening line of the first system of the *Agamemnon parodos.* One of the most doom-laden dances in all Greek tragedy, it starts with an exact hexameter, the most solemn meter of all (104, 122).

To conclude this general discussion, it is once again worth emphasizing that all the evidence, visual and verbal, demonstrates that the Greek dramatic choruses were displays of extremely complex, vigorous, and varied dance. They were not a matter of "movement" in the sense in which it is used by actors today when they arrive at an audition for a musical, are asked whether they can dance, and reply that they have done "Movement." Phrynichus did not twist his ribs till they creaked with a little "Movement" but with very vigorous, precisely choreographed dance. Perhaps there were occasions when a Greek chorus sang relatively still, moving mainly with their hands only. But such *cheironomia* to the exclusion of all other dance must have been rare. All the evidence makes it very clear that the normal chorus work required drilled precision and great agility. You would look very silly standing still to sing:

> High in the air like a fawn
> Leaping with splendor.[14]

The System

The system is easily defined. It consists of two matching stanzas, the first called *strophē*, the second called *antistrophē*, which are rhythmically identical. The majority of Sophocles' choruses consist of two systems only. Aeschylus tends to have more systems, though as a general rule each system has fewer lines. The *parodos* of the *Agamemnon* has six systems.

Behind a great many theories about great poets such as the Greek dramatists we find concealed premises that imply they were idiots. As we consider the reasons for the system, it is surely best to start from the premise that these great poets were not idiots, that they knew what they were doing and had good reasons for doing it.

There is only one good reason for writing the majority of the sung and danced portions of drama in systems of matching *strophē* and *antistrophē;* both music and dance in the *antistrophē* were an exact repeat of the music and dance in the *strophē*. Systems are very hard to write. Of all poetic forms in all European languages they are probably the hardest, even harder than the sestina. If we discovered some hard-pressed lyricist with his show already in rehearsal writing sestinas for production numbers we could be sure that there were good reasons. Sophocles maintained an average of two plays a year over sixty years' professional life. We can be sure that there were many occasions when he was just as hard pressed.

The complex Greek lyric meters are hard to analyze. Unless music and dance worked with the meter all the time, then the point of the meter would be lost.

And if the point of the meter is lost in performance, then there is no need to torture oneself composing in that meter. We see in the case of the dochmiac how quickly the poets avail themselves of metrical flexibility as soon as there is certain to be no confusion about what is a dochmiac. The Greek poets were not idiots, and as very busy men of the theater they had no time to waste. It is not stated in so many words that music and dance of *antistrophē* was identical to that of *strophē*. But for someone to write this down in the time of Sophocles would have been so much to state the obvious that it is not surprising that no remarks to this effect survive.

As I have said, it is not known who invented the system, and in all Greek literature there is only one mention of it. Triclinius, who of course lived long after chorus dancing had ceased to take place, said that in the *strophē* the chorus moved to the right, in the *antistrophē* they moved to the left, and in the epode they stood still.[15] The meaning of *antistrophē* certainly seems to imply some sort of movement in the opposite direction, and in its metaphorical uses it comes to mean "counterpart," "converse," and "inversion." We may therefore assume that the movements made in the *strophē* were made in one direction, and that in the *antistrophē* the same movements were made in the opposite direction. Clearly, the chorus did not stand still in the epodes, but they may have tended to work more directly to the front. It is very often the case and certainly so in the later choruses of Euripides, that the epodes are climactic and require more excited movement. This point is discussed later in this section.

The main argument for saying that the movement of the *antistrophē* repeated the movement of the *strophē* in the opposite direction is that, if we assume this to be the case and look at the Greek choruses, we begin to see choreographic patterns that make sense. Once we know that one movement has got to fit two different sets of words, it is remarkable how often we can see that only one kind of movement will do, while there is no chorus in the entire extant corpus that does not offer some sort of suggestion as to its choreography.

I am not saying that we can rediscover the exact movements that Sophocles gave his dancers. But we can discover choreographic patterns; we can, as it were, choreograph in terms of x and y, without always being able to supply the values of x and y. We can see the kind of course the dance must have taken; we can see the climaxes; we can tell what was highly mimetic, what was partly mimetic, and what was more or less pure dance. We can often see the necessity for one dancer to emerge from the crowd as a temporary soloist. Time and again, as we consider the choreography, we are led to see why a particular word order, which may seem awkward on the page, makes immediate sense when sung and danced.

Good examples of the system at its clearest and most straightforward are found in Aristophanes' hymns. The *parabasis* of *The Knights* contains the usual sung and danced lyric with the usual speech in trochaic tetrameters in between *strophē* (551–64) and *antistrophē* (581–94). The system is divided very clearly into three sections, of five, five, and four lines. The first section presents an invocation, in the *strophē* to Poseidon, in the *antistrophē* to Athene. Both *strophē* and *antistrophē* require a figure of power to dominate a general restlessness: in the *strophē*, Poseidon dominating his horses and his ships; in the *antistrophē*, Athene and the power of Athens, dominating in war and poetry, that is, dance. Probably one dancer high above the restless crowd of the remainder.

The second section of five lines gathers to a climax: in the *strophē* to the image of chariot racing; in the *antistrophē* to battle. We notice at the beginning of the ninth line the *strophē*'s words are "Come here" addressed to the god, and in the *antistrophē*, "Victory" (559, 589). This combination seems clearly to imply a strong gesture of raised hands.

The third section, of four lines, is a relatively static moment of direct invocation. Words in both *strophē* and *antistrophē* imply that the movement has calmed down. What is required seems to be gestures of prayer, of receptivity for the respective gods, Poseidon in *strophē*, Athene in *antistrophē*, now both directly addressed.

A very similar pattern is given by the equivalent lyric in the *parabasis* of *The Clouds*, again split by the chanted speech in trochaic tetrameters (563–74, *strophē*; 595–606, *antistrophē*). The system is in four sections, each presenting an invocation of a different god of three, two, two, and four lines. The first section invokes Zeus in the *strophē*, Apollo in the *antistrophē*. The word *height* occurs with reference to both gods. The movement must present, if it is to fit both situations, a sense of height, of stretching up. The second section is much more violent. In the *strophē* it is the sea heaving and the earth quaking under the power of Poseidon; in the *antistrophē* it is the heaving dances of the girls of Lydia in honor of the unnamed goddess, the great mother.[16] In the third section the movement becomes calmer and clearer: in the *strophē* it is the air that is invoked, in the *antistrophē* it is Athene. The last section must convey shining glitter in its movements: in the *strophē* it is the Sun with his rays; in the *antistrophē* it is the torches of Dionysus.

These hymns give us a very clear idea of how near we can get to the movement patterns of the original. The *Clouds* hymn gives clear indication of when the movement changes because of the change in the god addressed. We can see the shape easily: stretching up, violent heaving, something calmer, ending with something shimmery. Direct invocation of gods in all cultures must imply a stretching up or spreading out of oneself. It is easy to see how the heaving sea and women's orgasmic dances in a fertility rite can be represented with the same movement. Nor is it difficult to imagine a movement that will fit both a chariot race and a battle, as in the *Knights* hymn. Furthermore, even when it is harder to see the exact movement, as for example at the end of the *Clouds* hymn, since the movement must be a metaphor of the poetic image—shining, glittery, shimmering movement—yet it is obvious that for both *strophē* and *antistrophē* the same movement metaphor is required. What is true of these two hymns can be found true of all the systems of Greek tragedy. It is simply a matter of looking, comparing, and imagining the only possible types of movement to fit both *strophē* and *antistrophē*.

Consideration of these two lyrics helps us to see how they were staged. But even without considering the staging, we know more or less their function in the play: reminders of the existence of the numinous powers without whom there would be no play, no bawdy farce—acts of acknowledgment in the center of the play that its first purpose is worship. When we come to examine the very much more complicated systems in Aeschylus and Sophocles, we can find instances where the necessary choreography of a lyric gives us the meaning of the lyric, and indeed the meaning of an aspect of the play as a whole.

Perhaps the greatest achievement of chorus dance is the *parodos* of the *Agamemnon*. It is far too complex to analyze here in its totality. In broad terms its function is to fix Agamemnon as a focus point for several stories whose scope is too wide for a play. Part of what will be shown in the *Agamemnon* is that the Trojan War, though part of a divine plan for the annihilation of Troy, was itself an evil. War means the slaughter of innocent people. Agamemnon, as the commander, is responsible. It is reasonable that he, the killer, will himself be killed. Further, the fact of this great and terrible war is a sign that the world is out of joint. The gods themselves are in disagreement. Agamemnon is caught in the middle of conflicting forces. On the one hand, he must go to Troy and smash it, since Troy is to be destroyed. On the other, though there are gods to will the destruction of Troy, there are also gods to rise in fury at the slaughter of innocent people. At the end of the *Oresteia*, there will be harmony: the conflicting gods will be working together. But that is a long way in the future. At this point it is a maelstrom.

The dance begins with the gathering of the Greeks under Agamemnon and his brother to attack Troy. It moves via the anger of Artemis at the slaughter of the innocent into the inscrutable savagery of Zeus, the ruler of heaven who overthrew his own father. Then, having widened the scope of the action immeasurably, it focuses again on Agamemnon's troubles. In the fourth system we are presented with the Greeks held in harbor by the adverse, stormy winds, and the terrible suggestion made by the prophet Calchas: the winds will be lulled if Agamemnon sacrifices his own daughter Iphigeneia. The dance has demanded that one dancer be separated from the rest to represent Agamemnon in his terrible dilemma. The tempo of the dance has been speeding up. A moment of climax is near.

The first line of the fifth system contains the crux. In the *strophē* it is Agamemnon: "When he had put on the yoke of necessity, his spirit veering into wickedness." (218). The *antistrophē* is concerned with the actual killing of Iphigeneia: "Her prayers, her cries to her father, made as nothing by the chiefs." (228). The necessary movement for this is clear: it is not an obvious mime of a man putting on a yoke. The central figure suggests a free despair; this is immediately crushed by the crowd who gather round him. The yoke of necessity for Agamemnon is the demand of his chiefs to wage war. Iphigeneia's instinctive cry is stifled. Agamemnon's action is allowing his instinctive cry to be stifled too.

We can certainly try to visualize the kind of movement that would do for this situation. The central figure, Agamemnon-Iphigeneia, might fling his arms outward in some gesture of desperation. Then the rest of the chorus might advance around him, with some gesture of menace, and force him to bring his arms in to cover his face or to lower his head. However near Agamemnon is to being compelled, he is not compelled; he acts of his own will. Iphigeneia's cries are "made as nothing"; they are not gagged. The chiefs hem Agamemnon-Iphigeneia in. Desperate, the figure succumbs.

This linking of Agamemnon and Iphigeneia in the one action has enormous visual and emotional force. It is also central to the point of the *parodos* and indeed of the whole trilogy. Agamemnon and Iphigeneia are both destroyed by war. The general is caught in the same trap as the innocent girl. That is what war does. Further, by linking Agamemnon and Iphigeneia, Aeschylus gives Agamemnon a kind of innocence too. It is not really innocence from Agamemnon's own point of view. Later in the play it will be established without a shadow of doubt that Agamemnon is guilty of killing his daughter. But in the time scale in which Aeschylus is working, Agamemnon is also a victim, and this fact implies the possibility of there being a solution at the end of the trilogy. In this way Aeschylus' theology depends on his choreography and vice versa.

As we look at the dances in Aeschylus we find that this linking of apparently different figures in the same movement recurs. It seems part of the way in which he imagined. Later in the *Agamemnon* there is a furious lyric dialogue between the chorus and Clytemnestra after Agamemnon's murder (1447ff.). The fourth system is a solo in lyric anapests for Clytemnestra (1497–1504, *strophē;* 1523–29 *antistrophē*).[17] In the *strophē* she presents herself as the *alastor,* the spirit of vengeance. In the *antistrophē* she presents Iphigeneia. Movement at the climactic point of the system, the fourth and fifth lines, links Clytemnestra's vengeance with the original death of Iphigeneia. Choreography must bring out this conjunction. The effect then will be to make Clytemnestra's vengeance, so to speak, Iphigeneia coming to life again herself.

A similar effect is seen in *The Seven against Thebes.* Eteocles has just lost his temper and rushed out to fight his own brother (720–91). There is a sense of doom. We feel that Oedipus' curse will be fulfilled. The chorus presents this curse. In the third system a figure emerges from the group to present in the *strophē* Oedipus, the patricide sleeping with his mother, and in the *antistrophē* a wave of trouble hitting the city. The similarity of the sex act and a breaking wave in choreographic terms need hardly be stressed (750–57, *strophē;* 758–65, *antistrophē*). The fourth system continues to focus on the central figure. In the *strophē* he is the curse; in the *antistrophē,* Oedipus (766–71, *strophē;* 772–77, *antistrophē*). In the fifth system the *strophē* returns to Oedipus and his unhappy marriage; the *antistrophē* returns to how he cursed his sons (778–84, *strophē;* 785–91 *antistrophē*). In this last system the fighting sons are linked through the movement pattern with the cursing father. At intervals throughout the chorus, the same movement represents the curse and Oedipus. The curse is made physical in an obvious way, and all the members of the family are linked as being under the curse. Before the chorus started we have just seen a man run out, and we know that he is doomed to die. After the chorus finishes a messenger will run on to tell us that he is indeed dead at his brother's hands. The chorus between these two events shows us how and why he has to be killed. In all these examples from Aeschylus, it is not only that choreography helps the point to be made more clearly. The *Gesamtkunstwerk* of poetry plus dance is saying something more complex and subtle than the poetry on its own. The dance is part of a total meaning.

The *Gesamtkunstwerk* of Sophocles is just as important to consider as that of Aeschylus. But whereas Aeschylus is a poet of striking images, and something of his purpose can be learnt by concentrating for a moment on particular images such as that of Agamemnon and Iphigeneia linked in one movement, Sophocles is more elusive. His is a poetry of total pattern, in which it is very difficult to extract moments to be considered in isolation. In the space available it is therefore more profitable to analyze a Sophocles chorus in detail from a play—the *Antigone*—that will also be considered in detail in the next section and in Chapter 8.

When we look at Euripides' choruses we feel a looseness compared to those of Sophocles or Aeschylus. His plays in general are jerky compared to those of Sophocles, in which the parts flow into each other. Such construction is not easily mastered. Euripides never mastered it fully, whether in the totality of a play or in the details of a chorus. As we shall see in the following section, Euripides helped to destroy the centrality of the system, and this is understandable. The dances became more ornamental than central to the whole play; within each dance the movements exist more for decorative than for structural reasons.

There is, for example, an apparently climactic chorus in the *Heracles* (348–441). It is a moment of suspense. Lycus has announced his intention of killing the wife and children of Heracles. After the chorus, just as death is imminent, Heracles arrives to save them. It is a long chorus, of three very long systems. It presents itself as a dramatic moment of importance. But all it really achieves is to emphasize the powers of Heracles, since it is a presentation of his twelve labors. Two-thirds of the length of the dance part of the *Agememnon parodos*, to say so much less, this chorus begins to reveal that the function of the dance in Greek tragedy was starting to change.

It is relatively easy to see the choreographic possibilities. The various monsters provide excellent opportunities for dance patterns and movements. But although we can see the kind of movement that would fit the images of *strophē* and *antistrophē*, there is no particular poetic or dramatic point about the linking of the two images. For example, the first four lines of the second system present in the *strophē* Heracles taming the horses of Diomede (380–83), in the *antistrophē*, Heracles and the singing Hesperides with the snake that guarded their apple tree (394–97). Choreography to fit both *strophē* and *antistrophē* demands that the central figure representing Heracles should be seen mounting above the rest of the group, whose tossing arms and bending bodies represent in the *strophē* the horses that Heracles tames, in the *antistrophē* the singing, undulating girls and writhing snake. There is, however, no poetic or dramatic reason for linking the taming of the horses particularly with the apples of the Hesperides, any more than with any of the other labors. Even in this relatively early play we are a long way from the precision of Aeschylus or Sophocles.

It is probable that the system was taken into comedy relatively late, at about the same time as the comic competitions, when the comic poets had been able to watch and adapt the techniques of tragedy for their own purposes. Hymns in Aristophanes such as have been discussed are constructed more or less exactly as one would construct a system in tragedy. But a great many of Aristophanes' choruses are much cruder, much more a matter of a dance around, without any particular mime, something much nearer to the use of most dance in a twentieth-century musical. In these choruses the words are not very significant; it would not matter too much if a few were lost. So there is no need to present the meaning of the poetry through mime. In such a chorus there is no great problem about choreography, because the dance is merely the means of creating a moment of excited movement to contrast with the scene that has just passed. But as this is arbitrary, it is clear that we shall not be able to infer very much about the details of such a dance, except for its general tempo and mood, usually fast. In each play there is usually one dance of this nature. The *parodos* of *The Acharnians* for instance (204–33) is a chase around the *orchestra,* as the old Acharnian veterans pursue Just-City for having made a private peace.[18] Words and movement combine effectively to create the result Aristophanes needs. Unlike the *Heracles* chorus, this is as structural as anything in Aeschylus. All that Aristophanes requires here is a crowd of old men chasing one old man and exclaiming against what he has done. In this case the meter, not the images, gives us the movement almost exactly. The first four lines are trochaic tetrameters, and therefore mean that the chorus ran around (204–7, *strophē;* 219–22, *antistrophē*). The second half of the system is cretics and resolved cretics and clearly implies kicks, a fast syncopated movement. But there is no moment involving particular mime. The purpose of the chorus is at this point pure dance.

The matching of gesture between *strophē* and *antistrophē* can be used for laughs. Later on in *The Acharnians* (665–75, *strophē;* 692–701, *antistrophē*) there is a line in the *strophē* which refers to sardines packed tight together (670). The matching line in the *antistrophē* refers to the battle of Marathon (698). Clearly, at this point the chorus were in line, and bunched together in some ludicrous way, parodying the tight battle line of the Marathonian hoplite, which is compared with sardines in a frying pan.

Aristophanes makes good use throughout his work of systems that involve interchange between a soloist and the chorus, which therefore involve the soloist in the chorus dance. An amusing development of this technique is found also in *The Acharnians*, near the end (1190–1227). It is hardly a system, though it involves two soloists singing and moving symmetrically.[19] The general Lamachus has arrived back from a campaign that has gone disastrously for him. He is wounded and supported by two attendants. Meanwhile, Just-City has been enjoying his party. He comes out with two girls. As Lamachus clutches his wounds, Just-City clutches the breasts of the two girls. The movements of Lamachus and Just-City are not exactly the same, but for every movement the one makes, the other makes an equivalent. It is not the symmetry of the system, but it is a symmetry used for both comic and poetic effect, which depends for its form on the feeling for symmetry inculcated by the system.

A similar example of symmetrical action not in a system is found in the *Lysistrata* (530–40, 558–607). The women under Lysistrata are humiliating the pompous *proboulos*, the state official. In the first passage they put women's clothing on him; in the second, they dress him as a corpse. It is doubtful if there is an exact symmetry, because the line lengths are not the same. But it is not a song, only an anapest chant, which would mean that the symmetry need be only approximate. It is an example of the way the system's exact symmetry spills over into the rest of a play.

Since we do not even know who invented the system and since no Greek author wrote about it, we are forced into generalities when attempting to explain its hold on the mind of the Greek poets. We can talk of the Greek love of symmetry and think of the way they built their temples. Certain people and certain ages are freest within tight discipline. Such were the poets of the fifth century. Even Aristophanes, who has seldom been exceeded for fertility of imagination and variety of detail, so much enjoyed the apparent constrictions of the system that he made use of its symmetry even in places where he did not need to. We cannot explain the system, but we must acknowledge its dominance. If we do not understand it we shall understand nothing of the form of fifth-century drama. The system was the most important device in creating that form; when Euripides loosened the system, the whole form fell to pieces. Before considering this breakdown, however, it is worth spending time to consider one chorus in detail.

The First *Stasimon* of the *Antigone*

The first *stasimon* of the *Antigone*, which is often referred to as the "Ode to Man," is a useful example through which to amplify these theories of choreography. It is sometimes said that this *stasimon* is more of general application than of particular application to the moment of the play in which it occurs. Any great lyric can have a certain existence outside its immediate context. But this stasimon can be shown to have detailed application to the moment of its performance, and to obtain this application not least through the choreography.[20]

Chorus of Veterans
SYSTEM I.
Strophē Miracle nature, then a man,
Rarest miracle nature owns.
Watch him crossing the sea's expanse,
Oceans grey with the winter wind,
Row, sail on depth-tossing rollers
Beyond, beyond the waves. Then first
Of gods, and womb of gods—Earth,
Ageless, invincible earth he is grinding at,
Year after year shoving plow furrows into her,
Horse-plod turning loam-clods over.

Antistrophē Light-witted species, chirping birds,
The noose whirling, he runs, he traps,
Hunts down beasts of the woods and hills,
Drags sea fish in a swarming catch.
Those nets, that well-twisted rope-work,
The mastermind—a man, who rides,
With harness well devised, wild
Beasts of the mountain, obliges the mane-tossing
Stallion to stoop to a collar that breaks him in,
Yokes hill bull's untamed endurance.

SYSTEM II.
Strophē And words, and the winds of a plan,
And codes of behavior with rules,
All this he has taught to himself, with hearthstones,
Walls, roofs, to arch skies away
That threaten rain, sleet and hail,
Omnisufficient. Insufficient never, caught off guard
No, never. Death, death alone,
That one never lets you go,
Although incurable disease
Has been treated.

Antistrophē Some wisdom, some technical sense
Beyond what a man can expect—
Progress can be evil, but *can* be noble,
When law's obeyed, contracts kept,
In awe of God's Natural Law,
Citizenhood. Citiless away, away with you.
You love the wild life for kicks.

You shall never share my hearth,
Nor ever share my thoughts, my dreams.
'Ware such people.

(332–75)

The action of the *Antigone* is Creon's denial of burial to the dead Polyneices, who has traitorously led an army to attack Thebes. Creon's action is an affront to every decent human instinct; it is, in Sophocles' terms, an affront to *Dikē*, to the gods. To deny burial to a dead body is to dishonor death itself, which is the most obvious way in which a human being can overstep the bounds of right action for a human being. For death is the most obvious limit to a human's mastery of his own destiny. A proper respect for death is the center of *Sophrosynē*, which is the center of archaic Greek morality. To know one's limits is the most necessary thing either for man or for city.

That is the thought behind the *Antigone*. It is also contained within this *stasimon*, in distilled form. The *stasimon* occurs after we have heard Creon say that there will be no burial for Polyneices, and, in natural reaction, Antigone, Polyneices' sister, has buried the body. The burial has been discovered by a guard, who has also reported that there are signs of a small miracle at work: the burial is only a token handful of dust thrown over the corpse, but no dogs or carrion birds have touched it. Perhaps the spirits are at work protecting it. It is at this moment that the chorus sing the first *stasimon*.

The *stasimon* is in two systems, each of ten lines. In each there is an obvious pause during the sixth line, at a climactic point. The basic structure of the dance is very clear. Both systems seem to build toward line six, then change to different movement, and both systems seem to end relatively quietly.

Both systems describe the activities of man, first in relation to the rest of nature, and then in terms of social organization. Choreography must isolate a dancer, or a small group of two or three, to represent Man. This isolation will be obviously created and emphasized at the beginning of system I, by the activity required of the Man-figure: in the *strophē* sailing the sea; in the *antistrophē* catching creatures.

System I starts with a two-line introductory section, with a slight pause at the end of line 2. The key syllable seems to be the last in line 1: in the *strophē* "man," in the *antistrophē*, "birds." Out of the delicately fluttering group movement that suggests in the *strophē* the wonders of nature, in the *antistrophē* the light-witted birds, the Man-figure springs up with some definite action, which will serve in the *antistrophē* to represent the catching of the birds.

Lines 3–6 build to the climax in line 6. The main group's movement turns into some kind of heaving and swaying, to represent, in the *strophē* the sea, in the *antistrophē* first some undefined wild beasts and then fish in the sea. It is not difficult to visualize the kind of movement that would fit both these images. Through the heaving and swaying goes a Man-figure in a movement that suggests crossing the sea for the *strophē*, and catching beasts and fish in nets for the *antistrophē*. The climax of this movement occurs in line 6: in the *strophē*, "Beyond, beyond the waves"; in the *antistrophē*, "The mastermind—a man."

The last two syllables of line 6, and the rest of the system, present a new image; in the *strophē*, the taming and ploughing of Earth; in the *antistrophē* the mastering of the wild beast of the mountain, the yoking of the horse and the bull. Some massive and heavy shape confronts the Man-figure at the end of line 6, only to be pressed down by him. Perhaps during line 6, as the Man-figure rises in the triumph of having crossed the waves, the main group of the chorus gather fast together and form into some dense, heaving mass, representing the goddess Earth for the *strophē*, and for the *antistrophē* the succession of beasts.

This, then, is the movement of the first system. It would seem that the chorus is relatively scattered at the beginning, and ends in a tight group with the Man-figure dominant over a heaving mass sinking to the ground. It is remarkable how quickly dancers can change their formations completely, and we must presume that there would be a moment between *strophē* and *antistrophē* in which they could get up and regroup in their opening positions.

System II presents social systems and community life. The movement pattern seems to suggest a more and more clearly defined, more and more elaborately contrived grouping for the climax at line 6. It seems that the beginning of the system requires the chorus to be scattered, so that the Man-figure may organize them, whether by going around them, or, more probably, by performing certain movements in the center, to which all the other dancers correspond. Most of the poetry is relatively abstract. The only colorful imagery is in lines 4 and 5 of the *strophē:* the pelting rain and hail, which he has learnt to keep off his head. Some sheltering movement must be required. It would seem that all the chorus, for example, must put their hands above their heads to form some roof beneath which they can cower safely. This, then, will be the movement they make as they sing, "In awe of God's natural law," "natural law" being the nearest a translation into modern English can come to *Dikē*. *Dikē* is something to cower from. If we had not had the colorful imagery of the *strophē*'s rain and hail, we could have choreographed the *antistrophē* in many ways. But with the *strophē*, only this way will do. It is a very important insight into Sophocles' theology. *Dikē* is something that we would like to get away from—like hailstones. We cannot. But we can protect ourselves from it, if we take care.

The first half, then, of system II will have in some way organized and collected the entire chorus, focusing on the Man-figure. After the crouching and cowering of lines 4 and 5 comes the climax: Man, omnisufficient, in the *strophē;* Man in the exalted heights of civilization that is the city-state in the *antistrophē*. What we must notice is not only the obviousness of the climax, but also its abruptness. We must also note the exact matching of syllables between *strophē* and *antistrophē*, something much more exact in Sophocles' original than an English translation can manage. Both pairs of words convey what is in effect a pun. All these things point to the precision with which Sophocles created this moment. It is here that we must look to discover a clue to the total mood of the *stasimon.*

After the climactic word, we must immediately become aware of another figure. For in the *antistrophē* the chorus sing: "Citiless away, away with you." Clearly there is a dancer somewhat separate from the organized group who at this moment pops up with some wild, instantly remarkable movement that will suitably reach its first climax at the end of line 7, to illustrate the first mention of death for the *strophē,* and in the *antistrophē,* the phrase I have translated as "You live for kicks," which is certainly the meaning of the Greek and fits with what I believe to be the mood of this *stasimon.*[21]

What is the dance movement for the second half of the system? In the *antistrophē,* the chorus are singing to the intruder to go away, disclaiming any connection with him. It is not clear from the words alone whether they are in control of the intruder, telling him to go away from a position of strength, or dominated by him, begging him to go away from a position of weakness.

In the *strophē* they sing at first that Man is never insufficient, but then say that there is no escape from death. Death destroys all Man's pretensions and pretences. The dance must surely therefore show death dominating Man. Then in that case, of course, the intruder figure dominates in the *antistrophē;* the form of the dance is given by the *strophē,* and the *antistrophē* fits to it.

The last two lines of the *antistrophē* continue to refer to the intruder figure. Therefore he is still very much in evidence. Therefore death is very much in evidence during the last two lines of the *strophē.* But if death is still in evidence, then to sing that Man has cured disease is to boast of a little achievement, with the major achievement undone. For to cure a few diseases is a very small thing compared to the fact of death, which comes to all alike.

This being so, the movement of the second half of the system seems clear. At line 6 the Man-figure is in triumph. Immediately, however, a strange, wild figure emerges, and very rapidly the Man-figure cowers away from the intruder, who flourishes his dominance of the scene by the end of line 8. For the last two lines the Man-figure attempts to assert his independence, but we know that this assertion is ludicrous and meaningless; it is the assertion of the weak in the presence of the strong.

At no point in the second *antistrophē* has it been made clear who "lives for kicks," except that the intruder has more or less been defined as someone who will not obey the laws of the land. The dance has, however, connected this law-breaking figure with death itself. As the dance ends, we see the guards enter with Antigone. Now, if there is a clear act of identity made by some sort of physical contact between the dancer performing the Death/intruder figure and the actor entering as Antigone, then everything becomes clear. Antigone is the person who has broken the law of the land. But by breaking this wrong law she reminds us all of the respect we owe to death, reminds us of our mortality, the necessary background to all *Sophrosynē.* The conflict between the Man-figure and the Death/intruder figure is the conflict of the play between Creon and Antigone.

This suggests a further sense to be conveyed in the movement. At this point of the play, Creon will appear to be in command. Man is at this moment unaware of death. Therefore perhaps the Man-figure, though made to shrink in comparison with the dominance of the Death/intruder figure, should have no contact with the Death/intruder figure. It is Death upstaging Man, rather than knocking him down. It is perhaps Death making Man's organization look ridiculous.

The movement pattern, then, of this *stasimon* has shown us the meaning and also fitted the song very clearly into its context in the play. Whatever merits, and these are considerable, that it has as a lyric away from the play, it is first and foremost a perfect dramatic lyric embodying the center of the play itself.

Further, we can see how the lyric forces a choreography that will convey Sophocles' point in such a way that much of his sense would come over even if we missed most of the words. For if we hear "man" so that we identify the Man-figure, we shall then be shown by the dance that the first system presents man's dominance of other heaving bodies. The different movement of the first half of the second system will then convey man's organizing ability, developed to some climactic tableau at the beginning of line 6. For the rest of the system the tableau shrinks, while another dancer asserts himself over the organization. We have only to hear the word *death* to know that the point of the *stasimon* is to show that death mocks all man's civilization. The words of this lyric are so brilliantly constructed that they insist on a dance that acts as the backbone of the lyric, the main structure of what Sophocles is saying.

I have deliberately left to the end the question of the mood of the *stasimon*. What is the emotional relationship between Man and Death? Man attempts to assert himself in the last two lines of the *strophē*. That is ridiculous. No man may assert himself against death. The natural relationship would seem to be the mockery of Man by Death. If we came across the lyric translated into German, entitled "The Song of the Cosmic Joke," with its authorship ascribed to Brecht, we should have no hesitation in recognizing its mood: a kind of bitter comedy, the mood of the moment in *Everyman* when Death greets Everyman at the party, making mock of all his activity.[22]

The key to the mood lies in the matching pairs of words at the climactic point at the beginning of line 6. The first word is an adjective of intensification agreeing with Man; there is then a stop, and then the exact opposite, the negative adjective. In the *strophē: pantoporos, aporos*. In the *antistrophē: hypsipolis; apolis*. Both *pantoporos* and *hypsipolis* are *hapax legomena*, words that occur nowhere else in Greek, and therefore words we may presume Sophocles to have invented for this context. The word *poros* means "ways and means," "resources"; *panto* is "all." *Pantoporos* could be translated as "Complete provider"; it certainly carries the sense of "Full of resources." I have therefore translated it "Omnisufficient." Jebb in prose translates it as "Yea, he hath resources for all."[23] Kitto in verse translates it "Full of resource against all that comes to him."[24] Even in the face of these two great scholars, I feel that the word is more all-embracing: "all-resourceful," "all-provider"—without qualification. Liddell and Scott translate it as "all-inventive."[25] It is almost the equivalent of "almighty." In other words it is an exaggeration, a grotesque word, as I hope "omnisufficient" is also. In the same way *hypsipolis* has a flavor of grotesque: "height" and "city." Possibly "In the exaltation of his citizenhood." I am more confident that there is meant to be something slightly comical about this climax because of the rhythmic pattern, which is impossible to reproduce exactly in English because a run of unaccented syllables never occurs in English. Line 6 has these note values:

That rhythm on its own certainly suggests something toppling, insecure, perhaps teetering.

All these things together combine to suggest that the mood is that which would be suggested by entitling the *stasimon* "The Song of the Cosmic Joke." The mood is nearer to what would now be called comedy than what would now be called tragedy. Although I am not saying that Sophocles would have choreographed it for laughs, yet I am not sure that the mood would be far wrong if the movement in the second system was humorous.

What is abundantly clear is that the meaning is deeper and more subtle when we consider this *stasimon* as *Gesamtkunstwerk* than when we consider it purely as a poem in a book. What is also clear is how much the text reveals in terms of choreographic instructions. And these are as detailed and precise as Shakespeare's built-in instructions to actors as to how to speak his blank verse. Once we understand what Sophocles requires to be represented, our movement patterns need not be very far from his. The human body has not all that many types of movement at its disposal. There are not very many ways in which one can show man crossing the sea simply through a group of moving human bodies. I think therefore that a modern choreographer might sometimes hit on a movement pattern that could be very similar to the one Sophocles himself used. I think that we can nearly always recreate the movement structure of the dance of Greek drama, so that, if a habit of performing them in the theaters was formed, we would be able to judge whether particular movement structures fitted or did not fit with what we understood of the meaning of the play in general or the *stasimon* in particular. In other words the fifth-century poets have left enough choreographic instruction in their choruses for us to be able to perform them and know whether we are performing them right or wrong. This statement of mine, however, can be properly checked only after such performances have become a regular thing.

The New Music

Gesamtkunstwerk is a very precarious balance. And perhaps poet's *Gesamtkunstwerk* is a harder balance to maintain than composer's. For it is natural for music to dominate words, and it requires self-denial on the composer's part to allow words to remain dominant. I have tried to indicate how much we are able even now to appreciate the way in which words, music, and dance work together to create *Gesamtkunstwerk* in Aeschylus, Sophocles, and Aristophanes. I have hinted already that this *Gesamtkunstwerk* is less precise in Euripides. We know that very soon after the death of Sophocles the chorus had become merely a decorative adjunct to the drama, rather than the medium of the dramatic action itself. It would be surprising if we could not see the beginnings of this very abrupt change somewhere.

If a short discussion such as this may be allowed to summarize, then one might say that Sophocles, excellent dancer as we know him to have been, refined the technique of the system to such a degree of clarity and subtlety that it is difficult to conceive of any further advance. It is an altogether exceptional mind that can create for the theater in such a tight form as the Sophoclean system. Euripides probably did not have this kind of mind. Also it is natural when confronted with an older, very successful predecessor to attempt to do something slightly different. Since Sophocles had also developed the dialogue scenes into a subtle and speedy medium for carrying the story, and since it is much easier to write dialogue verse than lyric, and since Euripides was anyhow interested in analysis of motive, in showing underlying mental and emotional tendencies, there was every inducement for Euripides to give more and more of the main elements of his story to the dialogue, less and less to the chorus. Naturally, with this went a tendency to develop purely decorative qualities in the choruses.

If we study the formal perfections of the *Antigone*, or indeed any of Sophocles' seven masterpieces, whose every syllable seems to indicate dramatic movement created with exact precision, we are aware that the form is carried by the dance drama of the chorus with complete coherence, and also that the form is realized in the system of matching *strophē* and *antistrophē*. Always, this matching has precise meaning in the total *Gesamtkunstwerk*. Always, one image leads on to another. In Euripides this is no longer so. The chorus is no longer quite so central to the form of the play; the system is no longer central in the choruses.

Confront a modern composer and choreographer with Sophocles' system and they will suffer greatly. If we look at the system from our point of view, all we can see is the fact that every musical and choreographic effect must be repeated, exactly. This is because we have no general tradition of sung poetry. All we have are various media in which music uses words as the starting point for creating its own form. Opera and *Lieder* distort words as much as rock does, as is witnessed by the extraordinary vowel sounds that English classical singers are allowed to utter by an audience that has come to listen not to the setting of English but to a vocal tone poem. Only in the folk clubs is there an audience prepared to listen to sung poetry, where a tune serves words and does not dominate, where a musical climax can be repeated forty times in the singing of a traditional ballad, because the point of the exercise is not to listen for musical climaxes, but to hear a poem story, which, however, needs music for its full nature to be realized. Somehow or other, both music and dance in Aeschylus and Sophocles were more like the music of folk songs, a clarification and deepening of the poetry, not a medium in which one looked for independent climaxes. But at the end of the fifth century there were musicians who started to feel constricted by this repetition, started to feel more as a modern composer would. A typical Euripides chorus consists of short systems and longer epode—a piece of free music and dance that will not be repeated.

I have deliberately committed the eccentricity of titling this section "The New Music" and putting it in the chapter on dance. For we have to study what happened by looking at Euripides' choruses in comparison with those of Sophocles. If we do this we find a great elaboration of meters, which suggests vastly more complicated music and dance. It seems, however, that while the music did develop much greater complexity, the dance did not, and indeed in order to sing the much more complicated music, the dancers did less dancing. Sometime in the 420s the pirouette was introduced: that is what is being caricatured as modern dance in the finale of *The Wasps*. The sons of Carcinus do their pirouettes, while old Friend-of-Cleon, as we have seen, does the "Phrynichus crouch," leap, and kick (1482ff.). After that it seems that there were no new dance movements.[26] If the finale of *The Wasps* gives us a good impression of the vigor of the old dancing and a modern choreography inventive enough for Aristophanes to caricature with enjoyment, Plato the comic poet, who is younger than Aristophanes, gives a sad picture of the dance in his time.

> Those days, good dancing—hey what a sight!
>   they don't do anything now.
> They stand stock still as if they'd had
>   a lethal stroke, and howl.[27]

Although it is clear that the choruses of later Euripides have a high proportion of unrepeated epode to repeated system, there is also a far higher proportion of solo singing, and the solos are even more elaborate musically than the choruses. It is therefore reasonable to see the later Euripides as the beginning of what we may describe as an operatic style, with all the modern connotations of that word.

About 450 B.C. was born Timotheos, the poet-composer of dithyrambs and their solo equivalent, *nomoi*. He was one of the most influential of the creators of the New Music—astrophic songs in many types of meter, that is, in many different tempi. Euripides was clearly influenced by his work.

It is well to emphasize that, though this New Music was partly responsible for and partly a symptom of the beginnings of the breakdown of fifth-century drama, yet it too could produce its triumphs. For instance *The Trojan Women* is a great play by any standards. It is a lament, and an operatic style contributes to the intensity of its passions. We may regard the Cassandra sequence as providing a new kind of successful theatrical balance, operatic but appropriate. Cassandra is mad. There is little to establish in her scene except the monstrosity of the Greeks in taking the virgin priestess and giving her to be the general's concubine. It is a scene where naturalistic drama could only present horror-struck silence. Aeschylus and Sophocles would set its significance in the context of past action with a dance opening vistas on to the past and the future, as indeed Aeschylus does in the Cassandra sequence in the *Agamemnon* (1072–1177). Euripides, with more elaborate music and consequently words that will be less intently listened to, can develop what is more or less an extended scream. Cassandra enters with an astrophic solo, a free aria, of thirty lines in a great variety of tempi, excellently suited to the high emotion of her prophetic madness (308–41). She has one long speech (353–405) and one moderately long speech (424–44) and then breaks again into chant, to perform the running dance of the trochaic tetrameters for another twenty lines before going out (444–61). The scene's effectiveness now depends more on the music than on the words. But it is the kind of scene, the displaying of one uncomplicated emotion at extreme pitch, for which music is a more suitable medium than words.

Two examples will show how Euripides developed to this control. The end of the *Hecuba* is monstrous. Polymestor has been blinded by Hecuba and the other women in revenge for his murder of Hecuba's son. Although there is no excuse for Polymestor, the bloodthirstiness of Hecuba is almost unbearable. The scene with the blind Polymestor is made into a musical sequence. When Polymestor crawls out of his tent, he sings an astrophic solo of thirty lines (1055–84), immediately followed by another, shorter one (1089–1106). The main meter, however, is dochmiac. From its use elsewhere in Greek drama, dochmiac seems to have been a violent dance movement, but not very complicated musically. The strong syncopation, and the fact that dochmiacs occur like anapests in short interjectory passages, suggest that their effect was percussive, somewhere between song and shout, more like Lotte Lenya than Maria Callas. Musically effective in the right context, it is yet, as pure music, relatively limited.

A little later than the *Hecuba* was *The Suppliant Women*. After Theseus has won his battle on behalf of these women, while their leader Adrastus is preparing the funeral of the bodies of their husbands, which Theseus' battle has been fought to recover, there is an interruption. On the roof appears Evadne, wife of Capaneus, one of the dead heroes, crazed with grief. After a brief scene with her father Iphis, she leaps from the back of the *skēnē* down from the audience's sight on to the funeral pyre. A shattering theatrical interruption, and, if produced effectively, a moment to fill us with a thrilling horror at what war can do to innocent people. But not a moment on which to dwell too long; not a scene to make the audience think. Euripides again makes this primarily a musical sequence. He gives the actor a long solo system to sing, twice nineteen lines (990–1008; 1012–30). After a horrified reaction speech by Iphis, there is a sequence in stichomythia, which, as always, combines formality and speed (1045–71). Then Evadne disappears, not to be mentioned again. The actor has sung thirty-eight lines and spoken only sixteen. A scene that would not be credible as dialogue is made acceptable, and indeed effective, as opera. But it is effective only if we do not attend to it with the intelligence with which we are asked to attend to other parts of the play. It is emotional and musical excitement at the expense of *Gesamtkunstwerk*. Such a sequence can work fully only on very rare occasions, when the *Gesamtkunstwerk* is itself not founded on an intellectual conflict or a moral dilemma but is simply a cry of pain, as it is in *The Trojan Women*.

In several aspects of our attempts to understand Euripides it is right and proper to regard *The Trojan Women* as a watershed, the climax of a particular kind of development. So in this we may say that the Cassandra sequence is his finest example of opera integrated into the *Gesamtkunstwerk*. In his later plays the operatic element takes over more and more. This is something that we sense Euripides and Aristophanes to have explored together. The Hoopoe's monody (*The Birds* 227–59) has a different tempo for each bird summoned and imitated. In musical circles this may well have been the subject of excited gossip for the next few festivals. By 412 Euripides was able to respond with Helen's solos in the *Helen*, (167–251, chorus interspersed; 330–85, chorus interspersed; 625–97, duet with Menelaus); and then in the *Ion* with Ion's (112–83) and Creusa's (859–922) solos. But *The Phoenician Women* and *Orestes* go far further. In *The Phoenician Women* there are three major singing roles: the biggest is that of Antigone, who has a fifty-line solo aria (1485–1538) leading immediately into another nearly fifty lines of duet with Oedipus. (1539–81). The finale is also a duet between Antigone and Oedipus, and Oedipus' part has almost as many tempo variations as that of Antigone (1710–57). Antigone has also an earlier scene, (103–92) where she sings while the tutor answers in chanted iambics. There is even an aria for Jocasta (301–54). In other words, we are a long way from the *Hecuba*. Now both leading and second actor are required to sing what is musically very complicated. *The Phoenician Women* was one of the plays of Euripides popular in later antiquity, in what we call the age of the great actor. Provided that we realize that the so-called great actors of the Hellenistic and Roman periods were opera singers, then the popularity of this play is obvious.

Electra in the *Orestes* is a major singing role. Though some of her solos involve systems, the system is dominated by a longer astrophic epode (e.g., 960–1012).[28] The largest aria, however, in all Euripides' extant work is given to the Phrygian eunuch slave, who acts instead of a messenger and tells of the killing and magical disappearance of Helen. Broken five times by one-line interjections in chanted iambics, it lasts for just under one hundred and fifty lines (1369–1502) and is therefore much the same length as the sung part of the enormous *Agamemnon parodos*. Its tempi match its length in complexity. Even

Aristophanes could not top this. His most complicated aria is, needless to say, the parody of a Euripides aria that he gives to Aeschylus in *The Frogs* (1331–63), a mere thirty lines. The *Orestes* aria is anyhow itself comedy, if coloratura comedy; a Queen of the Night played for high camp. It cannot be parodied because it contains its own parody. It is a moment totally of the theater. But it is something very far from the *Gesamtkunstwerk* of Sophocles.

This then is the dominant development of Euripides, from the system that he inherited from Sophocles, which he handled always with less skill, to the solo aria in which, especially in moments where he was able to use comedy and theatricality for theatricality's sake, he developed his own mastery. The aria of the Phrygian slave is as great a theatrical achievement as anything in Sophocles. If we ask of our theater only to be theatrical then there is no reason why we should acclaim Euripides any the less than Sophocles. But if we ask more, Sophocles gives us more. His great moments are poetic, dramatic, and theatrical climaxes together. And this unity of purpose seems intimately connected with his reliance on the apparent constriction of the system.

The Bacchants is often described as one of Euripides' most "Sophoclean" plays. It does indeed present much more obviously a "dance of *Dikē*" in the metaphorical sense in which I shall use it in the next chapter. But the action of the play is not carried by the chorus as it is in the *Antigone* or either *Oedipus*. The chorus of bacchants are not significantly changed by what happens during the play, as the chorus are in the three Sophocles plays referred to.[29] The chorus are merely there to express adoration of Dionysus. Even after Pentheus' death, they are given no chance to react; for instance it is Cadmus, not the chorus, who forces Agave to see the truth that she has murdered her son. Similarly, the choruses in *The Bacchants* are not different from other late Euripidean choruses in shape. In the *parodos* and every *stasimon*, the system is dominated by an epode, except for the invocation of Holiness (370–432). In *The Bacchants* the dance is far more integrated with the action than in most of Euripides. But on the one hand, it is not dramatic like the dance of the *Antigone;* one dance does not lead to another in dramatic progress. On the other hand, it does not have the taut system pattern of Sophocles.

We can trace this kind of development in the plays where the chorus is important. For instance we can see the beginnings in a chorus from the *Hecuba* (905–52). This comprises two systems and an epode, but we can feel the dance building in excitement so that the epode is climactic. Obvious choreography for the first system would be to put the chorus on the ground; in the *strophē* they are lamenting the fall of Troy; in the *antistrophē* they are describing how it happened when people were asleep at midnight. The second system has two sections. In lines 1–4 they are still in some relation to the ground. The *strophē*'s words refer to them preparing for bed (923–26); the *antistrophē*'s to them having risen from bed to pray (933–36). The second half of this system is more violent: in the *strophē* they sing of the noise hitting the city and the Greek orders for attack; in the *antistrophē* of seeing their husbands dead, and of themselves being dragged away. In other words, this second half suggests much more movement, with grabbings and draggings about the stage. The words of the epode are a curse on Helen, and they were no doubt accompanied by the most violent dance movement as they sing to the sea to prevent her homecoming. Such a storm movement would provide a good climax to a dance that had started on the ground.

This tendency is further developed in *The Trojan Women* in a chorus on the same theme, the night of the fall of Troy (511–67). Throughout the system there is nothing very specific; the mood is excited anticipation. Nothing actually happens until the epode, which presents a great shout, terrified children fluttering round their mothers' dresses, the fighting, the slaughter, the rape of the women. A very clear picture; but one where the system is no longer adequate to express the dance.

In the lighter plays Euripides was able to go much further. In the *Ion*, after Ion's long solo, the chorus of Creusa's servants enter. The dance is a musical comedy number with lighthearted reference to the temple sculpture. An eleven-line system is followed by over thirty lines of free music (205–37). Almost certainly this provides one of the few examples of individual *choreutai* singing short solos.[30] There are three more main choruses in the play. Two of them, like the *parodos*, have extended epodes. As if to compensate for the one that is only two systems, there is also a short, completely astrophic dance (1229–43). The *Iphigeneia at Aulis* contains an even higher proportion of astrophic music for the chorus. It is easy to see that these lighter plays, less intimately connected with the rite of Dionysus for which the dance drama with its systemic construction developed, should tend to break away from the system's confines.

In spite of the fact, then, that the last decade of the fifth century saw some of the greatest plays, the elements of the *Gesamtkunstwerk* were beginning to get out of balance with each other. In the despondent mood of the postwar years, with no poets of the stature of Sophocles, and above all in the growing disillusionment with the worship of the Olympian gods, who had not been able to prevent the defeat of Athens, the minor element of the music was able to override the control of the poetry. For if there are to be no good poets, then it is better to be entertained by music than bored by bad poetry. Opera, however, is not *Gesamtkunstwerk*, and once we are aware of the exact nature of that precarious balance that was the achievement of fifth-century drama, we cannot but be saddened by its loss for ever.

Notes

1. Lucian *On the Dance* 25.
2. Gabriel Germain, *Sophocle* (Paris: Éditions du Seuil, 1969), p. 121. "The laws of the lyric require it to express itself in reminders of the great myths or in words of wisdom rather than in outpourings of humanity. At all events there is the tone. It is the warmth in the voice that is lacking in the old men of the *Antigone*."
3. Walther Kranz, *Stasimon* (Berlin: Weidmannsche Buchhandlung, 1933), p. 138. "The riddling unity of word, thought, rhythm, gesture, dance, song, instrumental sound, that is the womb of tragedy."

4. Cf. Athenaeus *Deipnosophists* 4.134A.

5. Ibid. 4.134B–D.

6. Plutarch *Table Talk* 8.9.732F.

7. Scholiast to Aristophanes *Clouds* 540.

8. Athenaeus *Deipnosophists* 14.630B–C.

9. Cf. Sir Arthur Pickard-Cambridge, *The Dramatic Festivals of Athens*, 2d ed. rev. John Gould and D. M. Lewis (Oxford: Clarendon Press, 1968), fig. 49.

10. Pollux *Onomastikon* 4.103–5; Athenaeus *Deipnosophists*, 14.629–31.

11. Frag. 304. Athenaeus *Deipnosophists* 14.629F.

12. The key book to study is T. B. L. Webster, *The Greek Chorus* (London: Methuen, 1970). Webster has collated all the pictorial evidence for dances, dramatic and nondramatic, with what we can infer about the movement from the meter of the lyrics. His argument is basically very straightforward: if a particular dance movement over a long period is constantly pictured on vases, then it is reasonable to assume that it was constantly danced; for otherwise the artist would not have seen it. If it was being constantly danced, then it is reasonable to assume that the meters used in the lyrics for moods and situations equivalent to a particular dance, as pictured, were indeed constantly employed for this purpose. We are therefore entitled to infer choreographic information from meter. The more we do so, the more the dances seem to make sense.

13. See Appendix 4 for notes on meters and Appendix 3 for meanings of terms used.

14. Euripides *Electra* 860–61.

15. Quoted as *scholion* to Euripides *Hecuba* 647.

16. Sometimes this goddess is named Artemis in Greek, but she is very different from Artemis the chaste huntress. It is better to think of her as one of the Eastern mother goddesses like Astarte, probably depicted with many breasts.

17. The Oxford text line numbers reflect textual problems.

18. The first four lines of the system are straightforward trochaic tetrameters. It is an interesting combination of system dance and traditional running dance, entirely suitable for this moment.

19. Rogers marks the opening, lines 1190–1203, as a system, *strophē* for Lamachus, *antistrophē* for Just-City. The Oxford text does not. The two stanzas do match in rhythm, but there are more substitutions of ♪ ♪ ♪ for ♪ ♩ than would be allowed in a genuine lyric.

20. Luckily there are no great problems over the text. This passage is also discussed in Chapter 8.

21. There will be those who object to the use of a slang expression in a translation of Sophocles. To reproduce the exact connotations of a great poet living in an age very remote from our own is almost impossible. What impresses me perhaps most of all about Sophocles is his pace, his *gestiches Sprach*, and the pungency with which his language works in the given context. To translate him into falsely smooth, archaizing English does him little justice in the late twentieth century, when all the great living poets make use of slang. I am not claiming to know that Sophocles' phrase *tolmēs charin* was as slangy as "live for kicks." I am claiming that in a poetic culture less slangy than our own, it had the same abrupt punch that we can obtain only by means of slang. For those who wish to pursue the matter further, there are many poets in all major Western languages who have used slang frequently: for instance, W. H. Auden, Pablo Neruda, Hans Magnus Enzensberger, Andrei Voznesensky, and Jacques Brel. In general, this use is on the increase.

22. *Everyman*, 85–86.

23. See lines 347 and 360 of *Antigone*, in *Sophocles: The Plays and Fragments*, trans. R. C. Jebb (Cambridge: Cambridge University Press, 1883–96), pp. 74–75.

24. H. D. F. Kitto, *Sophocles—Three Tragedies* (London: Oxford University Press, 1962), p. 14.

25. Henry George Liddell and Robert Scott, *A Greek-English Lexicon*, new ed. rev. Henry Stuart Jones with the assistance of Roderick McKenzie (Oxford: Clarendon Press, 1940), p. 1300.

26. Cf. Webster, *The Greek Chorus*, pp. 30ff. and passim.

27. Frag. 130, from the *Skeuai*, perhaps to be translated "Things."

28. Here a relatively short system of eleven lines is followed by a free monody of thirty-one lines.

29. See the discussion of the *Antigone* in Chapter 8; of the *Oedipus the King* in Chapter 6, "Form as Dance"; and of the *Oedipus at Colonus* in Chapter 10.

30. The Oxford text can be followed in its allocation of solos in this section. There has been, however, some strange aberration on the part of the editor, who has marked the passage as *strophē* and *antistrophē* though there is no correspondence between the two stanzas.

6

THE FORM OF FIFTH-CENTURY DRAMA

Form as Dance

I remember, when I sang under Sidney Watson in the Oxford Bach Choir, hearing him make a remark that I have always found useful when considering the form of major works such as the Greek plays. He was making a comparison between Bach's Mass in B Minor and the Missa Solemnis of Beethoven. The passage in question was the part of the Credo that deals with belief in the Holy Spirit, the Holy Catholic Church, and so on. All this section is so difficult to set, he pointed out, so theological; it is a major problem to a composer. Beethoven got over the difficulty by setting each theological phrase as a rapid chant more or less on one note, and punctuating these phrases with thumping reassertions of the opening "Credo, credo". Bach, on the other hand, said Dr. Watson, chose to set them to a tune so ravishing that we would not notice the difficulty of the words. The contrast between the two settings is indeed marked. But the more I consider Bach's "Et in spiritum sanctum," the more I feel that it is not just a ravishing tune. It is surely theologically significant that Bach sets his expression of belief in the Holy Spirit to a delicate dance with the oboe d'amore. It is also significant that he uses the same tune to set his expression of belief in the Holy Catholic Church. For to him the Church is nothing but the dance of the Spirit. Ravishing tune it certainly is, but the repetition affords theological insight and opportunity for meditation.

Modern drama is constructed on different principles from the drama of the fifth century. It is through hints such as that given by Bach's "Et in spiritum sanctum" that we are best led to appreciate the form of Sophocles. And I have mentioned Bach deliberately. Of all post-Renaissance art there is one form par excellence with which to compare Greek drama, and that is fugue. Whatever surprising developments Bach may have in store for us in the course of a fugue, even if he introduces a second or third subject in apparent contrast, there is a sense in which the end of a fugue is implicit in its beginning, in which the total fugue is the working out of implications contained in its subject. Secondly, there are minds that delight in complex pattern, indeed that feel liberated by strict discipline. This is partly a matter of temperament; some people feel the world as a pattern, a dance. But with Bach it is more than merely a personal delight. It is a philosophical and theological sense that the world is indeed a contrapuntal pattern, moving to a climax like a fugue, with great diversity making a unity. It is easier for us to understand Bach's delight in fugue than it is to understand Sophocles' delight in his medium. It is certainly almost impossible to imagine anyone who cannot appreciate Bach fugues making much headway with Sophocles.[1]

Analogy is a risky means of discussion, but not therefore something never to attempt. It is worth noting that in the analysis of a fugue we distinguish between those parts of it that are statements of the subject, whether straightforward, inverted in some way or in stretto, and passages without the subject present in any form, which are called episodes. I have always thought it significant that the dialogue scenes in Greek drama are also called episodes. It is not that they are less important than the statements of the subject; they are, however, in contrast with it. And it is the cumulative effect of subject statement after subject statement that builds the main weight of the fugue, just as it is the cumulative effect of chorus dance after chorus dance that builds the main weight of an Aeschylus or Sophocles tragedy. The episodes on their own, away from the chorus, certainly have life. They do not, however, necessarily have a self-sufficient life. They live in contrast to and in conjunction with the choruses.

I naturally do not wish to imply any pat resemblance between the form of Greek drama and that of fugue, only that it may be helpful to remind ourselves of the way in which we approach fugue before approaching Greek drama. Although in a sense fugue is governed by very strict rules, there are no rules for what comes when, no rules for the number of entries of the subject, and so on. The theoreticians have tried to formulate rules, but these bear little relation to the actual practice of Bach. To make a fugue is successfully to develop the implications of its subject with driving rhythm to a climax. May a method of analogy be allowed to make use of pun as well and suggest that this definition of making a fugue could, without changing a word, be used for the making of a documentary film: successfully to develop the implications of a subject with driving rhythm to a climax. But considering both the form of fugue and the form of documentary as opposed to story film, we may be led to a deeper understanding of the form of Sophocles. Documentary rhythm is based more on the intensification of an idea or image rather than on telling a story.[2] There are no rules for what comes when, as there must be in the telling of a story. If we attempt to analyze Greek drama, whether tragedy or comedy, in terms of rules for what comes when, then we shall find almost every play full of awkwardnesses in construction. To attribute such to Sophocles is absurd; the rules can be wrong, but not Sophocles.

We cannot apply externally derived rules of structure to the fifth-century plays. We certainly cannot apply rules derived from the theater of plot, which is what much formal criticism has done in the past. All we can do is to try and sense each play's own rhythm as a totality. All we can do is to sense smooth flow from chorus to episode to chorus, and consistent building of tension. And in some plays we feel slight awkwardnesses, slight failures to build as well as possible. We feel them, as we feel awkwardnesses in film editing, not as the breaking of external rules but as the breaking of the work's own internal rhythm. In this sense I can say with confidence that the *Antigone* is formally perfect and Euripides' *Medea* is not.

With these principles, it will be obvious that I can talk satisfactorily about form in terms only of complete plays, and therefore this chapter can be only a preliminary outlining of principles and a brief mention of analogies, in preparation for the fuller discussion of complete plays.[3] There is no one way of discussing form. There are only various analogies for illuminating rhythm.

In a book written now, it is necessary to emphasize and reemphasize that the Greek dramas are dance dramas. First—the dance is extremely important in itself. Second, the dance provides a focus, a means of concentrating the development of an entire play into one short song, as the first *stasimon* of the *Antigone* serves so to concentrate the entire play. Third, the plays are most satisfactorily analyzed in terms of a dance rather than of a story. This is perhaps repeating in a different way the analogy with the fugue. Greek tragedy is the "dance of *Dikē*". An action provokes a counteraction, and this in its turn provokes another counteraction, until the pattern has worked itself out. This metaphor implies, first, that there is a pattern into which human actions fit, a statement about the metaphysics of the poets who wrote the plays; second, that the performers in the drama are in a sense isolated by the dance; we are not concerned with them as complete human beings, only with their function in the dance. The first point has been dealt with in Chapter 4. The second is best amplified later, with regard to the way in which the poets portray character. Rounded characters are shown only if the situation requires a rounded character. Character is subsumed to the dance.

It is perhaps as well at this stage to include some definition of Greek tragedy, not because definition is in any sense exhaustive, but simply to state another of the guidelines that I use as I try to feel the rhythm of a particular play. It may be of use to refer to Aristotle's famous definition (*Poetics* 6. 1449B.24–28), which I would paraphrase as follows:

> We could say of every Greek tragedy that it was a lively meditation, conducted in public, into some issue of permanent significance, using song and dance and verse dialogue to represent an event in ancient history which embodied the particular issue, so that the audience's understanding of the issue should be deepened.[4]

To say that tragedy represents an action, rather than that it is the story of certain people, is to say something not very different from saying that it is a dance of *Dikē*. For in the representation of the action, each person has a part, and his character is interesting only as it affects his part in the action. And to describe tragedy as the dance of *Dikē* is more than a metaphor. For what is better able to represent action than dance? A moment such as Agamemnon's decision presented in Aeschylus' dance drama, which was discussed in Chapter 5, is much more precise than such a decision presented through dialogue (*Agamemnon* 218). We might say that all theater is patently artificial, a distillation of life. A form, then, that acknowledges such artificiality the most openly may well be the freest of all.

The following examples will, I hope, illuminate certain aspects of the above definitions and analogies. Using the analogy of the fugue, with its entries of the subject, and, in contrast, its episodes, I have suggested that the action is carried by the chorus. It is often thought that the *Oedipus the King* is very much a play about Oedipus. Much criticism almost ignores the large part of the play that is chorus song and dance. It is proper to take note especially of one *stasimon* at a climactic moment (863–910). An underlying idea of the play is that things are not what we expect. The action is Oedipus' flight from the consequences of the oracle, in which he heard about killing his father and sleeping with his mother (794–97). The development of the play is the verification of the oracles because what Oedipus did, through his ignorance of all the facts, fulfilled rather than avoided them. At the moment of this crucial *stasimon*, a suspicion has been roused that Oedipus has in fact killed his father. After the *stasimon* is over, Jocasta comes out to pray and offer incense to Apollo. What is she praying? (919–23). In effect, that Apollo make his own oracles not come true. This is something that the gods cannot do, just as Poseidon cannot revoke the curses that he has given Theseus, even though Theseus uses this gift to destroy his innocent son. After Jocasta's prayer the metaphorical dance of *Dikē* is continued by the arrival of a messenger to announce the death of Oedipus' supposed father. Apparently the oracles are false, though a little later this will turn out to be a part of the proof that the oracles have been fulfilled.

The *stasimon* has two systems. In the *strophē* of the first system the chorus sing a prayer that they may remain reverend and pious. In the *antistrophē* they sing of how violent arrogance begets the tyrant, and of course the word that I translate "tyrant" is the word applied to Oedipus.[5] The dance gives us the moral position of the chorus. The *strophē* must be danced with humble movements of prayer. Therefore so must the *antistrophē* be a humble prayer, the chorus by their movements praying to avoid such arrogance, such tyrannical behavior. Without the *strophē*, the *antistrophē* could be choreographed with arrogant struttings. As it is, the humble movement clearly shows the chorus starting to detach themselves from the tyranny and therefore the inevitable crash of Oedipus.

The second system continues in the *strophē* with a prayer that the man who does not reverence the shrines of the gods may fall. For if this does not happen, what is the point of dancing? The *antistrophē* presents the thought that if oracles are not fulfilled, then there is no point in worship. The dance mood of the second system is of a weakening, a falling, a shriveling up, but above all there is a mood of fear; for the chorus in the first system have firmly aligned themselves with pious worship. For this to turn out to be pointless is to destroy the purpose of their life. After this *stasimon* we are aware that their spiritual lives depend on the truth of the oracles. The death of Jocasta and the blinding of Oedipus are indeed horrible, and there is no mitigation of the horror. But nevertheless this horror is the result of two people's headstrong and impulsive actions; Apollo did not say that Jocasta must kill herself, or Oedipus blind himself. The horror is confined to the strange family of Oedipus. The ordinary people, who have been suffering plague, the effects of Oedipus' pollution, are now free. For them *Dikē* has performed its dance. And they have played their part of *Sophrosyne*. This *stasimon* has firmly aligned them with simple piety. The implications of the *stasimon* are: first let the oracles be fulfilled, even if it is our king who is destroyed; and second, if it is a matter of choosing between my king and my gods, I choose the latter. This is the sense of the declaration of faith in the last line of the first *antistrophē* (882). At this point in the action, the crucial choice is: which would you rather have, the oracles true or Oedipus safe? This choice is faced and answered by the chorus. In this sense the chorus is central to the development of the action. Episodes refer to and acquire their meaning in the totality of the play with reference to the *stasima*, not vice versa.

In Kitto's analysis of the *Philoctetes*,[6] he points out that Sophocles in the course of the play allows Neoptolemus to acquire more information on the question he is having to decide—whether to deceive Philoctetes and trick him into coming to Troy. In terms of plot there is no justification for Neoptolemus' further information. It is wiser, however, to regard the *Philoctetes* not as a plot, but as the exploraton of a dramatic situation in ever increasing depth. As such it makes excellent sense to give Neoptolemus more and more awareness of the nature of what he is choosing, at the same time as the choice itself is being delineated with ever greater clarity. In this too, it is helpful to use the metaphor of the dance. As the climax of the dance approaches, the dancer's movements are made with ever greater definiteness. We may also use an analogy with film: We see the action in larger close-up. And the progression from long shot to close-up is inherently rhythmic.

Neoptolemus develops not in terms of plot but in terms of Sophocles' pattern, the total dance of his mind. Such a development in terms of dance, but this time actual, not metaphorical dance, can best be seen in *The Libation-Bearers*. The play is 1076 lines long. Two hundred lines, that is, one-fifth of the play, are taken up by the *kommos*,[7] the invocation of the power of the dead, a prayer in song and dance for Orestes, Electra, and the chorus, followed by further prayer in spoken verse. Before the *kommos*, Orestes is undecided as to his course of action. After it, his plan and its activation follow with speed. Before the *kommos*, we have a sense of not knowing what will happen; after it, we know that Orestes and Electra will succeed in their terrible scheme. The events that follow, the actual killing of Aegisthus and Clytemnestra, in a sense can be regarded as the appendage of the dance. Sir John Sheppard was not particularly concerned to emphasize the role of the dance, and yet he writes as follows of this *kommos:*

> At the beginning, Electra is a gentle child, and Orestes a young, buoyant soldier, enlisted in a brave cause, ignorant of life and war. Before the end, Electra has grown hard, and Orestes is transformed into a ruthless instrument of vengeance. The dead man's spirit has possessed him. When he meets his mother, he will be implacable.[8]

This emphasizes that the justification of the dance for the fifth-century Athenians was that it was a way to divine possession. As in the example from the *Oedipus the King,* what is the point of dancing if there is no meaning in life? Conversely, if there is a meaning in life, we shall find it out through dance.

As we consider the form of Greek drama, it is inevitable to use one or other of the poets as central and explain the others' form in terms of his. I myself choose to regard Sophocles in this central light, and I think it is possible to make comparisons between his form and that of Euripides to the detriment of the latter. Choosing Sophocles rather than Aeschylus is not, however, to say that Sophocles' form is better than that of Aeschylus. It is more that with Aeschylus we are hampered by possessing only one complete play intended to be judged as a play on its own, *The Persians,* and one trilogy, the *Oresteia,* which still lacks its satyr play. The *Prometheus Bound* had at least one other play to go with it, and both *The Suppliants* and *Seven against Thebes* are parts of tetralogies. We can see from the scope of the *Oresteia,* and from our sensing of the scope of the other incomplete large works of which we possess only one movement, that Aeschylus' imagination was most happily employed on the large scale that such tetralogies entail. Since we possess not even the complete *Oresteia,* and no other linked plays at all, it is less practical to extrapolate generalizations about form from Aeschylus.

Apart from the question of scale, we may say that Aeschylus is a poet of striking image, while Sophocles is a poet of pattern. I have discussed elsewhere the way in which Aeschylus seems to build his drama around the development of a central image.[9] In *The Suppliants* it is the image of predator bird or beast and its prey, such as the hawk and the dove. In the *Oresteia* it is the image of the robe or net, and, even more central, the image of light or fire. These are not merely devices of verbal poetry. Their use in speech or song creates a tension in the audience, a desire that needs to be fulfilled. References to the image are such as to make us visualize it in our minds. Constant repetition of this act of visualization leads us to expect the image to appear physically on stage; eventually it does, and we are satisfied.

In the *Oresteia* the sense of doom is referred to in the image of the net, the robe in which Agamemnon was smothered in his bath. There are so many references to this net of doom that we cannot but have some strong picture in our minds. Then, at the moment of greatest despair, when Orestes has killed his mother, we are shown what we have been imagining. Orestes holds out the net to us and goes mad before our eyes (*The Libation-Bearers* 997 ff.). Another way of describing the form of the *Oresteia* is by saying that it is a question: Can light come out of darkness? All the way through the trilogy we think that light has come; we are bombarded with images of light. But the light only deepens the terror. Finally, however, right at the end, when the action has passed through the humans and is being completed by the gods, the light does come. Athene and the Furies are reconciled, and the Furies are escorted to their new home with torches. Just before the procession, the Furies have been given scarlet robes, and so we are reminded of the earlier image of the robe-net. In the light of the ending, the doom image of the robe-net and the hope image of the light become one, embodied in the events that we can now see physically happening onstage. This embodiment of images is something unique to Aeschylus. It has always surprised me that no other playwright has used this technique since it is one so appropriate to the theater. One can analyze the effect of such a development as the image of light in the *Oresteia* only in musical terms, treating the occurrence of the images as if they were musical themes. This again relates to the notion that Greek drama is the intensification of a dance rather than the development of a plot.

I have analyzed the form of Greek tragedy by talking in terms of an action that breaks the pattern of *Dike*, and its consequences. Xerxes, king of Asia, invades Europe, which is not his kingdom; *The Persians* shows the consequences. The Danaids flee marriage with their cousins. The *Suppliants* trilogy presents the consequences of this mistaken action. Prometheus gives fire to mortals and is chained to the rock. Ajax decides to kill all the Greek chieftains and is struck mad by Athene. Creon decides to refuse burial to Polyneices, which causes Antigone to react in such a way that Creon will lose everything. Heracles brings home Iole, which provokes Deianeira to an innocently intended reaction, which, however, will destroy both Deianeira and Heracles. Oedipus runs from the consequences of the oracles and, by apparently running away from them, fulfills them. Aeschylus' and Sophocles' plays can be analyzed in this way. So can most of Euripides'. But there are some that I have called "pathetic drama."[10] If the nature of *Dike* is such that a break in the pattern of *Dike* provokes reactions until equilibrium is restored, then innocent people will be hurt. Euripides' concern was often more to arouse sympathy for the victims than to understand how the initial action had happened. In his *Suppliant Women*, the initial action is far in the past, and not really the center of the play's form. What we are presented with is a series of incidents designed to arouse our pity for the victim. *The Trojan Women* is again a series of incidents, connected only in terms of their piteousness. It is the results of action—suffering. It is admittedly the third play of Euripides' only trilogy. We should compare what Aeschylus does in *The Seven against Thebes*, also the third play of a trilogy. The invasion of Thebes is the result of Oedipus' curse against his sons, which was presented in the preceding play. But Aeschylus does not merely show victims of this curse. He also shows one of the sons clearly choosing to go out and fight his brother (709 ff.). It is a headstrong action, against the advice of the chorus, not the right action for a commander. Eteocles' death is shown by Aeschylus to be the result both of previous wrong actions and of his own wrong action. In Euripides' *Suppliant Women* and *Trojan Women*, there is no equivalent to Eteocles' action.

One play of Sophocles, the *Oedipus at Colonus*, could in a sense be called pathetic drama. There is no action, as I have defined the concept. For unlike what he presents in the *Oedipus the King*, in this play Sophocles makes Oedipus, if not innocent, then at any rate purified, more a victim of the terrible pattern of *Dikē* than a breaker of *Dikē* himself (266 ff., 539–41). Admittedly, the assertions of Oedipus' innocence are made by Oedipus himself. But the whole poetry of the play is such that we think of Oedipus more as victim than agent. The *Oedipus at Colonus*, however, is anyhow a unique play, an extension of the form as Beethoven's C sharp minor quartet is an extension of sonata form, quite irrepeatable. Although there is no action, yet the play is by no means passive, as is *The Trojan Women*. But the form of it can be described only as the gathering of Oedipus' power, the transformation of his dying body into a *theos*, a power in the ground. The chorus has an active, developing role. From detached spectators of a helpless old man they become struck with horror when they discover who Oedipus is, but from then on they are drawn into closer and closer involvement with his impending death, until the final *stasimon* is an incantation, pure and simple, to that death (1556–78).[11] The *Oedipus at Colonus* is unique among extant Greek tragedies. But it could still be defined as a manifestation of the dance of *Dikē*; it is par excellence dance drama, and a performance of the rite that was fifth-century drama.

Apart from his pathetic drama, Euripides has, even in his plays of action, a less coherent sense of form than Sophocles. He gives us a feeling of dislocation. Instead of the flow of one event into another, we are presented sometimes with an arbitrary series of events. Taken all together these events do form a unity. But it is more the unity of an intellectual idea. It is easier to say what a Euripides play is "about," and the dislocation helps to make this easier.

The *Medea*'s action is clear. Jason, by neglecting his first wife, Medea, and marrying the daughter of the king of Corinth, drives Medea to extremes of rage. Since she is a sorceress she is able to achieve horrible revenge, first murdering the girl and her father with a poisoned dress, then murdering her own children to spite Jason. It would have been possible to write this play without awkwardnesses. But Euripides wished to push the idea further. There is something divine about passion as great as Medea's. A woman like her, wronged, hits back like a god, like Aphrodite in the *Hippolytus*, or Dionysus in *The Bacchants*. This idea is emphasized by certain abrupt transitions. There is emphasis on Medea's need to find a place to live in her exile (386 ff.) and a scene where she quarrels with Jason and refuses any help from him for her journey into exile (609–22). After a short chorus expressing fear of exile, Aegeus arrives, without preparation. He will give Medea a home in Athens. Sophocles would have integrated Aegeus into the action, either naturalistically or in terms of a chorus. Euripides is less in control, and also prefers to shock his audience. Medea is the sort of person for whom help always arrives. The more sudden the arrival, the more acute the demonstration.

The *Heracles* is in many ways a crucial play for the study of Euripides' development. It is his most violent protest against the way things are. For the first part of the play, he presents the sufferings of Heracles' dependents, whose sufferings derive from Heracles' noble action in taking upon himself the atonement for a killing done by his father. The second part of the play, the madness of Heracles, is brought about by the direct intervention of Hera. There is a moment of apparent triumph. Heracles has arrived in the nick of time to rescue his family. Then Iris, the messenger of the gods, arrives, accompanied by the figure of Madness. It is the first use of an abstraction onstage.[12] And this abstraction protests at the cruelty about to be inflicted on Heracles (854). The idea of the play is clear. At the moment of triumph we are brought low. The abruptness emphasizes the idea.

Madness protesting at the way the world is run, in the name of decency; it is an odd situation. Euripides emphasizes the oddity. After Madness has made her protest, Iris takes command. The meter changes. From spoken iambic trimeters they go into chanted trochaic tetrameters. It is likely that these had not been used in tragedy for about forty years.[13] They would therefore be associated in the audience's mind with comedy. Whether Euripides intended comedy or not here is very hard to tell. The natural way to present this scene today would be to exaggerate its grotesqueness and play it for black comedy. The situation is too horrible for anything but grim, beastly laughter.

The rest of the *Heracles* does not continue in this vein. But one of the lines of Euripides' development was certainly in this direction. For all the elements that I suggest may be present in this sequence are present throughout the *Orestes*, which is one of Euripides' greatest achievements. In the *Orestes* he found a perfect form to fit his ideas: a mixture of black comedy, grotesque theatricality, and constant sudden surprises. However we take the sequence in the *Heracles*, it is sensible to regard it as a preparation for the much more consistent inconsistency of the *Orestes*. This is discussed in Chapter 7.

The sequence in the *Heracles* has no reality except in terms of the theater. An abstract figure of Madness dancing a jog-trot on the roof—that is absurd. In the theater it can be absurd and yet have some strange reality that we cannot define; not the reality of ordinary life; not the reality of a religious rite; something sui generis. In the last ten years of his life, it was this pure theatrical reality that Euripides was exploring. In this exploration we can see how he and Aristophanes worked together. But whereas Aristophanes used the different levels of theatrical reality to deepen our sense of the rite that was the comic festival,

with such plays as *The Women at the Thesmophoria* and *The Frogs*, Euripides
was moving away from the rite that was tragedy. *The Frogs* is the most central
of all Aristophanes' comedies. The *Orestes* is the least central of all extant
tragedies.

In editing film one can reach a sense of what is the right sequence, the right
rhythm, only through seeing what does not seem to work. So, as we consider
the form of Greek tragedy, it is sensible to increase our understanding of the
best examples by examining those plays and sequences within plays that seem
to have an odd rhythm. Sometimes we discover the purpose of this oddness;
sometimes we are left with a sense that the transition is unnecessarily abrupt.
We learn therefore about Sophocles' form by comparing his work to that of
Euripides. It would also seem likely that we can learn about an artist's form by
sensing his own development, by comparing earlier work to later. We cannot,
however, progress very far with this enquiry with either Aeschylus or Sophocles. For we possess no early work by either. *The Persians* was written when
Aeschylus was fifty-three and the *Ajax* when Sophocles was about fifty. Both
wrote their greatest work at the end of their lives, but we cannot treat earlier
plays as if they were written by poets not yet in control of their medium.[14] Such
development as we see in Aeschylus is that of a mind reaching after larger,
richer, and more complex themes, a man taking ever greater delight in six-part
as opposed to three-part counterpoint. In Sophocles we are aware of a movement inward, into more and more unknowable depths. Why and how Ajax?
Why and how Creon of the *Antigone?* These are relatively easy questions to
answer. Why and how Electra? Why and how Philoctetes? These pose far
deeper problems about the nature of the world. And with the question posed in
his last play—Why and how Oedipus?—we are on the edge of language.

We do not possess any early work by Euripides either. The *Alcestis* was
written when he was over forty. But in so many of his plays we have the sense
that he was unhappy with his medium, constricted by doing what Sophocles
was doing more successfully. There are many ways in which to consider
Euripides' development. We can think of his frustrations with the Sophoclean
form and emphasize the awkwardnesses as discussed with regard to the *Medea*
and *Heracles*. Such an analysis of his development will end with the climax of
The Bacchants, a play in which the form is as smooth and flowing as any
Sophocles play, and the action is a breaking of *Dikē* and its consequences, as in
the Sophoclean structure. This is a fair analysis of Euripides. But it makes him
out merely as a second-class Sophocles. It is equally sensible to trace his development as that of a poet finding a new medium all of his own, in which the
only rhythm is the rhythm of theatricality. In this analysis the *Medea* and
Heracles are stages of his development toward the mastery of the *Orestes*. This
analysis does much more justice to the unique greatness of Euripides. It is,
however, a digression from the main line of argument in this book, since this
aspect of the achievement of Euripides bears little relation to the rest of fifth-
century drama. In general, however, it is helpful to be reminded that there is

more than one "Euripidean form," since we should also remember that no one kind of analysis, no one set of rules, totally embraces such a complex subject as the form of Greek tragedy.

The Form of Aristophanes' Comedies

Of the four fifth-century poets, Aristophanes is the only one in whom we can see a clear and obvious development in mastery of his medium. Our first extant play was written when he was twenty-one. Although *The Acharnians* is a very funny play and full of beautiful moments, it is not as tightly integrated as *The Women at the Thesmophoria,* or *The Frogs.* Clearly, formal integration is not the first requirement of a comedy, where more important than anything else is the getting of laughs. But because of this it is especially interesting to study Aristophanes' development, since his most mature work does show such an advance in formal coherence. He was even willing to risk vitality of invention in order to achieve it.

Aristophanes' center is a poetic vision, an image of lyrical intensity that cannot be paraphrased into anything other than itself. It is also totally comic, an absolute of fantasticality, a total topsy-turviness. From the Renaissance till the Marx Brothers and the Goons, Western comedy has been derived from New Comedy, not Old, from Menander, not from Aristophanes. New Comedy is comedy of plot, where the story is relatively logical and the characters are governed by the same laws as we in the audience are governed by. The comedy is incidental—amusing situations in which the characters find themselves, amusing remarks that they make when they find themselves in these situations. In contrast, the comedy of Aristophanes is total. We never know from one moment to the next at what level the fun is. At one moment we are presented with details of ordinary life portrayed with a documentary precision that makes them far closer to our own experience than the stereotype situations of most New Comedy from Menander to Noel Coward. At the next moment we are asked to soar into the wildest flights of fantasy. The only thing that holds the play together is Aristophanes' rhythm and our laughter. Without laughter Menander is still a play. Without laughter Aristophanes' rhythm falls to bits. That is perhaps why there is not a single device for making audiences laugh in the theater in the entire history of the comic stage of which we cannot find an example in Aristophanes.

One way therefore of describing Aristophanes' development is in terms of this topsy-turviness. The most perfect of his plays is *The Frogs,* whose central action is so upside-down and inside-out that it needs a long explanation to analyze it, though as theater, as I shall show in Chapter 8, it makes instant sense. The action of *The Birds* or *The Women at the Thesmophoria* is much more topsy-turvy than that of *The Acharnians,* or indeed the *Lysistrata.* The central action of the last two is straight: make peace. They are therefore plays that move on fewer levels, less complex as poetry in the sense of the word that includes theatrical as well as verbal images. I have indicated how every Aristophanes play contains an implicit philosophical dialogue. The implicit dialogue in *The Acharnians* or *Lysistrata* is much less complicated, much less far-reaching. *The Wasps* is formally less coherent. Its central topsy-turviness is the creation of a private court of justice, just as that of the *Acharnians* is the creation of a private state of peace. But Just-City[15] performs the action and creates his peace for himself. Friend-of-Cleon has his private court created for him, as a compensation for having lost the *agōn*, having lost his raison d'être as a juror. There is no philosophy behind the creation of his private court, and therefore the idea is not sustained throughout the play. The finale, which is climactic theatrically and which, as we saw in Chapter 5, demonstrates the triumph of old Friend-of-Cleon as a dancer, has nothing to do with the idea of justice. The chorus of old jurymen are done out of a job once the *agōn* is over and Friend-of-Cleon will have nothing to do with the courts anymore. On the other hand, although it is obvious that Just-City has obtained his peace, yet the presence of the old soldier chorus of Acharnians leaves an atmosphere of some tension: will something happen to disturb that peace? The tension is relevant: a necessary part of what the play is about. And the finale is completely relevant: the final triumph of Just-City over the general Lamachus.

Aristophanes was still only twenty-four when he wrote *The Wasps.* It may have won at the *Lenaia* or it may have come second; but it is full of excellent moments. I am, however, sure that Aristophanes wrote both *Acharnians* and *Wasps* without full understanding of the principles on which he wrote, and that as he came to understand his own principles, he chose to order his development in the direction of greater coherence, in the form to which *The Acharnians* rather than *The Wasps* pointed.

As one way of analyzing the form of tragedy is in terms of the central, *Dikē*-breaking action from which every event in the play develops, so there is an equivalent way of analyzing Aristophanes. Each play has a central idea, which we can express as a political or philosophical problem. The form of the play, however, depends on a central action that is a fantastical solution of this problem. The idea of the *Acharnians* is the question of making peace. The action is the private peace treaty negotiated by Just-City with Sparta. All the play is a true development of this action, though there is perhaps a sense of contrivance about the way the final climactic feast is held back by a series of interruptions, in particular the scene with the farmer who has lost his oxen (1018–47) and the scene in which the Best Man gets Just-City to give him ointment of peace for the bride to smear on her husband's cock and keep him from leaving her for the war (1048–70). But although there is a certain arbitrariness about the latter part of the play, we do need a sequence of such scenes to demonstrate in full Just-City's triumph.

The problem of *The Knights* is the problem of politicians whose raison d'être is to stay in power. The fantastical solution is to depose Cleon, currently the most powerful politician in the state, by persuading the sausage seller to outbid him for the favors of the Man-in-the-Street. The action is initiated by the two slaves, generals Nikias and Demosthenes, but they soon cease to play any part in the proceedings, and almost all the play is taken up with the contest between Cleon and the sausage seller, which is only resolved at the end. To topple Cleon at this time, when he was at the height of his power, gave a feeling of fantasticality to the play. Once the process of time has turned Cleon into just one more politician, the balance of the play is disturbed, and for this reason it is the least repeatable of Aristophanes' plays.

The action of *The Clouds* is the decision by Twister to study the new learning in order to argue his way out of paying his debts. The central action is therefore less fantastical than in any other play, and therefore several plotlike developments have to take place. The play is not simply the consequences of the action. Twister is thrown out of the think-tank and has to send his son to study instead. The creditors are discomfited, but Twister is then beaten up by his son and afterwards out-argued in a second *agōn*. Furious at his defeat, he finally burns down the think-tank. The complications of the events in the play are not entirely connected with its dialectic, which is a confrontation of old ways and new ways.[16]

The action of *The Wasps* is the decision of Friend-of-Cleon's son, Bdelycleon (Hater-of-Cleon) to let his father hold a private court of justice at home. But this fantastical act does not occupy the whole play. The first half is, as it were, naturalistic: Friend-of-Cleon's attempts to escape from his house-imprisonment to court, followed by an argument as to whether it is worthwhile serving on a jury. Although full of farce, this argument could be rewritten straight. This is an *agōn* that is not fundamentally topsy-turvy and is not consequent on the central action, but prior to it. This may explain why the end of the play also goes off in a different direction, into a general contest between young and old, the matter of justice and the courts forgotten. It could fairly be said that the play ends at line 1121, at the end of the *parabasis*, and that the final four hundred lines, marvellous farce though they are, are only a series of sketches.

The idea of *The Peace* is again the making of peace. The fantastical solution is the flight of Trygaeus (Vintage) to heaven on a dung beetle in order to drag Peace out of her cave. The play is the consequences of this action, but there is little conflict. War and Riot are dismissed peremptorily. The scene (236–88) is not even an *agōn*, merely an episode in dialogue iambics. Where we would expect an *agōn*, we have instead Hermes telling us the story of how Peace was shut away (603ff.). *The Peace* is Aristophanes' least good play, if we judge it in modern terms, for it has little dramatic tension. It is a useful play to study, however, if we wish to discover more about the fifth-century theater. For, as we shall see in Chapter 7, it demonstrates well that the purpose of Old Comedy was not just to create a play with dramatic tension but first and foremost to create a rite of laughter.

The Birds is often judged to be Aristophanes' greatest play. Its idea is enormously complex; the central character is splendidly ambivalent; we cannot be sure whether he is hero or villain. The action is highly fantastical. Persuader decides to leave the big-city rat race for the free air of the birds. Having arrived there he quickly turns the free air into a big-city rat race even worse than the one he has left. Democratic freedom in Aeschylus, Sophocles, and Euripides is connected very closely with the rituals of the city's worship of its gods. The freedom of Persuader's Cloudcuckooland is based on denying the gods their due. His action is blasphemy, but on the other hand it is impossible. So perhaps the blasphemy should not be taken too seriously. The form of *The Birds*, like the form of *The Frogs*, defies analysis.

The thought of the *Lysistrata* is the thought of peace. The action is the decision of Lysistrata to make the women refuse to make love to their husbands until the husbands bring the war to an end. Every part of the play is very much a consequence of this action. Conflict is maintained to the end with the double chorus of Athenian men and women who unite only to be confronted with a chorus of Spartans, who also finally unite with the Athenians. On the level of the implicit philosophical dialogue the *Lysistrata* is not nearly as deep as the *Birds, Women at the Thesmophoria* or *The Frogs.* Nor does it contain any such moments of intense lyrical beauty as the *parabasis* of *The Birds* (676ff.), or the confrontation of Dionysus with either chorus in *The Frogs* (209–69, 316–459), or even a moment such as the entry of the Clouds (263ff.), or the confrontation of the Acharnians and Just-City's Rural *Dionysia* (241ff.). The poetry and the ideas of *The Acharnians* are more complex, because at the time when the play was written the question of peace was something to debate seriously. By the time of the *Lysistrata*, no one of Aristophanes' sensitivity could debate about peace or war—one could only cry for peace. Climactic in both *The Peace* and *Lysistrata* is the rite of peace with which both plays end. And in both, this rite is celebrated in terms of sexual enjoyment. The rite is no less central, though neither poetry nor ideas are so intense.

The idea of *The Women at the Thesmophoria* is a reexamination of the status of women. Euripides, the poet who did so much to advance the cause of women, is presented in the play as a misogynist, against whom the women are plotting. Euripides' action is to send his uncle Mnesilochus disguised as a woman to the women's festival of the Thesmophoria, where the plot is being hatched. Mnesilochus is admittedly a second best for the effeminate Agathon, whom he had hoped to persuade instead. The play then develops more like a play of plot, like the plays of Euripides that it parodies.[17] Mnesilochus is captured. Euripides then attempts to rescue him in parody scenes from Euripides plays. These attempts fail. When, however, Euripides appears himself as a woman, a bargain is quickly struck. The women agree, and the one male figure left, the Scythian guard, is quickly put to confusion by a nude dancing girl. Central to the form of the play is that the events take place at a women's festival. The chorus continues to stress this during the play. The form is an image of the whole of Greek drama—a rite during which there is acting. There are many ramifications of paradox: it is very much part of the point that the poet's poetry, the scenes from Euripides plays, achieves nothing, only the poet's appearance in person. It is also part of the point that Euripides, who supports women, is treated as a misogynist, and that Euripides the man can finally rescue his uncle only after putting on women's clothing. It is also the point that the women employ a male guard, the Scythian, to watch Mnesilochus, and this guard is finally disposed of in the most obvious way in which a woman can render a man harmless, that of exciting him sexually. We can say that the play offers thought-provoking images as to the nature of poetry, and the relation between men and women, and the interconnection of the two. But we cannot analyze these images further.

The action of *The Frogs* is likewise very complex, and will be discussed in detail in Chapter 8. The two last plays are somewhat unsatisfactory in form, largely because there is about them a thinness and a tiredness. The action of *The Women at the Assembly* is the decision of Praxagora to take over the Assembly and give it to the women, and therefore change society. The action of the *Wealth* is the decision of Chremylus to restore Wealth's sight, so that he has once again the power to choose with whom he consorts, and so to reward merit. Both are good ideas, capable of unlimited development. But Athens was impoverished, and afraid; Aristophanes, we may suspect, was a broken man. There is no proper chorus; scenes are left in the air. The fantasy has deflated, and we are no longer borne along on a rhythm of laughter.

Another way of discussing Aristophanes' form is to examine the way in which he makes use of the traditional comic mold, the *parodos, agōn,* and *parabasis,* which seem to have derived from the original *kōmos.* First, we must note that Aristophanes is very free in his use of them. It is arid scholarship to create from Aristophanes' living form a dead mold to which we then relate the plays. It is more profitable to think of three traditional elements, a chorus entrance, a contest and a moment of direct confrontation between chorus and audience, and to notice that Aristophanes uses these elements in a slightly different way in each play. For instance, the actual *agōn* in the *Lysistrata* is between the *Proboulos* (Magistrate) and Lysistrata (486ff.). But this is much less important than that all the choruses are in the nature of an *agōn* from the *parodos* onwards simply because there are two opposing choruses. We might say that in the *Frogs, Lysistrata,* and *Knights* the *agōn* has spilled over into the rest of the play, and notice that all these plays have tight structures. Further the *agōnes* of these three plays clearly present the two sides of the basic question about which the play has been written. So does the *agōn* of *The Clouds.* But this *agōn* takes place between the Just and Unjust Logics, two characters who take no other part in the play and are anyhow abstractions. In this sense the play is less tightly structured.

The *parabasis* is so often treated by critics as if it were merely an excuse for the poet to talk directly to the audience. This is certainly the case in the *parabasis* of *The Knights*, for example. Almost nothing of what is said there belongs to the character of the chorus as knights, rich young men of the cavalry class. At the other extreme is the *parabasis* of *The Birds*. Here the confrontation at all levels is very much between the chorus in character as birds and the audience. The beginning of the first *parabasis* creates a bird world in fantastical terms (676ff.). But even the request to the judges to vote the play first stays within this bird world. If you judge against us, they say, never wear white again; for all the birds of the air will shower you with droppings (1116–17, in the second *parabasis*). The *parabasis* of *The Frogs* appears to be the poet talking directly to the audience. But to think this is to miss the full point. The great speech of reconciliation, which was to win the play a second showing, (686ff.), has far greater strength if we take it as a speech by the chorus completely in character as the initiate dead, the people who really know. The play is about a bringing back from the dead, and about the use of poetry to save the city. The *parabasis*, at the center of the play, is the confrontation of the living audience with the living dead. It is the most subtle use of the traditional mold in all the plays, the one where the elements of the *kōmos* have been most perfectly blended into the form of the play.

There is a further way to regard the development of Aristophanes' form. This bears a relationship to what I describe as the theater of plot.[18] In comedy of plot it is above all the task of the author to keep us guessing. This is not essential to the Old Comedy, but it is an aspect of play making whose advantages became apparent to Aristophanes as he developed. In *The Acharnians* Just-City is in control of the situation quite early on. In *The Knights* the sausage seller constantly defeats Cleon. Though admittedly there is a surprise ending to *The Clouds*, it is in the later plays—the *Birds*, *Lysistrata*, *Women of the Thesmophoria*, and *Frogs*—that the issue is really kept open to the end. We may therefore conclude that this exploitation of suspense was an aspect of comic structure that Aristophanes developed for himself within the context of a structure in which it was not an inherent part.

In most modern writing about Aristophanes we read that his form is a loose one, apart from those parts of the play that derive from the *kōmos*; the *parodos*, *agōn*, and *parabasis*. After the *parabasis*, we are told, his plays degenerate into a series of revue sketches. This is criticism based on the belief that the only good dramatic form is the well-made plot. Certainly, we can describe the iambic scenes at the end of the *Acharnians* or *Birds* as revue sketches if we wish. But such a description does not help our understanding of Aristophanes or explain our sense of enjoyment of the way in which the events build to a well-constructed climax. A state of triumph is reached. Just-City has made peace. Persuader has founded Cloudcuckooland. Before the final triumph is consummated, in the first case by Lamachus' discomfiture and Just-City's feast, in the second by Persuader's marriage to Zeus' mistress, Majesty, there are a series of quick scenes that illuminate farcically the state the two characters have reached. They do not follow one another with the inevitability of a well-made plot.

They build from one another in a rhythm of increasingly hysterical laughter. It is a rhythm easy to understand if we think of the cutting of a film. They are the equivalent of Tati's documentary montages, such as the series of shots of motorists, all picking their noses in traffic jams.[19] Aristophanes manipulates the rhythm of his audience's laughter like a good film editor. That is not an example of loose form.

It might be thought that, though all talk of a tragic hero in fifth-century drama is out of place, yet there is some sense of talking of a comic hero, since in many of Aristophanes' plays the character played by the leading actor is more central to the form of the play than in any tragedy. But a closer examination does not bear this out. Conclusive proof that this is not the way in which Aristophanes structured his plays is provided by his last one, the *Wealth*. Which part in this one is the most important, Chremylus or his slave, Cario? It is very hard to say. And in a sense there is no need for both Chremylus and Cario. What is divided between them could all have been done by one of them, which would have given more unity to the play. Without a chorus around which he could structure what happens, Aristophanes could have been expected to use the central character more centrally. That he did not is proof positive that his plays are "representations of an action," not plots about a hero.

Although it is the character played by the leading actor who acts so as to set the play in motion in the *Acharnians, Clouds, Peace, Birds, Lysistrata,* and *Frogs,* he does not do so in the *Wasps, Knights,* or *Women at the Thesmophoria.* In *The Knights* the action is initiated by the two slaves, Nikias and Demosthenes, who then take no further part. In *The Wasps* Friend-of-Cleon is merely a reactor, not an initiator. In *The Women at the Thesmophoria* the action is initiated by Euripides, but the leading actor must play the more important part of Mnesilochus. And in *The Frogs,* whose form is the most subtle and well built of all the plays, and where the relationship between the character of Dionysus, played by the leading actor, and the chorus, both of frogs and then of initiates, is the most complex and the most delicately drawn, the leading actor has almost nothing to do for the second half of the play, merely sitting as an almost mute spectator. If Old Comedy is a play with a hero, then *The Frogs* is not a well-written play. Since this is obviously nonsense, then Old Comedy is not a play with a hero.

This brief discussion has perhaps been sufficient to show that there is no one way of analyzing Aristophanes' form exhaustively. His medium had a fluidity that no dramatic form has possessed since until the age of film, and we are forced to discuss it in subjective terms like pace and rhythm, and the placing of laughter, rather than in the more easily classified terms of normal literary criticism. But pace and rhythm and the pacing of laughter are perhaps the most essential aspects of the comic poet's craft to master. It is helpful that analysis of Aristophanes in literary terms gets us such a little way, since we are reminded that he and his tragic colleagues were first and foremost practical men of the theater, engaged in winning the approval of a tough and critical audience. In one sense everything they wrote had a very crude purpose: to win first prize.

Theater of Plot

I have drawn a rough distinction throughout this book between the method of construction of fifth-century drama and "theater of plot." The former I have described by analogies with fugue, with documentary film, and above all in terms of metaphorical as well as actual dance rhythm, while maintaining also that it is sui generis, and ultimately indescribable except in its own terms. The latter I assume to be a familiar concept, and I intend no subtleties by it. In it the primary purpose of the play is to tell a story through the interaction of the various characters by means of dialogue. We say that it is a good plot if the characters behave consistently and naturally, and yet events surprise us, though after the event we are still able to say it was consistent with the characters in question to have acted like that. If the purpose of such drama is to create surprises within a framework of consistency, then it will tend toward naturalism, a style that attempts to put more real life on the stage than the theater of the previous generation. For, since all theater is artificial, there can be no absolute naturalism. It has been, however, the assumption for a long time that this tendency toward naturalism was also a tendency toward greater reality. This we can now see easily to be a fallacy. For on television each night we are able to see at least one example of plot construction in some serial of everyday life, and at least one example of montage construction in some documentary or TV commercial, the latter being probably a more extreme example. Both are equally artificial forms, to be chosen according to the subject and purpose of the maker.

In terms of this rough distinction, the New Comedy, which we possess in the works of Menander, Plautus, and Terence, is theater of plot. But New Comedy is formula writing, very much the writing necessary for series and serials in television today. Nothing originated with New Comedy. As with almost everything else theatrical, so with plot. The fifth century saw its invention by Euripides. This is a bald statement, but in terms of our rough distinction, a valid one.

I do not wish to imply that Euripides claimed one day that he had invented the idea of a play plot. We can, however, point to a general tendency to rely more on the intervention of characters in dialogue throughout the fifth century, and then to a moment when Euripides started to construct his plays very much more definitely on this principle than had been done before. We can date this precisely. It was after the unsuccessful production in 415 of the trilogy in which *The Trojan Women* was third play. His next plays were to have a very different feel; they are more light-hearted, more romantic; their construction is, in terms of the criticism of the last hundred years, much better; a way of writing had been discovered that could be made into a formula by the less inventive writers of the next century; and the theater of well-made plots had begun.

To describe the background to this, we must refer to the use of the dialogue scenes by Aeschylus and Sophocles. Once again Sophoclean practice appears as a norm. With three actors Sophocles is able to create extremely flexible dialogue scenes. There is something unstable about tragedy written with two actors, of which we possess only two or possibly three examples.[20] Aeschylus, who had pioneered two-actor tragedy, was very quick to adapt Sophocles' practice of the third actor, even though he was in his sixties when the new regulation was introduced.

There is an obvious clarity of form in one-actor tragedy. There are no problems about entrances and exits. The chorus creates a need for a certain character to appear; the character appears, says his piece and goes. Once there are more than one character on stage at once, entrances and exits become a problem. One may go, or both may go; one may stay or both may stay. Reasons have to be given for their actions. And reasons for entrances and exits are part, if a small part, of plot construction.

With only two actors, it may not be possible to allow an important character to return later in the play. We cannot but feel an awkwardness in the disappearance of the old queen, Atossa, from the last part of The Persians (852ff.). We have seen the disaster so much from her point of view; she is the person with whom we sympathize. As it happens, the final lament (907ff.) is sung by Xerxes and the chorus only. There is no dramatic reason why Atossa should exit at 851. We must imagine that Aeschylus himself as leading actor was the only one capable of singing and dancing Xerxes' part, and as leading actor he would also have played Atossa. It is possible that an extra could have put on Atossa's costume and mask, come out and watched the final lament. But there is no reference to her.

Aeschylus was not writing the kind of play where it matters that Atossa should be in relationship with Xerxes onstage. Atossa has had her say, and now it is Xerxes' turn to perform with the chorus. Two-actor tragedy is only an amplification of one-actor tragedy. The actors are not there to present characters who will interact with each other so much as to expand and explain the situations that the chorus dance.

These considerations notwithstanding, Aeschylus does seem to show awareness of the awkwardness in The Suppliants. This was probably one of the last works he wrote for the old regulations of two actors, possibly even after Sophocles had produced a play using three. At the moment of impending crisis, when the Egyptians are about to seize the Danaid girls, their father, Danaus, leaves the stage (775). His exit has been carefully prepared. He must find a guard of soldiers (726). But this guard will not appear, and it will be the king of Argos who rescues the Danaids from capture. Similarly, Danaus' reentrance is also accounted for (980). But we feel the need for his presence onstage during the crisis, and perhaps Aeschylus' careful plotting of his entrances and exits reveals that he too was beginning to sense the need for important characters to stay near the center of action onstage.

But it is wrong to treat a work of Aeschylus' maturity, such as *The Suppliants*, as though it were formally inadequate. By referring to awkwardnesses I am more outlining the different standpoint in our own outlook than denigrating that of Aeschylus. We can see this best by means of an example of how Aeschylus makes use of the technique of one-actor tragedy in his later plays. In *The Persians'* first episode (155ff.), Queen Atossa appears to tell the chorus of the dream she had last night. The dream foreshadows in miniature the entire course of the play: the defeat of Persia and the humiliation of Xerxes. It is a perfect piece of dramatic structure, and of course it is the technique of one-actor tragedy. No modern critic has ever found any difficulty with it.

The same technique, however, is employed in the *Agamemnon* on the occasion of Agamemnon's first entrance onstage, in his chariot, back from the Trojan campaign (810ff.). On his arrival Agamemnon addresses a long speech to the chorus. Then Clytemnestra comes out of the *skēnē* building and she too addresses a long speech to the chorus. Much paper has been spent on discussing the question as to why Clytemnestra does not address Agamemnon directly.[21] All sorts of judgments about the marriage between the two are made on the basis of this arrangement of the scene. The existence of these two speeches, however, has nothing to do with the characterization of either Agamemnon or Clytemnestra. At this point in the play Aeschylus needs to convey as much as possible both about Agamemnon and about Clytemnestra's reaction to the long wait. Much the quickest way of doing this is to give Agamemnon a long speech, and then give Clytemnestra a long speech. It is the technique of one-actor tragedy; the actor addresses the audience through the chorus. It is a technique useful for certain purposes. For its employment it is necessary that the actors' function must not solely be to interact in character with each other. Sophocles did without it almost entirely. Euripides reintroduced it, but mainly at special places in the play, such as at the beginning and end. Even New Comedy tolerates prologues delivered direct to the audience, and occasional asides. But Aeschylus and Aristophanes use the technique at will, taking advantage of the fact that their plays' construction does not depend on the interaction of character.

Sophocles, we may say, succeeded in creating the maximum possible interaction between his characters during the episodes, without breaking out of the dance drama form. A good example of this use can be found in *The Women of Trachis* (180–204, 225–496). At the beginning of this sequence, an old messenger arrives to tell Deianeira, who is worrying about what may have happened to her husband Heracles, that there is no need to worry; Heracles is on his way home, victorious. The chorus sing a paean, and Lichas enters. Lichas has actually been with Heracles but has been delayed by questioning crowds, so that the old man has arrived first with the news. Lichas is accompanied by captured girls and explains that they are the spoils of war. Heracles has been

enslaved through the influence of King Eurytus, and Heracles has sacked Eurytus' city in revenge. As Lichas tells his story, we are aware of a certain obfusca-
tion of Eurytus' part in the affair; we are puzzled and want to know more.
Deianeira is fascinated with the beauty of one of the girls, but Lichas says that
he does not know her name and then goes inside with the girls (334).

The preceding conversation makes the old messenger determined to tell the
story that he knows Lichas to have concealed from Deianeira. The beautiful
girl is Iole, daughter of King Eurytus. Heracles had fallen in love with her,
asked for her from Eurytus, but was refused. So he sacked the city and killed
Eurytus, all for the love of Iole. No wonder Lichas did not tell the complete
story. As Deianeira prepares to go inside and question him, Lichas comes out
again, about to return to Heracles, and prepared to carry Deianeira's message
to her husband (392). The old messenger now tries to make Lichas tell the
truth, while Lichas sticks to what he said before. When Deianeira charges him
by Zeus (436ff.) to tell her everything, making it clear that she knows who the
girl is anyway, Lichas admits the truth. The use of the three actors is very
exciting. It has created suspense: who, we wonder, is that silent girl who goes
into the house before we know her identity. It has illuminated the character of
Deianeira: she is brave when it comes to facing facts, magnanimous toward
Iole, and will not take advantage of a girl who is now a slave, while at the same
time she is clearly the weak and lovable woman whom a sensitive man like
Lichas would wish to spare pain. The episode leads to its naturalistic climax in
Deianeira's speech already mentioned (436ff). She implores Lichas to tell the
truth, saying she is a woman with experience of male fickleness. I know, she
continues, the impossibility of fighting love:

> Love lords it over the gods at whim,
> As well as me.
>
> (443–44)

This is one of the centers of the play, and Sophocles has presented it entirely
through the subtle use of characters interacting by means of dialogue.

A rough way of describing the best theater of plot is to say that it is the
presentation of growth of a relationship: the growing, changing, developing
relationship of the three sisters in Chekhov's play, the family relationships of
the Blisses in contrast with the development of outside relationships in *Hay
Fever*. The central relationship of the *Women of Trachis* is that between Heracles
and Deianeira; since these two characters are never seen together, the play as a
whole is obviously not theater of plot. Furthermore, fifth-century tragedy is
the representation of an action from history. The ramifications of the dance
drama make sense only in terms of an event that has happened. For if one made
that sort of a play about a fictional story, there would be no limits within which
the form could develop. If the center of a play is a developing relationship, then
there is no reason why the story should not be fictional. Fact or fiction makes

no difference. All that is important is the richness and reality of the relationship.

Three of Euripides' plays serve as examples of what is meant by saying that he invented plot: the *Iphigeneia in Tauris, Helen,* and *Ion.* None of these plays is based on an invented plot, but the first two are based on alternative versions of an accepted story, so prettified as to have the feeling of fairy tale. The appearance of Iphigeneia onstage, announcing that she was not sacrificed by her father Agamemnon, or of Helen announcing that she never went to Troy, must have immediately given the audience the feeling that they were watching fantasy, not fact, even though both alternative versions were current as stories.[22] Probably it was soon after these plays that Agathon wrote his *Antheus,* the first play with an invented plot.

These three plays of Euripides are concerned with the development of a central relationship: the *Iphigeneia in Tauris* with that between brother and sister, Orestes and Iphigeneia; the *Helen* with the marriage of Menelaus and Helen; the *Ion* with the complicated triangle of Ion's wonderings about his parents, and his mother's discovery that Ion is her child, while her husband is led to adopt Ion in the belief that he is his own child. The plays depend on our identification with the central characters of these relationships; the fantastical elements cause us no trouble. What is important is the element of suspense: will Orestes and Iphigeneia, having discovered each other at last, manage to escape? Will Menelaus and Helen, having discovered each other at last, manage to escape? Who will turn out to be the real parents of Ion? The success of these plays stems from the surprises in the plots combined with the vividness and consistency of the character drawing.

The *Iphigeneia in Tauris* is based on the alternative story of the death of Iphigeneia, in which, at the last moment, she was spirited away by Artemis, and a deer substituted. The play starts with Iphigeneia, now priestess of Artemis in Tauris, a place whose custom it is to sacrifice to the goddess any foreigners who arrive. Orestes has been told by Apollo to go to Tauris, find the ancient statue of Artemis, which fell down from heaven, and bring it back to Athens. By this action he will be cleansed of guilt for his mother's killing. Orestes and Pylades are arrested on landing at Tauris and brought to Iphigeneia. In the course of a long and complicated dialogue Orestes and Iphigeneia discover their relationship to one another. Their plan is to escape— all three of them. Iphigeneia will announce that before the foreigners can be sacrificed they must be purified in the sea from their matricide. The goddess, who has come into contact with them, must also be purified. Iphigeneia convinces the barbarian king, Thoas, who respects her greatly, and he allows her to do this. Once they have gone, a messenger arrives to tell the king that the Greeks have escaped with the statue, but the sea is too heavy for them and they cannot clear the harbor. King Thoas is about to give chase when Athene appears to tell him that the statue belongs in Athens, and that the whole escape has been ordered by Apollo. Orestes must found a festival in honor of Artemis that alludes to the human sacrifice by shedding a drop of human blood.

The *Helen* opens with Helen speaking the prologue and telling how she did not go to Troy but stayed in Egypt, faithful to her husband, Menelaus, while Paris went to Troy with a wraith of Helen. Helen has been well looked after and treated with great respect in Egypt as long as King Proteus was alive. But now he has just died. The new king, Theoclymenus, is determined to force Helen into marriage. She has taken refuge at Proteus' tomb and waits in longing for Menelaus to come and rescue her. Teucer is the first to arrive. He tells her of the destruction of Troy and the capture of "Helen" without recognizing the real Helen in front of him. He has come to consult the blind prophetess Theonoē, sister of Theoclymenus, about his return home. Helen has also entered to ask Theonoē about her husband, when Menelaus enters, shipwrecked and in rags. There is a scene for laughs as he begs at the palace and is given short shrift by the portress. But, after a scene where he is told by his servant that the phantom Helen has disappeared, he is at last reunited with his real wife. Theonoē appears and, though blind, recognizes him. She decides that she will let them escape. Helen tells Theoclymenus that Menelaus is a sailor shipwrecked in the ship commanded by Menelaus, which has been destroyed with all other hands. So now, she tells Theoclymenus, she is free to marry him, once she has conducted a funeral ceremony for Menelaus at sea. Theoclymenus does not suspect, and, as in the *Iphigeneia at Tauris*, they succeed in sailing off. A messenger arrives to tell the king that the stranger was Menelaus himself, that he embarked all his own shipwrecked sailors, and that they have killed the Egyptian crew and escaped. In rage Theoclymenus is about to kill his own sister Theonoē for having allowed this, when the *Dioscuri* appear above to tell him that he was wrong to try and keep Helen from her proper husband, and that Helen will eventually become a god.

Hermes speaks the prologue of the *Ion*, telling of how Apollo slept with Creusa, the daughter of the king of Athens, who became pregnant and then exposed her child. Hermes, at Apollo's request, rescued him, took him to Delphi and gave him to the prophetess to raise as a kind of temple servant, a kind of sacristan. Creusa has married Xuthus, a distinguished alien, resident in Athens, and they have come to Delphi to consult the oracle about their childlessness. Ion and Creusa meet, and Creusa declaims against the cruelty of Apollo, telling her own story as if it had happened to another girl. Xuthus meanwhile has been told that the first person he sees on coming out will be his son. He then meets Ion. It turns out that Xuthus once slept with a Delphian girl at a festival, so he assumes that Ion is her son, who has been brought up by Apollo, and determines to take Ion back with him to Athens. An old servant tells this to Creusa and encourages her to feel so slighted that they plot together to poison Ion at the feast Xuthus is giving to celebrate finding his son. The plot is discovered, and Ion is about to stab his mother in revenge when the prophetess comes out of the temple to stop him, and she shows him the cradle in which he was brought to Delphi. This is recognized by Creusa, and the whole story comes out. But Ion is inclined to think that she made up the story about sleeping with Apollo. He is about to consult the oracle when Athene appears to confirm the story and to say how Ion will found the race of the Ionians, of which the Athenians regarded themselves as a part.

What shocks us about these plays and makes us realize that they are not musical comedy is elements of brutality. They are stronger meat than the later plays with which we are inclined to compare them. Menelaus butchers an entire ship's crew of Egyptians. Creusa is about to murder Ion, and Ion to murder Creusa, though admittedly these killings do not actually occur. Such small examples should serve to warn us against treating even these plays as if they were written for a proscenium stage and required audience identification with the hero and heroine. Even as compared with New Comedy there is a greater sense of detachment, remnants of the old detached philosophy of *Dikē:* if you mistreat a woman like Helen, then certain consequences will follow, such as her husband committing havoc with your subjects.

The function of the chorus is different in these plays from the function in Sophoclean tragedy. The form of the play is not developed by the chorus, but the chorus is not in the way, as it sometimes seems to be in plays like the *Medea* or *Hippolytus.* The *Iphigeneia in Tauris* is created round Iphigeneia's longing for her brother and her home in Greece. The chorus provide an excellent balance to this. At first we see them merely as temple servants, devotees of the goddess. Gradually it turns out that they, like Iphigeneia, are captured Greeks, also longing for home (447–55). Later there is a most moving scene when Iphigeneia has to ask them to stay behind and back up her story to the king (1056–78). This they agree to do, though it makes them long even more for escape (1089–1151). Instead of escape they meet with the threats of the king. But finally Athene gives orders that they too must be sent back to Greece. Their relief is our relief. With this play a new role has been found for the chorus, that of sympathetic, involved spectators.

The chorus of the *Helen* are captured Greek girls, and a similar role would be applicable to them. But many of the chorus songs are merely decorative, and they are not involved in the action of the play. Their future is left in the air at the end, and we are not concerned about their fate.

The chorus of the *Ion* are Creusa's servants, and their function is to amplify her desires and intentions, whether in the decorative exclamations at the beauty of the temple (184–237), or more specifically as they support her prayer for children (452–509), pray for the defeat of Ion (676–724), and even encourage the attempted murder (1048–1105). They share in Creusa's panic when her plot is discovered, but after the confrontation between her and Ion, are silent. During the last four hundred lines of the play (1261–1622) they are spectators, except for two lines of dialogue from the chorus leader, and the final four lines of the play, chanted in trochaic tetrameters, the dance rhythm already started ten lines before by Ion, Creusa, and Athene. It would have been so easy to create a dance, if only a short one, in which the chorus could share in Creusa's rejoicing as they had shared in her plotting and her terror. This demonstrates very clearly the formal unimportance of the chorus at this time. Their role of sympathetic spectators is worked out only in the first of the three plays, because working out the role of the chorus was now only a relatively unimportant incidental.

What is left of the sense that tragedy is a rite? An elusive feeling of a numinous which can no longer be expressed except very obliquely. We cannot but be reminded of the last plays of Shakespeare: *Cymbeline, The Winter's Tale, The Tempest.* There is the same sense of a great poet, full of passionate religious, moral, and political concern, turning away from a direct expression of this concern to fantasy. In these three plays Euripides presents consecrated characters: Iphigeneia the priestess, Helen the wife waiting under the protection of the gods, Ion the servant of Apollo. We are reminded of the aura round Hermione or Prospero.

There is also a strong sense of the exploration of theatrical reality and the different levels of truth. This is something with which Aristophanes was to concern himself a few years later in the *Women at the Thesmophoria* and *Frogs,* and an exploration that Euripides was to take further in the *Orestes.* Here again we think of *The Tempest.* But we must remember that Euripides' age did not yet possess the categories fact/fiction, for Plato was to base his attack on the poets on a confusion between fact/fiction and truth/falsehood.[23] This is an exciting world for a poet of the theater to explore. But it is a realm particularly of the theater, and we cannot account in the language of analysis for the hallucinogenic quality of the parody scenes in the latter part of *The Women at the Thesmophoria;* we can only acknowledge that this hallucinogenic quality is one of the most important things about them. The beginnings of this exploration occur in the *Iphigeneia at Tauris,* with the prologue in which Iphigeneia states that she is, as it were, a legend. This also is a mystery, part of the way in which the theater secularized can still be a rite.

It is worth noticing that Sophocles was not unaffected by Euripides' developments toward plot. The *Philoctetes* should not be described as a play of plot, but it is a stage toward it. Instead of focusing our attention solely on the dance of *Dikē,* Sophocles is also concerned to depict the changing reactions of one man, Neoptolemus, or, alternatively, to show the growth and development of the relationship between Neoptolemus and Philoctetes. It is possible to analyze the play as a dance of *Dikē,* as Kitto does in *Form and Meaning in Drama.*[24] But if all Sophocles' work was like the *Philoctetes,* we might have to analyze his structures by different concepts much nearer to those of post-Renaissance drama.

The prologue establishes the relationship of Odysseus and Neoptolemus: the hardened and cynical politician and the eager boy. "Do wrong, just for one day," says Odysseus (83–84), and manages to persuade Neoptolemus to try and trick Philoctetes of his bow, which is known to be necessary for the Greeks if they are to defeat Troy. The chorus of Neoptolemus' sailors enter, in a *parodos* that establishes their relationship to Neoptolemus and their sympathy for Philoctetes' loneliness and suffering. The first episode is Neoptolemus' pretence not to know about Philoctetes, and his resultant hearing of Philoctetes' story. Mutual sympathy is created by the account of Philoctetes' wound and his desertion by the Greeks, and by Neoptolemus' faked story of how he has been cheated of his dead father's god-built weapons. Philoctetes' trust in Neoptolemus is developed to the point when he is prepared to leave the island, thinking that Neoptolemus will take him home to Greece. At this point Odysseus's servant arrives, pretending to be a merchant, with the news that Odysseus is coming himself in command of a force. This makes Philoctetes even more anxious to leave with Neoptolemus, but now Neoptolemus says that the winds are not quite right and that they must wait a little (639). It seems that Neoptolemus is starting to hesitate, now that he has almost achieved his objective. They go into Philoctetes' cave, however, to collect his few possessions, while the chorus sing a *stasimon* on Philoctetes' sufferings (676–729). As Philoctetes comes out with Neoptolemus, he is racked by pain, and helplessly asks Neoptolemus to carry his bow (762), however charging him by the gods not to give it up to Odysseus (770). The chorus then sing Philoctetes to sleep, and urge Neoptolemus to action. In the middle of this song there is a mesode, (839–42) where Neoptolemus suddenly chants in the sacred dactyls that it is no good merely taking the bow; they must take Philoctetes as well. When Philoctetes wakes up, Neoptolemus, out of pity, tells him the whole plan. He still asks Philoctetes to come to Troy to help the Greeks, but he is not surprised when Philoctetes refuses. Neoptolemus is now in a dilemma. When Odysseus arrives Neoptolemus goes with him, still holding the bow. But after Philoctetes has sung a lament, Neoptolemus returns. He cannot bear to abide by the results of what he regards as treachery. Odysseus returns, now to be threatened by the bow in the masterful hands of Philoctetes, and retreats. Neoptolemus then tells Philoctetes that his sickness is god-sent, and that it derives from his assault of the god-protected girl Chryse. The sickness will be cured only if he comes willingly to Troy. Even then Philoctetes refuses to come. Neoptolemus is now bound by his promise to take Philoctetes home, and they are on the point of leaving when they are stopped by the appearance of Heracles, now a god, and a particular patron of Philoctetes, who changes the latter's mind.

This is not a sufficient analysis of the play, but it serves to convey how much of it is the development of the character of Neoptolemus. A playwright no longer bound to take seriously the rite that was the center of fifth-century drama could read the *Philoctetes* and learn many things about making a naturalistic play of plot, whose raison d'être is to present a life onstage through characters who grow and develop and about whose lives offstage we speculate. It is possible to conceive of a fourth-century *Philoctetes* for which the above analysis might be sufficient.

With this play too there is a sense of the same mysteries as in the late Shakespeare, although here it is more a sense of the strangeness of time, as in *The Winter's Tale*. Here also there is a slight hallucinogenic quality about such a scene as that of the false merchant who arrives with a false message about the arrival of Odysseus and who is followed shortly by the actual arrival of Odysseus. By faith unfaithful he is kept falsely true.[25] There is also a sense of the numinous power of suffering. Philoctetes by his suffering is turned into a *theos*, just as his magic bow is a *theos*. It is the same preoccupation with the consecrated person as in Euripides, but, as we might expect, expressed more forcefully by Sophocles with his more deeply developed mystical sense. In this aspect it is very much a preparation for the *Oedipus at Colonus*.

The above discussion has been designed to show that Euripides succeeded in changing the center of a play's form from the representation of an action to the development of a plot. This development was necessary if drama was to survive when it was no longer history and no longer worship. None of the plays I have discussed in this section have totally lost their connection with the roots of fifth-century drama. Their strength and their mystery derive from those roots. Both Sophocles and Euripides grew up nourished poetically by the rite of Dionysus. But while plays such as the *Oedipus the King* or *The Trojan Women* directly present the rite, a play such as the *Ion* presents it only through a poetic treatment. The next generation of writers would lack the direct connection with the rite and would mistake the poetic treatment for the reality of Dionysiac worship.

Notes

1. This statement is most easily expanded with reference to some of the stupider criticism of Sophocles. Waldock, for example, in effect dismisses the *Ajax*, *Antigone*, and *The Women of Trachis*, as "diptych" plays—plays in two halves—because he does not consider the chorus to be important, and so notices only that the principal character dies halfway through each play. If a modern scholar's criticism, dressed in whatever fancy terms he chooses, imputes what any ordinary playgoer would call manifest incompetence to Sophocles, I prefer to assume that the modern scholar is not only wrong, but also using the wrong set of criteria. See A. J. A. Waldock, *Sophocles the Dramatist* (Cambridge: Cambridge University Press, 1951).

2. Perhaps I may be allowed to invent two silly little scenarios:

I. Man eats boiled egg.
   Man gets up from breakfast.
   Man goes out of house door with briefcase.
   Man catches bus.
   Bus explodes.

II. Man eats boiled egg.
   Another man eats boiled egg.
   Fat woman eats two boiled eggs.
   Grotesquely fat woman eats half a dozen goose eggs.
   Camera Pans down railway buffet, where everyone is eating boiled eggs.
   Man swallows glassful of a dozen raw eggs.
   Quick Montage of Big Close-Ups of spoons tapping egg tops, lips parting to admit spoonfuls

of egg and so forth.
Montage builds in speed.
One ostrich egg alone in an empty desert.

They will, I hope, suffice to serve as examples of what I mean by, in the first case, story rhythm or plot rhythm, and, in the second case, montage construction or documentary rhythm.

3. I am obliged again to refer to my fuller discussion of the form of most Greek tragedies, considered one by one in my earlier book: Leo Aylen, *Greek Tragedy and the Modern World* (London, Methuen, 1964). In such a discussion I must again acknowlege my indebtedness to Kitto. See H. D. F. Kitto, *Greek Tragedy* (London: Methuen, 1961); H. D. F. Kitto, *Form and Meaning in Drama* (London: Methuen, 1956).

4. Aylen, *Greek Tragedy and the Modern World,* p. 148. For further discussion see pp. 148–50.

5. It might be better to translate *tyrannos* on all occasions as "dictator" and therefore to entitle the play *Dictator Oedipus.* By referring to *Oedipus the King,* the normal translation, we call up inevitably the mediaeval associations of the word *king,* which are not at all the associations of the word *tyrannos.*

6. Kitto, *Form and Meaning in Drama,* pp. 87–137.

7. See Appendix 3 for meanings of terms used.

8. Sir John Sheppard, *Aeschylus and Sophocles. Their Work and Influence* (London: G. G. Harrap, 1927), p. 34.

9. Aylen, *Greek Tragedy and the Modern World,* pp. 36–39, 54–55, 58–60.

10. Ibid., p. 132 and Appendix, p. 355.

11. This passage is translated at the end of Chapter 13.

12. We might think that the figure of Death in the *Alcestis* was such an abstraction. Almost certainly, for the original audience, Death was very much an entity with some sort of personality.

13. None of our extant plays between *The Persians* and the *Heracles* contain trochaic tetrameters.

14. Though see below, "Theater of Plot," for a small example of lack of control in Aeschylus.

15. For translation of Aristophanes' character names, see Appendix 2.

16. Discussion on the form of *The Clouds,* however, must be tentative. What we possess appears to be a partial rewrite for a second production, after failure of the play to win first prize.

17. See Chapter 7.

18. See the following section.

19. Cf. Jacques Tati's film, *Traffic,* or, on a lower level, the scenario in note 2.

20. The *Persians* and *Suppliants.* The end of *The Seven against Thebes* requires three actors. Many scholars think this passage is spurious. The play was produced in 467 B.C. Sophocles' first competition was in 468. It is unlikely that he would have managed to change the regulation for the number of actors in the first year of competing, and therefore it seems sensible to conclude that Aeschylus' *Oedipus* tetralogy, of which *The Seven against Thebes* is the third play, was produced with only two actors, and that the last hundred lines were added later, probably by another writer.

21. It is surely a basic rule of theatrical production that any magnificent entrance, especially one involving riding in a chariot, must be allowed to cover the maximum stage distance available. Otherwise the entrance will look cramped, and the magnificence will be destroyed. Agamemnon will have entered up one of the *parodoi,* and will have crossed the *orchestra* in his chariot to the other side. He will therefore be at the side of the *orchestra* when Clytemnestra makes her entrance from the *skēnē,* and so he will probably be forty feet away from her, which is a great distance in stage terms. Given this mise en scène, there is no need for her to talk to him immediately.

22. See Herodotus *Histories* 2.113–16, for the story of Helen in Egypt.

23. See Chapter 10.

24. Kitto, *Form and Meaning in Drama,* pp. 87–137.

25. Alfred Lord Tennyson, *Lancelot and Elaine,* 870–71:

> His honour rooted in dishonour stood,
> And faith unfaithful kept him falsely true.

7

FOUR GREAT POETS

The Poets and Their Time

I am grateful to Norman Lloyd Williams, writer and educational broadcaster, for a piece of advice that seems to me to sum up one task of the critic. We were discussing a schools art program that I was to direct for his department. "All you can really do," he told me, "is dance in front of the pictures." If the work of Aeschylus, Sophocles, Euripides, and Aristophanes is not such as to make us dance, then a history like this has not been worth the pains of writing. Conversely, the history of the ancient theater, even during its long period of boring mediocrity, well repays study if this can illuminate our understanding of the four great poets within whose visions its achievement rests.

Dancing in front of pictures is such an excellent image because it so frankly acknowledges that this aspect of criticism is bound up with the critic's own likes and choices. It also contains the suggestion that the excitement may change from one day to the next. At this moment, in this mood, I choose to point with delight at that movement, that color. Tomorrow it may be different. In a book such as this, some acknowledgment of the inexhaustible creativity of these master poets must be made. It cannot but be haphazard. Furthermore, there is a large critical literature in most Western languages about the work of each of the four. Many books have been devoted solely to the work of one poet. A work such as this could only summarize in tedious generalities, or select arbitrarily.

If one reads a selection of the penetrating studies that have been written on the work of the four poets, one is struck by the fact that, just as the great work of the turn of the last century was in the field of scholarship, with the greatest achievements belonging mainly to the Germans, outstandingly to Wilamowitz, so for most of this century the great work has been in the field of literary criticism, with the achievements spread much more widely over the Western world. Many of the best books have been published by people who were, even when not poets in their own right, yet able to translate the plays about which they wrote into good verse in their own language. However we may judge Gilbert Murray's poetry or his translations now, his critical insights have value because they were conceived by a man who wrote from a poet's viewpoint, in the same way that the excellence of Richmond Lattimore's criticism is bound up with the fact that he is also writing independently as a poet.[1] Though I do not know if Kitto has written poetry other than his translations of Sophocles, his critical writing insists that at all points the Greek tragedies are the work of poets. Though I do not know if Gabriel Germain or Quintino Cataudella have written poetry, to select arbitrarily two good critics working in languages other than English, yet the merit of their criticism is again due to their ability to put themselves into the mind of a poet at work.[2] Criticism of a poet is not the same as that of a prose writer. Since poetry depends upon an imaginative leap, the critic must be prepared to leave the safety of scholarship for what the scholar might call inspired guesses. From the point of view of poetry, however, scholarship's noncommittal attitude can itself also cause mistakes.[3] It has been on the whole the achievement of the last half-century of criticism to realize this.

I do not wish to deny this approach any way, but its tendency has been sometimes to emphasize the literary qualities of fifth-century drama at the expense of the theatrical. Accordingly, I have chosen to perform my dance in front of the fourth fifth-century masters by selecting, somewhat arbitrarily, a number of climactic moments in their plays, which seem to demonstrate either a particular achievement of the poet in question as total "maker" or a particular aspect of the fifth-century theater that is worth stressing, or both. More space is devoted to Aristophanes because the presentation of Aristophanes reveals more of how the Athenians regarded their theatrical experience, the moments of magic that it is the task and craft of the poet to provide. Conversely, less space has been given to Euripides, since, while Aeschylus, Sophocles, and Aristophanes were representative in their age, Euripides' achievement is much more personal, idiosyncratic, and unsupported by the work of his contemporaries.

It is no very exaggerated statement to say that not only does the achievement of Aeschylus, Sophocles, Euripides, and Aristophanes dwarf twelve hundred years of the ancient theater into utter insignificance by comparison, not only is their work, with the one exception of Homer, the outstanding achievement of three thousand years of Greek poetry, but also that the corpus of their forty-three extant plays represents an achievement unsurpassed in the history of all theater except by the work of Shakespeare. Before allowing his puny faculties to play on a few aspects of such giant achievement, the critic must pose the fascinating question, which, needless to say, he cannot answer: was this achievement exceptional in the fifth-century itself?

Aeschylus seems to have won the first prize 13 times and to have written between 70 and 90 plays. That is to say, out of that total number of plays, 52 won him the first prize. Sophocles was once refused a chorus,[4] but apart from that never came lower than second and won first prize 20 or 24 times; out of a total number of between 104 and 130 plays, about 90 won him first prize. We do not know Aristophanes' total number of prizes, but his proportion of first prizes in the case of plays where we do know the result is very high. Euripides was relatively less successful, since only one-fifth of his plays won first prize; he was first 5 times, with a total of 90–100 plays. But Euripides' plays were far the most popular throughout the rest of antiquity, and if posthumous fame is accepted as the criterion of greatness, Euripides is by far the greatest playwright ever to have lived.

It is salutary to remember, however, that the *Oedipus the King* was second to a play by the unknown Philocles,[5] and *The Birds* came second to *The Revellers* by Ameipsias, an equally unknown writer.[6] I myself would call *The Birds* the second greatest of Aristophanes' comedies, and many would think it his best. And while I do not regard the *Oedipus the King* as the greatest Greek tragedy, or even the greatest of Sophocles' tragedies, yet many people from Aristotle onward have so considered it. The question must be posed: Were there a considerable number of poets, both tragic and comic, whom, if their work had survived, we should regard as almost as good as the four whose work we possess?[7] It is an even greater testimonial to the power of the fifth-century festival that its service may well have developed unknown talents almost as great as Sophocles, and a further measure of its importance that, when the service of Dionysus became a less central function of the art of poetry, there were no more great poets.

We cannot, unfortunately, form any very clear judgment about the work of the two poets whose lives are not completely unknown to us: Phrynichus, an elder contemporary of Aeschylus, and the long-lived comic poet Cratinus. Both, however, we may suspect of considerable achievements. The climax of Aristophanes' most beautiful lyric pays tribute to the beauty of Phrynichus' lyric poetry, for the mysterious spirit-center of the woods, the home of the forest Muse, is the place

> Where Phrynichus once like a bee
> Knelt sucking nectar out of your melodies.[8]

And although Aristophanes has some rude words for Cratinus while the latter was alive and his rival, fifteen years after the old poet's death he would invoke Cratinus' name as the special poet of the Dionysiac rite (*The Frogs* 357), and furthermore would give Cratinus an epithet usually applied to Dionysus himself: "bull-champing." Could there be a higher compliment?

In this context it is worth alluding to one fragment of a play by an unknown author, now accepted as from the fifth century.[9] A recently discovered papyrus fragment contains a speech from a play that Herodotus must have used for his account of Candaules, the king of Lydia, and his successor, Gyges.[10] We are justified in taking the account of Herodotus as the synopsis of the play. Candaules, king of Lydia, was besotted by the beauty of his wife; so besotted did he become that he tried to persuade Gyges, a trusted member of his bodyguard, to see her naked. Gyges was horrified at the proposal but allowed

himself to be persuaded. Candaules arranged for Gyges to be placed behind the
open door of the bedchamber so that he could see the queen undressing, and so
that he could slip out of the door once she had finished undressing and was
getting into bed. The queen, however, noticed him as he was escaping. She said
nothing at the time, but in the morning summoned Gyges and told him that he
must either be killed or else kill Candaules and make himself king and therefore
her husband. Though Gyges implored her to reconsider, the queen was ada-
mant. He therefore decided to kill Candaules and was installed in the same
place behind the bedchamber door, but this time by the queen. When Candaules was asleep Gyges stabbed him to death. Enraged by the murder of their
king, the Lydians took up arms, but a truce was declared while they consulted
the Delphic oracle. The answer was that Gyges should be king, but that in the
fifth generation from him, vengeance would strike his heirs. This vengeance
was manifested in the conquest of Lydia during Croesus' reign.

    None of the play is likely to have taken place in the bedchamber. The speech
that we have is made by the queen, presumably to a chorus of her attendants,
on the morning after she has seen Gyges spying on her. The fragment ends with
her intention to summon Gyges. Clearly, the play belongs to the period of two
actors, and it offers confrontation scenes between Candaules and Gyges, the
queen and Gyges, and the queen and Candaules. We can assume that the death
of Candaules would have been conveyed in a messenger speech.

    It seems likely that this was the first play in a trilogy, which could have ended
with the fall of Lydia to the Persians during the reign of Croesus. Clearly, the
descent of such a curse through the generations bears a strong relation to
similar plays of Aeschylus. Clearly, the action of Candaules is an action of
arrogance that offends humanity and therefore breaks *Dikē*. It is a powerful
story, full of moral and political meanings, taken from an area of history with
which we do not usually associate Greek tragedy, though it is clear that both
Phrynichus and Aeschylus were fascinated by the splendor, power, and luxury
of the Orient, as we see in *The Persians*, and judge from the many titles of
Aeschylus' plays that imply oriental choruses.[11] The speech of the queen that
we possess has powerful language and reveals sensitive insight into the way in
which she reacts to this slight to her femininity. A great female role had been
created before Aeschylus created Clytemnestra in the *Agamemnon*. It is perhaps the best surviving image of the general vitality and variety of the fifth-
century Greek theater. I cannot help feeling that the work of some of the less
successful poets of fifth-century Athens would be greater than the highest
achievements of many poetic cultures, which, relatively, we may honor.[2]

    There is therefore a small amount of evidence to suggest that the fifth century
was a period even richer in poets than the small fraction of its output that
survives would suggest. Within the work of the four poets themselves there is
an abundance of poetic skills, which it would take at least four books to point
out. The following examples, however, may help to demonstrate not only how
much the poetry of all four was a total "making," in which characterization,

stage effect, verbal imagery, song, and dance are all integrated parts of the whole, but also that this total poetry derived from and was rooted in the rite of Dionysus, in which the poets were ministers of the god for the city, for the audience of people engaged in political action.

Aeschylus

The greatness of Aeschylus' poetry lies in the vividness of its images. He is the poet of vision, where Sophocles is the poet of understanding. He is a man whose thought easily encompasses an epic scale, whereas both Sophocles and Euripides prefer to look deeply into the decisions and sufferings of one man. He is perhaps above all the poets' playwright. For though Sophocles and Shakespeare are as great poets as he, they can use their understanding of human character like any prose dramatist. With Aeschylus the images are all; his characterization, great though his powers of observation and his sense of personality can be, lies within the image. I have alluded already to his use of embodiment, the creating of an image through dialogue and song in the minds of his audience, creating a need for this image to be seen onstage, and then finally satisfying it. In this mixing of verbal and physical image, he is like Aristophanes, who will make a pun and then bring the pun onstage in physical form, for whom peace is as physical as the wine poured at its celebration, and for whom therefore the pun of drinking Pledges has an almost sacramental quality.[13] Like Aristophanes too, he is a lover of the brash stage effect. Vividness is all. A discussion such as this, drawing attention to climaxes where thought and poetry have reached their peak in harmony, is most easily done with Aeschylus and Aristophanes, and least easily done with Euripides, where thought and theatricality are very often at considerable variance, and where it often makes less sense to talk of the poetry moving to its climax, because the poetry is a less total thing. It is possible to conceive even of performing a translation of Euripides with the dialogue scenes in prose; it is inconceivable to think of doing so with Sophocles or Aeschylus.

The Suppliants, *Climax*

Many otherwise excellent books on Aeschylus have paid less attention to *The Suppliants* than they might otherwise have done, since their authors regarded it as a very early play. Now that we know it was produced about five years before the *Oresteia*, we are compelled to take it much more seriously and in consequence can find all sorts of insights into the mature mind of Aeschylus that we would otherwise not possess. The action of this first play in the tetralogy is the flight by the fifty daughters of Danaus from marriage with their cousins. Throughout the play the Danaids present themselves as innocent victims of a terrible wrong, and Aeschylus builds this emotion of horror to a climax in the great dance when the fifty Egyptian soldiers, the suitors' attendants, attempt to drag away the Danaids (825ff.). The third system (885–902) builds tension to the maximum. "He's dragging me to the sea, like a spider, step by step; a dream, a dream, black," scream the chorus, ending on a cry to Zeus. The matching movement of the *antistrophē* presents "the two-footed snake, the viper biting me," and ends on the cry to Zeus, exactly repeated. But as the Danaids are being dragged away by the Egyptian soldiers, the king of Argos arrives, in the nick of time, with his soldiers, and saves them. The Egyptians retreat in confusion, and the rest of the play presents the Danaids preparing to settle in Argos, triumphant in their chastity.[14]

At one level this first play is a straightforward melodrama of innocent chastity rescued from rape. Luckily, however, we know the main event of the second play, *The Egyptians*, though virtually nothing survives. Some compromise had been reached, and the Danaids did have to marry their cousins, but, with the exception of one girl, they all murdered their husbands on the wedding night. With this information, which the original audience would have possessed from their familiarity with the story, the first play feels very different. To the Greeks there was nothing wrong with the marriage of cousins. Nor is any reason given why the Danaids should be fleeing this marriage. The king of Argos receives them as victims of persecution, accepting their version of the story. But to the audience the whole panic is merely an exaggeration of the inexperienced virgin's scream at the first mention of sex.

The emotional climax might be said to be the rape scene. But this is not the theatrical climax, which could be said more correctly to occur in the last few lines of the play. Our fear for the virgins about to be assaulted is certainly a strong emotion. But Aeschylus has more emotional experiences in store for us, and more theatrical tricks to emphasize his meaning. To study the end of this play is to realize the consummate theatrical and poetic genius of Aeschylus at this time of his life. Who else could ever dare to treat the rape of fifty girls by fifty men as merely one incident en route to his climax?

The play that we have is the development of a triple image: the predator beast and its prey, hawk and dove, wolf and lamb; the man pursuing the virgin he desires; and God pursuing man.[15] From the point of view of the dove, the wolf is an unjustified villain. From a wider point of view, it is natural for hawk to kill dove, wolf to kill lamb. Aeschylus starts from this image of the way in which nature's pattern is just, by virtue of its savagery; the hawk would not be a proper hawk if it could not kill doves. He goes on to infer the character of God from nature.[16] It is a concept totally original for its time, though it has become familiar to us through Christianity: God hounds us till we fall, shattered and broken, at His feet; an image at the center of *The Hound of Heaven* or *The Wreck of the "Deutschland,"* though it derives from Judaism and finds its greatest expression in Psalm 139:2, 6–9.

> Thou art about my path and about my bed:
> and spiest out all my ways.

Whither shall I go then from thy Spirit:
or whither shall I go then from thy presence?

If I climb up into heaven, thou art there:
if I go down to hell, thou art there also.

If I take the wings of the morning:
and remain in the uttermost parts of the sea;

Even there also shall thy hand lead me:
and thy right hand shall hold me.[17]

The image Aeschylus uses to join the virgin's fear of sex with man's flight from God is the story of Io. Io rushed in panic from her home because she could not bear the thought of sexual intercourse with Zeus. She fled in pain and fear across the world, driven mad by bitings and noises in her ear. Finally, when she collapsed exhausted at the mouth of the Nile, Zeus came to her, and with a touch only, made her pregnant, in a moment of utter gentleness.

Io is invoked in the *parodos* with which the play opens, and is central to the great invocation of Zeus/God in the middle of the play (524–99). The Danaids are descendants of Io, fleeing like Io from sex. In the first *stasimon* (348–406) the first three systems contain dochmiacs and therefore would have involved very vigorous dancing, full of kicks. In the second line of the third system (393, *strophē;* 403, *antistrophē;*) there is an obviously climactic dochmiac. The *strophē*'s words refer to the "male strength," the *antistrophē*'s to "the counterbalancer Zeus." The movement of assertive vigor definitely links male strength with the power of Zeus/God.

The word, however, that I have translated "strength" is not translatable into one modern English word. It means physical strength, power, sovereignty, and victory all together. The archaic word *sway* is perhaps the nearest, though this does not include the very important sense of physical strength. This ambiguity is at the heart of the play's final climax. The Egyptian soldiers have been beaten off, and the Danaids have danced in triumph. Danaus has made a long speech of advice to them (980–1013) in which he stresses how they must value *Sophrosynē* more than life itself (1013), and *Sophrosynē* in this context means virginity. This is not a natural attitude for a Greek. While a man prizes the fact that his bride is a virgin when he marries her, there is no value in virginity as such, which is a Christian notion entirely. The Danaids' avoidance of sex has by now been shown to be an unnatural fear.

At this point the Danaids' finale of triumph is interrupted by the song and dance of the handmaidens. Aeschylus has given his audience the shock of seeing a chorus of fifty; he has then shattered their theatrical sense by bringing on his second chorus of fifty for the attempted rape scene. All the time there has been a silent group of fifty handmaidens reflecting the fears, hopes, panic, and final relief of the Danaids. But the audience knows that they will say nothing, because they are only extras. But this is a time when Aeschylus dominates the theater, and Athens is becoming enormously rich. This year

Aeschylus must have found a very rich and lavish *choregos,* and he was able to train yet another group of dancers. With a trick of which he was apparently fond, he makes the so-called mutes break silence.[18] The theatrical surprise ensures that the audience will pay maximum attention to the words with which the mutes burst into sudden song, just as the words of Pylades at the crux of *The Libation-Bearers* are the more formidable for being spoken by a personage whom we had imagined was not allowed to speak.

But there is more still. The first system of the finale (1018–33), sung by the Danaids, while the handmaidens wait at the side, still apparently extras, is in the languid and sensual Ionic tempo. What on earth are the girls doing, celebrating their victory with such a luscious dance. We think of their father's recent speech in which he compared their beauty to the ripeness of summer fruit (998), and we know that summer fruit must be picked, or it will rot. Now they are flaunting their attractiveness, and we might guess that the Greek audience would agree with the judgment of Azdak in Brecht's *Caucasian Chalk Circle* that a woman who flaunts her sex deserves to be laid.[19] It is in this tempo that the handmaidens answer with their song that the goddess of love, and Hera, goddess of childbirth, must also be honored. The second system ends with probably the happiest tempo in Greek music, that variant of Ionic, the anacreontic, which is the tempo of drinking songs (1042, *strophē;* 1051, *antistrophē*). The words of the *antistrophē*'s end are simple: "marriage is the lot of women." The words of the corresponding line in the *strophē* contain a pun: "the *tribos* of whispering loves." The word *tribos* means a path, but the root of the word is "rubbing," and in later medical writers it can mean a "joint or socket," part of the human body; it can also mean "physical exercise." An apparently innocent word, it is full of rich and devious sexual connotations.

A system follows in the same Ionic tempo, in which both choruses alternate. The Danaids sing their triumph and refer it to Zeus. But the handmaidens sing that they must not be excessive in their demands. The final system (1062–end) changes tempo. It is in syncopated iambics and would appear to be musically climactic. The first three syllables contain the kernel of the play. The syncopation of the iambic meter forms a cretic, which therefore may well have involved a kick in the dancing. Whatever was danced, it must have been violent and climactic. In the *strophē* (1062) these first three syllables present "Zeus the lord." In the *antistrophē* (1068) the matching movement goes with the shout of "kratos," and with this we are reminded of the earlier equivalence of *kratos* with the power of Zeus, in the third system of the first *stasimon* (393, *strophē;* 403 *antistrophē*). But this time the chorus goes on to sing the prayer that this *kratos* be given to the women. I have commented elsewhere on the interesting mistranslation in Weir Smyth's normally excellent prose rendering of the play.[20] He translates: "And may he [i.e., Zeus] award victory to the women." But *kratos* implies mastery as well. And for women to pray for mastery over men was an obvious wrong to fifth-century Athenians. Furthermore, this mastery for which they pray is choreographed with a gesture that also presents Zeus/

God himself. It is, as it were, a gesture of blasphemy, containing many of the ambivalences of the gesture with which Aristophanes ends *The Birds* (discussed in a later section of this chapter). A few lines after this blasphemy, the dance stops, not with a quiet cadence, but triumphantly. There is no anapest chant for the chorus to exit singing. Therefore the dance must stop, and they must hold their final tableau. And then the tableau will dissolve and they will walk off in silence. Nothing must interfere with Aechylus' tableau of blasphemous, triumphant, provocative virginity.

I referred above to the last system being sung by "the chorus." This is how it is marked, and it is usually, if not universally, taken that the two choruses of Danaids and their handmaidens unite to sing this last system. This would make nonsense of the function of the handmaidens, who have been counseling the naturalness of marriage and sexual intercourse, and the need to submit to the gods. The last system must be sung by the Danaid chorus alone, while the handmaidens retreat somewhat from them. Once again, Aeschylus will use their silence to make a theatrical point. The two choruses have not joined together, as we might expect, because there is much to come before the pattern of *Dikē* can flow smoothly again. Fifty girls demonstrate triumph, while fifty others stand back to show quietly that the triumph is temporary, and almost certainly misguided.

To have suddenly created a double chorus of one hundred, then not to use more than fifty to sing and dance the final phrases, presents a gaudy, instantly visible theatrical image of instability. Aeschylus is the master of image, the master of making the image manifest in brash staging, but also the master of silence. The idea that the man's penetration of a woman should stand in some way for God's penetration of man may not be an idea to appeal to the age of women's lib. But it is an interesting theological speculation and a profoundly reverberant image. Through poetry, dance, and mise en scène, Aeschylus has led us into his speculation, using our basic emotions of fear and relief and sexual desire, to leave us men suddenly confronted with girls standing over us in triumph, flaunting their untouched sex as though it were a weapon instead of a fruit to be enjoyed. Poetry, dance, and theology blend in a moment that is all three at once, which both sums up everything that has happened onstage so far and also looks forward to the three remaining plays, which unfortunately do not survive.

The Oresteia, *Climax*

Of all Greek plays, perhaps indeed of all plays ever written, it seems most impertinent to discuss the *Oresteia* with anything less than a complete book. So much has been written, and so much remains to be written about the complexity of its rhythms and the simplicity of its pictures, the intricate depths of its thought, the glittering brightness and stark blackness of its poetry. From such richness it would be easy to select many climaxes similar to the end of *The*

Suppliants in unity of thought, poetry, and theatricality. I have chosen to consider only the last climax of all, the final two hundred lines of the *Eumenides* (778–end), partly because it is important again to emphasize the way in which Aeschylus the unabashed genius will confidently top what any normal theatrical talent would regard as untoppable, partly because this last climax is the one to bring the play into relationship with the particular audience at that particular year's festival, and partly because the end of the *Eumenides* has been widely misunderstood.[21]

Many critics, full of their own ideas of tragedy, have found that the end of the *Eumenides* conflicts with these ideas, and have dared to say that what the highly critical fifth-century Athenian audience regarded as the finest tragedy ever written was "not quite tragedy." Sir Richard Livingstone could write: "The last three hundred and fifty lines of the Eumenides are not an integral part of the trilogy. They are a loosely connected episode, stitched on its outside."[22] For a playwright to end his largest-scale work with a "loosely connected episode" would be an act of the grossest play-making incompetence. I prefer to attribute the incompetence to the deficient vision of the critic.

Now, it is true that in anyone's hands but Aeschylus' these last two hundred lines would be an anticlimax. So much has already happened. There have been the four actions of the first two plays: the action of Agamemnon, that of Clytemnestra, that of Orestes, and that of the Furies.[23] The action of Agamemnon was performed in collaboration with Zeus; he avenged the wrong done by Paris and rightly destroyed Troy, but in order to do this he sacrificed his daughter Iphigeneia—a filthy wrong that cries for vengeance, not only because of what he did to his own daughter, but also because he and his war destroyed innocent victims. The second action of Clytemnestra is also in a sense in collaboration with the gods, for we have already seen that the gods themselves are at variance. Clytemnestra is the *alastor,* the spirit of vengeance for the wrong done to Iphigeneia and to all the other innocent victims of the war, of whom Cassandra, the virgin priestess of Apollo, now forced to be Agamemnon's whore, is the example brandished at us onstage. But though Clytemnestra's action is in a sense justified, and though she acts in collaboration with Aegisthus, who is the avenger of the wrong Agamemnon's father did to his father, yet Clytemnestra's action is even worse than Agamemnon's. For he had the excuse that the killing of Iphigeneia was necessary for the success of his military expedition. Clytemnestra killed her husband, the king, because she had been making love with Aegisthus and wanted Agamemnon out of the way, just as Aegisthus wanted to enjoy Clytemnestra in peace.

The third action, that of Orestes, is performed in a very different spirit. Orestes has been told by Apollo that he must restore order in his father's kingdom and kill his father's murderers. Orestes performs his task throughout with constant awareness that he is engaged on a sanctified mission, in constant touch with the god who ordered it, and with clear, unhypocritical realization of the horror he is forcing himself to commit. For to kill his father's murderers means to kill his own mother. The right and proper consequences of this action are for him to be hounded and driven mad by the avenging Furies.

This has been the end of *The Libation-Bearers* and the beginning of the *Eumenides.* We have now just seen the fifth action, by Athene in collaboration with an Athenian jury. This action is also justified. Confronted by a just, though guilty, man—Orestes—hounded by terrifying goddesses of darkness, they have put him on trial and then acquitted him by a narrow margin. The sacred representatives of Athens, the court of the *Areopagus,* with Athene herself, patron goddess of Athens, sitting as president, have acquitted Orestes of guilt for his action in the way that Apollo, speaking in his defence, had asked. This action of Athens's high court, of Athens's patron goddess, with all due consideration of justice, is still a violation. It is right and proper that the Furies should hound a matricide to madness. How can a man kill his mother, for whatever reason, and ever feel free?

This is the skeleton of what we have so far witnessed. The mise en scène has been equally awe-inspiring. After the searing long dance of the *Agamemnon parodos,* we have been led with gathering excitement to the arrival of Agamemnon himself. We have seen clearly how he allowed himself to be persuaded by his wife to walk on the purple carpet, behaving like an oriental despot, not a sensible Greek commander. We have been shown by this image, as we were shown in the dance of the *parodos,* that he is by now in some sense the monster whom Clytemnestra will rightly kill. We have seen Cassandra the prophetess, apparently the innocent victim of the Greek rape of Troy, flaunted by Agamemnon as his mistress before the eyes of Clytemnestra and therefore clearly marked out for murder as well. We have seen her, after staying silent under Clytemnestra's taunts until we think that she cannot speak, suddenly burst into song to reveal Apollo's hand in her own moral as well as physical destruction, and lead us by her clairvoyance to see in advance the death of Agamemnon. We have seen the arrival of Aegisthus and been reminded by him of the monstrous behavior of Agamemnon's father, a reminder that demonstrates the depth of the roots of evil in the family. We have seen the deep grief of the innocent Electra, daughter of Agamemnon, waiting without hope. We have seen the arrival of Orestes to give her hope. We have entered the invocation of the dead in the great *kommos* and seen how through this dance Orestes and Electra draw strength from the dead and the gods. We have had one moment to laugh and cry a little, as, just before the terrible confrontation of Orestes and his mother, we have been presented, as it were, with a flashback of that same Orestes—a little baby in his nurse's arms, wetting his diapers. We have heard the momentous three lines, spoken by Pylades, whom we thought was being played by a mute extra, and received his words as though they were the words of Apollo himself, so that to all of us in the theater Clytemnestra's death has acquired inevitability. We have seen the equally inevitable horror strike Orestes, as he runs offstage going mad at the end of the second play. With the beginning of the third play, we have seen the pursuing Furies, now horribly manifest, able, if we believe the story, to give the women in the audience miscarriages, and our hearts have been beating faster as Orestes manages to outrun these Furies to what is now presented as Athens itself. We have experienced the excitement of the trial scene and watched in suspense as, one by one, the jurors go up to the urn and drop in their voting stones. At last we see Athene declare Orestes acquitted. Our poetic imagination has been teased by the repetitions of the two images—that of the robe or net, and that of light. The one character for whom we feel sympathy—Orestes—has been through so much, and now he is free. Surely that is enough for one day's theater. How can Aeschylus top it?

The first action has been performed by Zeus and Agamemnon; the second action by Zeus and Clytemnestra; the third by Apollo and Orestes; the fourth by the Furies; the fifth by Athene in collaboration with the representatives of the people of Athens. Aeschylus achieves his climax by the final coup de theatre: the sixth and last action is performed by the people of Athens themselves, en masse, with their patron goddess acting as representative. It is the perfect climactic expression of the power of the theater of Dionysus in Athens: the people of Athens and the trappings of the festival itself become part of the play; the play is linked utterly with the rite out of which all drama grew.

All through the play the horror of the Furies has been emphasized. But they are also magnificent. We must remember that to Aeschylus the hawk hunting the dove was an image of God. Aeschylus' poetry rings throughout with agreement for Rilke's definition of beauty:

> Denn das Schöne ist nichts
> als des Schrecklichen Anfang, den wir noch grade ertragen,
> und wir bewundern es so, weil es gelassen verschmäht,
> uns zu zerstören.[24]

Aeschylus was, however, even stronger than Rilke and could see beauty in pure, unmitigated terror. As soon as Orestes has been acquitted, made a quick speech of thanks, and left, not to be mentioned for the rest of the play, the chorus of Furies burst into a wild dance of anger at the "younger gods" who have insulted and tricked them. In this dance our sympathy is enlisted for these savage beings. From their point of view matricide could never be condoned, and therefore from their point of view they have been tricked, by the people of Athens. Compared with the primaeval force of the spirits of darkness all civilized powers seem frail. Even Athene, the goddess of wisdom, can surely not protect us from the instinctive unreasoning power of their rage, as the chorus of Furies now spit their hatred at the audience, kicking curses of poison and sterility at Athens and threatening to blight the earth itself. Athene can only speak in quiet dialogue iambics, while the chorus, magnificent in their power and hate, wronged in the center of their nature, rear and leap and kick in a climax of violent choreography. But the two systems that they sing are not normal systems. *Strophē* and *antistrophē* carry identical words. It would be natural, therefore, to assume that the movement of the *antistrophē* was exactly identical to that of the *strophē*, rather than matching it with identical movement but in the opposite direction. The feeling of this sequence (778–891) is that although Athene is weaker, yet she can reason, while they can only scream, she can develop and grow, while they are not progressing. Athene quietly continues to suggest that the dishonor they feel is only in their minds. This crisis could be the occasion for them to receive far greater honor than anything they have ever known before.

There is a moment of pause, and then the chorus leader starts to ask Athene questions about this honor they will receive in Athens. Athene tells her that it will be such power that without a Fury's blessing no home will ever thrive (895). This is an enormous power over the city. What will it mean for the inhabitants? The chorus leader continues to ask further questions, suggesting that peace may have been achieved: what kind of blessings does Athens require? And Athene replies, blessings of earth and sea and sky, fruit and growth and freedom from sorrow. Apparently these are blessings she cannot give. Her realm is in men's minds, not in the darkness where seeds take root.

During this passgae of stichomythia and Athene's longer speech (892–915), the rest of the chorus must be in a tight group by the altar in the center of the *orchestra*. For this is the position that commands the *orchestra*, and the end of the previous system has presented the Furies defiantly raging against Athene and her city. During the stichomythia the chorus leader will have to approach the actors' terrace, on which Athene is standing. Clearly, this should happen after the vital sentence in which Athene states that no home will prosper without the Furies (895). During Athene's speech (903–15) the chorus leader must remain by the terrace, while the rest of the chorus remain by the central altar.[25] Before the next chorus dance, (916ff.) there will have to be a pause while the leader rejoins the rest of the chorus by the central altar, a walk across the radius of the *orchestra* circle, a walk of thirty feet.

And so in the audience we wait breathlessly for the next move. The chorus have been absolutely still; their last move was screaming defiance. What will happen next?

What happens is a happy dance by the terrifying monsters, fanning out from the central altar and approaching the edges of the *orchestra*, a sudden dance of blessing from the spirits at whose wrath we had been cowering a moment ago.[26] The power we had felt in these goddesses of darkness, which we had thought was to be unleashed in a fury of curses that would destroy our land, is as suddenly unleashed in a stream of blessing.

Chorus of Furies. Strophē I shall join, Pallas, your community.
I shall not abuse this land,
Where, with Zeus the lord of all and Ares,
You have built a fort for gods—

Glory guards the altars,
Guards the spirit powers of Greece.
Now I do begin to bless,
Prophesying favourably.
So may the city feel a burst
Of happiness.
May earth swell, ripen, gush,
Nourished by the beaming sun.

Athene (chanting in anapests).   So for my city, readily
I shall enact, establishing here
These powers you'll not charm easily,
Whose province will be to oversee
All human affairs.
He who meets them when they are hard
Will not know how his wounds appeared.
All that his ancestors transgressed
They add to his acts, and for all his boasts,
Silent, unsmiling, they level him to the dust.

Chorus of Furies. Antistrophē   Not a breath, blight and rot, to harm these
trees—
Now I start to give the blessing—
Cankers, moulds that blind the eyes of flowers,
Do not cross the boundaries.
Creep away for ever,
Crippling sick sterility.
May the goatskin god of beasts
Fill to bellyful your flocks
To give a double lambing time,
And underground
May earth's deep rocks disclose
God and fortune's treasure trove.

Athene (chanting in anapests).   Hear this, you, my city's watchtower,
This which is coming to pass.
Great is the lady Fury's power
Among the immortals, down in the depths,
Over the lives of men.
Manifest, final the way they apportion
Some lives to song,
Some lives to tears,
Stunting them to an abortion.

(916–55)[27]

In between *strophē* and *antistrophē* Athene intervenes, now chanting in
anapests. There is only one way in which to stage this. Athene must come

down from the actors' terrace and march to the central altar, to which the Furies return, so that at the end of her chant they can start again from the altar to dance forward to the edges of the *orchestra* in a second blessing. So at the end of Athene's first chant (937) she and the Furies are together at the central altar of Dionysus, and the Furies are now installed as members of the Athenian community. Their powers are in no sense diminished, and they are still in every way the hounds of hell. But they are hounds of hell in the employment of the Athenians: spiritual policemen, not spiritual leaders of vendetta.

This chant of Athene is an echo of something we have heard earlier in the play. Threatened by the prospect of the trial of Orestes, the Furies sing that if they are defeated it will be a catastrophe (490ff.). For a city that dishonors the hounds of hell is bound to fail. At that point in the play they thought that if they were defeated, they were automatically dishonored. But Athene has now found a way whereby both Orestes may be acquitted and the Furies may be honored. The acquittal of Orestes is a special case. The Furies concede the special case because their natural right has been confirmed by Athene as part of her civilized community forever. At this moment Aeschylus' theology may be translated almost exactly into Jewish or Christian terms. What the earlier chorus affirms from the point of view of primitive, irrational intuition and instinct, and what Athene now confirms with the full rationality of her divine wisdom, is that there can be no democracy without the fear of hell. Passionate believer in democracy though Aeschylus was, it was a democracy dependent on a condition of awareness of the numinous.[28]

It is on this condition that the image of the robe-net, the image of doom, joins with the image of light. For the Furies will now be dressed in the scarlet robes of resident aliens and take their place in the torchlight procession that is the beginning and the heart of the Dionysiac festival. And it is this procession that is the final embodiment of the image of light. All the five preceding actions of the epic drama have led to the sixth action of acceptance by Athens of these hounds of hell, who are now given the place of honor in the procession that is the central act of the city's worship. And as this takes place we realize that it is we in the audience who have taken this sixth and last action, for from the audience are rising our representatives, the *propompoi,* the actual attendants from the procession itself. Is this part of the play or part of the procession? We can no longer tell. But it is the center of the festival, as the festival has never been celebrated before nor will ever be again. The city's representatives lead the powers of darkness as resident aliens in a procession that circles the central altar where Athene stands, and, now with Athene bringing up the rear and walking with the leader of the chorus, circles the *orchestra* once more and marches out into the city. In the last verse of the hymn, the Athenian representatives are singing of how Zeus is now at one with the dark primeval power of Moira, whose ministers the Furies are. In this moment the poet has united the old and the new gods, the spirits of passion and the spirits of reason. He has done so by making all at one: drama and theatricality, action and ritual, stage and audience, festival and play presented at that festival. It is the moment of all Greek drama with the widest possible implications; it is the moment of all Greek drama most particularly private for Athenians of that time. It is the center and the crowning glory of the Greek theatrical experience. It is the moment of all moments in the theater when the empty space is at its fullest with the spirits that every play attempts to conjure up. It is the moment of all moments that encourages our feeble imaginations to hope that somehow, somewhere, someone working in our craft of tinsel and painted papier-mâché will dare to challenge the world again with Aeschylus' challenge that great theater can make a great society, and that society will be truly great only by possessing and cherishing a truly great theater.

Sophocles

I have said before that Sophocles was less parodied than the other great poets because he was, like Pope, in such control of his language that in everything he wrote every implication of each word is indeed implied, and so there are no implications left for the parodist to develop. I do not wish to suggest any other similarities between the fifth-century Athenian and the eighteenth-century Englishman. Be it far from this study to suggest any connection between the impassioned rituals of the dancer-priest of Asclepius and the cool, cynical observation of the deformed poet of the age of reason. But given the vastly wider emotional canvas of Sophocles, as we try to summarize his poetry we fall back on phrases such as "perfect rhythm," "complete control of every word, every syllable, every connotation." He is a poet's poet, because everything in him is poetry and seems to disappear when analyzed. He is a poet's poet because one's understanding of him depends upon one's own poetic maturity. He is a poet's master poet, because there are things that he can do— untranslatable, unanalyzable things—that no one else has ever been able to do. Ezra Pound persuaded T. S. Eliot to tear up a set of heroic couplets with which Eliot was feeling quite pleased because, said Pound, Pope has done all that better. Across a gap of twenty-five hundred years Sophocles still has this kind of quality. His technique forces poets today to admit that there are certain skills in which the highest achievement can only be to reach as near to his attainment as possible. No wonder that his own contemporaries walked in his shadow.

A sense of brilliance and excitement might be how we would sum up our reactions to the climaxes in Aeschylus. A sense of clear mystery is a possible reaction to the climaxes of Sophocles. Everything appears to be straightforward, but it is not. Part of the pattern of Sophocles' thought is irony: things are not what they seem. This irony has been much discussed as central to the way in which Sophocles' mind works. It could be described as the pattern of the *Oedipus the King:* Oedipus by his deliberate action brings about the opposite of what he intended. Similarly in the *Electra*, Clytemnestra and Aegisthus bring about exactly the opposite result to the one they intended. I prefer, however, to define this irony, important though it is, as being part of a more general sense in Sophocles that we move in a mystery we do not understand. At the center of this mystery is the fact of death, and it is in the relationship of death to life that we are confronted most clearly with Sophocles' mystery.

I have, I hope, emphasized enough in the course of this book that Sophocles wrote dance dramas in which every aspect of play making is subsumed to the total pattern, the total rhythm, and that characterization was only one aspect of this totality to be used or not used as necessary. Such emphasis is necessary in the current state of writing about the Greek plays, which underestimates the chorus and tries to treat them as plays of the same order as the plays of naturalism. But given that this is misguided, and that Sophocles is a poet of a completely different order, we must acknowledge also his ability to present human personality in its complexity onstage. And so, in these two examples of his genius, I shall concentrate more on the character and the actor, and less on the total dance.

Ajax, *the Suicide of Ajax*

The suicide of Ajax is a well-known point of dispute among scholars, both in terms of its staging and in terms of its interpretation. The points disputed, however, are relatively small, and I shall not discuss them in detail. What seems to me important is that the sequence is clearly meant to contain a deep ambivalence, because it presents a great mystery.

The central action of the play is Ajax' monstrous decision to kill the entire company of the Greek leaders, on account of his anger at having been passed over by them in favor of Odysseus as the inheritor of Achilles' armor. Athene, however, drove Ajax mad. While it seemed to him that he was attacking the Greek chiefs, he was actually attacking sheep and cattle, killing some and capturing others to torture at leisure. Ajax' act of arrogance and violence is transformed by the goddess of wisdom into the vicious action of a petulant child. The play opens with an extreme presentation of this transformation. The goddess Athene, for whom Athenians felt some of the special love and veneration that Catholic Christians feel for the Virgin Mary, is presented by Sophocles urging Odysseus to come and watch Ajax in his ludicrous delusion, and then to mock him (79). Ajax' act is so monstrous that even the figure of all that is most holy in Greek sanity will ask men to laugh at him before she makes him realize what he has done.

Ajax' action is the action of a spoilt child, unfit to be a chief. His requital is to be made a fool. That is all. There is an important episode later in the play (719–83), where we learn that Calchas the seer has revealed that if Ajax stays inside his tent for the day, surrounded by the corpses of the sheep and cattle, which he can now recognize, he will be saved and live. But Ajax is not the sort of person who can endure humiliation. He commits suicide as an act of extreme irresponsibility. His wife and son need him to protect them; but he deserts them. He gives instructions to his brother Teucer to see to his burial, but in the latter part of the play we shall see that Teucer is powerless to bring this about. The Greek chiefs are determined to dishonor Ajax in the only way left to them, by dishonoring his corpse. The burial finally takes place only through the insistence of Odysseus, whom Ajax conceived as his arch enemy; for Odysseus is too wise to insult a fallen foe and knows that to refuse burial to a corpse pollutes the man who refuses it. The action of Ajax is in intention monstrous villainy, committed out of overweening arrogance, in order to assert his sense of his own importance. It is a total failure. Without the intervention of Odysseus, Ajax' corpse would be lying, lower than nothing; an unburied corpse; rotting offal.

To make a snap comparison, Ajax is the greatest villain in Sophocles, just as Macbeth is the greatest villain in Shakespeare. But neither is his author's most evil character, this latter achievement being Creon in the *Oedipus at Colonus* and Iago in *Othello*. Ajax and Macbeth commit the most monstrous action but are not in themselves totally evil; the sad thing is that we can see what great men and what great leaders they can be, and indeed for the most part are. Shakespeare gives Macbeth some of his finest poetry to speak; so does Sophocles to Ajax. In both plays we are asked to see very clearly both the sinner and the sin, and to distinguish one from the other, even at the moment when we are being shown the former swamped by the latter.

The prologue is a clear exposition of Ajax' monstrous action. At the instigation of Athene he comes out of his hut to demonstrate what he thinks is his bullying dominance of the Greek chiefs, whom we can see to be only beasts. But the following sequences develop our sympathy for Ajax. The chorus are Ajax' sailors from his home of Salamis; they depend on their captain and hero. So does the weak and gentle Tecmessa, his wife. Then Ajax is presented on the *ekkyklema* with the slaughtered beasts, regaining his right mind. After a lament for his disgrace, a scene follows in which he ignores Tecmessa's pleading and announces that he will commit suicide. The *stasimon* that follows (596–645) continues the sense of the preceding episode. The first system links the chorus's love of their home, Salamis, and their fear of dying far from it in obscurity, with the fall and disgrace of Ajax. The second system links Ajax and his sorrowing parents. The whole *stasimon* is a strongly lyrical outpouring of grief, a passionate declaration of dependence and a plea on behalf of those who are dependent on Ajax.

Ajax' suicide has now been prepared. But it does not follow immediately. Instead there follows a long and acutely ambivalent speech by Ajax (646–92) about time and mutability and the strangeness of how he possesses Hector's sword, which had killed so many Greeks. For someone like Tecmessa, wanting desperately to believe that Ajax will change his mind and not kill himself, it appears to offer a kind of hope, and some critics have wondered at Sophocles for making Ajax appear to change his mind. Sophocles is much cleverer than that. The speech is perfectly compatible with its being made by someone about to commit suicide, but by someone who sees his suicide as part of a total pattern far bigger than himself. It is as if Ajax was hypnotized by the prospect of his own death, and, while almost in a trance, his words do indeed have a kind of total mysticism, reverberating far beyond his own death.

The following short, one-system *stasimon* (693–718) is the perfect foil for the preceding speech. It expresses an almost orgasmic excitement, an emotion also naturally aroused by the imminence of death. The opening line means: "I shuddered with sexual desire; joyously I flew aloft." It is an invocation to Pan, and the best explanation for the introduction of this otherwise irrelevant god is the folk belief, current in Greece until almost the present day, that Pan slept at noon and was terrible when woken. The scholars who have tried to take the preceding speech of Ajax as the expression of his change of mind have also tried to take this *stasimon* as the expression of the chorus's relief. It is certainly not an expression of relief. Everything is ambivalent. In the *antistrophē* there is reference to the clear light of day (708–9), but that is the time when Pan is dangerous. The opening line of the *antistrophē*, danced to a movement that must also be used for the "shudder of sexual desire," means: "The god of war has loosened the terrible pain from his eyes." (706). The only way in which the god of war ever loosens pain is by death. The detached trance and the shuddering orgasm. Both are part of the mystery of death. The power of this sequence is that Sophocles presents very clearly what is going to happen through the actions of people who do not really understand what is going on. By this means we see clearly, but at the same time we realize that we are witnessing a mystery far beyond our complete understanding.

The rest of the suicide follows with no hesitation or difficulty. The messenger enters in the episode already alluded to (719–814). If Ajax has left his hut, then he is in great danger. Chorus and actors then leave the stage to look for him. After a moment in which the stage is empty, Ajax appears on the *ekkyklema*, (815), now made to look like an exterior. On it is fixed the sword of Hector, by which he stands to make his dying speech as a soliloquy direct to the audience. Finally, having invoked death itself, Salamis, his native earth, Athens, his audience, and then the land of Troy, where his death is set, he falls on the sword. The *ekkyklema* is rolled in. The actor gets up and changes into Teucer's costume and mask, while the stage staff substitute a dummy on the *ekkyklema*, which will be revealed again at some point during the succeeding dance presenting the chorus and Tecmessa's search for Ajax (866ff. Tecmessa sees the body at line 891.). For the rest of the play the dummy will remain in view with the sword sticking into it, until, in the last few lines, Teucer's attendants bear it away and the *ekkyklema* is closed while the cortege moves out down the *parodos*.[29]

I suggest that the main difficulties that have been encountered in analyzing this episode have been of the critics' own making. If we do not theorize with inadequate evidence that the Greeks never showed a death onstage, and if we

do not attempt to translate Sophocles' highly ambivalent poetry in the long
speech of Ajax and the *stasimon* to Pan as unambiguous prose, then it is clear
what happens, and we can absorb the event's reverberations without letting
theories get in the way.

I have deliberately left to the last the central potential misconception for a
modern audience—the attitude to the act of suicide. We have been bludgeoned
too much with the Stoics and their successors, who taught that suicide could be
noble. We do not ourselves believe that suicide is other than a pathetic waste of
life. For a commander of men, for a husband and father with dependents,
suicide is the ultimate selfishness. His death deprives the people who depend
on him. But when we go to some plays and certainly to some operas, we allow
our own judgment to be set aside in favor of a misguided and socially perni-
cious romanticism that presents suicide as a noble action. If we are to watch the
Ajax properly, we must forget such rubbish and follow the drama with our
own common sense alert. Ajax is a selfish, vainglorious man, and his suicide is
the culmination of his selfish, vainglorious career. It is especially reprehensible
in a man supposed to be a leader, in charge of men who look to him for orders,
and in charge of a weak, devoted wife and a young child who need his protection. His death is a stupid, unnecessary waste.

And yet, in spite of all this, Ajax is magnificent. The unthinking passion with
which he refuses to contemplate any alternative to suicide is the power that
makes him a leader whom his men will follow anywhere, and whom his wife
will love whatever he does. However wrongheaded, his death has a
magnificence about it. We are asked to witness it as we might be asked to
witness a storm or an explosion, an event that destroys people but in itself is
beautiful. The center of the speech contains an image whose ambivalence focuses the ambivalence of the play in one word. Its apparent imprecision is the
height of precision, the master use by a master poet who never put a word out
of place.

>   the snowy
> Winters move out of fruitful summer's way.
> The endless wheeling of the night stands back
> To let the white-horsed day kindle its light.
> The blast of awful winds has put to sleep
> The troubled sea; and that all-powerful slumber
> Binds, and then looses, grasps, but holds not always.
>
>   (670–76)

The last word of line 674, which I have translated "put to sleep," is the key. Of
course winds do not put the sea to sleep; they rouse it into storm. It is a piece of
nonsense, but spoken by a man who is about to die—to undergo the all-
powerful slumber that binds and does not loose, grasps and does hold always—
and whose death will be a kind of storm, it has an awful sense. The character's
nonsense speaks far beyond what the character knows, to touch some deeper

and more total pattern, in which wind and sea are not at variance, but are sleeping partners in the unsleeping total rhythm, which does not die.[30]

Electra, *the Revenge of Electra*

The death of Ajax has indefinable ramifications. The climax of the *Electra* is a moment of unambiguous simplicity. Clytemnestra committed adultery with Aegisthus and then killed her husband Agamemnon. She and Aegisthus bring up Electra, her daughter by Agamemnon. Electra, thus raised by murderers attempting to suppress their feelings of guilt, grows into a warped and re-pressed woman. Their act of murder causes their own destruction, by produc-ing the natural reaction that Orestes will avenge his father's murder and kill both his mother and her lover with the help of Electra. Things turn out the opposite way from the murderers' intentions. Their actions have been gov-erned by fear that Orestes, who had been sent away from home by Electra as a baby, will return and kill them. Their hope therefore is that Orestes will die before he can return. One of the turning points in the play is a moment when Clytemnestra prays to Apollo for what amounts to the death of Orestes, though she does not make this quite explicit (634 ff.). As soon as she finishes her prayer it appears to be granted, for the old tutor enters with the false message that Orestes is dead (660 ff.). The climax of the play is the climax of this false hope. Aegisthus has been told that Orestes is dead, and that his body is being brought home. He arrives to see Orestes and Pylades, neither of whom he recognizes, standing on the *ekkyklema* over a shrouded corpse. Aegisthus exclaims ambiguously, "Oh Zeus I behold a vision not without malice havng fallen. If there is vengeance here, I make no mention." (1466–67). I have used this overliteral rendering to bring out all the ambiguities of the Greek. The shroud is then lifted, and he sees that the corpse is not Orestes but Clytem-nestra, his mistress and fellow murderer. He looks up and realizes instantly. "The dead are alive," says the living Orestes. "I understand," says Aegisthus (1477–78). It is the most concise image of the Sophoclean irony. Things are not what they seem, and if you do not live in humility, they will certainly turn out very much the opposite of your guess. Morality, drama, and theatricality meet here in what is in a sense a crude theatrical trick, but used with such consum-mate skill that it is one of the greatest moments in the history of the theater.

This is the climax of the play, but it is shortly preceded by the most remark-able throwaway in the history of the theater. Aeschylus and Euripides present the murder of Clytemnestra by her son as the climax of their respective plays—naturally, since that is by far the most horrific killing. Sophocles is concerned to build his events toward the climax of irony described in the previous para-graph. The confrontation between Orestes and Aegisthus takes place onstage. Orestes kills his mother offstage, and all we hear are her cries from behind the *skēnē*. What we see is Electra, onstage, shouting without the slightest hesitation or remorse, "Hit her again" (1415). The death of Clytemnestra is treated as an apparent incidental. This has led some critics to think that Sophocles is not interested in morality, since he appears to approve of matricide. Sophocles was more sure of his own audience. Knowing that they would shudder in horror at the matricide, he also knew that they would shudder even more at the sight of Electra screaming, "Hit her again" without the slightest sense of pain that the victim of this blow was her own mother. Electra's punishment is her triumph. Her triumph is her punishment. For what horrors must have taken control of her mind if she can simply stand and shout, "Hit her again," while her own mother is stabbed to death.

The morality of the Electra is the statement that if you do what Clytemnestra and Aegisthus do to a person like Electra, you will turn her into a fiend. And this process is very much a part of the total pattern of *Dikē*. To present this in essence is the function of the *parodos,* which, if we include Electra's opening anapest chant, is the longest piece of continuous music in Sophocles (86–250). It is a duet for Electra and the chorus. Most of what Electra sings is in anapests, which suggests that this year Sophocles did not have a leading actor who was a great singer; no doubt his first effort was to find an actor capable of this enormous female role. For the earlier part of the *parodos,* therefore, the chorus dominate Electra musically. But in the final epode Electra sings a proper tune and clearly dominates the chorus.[31] The effect is a miniature of the whole play. Out of the invocations of the gods, out of Electra's grief and the loss of Agamemnon, out of the exile of Orestes and the power of Zeus, who looks after Orestes, out of the horror of that day of death for Agamemnon and the sullen, unappeasable hatred with which Electra waits to avenge him, out of all this will rise Electra like a Fury, a minister of *Dikē,* herself an angel of revenge. At the climactic moment of the long *parodos,* as her chant turns into a fully musical song, her personal hatred is generalized. She is part of the pattern of *Dikē:*

> For if this poor corpse lies here
> Mere earth and nothingness,
> While they
> Never repay,
> Never receive their punishment of death.
> Then throughout all the world the sense of dread
> And holiness will utterly disappear.

> (245–50)

The course of the Electra is the demonstration of how Electra is turned by the actions of her mother and Aegisthus into the divine instrument of *Dikē* who is also the Fury who can scream over her dying mother, "Hit her again." Such a form is interesting only if the character of Electra is interesting. Just as the action of the *Antigone* could not take place if Creon were not the man he was, unsure of himself and not up to his job as supreme ruler, so the *Electra* can move us only if we are able to see the kind of person Electra would have been if she had not been turned into a Fury. Accordingly Sophocles has created one of the greatest roles on the Greek stage. Possibly he asks more of his leading actor in *The Women of Trachis,* when he requires first the portrayal of the weak and gentle woman whose beauty is fading, then the tough hero to whom she gave her heart. But the *Electra* certainly offers the greatest task for a leading actor while portraying only one character. The gamut of every emotion is run to show how such a warm and loving girl of volatile and varied moods could become the sullen and obsessive monomaniac whom we see. She has all the womanly desires for the husband and children she will not possess (164–65). But in the joy of confrontation with her brother she can forget that she is a woman (1238–42). She is brave and she is intelligent. Above all she is capable of boundless love, because it is only a woman with such a capacity for love who could hate so deeply as Electra has come to hate her mother. During the course of the play, the leading actor has to demonstrate every major human emotion from the height of joy to the depths of grief. The climactic expression of her love and grief, the moment that sums up the power of the person Electra might have been, is the speech she makes while holding the urn supposedly full of the ashes of Orestes.

Electra.   This was the man that of all the world
I loved the most. And here's the scraps,
What's left of Orestes. Look how I welcome you,
Look at my greeting—different from when
I waved you goodbye. I pick you up
In my hands, a nothing. Oh I sent away
All the brightness out of our home, boy.
Oh if only you'd passed away before,
Before I let you slip through my fingers
On to foreign earth, protecting you
From the murderers here. But on that day,
At that moment, you should have died
And received your place in our father's burial.
Now it's away from home, it's a foreign country,
It's a mean death, it's away from your sister.
Not with my hands to love you, to hold you,
To adorn you with water, raise from the ashes
Your sad small corpse in the proper ritual.
Hands of strangers attended you, boy.
Miserable weight in a miserable pot.
No.
Oh how I cradled you once upon a time
Uselessly, uselessly. . . .
Oh how lovely it was to look after you.
I was the mother who loved you—not her.
I was your servants, I was your nurse.
I was the sister you always called for.
Aii gone, in one day.
You're dead. You've snatched it all.

Like a storm, gone. Father's dead.
I'm dying with you; you're gone, you're dead.
Enemies laughing. Mad with joy
Our mother unmother—and so often you promised
In your secret letters that you'd come back
And break her. Oh you and me—
We've got an unlucky spirit that crushed you.
Look how you . . . arrived to meet me
Not in your lithe young body, but ashes.
Dust, a shadow. Useless—oh no—
No. . . .
What a stupid shape. No. No.
What an awful thing. Oh no. . . .
I sent you away and you've killed me, boy.
You've killed me, my dear brother.
So come on, let me in to your little hut,
Your little nothingness, I'm your nothing sister.
I'm coming to live with you for ever.
When you were here we shared everything.
So now don't stop me from sharing your grave.
For the dead, I don't see them suffering pain.

                                                    (1126–70)[32]

It is perhaps typical of Sophocles' complex irony that this greatest funeral
speech, which takes itself out of the immediate context of the play by the sheer
power of its compassion, should, in the context of the play, be based on a
falsehood. For Orestes is not dead, and the fact that he is alive and coming in
vengeance will mean that Electra will become the Fury incapable ever again of
such compassion. But Electra's cause is such that, horrible though its outcome
be, yet we do not grudge her the chance to express such love, any more than we
grudge Ajax, selfish and petulant though he be, the chance to see through the
trappings of death to something of its central mystery. For of these paradoxes is
human nature composed. It is worth remembering the story of how the great
fourth-century actor, Polus, spoke Electra's urn speech while holding the ashes
of his own recently dead son.[33] For perhaps it is essentially part of the complexity of the theater that what is most specially suitable for a moment in a play
fixed with the utmost particularity of context should acquire by the intensity of
its particularity the widest possible general application. The speech—which, as
it happens, is pointless—for a particular, wasted death, becomes a general cry
of lament. For, after all, all death is waste, and all speech over death is pointless.

Euripides

In a book such as this it is necessary both to summarize the work of the great
poets whom I discuss, and to present examples of their work in relation to
work of the others. If we consider Euripides in relation to the other poets and

especially to Sophocles, we sum up his work with words like "jerkiness," "shock," "vivid detail," "speeches that detach from their context," and sometimes "what appears to be sheer perversity." This does much less than justice to the smoothness and control of a play like the *Ion*, but it seems fairer to judge Euripides by looking more closely at the plays that are jerky but also are works where he appears to be more passionately involved.

The play of Euripides that moves me most is *The Trojan Women*. In this searing condemnation of war, there are many beautiful, heart-rending moments, but somehow the scene between Hecuba and her daughter Andromache sticks most in the mind. Andromache, the gentle, the good wife of Hector, is now going to be the mistress of Neoptolemus. Andromache wants to die, because she fears that she will come to love her new man:

> And yet they say one night can soften
> A woman's hate into bed with a man.
>
> (665–66)

But Hecuba tells her not to worry; she is to go with Neoptolemus and love him, and bring up Hector's and her son so that one day perhaps there will be another Troy (702–5). And at that moment the Greek herald arrives to say that the child is to be thrown from the battlements, because the Greeks fear the possibility of another Troy. We talk of Euripides as abrupt and jerky. This example is the abruptness of great grief and rage; it is abruptness totally appropriate.

With less passion involved, the abruptness often appears merely abrupt. There is about Euripides often an air of the intellectual flitting from topic to topic, rather than the poet dancing through dream after dream. Much of his work touches us at a more conscious, less deep level. Scenes such as those between Jason and Medea (446–626, 866–975) reveal a knowledge of human sexuality that shows Euripides did not need to read his Freud nearly two and a half thousand years later. But modern critics who have noticed this have sometimes written as if the age of Sophocles was like middle-class Vienna in Freud's day, a society needing liberation. Sophocles needed no liberation; his awareness of sex was without inhibitions. The sense of human sexuality is all the stronger in his work for not being intellectualized, for sexuality and talk do not go very well together.

I referred to Euripides' perversity. There are occasions in his plays where he seems almost deliberately to make things hard for his audience, confuse them as to where their sympathies should lie. This, I cannot help feeling, spills over into his poetry. Sophocles, as Shakespeare or Aeschylus, seems always to have some great lyricism ready for the moments when he needs to soar. Some of Euripides' best poetry seems to come at the wrong moments. Euripides is a great writer of messenger speeches, and in these speeches of vivid narrative his powers of detailed description have full play. But one of his greatest messenger speeches is that from the *Electra*, whose climax is Orestes' revenge. Received with hospitality by Aegisthus, Orestes struck him in the neck with a meat axe as his back was turned (774–858, especially 839–43).

The desire to shock his audience with the message of his plays; the intellectual's tendency for discursive talk rather than single-minded direct passion; sheer perversity; such a summary does not do total justice to the variety of Euripides and certainly does not prepare us fully for the single-minded passion of *The Bacchants,* most usually acclaimed as his greatest play. I have concentrated in this study, however, more upon showing the ways in which Euripides was a transitional artist caught between the old Dionysiac rite and the new self-sufficient theater. It is the awkward qualities of Euripides that fitted him so well to write extraordinary plays applicable only to the moment in history when the archaic Greek consciousness was dissolving into something else. It is the genius of Euripides that these plays, which fit with no tradition, should be masterworks lasting until our own day and beyond.

Orestes, *the Phrygian Eunuch's Aria*

Of these plays the *Orestes* is the richest, most complex, and most successful. Modern theater has not yet caught up with it, and modern critics have tended to treat it with less attention than the rest of Euripides' corpus.[34] Part of the reason for this may be that, unlike most of his plays, the *Orestes* cannot be analyzed in terms of an idea. It is itself, and nothing else: a poem for the theater, as much a whole as any play of Sophocles, as full of paradox within paradox as any of Aristophanes. It is not theater of plot, but it is constructed in terms of purely theatrical rhythm; it is like the *Iphigeneia in Tauris* or *Ion* in that it does not depend on the sense of the Dionysiac rite or on the historical events around which a traditional tragedy was normally built. It is not theater of plot, but the mastery of a rhythm such as Euripides demonstrates here could have been acquired only by work in theater of plot. Instead of depending on history, the *Orestes* depends on previous plays on the Orestes theme, just as the more obvious parody of Aristophanes so depends, to such an extent that the structure of *The Women at the Thesmophoria* rests upon the structure of the plays it parodies. It is difficult to imagine the *Orestes* ever being written if Euripides had not been able to watch the development of Aristophanes.

The climax of the *Orestes* is certainly a moment as paradoxical as anything in Aristophanes. The performance given the most theatrical attention is undoubtedly that of the Phrygian eunuch slave. His aria lasts almost a hundred and fifty lines (1369–1502) and is therefore almost as long as the sung part of the *Agamemnon parodos.* It is metrically, and therefore musically, extremely complicated. Its function is to substitute for a messenger speech, and it therefore comes at a moment of dramatic tension. The Phrygian has no spoken dialogue at all. After the aria, Orestes comes out and there is a short sequence of chanted stichomythia in trochaic tetrameters, while the cowardice of Orestes threatens the shrill panic of the eunuch. The eunuch is chased off and is not mentioned again.

The play is based on a paradoxical idea, that of presenting the story of Orestes, a story dating from the time of blood feud, in a contemporary setting. There is no point in this play to the murder of Clytemnestra. Orestes could have prosecuted her in the courts (491–541). This is part of the sense of Euripides' *Electra*, but there the anachronism is something felt rather than stated. In the *Orestes* the anachronism becomes part of the setting: the play takes place in the never-never land of the theater, and in no other place.

The play emits a sense of disgust—disgust with Athens, disgust with the old attitudes of morality, disgust with the old objects of veneration of which the Orestes story provides its fair share. For to Euripides in 408 B.C., these attitudes, which had "made Athens great," had now brought Athens to the edge of humiliating defeat and had left the city Euripides loved split by civil strife after two coups d'etat. There is the same sense of universal corruption and disintegration that we find in the work of the Jacobean dramatists, such as Webster. But much of the play is for laughs. There is also the feeling of black comedy, the sense that what we are confronted with is so horrible that tears are inadequate, and that laughter expresses our bitterness better.

A changing philosophy of life, a disintegrating society; Euripides expresses this background in a play that alternates scenes to be played for pathos, scenes to be played for melodrama and scenes to be played for laughter, with the control and rapidity of Aristophanes. Our own uncertainty as to the tone in which we are to accept each successive scene contributes to the total rhythm of the play, just as our laughter contributes to the rhythm of a play by Aristophanes.

The prologue presents Electra, watching over her sleeping brother Orestes, who has collapsed with hysteria after having killed his mother. That was six days ago, and he is now virtually mad. The people of Argos hate Orestes and Electra for what they have done and are proposing to put them to death. The only hope of rescue is Menelaus, who is supposed to be arriving this very day. He has sent Helen on ahead by night, frightened that the Argives might stone her in revenge for all their men who died in the war to win her back.

At this point Helen joins Electra and tries to persuade her to go on her behalf to the tomb of Clytemnestra and lay her offerings. Electra refuses, suggesting that if Helen does not dare venture out, surely her daughter Hermione would be the best substitute. The scene is full of sly humor, as in Helen's protest at this suggestion: "It's not good for girls to walk about in a crowd" (108). This from Helen, who has done somewhat more than walk about! Helen is beautifully characterized. We notice how she has cut off only the tiniest tips of her hair as offering (128–29). Middle-aged as she is, she is as vain as ever. Her opening address to Electra displays the contempt of the sexually satisfied for the frustrated in a couplet of delightful bitchiness:

> Daughter of Clytemnestra . . . and Agamemnon,
> Virgin a great length of time, Electra.

> (71–72)

After this sequence comes the *parodos,* a dance for Electra and the chorus of women of Argos. It is pure musical comedy, with almost exactly the humor of the elephantine pirates in *The Pirates of Penzance* singing, "With cat-like tread" and clumping around the stage thunderously. The ladies of Argos dance around the mattress where Orestes is supposed to be sleeping, singing, no doubt at the tops of their voices, "Don't make a noise." Needless to say Orestes wakes up, as the chorus ask Electra to "see if he's died while we were mourning him" (208–10). A sequence of farce follows. Orestes sits up and then immediately lies down in bed, and then immediately sits up again (217–36). There is then a grotesque sequence in which he chases invisible Furies with his bow (268ff.) and in general has carte blanche to "play his mad scene." Electra goes into the palace, while the chorus sing, at a much more genuine level, a prayer to the Eumenides to free Orestes of his madness (316–47). Somewhat as with the dances of prayer and invocation in Aristophanes, the genuine ritual takes over from the theatrical situation.

Menelaus then arrives; as in most plays of Euripides he is a thoroughly contemptible person. Orestes begs his help, but Menelaus carefully refrains from committing himself to any action. Before anything is decided, Tyndareus arrives, the father of Helen and Clytemnestra. He does not excuse Clytemnestra's adultery and murder of Agamemnon, but roundly condemns Orestes for murdering her in return instead of committing her to trial. Obvious use of anachronism such as this is an easy way to get laughs, and Orestes' answer includes a parody of Aeschylus (551–54), since his "defense" that murdering a man is more serious because the man is the true parent must be a dig at Apollo's defence of Orestes in the *Eumenides* (657–73). Orestes' defence so enrages Tyndareus, that he, who had defended law and the reasonable course, now hurries to urge the Argives to stone Orestes and Electra without bothering to wait for a proper trial (612–14). Tyndareus, who had appeared to be more honorable, now shows himself as bad as the rest. Menelaus then also leaves for the meeting of the Argives, making feeble excuses for his inability to do all that he would like to do toward helping Orestes. We can see that he will in fact do absolutely nothing.

At this moment Pylades arrives. The scene is a chanted dance in trochaic tetrameters, expressing the excitement and relief that he is there to help. Pylades has been banished by his father from home for aiding the crime of Clytemnestra's murder. He encourages Orestes to go to the Assembly. After an excess of mock heroics and time wasting, Pylades calls for haste, since "they may have taken the vote already" (799). As they leave, the chorus sing sadly of the family's gathering troubles, culminating in the horror of Clytemnestra's murder. Electra comes out of the *skēnē* to meet a messenger arriving from the Assembly to say that all is lost and that she and Orestes must kill each other within one day, in lieu of being stoned by the people. Electra sings an aria of lament, whose effect seems straight. It is a change of mood, ending quietly with a section of anapest chant.

Pylades and Orestes return, and there follows another scene of fake heroics, each outprotesting the other in nobility. Suddenly Pylades proposes the daring stroke of murdering Helen in revenge for the way in which Menelaus did nothing to help them. All they have to do is to overpower her Trojan slaves. The cowardly Orestes' courage is roused at last: even he can face Trojan slaves. The plot is elaborated when Electra suggests that they also capture Hermione as a hostage. There then follows the second parody of the *Oresteia*, this time of the *kommos* in *The Libation-Bearers* (306–478), as Orestes with Electra and Pylades calls upon his father's ghost to help his enterprise (*Orestes* 1225–45). The mood of this parody is extremely complex. It is not simply a piece of theatrical fun. There is a feeling of blasphemy as Orestes invokes the aid of Zeus in what is an obviously cheap, unjustified act of revengeful murder. It is as if Euripides was pointing to the way in which the spirit of Aeschylus has been abused in order to justify the aggression that had brought Athens to her present disastrous condition.

Orestes and Pylades go into the house, while Electra and the chorus sing another *Pirates of Penzance* number about keeping watch. We hear Helen's dying screams, and then Hermione arrives to be told by Electra to go into the house and plead with Helen for the lives of Orestes and Electra. As she enters, we hear her cries at her capture. There is a short dochmiac dance of triumph as the chorus sing of the vengeance that has overtaken Helen, and at this moment the Phrygian slave enters to sing of how Orestes locked up the slaves, and then Pylades killed them, and of how they then caught Helen and struck her mortally, but that as she was dying, and as Orestes paused to seize Hermione, Helen disappeared. A short grotesque dance follows in trochaic tetrameters as Orestes runs out to threaten and stab at the Phrygian slave, who manages to escape. As Menelaus hurries up, having heard the news, Orestes appears on the roof, holding his sword to Hermione's throat, demanding that Menelaus make him king in Argos, or Hermione will die. As Menelaus is brought to admit that he is trapped, Orestes gives orders to fire the palace. The bargain is forgotten; they are all going up in flames. At this moment Apollo appears above in the *mēchanē*, and everything is quickly tied up in a happy ending so neat and pat that it is ludicrous. Helen is with Apollo; she is becoming a god. Orestes must take his sword from Hermione's throat and marry her, after doing a year's pilgrimage and being acquitted at Athens. Pylades shall marry Electra so that everyone can live happily ever after.

There has been one further occasion for Euripides to parody the *Oresteia* just before Apollo appears: it in the sequence on the roof, Pylades is played by a mute since the three actors are required for Orestes, Menelaus, and Apollo. Menelaus is made to shout at Pylades asking him where he stands in the business. After, no doubt, a significant pause, in which we register that Pylades is played by a mute, but, unlike the mute in *The Libation-Bearers* (900–902) one who will not break silence, Orestes says: "His silence talks; I'll speak for him" (*Orestes* 1591–92). But the whole sequence on the roof is a kind of parody. It is, as it were, the most complex crisis of melodrama tied up in the most obvious way by the device of the god in the *mēchanē*, which was now becoming famous as an easy way to resolve a complex plot.

If we think of the end as Euripides parodying himself, then we can think of the Phrygian slave's aria as also a piece of self-parody. It is as if Euripides knew that Aristophanes was going to parody his monodies in *The Frogs* (1309–63) and determined to get in first with a parody of his own work so outrageous that even Aristophanes could not top it.

Throughout the play people say one thing and do another. At the beginning Electra says that she will never leave Orestes and leaves him within five lines (307–8, 310–11). Orestes and Pylades leave for the Assembly announcing that they will die fighting (781–82) and return not having even drawn their swords. This is laughable, and in the theater will get laughs. But it is the more effective at getting laughs, as is also the element of parody, because this bitter humor is based on a serious appraisal of human life. People do not do what they say they will do; things do not turn out as one expects. Orestes says that Apollo has destroyed them (955–56). But it is Apollo who rescues them in the nick of time. It is a play about misunderstanding, like the *Ion*, though its tone is far more violent than the *Ion*'s gentle humor and lighthearted melodrama.

Part of the secret of the play is that Euripides is continually changing its genre. Part of the suspense is that we are kept guessing not only as to what will happen, but also as to whether the play is tragedy, melodrama, or farce. The function of the chorus is important; it serves to change the mood from one extreme to the other, very much as the chorus does in Aristophanes. A central climactic moment to this kind of a theatrical form is the aria of the Phrygian slave. The character of the slave is ridiculous, a pathetic, flabby, cowardly eunuch. The idea of having a messenger speech, which is normally full of realistic detail, sung as an extremely florid aria, is even more ridiculous. And yet, because of the viciousness of Orestes, we are more sympathetic toward the Phrygian slave than toward any other character in the play; he is the only person who is not actively evil. And at the same time he cannot but dominate the stage because of his music.

I have said that the chorus has an important function in the play. But they are not the central focus of the action as they are in a play of Sophocles. The chorus are not involved in the events, because they are not in danger themselves. And there is no principal character with whose fate we can feel any involvement at all. In the *Iphigeneia in Tauris* and *Ion*, Euripides started to create the theater of plot, part of whose essence is that the audience be emotionally involved with the principal characters. In the *Orestes* Euripides has gone beyond such involvement to a new detachment. We can call the *Orestes* black comedy in the sense that it is the story of villains, who, as villains so often do, triumph.

A play about the difference between appearance and reality, a play in which Euripides parodies himself, a play where the most farcical moments are the most seriously savage. There is no one way to analyze the *Orestes*, and as we watch it we will be struck by apparently conflicting moods at the same time. In analysis these moods appear to be totally contradictory, but in the theater they can coexist as mutual counterpoint. In analysis we must try to decide the mood of the Phrygian slave's aria. In the theater we are simply aware of several moods combining together in one exciting climax that we cannot analyze.

It is certainly right to dwell on the three moments of parody of the *Oresteia*. Part of the center of the *Orestes* is disgust with Athens, and so the story of Athens's greatest drama, the highest achievement of the Athenian mind, is presented as something sick and beastly. This paradox calls into question the whole basis of the theater. If its greatest achievement is the elevation of a sick delusion into great art, then the art is a sick delusion. The *Oresteia* presents us with the challenge that great theater can make a great society, and society can be truly great only by possessing and cherishing a truly great theater. In the *Orestes* Euripides hurls at the Athenians the decadence of the theater and the sickness of the society, and the fact that the two are still dependent on each other. The *Orestes* is more appropriate a play to consider as the end of fifth-century drama than those three great, coherent rituals, the *Bacchants, Frogs* and *Oedipus at Colonus*. For when those supreme plays could appear within a year of each other, it must have been hard to think that some intangible mystery was about to leave the theater and never return. It is right that a study such as this should focus on the *Orestes*, for though it is a magnificent achievement in theatrical emotion, it is the end of a line. In the bitter parody of its ludicrously artificial ending, it celebrates the impending departure of the gods from a theater whose raison d'être was to worship the gods.

But at the same time the *Orestes* is worth studying because Euripides uses it to have the last laugh. The mystery is leaving the theater, the society is crumbling. But it is part of the perversity of the theater that, as long as it can laugh at itself, as long as one clown can get up on stage and make a fool of himself, then the theater can triumph. The greatest aria in Greek drama is given not to some great hero but to an utterly worthless, cowardly, eunuch slave. It is the climax of Euripides' development in purely theatrical terms. Its combination of shock, farce, pathos, and magic make it one of the most complex moments in all his plays. And yet at the same time it is a triumph of the poet's compassion. Because what we shall take away from the play is not so much the butchery and false heroics of the psychopathic central characters; not even the generalized sense of disgust at the degenerate society depicted, which hammers such echoes into us of our own; but this strange, flabby, effeminate creature, scuttling about in pathetic, ridiculous terror, and yet at the same time soaring through top notes in a coloratura triumph.

Aristophanes

If we produce a play by Aristophanes today, we must get laughs. For the worst disservice one could do to a comic poet is to present him in such a way that he is not funny. Some modern adaptations have successfully shown us how funny Aristophanes is, but sometimes at the cost of showing that he is also a great poet. Conversely, those critics who have enlarged our understanding of his poetry have not necessarily had to make us laugh. Aristophanes is a great poet who works with laughter; the poetry and the laughter are one. As we approach the tragedies we must at all times make the effort of imagination to put ourselves inside the unity of poetry, religion, politics, and morality that is the rite of tragedy. With comedy we need to make the same act of imagination, but in addition put ourselves into the audience laughing at the jokes.

It is also the case that many critics in the West have acted as if the "high seriousness" that Matthew Arnold considered necessary to a great writer excluded a poet who was full of laughter. In spite of the fact that English literature contains Chaucer, Shakespeare, and Dickens, far too many critics writing in English have implicitly equated high seriousness with hard solemnity. From such an attitude Aristophanes has suffered. In a short study such as this it would be hard to establish fully the greatness of Aristophanes in every aspect of what it is to be a poet. But it is necessary to make the acknowledgment that he is indeed a master to be reckoned among the great masters, someone to whom every age can return and find something for itself, someone whom no age will ever define completely.

Although he is very much a total "maker," someone for whom verbal imagery, characterization, theatrical effect, and ribald slapstick blend into an unanalyzable whole, yet he is at the same time a master of every skill with words alone:

Aristophane est l'enchanteur de sa langue; il en tire des accords inouïs, des métaphores qu'on traduirait par des arabesques. Il fait battre les mots, comme les jeunes Athéniens de son temps faisaient battre les coqs et les cailles. . . . Mille images opposées se heurtent dans un désordre magique.[35]

Of the four poets it is Aristophanes who is the hardest to summarize in a paragraph. Most critics would probably agree with the following three generalizations. First, like Aeschylus', his is a very physical poetry. He presents us with concrete and colorful images, many of which appear actually onstage after they have been introduced to our imaginations through language. Aristophanes has the same delight as Aeschylus in mixing the reality of an imagined picture and the reality of an object before our eyes onstage. Second, we notice a kind of rhythm about his humor, which takes account of our laughter. We may notice, for example, how he sets up his good jokes by preparing them with bad jokes. To laugh at bad jokes is an indulgence we all enjoy, but we are slightly ashamed of doing so. Once we have done so, however, we are relaxed; our buttons are now undone, we have let out our belch, and we might as well forget appearances, since we have disgraced ourselves already. If I may be allowed to be personal, I have often found myself giving a poetry reading to an audience for whom poetry is something to be approached in a spirit of frozen sanctimoniousness. With such an audience I try as soon as possible to give them something that will make them laugh. Once they have laughed they slightly despise my poetry; I can almost see them saying to themselves, "Ah, he's not a poet, merely a writer of humorous verse." As they do this, they relax. They are then free of presuppositions, and the poetry can work on their total personalities. Similarly, if a clever audience is watching a play, they can be relaxed by terrible jokes, until they are ready to be swept off their feet by either poetry or laughter. Third, we find that the best "bad" jokes are puns. Shakespeare is full of "bad" puns. So is Aristophanes. Whether the audience of Shakespeare or Aristophanes were as complicated as we, who are inclined to applaud an outrageous pun with a groan rather than a guffaw, we cannot tell. But whether one applauds the pun or despises it as we affect to do today, puns have a noticeable loosening effect on one's conscious control. In a world full of bad puns, anything can happen. In other words, I am suggesting that the ability to create bad puns is a great quality in a comic, but that in Aristophanes, who is perhaps the greatest master of the pun who ever lived, the pun becomes a kind of philosophy of life. Things are not what they seem, and all things are connected in ways we do not understand. The center of Aristophanes' laughter-poetry is the pun, which is, after all, the natural activity in which poetry and laughter become totally intertwined.

All three of these facets of his writing can be seen on a small scale in a silly little example from *The Wasps*. As Hater-of-Cleon[36] prepares the private law court in which his father will sit in judgment, he is careful to bring out a chamber pot for the old man (807). Chamber pots are a cheap laugh, a schoolboy joke. As Hater-of-Cleon hangs up the object, which for the Greeks was a bottle more like what is used today in hospital, there will be a laugh of the most vulgar sort, merely at the presence of the object. Later on, however, the actors look around to see if they now have everything necessary for conducting the business of the court. Hater-of-Cleon exclaims that he has forgotten the clock for timing the speeches. In Athenian courts this was like an hourglass, but it used water instead of sand. Quickly Friend-of-Cleon answers: "Water-clock? What about this?" and holds up the chamber pot (857–58). The cheap bathroom joke has now developed into a pun, an amusing instance of image manifest in physical object. Later still (940) the joke elaborates into a full poetic conceit. Friend-of-Cleon stops to use the pot. Hater-of-Cleon exclaims at how long he is taking: "Won't you ever sit down." In a water clock, time is water. Therefore to make water is to make time. Furthermore, of course, there is an allusion to the rule about sitting down when the time for speaking has run out. Friend-of-Cleon continues to stand while the water is pouring into the "clock." The pun has turned metaphysical, as puns do in *Alice in Wonderland*. The joke has developed from a cheap bathroom crack that anyone can make for a quick laugh into a metaphysical joke with many levels of reality, a small but manifold poem of laughter.

The Clouds, *Denouement*

Such punning is the stuff of Aristophanes' thought. A pun is certainly at the center of the denouement of *The Clouds*. Twister has had a lot of trouble. It all started when he wanted to cheat his creditors, and so tried to persuade his son, Horsey, to enroll as a student in Socrates' think-tank, where one learns the Unjust Logic by which one can evade debts. Horsey refusing to enroll, Twister entered himself. He gets a short course of metaphysics, in which he is told that Zeus is no longer the controlling god, but that Dinos rules the heavens: Dinos—a whirling of air. He is given some useless grammar, but soon he is expelled as too stupid. Eventually Horsey is persuaded to enter instead and sees the contest of the two Logics, the Just and the Unjust, won, needless to say, by the Unjust. Twister having met his son, pale as an intellectual on completion of his course, acquires one piece of dubious logic with which he chases away the creditors. Father and son go in to a celebration dinner, while the chorus of clouds sing a song mocking the old man in advance (1303–20). "So he thinks he's cheated his creditors. Just you wait. He'll soon wish his son had not learnt to speak." Up to this moment we had thought that the clouds were Socrates' goddesses, patrons of the think-tank. Now we begin to wonder whose side they are on. As the song finishes Twister rushes out screaming, "Ow! Ow!" (1321). This, we remember, is one of the devices of crude comedy that Aristophanes has protested his plays do not contain (543). Horsey chases his father out, beating him up in a scene of crude slapstick. The clouds find out what happened and preside over a second *agōn*, in which Horsey proves conclusively to Twister that it is right to beat one's father, and is about to prove that it is right to beat one's mother also. Twister turns to the clouds accusingly. "Why did I put my affairs in your hands?" he asks (1452–53). The clouds, however, tell him that it is all his own fault (1454–55). Twister immediately acknowledges that they are right and tries to persuade Horsey to join him in destroying the think-tank, to reverence Zeus, not his teachers. Horsey replies that there is no Zeus. "Dinos reigns." (1471). Twister says that it was all his mistake. He goes to the central door of the *skēnē*. On one side of it there is a large earthenware jar, presumably a kind of trash can. The word *dinos* means both "jar" and "whirlwind." Twister now points to this *dinos* and exclaims what a fool he was to think that a pot was a god. Horsey merely replies, "Rave away" and takes no further part in the proceedings. We have now been made aware that the *dinos*, which we had thought was merely set dressing, has a part in the play. On the other side of the door is a herm, one of the fertility statues that every house had as its icon. Twister now bends down to it and whispers in its ear, asking for pardon for his wickedness and instructions as to what to do now. The swift result of this conversation is that he attacks the think-tank with torches, and the finale of the play is a confusion of bangings and fallings, waving flames and Socrates dismayed. The clouds leave chanting, "We've had a fair old dance today."

The end of *The Clouds* is fast and funny. It is also a moment of theatrical complexity. First there is the question as to the nature of the clouds. We had thought that they were symbols of the new religion, which defined the world in terms of physical forces—meteorology and astronomy—instead of the personal forces of the old Olympian gods. They seem to be spirits at the beck and call of Socrates, who in this play is shown as the leader and type of these new thinkers. We had enjoyed the joke of their entry, when Socrates invokes these impersonal forces as if they were personal gods, in the intense lyricism of the preliminaries to the *parodos* (263–74) and in the even more intense lyricism of their opening song (275–290, *strophe*; 299–313, *antistrophē*). But we now see that we were tricked. We thought Aristophanes was pulling our leg with a ritual invocation of impersonal forces. We noticed that they had personal masks, that they looked like girls, but we accepted the joke by which he accounted for these masks (344–55). Now, in the denouement, we see that they were personal goddesses after all, members of the pantheon about whom we did not know, a sort of mischievous nymph, as keen as any traditional god upon the fact that the gods must have their due. In the confrontation between them and Twister to which I have already referred (1452–61) they say what their function is:

> Whenever we see a man in love
> With wickedness, with wickedness,
> This is the way we always act,
> Always act, always act,
> Till—with a push—he's gone to the bad,
> Where he shall learn the fear of God.
>
> (1458–61)[38]

Traditional Greek religion had no limit on the number of its gods, and no definite theology. There was therefore nothing much to prevent a man adding new gods to the old ones. Throughout Aristophanes there is a delight with the joke of making those who invoke the new impersonal gods do so with all the old traditional, personal forms of worship.[39] This is part of the total joke of *The Clouds*, that not only are these new gods treated like old gods, but they also behave like old gods themselves.

A further element in the total topsy-turviness of the play is the character of Socrates. As we can see from the Platonic dialogues, Socrates was conspicuous for his traditional piety and his respect for the elements of traditional religion, such as oracles, sacrifices, libations, and so on. Certainly, Socrates was a "new thinker." But it may well be that the central joke of *The Clouds* is in making Socrates, who was famous for his piety, into an "atheist," just as it is Euripides, who was notable for his sympathy with the cause of women, who is characterized as the enemy of women in *The Women at the Thesmophoria*.

The paradox reaches its most acute in the confrontation with the herm outside Socrates' door. Socrates in the play speaks as a fashionable atheist. But outside his door he keeps a traditional phallic icon. This icon is made to tell

Twister to burn down its own house, the house whose protection is the icon's special duty. Would Socrates' house have been burnt down unless he had an icon at its door to tell Twister to do the burning? Therefore is Socrates being burnt for his piety or his impiety? Provided that our logic remains the logic of Humpty-Dumpty or the Mad Hatter, we are encouraged by Aristophanes to take off from this sequence into such a discussion. We will not, however, get any answers.

This sequence at the end of the play is a fitting climax. Implied in what we have been shown is a dialogue about religion, about different ways of analyzing phenomena, about the changing attitudes of Aristophanes' generation. This opposition between new and old is finally crystallized into an opposition between two objects: the trash can and the icon. The icon wins. But it has really been winning all the time. The spirits we thought were spirits of the trash can are really spirits of the icon; the man who invoked the spirits of the trash can possesses an icon, and in his invocation of these spirits of the trash can treats them exactly as spirits of the icon. That is the holy joke of the play: atheist Socrates, invoking the clouds as if they were goddesses, until the denouement of the play shows them to have been goddesses after all.

The Peace, *Presentation of Theoria to the Council*

Fifth-century drama was a fertility celebration with political content. The climax of *The Peace* presents these two elements in about as intense a counterpoint as anything we can find in any play from any period. It also provides a vivid example of what is on one level an extremely intense piece of political activity through poetry, and on another level a piece of the crudest erotic theater possible.

The Peace was performed at the City *Dionysia* in March 421. Negotiations for peace between Athens and Sparta were being discussed, but at the time of the production nothing definite had been concluded, though, later in the year, peace was indeed signed. The play is a celebration of the peace that Aristophanes could feel was in the air. It is often accused by critics of lacking conflict in comparison with Aristophanes' other plays; and this is certainly true. There is, however, the tension of strong conflict during the central passage about to be discussed, and this conflict has not been fully recognized, partly because it is such an overtly sexual sequence and modest critics have fought shy of explaining it in detail (856–921).

At this point in the play most of the action is over. Vintage has flown up to heaven on the back of his dung beetle and discovered where Peace is hidden in a cave. After a brief moment of fear at the appearance of War and Riot, Peace has been pulled out of her cave by the chorus of Attic farmers, and after a few digressions Vintage has returned to earth, while the chorus have presented the *parabasis* in praise of Aristophanes. The latter part of the play will be Vintage's feast of peace and victory, delayed by a few farcical interruptions and finally taking place in triumph.

Vintage has two companions as he returns from heaven, two lovely girls. One is called Opora and the other Theoria. Opora's name is straightforward: it means "harvest" and "ripeness." This girl, whom we see very scantily and provocatively clad, is to be Vintage's wife. Hermes tells him to "make love to her in the fields and beget bunches of grapes" (706–8). It is the same straightforward image of peace as sexual satisfaction that Aristophanes used in *The Acharnians.* The other girl is completely naked. *Theōria* is rightly translated "spectacle," but there are many more meanings in the name, and the whole sequence involving her is an elaborate pun. She is to be given to the Council of Athens.

What exactly would naming a naked girl Theoria suggest to the Athenian audience? It is worth summarizing the various meanings given in Liddell and Scott. *Theōria* is the act of sending state-selected ambassadors to consult an oracle or to attend festivals such as the Olympic games as representatives of their city. It is therefore the act of being a spectator at games or theater. It is also in quite general terms the act of seeing itself, and by extension the act of contemplation.[40] It is also used to mean "sight" or "spectacle." Her name therefore includes the sense of the embassy and therefore reminds us of the embassy that Aristophanes hopes will soon be sent to Sparta; it includes the sense that we are watching a show in the theater; it also includes the sense of seeing, vision. Should we translate her name as "Miss Embassy Open-youreyes"?

The sequence is in effect remarkably straightforward. But until very recently Western theater has seen nothing like it for flamboyant eroticism. The sequence consists of a system of song and dance for Vintage, Theoria, and the chorus with an episode in between *strophē* and *antistrophē* (856–67, *strophē;* 868–909, episode; 910–21, *antistrophē*). Before the *strophē* Opora has been taken inside to be bathed and got ready for her wedding with Vintage. During the system Vintage dances an erotic dance with Theoria, ending with a simulation of the sexual act. During the episode he uses her to rouse the Council members, sitting in their front-row seats, to such a pitch of erotic excitement that one of their number is starting actually to make love to the beautiful naked girl in his seat. At that moment Vintage snatches her away and performs the *antistrophē* of the dance, at the end of which the girl runs into the *skēnē* and disappears.[41]

It is worth comparing the basic pattern of the *strophē* and *antistrophē*. The following tabular summary may help to make this clear:

	STROPHĒ (856–67)	ANTISTROPHĒ (910–21)
1–3	Chorus Lucky you.	Chorus Lucky you. Well done.
4	Vintage What about when I'm wed.	Vintage When you're harvesting your grapes you'll know how well I've done.
5–7	Chorus Old man you're young again.	Chorus Well you've certainly saved us.

8	Vintage
	Wow! What about when I grab hold
	    of her tits.
		Vintage
		What about when you're drinking
		    the new wine.

9	Chorus You'll be happier than a pirouette dancer.	Chorus We think you're the greatest.
10–15	Vintage	Vintage
10–11	How right I was to ride the beetle	I'm a fine fellow
12–14	Saving Greece so that in the fields you all	for freeing you all from troubles
15	can fuck and sleep.	and doing down Hyperbolus.

There is surely only one possible choreographic plot for such a dance. The chorus must dance round Vintage, who is in the middle with Theoria. Vintage must preen himself with growing sexual excitement. Line 8 in the strophē obviously suggests that his hand is on the girl's breasts. Such an action fits so obviously with the sense of fertility in the equivalent line in the antistrophē about drinking the new wine. Line 9 suggests that Vintage's movements are becoming even more excited. The last five lines inevitably point to a simulation of the sex act. Vintage must ride the girl as he rode the beetle, and the dance must end with them both falling down together as if exhausted. This movement will fit with the words of generalized triumph in the antistrophē. Well may Vintage claim to be a fine fellow while riding such a beautiful girl. The movement in the last line, which represented orgasm in the strophē, now represents the wrestling with and overcoming of the warmongering politician Hyperbolus.

The intervening episode is almost entirely erotic in feeling. It begins as Vintage's slave comes out to say that Opora is ready. "The girl's had a bath. All's fine round her fanny. The cakes are baked. All we need now is a cock" (868–70). Vintage, however, says that they must take Theoria to the Council. The following scene starts to define her character and the pun that is her character. Up to this moment she has just been a sexy naked girl. "Is this Theoria?" says the slave. "Why, we made her all the way to Brauron. We were stoned out of our minds" (874). The slave goes on to say that she "has the buttocks of a five-year-old," presumably slapping them (876). Brauron is a village of Attica noted for a five-yearly festival of Artemis, presumably a fertility festival and therefore one much looked forward to as the five-year cycle draws to its close. A village festival may well not have taken place during the war, when rural Attica was overrun by the Spartans. Theoria's name now identifies her with the goddess of fertility, and with the act of attending the festival, which was no doubt an excuse for sexual indulgence. Vintage then notices that the slave is touching the girl up. He shouts at him a word with multiple meaning: *perigraphō*. This can mean "draw" or "bring to an end" or "cure a disease."[42] The disease the slave would be trying to cure as quickly as possible would be that of sexual abstinence. He answers, however, to the meaning of "draw." "I'm marking out a tent for my cock to grab at the Isthmian games." With this the meaning of *theōria* as an embassy is introduced. The Isthmian games are mentioned, because, for obvious reasons, an isthmus can also mean a woman's private parts. Vintage reacts by taking the girl away from the servant and leading her down to the front of the *orchestra* by the front-row seats reserved for the Council. "Lay your vessel on the ground," he tells her (886). He then invites the Council to look at her, while he gets her to demonstrate her sexiness. He describes her as if she were a festival of athletics. But each competition mentioned refers to a different position for the sex act, each of which she demonstrates. The climax is approached in terms of the horse race, the word also referring to the position for intercourse in which the girl rides the man, and the final description is in terms of charioteers fallen at the bends (905). Vintage then raises the panting and sweating girl, and leads her actually into the front row. "Receive her, Councillors," he says (906) and goes on to remark at one councillor's enthusiasm, who presumably is now holding on to her, ready for action.

The last two lines of the speech are full of pun and multiple meaning (908–9). They must provide the climactic joke. Laughter will have built up during the preceding speech. But it will have been the laughter of nervous excitement since there could not be any man in the audience who was not being considerably stimulated sexually by Vintage's words and the girl's actions. The end of the speech must be a punch line, which will relieve the audience's sexual tension with a guffaw.

The first word with multiple meaning could be translated by "for nothing, freely." But the word also refers to a marriage portion. The accompanying verb has several rather general meanings, and also contains the meanings of introducing a proposal and making advances to a woman. The last line ends with a word that can mean "hand-out," that is, "allowance" or "bribe," but it can also mean "abstinence." The verb in the last line can mean to hold out in the literal sense and also, as in English, to endure. The last line therefore refers both to the councillor's holding out his hand for his allowance, which he would draw as he went on the embassy to treat for peace, and to his having to endure sexual abstinence; and it presumably also refers to his putting out his hand for his bribe, that is, for the girl. The two lines are full of contradictions. To translate them is impossible. But their reference is absolutely clear. The Council are not going to be allowed to enjoy the girl, because she is not for grabs—or not yet at any rate. First they must organize themselves into a *theōria*, go to Sparta, and treat for peace. The punch line of the speech is a joke at the politician's expense. The gesture implied in the speech's ending is of course very clear. Vintage grabs the girl back from the rampant councillor, and the audience roar with laughter at his discomfiture, as Vintage starts to dance the *antistrophē*.

This, then, is the climax of *The Peace*, a moment thoroughly appropriate to a festival of eroticism, and yet a moment in which the poet plays very active politics. Aristophanes quite deliberately arouses the audience, especially the Council members in the front row, with an extensive flaunting of the lovely girl's full sexual equipment. A councillor is actually invited to make love in the theater, in full view of everyone. If the production had only a small fraction of the power of the language, there must have been many councillors ready to oblige without any hesitation. At that moment Aristophanes whisks the girl away. You're not ready, he says. You haven't even sent off your peace embassy. Pass that resolution, and then make love. She is only for those who remember her name, Miss Embassy Openyoureyes. Open your eyes, and act, and you shall have her. Perhaps this is what caused the play to be voted only second. The jury could not endure the sexual frustration. They sat in the front rows too.

The Birds, *Finale*

The Birds is encapsulated in its last line. Persuader, the Athenian confidence trickster is hailed by the chorus of birds as "highest of gods" in a mock paean. Athenian man has outwitted the gods at all points. Its representative stands with his arms round Majesty, the girl who used to be the mistress of Zeus himself.

What is the meaning of this finale? First, there is no doubt that we are sent out of the theater with our spirits raised. The finale is undoubtedly a triumph, an exuberant fling. We enjoy Persuader's victory. But although he is a loveable rogue, he is less at the heart of this play than, for example, Just-City is at the heart of *The Acharnians*. Persuader has no beautiful songs to sing. The lack of lyric intensity is a sure sign that we are not to identify with him as closely as with some of Aristophanes' principal characters, especially as *The Birds* is Aristophanes' most lyrical play, with the most beautiful songs.

The story of *The Birds* is easily summarized. Persuader and his friend Optimist (Euelpides) set off from Athens to find a new life with the birds. As soon as they have been accepted, they found a city and cut off all sacrifices from going up to heaven from earth. Accordingly the gods are starved into submission. After an ineffectual effort by Iris, the messenger god, which ends with her narrowly escaping rape by Persuader, there is a major embassy of Poseidon,

Heracles, and a gibberish-speaking god from the barbarous north. Heracles' gluttony quickly causes the embassy to capitulate to Persuader's terms, which are that he should be recognized as supreme, and enjoy Zeus' mistress.

Persuader behaves as the typical colonialist, exploiting the subject peoples. Having persuaded the birds to accept him, he then takes complete command. The great songs of the play are given to the bird chorus, and to the Hoopoe, the pathetic, bedraggled king of the birds, who is dispossessed by Persuader and disappears half way through the play. Aristophanes' sympathy is clearly shown by his lyrical intensity. It is with the underdog. We must remember the lost play, *The Babylonians*, for which Aristophanes was prosecuted because he showed the subject allies as the slaves of Athens. Persuader behaves to the Hoopoe just as an Athenian general might behave to a weak state that he was "putting under the protection of Athens."

The play was produced less than a year after the expedition to Sicily had left Athens on the most grandiose and nakedly imperialist act of invasion that Athens had ever undertaken. Persuader is very obviously a comic poet's version of the rough diamond who wins empires for the folks at home, adventurous, resourceful, none too scrupulous. There is a very strong allusion to Athenian aggressive imperialism. As they plan to starve the gods out, Persuader refers to them suffering from "Melian hunger" (186). At this reference the laughs would have stopped abruptly, and there must have been a deadly silence in the theater. For, just over a year before, there had been the unprovoked invasion of Melos, followed by the massacre of all the men. It was the worst Athenian atrocity of the war, and the Athenians, who had changed their minds and sent out, too late, a ship to countermand the massacre order, would not like to be reminded of it. It is possible after all that *The Birds* failed to win first prize for political reasons.

The other topic of conversation for the year previous to *The Birds*' production was the mutilation of the herms, the household fertility icons with erect penises. We should notice that the play refers to stopping the gods' power in very strongly sexual terms. For example Persuader tells the birds (557–60): "Don't let these gods go through your territory in a state of erection, looking for mortal girls to commit adultery with. Put a seal on their cocks, so they can't fuck."[43] It is important that the preliminary climax of the play is the very crude sexual assault on Iris. Persuader thrusts his phallus at her and chases her off, shouting exultantly, "I've got a hard like the prow of three warships." (1256). The tables are beginning to turn; now, the mortal is after the immortal girl, instead of the other way round. It is significant that the final image of Persuader's triumph is that he will enjoy the object of Zeus' sexual enjoyment.

So the play is about imperialism and blasphemy. But the blasphemy at one level need not be taken too seriously. To sing that Persuader is "highest of gods" is not fully blasphemous because it is an impossibility. Two small examples demonstrate that Aristophanes wanted us to realize this too. In the scene with Iris, Persuader tells her that she deserves death for her daring. "But I'm immortal," she replies. "All the more reason for you to die," he counters (1223–24). A little further on, Persuader says: "Birds are the gods now. Men must sacrifice to birds. Not to Zeus, by Zeus" (1236–37). His action and his final triumph are ridiculous, because impossible. The impossibility is more central to *The Birds* than it is to the other plays. We accept the impossibility of Just-City's private peace or Vintage's flight to heaven on the dung beetle as part of the play's reality. But with *The Birds* it is almost as if Persuader was performing a logical impossibility like making square circles. In this play we are to be aware the whole time of the impossibility, instead of losing the impossibility in a make-believe where all things are possible. Here the impossibility of the action is part of the fun of the action.

Fundamental to the point of the play is the scene immediately preceding that of the embassy of the three gods (1494–1552). Persuader is visited by a strange creature, very frightened and wrapped up in a number of blankets. When the blankets are taken off, we are told that this is Prometheus. But instead of the archetypal heroic being, the Titan who braved the wrath of Zeus, the tough representative of humanity who dared defy the gods, the equivalent in actual myth to Persuader, we see a wildly farcical figure in drag, gossiping campily about troubles in heaven, and so terrified of Zeus catching a glimpse of him that he leaves the stage hiding under a parasol so that he can be mistaken for the basket-bearer girl in the festival procession. There are British camp comics working now who can reduce their audience to hysterics simply by saying: "Look at me—Butch." In Greek mythology Prometheus is the most butch character of all. Here he is presented as the extreme of camp. A very funny scene, but also a very necessary part of the general topsy-turviness. Persuader's Promethean act must be seen in conjunction with a Prometheus who is the total opposite of everything Promethean. It is a sign just before the finale that the finale should be taken turned upside down. The *Birds, Frogs,* and *Women at the Thesmophoria* contain most of Aristophanes' most beautiful lyric poetry. They are also the plays whose totality is the most complex topsy-turviness. These two things should be seen as inextricably linked. This is very much what is meant by saying that Aristophanes is a great and complex poet.

The Women at the Thesmophoria, *Denouement*

I have said that the pun is at the heart of Aristophanes' laughter-poetry, and that for him pun is a kind of metaphysic, in which language mirrors the world as it was to do for Wittgenstein and the Logical Atomists. Parody, then, is a kind of subspecies of the general pun. Of all plays ever written, *The Women at the Thesmophoria* seems to take parody farthest into its function as a general metaphysic of topsy-turviness. At the time when this play was written, the philosophers were beginning to enquire into categories of meaning and truth, and it was natural that theatrical reality should provide topics for discussion. Plays like the *Helen* and the *Ion* start to pose the question as to what is theatrical reality, what is the life that takes place on the stage and ceases when the play is over. If theatrical life is real, then the poet is truly a *daimon*, a creating spirit, superhuman. For Aristophanes the question of the poet as superhuman, and the question of theatrical reality, come together as we consider parody, which is the extreme example of a reality purely theatrical, which has no reality outside the theater.

Given what we possess of the dialogues of Xenophon and Plato, it is very easy to imagine these kinds of topics being discussed with wit and seriousness at the drinking parties in Athens during the last twenty years of the fifth century. As the political situation became worse and worse, it was natural that the poets should have turned inward to consider the nature of their own art independently of its effect on society. The two plays in which these kinds of speculations are crystallized are *The Women at the Thesmophoria* and *The Frogs*. But of course we must not expect philosophy; we are given Aristophanes' best pun and parody and most complex topsy-turviness.

The paradox of *The Women at the Thesmophoria* is easy to describe. Its implications reverberate almost without limit. Euripides has persuaded his cousin Mnesilochus to dress up as a woman and attend the *Thesmophoria*, the solemn festival of fast, to which only women may go. Mnesilochus has been caught, and the second half of the play, after the *parabasis*, will consist of his attempted and finally successful rescue by Euripides. In the first scene (846–927) Mnesilochus "plays" Helen, and Euripides enters as Menelaus. The scene contains many lines of dialogue directly lifted from Euripides' own play, produced the year before. During this scene Mnesilochus' guard has been one of the women. But she is replaced by a Scythian guard, type of the uncouth barbarian and of course very obviously male. Mnesilochus is taken inside by the guard, and a long dance for the chorus follows, an invocation very much of the festival. Instead of the first system, there are three short identical stanzas, exactly as in the traditional hymns. Apollo, Artemis, Pan, Hermes, the Nymphs, and finally Dionysus are invoked to join and bless the festival of fasting (947–1000).

At the end of the dance, Mnesilochus is revealed on the *ekkyklema*, tied to a wooden structure representing a rock.[44] Mnesilochus now represents Andromeda and the ensuing scene is obviously a close parody of Euripides' *Andromeda*, probably produced with the *Helen* the year before, and a popular success. Euripides flies in on the *mēchanē* as Perseus. Mnesilochus then sings Andromeda's lament and is answered by Euripides, now playing Echo, with whom Andromeda has a sad dialogue. No doubt Euripides swung in and out on the *mēchanē*, and the scene with an echo has obvious comic possibilities as the stupid guard is bamboozled by the voice that comes from nowhere. Euripides then comes on as Perseus (1098), perhaps simply putting on a special Perseus helmet, and the scene continues as parody of the Andromeda-Perseus scene from the Euripides play. Perseus-Euripides achieves nothing, however, and goes out again, while the chorus dance an invocation, this time to the goddesses: to Athene, to the nameless ones, and to the two special goddesses of women, patrons of the festival, Demeter and Persephone, though these also are not named openly (1136–59). As this ode ends, Euripides appears as an old woman, and peace is concluded between him and the chorus in eleven lines. There is no triumphant finale as in *The Birds*. The last scene of the play is the seduction of the Scythian by a girl who comes on with Euripides. She "practices her dance," then takes off her clothes and sits on the Scythian's knee as the music plays faster (1181–88), all on the instructions of Euripides, now acting the old crone bawd, the madam of a brothel. The Scythian is beside himself; Euripides takes the girl away, then offers her to the Scythian, who goes to fetch his money. While he is gone, Euripides frees Mnesilochus, and the play ends with a slapstick chase as the Scythian tries to catch the naked girl while the chorus send him in the wrong direction and march quickly out themselves.

The main problem is the very abrupt truce between Euripides and the women of the chorus. I believe very firmly that this entrance of Euripides, dressed as the old madam, was also on the *mēchanē*. When Euripides left at the end of the *Helen* scene he said that he possessed many *mēchanai* (927). Admittedly this has metaphorical meaning: many tricks. But Aristophanes would always intend to suggest both the strictly physical and the metaphorical meanings. I therefore conclude that Euripides must make more than one entry on possibly different kinds of *mēchanē* during this part of the play.

If on the *mēchanē*, then Euripides' entry as the old madam (1160) is a parody of the Euripidean fondness for bringing on a god at the end of his plays in the *mēchanē*, and tying the ends of the story up very quickly. It could be very funny indeed if he spoke his speech very fast, in an obvious parody of all "neat" endings that tie up complicated plots. If this entry is on the *mēchanē*, then he will have to leave it eleven lines later, after the bargain with the chorus, and before starting to organize the seduction of the Scythian (1171). This will be possible if he appears in some kind of god-chariot, out of which he can step easily once it is on the ground. If he does enter as an old woman but in a god-chariot swung on by the *mēchanē*, then this entry will be his most theatrical of all and will therefore suitably top all that has gone before.

The play then presents an image of the poet attempting to influence events through his poetry, and failing. When he appears in his own person, he is god, and immediately achieves what he wants. But because things are upside down in Aristophanes, his entry in his own person is an entry as a woman. The poet is able to achieve anything with his audience only by becoming one of them. Furthermore, women are the weakest of humans, and old women are weaker than young women. The poet must become weaker than the weak in order to achieve his end, and be a god who can tie up a story.

The image is further complicated in its topsy-turviness. Euripides is the poet who did most for the cause of women, and his poetry is most full of sympathy for their weakness. Is it merely Aristophanes' sense of paradox that makes it Euripides who is attacked by the women, a simple topsy-turviness—Euripides the woman-lover shown as the woman-hater? Or is Aristophanes also saying that in life it is often the people who love and exercise sympathy who receive hatred in return, and that as often as not a poet's words are taken in exactly the opposite sense to what he had intended? Euripides after all was abused for having given Hippolytus the famous line: "My tongue swore; my heart remained unsworn" (*Hippolytus* 612). The line was taken as if Euripides had uttered approval of perjury, but the play showed Hippolytus as a man who died rather than break that particular oath, and so the total poetry meant exactly the opposite to the catchphrase. Both meanings are part of the total meaning of *The Women at the Thesmophoria.*

We now no longer know the full implications of the *Thesmophoria.* There may be some sense of paradox in the festival itself. For it is a festival of fast, and that is in itself a paradox. At any rate one implication is obvious. The festival to which men are not admitted is the moment of the year in which women have power. And the play is about the mysterious power of women, without whom men can achieve nothing. The last two *stasima* of the play are clearly very important (947–1000; 1136–59). For these are full invocations of the gods in a part of the play where normally the *stasima* are light-hearted, sometimes little more than revue songs. It is important that the first invocation to the gods achieves nothing. It is only the second invocation to the goddesses that immediately brings on Euripides as old woman-god in the *mēchanē.* Nothing is achieved except by the female.

The last scene stresses as crudely as possible the power of woman over man. The tough, rough, masculine Scythian is rendered helpless by a pretty stripper. A woman who excites a man, and then refuses to let him consummate, has that man at her feet. The greatest powers are tamed by sex: it is a thought that occurs continually in Greek literature. In this play, as in the *Lysistrata,* Aristophanes has gone further and suggested that women could use their power for political ends. The women of Athens did not make use of his suggestion, which has not ever been followed until the present day and the age of women's lib. *The Women at the Thesmophoria* makes sense in Aristophanes' terms because it is an impossibility for his age that women should use their power. The paradox of the play depends on the practical impossibility of Athenian women seizing power. But nevertheless Aristophanes' impossible paradox has very real political implications.

So on the one hand, the play is an exercise of delight in the odd and crazy reality of the stage as stage, using parody as the central aspect of that odd reality. On the other, it is an image of what is to be a poet and to try and achieve some end through poetry. As such its implications are explored further in *The Frogs.* But if such an analysis has given a somewhat portentous feel to this feather-light poem of fun, then let us take note of its ending. I am prepared to hazard that, in all literatures the world has ever known, there will not be found another poet who is able to give his audience in one hundred fifty lines only, without the slightest sense of incongruity or overabrupt transition, the intricate details of literary parody, a devout dance of prayer to nameless female spirits, and a naked girl being chased all over stage.

Notes

1. E.g., Richmond Lattimore, *The Poetry of Greek Tragedy* (Baltimore: Johns Hopkins University Press, 1958).

2. Gabriel Germain, *Sophocle* (Paris: Éditions du Seuil, 1969); Quintino Cataudella, *La Poesia di Aristofane* (Bari: Gius. Laterza & Figli, 1934).

3. It is in this spirit that I have dared to question the near omniscient scholarship of Pickard-Cambridge in such matters as the fundamental unity of the *Anthesteria* as a drunken revel and an All Souls' Day (see note 8 to Chapter 3), or the natural connection of the dance of the fertility spirits with the religious seriousness of tragedy (see Chapter 3, "The Beginnings of Greek Drama").

It is in this same spirit that I would dare to question even the accuracy of some of Jebb's translation of Sophocles. His scholarly mind insists on reproducing words and phrases which in Sophocles have multiple significance with an English translation including all the meanings but lacking the reverberations of the Greek. In certain lyrics especially this can be very misleading.

4. Cratinus frag. 15.

5. 2d *Hypothesis* to the play.

6. 1st *Hypothesis* to the play.

7. See Appendix 6.

8. *Birds*, hymn from the *parabasis*, 748–50. The complete hymn, lines 737–51, and 769–83. These two lines are taken from a translation in slightly freer style than the ones in this book, and published in a collection of poetry: Leo Aylen, *I, Odysseus* (London: Sidgwick & Jackson, 1971), p. 49.

9. See D. L. Page, *A New Chapter in the History of Greek Tragedy* (London: Cambridge University Press, 1951). My account merely summarizes Page's.

10. See Herodotus *Histories* 1. 8–13. The arguments for this identity are set out in Page, *A New Chapter in the History of Greek Tragedy.*

11. E.g., *Phrygians, Egyptians, Thracians, Carians, Mysians, Lydians.*

12. We might allow ourselves the speculation that the author of this trilogy was Phrynichus.

13. In *The Acharnians*, line 186ff., Just-City has ordered samples of peace treaties with Sparta. These are now brought to him. The word for a peace treaty means "libations," because libations were poured as a ritual act at the signing of such a treaty. Just-City samples each type of treaty as if at a wine-tasting. This pun, however, is not the complete joke. It is not only the presentation of the abstraction of the peace treaty as a concrete mouthful of wine. It is that Just-City is drinking what should be poured out on the ground. This pun's central paradox is untranslateable.

14. Scholars do argue as to whether the chorus was really fifty. Dithyrambic choruses were fifty, so that Aeschylus would have had some precedent. Also, the size of the chorus presumably depended on the purse of the *choregos*. By 463, Athens had become very prosperous, and Aeschylus had become very famous. I do not think it is inconceivable that there should have been a *choregos* willing and able to pay the very large bill that production of this tetralogy would have involved.

Ultimately, we must choose between probabilities. Would the Athenian audience have accepted a chorus of twelve people representing fifty? I conclude myself that they would not, and that therefore Aeschylus was able at this time to ask for and obtain a very, very large production budget.

15. For more detailed discussion, see Leo Aylen, *Greek Tragedy and the Modern World* (London: Methuen, 1964), pp. 51–56; Leo Aylen, "The Vulgarity of Tragedy," in *Classical Drama and Its Influence,* ed. M. J. Anderson (London: Methuen, 1965).

16. Theologically, with this play, Aeschylus is looking beyond his polytheism to a single controller of phenomena. It seems best here to translate "Zeus" by "God."

17. Psalm 139:2, 6–9 (Version taken from *The Book of Common Prayer.*)

18. Aeschylus apparently delighted in the theatrical trick of bringing a character on stage who would then remain silent for a long time. The character's first words would naturally cause surprise in the audience, who by this time would have assumed that the role was being taken by a mute. His

most famous use of this trick was apparently in the lost play about Niobe, with the character of Niobe herself. This is satirized by Aristophanes in *The Frogs* 912–13.

19. Bertholt Brecht, *The Caucasian Chalk Circle*, 2.5. The play has been translated into English by James and Tania Stern with W. H. Auden. See Bertholt Brecht, *Plays*, vol. 1 (London: Methuen, 1960), pp. 75–76.

20. *Aeschylus, with an English Translation by Herbert Weir Smyth*, vol. 1, Loeb Classical Library, (London: William Heinemann; New York; G. P. Putnam's Sons, 1922), p. 105. See Aylen, *Greek Tragedy and the Modern World*, p. 54.

21. The lyric in which the Furies change direction is translated and discussed later in this section.

22. Sir Richard Livingstone, "The Problem of the Eumenides of Aeschylus," *Journal of Hellenic Studies* 45 (1925); 123–24.

23. The name *Eumenides*—"Kindly Ones"—is the normal euphemism for "Furies," an exactly equivalent euphemism to calling the fairies "the Good People."

24. Rainer Maria Rilke, *Duino Elegies*, trans. J. B. Leishman and Stephen Spender (London: The Hogarth Press, 1952), 1.4–7:

> For Beauty's nothing
> but beginning of Terror we're still just able to bear,
> and why we adore it so is because it serenely
> disdains to destroy us.

25. I do not propose to waste words justifying my mise en scène for this sequence, since it seems to involve such basic use of the space available that any other groupings and movements are frankly inconceivable. The interpretation of Aeschylus' climax, however, is not affected by the way in which it is staged, since this interpretation does not depend on movement patterns. I have included a description of the movement patterns only to help a reader visualize the scene.

26. The only conceivable movement during this system can be a fanning out in order to embrace the whole audience. Perhaps for the whole of this three-system sequence the movement in *strophē* and *antistrophē* is identical in direction as well as gesture, just as it was in the two previous systems of rage, when the words of *strophē* and *antistrophē* were identical.

27. Athene's chant is not in matching stanzas. The translation of lines 927–37 is reproduced from Aylen, *Greek Tragedy and the Modern World*, p. 61.

28. Also contained in the chorus, 490–565, is direct political reference. Four years before, the *Areopagus* had been deprived of its powers except as supreme court. Aeschylus clearly approved of this triumph for the radical movement. But, since the reforms, there had been political violence, of which the killing of Ephialtes was only the most conspicuous example. There are indications in this chorus that Aeschylus is saying, "Enough is enough; do not go too far." But for us now, the specific political point is absorbed by the wider moral and religious one.

For further discussion see Antony J. Podlecki, *The Political Background of Aeschylean Tragedy*, (Ann Arbor: University of Michigan Press, 1966), pp. 80–100.

29. Scholars will continue to argue about this staging. The *ekkyklema* must have been used early in the play at the moment when we see Ajax surrounded by the slaughtered beasts, most probably after the chorus's call to "open" at line 344. Without the *ekkyklema*, it is difficult to explain the sudden appearance of Ajax at line 815 with an obvious implication that the scene has changed. If Ajax appears on the *ekkyklema*, but with some indication of exterior setting also on the platform with him, then there is no difficulty. Equally, the entrance of the two semichoruses after Ajax' death would be very awkward if his body were visible. But for Ajax to walk back inside the *skēnē* at the end of his death speech (865) seems quite wrong. The whole point about Ajax' suicide is that it is in the open, away from his hut. If he had stayed inside he would have been safe (see lines 752–57).

Next, there is the question as to whether the actor performed the suicide on stage. Arnott discusses the evidence. See Peter Arnott, *Greek Scenic Conventions in the Fifth Century B.C.* (Oxford: Clarendon Press, 1962), Appendix 2 "The Suicide of Ajax," pp. 131–33, and Appendix 3, "Death on the Stage," pp. 134–138. Arnott, however, reaches the opposite conclusion to mine. There are three main pieces of evidence. First, the scholiast on the beginning of the suicide speech (815ff.) says that events such as this were rare on the old stage and usually reported by messengers, and therefore implies that he thought the death was actually staged. Second, the scholiast on line 864 also refers to an actual falling on the sword, but implies that it took a powerful actor to carry the audience with him for such a moment. Third, we learn from Plutarch, *On the Eating of Flesh*,

2.5.998E, that in Euripides' *Kresphontes,* Merope was threatening her son with an axe, and the audience was terrified lest help should not arrive in time and she should actually kill him. These seem to show that death on stage did sometimes occur. The context of the *Ajax* does require his suicide, and that it should take place in the open air. I see no need therefore to attempt to explain away this death onstage.

30. See Aylen, *Greek Tragedy and the Modern World,* pp. 79–84, for further discussion, where the above translation is quoted on p. 81.

31. This sequence is also discussed in Chapter 4, "Music."

32. This passage is reproduced from Leo Aylen, *I, Odysseus* (London: Sidgwick & Jackson, 1971), pp. 56–57.

33. The story is told by Aulus Gellius, *Noctium Atticarum,* 7.5. Polus flourished in the latter part of the fourth century, lived to a ripe old age when he acted eight tragedies in four days. He was equally famous for his portrayals of Oedipus as the king, and as the poor beggar of *Oedipus at Colonus.* For details of the evidence, see R. C. Jebb, trans., *Sophocles: The Plays and Fragments* (Cambridge: Cambridge University Press, 1883–96), *Oedipus Tyrannus,* p. xxxi.

34. I include myself among these critics. Though the play is not central to the subject discussed in my *Greek Tragedy and the Modern World* and I had therefore reason for ignoring it, at the time of writing that book I had certainly not understood what an important play the *Orestes* is.

35. P. de Saint-Victor, *Les Deux Masques,* tome 1 (Paris: 1882), p. 520. "Aristophanes is the magician of his language; he draws out unheard-of harmonies, metaphors that should be translated by arabesques. He makes his words fight, as the young Athenians of his day made their cocks and quails fight. . . . A thousand images jostle each other in a disorder that is magical." The passage is quoted by Taillardat as an opening to his book: Jean Taillardat, *Les Images d'Aristophane* (Paris: Societé d'Édition "Les Belles Lettres," 1965). Taillardat analyzes every image in Aristophanes. Necessarily somewhat pedantic, it is an invaluable book by which to understand that at the center of Aristophanes' great theatrical craft was a total command of every aspect of language.

36. See Appendix 2 for translation of Aristophanes' character names.

37. Translated and discussed in Chapter 3, "Drama for the God of the Theater."

38. These repetitions are not in the Greek. They seem, however, to fit with the tone of this revelation of the clouds as mischievous spirits. Having done this translation, I looked at Rogers's version and noticed that he had had the same instinct. Benjamin Bickley Rogers, trans., *Aristophanes,* vol. 1, Loeb Classical Library (London: William Heinemann; Cambridge: Harvard University Press, 1924), p. 397. In the middle of the blank verse that he uses normally to translate Aristophanes' dialogue verse, he interposes a four-line ballad jingle. The Greek, however, could be translated:

> This is the way we act, as soon
> As we know a man is in love with evil,
> Until we cast him down to Hell,
> Where he shall learn the fear of God.

(1458–61)

This could be the speech of a Fury, straight out of tragedy. Whichever is the best translation of the poetry's tone, there is no doubt that this is a moment for truth to be revealed. Suddenly we see that the clouds are indeed spirits of power.

39. E.g., see Euripides in *The Frogs* 892–94.

40. The first example of *theōria* meaning "contemplation" that we possess occurs in Plato. It is possible therefore that Aristophanes and his audience did not include this meaning. See Henry George Liddell and Robert Scott, *A Greek-English Lexicon,* rev. Henry Stuart Jones (Oxford: Clarendon Press, 1940), *theōria,* 3.2.

41. Such a mise en scène may provoke argument. I base this staging on the fact that Opora is taken into the *skēnē* at line 855 for her bath. Theoria stays onstage as the dance starts. Now, no director could leave a naked girl standing onstage, and carry on as if nothing was happening. If she stood still she would be the focus of attention, distracting us from any antics Vintage might be performing in the dance. Therefore she must take part in the dance. Therefore, at the end of the episode, she must be whisked away from the councillor's seat in order to take part in the *antistrophē,* which must match the *strophē* in movement.

Furthermore, if she does not take part in the dance, what does she do at the end of the episode? She can hardly stay naked in the councillor's seat. Apart from the fact that, even in Greece, March is too cold to be naked for long, can we imagine Aristophanes allowing the distraction of a naked girl and a sexually aroused politician in the front seat of the theater for the rest of his play?

42. See Liddell and Scott, *A Greek-English Lexicon, perigraphō*. The medical meaning occurs only in late medical writers. But the only medical writing we possess is late. There is no reason why it should not have been part of the conversational meaning of the word in the fifth century. Unfortunately we possess no fifth-century colloquial writing except Aristophanes.

43. I am not exaggerating the Athenians' preoccupation with the herms. Even four years later this was a topic of conversation. See *Lysistrata* 1093–94. The sex-starved men are being warned to wear cloaks, and cover up their erections in case "the Hermchoppers see them." These icons were fertility spirits; the penis was the center of attention.

44. The word *sanis* is often translated "plank," and it is therefore sometimes suggested that Mnesilochus is merely bound to an upright plank or post, and that therefore he could have walked out with it on his back. See Arnott, *Greek Scenic Conventions in the Fifth Century B.C.*, pp. 97–98. This problem of staging is the same as that of Prometheus' rock in the *Prometheus Bound* and is discussed in greater detail in Chapter 8.

8

THREE PLAYS

Aeschylus: *Prometheus Bound*

If the *Oresteia* is the climax and the crowning glory of fifth-century drama, and the figure of Oedipus symbol of its strangeness, the figure of Prometheus has dominated the minds of Western man for centuries. For Prometheus seems to stand for all that the West admires, arrogant and restless curiosity, the spirit of discovery and adventure. For those generations before us who have treated man's scientific ambitions as a right and his increasing dominance over nature as progress, the *Prometheus Bound* has always appeared an unbalanced play. How dare Zeus bind Prometheus to a rock in the Caucasus. Our generation, confronting as a serious possibility the destruction of the world by Western man's Promethean spirit, can accept more easily what Aeschylus has set before us.

Almost certainly the *Prometheus* plays were the last that Aeschylus wrote, very shortly before he died. They were therefore written in Sicily, and it is most likely that they were produced at Gela, which had been governed by a tyrant but had recently become a democracy.[1] We possess some fragments from the sequel play, the *Prometheus Unbound,* but nothing else, except for the title of a play *Prometheus the Fire-Bearer.* All attempts to reconstruct a trilogy or tetralogy have left serious problems unsolved. I now wonder if we need make the attempt. If the play was produced at Gela, four plays, as required by the Athenian festival, may not have been necessary. We may presume also that if the greatest poet of the Greek world, on a visit to a relatively unimportant city in an area still felt to be colonial, offered to produce one of his latest plays, the authorities would be so delighted that they would waive any rules they might normally enforce. I am therefore now inclined to believe that what Aeschylus produced at Gela in 457 B.C. was a pair of linked plays, *Prometheus Bound* and *Prometheus Unbound,* only, and that the title *Prometheus the Fire-Bearer* applies to another work altogether, possibly the satyr play produced with *The Persians* and called *Prometheus the Fire-Kindler.* I shall therefore discuss the *Prometheus Bound* as being the first half of a pair of plays, of which we know more or less the complete outline.[2]

There would have been another important consequence of the *Prometheus* having been written for Gela; the standard of dancing would have been much lower than that in Athens. Scholars have suggested that Aeschylus failed to finish his choruses and that they were finished by his sons. I think we can see that the choruses fit perfectly into his scheme of dance drama, but that the scheme is boldly straightforward, much less complicated than that of the *Oresteia*. Aeschylus, the greatest choreographer of the time, cut his coat according to the cloth.

The action of the *Prometheus* is simple. Prometheus stole fire from the gods and gave it to mortals. For this usurpation of the gods' privileges, he is chained to a rock in the wildest part of Scythia. He still remains defiant, however, proclaiming that he has a secret that will be the eventual downfall of Zeus. For this defiance, at the end of the play he is destroyed in a cataclysm. The events of the *Prometheus Unbound* can be reconstructed from the fragments. Prometheus is now chained to a rock in the Caucasus. Thousands of years have passed, and the chorus of Titans who have been imprisoned by Zeus are freed. They come to visit Prometheus, who also longs to be freed from his pain. The cast list includes the goddess Earth, mother of Prometheus, and it may be she who persuades Prometheus to give up the secret, which must now seem pointless to keep. Heracles then arrives and shoots the eagle torturing Prometheus. The play ends in reconciliation, and it is suggested that there is some presentation or at any rate reference to the feast of the *Prometheia*, the sign of the alliance between Prometheus and Zeus.

Aeschylus' earliest years were spent in an Athens that was developing fast in power, beauty, and intellectual attainments under the government of the sons of Pisistratus: Aeschylus' earliest political memory would have been the expulsion of Hippias, following the four years of his growing despotism after the assassination of his brother Hipparchus. It is important to remember that the tyranny of Pisistratus and his sons was thoroughly beneficial to Athens. It is also important to remember that Pisistratus obtained power through the ordinary people and deposed the aristocrats. The middle classes, such as the family of Aeschylus, were probably better off and probably felt more involved in the process of government than they had before. Certainly, after the expulsion of Hippias, Athens was ready for democracy. Aeschylus was old enough to realize that a spell of tyranny had been necessary to turn Athens into the best-governed state in the world, as he would certainly believe it to be. For Aeschylus, tyranny could be a harsh good, leading to a better good. It is not difficult to see how the request to write for Gela, recently rid of its tyranny, might revive the thoughts inspired by the political atmosphere of his youth.

But Aeschylus was not making an overtly political play. It would be hardly likely, if the play was to be produced away from Athens—the only place where Aeschylus would want to engage in political activity. It was Aeschylus' special vision to see the political development of human society as a type of the total development of the world order of gods and men. The *Oresteia* presents an opening where the gods are at variance with each other, and an end where the gods are in agreement, reached in terms of the human city. There can be progress in human affairs, Aeschylus believed, because Zeus himself can learn. He knows the art of persuasion, by which gradually he has been able to get all powers to work for him, and for his order. The end of the *Oresteia* shows the Furies agreeing to work with Athene and Zeus, because if they do so they will receive greater honor than before.

The stories of Greek religion contain the idea that the world evolved from chaos, and that the rule of the world has involved revolution. The first ruler was Ouranos, the second his son Kronos, who overthrew his father and in turn was overthrown by his son Zeus. In the story of the *Prometheus,* the Titans were members of the old order who supported Kronos and were overthrown with him. Prometheus, although a Titan, knew that Zeus would win, and therefore took his side, thus helping him to an assured victory.

Aeschylus is treating this story from a viewpoint that sees the strife in heaven as something of the far distant past. On the whole, the world works according to rules; the alternative would be chaos. As at one point absolute rule was necessary for Athens, for the alternative was chaos, so now absolute rule is necessary in heaven; the alternative, chaos, would be too horrible to contemplate. Therefore all those who oppose such rule must be persuaded to obey, and if they will not be persuaded, they must be crushed.

It is a harsh philosophy, but it is realistic. Which is the more cruel, the harshness of Aeschylus, which tolerates the idea of Prometheus crushed into submission, or the sentimentality of Shelley, who would overthrow the world order, upon which overthrow what unimaginable sufferings would result? Aeschylus would certainly regard the defiance of the speech that closes Act III of Shelley's poem as dangerous, with its suggestion of man "exempt from awe, worship, degree."[3] But he would also regard it as ridiculous. How can one overthrow the order of the world. Shelley viewed from the standpoint of Aeschylus is like someone raging at the constrictions of the law of cause and effect, without accepting that it is only through this law that he himself is able to cause a few small events and so to achieve something. Without that law he could cause nothing at all.

Prometheus gave mortals greater power than they had had before. He it was who started them on the way to knowledge, literacy, numeracy, and science (436–506). In terms of Aeschylus' theology it was perhaps that Prometheus acted too soon. For it could not be part of the theology of the poet who wrote the *Oresteia* to suggest that Zeus would have kept men permanently in the confusion of a dream world (449–50). Prometheus acted before Zeus was firmly enough established in his power to give power to any other being. And so Prometheus is crushed. Later Zeus can afford to release him, and can afford to have mortals more powerful too. Whatever happens, nothing will overthrow the world order. To rebel against it is therefore silly, and often dangerous.

It is hard for Prometheus. But life is hard. Many people are put in intolerable positions by God. And at least we know that Prometheus is an immortal, and that now he is worshiped at his own festival. We may sympathize with the pain and the humanity of Prometheus chained to his rock, we may applaud his courage. But we know that it is useless. The world order will not change and he will have to give way. As soon as he surrenders everything, he will be rewarded. One cannot argue with God. The feeling of the two plays must have been remarkably similar to that of the Book of Job. Of course we sympathize with Job's horrible sufferings, of course we applaud his defiance. But our reason supports the fact that he will be free only when he collapses totally. One cannot argue with God; one can only collapse before Him. And this is true whether our God is personal or impersonal; the God of Love, or the force of gravity, or Marx' economic determinism. However much we may have a childish desire to shake our fists at Niagara Falls, it is silly, and we will be hurt. The point that Aeschylus drives home to us is that, however much we sympathize with Prometheus, he is still wrong, and he will be crushed.

The feeling of the play is similar to that of *The Suppliants*. Both make extensive use of the story of Io. Io fled from Zeus because she was frightened of sex. In her flight she suffered very greatly. When she finally gave up, Zeus touched her, and with the utmost tenderness gave her a child. It is important that Heracles, Prometheus' eventual rescuer, will be a descendant of Io, and also a descendant of the one Danaid who did not resist marriage with her cousin and refused to kill him on the wedding night (865–73). The *Prometheus Bound* is connected to the *Suppliants* tetralogy even by its employment of the image of hawk and dove (857). Io, Prometheus, and the Danaids fleeing in panic from a perfectly reasonable marriage, are all the same—suffering mortals fleeing from the terror of God. We weep with them for the pain they suffer, but we see that their pain is the result of their own misguided attitude.

The form of the play is very simple. Aeschylus wishes to exercise our sympathies more and more for Prometheus, while leaving enough indications for our intellects to grasp that what Prometheus has done is foolish and what he is suffering is unnecessary. Essential to this is the treatment of the chorus. They must involve our sympathy completely. At the end of the play they identify totally with Prometheus' destruction. It is a pointless gesture, but it is one that moves us very much by their kindness and courage. The form of the play, then, is the ever-increasing involvement of the chorus in Prometheus' imminent, and finally actual, destruction.

With a simpler form than usual, in which less happens, and with less than expert dancers, Aeschylus solved the problem of how to keep his audience's interest by very bold use of theatricality. For his chorus he created a sensational *parodos* and *exodos*[4] in both of which the surprising theatrical effect would have obviated the need for too elaborate dance. For the rest of the play he varied the theatrical texture more than usual, and in particular created two humorous scenes, one almost farcical and one of black comedy.

One of the easiest ways in which a critic can misunderstand a play is by missing humor. It is not generally accepted that some of the *Prometheus Bound* should be played for laughs, but there seems no other way of interpreting the text. The most obviously funny scene is that with Oceanus (284–396). Oceanus plays his whole scene riding an articulated dummy, clearly made to look like a grotesque beast, a sort of griffon with four feet and wings. He would therefore be gently swinging for the entire scene as he dangled on the *mēchanē*. There is absolutely no need for him to enter thus. It is Aeschylus enjoying gratuitous theatricality; unless it is funny, it has no point at all. After Oceanus' opening chant, his first piece of serious advice is ludicrous. "Adapt to the new ways," he tells Prometheus (311). What possible adapting can Prometheus do, chained to a rock in the wilderness? Prometheus starts to laugh at Oceanus too, as, for example, when he praises Oceanus for having "shared and dared everything" with him (331). Oceanus has shared nothing, and dared nothing. Oceanus' answer is to play the car salesman. "Zeus will do it for me," he says. "I can fix everything," is the implication (338–39). By now it is patently obvious that Oceanus can fix nothing. Zeus would only laugh at him, even if Oceanus could ever come near him. Prometheus' next speech (340ff.) starts in mockery as he praises Oceanus for being in no way deficient in enthusiasm. The speech then turns to horror as he describes the sufferings of his brother Titans. He ends, however, by telling Oceanus, "You're a man of experience," (373) and advising him to look after himself. Oceanus' reply is the ludicrous and, in the context, tasteless remark, "words can cure a sick temperament." (378). Unless this was made to get a laugh, it would turn Oceanus into a monster. Words, as a cure for metal driven through Prometheus' body! The scene then ends very quickly, once Prometheus has suggested that there may be danger for Oceanus in associating with him, though Prometheus adds (383) that the only danger is "excessive trouble and stupidity." But Oceanus is now bustling home on the patently thin pretext that his griffon wants to get back into its stall. The language he uses of this bird is also, surely, ridiculous. "The smooth path of the air being stroked by the wings of my four-legged bird." (394–96). Let us imagine for a moment the movement of the dummy's wings during that speech; hardly the gentlest of flutters, as the word used would suggest. Arnott asks of Oceanus' articulated dummy whether it will "suit the high tone of tragedy."[5] Clearly, it will not suit the high tone of tragedy conceived in the mold of Racine or Wagner. But the episode of Oceanus, starting in farce, moving into bitterness, and ending as farce, is a very suitable episode in the morality play that is the *Prometheus Bound.*

Once we have realized the farcical nature of this one episode, we can see other moments in the play that demand a tone very different from the high tone of tragedy. The last scene of the play (944ff.) is not farce, but it is helpful to remember the earlier farce as we consider the character of Hermes, the messenger of Zeus, arriving to bully Prometheus. He starts with a wisecrack (944), and uses sarcasm:

> For I think it is better to serve this rock
> Than be the loyal messenger of Zeus.
>
> (968–69)[6]

The bullying servants of late medieval drama, ultimately derived from the devils in the mystery cycle, give us a reasonable model for this characterization: a little demon with bitter jests.

Most important of all, the play opens with rough, black farce. A weak man being made to do something against his will by a tough guy who does not have the skill to do the job himself is a basically funny situation. The two tough guy giants, Force and Violence, drag Prometheus on stage. They also drag on the little, lame Hephaestus and order him to nail Prometheus to the rock. Hephaestus' first remark is a weak attempt to make the giants leave: "There's nothing to keep you; you've done what you were told to do" (12–13). Clearly an ineffectual attempt like this has humorous possibilities for staging. Hephaestus says, "I haven't the courage to bind a fellow god" (14–15). But the fact is that Hephaestus hasn't the courage to do anything else. The pity that he is starting to express for Prometheus is quickly checked. "But in all respects these people provide the necessary means for me to summon up courage" (16). We can feel clearly through this line the giants' movements as they loom over the little god. Hephaestus' opening speech offers three chances of a laugh in six lines.

After some lines in which Hephaestus has been allowed to develop a lyrical compassion for Prometheus, the giants move in again. Hephaestus can say, "What a terrible and powerful thing is kinship." But Force will reply, as it were slapping Hephaestus on the shoulder, that it is much more terrible to disobey Zeus. Some rough banter follows about Hephaestus' craft, and then Hephaestus prepares to fix the fetters (54ff.). Fixing and climbing up and down the rock can provide plenty of grotesque farce. Half-way through the fettering, Hephaestus says: "No one should blame me, except for him." (63). This must be ludicrous. The only person in whom we are interested is Prometheus. After Prometheus' arms have been fettered, a great wedge is to be driven right through his chest. Clearly this is a complicated movement involving elaborate production. Hammering the wedge in, Hephaestus says, "Oh Prometheus, I groan for your sufferings" (66). Hephaestus is a pathetic little creature, not a monster. If this is not laughable, then Hephaestus becomes a monster. Finally, after more climbing round, Hephaestus says, "The job's done without too much trouble" (75), though the word which I have translated "trouble" also means "pain," and is the word used for the pain of Prometheus as the wedge goes through his chest. Again, unless this gets a laugh, it is the remark of a totally insensitive monster.

The effect of this scene is of a pathetic little man being made to get on with a job that is unpleasant but not particularly personal, like a man unblocking sewage and not liking the smell, while a tough stands over him to see that he does not shirk it. It is as if the three of them were manhandling a dummy. For all his personality, and his relationship with Hephaestus, Prometheus is treated like a lump of wood.[7] After this scene is over the dummy comes to life and speaks. It is a great theatrical moment, and one of the most beautiful sequences of pure lyricism in dramatic speech:

Oh brilliant air, swift wings of the wind,
Springs, streams, rivers and ocean waves'
Infinite laughter, and earth the All-Mother,
And all-seeing whirl of the sun I call you,
Look how the gods rack me—a god.

(88–92)

But, it will be said, this is stupidly fanciful. Present Prometheus, this tragic figure suffering untold misery at the hands of God, as a piece of knockabout farce. This is like making a farce of the Crucifixion. It was such a consideration that made me see why and how the opening scene of the *Prometheus Bound* is indeed the black, bitter farce I have described. It is so similar to the play of the Crucifixion in the mystery cycles. For example, in the York play of the pinners and painters, the first half is rough farce as the soldiers fix Christ to the cross and raise it with considerable effort into its position (*Play of the Crucifixion*, 1–252). There is plenty of business climbing up and down the construction, just as in the *Prometheus Bound*, and just as in Aeschylus' play we are concentrating on the soldiers. The figure of Christ is merely part of their job, something they have to fix on a structure of wood and raise in the air. Once the cross is in position, the soldiers stand back to admire their work. In an equally breathtaking moment of theater, Christ speaks:

All men that walk by way or street,
Take tent ye shall no travail tine;
Behold my head, my hands, my feet,
And fully feel now, ere ye fine,
If any mourning may be meet,
Or mischief measured unto mine.

(253–58)

The effect of the two moments is so similar, we would say that the Christian poet had copied the Greek, did we not know that it was impossible for him to have read Aeschylus.

It was necessary to discuss the theme and theatrical tone before considering the detailed problems of staging, since this discussion must depend on the earlier one. The two main problems are the entrance of the chorus, and Prometheus' rock, involved with which is the question as to how the play ended. The words of the finale imply that the rock will be broken and Prometheus buried (1016–19). Prometheus' last chanted cry implies that what Hermes promised is actually happening—the earthquakes, thunder and lightning (1080–end), and his first words of this cry are that it is happening actually, not just in words (1080–81). Whatever happens at the end of the play must happen to Prometheus and the fifteen members of the chorus too. For the dramatic climax of the play comes when Hermes tells the chorus to leave Prometheus and save themselves from involvement in his destruction. In anapest chant (1063ff.) they defy him and cluster around Prometheus.

Some critics suggest that nothing physical happened at all, merely that Prometheus' final chant reached a climax of passion, and then he and all the dancers "froze" in their positions. But this does not seem to fit with Prometheus' words that things are really happening. Furthermore, the Athenian theater had no blackout. After a pause, the actor and the fifteen dancers would have had to get up and walk off in full view of the audience cracking nuts and waiting for the next play. Would the Greeks have tolerated this?

The most likely solution seems to be that, before the play started, the *ekkyklema* was rolled out, on which was erected a wooden structure to represent the rock. This would be large enough to allow Hephaestus to clamber up and down in the prologue with plenty of opportunities for business. It would be large enough to allow all fifteen members of the chorus to cling to it as they make their final gesture of identification with Prometheus. During Prometheus' last chant the *ekkyklema* would then move slowly back inside the *skēnē*. If Gela possessed thunder and lightning machines they would have used them, and, as I have suggested earlier, I see no reason why these machines should not have been in use in Aeschylus' time. This would not be naturalism, but it would provide a theatrical representation of what was meant to be happening, in a convention that the audience could easily accept.[8]

The problem of staging that has aroused the most controversy is that of the entry of the chorus. At their entry they are "in the air," and they stay in the air for a hundred and fifty lines until Prometheus asks them to "walk on the ground" (272). This request is answered by seven lines of anapest chant as they describe themselves "with light foot leaving their swiftly rushing seat and the air" (278–80). During the scene with Oceanus that follows this descent, there is no mention of the chorus, which is odd since they are his daughters. They must therefore be out of the way of what is happening on stage. After Oceanus has been swung off, they reappear in the *orchestra*, immediately dancing. There are no lines of anapests to get them into position. Finally, we should notice that the initial entry of the chorus takes a long time. For nearly fifteen lines Prometheus is chanting of noises and scents and rushing wings approaching his rock (114–27). Whatever the means of the chorus's entry, they perform it to this chant of Prometheus, for what follows is regular dance in two systems.

Various theories have been suggested. First, some critics say that they entered in the normal way up the *parodoi*, and merely conveyed flight through the air by the kind of dance movements they made. But if so, it is very odd that they take seven lines to "leave the air" (277–83), and even odder that there is no recognition of them by Oceanus. For on this theory they must remain in the *orchestra*.

Second, it is suggested that they are swung in on the *mēchanē*. This would explain why they are absent from the Oceanus scene: as he is swung on, they are swung off by the counterbalancing mechanism. But there is no evidence of a *mēchanē* bearing the weight of more than two or three actors. Fifteen men is far more than it is required to carry on any other occasion in the extant plays. Also, it creates an extraordinary movement with which to reply to Prometheus' request to leave the air and listen to his full story. As the chorus are "leaving the air" they chant, "I shall approach this rocky ground" (281). On the *mēchanē* theory they would have to chant this at the moment when they are almost disappearing over the top of the *skēnē*, as far both from Prometheus and the ground as possible. Furthermore, it is inconceivable that they could have danced a strophic system while dangling on the end of a crane. If Aeschylus had wanted such an entry, he would surely have written an astrophic, irregular *parodos.*

The third suggestion is that they are drawn along the balcony of the *skēnē* in a winged car. During the Oceanus scene they would then descend through the *skēnē*, and emerge in time for their next dance when he had gone. The main disadvantage of such an entry is that it would look so cramped. At the moment of their entry Prometheus is chanting, "The air whistles with the light whirlings of wings." Fifteen men sitting tightly together in a car drawn relatively slowly along the balcony would hardly fill the vision of someone sitting at the back of the theater, a hundred yards away. Whatever the method of entry, it must fill the stage with sudden movement, more especially since we have been asked in the previous scene to concentrate closely on the lone figure of Prometheus. Since the mood changes, it would be natural to change the focus of the audience's gaze.

The conclusive argument against the winged car also gives a suggestion for the final theory. Almost the first words of the opening chorus lyric refer to their having approached by "swift races of wings." This must imply that they entered individually, which is supported by the long chant of Prometheus before they are ready for their first dance. A theory accepted by some scholars is that the chorus entered by one of the *parodoi* as usual, but each *choreutes* rode on an individual scooter decorated with wings. This could certainly represent movement through the air; it would account for the phrase "swift races of wings," and also for the irregular entry during Prometheus' long chant. It would also account for the phrase with which they describe their descent from the air: "With light foot leaving my swiftly rushing seat" (278–79), and suggests an obvious movement, that of swinging the leg over the seat, the natural way to dismount from bicycle or scooter. It also accounts for the first words of Prometheus at their approach: "What is this sound?" Scooters could not have been silent, certainly as they approached fast up the *parodos.* Some reference to the sudden sound is natural.

I can well remember the first time I heard this theory advanced in a lecture at Oxford by Maurice Platnauer. Most of his student audience, myself included, laughed at the idea, thinking it typical of a scholar totally out of touch with the theater: winged scooters—how ludicrous. How unsuitable for the *Prometheus Bound*, that great tragedy of noble suffering. The theory may not have come from people aware of its theatrical implications. But I am sure it is right. The play has started with the black farce of the binding. There has then been a complete change of mood with Prometheus' solitary lyrical outburst. Then, to follow this moment of stillness, the *orchestra* is suddenly full of tender-hearted spirits, whirling around on winged scooters, kicking their bare feet in the air. Scooters offer marvellous opportunities for unusual and beautiful movement. The daughters of Oceanus are the most innocent and lovable of all the spirits presented in the entire corpus of extant Greek tragedy. As a theatrical presentation of these sweet and playful young girls, an entrance on winged scooters could be a moment of outstanding theatrical rightness, presenting us with a picture appropriate to the poetic meaning of this moment in the play, and one appropriate to the character of the girls.[9]

The structure of the dance drama is a natural development from this widely dispersed, fast moving entrance, to the quiet seriousness with which the chorus cluster around Prometheus as the rock moves under the wrath of Zeus. The *parodos* expresses very little except the chorus's sympathy for Prometheus. Aeschylus would hardly have written elaborate words for a dance on scooters. Naturally, the scooters would demand full use of the *orchestra*.

The first *stasimon*, after the scene with Oceanus (397–435), presents the whole world lamenting for Prometheus. The second system (415–24) is trochaic. This meter suggests running, and the words refer to far-flung peoples. The impression we receive is of the chorus running to the edges of the *orchestra*, well spaced out.

The second *stasimon* (526–60) is more solemn, in dactylo-epitrites. The girls pray that they may pass their lives in reverence of Zeus. At the beginning of the second system (545–46, *strophē*; 553–54, *antistrophē*) there is a direct address to Prometheus, and therefore a movement towards him. But their involvement with him is interrupted by the arrival of Io.

The third *stasimon* is the last dance in the play (887–907). It is short, only one system and an epode. It is a prayer by the chorus that they may marry beings like themselves. The natural way to choreograph it would be to create a very symmetrical pattern near the altar in the exact center of the *orchestra*. The meter is again dactylo-epitrite, and therefore the movement is relatively quiet.

This would then present a clear and simple total dance pattern: the *parodos* utterly surprising, *allegro scherzando*, with fast movement all over the stage; the first *stasimon*, *allegro*, whose effect rests on the simple device of making the dancers run to the very edge of their performing space; the second *stasimon*, *andante*, with some movement approaching the center of the *skēnē* at the rear of the orchestra where the *ekkyklema* stands with Prometheus on it; the third *stasimon*, also *andante*, in a relatively static grouping in the center of the *orchestra*; the *exodos* full of noise and screaming, but with the chorus bunched in as tight and fearful a group as possible, frozen into immobility with fear as the rock dissolves into the *skēnē*. An unusual opening, and an unusual close; and for the rest, simple dances and masterly use of simple groupings; this seems to be the pattern of the *Prometheus Bound*, one appropriate to production in relatively unskilled Gela, appropriate to the meaning of the play, whose aim is to focus sympathy on Prometheus, and appropriate to the fact that this mise-en-scène is the last work of a great master, equally at home in all aspects of the theater. The *Prometheus Bound* is often described as a dramatic poem rather than as drama. Certainly there is little if no interaction of characters in conflict. There is no harm in calling it a dramatic poem provided that we are always aware that it is a poem orchestrated with a wide variety of theatrical effects.

The simplicity of the form is demonstrated by the way in which the prologue mirrors the form of the whole play. The first part, as already discussed, on the one hand creates a mood of black farce as the smith god Hephaestus works at his job, the living Prometheus, who is being treated like an object, and on the other hand prepares our sympathies for Prometheus when he does eventually break silence in his great cry to the elements. The solitary concentration of his lonely pain is answered by the rushing wings of the scooter-riding chorus, rising and crouching on their machines. One line's demands for movement that will fit both *strophē* and *antistrophē* give us a good picture. The last line of the first system (135, *strophē*; 151, *antistrophē*) presents two images that at first reading appear to be very unlike each other. In the *strophē:* "I rushed without shoes in my winged car"; in the *antistrophē:* "The monsters of old he destroys." If, however, the line began with a violent kick high in the air, this could both draw attention to bare feet and also suggest some sort of monster. If this kick was followed by a low crouch, this would emphasize the car for the *strophē,* as the human being sank into it, while for the *antistrophē* it would demonstrate the destruction of the monsters.

There then follows a dialogue episode (193–276) between Prometheus and the chorus leader. They learn the story of how Prometheus had helped Zeus overthrow Kronos, and how, after he had won, he had wanted to destroy the entire race of men. Prometheus alone had taken their side and for this was punished. As the chorus leader continues, however, she implies that Prometheus did act wrongly. In order to discuss the matter further, the chorus must leave their scooters, but they are interrupted by the arrival of Oceanus, who offers his fussy advice and is sent packing.

As Oceanus is swung over the *skēnē* on his griffon, the chorus, having left their scooters in the *parodos,* take their places in the *orchestra* for the first *stasimon,* invoking the whole world to join in sorrow for Prometheus, especially all the men whom he has helped with his techniques and advice (397–435). This leads naturally into a long description by Prometheus of the various benefits he has bestowed on the human race, the sequence ending with a suggestion that the power of Zeus will not last forever (436–525). We have heard this before, in the chant with which Prometheus replied to the song of the chorus in the *parodos* (168–77), but at that moment it had seemed like mere raving. Now there is a coherence about the way in which Prometheus assures them that Zeus will fall, although he must not yet tell them how.

The reverence of the second *stasimon,* in which the chorus acknowledge their weakness before Zeus and think with longing of the time they attended Prometheus' marriage (526–60), is shattered by the mad entry of Io (561). She rushes on chanting anapests, and then performs a system of solo dance mostly in dochmiacs. In the tenth line of the *strophē* (583) she shrieks: "Throw me to sea monsters as food." The matching line in the *antistrophē* ends with a wordless scream (602). It would be appropriate if at this moment the actor threw himself to the ground, and continued there for the next few lines, writhing and gradually rising again. All that we receive from this dance is a sense of madness and frenzy and that she is being persecuted by Hera.

A short sequence of stichomythia reveals who Prometheus is; this prompts Io to ask him to tell her how her wanderings will end (609–30). The chorus, however, interrupt and ask Io first to tell how she came here, which she does in a long speech (640–86). After a brief outburst from the chorus (687–95), Prometheus tells of her wanderings from the moment she leaves him to the time when she will leave Europe (700–741). Io's exclamations of horror lead to a sequence of stichomythia where Prometheus reveals the secret that Zeus will contract a marriage with a girl whose son will be more powerful than Zeus himself and will dethrone him (764, 768). Prometheus also reveals that it will be a descendant of Io who will be his own rescuer (772). He then goes on to offer Io a choice of two stories: either the story of her wanderings from the point at which he broke off, or that of his own rescuer. The chorus, however, interrupt and ask him to tell both. Prometheus then takes up the story of Io's wanderings, a speech full of monsters, and tells her that finally she will settle at the mouth of the Nile (786–818). Then, instead of telling the second tale as he had proposed, he says he will now tell how Io came where she is now, in order to prove his clairvoyance. He then changes his mind, giving only a summary account of her previous wanderings and mentioning only two things of substance, that the talking oaks at Dodona hailed her as the bride of Zeus, and that the Ionian sea will be named after her (823–43). He then goes on (844–76) to describe the city of Canobus at the mouth of the Nile, where Zeus will eventually restore her sanity, and then describes the Danaids, fifth in descent from her son by Zeus, Epaphus. The Danaids will flee the marriage with their cousins, will be received in Argos and will murder their husbands on their wedding night. The one girl who does not murder her husband will be the ancestor of Prometheus' own deliverer. He finishes by saying that there is no point in Io hearing the means of his deliverance, as Io, stung again by the gadfly, rushes madly around the *orchestra,* chanting ten lines of anapests, and runs away.

If we think of this sequence as naturalistic dialogue, it seems very awkwardly constructed. Why does Prometheus offer Io the choice of two stories? And then why, when persuaded by the chorus to tell both, does he not tell both? The scene make sense if we think of it in quasi-musical terms, in terms of a sequence of emotion that Aeschylus wishes us to feel. The first part of the scene emphasizes Io's suffering and skates over the fact that the suffering will have an end. The next long speech of Prometheus (790–818) is supposed to describe the end of her wanderings, but by its mention of all the monsters, the effect is more horrific than what has preceded it. When, however, he does not do what he said

he would do (823 ff.), we begin to be suspicious of his total control of the
scene. Is Prometheus' point of view the only one to trust? Now we hear of Io's
previous wanderings, but all we hear is that she was hailed as the bride of Zeus,
and that the Ionian sea will be named after her; two marks of her honor. We
start to wonder if this so-named tyrannical behavior of Zeus is quite as tyrannical as it has been made out. Then Prometheus goes on to tell us—quite unnecessarily in dramatic terms—about the Danaids, the girls who were naturally
frightened of sex, but who carried this fear to quite unnatural extremes—the
Danaids, who are the type of man's wrong-headed flight from God. The
deliverer of Prometheus will be the descendant of the one girl who did submit.
The solution of the second play is hinted at: eventually Prometheus too will
submit like Io, or like the submissive Danaid, and he will find, as they do, that,
once he has submitted, Zeus has a gentle touch. However, we are not allowed
to dwell on this hint of the reconciliation to come. Io is racked again with
madness and rushes out. Our last impression from this scene is not the eventual
peace, but the present torture.

   The following chorus, the third *stasimon*, fits subtly into place. The
Oceanids sing their humility in the face of Zeus with a dance of demure
marriage, so exactly the opposite of Io's wild panic. Prometheus replies to their
quiet reverence with defiance. He abuses Zeus, thus preparing the entry of
Hermes (944). Hermes' threats will not make Prometheus give up the secret.
Both grow more violent in their mutual defiance, until there is nothing left for
Hermes to do but prophesy the cataclysm that is about to strike Prometheus.
The chorus advise Prometheus to be less stubborn (1036–39) but he breaks into
chant (1040ff.), declaring that the new torture is not unexpected. Hermes
replies, advising the chorus to leave Prometheus, who is now mad. This they
refuse to do and huddle on the rock for the finale of destruction. All the last
fifty lines are chanted anapests.

   A dramatic poem orchestrated by theatrical effects; the lyrical development
of a single situation; a dance drama moving from whirling activity to tense
stillness; all these formulae help to summarize the form and movement of this
play. Its power, however, rests on the force of Aeschylus' compassion for the
giant sufferings of Prometheus, and the delicacy of the relation between the
towering figure of the defiant Titan and the uncomplicated, innocent sea-
nymphs. The choice of chorus is apparently illogical; why should these spirits
visit the waste places of Scythia? But it is poetically appropriate. Their entrance
bears no relation to any reality except the theatrical, but in terms of the surrealism that we associate more often with Aristophanes than with the tragic poets,
it works. The *Prometheus Bound* fits no easy categories. For those who have
tried to confine the imagination of the Athenian poets, it is an excellent example of the tricks Aeschylus had at his command—colorful, surrealist, and
always surprising. It is also a good example by which to understand that the
wildest effects were always to be employed in the service of a poetic enquiry
driven as deep as possible into the meaning of what it is to be alive.

Sophocles: *Antigone*

Anouilh, Brecht, and the Living Theatre have all contributed modern versions of the *Antigone*. Twentieth-century audiences find it the most easily accessible of all Greek drama. The theme of rebellion, the confrontation between two conflicting ideas of politics, which are central to all the modern versions, are not the central concern of Sophocles. The apparent familiarity of the ideas to us must not allow us to turn Sophocles into a twentieth-century writer. Like all of his plays the *Antigone* is a celebration at the altar of Dionysus, a presentation of the pattern of *Dikē* working itself out through the dance.

The *Antigone* is about an insult to death. Death is the focus of life. Any attitude that ignores this is a wrong attitude. The ceremonials with which we surround death are a proper acknowledgement of death's centrality. The action of the *Antigone* is that Creon refuses burial to a corpse. As a result of this insult to death, this affront to a fundamental human instinct, he loses everything that gives meaning to his life: the loyalty of his subject citizens, over whom he has just assumed command, the love and the life of his wife, and, above all, his adored son.

Our generation has become so coarsened to death. But almost no generation except our own would leave the bodies of soldiers to rot. Even as recently as World War I, army chaplains performed heroics under shell-fire in order to enact the burial ceremony over the dead soldiers. For them, as for Sophocles, the ritual was necessary.

We can see very clearly Sophocles' attitude to this. The *Ajax* also involves the question of burial. Ajax, who has plotted the murder of all the chiefs, and would have achieved this murder if he had not been struck mad by Athene, has now committed suicide. Agamemnon decides in the name of the army that the body of Ajax should be refused burial. But Odysseus, the man who was most hated by Ajax and had most to suffer from him, opposes Agamemnon's decision. He argues:

> Not this man, but the laws of God
> You would be destroying.

> (1343–44)

An action such as this corrupts the person who performs it, the city in which it is performed. It is an affront to *Dikē*, and *Dikē* affronted will automatically right itself.

It is necessary to emphasize this point, because Anouilh for instance makes Antigone's burial of the body an *acte gratuit*—an existentialist act of defiance. Anouilh's play is about two different attitudes to life; we sympathize with one or the other as we feel. With Sophocles there is no ambiguity; Creon is wrong. He has performed a monstrous act, and if he does not change his mind, he will be crushed.

The *Antigone* begins at the moment when the two sons of Oedipus have just fulfilled their father's curse on them. Polyneices has led an Argive army of invasion to attempt to take Thebes and drive his brother off the throne. Eteocles and Polyneices have met in single combat and killed each other. The Argive army has retreated. Creon, the uncle of Oedipus' children, has taken command of the city. His first action as commander is to insult death, and so the god of death. It is effectively his first, and his last, act as commander.

I emphasized in Chapter 3 that Dionysus is the lord of death, and that, as it is central to the *Anthesteria* that celebrations of wine, fertility, and drunkenness are part of the same festival as an All Souls' Day, so in the *Dionysia* both these aspects of Dionysus are equally important. The celebration of Dionysus is very much in evidence in the dance drama of the *Antigone*.

The form of the play emerges very clearly from the dances. The chorus, men past military age, men of the age of Sophocles himself at the time of writing, represent the mature citizen body. At first they support Creon as their new leader, but then they try and dissuade him, and finally they tell him openly that he is wrong. At the same time the dances become gradually less equivocal, until the last one calls down destruction on Creon.

The *parodos* is a war dance of triumph (100–162). Thebes has beaten back its invaders. But just as the invader has fallen with a crash, so all big-mouthed boasting is hateful to God. The dance is followed immediately by Creon's opening speech, big-mouthed and boasting. The *parodos* ends with a cry to Dionysus. A natural cry to the god of the festival, we might think. But Creon's opening speech will touch on the realm of Dionysus less as lord of the festival than as lord of death.

The first *stasimon* (332–83) is the so-called Ode to Man, which is analyzed in detail in Chapter 5, and which I have suggested, not altogether light-heartedly, should be renamed "The Song of the Cosmic Joke." Although it appears to have application to many other situations than this play, it yet fits perfectly into its place between the episode in which we become aware that the gods are helping Antigone's act of burial, and the actual appearance of Antigone to begin her confrontation of Creon.

The second *stasimon* (582–630) is about choice. As so often with Sophocles, the relevance of the dance appears only at its end. The first system appears to be a lament, both general and for the house of Oedipus. It follows neatly from what has gone before, when Ismene has identified herself with Antigone and been put under guard. The *strophē* of the second system continues what appears to be a generalizing tendency, with a reflection on the power of Zeus and the precariousness of man's life. The *antistrophē*, however, refers to the man who thinks good is evil, and how this is the sign that God is about to ruin him (622–24). We thought that the *stasimon* had been about Antigone's choice. Now we realize that it is about Creon's. In the next episode he will have one more chance, to listen to the reasoned arguments of his son Haemon. He will turn his back on Haemon in hysteria, and from then on we know that there is little hope for him.

Haemon may do something dangerous because he is in love with Antigone. He rushes out, and *stasimon* 3 follows, the song of the power of love (781–801). This leads straight into a *kommos* for Antigone as she is led to death in a kind of parody of a wedding ceremony where death is the husband (802–82, including linking chorus anapests).

After Antigone has been taken away to be immured, there is the most complicated *stasimon* in the play. Its function is twofold: first, to foreshadow the destruction that is coming on Creon for the action he has just completed and to identify that action not only as cruelty to a girl but also as an insult to Dionysus; second, to link Antigone's exit with the entrance of Teiresias that follows (944–87).[10]

The fifth and final stasimon (1115–52) is a direct invocation to Dionysus. It builds in excitement and ends with a cry to him to appear. Instead, the messenger appears, as if he were the god, with the news of retribution. The finale is mostly a *kommos* for Creon—agonized twistings on the rack of his own self-inflicted agony, ending, as so often with Sophocles, with the resignation of calm, clear, and total despair.

A musical analogy might help to give an idea of the general rhythm of this impeccably conceived dance drama: *parodos, allegro con brio; stasimon* 1, *allegro moderato scherzando,* an apparently light scherzo with sinister implications; *stasimon* 2, *andante,* a quieter, more reflective piece, using dactylo-epitrites; *stasimon* 3, *allegro maestoso,* the song of love's power, leading to *maestoso,* Antigone's *kommos; stasimon* 4, *andante mysterioso,* the strange transition from Antigone to Teiresias; *stasimon* 5, *allegro* leading to *presto,* the invocation to Dionysus; finale, *allegro ma non troppo,* the violent syncopations of Creon's twisted cries of pain, ending on the anapest chant of the chorus's exit, which sounds like a quiet chorale. The *parodos* and the invocation to Dionysus involve the most violent dancing. *Stasima* 1 and 4 involve the most complex mime.[11]

The distribution of parts has great significance for the meaning of the play.[12] The leading actor plays Antigone, Teiresias, and the messenger. The second actor plays Creon throughout, and the third Ismene, the guard, Haemon, and the queen, Eurydice. Antigone, Teiresias, and the messenger are the three manifestations of *Dikē* as it strikes Creon. Antigone and Teiresias are very strongly linked by the *stasimon* between the former's exit and the latter's entrance. It no longer needs stressing now that Sophocles' play is not "about" Antigone, nor is it a conflict between Creon and Antigone, as Anouilh's play is. If it were either of these two, then it would be manifestly incompetent, since Antigone leaves the stage two thirds of the way through. The play is the dance of *Dikē* recoiling on Creon, and Sophocles underlines this by giving his leading actor three roles that are in a sense not so much three identities as three aspects of one identity.[13] In every aspect. Sophocles is totally in control of his form.

As we compare the tasks of leading and second actor, we learn an important truth about the nature of the fifth-century theater. The role of Creon involves a most complex display of character. He must demonstrate almost the entire range of emotion: joky, patronizing, bullying, indecisive, deeply loving, terrified, lashing out wildly, in paroxysms of grief. In contrast the leading actor does not have much character to display. There is no need for Antigone to be fully characterized. She is an instrument of the situation, and the writing allows us no opportunities to see what she would be like away from the crisis. Similarly, Teiresias has to convey the prophet's power, but does not develop or change or show ordinary human emotions. The leading actor's speeches are better than those for the second actor, but they are not displays of character. The finest speech in the play, as so often in Greek tragedy, is that of the messenger (1192–1243), which is of course purely descriptive. Both the leading and the second actors have to sing and dance. But Creon's *kommos* is nearly all dochmiacs, suitable to the jerky desperation of his near madness. As we have seen elsewhere, dochmiacs do not seem to have involved such elaborate music. Antigone's *kommos*, on the other hand, appears much more obviously as a musical climax. Its function in the play is primarily to arouse sympathy for Antigone as she is about to die; it is, with perfect appropriateness, a tearjerker. In terms of the performing task, the job of the leading actor is harder and more rewarding than that of the second. It is a very clear demonstration that characterization was not the most important part of the actor's task, and certainly a clear indication that the plays of the fifth century are not constructed on the interaction of characters.

Given that the *Antigone* is a dance drama, not a play built upon the interaction of character, Sophocles is a writer able to convey the intricacies of character as well as the greatest writers. Characterization is subordinate to other elements, but when detailed characterization is required, Sophocles can supply it. The action of the *Antigone* can be committed only by a very special individual. And so Creon is defined with great individuality and precision. Sophocles' Electra is the most dynamic personality portrayed in Greek drama, but Creon and Neoptolemus offer the greatest growth—Creon from an apparently sensible commander into a screaming hysteric, sobbing like a child, Neoptolemus from an unthinking boy into a potential commander. Creon lacks judgement, lacks a sense of the way things are. That is the summary of the long messenger speech (1242–43). His failing would not be serious if he were not in command. As ruler, his failing is disastrous. Creon is a man too small for his office. His opening speech declares his contempt for the man who panics and will not take advice (179–81). Very soon he will panic and ignore all advice. He is a weak man, with all the stubbornness of the weak. He says that the only thing for which he cares is the well-being of the state (187–90, 663–67). But when his son points out (692 ff.) that the majority of that state are horrified at the thought of putting Antigone to death, he retreats into irrational screaming. Creon's weak obstinacy is dangerous, because he persists in his wrong course of action in order to show that he is strong. By this wrongheaded persistence he destroys himself.

Part of the drama, then, is the development of Creon's obstinacy as he traps himself more and more in his wrongheadedness, in opposition to the more or less unmoving manifestations of the recoil of *Dikē:* Antigone and Teiresias. The only moment in the play that is complicated for us to interpret is the transitional chorus during which, on a poetic level, Antigone turns into Teiresias in just as real a sense as, on a technical level, the leading actor is changing from one mask and robe to another. This *stasimon* is of enormous importance for the structure and interpretation of the play.

If we read it on the page it seems almost impossibly obscure. Its point lies in the relation of what is sung to what is not sung but would be known to the audience. The effect is similar to film superimposition. More than one picture is presented to us at once. We notice that the words convey very clear instructions for mime. The mime simplifies the stories presented into the schematic essentials that Sophocles needs in order to relate them to his play.

The *stasimon* is in two systems. It presents what might appear to be three totally disconnected stories in a very oblique fashion: in the *strophē* of the first system the story of Danae; in the *antistrophē*, that of King Lycurgus; in the second system, that of King Phineus.

Chorus of Veterans
SYSTEM I
Strophē Patient Danae waits. Heavenly sunshine
Darkened. Prison has shut. Bronze-fitted chains.
Walls, walls. There on the bedrock
Secret forging of links occurred. Couplings.
Oh! There! Family honor!
What a thing! Child! Child!
She took charge of the golden . . .
Of the seed raining from Zeus.
Oh how destiny takes you
With its awesome strength.
Neither by fighting, nor by wealth,
Nor castles, nor black ships that pound
The oceans, may you flee what's fated.

Antistrophē Second forging of links. Easily angry
King Lycurgus of Thrace. Mocking the god.
Struck mad by Dionysus.
Walled up tight in a rocky, dark, blind hole.
Now his madness dispersed, trickling away his strength,
His fine, flourishing strength. He
In his madness had a feel—
God felt back, and he crumbled,
And his laugh choked dead.
For he'd checked girls possessed by God,
Put out the holy Bacchic fire,
And angered all the dancing Muses.

SYSTEM II.

Strophē   And by the dark-coloured rocks that are dashed by the
    twin-channeled
Sea where Bosporus shore and the Thracian cliffs confront
Salmydessus, the War-God was on guard
Watching the curse and the wound
Strike the two sons of Phineus.
That blinding! Wife! Newly-bedded woman!
Savage as the hollow socket holes that once were eyes,
The blood-stained blind revenge in darkness.
Hands feel for blood. Blood is on the needle.

Antistrophē   Nothing but melting in tears and a sob for the death-sob.
Cry, Birth *not* to be born, and a marriage *not* a marriage.
Though she boasted a long family tree,
Athenian royal descent.
Far from her home, in stone caves
She learns the snow-clouds her father handled,
Gallops up the wind and hurtles down the crags, a storm,
A storm-god's child. At last however
Th' abiding Fate ends her story, Child! Child!

(944–87)

The gist of the story of Danae is that King Acrisius was warned by the
Delphic oracle that his daughter Danae would bear a son who would kill
Acrisius. He therefore immured Danae, so that no one should make love to
her. But Zeus visited her as a shower of golden rain, and she bore a son,
Perseus, who eventually caused the death of Acrisius.

We might render this story schematically: a king, being warned that a girl is
dangerous, immures her. She is, however, visited sexually by God, and the
result is disaster to the king.

The connection of this story to that of the *Antigone* is obvious. All that
Sophocles presents is Danae, shut in the prison, visited sexually by Zeus, and a
feeling that there is no escaping from what is in store for us.

The second story, of Lycurgus, is one like that of Pentheus as shown in *The
Bacchants.* King Lycurgus was driven mad by Dionysus because he restrained
the bacchants. In his madness he killed his son and wife. He was then blinded
by Zeus.

Schematically the story might be rendered: a king checks girls who are acting
with God, is driven mad, and destroys his son and wife. All that Sophocles
presents, however, is a suggestion of the story, more or less in reverse order.
Lycurgus, raging, struck mad by Dionysus, and imprisoned, as he was, in a
cave. His strength dissolves as his madness ebbs. There is an allusion to how he
restrained the bacchants, and how he has angered the Muses, who are closely
associated with Dionysus.

With this second story the meanings multiply considerably. On the most superficial level, there is a connection between Danae and Lycurgus because both are immured in a cave. But the function of the Lycurgus story in Sophocles' pattern is more to hint at how Creon will destroy his son—Haemon—and wife—Eurydice—and, how, in addition, his offence is an offence against Dionysus. We shall remember this when the chorus invoke Dionysus in the fifth *stasimon* and when, after that final cry to Dionysus, the messenger arrives to lead into the death of both son and wife.[14]

Another thing we notice is that the movement must consist of a central figure, representing Danae in the *strophē*, Lycurgus in the *antistrophē*, immured, performing some orgasmic movement to represent in the *strophē* the act of sex, (949–52) in the *antistrophē* the collapse of Lycurgus (960–63). The *strophē* focuses on the girl, the *antistrophē* on the king. But the two are linked in disaster. To be prosaic we could say that Antigone's destruction is Creon's destruction.

The third story is that of Phineus, another king. He divorced and imprisoned his wife Cleopatra, by whom he had had two sons. He then married Eidothea, who put out the two sons' eyes and then imprisoned them. Phineus was then blinded for his cruelty.

Sophocles presents the story backwards: in the *strophē*, the destruction of Phineus, in the *antistrophē*, the imprisonment of Cleopatra. Schematically, it runs: as a result of imprisoning a girl, the king destroys his family and is blinded. The girl's imprisonment is a gathering of God's power. The presentation is much more oblique and surrealistic than in the first two stories. There is a resonant vagueness about the language, combined with an excitement created by the sense of wild landscape. The wild landscape leads into the wounding of the two sons of Phineus by the new wife. The *strophē* ends with a stress on blood and revenge. Whose blood? Whose revenge? Sophocles is perhaps the most precise poet who has ever lived. If he is vague, we can be sure that he means to be ambiguous. The *antistrophē* refers to Cleopatra, but she is never mentioned by name. There is mention of her marriage, which is no marriage. Then her childhood is referred to, her upbringing in mountain caves, learning the storms that her father, the North Wind, rides. The imprisoned girl ends by being a creature of power.

Once again there is clearly a central figure in the dance. In the *strophē* he will represent the king, in the *antistrophē*, the girl. Once again there is a linking of Creon and Antigone. In poetry like this, I do not think we need worry that the son destroyed is portrayed by the two sons of Phineus. A slight lack of precision in the references helps the sense of surrealism. It is the poetic equivalent to dim lighting. The second system is a repeat of the first: a foreshadowing of Creon's downfall with death in his family; and a return to the girl he has condemned, emphasizing that she is a creature of power, with the power of gods behind her.

In other words, the figure of Antigone is superimposed on the dance of the *strophē* in the first system, which presents Danae; the figure of Creon is superimposed on that of the *antistrophē* presenting Lycurgus. Creon remains superimposed on the *strophē* of the second system presenting the destruction of Phineus, but in the filmic sense he dissolves into the figure of Antigone for the *antistrophē*. We are prepared for Antigone to re-enter in power. And as the dance ends, that is precisely what happens. Teiresias enters, as it were the reincarnation of Antigone.

As Teiresias enters, the thing that has been puzzling us is made clear. Why in the stories was there this harking on the theme of blindness: Lycurgus, the sons of Phineus, and Phineus himself? With the appearance of blind Teiresias, the leitmotif of blindness during the preceding dance makes sense. It is a kind of preparatory resonance, again linking Teiresias very firmly with what has gone before.

Before tracing the development of the play as a whole, it is worth noticing a so-called problem upon which much printer's ink has been spent. It concerns part of the last speech of Antigone as she is about to go to her death (905–15). Scholars accept that our text of Sophocles is free of interpolations; but a number of scholars have made this passage a sole exception. Page, for example, cuts it out of his text as an actor's interpolation.[15] Antigone is giving the reasons why she acted as she did. She says that she would not have performed the burial for her children or for her husband. Only for her brother would she have done it, since with her father and mother dead, she will never have another brother. In the context of theatrical production there is no problem about this passage at all. Antigone's incoherence is theatrically effective and dramatically appropriate: at this point she is somewhat hysterical. The point of the passage is that she is attacking Creon with his own coarseness. Earlier in the play Creon had referred to the great love between Antigone and Haemon with obscene brutality. Ismene has asked him if he will kill his son's marriage. He replies:

There are plenty more fields he can fertilize.(569)

Antigone's farewell speech to Creon takes up his filthy-mindedness:

> Wise men should approve this respect I've shown.
> If I'd been a mother and lost my children
> Or my husband had died and was laid out rotting,
> I wouldn't have bothered to offend the citizens.
> By what principle d'you think I'm acting?
> One husband dead—you can find another.
> Miss with one child—have a go with a new man. . . .
> But with mother and father both in their graves
> No more brothers will ever grow. . . .
> That's the principle of your special treatment
> Which has so offended Creon with its . . .
> Excessive audacity. . . . My heart. . . . My brother. . . .
>
> (904–15)

A frightened virgin, desperate with first love and fear of death and hatred of the man who has spat on her love and is sending her to her death, she turns to the corpse of her brother, disgraced and thrown away, as the only focus of the tangle of her emotions. It is a beautiful speech for an actor, and the only moment in the play where the leading actor must display really complex characterisation and emotional content.

The scholars have been unhappy about this passage largely because they feel that at this point Antigone should be able to give a better reason for her action. This is to miss the nature of Sophocles' poetry. There is no need for Antigone to give any reasons at all. The dance drama shows perfectly clearly that Antigone is justified. Everything is contained in the first *stasimon* and the fourth, the dance preceding her arrest and that which follows her entombment. To feel that Antigone ought to justify herself is to confuse Sophocles with a writer of naturalistic drama of plot where everything must be conveyed in dialogue by the characters of the story. The central meaning of a play does not appear in the dialogue but in the choruses, so that Sophocles does not have to overload his dialogue. Here he is merely creating emotional embroidery. That is not to say it is not important. It is extremely important that our hearts should be wrung with pity for Antigone, because, in the earlier part of the play, Antigone's very rightness has made her seem somewhat cold. But our emotional involvement is not structural; the play would exist even if we detested Antigone. For the point about her action is that it is right, even if she cannot justify it.

With these preliminary considerations, we may summarize the development of the play. The prologue is a scene full of urgency as Antigone meets Ismene and tells her about Creon's edict. We learn that the penalty for disobeying the edict and burying Polyneices is "death by community stoning in public" (36). Ismene at first fails to catch the drift of what Antigone intends. When she does, she is horrified at the risk involved and fumbles for excuses to do nothing. Antigone announces her intention of going on alone. The scene ends almost in hatred as Antigone hurries off to perform the burial.

A normal reaction to this scene, and one perfectly consistent with it and the rest of the play, is to make Antigone a pale, set person, not especially strong, but with total determination; and to make Ismene a more normal, feminine girl, with ordinary weaknesses and vacillations. There is no evidence for this, however. Antigone for Sophocles is merely a girl who has made up her mind. Through the sufferings that come to her, she may become hysterical, but she does not change her mind. Ismene is a girl who, from fear, in the prologue refuses to act and then, later on, acts with courage in spite of her fear by offering to share the punishment as if she had so acted. It is annoying for us that Sophocles, who can illuminate character so brilliantly, does not bother to do so for the two girls. The scene is a great challenge to actors. But, unlike a scene in Chekhov, it does not require knowing all there is to know about the lives of Antigone and Ismene away from the particular situation in which we see them.

Antigone and Ismene exit in opposite directions, and the chorus march on without singing. The *parodos* starts as a strophic dance. It is in two systems, but after each *strophē* and *antistrophē* there is a stanza of anapests. Those attached to the first system match rhythmically, contain Doric dialect and so were sung. They are really part of the dance, a kind of variation of texture. The march rhythm suits what is sung to it, in the *strophē* the march of the invading army (110–16), in the *antistrophē* the doom of Zeus (128–33). Only the final stanza of anapests is the normal linking chant to announce the entrance of Creon.

The dance is obviously vigorous. The ninth line of the first system is full of short syllables. The pattering speed of this rhythm fits very well the *strophē*'s panic (108) and the *antistrophē*'s clatter of battle (126). At a moment for climactic vigor in the fifth line of the second system the line is two cretics, and therefore presumably involved kick steps (138, *strophē*; 152, *antistrophē*).

The mood of the *parodos* is triumphant, but it contains a note of warning. The first line of the second system presents in the *strophē* the crash of the attacker (134), in the *antistrophē* (147), the arrival of victory. If we had only the words of the *antistrophē*, we might think that this was an unconditionally triumphant moment. But if the dance is to fit the words of the *strophē*, at any rate some of the chorus must be on the ground, representing the crash. They will therefore sing of the arrival of victory from this position of humility. This of course makes an enormous difference to the mood. The *Gesamtkunstwerk* expresses the moral attitude of the play, and indeed of Sophocles in general: victory is to be received only on our knees.

As the dance ends Creon enters. He announces that with the death of Eteocles and Polyneices he has taken command of the state as next of kin. The real test of a man, he proclaims proudly, is what he does when he is in power (175–77). This is the test that he himself will so soon fail. His speech is the overemphatic protest of a weak man.

In contrast to the presentation of Antigone and Ismene, the actor playing Creon is required to think extensively about the character of Creon away from the situation of the play. All kinds of character quirks round out his personality for the actor who can find them. Creon is a man who has been second-in-command too long, a man used to the privileges of office without the pain of responsibility. We see from this opening speech that he is a man who laughs at his own jokes. What makes the situation unusual for him is that now other people will have to laugh at his jokes too. This sudden unexpected popularity unbalances him. This speech contains two jokes—weak puns. It is a trait of Creon we shall notice at other places in the play. All his puns are weak. After his opening general remarks he starts the meat of what he has to say as follows:

> Now, here's the *pair* of orders I've issued
> About that *pair* . . . the sons of Oedipus.
>
> (192–93)

And a little later he refers to Polyneices:

> But his *blood*-brother . . . I mean Polyneices.
>
> (198).[16]

With these two jokes Creon announces his monstrous revenge on the defeated
attacker. The chorus accept his authority and do not exclaim at the horror. But
they are not eager to be involved in the guarding of the corpse (216).

At this moment the guard arrives, one of the men detailed to watch the body.
His entrance is obviously comic. He makes a great show of breathlessness, but
he is going very slowly. A man panting excessively but moving very slowly is
bound to get a laugh. It is the breathlessness of fear; but as the scene progresses, we see that he's the kind of cocky peasant whom nothing can really
keep down. The breathlessness is the exaggeration of a put-on. The whole
introductory speech is garrulous (223–36). At this moment, as the tension of
the situation is gathering, Sophocles allows us to breathe a little with some light
relief. The first exchanges involve Creon in the humor:

> How well you marshal your facts, without
> Going beyond the evidence. Now—
> Let me guess—you're about to . . . tell me something.

This seems to be the sense of one of Creon's baffled remarks in reply to the
guard's blather (241–42).

The audience and Creon are enjoying the joky atmosphere. But eventually
the guard has to blurt out that the body has been buried. Creon shouts out a
line of rage (248) and then listens in frozen silence, while the guard describes
the details. The corpse has had a thin film of dust sprinkled over it, but no dogs
or birds have mauled it. After he has finished, the chorus leader suggests—very
tentatively, if we follow the word order—that "possibly" this is the work of the
gods (278–79). A handful of dust is not enough to protect a body from dogs in
a hot climate. But as an act of *Dikē*, it is sufficient. The gods help the action.
Creon will be destroyed by Antigone's gesture even though it was not fully
effective.

There is no enormous originality in the character drawing of the guard,
though he may well have been a great achievement at the time of the play's first
production. He is a fairly stock, low-class figure, intent only on his own safety
and well-being, remarkably callous to all those around him. What makes this
scene such a perpetual lesson in theater poetry is the use to which Sophocles
puts him. At the end of this long speech there are ten lines of empty chat (268–
77). The guard is talking to fill a gap. Sophocles has put them in for the actor
playing Creon to show his inability to react. The guard's frightened cockiness
calms the tension, and when he finally peters out, still Creon does not speak. It
is the chorus who interrupt with the remark about the gods. This finally rouses
Creon to anger. For the first twenty-four lines of his speech he addresses them.
It is a speech of wild accusations, thrashings about, paranoia. It is the speech of
a man quite incapable of command. Eventually Creon turns to the guard with
filthy threats of hanging him alive (309). But the guard knows that this is
bluster. The scene ends with the guard quipping back at Creon (315–26),
carefully deflating him, defusing his anger. The final dialogue is bathos, delib-

erately used. It is theatrically entertaining because it provides comic relief. It is
dramatically useful, to show Creon's inadequacy. The guard outwits him, and
Creon is shown as unable to face the consequences of his own order.

Creon goes into the palace and the first *stasimon* follows: the dance of man's
control over nature, and the triumph of the city, but containing the warning
that the highest civilization is upstaged by death, just as this city is being
upstaged by Antigone. At the end of the dance Antigone appears, the figure
who by breaking laws makes us aware of the nature of death. She is marched on
by the guard, and Creon appears as they are about to call for him. Creon is
unable to face the fact that it is Antigone who has performed the burial. To the
guard it is all so simple. He has caught the person he was told to catch, and so
he is in the clear. Creon can only ask the guard if he means what he says (403).
Such a remark is again the sign of an inadequate commander, refusing to accept
evidence. The guard takes the opportunity to describe the whole story in detail
(407–40). They went back, uncovered the body and waited. After a great dust
storm, they saw Antigone returning to finish the task of burying in which we
must assume that she had been interrupted.[18]

The guard leaves, and Creon has to face Antigone. The crunch comes
quickly. Antigone says that she knew all about his order. Creon blusters, "And
yet you dared contravening the laws" (449). Antigone replies, "It wasn't Zeus
who issued your order." She simply says that to leave her brother as an unburied corpse is more dreadful than anything Creon can do to her. The chorus
at this point stand with Creon, referring to her speech as "violent" (471–72).
Creon's reply is only bluster. But included in his blustering attempts to frighten
her comes a sudden command to fetch Ismene and include her in the charge.
With this arbitrary action he reveals himself as even more obviously a tyrant.
After this long speech of loud-mouthed emptiness, Antigone simply says,
"D'you want to do more than take me and kill me?" Creon is taken aback and
can only reply, "I? No. . . . If I do that, I've done quite enough" (497–98).
From that point Antigone is seen to be completely in command of the scene.
Alone certainly, fearful perhaps, but right. Creon rages around the still center
of her conviction.

Ismene is then brought in (526), and Creon, again with exaggeratedly violent
language, accuses her of being a party to Antigone's action. Ismene tries to
claim that she is, and a very moving scene between the two sisters follows as
Ismene offers to share Antigone's fate, while Antigone insists on suffering
alone. Creon takes it that Ismene is involved, while she pleads for Antigone as
the future bride of Creon's son Haemon. Creon pushes aside their great love as
mere sexual desire, and, what is more, by so insulting his son's feelings for
Antigone, insults Haemon in the deepest part of his nature. As far as the play is
concerned, Creon has only one noble trait, his love for his son. This he will
destroy as a result of his paranoiac obstinacy. The chorus are astonished and
ask if Creon really means to take Antigone away from his son (574). We may
assume, therefore, that it is not until this moment that they can believe that

Creon will really kill Antigone. Perhaps even now Creon has not yet made up his mind. The scene could end with him giving orders for their execution. But all he says to the guards is, "Take them inside." Again it is bluster, not the quick, resolute decision of a leader.

The girls are escorted inside, while Creon remains onstage during the second stasimon,[19] which ends with reference to *Atē*—the destruction that is also delusion—and its veiled allusion to Creon. Four lines of chant introduce Haemon, whom Creon greets nervously, hoping for his son's support (631–34). Haemon is a stronger, wiser man than his father. He is passionately in love with Antigone, but he also loves his father. He has determined to keep the discussion calm, and his opening speech is a politician's speech: all I want is that my father make the right decision (635–38). Creon is so relieved that Haemon has not attacked him that he overreacts and treats Antigone with open contempt:

> Spit this girl out, treat her as enemy,
> Send her away to bed someone in hell.
>
> (653–54)

The speech continues with hollow rhetoric. Haemon remains calm and replies with a long speech in which he describes the remarks of the citizens that he has overheard. The city does not think Antigone is worthy of death (693–95). Creon should be truly strong, and not afraid to change his mind. We are shown a beautiful little hint at the normal relationship between father and son, when Haemon uses the same kind of weak pun that his father uses at intervals throughout the play:

> In my opinion—though I know I'm too junior—
> I think that the man who should have seniority
> Is the one with complete knowledge of everything.
>
> (719–21)

The wordplay continues, as their argument becomes more violent. There are several more punning exchanges in the next twenty lines (729–30; 740–45). We are given to imagine the normal conversation between father and son, full of puns and wordplay. But now the tension is building. Haemon remains calm for a long time. He tries to argue that the city agrees with him, and that a good ruler respects the city's opinion. Creon takes this as an attack on his own authority. He shouts that Haemon is siding with the woman to attack him. A climax is reached:

> *Creon.* All your arguments are only for her.
> *Haemon.* For you. For me. For the gods of death.
> *Creon.* Not for her. You won't . . . marry her alive.
>
> (748–50)

At this point Haemon realizes that he has lost. The end of the scene comes quickly. Both men are out of control with anger. While Creon shouts to the guards to bring Antigone out and kill her before her bridegroom's eyes, Haemon rushes out, shouting that he will never allow that to happen, and that Creon will never see his face again. The chorus has tried to keep the balance between father and son. They try to calm Creon by referring to Haemon's youth. Creon replies that nothing will stop the two girls being killed. The chorus exclaim at the thought of killing Ismene, who has had nothing to do with the breaking of the law (770). In one line Creon admits that they are right (771). This casual vacillation between life and death is another example of how Creon is caught in the delusion of *Atē*. The chorus persist with Creon. How is he going to kill Antigone? We remember the prologue, where we learned that disobedience to the edict meant public stoning. Creon announces that Antigone will be taken to a remote cave, and there walled up with some food, so that the city cannot be deemed to have killed her, and therefore will not incur pollution.

There is no answer from the chorus except to start the third *stasimon*, the song of the power of love, before which even the immortals succumb. Creon is resisting an irresistible force. The mood of this leads into the *kommos* for Antigone, where she sings of her marriage with death. The chorus sing anapests between each of her stanzas. They reveal some sympathy for her, but are not totally on her side by any means. Their final judgment is that she has brought this on herself (875). Her only reply is a last pathetic epode:

> No tears, no friends, no marriage song.
> Down I am dragged, down, down that path
> That will wait no longer.
> Never again the blessing of light,
> Holy sunlight feeling my eyes.
> None of my friends shedding a tear
> For my despair.

> > (876–82)

Two speeches follow, a short one from Creon in which he checks her lament, and the long one from Antigone, discussed earlier in this section, in which she expresses her desolation. Quickly she is hurried out, chanting a short sequence of anapests:

> Buildings and soil of Thebes,
> Gods of my fatherland,
> His orders are, "No more delay.
> Drag her away."
> Look at me, princes of Thebes.
> I am the last of the kings.
> Look at my sufferings.

Look at the man my sufferings please.
Reverence demands obedience, and I obeyed.

(937–43)

Immediately there follows the surrealist transitional *stasimon* already discussed, the song that shows how this girl's imprisonment will be the king's destruction. Meanwhile the leading actor changes his mask to reappear as Teiresias at the end of the dance. The scene is straightforward. Teiresias has come to tell Creon that because of the unburied body there is pollution in the city. This pollution is the direct result of Creon's action. He must take advice and cease to be stubborn. Creon flies off into the ravings of a paranoiac. He accuses Teiresias of having taken a bribe. He knows, as we know, that Teiresias is incorruptible. He also knows that Teiresias is his true friend. The opening lines of the scene have shown that (991–97). Creon has been in the habit of treating the prophet as a kind of father figure. And now he says that he has taken a bribe to conspire against him. This obsession with bribery has come out before, in the scene with the guard (294ff.). It is one more indication of paranoia, or, as the Greeks would say, *Atē*.

After some fencing in stichomythia, Teiresias is provoked to tell Creon openly that for the corpse he has insulted he will have to give a corpse "from his own guts" (1066). He sums up the theology of Creon's wrong action:

An above-life you've thrown below,
Colonizing graves with a person still breathing.
And you hold up here what belongs down there.
A corpse without rites violates death.
That body's not yours, nor the powers above.
Your action's a rape of the air itself.

(1068–73)

For this, revenge will come quickly. Teiresias does not wait for Creon's answer. He leaves, in total command of the scene.

The chorus leader breaks the silence. Teiresias has never been wrong, he says. There follows a moment of surprise: Creon changes his mind. He who had boasted of his independence now puts himself in the hands of the chorus. He asks them to tell him what to do (1099). They say he must fetch Antigone immediately and give Polyneices burial. Creon rushes out to do so. Theatrically, the sudden panic of Creon is enormously effective. Dramatically, it opens a whole new aspect of his character and shows how Sophocles could create the sudden and yet properly motivated changes in plot that later naturalistic theater would regard as the be-all and end-all of playwriting. In the totality of the religious poetry that the prosaic call Sophocles' philosophy, it serves a major purpose, which will be revealed in a moment. Creon changes his mind. But we shall see it is too late. Affront *Dikē*, and *Dikē* reacts, like a crossed electric wire or a burst dam. This is not to say that Creon is a helpless puppet of fate.

Stasimon 2 and the scene with Haemon that follows stress that he could change his mind. But it is an important part of Sophocles' religion and poetry that there is a moment when you choose finally, and after which you are caught in the consequences of your choice. I myself think that Sophocles means Creon to be free to change during the scene with Teiresias. But his accusation of Teiresias as accepting bribes is the final refusal to face the truth.

Sophocles' vision of free will is much the same as that of orthodox Christianity: choose and then accept the consequences. But with Sophocles there is of course no concept of repentance. Creon does repent. But it is too late. We should notice that the chorus tell Creon to rescue Antigone and then bury Polyneices (1100–1101). Creon, we shall learn from the messenger, went and buried Polyneices first, then went to free Antigone. If he had done the two jobs in the order in which he was told to do them, he would have been in time to rescue Antigone and therefore save the lives of Haemon and Eurydice. Creon is caught up in *Atē*, and so his judgment in every detail is wrong.

Now the chorus have taken command, in full realization that Creon is wrong. Up to now they have wavered between support for Creon and sympathy with Antigone. The dialogue passages have suggested citizens full of doubts, trying to express what is best for the city. The songs have expressed an ambivalence between their poetic and dramatic meaning, between what they mean in the total context of the dramatic poem and what they mean in terms of the character of the chorus at that particular moment in the play. In the first *stasimon*, the dramatic meaning implies a brushing aside of the fact of death, which the poetic meaning puts clearly before us. In the second and third *stasima* the dramatic meaning of the words alone are generalizations. It is the *Gesamkunstwerk* that pinpoints them. But in the fifth *stasimon* dramatic and poetic meaning are completely one. The chorus call for Dionysus to come. It is unconditional acceptance of the god. The dramatic development of the play is over, the interaction of the characters, including the character of the chorus as Theban councillors, is over. The dance brings on the god of fertility and death, the god of the theater. The rest of the play is an expansion of that moment.

The *stasimon* finishes with a cry to Dionysus (1152). The leading actor enters again, this time in the mask of the messenger. *Dikē* has recoiled, first in the thwarted action of Antigone, then in the prophesies of Teiresias, and now in the actual disaster of the messenger speech. Creon has buried the body of Polyneices, but he was too late to save Antigone from hanging herself while the walling-up was still unfinished. Haemon has been discovered in the cave with his bride and has slashed at his father with his sword. Having missed his father, he has stabbed himself. Eurydice, the queen, who has appeared from the palace to hear the messenger's speech, now goes into the palace and hangs herself, cursing Creon as a murderer. This we shall learn later from the messenger who follows her into the palace as Creon arrives with the cortege, himself carrying his son's body.

Creon's *kommos* is a long one, of three systems, mainly in dochmiacs. The first system ends with iambic recitative, one line sung by the chorus. After the first *strophē* the messenger reappears with the news of Eurydice's suicide, which is amplified in short passages of iambics between the sung stanzas, probably all these iambics also being chanted. This finale has a certain liturgical quality. Because of this it is necessary to stress that there is no hint of some Christian reconciliation. Creon is humbled, abject, and repentant. But there is no help for him. Broken by despair, writhing in love for his son, he cries for his own death to come in an agonized song of pure dochmiacs (1328–32). That, however, is not to be yet.

> *Chorus.* That's for the future. What needs your attention
> Is the present. The future . . is in other hands.
> *Creon.* But what we're discussing is my sum total prayer.
> *Chorus.* Now, pray for nothing. You are a mortal.
> From your destined destruction there's no escape.
>
> (1334–38)

So the sequence continues in recitative. We may call the final *exodos* of the chorus a chorale. But we must remember that it is not a Christian chorale:

> Happiness only comes
> From a sense of the nature of things.
> In matters involving God
> There must be nothing but awe.
> Arrogance speaks so big,
> Arrogance suffers big wounds,
> Old age and wounds in the end
> May teach you to understand.
>
> (1347–53)

Understanding one's place in the pattern; that is the end for Sophocles. No reconciliation; no love. To try and make Sophocles a Christian before his time is to sentimentalize him. This final chant provides a few lines to remember as a summary of his philosophy, a useful preliminary to considering the final expression of his mystical vision in the *Oedipus at Colonus.*

Summary of a great poem is an oversimplification. The only way to sum up the *Antigone* is to perform the play from beginning to end. If we are to summarize with a catchphrase, we may say that it is a play about reverence. A leader without reverence is a bad and foolish leader. A city without reverence is a bad city. Sophocles makes Creon's offence, his insult to the dead, at one with Lycurgus' offence against Dionysus. Dionysus is the focus of the city's reverence. He is also lord of the dead. And to acknowledge this with ritual is for Sophocles common sense. It is sensible to honor the dead, for, as Antigone puts it in the most matter-of-fact way, "I have to spend much more time with the dead than with the living" (74–75). The implication of the play is that it is sound sense for us all to remember this.

Aristophanes: *The Frogs*

The Frogs is worthy of study as Aristophanes' masterpiece. We might also describe it as the fifth century's *Tempest,* the play most concerned with the nature of the theatrical experience itself. Although it is one of the funniest plays ever written in any language, behind almost every joke there is a sense of serious preoccupations. It is the one of all Aristophanes' plays where all the laughter contributes to the total topsy-turviness in a poetic rhythm as strongly controlled as any play of Sophocles. Paradox within paradox grows, changes, and vanishes. It can be studied as a great allegory of what it is to be a poet, a poem to compare with *The Tempest* or *Piers Plowman.* Let an Italian make the comparison with Dante:

> Aristofane passa in mezzo ai suoi contemporanei come in mezzo a un popolo di morti, su cui s'e impressa la condanna del poeta, in nome del passato e dell'avvenire; come Dante.[20]

Inevitably an essay such as this must concentrate on the deeper meanings of what Aristophanes presents to us. But it is necessary also to emphasize that the serious concern of the poet does not in any way hamper the laughter. It is more that Aristophanes is saying, as it were, "Let us make them laugh to their limit; for that will make them remember the image as long as possible. Let them laugh in the theater, and think about it afterwards."

The action of the play is the decision of the god Dionysus to dress up as Heracles and go down to Hades in order to bring Euripides back from the dead. For the good poets are gone, and the city needs a poet. Having arrived at Pluto's palace, Dionysus discovers that Euripides has lost no time and has just put in a claim to be nominated the greatest poet of the dead, with the privileges this honor entails. Dionysus is asked to judge the contest that follows this claim and at which Aeschylus defends his title against Euripides. In the course of the contest, Pluto advises Dionysus to take the winner back to earth. Finally Dionysus decides for Aeschylus.

The form of the play can also be expressed in terms of a serious thesis, with fantastical solution. The thesis is that the city is in a desperate situation and that what it needs is a good poet, not only to inspire it, but even to advise it. The fantastical solution is to fetch up a poet from the dead. Where, however, *The Frogs* is different from all other Aristophanes plays is that the action is not instigated by a typical Athenian, usually just a man-in-the-street character, while in *The Women at the Thesmophoria* it is Euripides, as the Poet. In *The Frogs* the action is performed by the god Dionysus himself. This gives the play a different flavor. Part of the point of Aristophanes' combination of serious preoccupation and fantasy is—in the rest of his plays—to leave the suggestion with his audience: You too can do something about the problem. You could make peace somehow, even if not by refraining from all sex with your hus-

bands. Behind the preoccupation of *The Frogs* is the suggestion that if the
solution comes from Dionysus, there is nothing that the audience can do. At
the back of the laughter there is a deep sadness, even a desperation.

The central image of the play is of course the figure of Dionysus himself. He
appears in the traditional fat-man costume associated with the worshipers of
Dionysus.[21] This is one paradox: Dionysus taking the form of one of his
worshipers. Another paradox is that Dionysus should need to go to all the
trouble that he does in order to reach Hades. For we must remember the
fragment of Heracleitus already quoted:

One is the Lord of Death, and Dionysus of the raving maenads.

(frag. 15)

Dionysus dresses up as Heracles, the god whose nature is most opposed to his,
and suffers great hardships in order to reach the realm that is his anyhow.

The personality of Dionysus, even without Aristophanes, is full of paradox.
He is the god whose strength appears weakness, and weakness strength. This
we see in *The Bacchants*, where Dionysus appears as a soft, effeminate man,
and where his power is demonstrated through women. There is also a tendency
to laugh at Dionysus in a way in which one would not laugh at Athene, simply
because Athene is a goddess of mental activity, and mental activity is not as
potentially funny as drunkenness or the act of sex. Aristophanes can add to this
foundation, because Dionysus is the god of the theater and must therefore
approve of all the violently contrasting images presented in the theater. Dionysus becomes a chameleon creature because the theater is chameleon. One of the
important moments in the total paradox is when Dionysus, dressed as Heracles, confronts the real Heracles, who splits himself laughing. At this moment
something is said about the relationship of theater and life. We cannot define it
further; but we recognize its significance.

Right at the beginning of the play, we are introduced to the idea of Dionysus
watching all the plays performed, and being bored by the bad jokes he so often
sees (16–18). This, however, should best be regarded as one element of a larger
paradox. Dionysus takes part in his own worship. The most important image
of this is the mere silent presence of Dionysus onstage as the procession of
initiates sing their hymn to Dionysus.[22] The paradox is all the stronger for not
being stated except visually. It is a theatrical representation of the fact that the
statue of Dionysus stayed in the theater for the performances. At every festival,
in a sense, Dionysus takes part in his own worship, because he is present in the
form of a statue. What is the difference between a stone or wooden representation and one that consists of a human being? We cannot answer or define
this question further, but it is part of the paradox of the play, which we
recognize and remember.

This paradox is underlined further by two very important jokes. Just before
the entry of the chorus of initiates, Dionysus is confronted by the imaginary

monsters of Hades. In terror he runs straight across the *orchestra* to the central front seat, where the priest of Dionysus sat in the place of honor. "Help me, priest," he shouts, "so we can have a drink together after the show" (297). Obviously this is a very funny moment, but it also leaves a very hallucinogenic sense of different levels of reality. In association with this joke is a moment in the procession of the initiates. After they have sung and danced their hymns to the traditional three gods, Demeter, Persephone, and Iankos-Dionysus, they sing the equally traditional satiric verses while the procession moves on. Into this traditional song Dionysus enters, asking the way to Pluto's house in a verse to the tune the chorus are singing. The natural thing for him to do is to approach the head of the procession to ask his way. At the head of the procession is the statue of Dionysus, which the worshipers carry. Dionysus accordingly asks the way of his own statue. It is a funny theatrical joke. But there is also a thought-provoking paradox. Dionysus does in a sense depend on his rituals and on his priest. Worship depends on worshipers. There are hints in the plays that the Greek gods are not self-sufficient. In the prologue of *The Trojan Women* (26–27), for instance, Poseidon says that as Troy falls, so the gods who have been worshiped in Troy themselves suffer.[23] In *The Birds* there is a frisson behind the joke of cutting off the gods' sacrifices (*Birds*, especially 186, 554–69, 611–26). The gods can be weakened. It is partly to do with the fact that unlike the Jews, the Greeks of the fifth century did not have the concepts to define the nature of the gods apart from their rituals.

Clearly, there is a relationship between the image of Euripides as the Poet in *The Women at the Thesmophoria*, and the image of Dionysus in *The Frogs*. The Poet is naturally connected with the god of poetry. One of the important things about the image in *The Women at the Thesmophoria* is the ineffectiveness of Euripides while acting in his own plays. The poet is unable to achieve things. In the same way Dionysus is ineffective, and this is part of the play. We can see this if we realize how everything that happens in the play either is, in a sense, unnecessary or achieves the opposite effect to that intended. Dionysus dresses up as Heracles in order to steal a poet away from Hades. But as soon as he is recognized in Hades he is treated with great honor and allowed to take whatever poet he wishes away with him. The Heracles act is quite unnecessary. In order to reach Hades, Dionysus must cross the dread lake by boat. Once he has done this, in considerable discomfort, he is met by his slave, who has walked around. There is an elaborate sequence in which Dionysus and his slave Xanthias are beaten to see which of them is the god. Afterwards they are taken inside so that Pluto can say instantly which is the god. The beating is unnecessary. Dionysus goes down to Hades to fetch up one poet. He ends by fetching up another. Pluto arranges a contest to decide which is the best poet among the dead. Dionysus is appointed judge and then told to take the winner back to earth. The contest is therefore pointless, since the winner will not sit in honor among the dead. The end of the play is Aeschylus bequeathing his seat of honor to Sophocles and saying that Euripides must never occupy it. But we remember that the reason for the contest was that Euripides had built up a faction to support his claim. This faction will support his claim against Sophocles, just as they had against Aeschylus. There may have to be a second contest. This unnecessariness is of course helpful in producing laughs. It is also part of the texture of the thought. We are being given images of the poetic process. Dionysus rows across the lake partly because Aristophanes has made him row.

The question the play asks is, Can poetry help the state? The question was especially important because at the time of writing Athens was in a condition of acute crisis. Four months before the play's production, in September 406, the Athenian fleet had won a major naval victory over the Spartans at Arginusae. But the victory had been spoilt. A storm had risen immediately after the battle, and the generals had decided not to risk picking up survivors of the wrecked ships, let alone the dead bodies. The generals were therefore attacked for neglecting their duty. Eight were prosecuted and found guilty. Six were executed, two having fled after the battle. The mood in Athens therefore was manic, rather than joyful. Arginusae had been a desperate effort. For the first time slaves had been drafted as rowers, and after the victory given their freedom. Athens was once again in command of the eastern Aegean. But money was short, and there can have been little sense of security. After Arginusae, the Spartans had offered peace on the terms that each side would keep what it had won, except that the Spartans would evacuate Decelea, their fort in Attica, which prevented any effective farming of the land and made it unsafe for Athenians to leave the city walls. These peace terms were the best that Athens could hope for. Even at this stage of the war, the Spartans were not fully determined to smash Athens completely. It seems incredible that peace should have been refused. But the demagogue Cleophon persuaded the Assembly to reject the Spartan offer. To a lover of peace like Aristophanes it must have seemed that Athens was completely mad, in the grip of _Atē_, the destruction which brings delusion. To the wise observer it must have been fairly obvious that if Athens was defeated once again at sea, it would be the end. That defeat was to come in the summer of 405, at Aegospotami, a few months after _The Frogs'_ production.

It appears from the song in the _parabasis_ (674–85) that there was some trial of Cleophon in process, or contemplated. Unfortunately we do not know any more about it except for this oblique allusion. At any rate, there is no mistaking Aristophanes' attitude. Much of _The Frogs_ is both elusive and allusive, paradoxical, topsy-turvy and thought-provoking on many different levels at once. But the references to Cleophon are baldly straightforward. Aristophanes begs his audience to get rid of him. The last words of the play are chanted in the sacred dactyls: "Let Cleophon fight if he wants to in his own country." He was a foreigner from Thrace, and no doubt it seemed to make matters worse that a foreigner should be leading Athens to destruction.

There was only one commander capable of saving Athens, the brilliant but unstable Alcibiades. In the summer of 407 he had returned to Athens after having won victories in the Aegean that had revived Athenian fortunes. It had been eight years since he had left with the Sicilian expedition, eight years since he had been exiled in his absence for the alleged blasphemy of the incident of the herms, eight years since his advice to the Spartans had caused the near total defeat of Athens. How could the Athenians not regard him with very mixed feelings?

Alcibiades' most notable achievement in 407 was to organize the proper celebration of the Eleusinian mysteries. Normally a procession along the Sacred Way from Athens to Eleusis was the main event of the festival, which took place every year in September. Since the Spartans had occupied Decelea, the procession had been unable to walk, and the participants had sailed instead. Alcibiades organized an escort, and the procession had taken place. To present a chorus of initiates in the Eleusinian mysteries a year and a half after this event must have had a profound emotional effect; it was also a political action, reminding the audience of what Alcibiades had done for them.

In the spring of 406, the Athenian fleet had suffered a minor defeat at Notion. Alcibiades was not there, but he was blamed and deposed from his office of general. Enraged at this, he had left Athens for his private fort on the Hellespont. Many Athenians must have seen him go with the feeling that now their last hope had gone. One of the important questions asked of the two competing poets (1422 ff.) is what the city should do about Alcibiades. The significance of this question is not so much the answers as the fact that they are irrelevant. Alcibiades has given the city up in disgust. It is the most painful image of the impotence of poetry that the play presents.

The presence of Cleophon and the absence of Alcibiades are the two most important features of the audience as political people. They help to provide the sense of desperation that is at the back of the laughter. We learn from the first argument that The Frogs had two choregoi instead of the usual one man. It would be natural that at this stage of the war, with Athens impoverished, there would be few Athenians left who were rich enough to undertake the duties of choregos. After the total defeat of Athens in 404, the city was reduced to bankruptcy and could not afford proper choruses. The choruses of comedy were more likely to be cut than those of tragedy. It seems clear from the two fourth-century plays of Aristophanes that the comic chorus was never fully restored. So perhaps the comedies of 405 were the last to have choruses in the sense in which Aristophanes would have understood the term. At the climax of the contest, Dionysus says that he came down to Hades to fetch a poet "so that the city could be saved and keep her dancing choruses" (1419). Contained in The Frogs is the feeling that Cleophon will not be driven out, that Alcibiades will not return, that the city will therefore not be saved, and that therefore the dancing choruses will disappear.

It was a strange time altogether. Euripides had left Athens after the production of the Orestes in 408. He had written The Bacchants at the court of Macedonia and probably produced it there. Disappointed with his relative failure in Athens, he had then died in Macedonia. Sophocles heard the news at the time of the spring festival in 406 and appeared with all his performers at the *proagōn*, without crowns and wearing black. It was probably at that festival that *The Bacchants* received its first Athenian production, for we know that it won first prize posthumously, produced with the *Iphigeneia at Aulis* and the lost *Alcmaeon at Corinth*. During that year Sophocles was writing the *Oedipus at Colonus*, his final masterpiece, his final incantation and offering of himself as dying poet in a last attempt to save Athens. During the year Sophocles also died. Aristophanes must have written *The Frogs* after the battle of Arginusae in September 406. He would have seen *The Bacchants*, and may very well have also seen the script of the *Oedipus at Colonus*. Sophocles and Euripides had made their greatest plays and died. Aristophanes also presents his poetic last will and testament. Three of the greatest plays of the fifth century belong within a year of each other.

Which was the more important event in Athens, the death of Sophocles or that of Euripides? We have only to ask the question to realize the answer. Sophocles was part of the council supervising the war effort. He was also the most universally praised of all the poets. We read in his life that the Athenians even sacrificed to him after his death.[24] Priest and ex-general, he was unquestionably the poet of all poets to be the savior of Athens. However much Aristophanes might enjoy Euripides' work, as the excitement of *The Women at the Thesmophoria* vividly demonstrates, there could be no doubt as to which poet would seem the greater to the vast majority of the audience.

Our interpretation of *The Frogs* depends very much on our interpretation of the contest of the poets, which occupies the latter half of the play. Remembering the topsy-turviness of the rest of the play, we should certainly not expect to take the poetry contest straight, particularly when we are confronted near the end with the fact that one of the crucial tests for the poets is to advise about Alcibiades, who has already left the city. The obvious poet for Dionysus to bring back from Hades to save the city is Sophocles. Sophocles is hardly mentioned in the play. Heracles is made to say to Dionysus that Sophocles is the poet to bring back (76), but Dionysus deliberately gives a silly reason for not fetching him by saying that he wants to see how Sophocles' son Iophon, also a poet, manages without his father's help. This remark of Dionysus would not get a very large laugh; it is just a silly thing to say. The audience would be made aware that Dionysus is acting wrongheadedly.

The contest finally results in a win for Aeschylus. Most scholars have assumed that Aristophanes disliked Euripides and have interpreted the contest as an out-and-out win for Aeschylus. But nearly all of the contest is drawn. Dionysus is in doubt until he poses the two final tests, the problem of Alcibiades, and a request for general advice to the city. The former is, as I have said, irrelevant. As for the latter, Euripides answers with indeterminate pedantries, seeing both sides of the case (1443–50); Aeschylus with oracular truism (1463–65). He produces the old advice of Pericles to rely on the navy. This sounds very like a stock joke, the kind of advice that might be offered by some old-timer out of touch with the reality of contemporary life. Athens has relied on her navy for years. Look where it has got her. A modern equivalent might be a play produced in America in the early 1970s, before an audience sick of the Vietnam War. Some great old-timer—an amalgam of Roosevelt, Hemingway, and John Wayne, but poet and thinker as well—is asked what he would do to save the nation. His answer: "Bomb the shit out of them."

Aristophanes was a devoted supporter of the peace cause. Athens was sick of war. The first achievement that Aeschylus claims for his poetry is that it helped to make the Athenians more warlike (1013 ff.). We must remember that Aeschylus made no mention of his poetry on his epitaph, only that he had fought at Marathon and Salamis. It was perhaps a stock joke in theatrical circles to laugh at Aeschylus' military pretensions. But at any rate, there can be no doubt that Aeschylus stands as the poet of war, and therefore is the least suitable poet for Athens in 405, when the main need is for peace.

One can guess that the natural verdict of a sensitive Athenian such as Aristophanes would be that Aeschylus is the right poet to hold the chair of best poet among the dead, and that Sophocles is the right poet to bring back to life and save the city, but that if a choice is to be made between Aeschylus and Euripides for saving the city, then Euripides, with his interest in sex, would certainly do less harm than Aeschylus, with his interest in war. Dionysus, then, chooses wrongly all along the line. Is Dionysus here the representative of Athens, since clearly Aristophanes is saying that Athens is choosing wrongly? Is Aristophanes making a point about the theater, saying that the judgment of the theater is wrong, in fact paying a surreptitious tribute to his friend Euripides, who was not enough appreciated by the theater audience? Such an implication could hardly have been primary. Aristophanes depended on the support of the audience, depended on being able to believe that their judgment was sound.

In nearly all his plays Aristophanes clearly approves of the fantastical solutions performed by Just-City or Vintage, Twister, or Lysistrata (Disband-the-Army). The most idiotic of his central characters is Dionysus, the god of the theater. The Frogs is the only play that, so to speak, ends in disaster. Of course it is not stated, because a comedy must end happily. But the implication of the end is that Aeschylus will return to Athens in triumph and urge the Athenians to war and so to disaster. Part of the meaning of this play is that the god of the theater, by taking part in the theater, brings about disaster.

The depth of these paradoxes is beyond us, because we shall never fully recapture the sense of what Dionysus was to Aristophanes. We are left with a frustrating sensation that Dionysus himself is eluding us. But it is not impossible that this also is part of Aristophanes' intention. Would he have put Dionysus unequivocally onstage in a comedy, particularly such an equivocal comedy as this?

We should notice that Dionysus is presented in totally ridiculous light only in the first half of the play. There are several undignified moments in the prologue. There is then Dionysus' encounter with the frogs, a sequence both lyrical and grotesque. Then follows the scene with the imaginary monster, in which Dionysus disgraces himself. Then there is the beauty of the procession of initiates, followed by the farcical scene in which Dionysus is beaten. It is almost as if Aristophanes was pushing a paradox as hard as possible. As he prepares to show the worship of Dionysus at its most beautiful, so he shows the figure of his Dionysus at its most grotesque.

The Frogs is Aristophanes' formally most perfect play. But there is an odd lack of integration of the chorus with the action. This again is significant for the meaning of the play. As Dionysus rows across the lake to enter Hades, he is met by a chorus of frogs. The song-and-dance sequence that follows provides one of the most memorable moments of lyrical-comical absurdity in the history of the theater. But as lyric poetry, it is as full of allusion as the most complicated *stasimon* in Sophocles, and depends for its complete understanding on a complex web of awarenesses which its original audience possessed, and which we do not.

> *Chorus of Frogs.* Brekekekex koahx koahx.
> Brekekekex koahx koahx.
> We are the pond-bogside kids.
> So blow that horn. We've arrived
> Hymn-singing. How d'you like this tune? Some rhythm!
> Koahx koahx.
> Once—oh what a beat we had.
> We sang for the Lord of Life
> Bogside Dionysus' shrine,
> Smashed as a blessed pitcher
> Pouring the blessed liquor,
> We'd rave to the shrine, and we were . . . alive . . . people.
> Brekekekex koahx koahx.
>
> *Dionysus.* At this with pain I start to gasp.
> Koahx koahx
> I've got a sore ass.
> But I suppose you couldn't care less.
>
> *Chorus of Frogs.* Brekekekex koahx koahx.
>
> *Dionysus.* To hell with you and your koahx.
> You're nothing but—koahx koahx.
>
> *Chorus of Frogs.* Serve you right for interfering.
> We are beloved by all music-loving spirits.
> Demon of the hoof-dance with his whistle-winds a-blowing—
> As for the Lord of golden harp—how they adore me . . .
> There is a musical instrument industry
> Out of the bamboo stems from ponds.

Dionysus. And I've got blisters on my—oh!
My ass is sweating ever so.
And soon it will pop up and go—

Chorus of Frogs. Brekekekex koahx koahx.

Dionysus. My dear musicians, do stop.
Less brio!

Chorus of Frogs. Certainly not!
We shall croak as we can croak
All day long in sunny summer,
Leaping through the rushes and sedges,
Leaping high, croaking for pleasure,
Plenty of plunge-plopping melody.
Rainy days we still go dancing—
Easy to shelter under water—
There we play our double forte
Pondbubble-an-splatsplashmachine.

Dionysus. Brekekekex koahx koahx.
I'll play your tune, take it from you.

Chorus of Frogs. That's a dreadful noise you're making.

Dionysus. Nothing to the noise when I start breaking.
Stop or I shall split in two.

Chorus of Frogs. Brekekekex koahx koahx.

Dionysus. Oh go to hell. I couldn't care less.

Chorus of Frogs. Yes, and we shall croak crescendo
Long as our throat can keep wide open
All the day from dawn to dusk.

Dionysus. Brekekekex koahx koahx.
You'll never get away with this.

Chorus of Frogs. Nor will your voice top me either.

Dionysus. Nor will you top my reprise.
Never ever. For I'll crescendo
Even if it takes all day.
Brekekekex koahx koahx.
Till I, sforzando, diminuendo your koahx.
Brekekekex koahx koahx.

I thought I stood a fair chance of stopping your koahx.

(209–69)[25]

The frogs refer to themselves as the ghosts of the worshipers of Dionysus who used to sing at the *Anthesteria* celebrations in the "Bogside" where the old temple of Dionysus stood. Clearly, this "Bogside" could not have been a real bog in Aristophanes' day. For one would hardly build a temple in a bog, or use it as the site of a winter festival. From the name, derived no doubt from a time long ago when there was a bog on the site, Aristophanes conceives of making his ghosts into frogs who would rightly live in a bog.[26]

Dionysus is crossing the *orchestra* in a ship-car similar to that in which the statue of Dionysus was carried in procession to his temple for the climax of the *Anthesteria,* the Sacred Marriage of Dionysus and the bride of the King Archon, at the moment when the festival changed from a day of drunken revel to an All Souls' Day. Clearly it is important that the ship-car would remind Aristophanes' audience of the Sacred Marriage, and of the moment when the festival changed. As the festival changes to the Day of the Dead, so Dionysus enters the kingdom of the dead.

The second day of the *Anthesteria* commemorated the dead, especially those drowned in Deucalion's flood, the catastrophe in Greek folk memory equivalent to the Jewish story of Noah. Clearly, it is also part of the joke of the frog chorus that they are the ghosts of drowned people. For frogs do not drown.

The sequence is both lyrical and grotesque. Its meaning is unanalyzable in straightforward prose terms. As a warning against taking its lyricism straight, Aristophanes presents us with a delightful image to show that it is nonsense also. The frogs dive into the water to escape getting wet in the rain (246–49). Medieval Christians contained the power of the demons they feared by sculpting them as gargoyles, making them into funny little creatures to decorate the columns of their churches. Aristophanes has made what is somewhat like a gargoyle: the terrifying Dionysus, lord of the lightning and death and fertility, is presented as a grotesque little fat man. The beautiful songs of worship, in which no doubt Aristophanes and his audience delighted, are presented as the croak of frogs. It is a charming sequence and one in which we do feel a sense of the mystery of Dionysus. But the picture, strong as it is, defies analysis.

There is clearly a relationship between the chorus of frogs and the later chorus of initiates. For one thing, the two choruses must have been played by the same people. In times of poverty, no *choregos* would have wasted money on two choruses when he could make one do both with a change of costume. The frogs are ghosts; the initiates are the living dead, the people who by their rites of initiation are able to continue to live after death. From the title of the play, the audience would be expecting the chorus of frogs but not the chorus of initiates, and we can imagine that the second *parodos* would have caused a hush in the theater with its simple lyricism (316–459).

The chorus of initiates have the most purely lyrical function of all Aristophanic choruses. We know that the Athenians were extremely sensitive about the Eleusinian mysteries and therefore any kind of mockery of the mysteries would not have been tolerated. As with *The Women at the Thesmophoria,* Aristophanes is very determined to keep his comedy from interfering with the rite. In the latter part of the previous play the chorus of women are mainly there simply to dance the hymns and keep on reminding us that we are indeed at the *Thesmophoria*. It is perhaps no coincidence that Aristophanes insists most on the fact that his plays are an element of worship in the two plays in which he is most concerned with the art of poetry.

The strongest image that the initiate chorus presents is a negative one. Why is there no relationship between them and Dionysus, no sign of recognition? There is only one occasion on which they become involved with Dionysus' adventures: as he reaches Pluto's house he is met by a series of characters who alternately love and hate Heracles. Those who hate Heracles threaten him, at which Dionysus is terrified and asks his slave Xanthias to change places with him, with the result that he is acting the slave at the moment when the friends of Heracles arrive to entertain their hero. There is one *stasimon* that delightedly applauds the rapid changes, celebrating first Dionysus and then Xanthias with apparent indiscrimination (534–48, *strophē*, Dionysus and chorus; 589–604, *antistrophē*, Xanthias and chorus). Here the joke lies in the fact that the chorus of initiates behave like anyone else. It is musical comedy; the chorus could be yokels and Dionysus could be any tricky dealer whom they applaud.

The dance of the initiate chorus was probably more a matter of ritual gesture than elaborate mime. The *parodos* does not suggest an elaborate mime choreography. The system in the *parabasis* is unfortunately very hard for us now to interpret, since it is concerned in the *strophē* with Cleophon, and in the *antistrophē* with another villain, Cleigenes, about whom we know nothing. Unaware of the exact nature of what he was doing wrong in Aristophanes' eyes, we cannot reconstruct this system in more than very general terms.

The most important song of the chorus in the latter part of the play is just before the poetry contest starts (814–29). This is a four-stanza hymn, mainly in dactylic hexameters, that is, in the sacred chant. The chorus present the two poetic styles of Aeschylus and Euripides in a delighted exuberance of language. It is an obvious moment for production to emphasize the centrality of the chorus. The initiates assert themselves. Their holy chant is as rich a language as the words of the poets. The initiates must appear as the true audience of the poets, the people whom the poets must satisfy before all others.

The holy chant of dactyls must imply that whoever chants it dominate the stage. This, I think, reveals the main purpose of the initiate chorus. They must take the audience by surprise at their entrance and dominate them by the lyrical beauty of their worship. They must reassert their position as the purified citizen community of Athens, the people to whom the rest of Athens should pay close attention, during the *parabasis* and before the contest of poetry. They are not to be involved in the ludicrous business of the comedy, because their most important function is right at the end of the play. For there is no normal *exodos*. The last lines of the play are a six-line chant, again in dactyls (1528–33). The chorus would not have marched during this; they would have stood still. The last words of the play are: get rid of Cleophon. Nothing must interfere with the impact of these words, delivered as if by an oracle. Having delivered them, the chorus will walk out in silence. It is a very strong ending, and the production of the chorus must be such as not to impair their strength.

Four actors are necessary to play the parts in *The Frogs*. But there is bound to be some argument about the distribution, since it would be feasible to confine the fourth actor to a very minor role. There can be no doubt that the leading actor played Dionysus, and the second Xanthias and Aeschylus. Xanthias disappears half-way through the play. Aeschylus has far more singing and dancing than Euripides. Indeed the double of Xanthias and Aeschylus gives the second actor much more singing and dancing than the lead.[27] But in comedy, as we see in *The Birds*, the lead does not always have the most singing. Technically, it would be possible for the third actor to take all the other parts except the corpse (173–79) and Pluto. With the exception of the finale, this would mean that the fourth actor's role was merely that of an extra. But in the finale (1500ff.) Pluto has twenty lines of anapest chant (1500–1514, 1524–27). It seems unlikely that this would be given to an extra, and therefore I assume that the fourth actor had more parts to play, and I allocate them as follows: leading actor, Dionysus; second actor, Xanthias and Aeschylus; third actor, Heracles, Charon, Aeacus, the landlady, and Euripides; fourth actor, the corpse, the servant girl, Plathanē, and Pluto.[28]

Aristophanes' prologues are all masterly demonstrations of pacey writing. But that of *The Frogs* is the best of all. Within two hundred lines we have been introduced to five characters; we are then confronted with the spectacle of the frog chorus. The play opens with a heavily burdened slave riding a donkey, while a fat man walks beside him. In the first two lines the slave, Xanthias, refers to the old stock jokes that always make an audience laugh. They continue with some broad digs at the tricks of the low comics, and we are settling down to enjoy a normal comic double act—such as we find in the opening of *The Knights*, for instance—when the fat man exclaims that it is a disgrace that he should be walking while his slave rides for he is "Dionysus, son of Winebottle." We are astonished. Is this Dionysus? There is some philosophical nonsense about whether Xanthias is actually carrying the baggage, since the donkey is carrying him, and they arrive at one of the side entrances, now deemed to be the house of Heracles.[29] The first major confrontation now takes place. Dionysus dressed up as Heracles meets Heracles himself. It is a ludicrous moment, turning our world topsy-turvy right at the beginning of the play (37ff.). Their conversation is full of gags. Dionysus has an unspeakable desire for Euripides, for a poet who can produce original phrases like "God's home, the air" or "the foot of time" or the phrase about "the mind not wanting to swear sacred oaths, but the tongue swearing independently" (100–102). The poets alive at the moment are twitterers who can only piss on tragedy (95). Dionysus is going down to Hades and wants some travel information from Heracles. Heracles tells him that there are three ways down. The sequence is a beautiful illustration of the way in which Aristophanes builds his laughter. The joke consists in the way that Heracles starts by describing a normal way of travel and then quickly changes the meaning so that it refers to a method of committing suicide. The humor is in the rhythm of the change. The first comes quickly (121). It is the way "by rope and bench," that is, by a boat of some sort, or rather—by hanging yourself. The second takes a little longer. It is a riddling sentence; its point depends on a pun, which, once guessed, changes the meaning of all the preceding words in the sentence. "There is a path, a short cut, a well-trodden one," says Heracles, "the way of the cup," though the last word can also mean "mortar." There must be a pause while the audience try and guess this one. Just before they succeed in doing so, Dionysus answers, "You mean hemlock." For hemlock is ground in a mortar and drunk from a cup, and the word that I translated as "well-trodden" could also mean "pounded." The laugh would have the feeling of black comedy. Hemlock poisoning had become a little too familiar an incident of Athenian life since the coup of the Four Hundred six years before, and the counterrevolution which followed (123–24). The third travel method takes longer to tell. There is more of a build to the joke. We can imagine Heracles playing with full histrionics and many overdramatic pauses:

> *Heracles.* Shall I tell you a quick way? Straight down?
> *Dionysus.* Good. I'm not the walking type.
> *Heracles.* First, creep down to the Kerameicus.
> *(Long pause).*
> [The Kerameicus was the burial place for important citizens. We wait, with
>   no idea as to what Heracles is driving at.]
> *Dionysus.* Then?
> *Heracles.* Climb the tower. The high one. . . .
> *Dionysus.* And do what?
> *Heracles.* The torch race is starting. From that spot. Watch it. Then, just as
>   the spectators are shouting "go-o-o-o" . . . you go too.
> *Dionysus.* Where?
> *Heracles.* Down.
>
> (127–33)

After the exaggeration of the build-up, the "death" must come as an anticlimax and get the laugh of nervous reaction to tension. This sequence will get three different kinds of laugh, in a perfectly staged rhythm. It is unimportant sequences such as we have here, as much as his more obvious stage effects, that demonstrate Aristophanes' mastery of his theatrical medium.

After this Heracles tells Dionysus that he can go the way that he went himself. He must pay the ferryman Charon two obols and be rowed across the lake.[30] Then he will meet all sort of monsters, and finally come to the initiates and the house of Pluto. During this scene Xanthias has been steadily interrupting to complain at having still to carry the baggage (87–88, 107, 115). Now, at last, he starts to unload himself (160). As soon as he has unloaded, five lines later, Dionysus tells him to pick the baggage up again (165). A simple joke, but again handled with perfect timing.[31]

They need a porter to carry their bags to Hades. Luckily a corpse is passing. Xanthias tries to bargain with him. But they cannot agree on terms. At Xanthias' final offer, the corpse exclaims, "I'd rather live" (177). Charon arrives with his boat, but he refuses to take slaves, except those who fought at Arginusae (191). We have already had one allusion to the battle (33). It is a constant background to the play.

Xanthias leaves to walk around the lake, while Dionysus sits in the boat. He is made to row, while Charon sits and watches, this reversal offering another laugh and another minor topsy-turviness. Almost immediately the frogs appear, leaping out from behind the *skēnē* (209–69).[32] Charon has told Dionysus that he must keep in time with the frogs' song. The sequence develops into a contest between Dionysus and the frogs as to who can sing the louder. How does the ship on wheels cross the *orchestra*? The only staging that makes sense is if the frog chorus pull the boat in different directions.[33] Naturally, the frogs' movement must keep time with their singing. If they pull Dionysus more and more vigorously, as they sing more and more vigorously, and Dionysus has to make a more and more vigorous show of rowing in order to keep up the pretence that he is rowing the boat, then there is point in his attempt to out-sing the frogs. Perhaps there is also a hole in the bottom of the boat, through which the actor's legs can come, so that he can also walk the boat across. Then the contest between Dionysus and the frogs is one of his trying to walk the boat straight across the *orchestra* while they pull him in different directions. Clearly it will be easier to pull the boat by ropes than it will be to walk it. The dance is astrophic, and the meter is mostly relatively simple iambics and trochaics, which suggest that the dance was not very elaborate. It does not take much imagination to conceive a choreography for leaping frogs.

After a hard-fought struggle Dionysus out-croaks, or rather out-runs, the frogs, reaches the other side of the *orchestra*, and gets out. He pays Charon for having sat and watched him and meets Xanthias, who has walked around with the bags. They mime their way through darkness and mud (273). "Where are the perjurers and parricides mentioned by Heracles," asks Dionysus. "Can't you see them?" Xanthias replies, pointing to the audience (274–76).

Dionysus makes great pretence of not being frightened of the monsters, which Heracles warned would be near them now. Immediately there is play with an invisible monster. Dionysus keeps trying to put Xanthias in between it and himself. Difficult, since the monster keeps coming from opposite directions. Is this a monster invented by Xanthias? Or a "real" monster that remains invisible? We cannot say. Such is the nature of stage truth.

At any rate, the climax of the scene is the moment, already mentioned, when Dionysus runs to his priest for protection (297). Once again the joke jolts our various levels of stage "reality." It is also a preparation for the devotional sequence that follows, though it is the kind of preparation that could have been conceived only by a great comic poet.

The initiates enter, presumably from behind the *skēnē*, which would be an appropriate place in this context, and also convenient if the frogs both enter and exit that way. They enter during conversation between Dionysus and Xanthias, and there is no anapest march. The first system is an invocation of Iankos. The music is in the Ionic rhythms associated with the dances of maenads, notable for the sinuous body-bending. Some of the language (especially 326–30) recalls the chorus of invocation preceding the palace miracle in *The Bacchants* (547–49). The dance must have been similar too, since both choruses are in Ionic rhythms. The effect of this opening system, as of all the *parodos*, is more dance than mime. Choreography is a matter of establishing a mood of lightness and fluttering delight. We can find clues from the matching of such phrases as "dancing down the meadow" with "light-bearing star" (326, *strophē*; 342, *antistrophē*); or "shaking fruitful branches" with "old men's legs leaping" (328, *strophē*; 345, *antistrophē*).

There follows an anapest chant similar to the opening section of a normal *parabasis*. When, later on (675 ff.), we come to the *parabasis* of *The Frogs*, there is no opening anapest section. That has been placed in the *parodos* instead. At any rate, by this stage of his career, Aristophanes enjoyed almost total freedom to do what he wanted with the traditional forms of old comedy. Here the anapest chant by the chorus leader, addressed, as in a *parabasis*, very directly to the audience, is in the form of the traditional warning to the profane to depart from the celebration of the rites to come. It starts in general terms, then becomes more specific. The tone hardens into an attack on those who stir up party strife, those who take bribes while in office, those who betray forts or ships to the enemy. Then he turns to particular people, such as Thorycion (363), about whom we know nothing except that from this passage he must have traded goods with the enemy. Others are also mentioned, though in more general terms. Tension in the audience is building as they start to wonder whom Aristophanes will attack next. But he lets us off the hook at this moment with an enormous belly laugh. The chorus leader continues that he also does not want to see "the man who shits on the Hecate shrines while singing a dithyramb" (367). The allusion, we learn from the scholiast, is to Kinesias, the much mocked dithyrambic poet[34] who was apparently taken short at one of his own performances. As the audience collapse with relieved laughter, the attack continues on the man who had proposed cutting the comic poets' pay, whom we learn to have been Agyrrhios. This would have got another laugh, and so, with the balance of serious invective and laughter restored, the chant ends with a direct invitation to all, chorus and audience, to join in the rites.

There follows a simple, apparently solemn, one-system hymn to Persephone, who is not openly named. It is mainly spondaic[35] in rhythm, and must therefore have had a slow tempo. But it is not a Lutheran chorale. The system ends humorously. The last line of the *strophē* encourages the participants: "Our lunch was really quite sufficient." The *antistrophē* refers again to the hated Thorycion: "Even if Thorycion doesn't want us saved" (377, *strophē;* 383, *antistrophē*). What possible connection can there be between those two thoughts? The only way in which I can think of connecting them is by ending the song with a belch, which will refer in the *strophē* to the excellent lunch, and in the *antistrophē* will signify contempt of the hated traitor.

There then follows a one-system hymn to Demeter. It is in iambic dimeters. The last line seems to demand climactic movement, perhaps a leap. The *strophē* refers to "sport and dance" (390), the *antistrophē* to "victory" in the competition (395). Here, incidentally, we notice an alienation device. We are not totally inside the celebrations of the initiates. Reference can be made to the competition, which Aristophanes had every intention of winning. His desire to win is expressed as part of the prayer to Demeter.

The third hymn is addressed again to Iankos. It is in three matching stanzas, with a refrain in the last line: "Iankos, lover of the dance, join the procession with me." The first two stanzas are straight, the third is a joke. The singers refer to a pretty girl they can see whose dress is so torn that her tit shows through.[36] To create a choreography that would represent the girl and also fit with the preceding stanzas is clearly impossible. We must therefore assume that an actual girl extra appeared at this moment, dressed in rags with her tit showing. The joke will then be that the dance and music take no notice of her, and the words that describe her are sung in exactly the same way as the hymn to Dionysus. At this point Dionysus himself starts to chant. But instead of answering the hymn that the chorus have been singing to him, he is only interested in getting his hands on the girl. Dionysus takes no notice of his own worship. All that interests him is some incidental sexy business.

The tone now lowered, the traditional song of mockery begins (420 ff.). First there are five identical short stanzas, obviously set to a traditional tune, poking bawdy fun at well-known personalities. Then Dionysus and Xanthias approach. Dionysus asks the way of his statue, the chorus reply, and Dionysus sets off, with Xanthias carrying the bags again. All this is done to three more verses of the traditional song. Dionysus has been involved in his own worship, but only in terms of jokes.

While Dionysus and Xanthias approach the central door, the chorus dance in the center of the *orchestra* a final system expressing their holy joy in their happy state. It would seem likely that this is the lyrical climax of the *parodos,* the most beautiful tune, danced with quiet radiance.

The tone is now abruptly lowered. Dionysus and Xanthias knock at the door, which Aeacus answers. He is here represented as a mere slave of Pluto, though in Greek mythology he is one of the highly dignified judges of the dead. He lets out a torrent of abuse at the fake Heracles for coming down and throttling Cerberus (465–78). He threatens Dionysus with assorted monsters. We notice that one of these is the Tartesian lamprey, which was a noted gastronomic delicacy—as if one was to include in a list of monsters the Maine lobster. While Aeacus rushes back inside to collect his monsters, Dionysus shits himself, only twenty lines after the holy Dionysiac dance. He describes what has happened with an untranslatable pun. During the rite of libation pouring, it was customary to say, "It is poured out; call the god." Dionysus says instead, "I have shat; call the god." The two words are very nearly the same: *ekkechutai* and *engkechoda*. The shit joke is rubbed in, in all senses of the word. Dionysus asks for a sponge to dab on his heart; so frightened is he (482). When Xanthias hands it to him, he uses it to wipe his ass. "Golden gods," says Xanthias, "D'you keep your heart there?" (483–84).

Dionysus then makes Xanthias wear the Heracles lion-skin and carry the club. Immediately a maid comes out of the house and is all over the supposed Heracles. She invites him to dinner, which Xanthias resists with difficulty, and then offers "freshly plucked dancing girls" (516), which he cannot refuse. As he is about to follow her in, Dionysus insists on changing back into the Heracles costume himself. Xanthias protests, calling the gods to witness. "What gods," retorts Dionysus, and has his way. The *strophē* of a system for Dionysus and the chorus follows, in which he congratulates himself (534–48).

But Dionysus' triumph is short-lived. Two landladies enter to attack "Heracles" for the amount of food he ate without paying. In panic, Dionysus begs Xanthias to take the Heracles costume again, promising that he will never again ask to change back. The *antistrophē* follows (589–604).

The dance is obviously straightforward. The trochaic meter suggests that the chorus perform a simple run around Dionysus in the middle for the *strophē*, Xanthias for the *antistrophē*. Just before the *strophē*, Xanthias has been told to pick up the baggage, a slave once more (525). The second half of the *strophē* is a solo for Dionysus. In it he sings of how awful it would be if Xanthias, as master, had been lying on the rugs, making love to a dancing girl, while Dionysus was standing by, watching the lovemaking and clutching his own phallus, and then Xanthias, angered at his slackness, had knocked his teeth out. During this song Xanthias must surely therefore be lying on the baggage, not picking it up, while Dionysus prances in the middle of the chorus, and at the requisite moment clutches his phallus (545). This movement pattern fits very well with the *antistrophē*, when Dionysus will have returned to the baggage as slave, but like Xanthias before him will lie on the baggage rather than pick it up. At the line that requires Xanthias to clutch his phallus, if the movement is to match the movement of the *strophē*, the words refer to "showing a virile spirit," a phrase amply suited to the necessary gesture. So we may see that the climax of this dance is a phallic flourish.

At this point Aeacus returns with a gang of his thugs to pounce on Xanthias. Xanthias protests his innocence and offers to prove it by letting his "slave" be tortured. Generously, he forgoes the right of compensation if the slave is damaged (625). At this Dionysus protests that he is a god. Xanthias retorts that if he is, he will feel no pain. Xanthias then volunteers to undergo the flogging himself as well. Whichever cries out first is not the god. Both are flogged and pretend not to notice the pain. As the flogging increases they have to invent wilder and wilder reasons for crying out. The climax is a scream from Dionysus to Poseidon (664), which he turns into an unrhythmical hymn, no doubt shouted to a nontune. Aeacus says that he will take them both inside so that Pluto and Persephone can establish which is the god.

The *parabasis* then follows (675ff.), consisting merely of *strophē, epirrhema, antistrophē,* and *antepirrhema.* The song is an invocation to the Muse of the holy dances. The meter contains many dactyls, though there are no exact dactylic hexameters. The tone is serious; the poetic and therefore choreographic content is detailed and dense. The general sense is clear; the *strophē* is a condemnation of Cleophon, the *antistrophē* of another warmongering immigrant, Cleigenes. But unfortunately, the lyric is as allusive as the fourth *stasimon* of the *Antigone.*[37] And since the allusions are to events contemporary with the production of the play, we are unlikely ever to discover their full significance and must rest content with a general impression only.

The *epirrhema* and *antepirrhema* present the reverse thought to that of the song. The *epirrhema* (686–705) is a call for reconciliation: Pardon those who were involved in the oligarchic revolution of six years ago. Make a strong gesture of unity, in the same way as you gave the slaves who fought at Arginusae their freedom. The *antepirrhema* protests the current habit of illtreating and failing to make use of the aristocrats, who are able to contribute much to the state. There seem to be no jokes at all in the entire parabasis.[38] It is a pure use of the rite as an occasion for reconciliation and an attempt to impose that reconciliation on the city.

After the seriousness of the *parabasis,* the tone is again lowered as Xanthias and Aeacus come out to indulge in a bit of below-stairs gossip, two slaves laughing behind their masters' backs. A noise is heard inside, and we hear that it is the two quarrelling poets. Aeschylus had held the poets' throne, the special seat in the Prytaneum, set aside for the acknowledged master of each craft and carrying with it the privilege of free meals at the public expense. This is an allusion to the normal Athenian practice of giving these dining rights to distinguished citizens who had performed some service to the state.[39] Aeacus describes how Euripides built up a claque of criminals who insisted that he should have the throne. Now there must be a contest, with Sophocles waiting to take on Euripides if Aeschylus is defeated. Who could be a better judge than Dionysus, god of the theater.

The chorus sing their dactylic hymn to language, contrasting the teethgnashing thunder of Aeschylus with the unwinding tongue of Euripides (814–29). As it ends the poets come out, yelling at each other. The first scene is in iambic dialogue, and the abuse is in general terms. The only point scored is in Aeschylus' claim that he is at a disadvantage since his works have survived him, while those of Euripides died with him and so have come down to Hades (868–70). Dionysus calls for fire and incense, Pluto comes out, thrones are provided for him and Dionysus, and the contest is ready to begin.

While Dionysus offers incense the chorus sing an astrophic prayer, mainly in dactyls. Its language seems strangely Euripidean: "Muses who look down on the little-word-understanding minds of the men who make the sayings" (876–77), which I would guess should be properly translated: "the witty, itty-bitty minds of the trendsetters." All through the contest there will be ambiguities. The song that will celebrate Aeschylus' victory (1482–99) is praise for the man of "sharpened understanding," a phrase surely more applicable to Euripides than Aeschylus. After the two poets give their advice on Alcibiades, Dionysus is made to say that one has spoken cleverly, the other clearly. But which is which is carefully left undecided (1434).

Part of the point of these ambiguities is that the contest consists of Aeschylus outsmarting Euripides, the poet of bombast outwitting the poet of wit. The nature of the contest, however, also demonstrates every culture's doubt as to what is the definition of the poet: is it that he is a man of special vision, or someone especially skilled with words? The general statements made about poetry, and the final judgment of the contest, imply that we are concerned with the former definition. But the actual course of the contest is concerned with the latter. Theoretically Aristophanes is inconsistent. In practice his inconsistency fits well with our own, or that of his original audience.

The contest in outline consists of a formal *agōn* in which first Euripides and then Aeschylus abuses his opponent; there are then two episodes in iambic dialogue in which they attack first each other's prologues and then each other's lyrics. The poetry is then weighed, and after Dionysus has declared a tie, the contest is then decided on the final two pieces of advice to the city. At no point is one or the other made to be obviously better than the other, either by the logic of ordinary judgment or in the topsy-turvy logic of Aristophanic comedy, except for when the poetry is weighed when, rather naturally, Aeschylus' comes out heavier.

The contest starts with prayer (885–94). Aeschylus prays simply to Demeter, strengthener of the mind, to make him worthy of her mysteries (886–87). Euripides insists on praying to his own gods: "Air my pasture, pivoting tongue; wit and sniffing-inquisitive nostrils" (892–94). There follows the formal *agōn*: chorus *strophē*, section in chanted iambic tetrameters mainly featuring Euripides, chorus *antistrophē*, section in chanted anapestic tetrameters mainly featuring Aeschylus. The chorus song is a straightforward piece of ringside encouragement. We should notice that Euripides is given iambics, while Aeschylus has the more dignified anapests, and recall the similar allocation in *The Clouds* where the Just Logic had anapests, the Unjust iambics (961–1088).

Euripides attacks Aeschylus for bamboozling his audience. He would bring on a character and keep him or her silent for scene after scene. Suddenly the character would break silence in a torrent of unintelligible words. Euripides goes on to claim that he himself made tragedy more logical, more a matter of ordinary talk. He ends with a *pnigos* about how he gave ordinary people ideas.[40] Dionysus takes up the *pnigos,* presumably rising from his seat to dance the knees-up. Everything's chat, he answers. Everyone does nothing but complain. Talk, talk, talk.

After the *antistrophē* Aeschylus is urged to counterattack by Dionysus:

> Thou first of Greeks, who built
> Those solemn towers of speech
> And decked the tragic stage
> With drivel, cheer up and spout.
>
> (1004–5)

Aeschylus makes Euripides admit that the poet should be praised not only for his skill, but also for making men "better in their cities" (1009–10). He then claims that he made men more warlike with plays like *The Seven Against Thebes.* "Certainly," interrupts Dionysus, "and that was disastrous. You made the Thebans too warlike" (1021–24). Aeschylus, however, goes on about the warlike qualities of his poetry. He never had a love interest. To this Euripides laughingly agrees, but Aeschylus stops his mockery with a reference to Euripides having been cuckolded, and he attacks Euripides for his love scenes, which drove virtuous women to suicide, and in general for his kitchen-sink drama. He ends with a *pnigos* on the disgusting Euripidean drama, full of incest, gossip, and unfit people (1078–88), which Dionysus caps with a description of the torch race at the *Panathenaea* where the runner was so unfit that he was hit by the spectators until he performed the only strenuous thing of which he was capable—a fart so enormous he blew out his torch.

After a vigorous dance celebrating the contest, the detailed criticism of prologues starts. Euripides attacks the opening lines of *The Libation-Bearers* as repetitious and obscure. Dionysus joins in the mockery of Aeschylus, and Aeschylus then abuses Dionysus (1149, 1150). Aeschylus finally loses his temper. He turns to attack Euripides' prologues, first fastening on the first two lines of the lost *Antigone* as nonsense, and then offering to demolish every single one of Euripides' prologues "with an oilcan." The point of the joke is that the straightforward Euripidean prologue comes to the cesura of a line, having given a subject and subordinate clause, and thus needing main verb and object. The sentence and the line therefore can always be finished with a phrase "lost his oilcan" which always scans and makes a kind of nonsense sense. Faster and faster Aeschylus brandishes his metaphorical oilcan, until Dionysus advises Euripides to concede and try criticizing melody instead.

A short astrophic song from the chorus exclaims at anyone daring to criticize Aeschylus, the greatest tune maker of all, but Euripides plunges into reducing all Aeschylus' choruses into a refrain of thunderous nonsense, and he then composes a second Aeschylus lyric made up of an unintelligible jumble of phrases with the refrain for an imaginary lyre—*phlattothrattophlattothrat.* Aeschylus retorts by saying that his own songs came from noble sources while those of Euripides are based on rubbish. He calls for a lyre but then changes his mind. He will demonstrate Euripides' music accompanied by Euripides' Muse. On comes a near naked girl playing the castanets.[42] Aeschylus then sings a nonsensical parody of a Euripides chorus set to the new music. One syllable has six notes to it, quite appropriately since it means "whirling" (1314). Otherwise we have a vague picture of seabirds, spiders, dolphins, and vines. The song acts as a warm-up for what follows: a thirty-line nonsense solo in the new style, recalling such Euripidean arias as that of the Phrygian slave.[43] It is a glorious monument to bathos, parodying the way in which Euripides sometimes uses inflated tragic diction to describe very trivial incidents. Aristophanes must have enjoyed creating it; it is magnificently banal (1331–63). It is the song of a poor spinning girl who has had a bad dream and wakes up to find her rooster has been stolen. Almost all the gods and goddesses of the pantheon are invoked to help her find the criminal. We can hear the melody building to heights of incongruous coloratura, sung of course by the military, bearded Aeschylus. No wonder Dionysus cries, "Stop" (1364).

The final test is that the poetry should be weighed. During another short astrophic song from the chorus, a great machine is brought in: scales in which to weigh the verse.[44] As we might expect, Aeschylus' verse weighs the heaviest. At last one of the poets appears to be definitely winning. Appropriately, it is at this moment that Dionysus declares himself at a loss to choose between them (1411–13). At this point there is a considerable pause while the scales are removed, either by the *mēchanē*, or carried out by extras. The silence is significant. We look around to see who will break the deadlock.

Then Aristophanes does his Aeschylus trick. The actor playing Pluto, whom we have now come to think of as a mute, since he has been on stage for so long without saying a line, now breaks silence to tell Dionysus that if he cannot make up his mind, his journey will have been wasted (1414). "What happens if I do make a choice," asks Dionysus, revealing himself as even more of an idiot. Pluto tells him that he can take the winner back to earth. Dionysus returns to business and asks the final test questions. First, what would they do about Alcibiades. Euripides is ambiguous but seems to be against him on the whole (1427–29); Aeschylus is in favor of Alcibiades but oracularly abscure (1431–32). Dionysus can only exclaim that he cannot choose; "one is so clever, the other so clear" (1434). Next comes the advice to the city.[45] Once again Euripides is pedantic and ambiguous (1446–50). Aeschylus replies with oracular nonsense again, though it seems to refer to the conventional advice of Pericles at the beginning of the war, which was now ringing very stale:

> Treat hostile soil as yours, your own as hostile;
> Your ships as means, your means as meaningless.
>
> (1463–65)

We are quickly distracted from serious consideration of the advice by Dionysus' verdict for Aeschylus and his altercation with Euripides, furious at being
passed over. The verdict is given in a parody of Euripides' well-known line
from the *Hippolytus* (612). "My tongue swore," says Dionysus, "but I'll
choose Aeschylus" (1471)[47]. Further parodies of Euripides follow, examples of
his so-called immorality and sophistry, ending with two lines from the missing
Phrixus, which ran in his play:

> Who knows if this which we call death is life,
> And life is dying?
>
> (Frag. 830, 1–2)

Dionysus twists them into his final sophistic justification for betraying
Euripides:

> Who knows if life be really death,
> Breath be a breakfast, sleep a sheepskin?
>
> (1477–78)

Pluto hurries them inside before the word play becomes too outrageous, so
that Dionysus and Aeschylus can be given dinner before they leave for earth.
While they are all inside feasting, the chorus sings its *strophē* in praise of the
witty poet, though its *antistrophē* attacks those who consort with Socrates. The
wit praised in the *strophē* is precisely the quality that one would expect to
develop by consorting with Socrates. The song is as contradictory as the
gnomic utterances of the poets.

The finale is an anapest chant by Pluto with good wishes for Aeschylus'
return to earth, and with various offers of death-dealing instruments to be
given to unpopular members of the audience, so that they will come quickly
down to Hades. Aeschylus replies, also in anapests, bequeathing his throne to
Sophocles until he himself comes back, and giving orders that Euripides is
never to possess it on any account. Dionysus, we notice, says nothing throughout the finale. Is this a final image of his ineffectiveness, and so of the ultimate
ineffectiveness of poetry—something similar to the climactic image of *The
Canterbury Tales*, when, alone of the pilgrims, Chaucer the poet is shouted
down, or to Dante's final inability to describe the beauty of his glorified
Beatrice[48]—the final silence that only the greatest poets reach? What should
Dionysus be doing onstage at this moment? At any rate, he says nothing, and
the play ends with the dactylic chant of the chorus already mentioned, praying
to the powers below the earth for the poet's safe journey and good advice to the
state, and ending with their plea to the city to banish Cleophon the warmonger so that the city may have peace.

Poetry can never persuade people to choose what they would not otherwise
choose. But it can enlarge men's minds so that they choose from the basis of a
clearer vision. Comedy must work even more indirectly still. What we are left

with after seeing *The Frogs* is many laughs, many pictures and many questions. Dionysus is at a loss to decide between the poets and finally chooses for nonpoetic reasons. Is Aristophanes saying that the Athenians do choose their winning poets for nonpoetic reasons, or that they should do so? Is Dionysus, depicted as an idiot most of the way through the play, supposed to be right or wrong in his choice at the end? Do the audience agree with his decision? Is Aristophanes denying that the theater can influence political events? Or is he pretending that it can? Whatever answers we give to these questions, they cannot be unequivocal ones. But if the purpose of poetry does not lie in giving answers but in posing questions as deeply, and also as memorably and enjoyably, as possible, then *The Frogs* is a great play. Since *The Frogs* is clearly a great play, then we may conclude that it is in the depth of the questions posed, not in the answers, in which lies the greatness of great poetry.

Whitman ends his book on Aristophanes with the sentence: "In Aeschylus, Aristophanes found a figure through whom he could say, 'Athens is falling; her meaning is immortal'."[49] I agree with Whitman that, in spite of all the laughs in *The Frogs,* there is a sadness of great depth. Aristophanes might agree with the last sentence. But he would not put it in quite such resigned terms. He would perhaps say, "Athens is falling. Her meaning, I hope, is immortal. But she is falling now, because you, Athenians, have chosen wrongly, and your choice will lead us to disaster." In some senses the end of *The Frogs* should be compared with the end of *The Birds.* There is a condemnation at one level in the choice of Aeschylus in *The Frogs,* just as there is a sense of impending disaster in the triumph of Persuader at the end of *The Birds.* But Aristophanes is richly human, and he admires with gusto the adventurous spirit of Persuader, just as he loves the exuberance of Aeschylus' thunder and lightning. May we allow Aristophanes the same kind of vision as Shakespeare at the end of his life, and grant that the writer of *The Frogs* realized as much as the writer of *The Tempest* that the present play was the end of an era? Then, perhaps, we could allow Aristophanes to rephrase the thought on which Whitman ends. "Athens is falling, because she has praised and encouraged flamboyance, grandiloquence, and adventure. These qualities have brought her into her present disaster, which she richly deserves; for it is all due to her own foolishness. But all the same, being an Athenian, that was quite something, wasn't it?" If the imaginary speech of Aristophanes is fanciful, at least it implies a sad chuckle as Aristophanes' final comment. And what other end could there be for a poet knowing that he had made Old Comedy's masterpiece, but also that with it Old Comedy had come to an end.

Notes

1. Georges Méautis, "L'Authenticité et la Date du 'Promethée Enchainé' d'Eschyle," *Université de Neuchâtel, recueil de travaux publié par la Faculté des lettres* (Geneva) 29 (1960).
2. There are a great many theories about the circumstances of this play's composition. Some scholars have even thought that it was not by Aeschylus. Perrotta, for example, came to the

conclusion that the *Prometheus Bound* was not by Aeschylus and the *Prometheus Unbound* did not follow its apparent predecessor. His main argument, however, was that the *Prometheus Bound* must have been presented in 469 B.C. at the latest, because the first play of Sophocles, the *Triptolemos*, which we know to have been produced in 468, contains long geographical passages, which he claims must be imitations of the passages in the *Prometheus Bound.*See Gennaro Perrotta, *I Tragici Greci* (Firenze: Casa Editrice G. D'Anna, 1931), pp. 8–9, 49–55. The study of this play abounds in ideas as fanciful.

Mark Griffith works in a different vein. See Mark Griffith, *The Authenticity of 'Prometheus Bound'* (Cambridge: Cambridge University Press, 1977). He musters a formidable array of metrical arguments to support his view that the *Prometheus Bound* was by someone other than Aeschylus. My own feeling is that this sort of analysis is not yet conclusive. We need to set up control experiments for this kind of testing. (Might one, for example, find that there were discrepancies in language and meter between *Sweeney Todd* and the rest of Stephen Sondheim's work?) Such experiments can now be done relatively easily with computers. When complete "maps" of the great poets have been made, we shall then be in a position to assess properly whether the apparent anomalies shown here are irrefutable proof.

It would not make much difference to my judgment of the play if it was proved not to be by Aeschylus. It is a magnificent play, whoever wrote it. And evidence such as the Gyges fragment, and the defeats of *Oedipus the King* and *The Birds* suggest that there were other poets capable of writing great plays. What makes me suspicious about attempts to prove the *Prometheus Bound* not by Aeschylus is that there has been a long history of worry about its content. Nineteenth- and early twentieth-century scholars were very unhappy with the theology of the play, with its demonstration of what they regarded as intolerable cruelty by God to man. Our generation, no doubt, has its own manifest delusions, which will make us equally laughable to our succesors. But at least we can hardly blind ourselves to the intolerable suffering men undergo, and can hardly fail to realize that whether we are Atheist Humanists, Jews, Moslems, or Christians, it is in the intolerable that our faith must be tested.

3. Shelley, *Prometheus Unbound*, 3. 4. 196.

4. For the meaning of terms used, see Appendix 3.

5. Peter Arnott, *Greek Scenic Conventions in the Fifth Century B.C.* (Oxford: Clarendon Press, 1962), p. 77.

6. The Oxford text marks a question. I take it as a statement, which seems to make better, stronger, sense.

7. It has been suggested that Prometheus was represented for the entire play by a dummy, while his lines were spoken from behind the *skēnē*. This triumph of the untheatrical imagination was achieved because it was believed that the play was relatively early and therefore before the introduction of the third actor.

Croiset says all that needs to be said: "Il n'est pas donné à tout le monde de croire à ce mannequin." See Maurice Croiset, *Histoire de la littérature Grecque* (Paris: E. de Bocard, 1928), 3:188 n. "It is not given to everyone to believe in this dummy." Kitto takes wry delight in Croiset's mockery. See H. D. F. Kitto, *Greek Tragedy* (London: Methuen, 1961), p. 56 n. 1.

8. I assume that a wooden structure of blocks was erected on the *ekkyklema* floor and that this served to represent the rock. To it Prometheus could be fastened with real fastenings. As in the modern theater, where a block or a rostrum might so easily represent a rock, I do not imagine that there was any attempt at realistic representation of a rock, which would not fit with the standard temple facade, whereas a plain block would be perfectly acceptable. Whatever we decide for this staging, it is best to assume that the same staging served for Euripides' *Andromeda* where Andromeda was tied to a rock, and therefore for the parody of the scene from *Andromeda* in *The Women at the Thesmophoria* (1001 ff.).

Arnott, *Greek Scenic Conventions in the Fifth Century B.C.*, pp. 97–98, argues that both Prometheus and Andromeda-Mnesilochus are simply bound to a pillar, and refers to several vase paintings where both Andromeda and Prometheus are shown thus. Arnott himself admits, however, that not all the representations of Prometheus and Andromeda merely show a pillar, though it is difficult to see why the vase painter should have ever shown a rock as a pillar if it was not a stage convention in use on some occasions. Naturally the pillar must be fastened to the *ekkyklema* floor. Possibly the structure necessary to support it will provide enough extra height, with perhaps two steps, to allow Hephaestus to make business clambering up and down in the fettering sequence (*Prometheus Bound* 52–81). Finally our choice must be partly a matter of our own temperament: either the simplest possible pillar, giving no physical help to the actors, but in keeping with one or two vase paintings; or, a larger structure, allowing Prometheus to be more spreadeagled in a position leaning back against his structure, though of course nearly upright. At the bottom of this structure there would be some steps, so that the chorus would not be on one level only for their final tableau as they cluster round Prometheus at the end (1063 ff.).

We might think to have found a clue in *The Women at the Thesmophoria.* At line 940 Mnesilochus is to be taken inside, and bound to a *sanis.* Then, after an intervening *stasimon,* he appears, obviously on the *ekkyklema,* with the guard telling him to moan outside (1001). Unfortunately we cannot be sure of the meaning of *sanis.* It can mean a "plank," but it can also mean a "platform," in particular the deck of a ship. There is a crucial passage in the *Odyssey* (21. 51). Penelope goes to a storeroom and walks "on to the high *sanis.*" Liddell and Scott translate this as a "scaffold" or "stage," and it is difficult to see how the word could be used for a floor with the adjective *high* unless it was some sort of raised platform. Henry George Liddell and Robert Scott, *A Greek-English Lexicon,* new edition rev. Henry Stuart Jones with the assistance of Robert McKenzie (Oxford: Clarendon Press, 1940), *sanis.* Hilaire Van Daele's translation in the Budé edition of Aristophanes (q.v.), suggests that it might be some sort of portable stocks. *Aristophane, texte établi par Victor Coulon et traduit par Hilaire Van Daele* (Paris: Societé d'Edition "Les Belles Lettres", 1946; Collection des Universités de France publiée sous le patronage de l'Association Guillaume Budé), *"Les Thesmophories,"* p. 57. But there seems no evidence for this at all. We must choose between Arnott's simple pillar and a construction of three or four blocks.

9. On this theory the chorus will retire during lines 277–83 into the *parodoi* and leave their scooters out of the way. They will then slowly return during the scene with Oceanus to take up their position in the *orchestra* for the *stasimon* at 397, but without appearing properly in the *orchestra* while Oceanus is on stage.

10. Translated and discussed below.

11. The chorus are supposed to be old men. Was there a concession to their age in the style of dancing? Probably not. We should remember that Aeschylus played his own leading roles. The role of Xerxes requires vigorous dancing, and when he played Xerxes Aeschylus was fifty-three. There are many professional dancers today in their late forties and early fifties who can perform movements more or less as vigorous as those of far younger men. All that is necessary is that the chorus should represent men over the age for being soldiers. They need not be dodderers. Athenaeus notes in his day how at Athens old men continued to dance (*Deipnosophists* 4. 134B–D).

12. Fortunately there is little argument among scholars about this distribution. The leading actor must play Antigone and Teiresias, the second Creon. And would any leading actor conceivably give the messenger speech to a third actor while he took the almost mute role of the queen?

13. It might be argued that a skilful Greek actor, in a mask, would so change his identity with each role that the audience would simply not be aware of the same actor playing different roles. Against this we need only to say that at any rate the leading actor, competing for his prize, would certainly make absolutely sure that everyone knew which roles he was playing. How, it may be asked? That might be to betray the secrets of the profession. Given permission to do so, any actor of experience can identify himself to an audience, even if wrapped in a winding sheet.

14. See Jebb's note to this passage (955–65); *Antigone,* in *Sophocles, The Plays and Fragments,* trans. R. C. Jebb (Cambridge: Cambridge University Press, 1883–96), pp. 170–73. The Lycurgus story is told in the *Iliad* 6. 130–40. Complete knowledge of the story depends, however, on vase paintings. Jebb describes a Neapolitan vase on which there is a picture of Dionysus in calm majesty stroking his panther, while on the other side there is a picture of Lycurgus in murderous rage with his son and wife. But Jebb does not quite see the point of this *stasimon.* He thinks that the vase painting represents "a version different from that of Sophocles." The point of introducing Lycurgus is not simply that he was imprisoned, as Jebb suggests. That is an incidental in the pattern of the *stasimon,* whose real point is to foreshadow Creon's destruction of his son and wife. The point lies in the relation of the words sung to the rest of the story conjured up in the minds of the audience.

15. D. L. Page, *Actors' Interpolations in Greek Tragedy* (Oxford: Clarendon Press, 1934), pp. 86–90.

16. The first translation is somewhat approximate. The pun word occurs only once, applied to the orders. So literally: "Here are the brother orders, about the sons of Oedipus." The second pun in the English is exactly the same as the Greek.

17. For a translation and discussion, see Chapter 5.

18. The problem of the double burial is in the theater less important than it seems when we are reading the play away from the stage. In the theater we need three things to happen: the announcement by Antigone that she will bury the body, as revealed in the prologue, the announcement that

the body has been buried and that the spirits are involved, as is revealed in the scene with the guard, and the actual capture of Antigone. In order for Antigone to be caught burying the body, after the burial of the body had been announced, Sophocles needed that Antigone should have to go back to finish off an unfinished work. The interrupted first burial gives Sophocles a chance to bring Antigone back to bury the body completely, and also to show that even in her unfinished act of burying the gods have taken a hand. To ask why she was interrupted is a question appropriate only to the naturalistic theater, and it simply does not occur to us as we are watching Sophocles' poem.

19. I accept Kitto's arguments that Creon remains on stage. See H. D. F. Kitto, *Form and Meaning in Drama* (London: Methuen, 1956), pp. 146–47, 165, 167–70. Sophocles usually indicates entrances and exits in the dialogue. Creon's entrance after *stasimon* 1 is clearly indicated at line 386. There is, however, no indication of exit before *stasimon* 2, and no indication of entrance before Haemon enters at line 626. The most reasonable assumption therefore is that Creon stays onstage from the end of *stasimon* 1 at 386, to his exit after the scene with Teiresias at line 1115.

20. Quintino Cataudella, *La Poesia di Aristofane* (Bari: Gius. Laterza & Figli, 1934), p. 17. "Aristophanes passes through his contemporaries as though through a populace of the dead, on which is imposed the judgement of the poet, in the name of the past and the future—just as Dante does."

21. For example, see line 200, where he is called *gastrōn*, "potbelly." There is another reference to his paunch at line 663. A man with a false paunch would inevitably recall the original fat men.

22. See the beginning of Chapter 3. We are, I think, justified in assuming that the Athenians of Aristophanes' day would take Iankos and Dionysus to be identical.

23. I found that these two lines provided such a strong thought and image that they led me to make a poem, for which they serve as preface. See Leo Aylen, *I, Odysseus,* (London: Sidgwick & Jackson, 1971) pp. 20–21, "The Departure of the Gods." For a critic to refer to his own poem may appear unorthodox, if not unethical. But the thought in Euripides has unusual resonances. It is perhaps as well viewed through poetry as analyzed by prose. To refer to my own work is not to claim special merit for it, but only to suggest that the practice of modern poetry may on occasion be as helpful a way to the understanding of ancient poetry as the practice of prose analysis.

24. *Life of Sophocles,* 17.

25. Although this sequence is an astrophic song, I have reproduced Aristophanes' original rhythms, since their precision has obvious musical significance. For a discussion of this lyric in context of the *Anthesteria* festival, see Chapter 3, "The Festivals of Dionysus."

26. I do not accept the *scholion,* which says that the frogs were rendered by singers within the *skēnē.* First, could Aristophanes have resisted the stage picture that the frogs would present? Second, could the play have been named after a group that never appears? Third, and perhaps most important of all, the frogs never identify themselves as frogs, except by the cry "Brekekekex." Four lines after this cry, they are describing how they sang at the *Anthesteria.* These words from an unseen chorus would be impossibly confusing.

27. Kenneth McLeish, *The Theatre of Aristophanes* (London: Thames and Hudson, 1980), pp. 151–52, argues persuasively that Xanthias and Euripides should be played by the same actor (he says the second) because they are the same physical type—the crafty one, just as Heracles and Aeschylus are the same—the big, bombastic one. He gives Heracles, Charon, Aeacus, and Aeschylus to the third actor. I would have thought that the musical demands of Aeschylus' part must have meant that this was a second-actor, if not a first-actor role. In the first half of the play Xanthias is the best role after Dionysus. Would not the actors have enjoyed playing opposite physical types?

28. It would be much easier to stage the sequence at the door of Pluto's palace (460–674), if the various characters popping out of the door were taken in turn by third and fourth actor. There are those who, objecting to the idea of the fourth actor being given a chanting part in the finale, suggest that the leading actor put on Pluto's costume and mask for the finale, changing during the last short *stasimon* (1482–99). The fourth actor would then appear in the Dionysus costume, which would explain the silence of Dionysus during the finale.

29. Those who do not accept more than one entrance in the *skēnē* must make Heracles appear in the main entrance, which will later serve for the door of Pluto's palace. From the evidence of other plays, I accept that there was more than one entrance in the *skēnē* at this time (see Chapter 4, "Setting"). This will then allow Dionysus to leave the house of Heracles and start his boat trip on one side of the *orchestra,* cross the *orchestra* by boat, and then, during the succeeding sequences, work back toward the center of the actors' terrace before he knocks on Pluto's door.

30. See the discussion of the fare in Chapter 3, "The Festivals of Dionysus."

31. I assume that the donkey has wandered off when Dionysus and Xanthias first arrive at Heracles' door. We hear no more of it, and the baggage joke would not work so well if it was still there. It is, however, possible that the donkey does not disappear until Xanthias' exit to "walk round the lake" at line 196.

32. Translated and discussed above, and in Chapter 3, "The Festivals of Dionysus."

33. At the *Anthesteria* the worshipers pulled the ship-car in which Dionysus rode. As the frogs are the ghosts of the worshipers, it is right that they should pull the car. Only, because the sequence is topsy-turvy, they should pull it in the wrong direction.

34. See especially *Birds* 1372–1409.

35. See Appendix 4 for notes on meters.

36. It was part of the Eleusinian tradition that one wore one's robe till it fell to pieces.

37. See Chapter 8, "Sophocles: *Antigone.*"

38. In the middle of the song there is possibly some bitter joke involved in the fact that Cleophon is accused not of being a mad militarist, but of being a foreigner, and Cleigenes is treated as a bathhouse-keeper (680–81 in the *strophē* for Cleophon, 711–12 in the *antistrophē* for Cleigenes).

39. We do not know if it was the practice in Athens to give such dining rights to the masters of the crafts. However it would seem very likely. If this was so, then we can have little doubt as to who would have had the poet's seat in Athens until his recent death: Sophocles. And he may very well have held it for forty years or so, since he had been the supreme poet for that length of time. This conversation therefore would further emphasize the sense of Sophocles' unmentioned but ever present involvement in the entire course of the play.

40. See Appendix 3, for the meaning of terms used.

41. Commentators who insist that *The Frogs* is unmitigated praise of Aeschylus naturally have a hard time explaining away this obvious mockery. See, for example, W. W. Merry, *Aristophanes, The Frogs* (Oxford: Clarendon Press, 1884), pp. 52–53.

42. The word for these implies that they were earthenware, though it is also used to refer to the shell of snails, mussels, tortoises, and even eggs. So the instrument may have been made of shells.

43. See Chapter 5, "The New Music," and Chapter 7, "Euripides."

44. It is usually thought that this is a parody of Aeschylus' play, *The Weighing of Souls*, in which Zeus weighed the souls of Achilles and Memnon in his balance, in a similar way to the description of the weighing of Achilles and Hector by Zeus just before Hector's death in the *Iliad* 22. 208–13. If this is so, then the balance was probably swung in on the *mēchanē*, since it is likely that Zeus would have appeared in the *mēchanē* for the scene in Aeschylus' play.

45. I accept the obelization of lines 1437–41 and 1452–53 by Aristarchus and Apollonius. See Oxford text *apparatus criticus*. It does seem necessary that each poet should give only one piece of advice. Aristophanis *Comoediae*, ed. F. W. Hall and W. M. Geldart, Tomus 2, "Ranas" (Oxford: Clarendon Press; Scriptorum Classicorum Biblioteca Oxoniensis, 1901), 1437–53.

46. *Poros*, which I have translated "means," has many senses: "ways and means," "revenue," but also "ford," "sea channel." The negative word, a noun in the Greek, *aporia*, which I have translated "meaningless," has the sense of "difficulty," "problem," "lack," "poverty." Perhaps the speech of Aeschylus is only meant to sound as if it might make sense, and actually to be nonsense.

47. Already parodied once in *The Frogs* 101–2.

48. *Paradiso* 30. 31–33.

49. Cedric H. Whitman, *Aristophanes and the Comic Hero* (Cambridge: Harvard University Press, 1964), p. 258.

9

THE SATYR PLAY

"Virtue," said Ion of Chios, "like the four plays of the tragic poets, should always contain a satyric element."[1] It was part of the way in which the Athenian mind worked to need a focus for unrestrained sensual abandonment. This the satyrs provided. Many people in many cultures would agree with Ion of Chios. Many religions contain a satyric element: both Hinduism and pre-Reformation Christianity for example. The two religions, however, that have most notably contained minimal satyric elements are Christian Protestantism and the Atheist Humanism or Rationalism that has grown out of Protestantism in the countries of Northern Europe and America. Many, however, of the great writers on Greek drama in this and the last century have adhered to one or other of these two religions and have found the idea of the satyr play almost incomprehensible. As a result they have distorted certain aspects of the Dionysiac festivals almost beyond recognition. "Tragedy," says Aristotle, grew "from a satyric thing," and, for all the great age of the fifth century, the satyrs were very much part of its festival.[2]

At the end of the sixth century, the poet Pratinas brought it about that every tragic poet's offering for the festival had to contain a satyr play, a dramatic celebration of Dionysus through the spirits with whom his worship was especially connected. This concentration in one play left the poet free to explore any story from history recent or distant in the other three plays. The presence of the satyr play ensured that no one forgot that the Great *Dionysia* was, like the other festivals of Dionysus, also a festival of fertility.

There is a possible analogy between the Furies and the satyrs that may help us to understand the function of the latter. Both satyrs and Furies relate very easily to primitive man's two most important emotions: the sense of gusto, the desire to grab hold of life and enjoy it; and the fear of doing unmentionable things that will bring disaster. A development of fifth-century tragedy can be pinpointed with reference to the Furies. The Furies are present at the end of the *Oresteia* and in the *Oedipus at Colonus.* But in the former play they are visible performers on stage; in the latter they are unseen spirits in the background. Both the *Oresteia* and the *Oedipus at Colonus* celebrate a power being brought into Athens, a power indefinable and acting in realms not controlled by conscious intellect. But in the *Oresteia* the point of contact between the human and the dark power is an act of city ritual; in the *Oedipus at Colonus* it is the secret burial of one body in the ground. Tragedy has developed inward. Part of this development is due to the collapse of the city-state from the glory and success of Aeschylus' last years to the disintegration and failure of Sophocles'. But partly it is a natural tendency for art and thought to move inward, from public celebration to private meditation. If I may be allowed to define the satyr play by a conceit, I would say that Pratinas, as it were, recognized that this development inward would take place and insisted on the satyr play so that one at least of the basic emotions of tragedy should be exposed as public celebration.

Otherwise we do not possess enough satyr plays to attempt a more comprehensive definition. One thing at least we might say: that the satyr play always contained a chorus of satyrs, and, probably, the figure of Silenus, the fat, drunken, and lecherous father of the satyrs. The *Alcestis* of Euripides, however, was submitted as his fourth play in the competition of 438. It does not have a satyr chorus and does not seem to be very like what the normal satyr play appears to have been. The satyr play was usually the fourth play in each poet's series, but not always. *The Net-Haulers* by Aeschylus presents the beginning of a story as the first play in a trilogy of which we know the outline.[3] We know the titles of the three other plays presented by Euripides in 438 but it does not seem as if any of those could be satyr plays.[4] We must therefore conclude either that Euripides for some reason was able to bend the regulations, or that by 438 the regulations prescribing one satyr play were no longer insisted on, or that the *Alcestis* in some way was able to qualify as a satyr play. We simply do not possess the evidence to decide between these three possibilities. Given the enormous variety of fifth-century tragedies, we should not attempt to define the satyr play with more precision than our evidence allows.

The satyr play has often been defined as a farce or as burlesque.[5] This definition cannot be acceptable once we see how much farce and burlesque were present in the tragedies.[6] Certainly the themes of many of the satyr plays whose outlines we can discover are more full of ribaldry than the tragedies. But while the *Cyclops* of Euripides is mostly farce and contains vigorous bawdy, *The Searching Satyrs* of Sophocles does not seem to contain much of either. The only satisfactory summary of the satyr play we can give in the present state of our knowledge is to say: that it nearly always contained a chorus of satyrs; that it was usually the fourth of the poet's four plays, and therefore probably lighter in tone on the whole; that its atmosphere remained nearest to the primitive fertility rite out of which tragedy grew; and that its function was to serve as a regular reminder of our joy in the life-force with which the worship of Dionysus is concerned.

Aeschylus was as much applauded for his satyr plays as for his tragedies. Relatively recent papyrus finds have added to our knowledge, especially with fragments of two plays. The best is from *The Net-Haulers*. This play presented the arrival of Danae with her infant son, Perseus, on the shore of the island of Seriphus. We know from other versions of the story that she had floated out to sea in a chest. We possess a scene in which this chest is being hauled out of the sea, presumably by the chorus of satyrs. We also have a scene in which Silenus attempts to seduce Danae, while acting the kindly uncle to the little boy. Beauty chased by the satyrs is a common theme for a satyr play.

This play presents an interesting problem in staging. The chest with Danae and the infant Perseus must have been dragged out of the central opening in the *skēnē*, just as the statue of Peace is dragged out by the chorus of *The Peace*. Presumably therefore the Athenian audience was happy to accept this opening in a temple facade as representing the sea.

Another new fragment is from *The Spectators* of Aeschylus. The scene we possess contains a confrontation between Dionysus and the chorus of satyrs. Dionysus is complaining that the satyrs abuse him for being no good at metal-work, and indeed for being a weak, womanly creature not to be counted as a man. He in turn abuses them for despising his dancing, and training so hard for the Isthmian games that they now have "little mousetail penises" (Frag. 276, 29). We can see that Aeschylus may have performed mockery of Dionysus similar to that of Aristophanes in *The Frogs*. At any rate, it is an expression of the ambivalent attitude to Dionysus that we find at all periods of Greek poetry: Dionysus, the apparently weak and effeminate god who is a power unimaginable.

One phrase, "ear-pads next to his ear-rings," is all that survives of the *Kerkyon* (Frag. 52). We know, however, the outline of the story, which was of Kerkyon, king of Eleusis, the son of Poseidon, who forced all passers-by to wrestle with him. The phrase that survives refers to the wrestler's ear-pads and gives a vivid picture of the rich wrestler's head. Presumably, since the only notable thing about Kerkyon was his wrestling, the play must have contained a wrestling match, or at least a dance representation of a wrestling match. Consideration of this tiny fragment therefore may add a little to our picture of Aeschylus' theatrical variety, and of what was possible on the fifth-century stage.

We possess the synopsis of the *Amymone*, the fourth play of the *Suppliants* tetralogy.[7] Amymone, one of the daughters of Danaus, was sent to look for a spring of water. As she was searching she threw a dart at a deer and hit a sleeping satyr. He woke up and tried to rape her. Poseidon intervened, but, having saved her from the satyr, he had sex with her himself and showed her the springs at Lerna. What is interesting about this story of sex escaped and then finally consummated is that it mirrors the story of the previous three plays in the tetralogy. And unless the satyr play did so mirror the action of the preceding tragedies, it is difficult to see why Aeschylus should have written linked tetralogies as he so often did.[8] At any rate, the erotic theme and imagery of the *Suppliants* fit very well with one important element of the satyric.

Lecherousness is one of the most important characteristics of the satyrs. It could hardly fail to be when their costume emphasized to the maximum their penis, most usually in a state of erection.

If there is one play whose discovery would illuminate the nature of fifth-century drama more than any other, it is the *Proteus,* the fourth play of the *Oresteia.* We cannot but wonder how Aeschylus could have followed the emotional climax of the end of the *Eumenides,* and it seems likely that it must have been a very lighthearted play. Presumably it concerned Menelaus' stay in Egypt, as described in the fourth book of the *Odyssey,* in which he encountered Proteus, the old man of the sea, who could change himself into a lion, a snake, a leopard, running water, and a tree. The ancient story about Proteus, we read in Lucian, was simply that he was a dancer and wonderful mimic.[9] Authors on the subject frequently refer to a dance called *morphasmos,* the changing of one's shape.[10] The play must at least have given good opportunities for a display of *morphasmos.*

We must, however, also mention another possibility. Euripides' *Helen* presents the story of Helen in Egypt, while a phantom Helen went to Troy and caused the Trojan War. Euripides makes his king of Egypt Theoclymenus, son of Proteus. The story, however, appears in Herodotus (*Histories* 2.112–20) where the king who entertains Helen is Proteus. Herodotus says that he heard the story in Egypt, which he visited about the time of the production of the *Oresteia.* It is possible, though not certain, that Aeschylus could have known the story. Would he have contemplated using it? Could he have constructed his fourth play out of a story that makes nonsense of the preceding three plays? Is that part of the purpose of the satyr element, that essential quality of virtue and the Greek mind? Proteus as the name of the king of Egypt must cause us to ask such questions. It is, I suppose, also possible that there could have been a story whereby Proteus, old man of the sea, was the king of Egypt. Otherwise the existence of two Proteuses is an odd coincidence. The questions roused by this play may perhaps open our minds to possibilities about fifth-century drama. But, alas, they cannot be answered.

Sophocles certainly used erotic themes in his satyr plays. *The Lovers of Achilles* contains a nine-line fragment, though unfortunately with a much mutilated text, that describes love as joy mixed with pain, like ice in bright weather that you can neither hold or let go. (Frag. 149). It has been suggested that the play was set at the cave of Chiron, where Achilles was brought up, and that the chorus of satyrs were the lovers of Achilles. It has also been suggested that this is the play to which Ovid refers when he says some tragedy is "mixed with obscene laughter" and contains indelicate language, because in the next line he refers to an author "who made Achilles a sissy." (*Tristia* 2.409).

Sophocles' *Pandora* was also called *The Hammerers,* which may mean that the chorus of satyrs helped Hephaestus to create the manufactured woman Pandora, whom Zeus sent to loose troubles on men in punishment for Prometheus' theft of fire.[11] The beauty of Pandora, once all the gods had given her their gifts, was conspicuous. It would have provided an amusing erotic sequence if the satyrs, having created her, then attempted to seduce her. One of the fragments (frag. 483) certainly contains a sexual meaning, though its exact translation is difficult and its context unknown.

In contrast we should notice the *Amykos*, of which only two lines survive. The Argonauts on their voyage came to Bithynia, whose king, Amykos, would not let strangers land unless they boxed with him. Polydeuces, however, was on the *Argo*, and managed to beat Amykos. The center of the play therefore must have been the boxing match, as that of Aeschylus' *Kerkyon* must have been a wrestling match.

Of Sophocles' *Searching Satyrs* we have about 306 complete lines. Our text covers probably about two-thirds of the play, though much of that two-thirds is unintelligible.[12] We possess almost nothing in lyric meters, but it appears that there cannot have been very much singing. We have enough of the text to experience the feel of the play, a simple story full of rather childish fun, with opportunities more for capering about than for highly organized dancing. But the action of the play is the stealing of Apollo's cattle by the infant Hermes, and we cannot fully analyze the structure because we do not possess the end of the play, in which Hermes must have appeared. We cannot therefore make firm judgments as to how this play fitted into Sophocles' philosophy or moral order.

The play presents the miraculous birth of Hermes, as described in the Homeric *Hymn to Hermes*. Of all extant fifth-century plays *The Searching Satyrs* has most of the feeling of primitive folk myth. The miraculous birth of Hermes and his rapid growth to maturity in six days, remind us of the Canaanite *Poem of Dawn and Sunset*, to which I alluded while discussing the prehistory of drama in Chapter 3. This element of primitive folk myth is perhaps one of the central ingredients of the satyr play.

Our text of *The Searching Satyrs* opens with Apollo talking to Silenus, father of the satyrs, and so presumably to the satyrs too. We do not have the beginning of the play, though it does not seem as if much is missing. Apollo has lost his cattle and is promising a reward to anyone who finds them. Silenus accepts on behalf of himself and his sons the promise of gold if he finds them. There is also a reference to another reward—freedom for them all (44–45). One of the important elements in the *Cyclops* is the fact that the satyrs have been made slaves of the Cyclops, which they should not be, since they are the attendants of Dionysus. A significant result of Odysseus' action in blinding the Cyclops is to release Silenus and the satyrs from slavery. It is tempting to wonder if such a freeing of the satyrs was a common event in the satyr play. Freeing the satyrs conveys a possible image from folk myth: freeing the spirits of fertility from slavery is a little like the return of Persephone from the dead, or other stories obviously derived from the return of spring. We have no evidence however to push this tempting conjecture further.

Apollo leaves, and the satyrs start searching under the guidance of Silenus. There are a few lines of lyric iambic for Silenus, but the rest of what we possess is ordinary dialogue. The satyrs discover the tracks of the cattle but are frightened by a strange booming noise coming from the cave in front of them, represented as usual by the central entrance in the *skēnē*. The panic gives the chorus opportunity for performing all sorts of antics like crouching, crawling, and monkey-running (90–94). Silenus abuses their cowardice in a strong speech, (111–134), but when he hears the noise he is just as frightened. The satyrs now jump and kick the ground in a series of leaps to make the creature come out of the cave (157–67). Surprisingly, this appears to have been done in dialogue iambics. We wonder why Sophocles did not create a lyric for this sequence.

The nymph Cyllene now appears from the cave and rebukes the satyrs for being so different now from what they were when they used to dance in Dionysus' train (168–89). The satyrs now appear to have a short astrophic song with which they enquire about the strange noise. This allows Cyllene to tell of the miraculous birth of Hermes, child of Zeus and Maia, whose whereabouts must be kept secret for fear of Hera's jealousy. Hermes is now a full-grown boy, though only six days old. The noise comes from the lyre, which he has invented from the shell of a tortoise. It also emerges that the strings are of cattle hide, and therefore that Hermes must be the cattle thief. The final details of the lyre's nature emerge in chanted stichomythia (236–56) in the unique meter of the iambic tetrameter acatelectic.[13]

At this point (257–65) the satyrs dance their accusation of Hermes in a short astrophic lyric containing cretics and dochmiacs. The tension builds between them and Cyllene for the rest of our text, which then breaks off.

The ending of the play presumably involved a confrontation between Apollo and Hermes, in which, as in the Homeric *Hymn*, Hermes gives the lyre to Apollo in compensation for the stolen cattle. Presumably the finale was the celebration by the satyrs of their new liberty, and perhaps a song from Apollo to the lyre.

The fact that we possess neither beginning nor ending, and almost none of the lyrics, leaves us unable to make any very significant judgments about this play. It does, however, convey a little of the lighthearted charm that we know to have been a characteristic of Sophocles from the personal anecdotes told about him, which the stern morality of the extant seven plays makes us inclined to forget.

It is much easier to be definite about the intentions of Euripides in the *Cyclops*. With a few minor alterations, mainly dictated by the conditions of staging, it presents the story of Odysseus and the Cyclops as told in the ninth book of the *Odyssey*. Odysseus, however, does not possess the character he possesses in the *Odyssey*. He is, rather, the crafty, unscrupulous, and brutal time-serving politician that he is elsewhere in the plays of Euripides. In contrast to him is the Cyclops, with no respect for law, and no respect for other people at all. His life is entirely devoted to satisfying his base desires. Such a way of life leads him to disaster, and his fate is sealed because his greed will not allow him to involve his fellow Cyclopes in what he thinks will be his supreme moment of sensual indulgence. Because he does not want them near to enjoy part of his pleasure, they will not be near to save his skin. The play presents a conflict between two unlikeable people, a conflict that is won by the more intelligent. The medium is on the whole a kind of black farce, which suitably distances us from both sides.

The action of the play is the cannibal greed of the Cyclops in eating two of Odysseus' men, which causes Odysseus to retaliate with the brutal action of burning out the Cyclops' one eye. The one major change from Homer's version makes Odysseus' action much more brutal. In the *Odyssey*, Odysseus cannot just kill the Cyclops in revenge for his dead companions because the Cyclops has closed the cave with a stone too big for humans to roll aside. The only chance for the Greeks to escape is by blinding him (*Odyssey*, 9. 299–306). In Euripides' play the action of Odysseus is much more brutal because it is not presented as the only option. This major change goes well with the total change of the character of Odysseus.

Silenus speaks the prologue, invoking Dionysus and reminding him of the help that he, Silenus, has given his patron god in the past. He goes on to say that his present trouble has come about because, when Dionysus was kidnapped by pirates, Silenus and the satyrs set sail to look for him, were shipwrecked on the coast of Sicily, and were enslaved by the Cyclops. Now they herd his flocks instead of dancing to Dionysus.

The *parodos* follows as the satyr chorus enters, dancing the *sikinnis* with exuberance (41–81. Line 37 tells us it is a *sikinnis*.). The dance consists of one system, probably with repeated refrain and an epode. It is a rounding-up dance of apparently real sheep. If there were real sheep onstage there cannot have been any very complicated choreography, though the fact that the dance is a *sikinnis* means that the individual movements were very vigorous. The epode, as so often in Euripides, suggests an increase in excitement. The words refer to the Bacchic dances that they are not allowed to perform (63–70). Presumably the dance presented some of this forbidden Bacchic movement, which would both be theatrical and create good dramatic tension, giving excellent motivation for the words of Silenus that immediately follow the dance: "Be quiet" (82).

Silenus has seen Odysseus and his companions approaching, and so orders the satyrs to drive the sheep inside. Stichomythia between Odysseus and Silenus establishes who the Cyclopes are. Odysseus gives Silenus a drink of wine from his magic flask, which continually refills itself, and arranges to barter some of the Cyclops' cheese and lambs for wine. Silenus is drunk and feeling lustful (169–72). All he wants to do is to dance and have sex, caring nothing—or so he says—for the Cyclops.

While Silenus goes into the cave to fetch out the lambs and cheese, the chorus leader asks Odysseus about the sack of Troy. Since all their trouble had been for the whore Helen, did everyone take advantage of the fact that she was a whore and each man lay her in turn? (180). This little sequence offers humorous production possibilities, allowing the satyrs to perform vivid movements with their phalluses, and is dramatically appropriate as expressing one of the worst aspects of their slavery, sexual frustration, on which they continue to harp (437–40). It also demonstrates Euripides' bitter preoccupation with the worthlessness of Helen, which is a feature of so many of his plays, and which seems to have been an image for him of the worthlessness of war in general.

Silenus' trading is interrupted by the arrival of the Cyclops himself, who catches them unawares. Odysseus refuses to run, preferring to "die nobly" (201). The Cyclops reduces the chorus to terror while Silenus slinks into the cave, whence he will emerge pretending to have been beaten up and forced to hand over the lambs and cheese. Silenus adds some colorful insults, which the Greeks are supposed to have uttered against the absent Cyclops, (232–40), and recommends that they be eaten. The Cyclops believes him, though the chorus say that their father is lying (270–72). The Cyclops then questions Odysseus and learns that he has just arrived from sacking Troy. What a shameful thing, he says, going to war for one bad woman (280, 283–84). Odysseus dismisses the war in one line:

> Some god's affair! No mortal is to blame.
>
> (285)

It is a classic remark of a politician, blaming his actions on the circumstances of the times, making out that he was merely a pawn of fate.

Odysseus now goes on to ask the Cyclops to behave in a civilized fashion. The Cyclops laughs him aside. "Wealth is the wise man's god" (316). He cares nothing for threats involving retribution from Zeus. Why, if Zeus thunders and rains he merely goes inside his cave, and has a big blow-out. "Eating and drinking and having no worries, that's Zeus," he says (336–38), and adds, "for the *sōphrōn*," the word used throughout tragedy for the man who understands and keeps to the limitations of his mortality, the man who is the very opposite in every way to the Cyclops. "Laws are merely the embroidery of life," he continues, snapping his fingers at them. He goes into the cave, followed by Odysseus after a short prayer to Athene and a rather peevish prayer to Zeus: "If you take no notice, Zeus, you're a nothing god" (354–55).

A one-system dance follows for the chorus, either with mesode, or possibly with repeated refrain. The satyrs invoke the Cyclops opening his vast jaws to gobble human flesh. Both *strophē* and *antistrophē* involve much the same eating action, offering obvious mime possibilities for a dance that revels in what it fears (356–74).

Odysseus then reappears to tell how the Cyclops ate two of his men, and how he gave the Cyclops some of the magic wine. Silenus has also been drinking it and, though he would like to escape, is now useless for action. Odysseus describes his plan to blind the Cyclops with a red-hot sharpened stake and tells the satyrs that he will take them away with him on his ship. The chorus volunteer with enthusiasm to help him.

Meanwhile the Cyclops and Silenus come out drunk. Chorus and Cyclops sing three identical stanzas in anacreontics, the standard rhythm of drinking songs. The dance was probably a simple ring dance around the reeling Cyclops. It leads into a scene of stichomythia between him and Odysseus, in which Odysseus praises the god of wine and persuades the Cyclops not to share the drink with any of his fellows. Farcical horseplay follows as the Cyclops and Silenus stretch out on the ground and each tries to keep the flask to himself. Finally Odysseus encourages the Cyclops to drink every drop. The Cyclops goes into an ecstasy, seeing the throne of Zeus and heaven mixed with the earth (576–84). It is a moment of almost Aristophanic topsy-turviness. The brutal Cyclops in his moment of greatest debauchery is almost beautiful because he is possessed. The lines that follow are the extreme point of the farce, as he starts to make love to Silenus and carries him protesting into the cave. But it is also the nearest to a romantic moment that the Cyclops can achieve. He sees the bloated Silenus as Ganymede, the beautiful boy beloved of Zeus himself. Gross farce as it is, it is also a moment of complex poetry.

From here the play moves quickly to its end. After a short prayer to Hephaestus, god of fire, Odysseus goes into the cave, while the satyrs invoke the fire in a brief astrophic dance. Odysseus reappears to tell them to be quiet and prepare to grab the red-hot stake. Naturally at this moment the cowardly satyrs start to make excuses, and Odysseus goes in to do the work while the satyrs do the shouting. The Cyclops emerges, blinded, blocking the entrance to the cave. As in the *Odyssey*, Odysseus has told the Cyclops that his name is Nobody. But the trick has less point here than in the *Odyssey*. Here it is merely used as a chance for laughs in an interchange between the Cyclops and the chorus (669–75). "Nobody blinded me." "Then you're not blind" (673). And so on. The Cyclops is searching for the Greeks. The satyrs baffle him by giving him wrong directions, and by making him run his head against the rock (682). The Greeks escape, and Odysseus reveals his real name. The Cyclops warns him that he will suffer for what he has done, but Odysseus laughs at him. The play ends with the Cyclops threatening to throw a rock and crush Odysseus' ship, while the satyrs say that they will enlist with Odysseus and take their orders in future from Dionysus.

The date of the *Cyclops* is a matter of considerable dispute. An ingenious theory solves the problem of its date and interpretation in one.[14] This suggests that it was produced with the *Hecuba* in 425, at a moment when Athens had suffered the plague and six years of war. There are remarkable parallels between the two plays. Both Polymestor and the Cyclops are brutally blinded. In both plays barbarous vengeance is taken on a barbarian, while we are left with a sense of sickness at the horrible way in which supposedly civilized Greeks can behave. The role of Odysseus is the same in both plays, the embodiment of the so-called civilized person, behaving worse than a savage. There is no evidence for this date, but there is no evidence for any other date. We have seen from the example of the *Amymone* that, in Aeschylus' tetralogies at any rate, the satyr play provided some kind of counterpoint to the theme of the previous tragedies. This kind of counterpoint must often have taken the form of a farcical version of the same story, and so given justification to the belief that the satyr play was merely a farce that relieved the tension built up by the preceding three tragedies.[15] Such a patterning could be said to rest on the sound principle that events in life can be seen as tragedy, comedy, or farce, depending on our point of view. It is a neat philosophical raison d'être for the satyr play, and perhaps it will help our understanding of what little survives. But with such limited material from which to generalize, all our generalizations must be guarded.

Should we consider Euripides' *Alcestis* as a play of the same category? In terms of Euripides' work it is better to think of it as the precursor of his later so-called tragicomedies, plays like the *Helen* or *Ion*. The *Alcestis* is not farce, but then nor is *The Searching Satyrs*. Much more important, there is no chorus of satyrs, no Silenus, no chance for dancing the *sikinnis*, and no particular reference to Dionysus. On the other hand, the rescue of Alcestis from death has the feeling of primitive folk myth that we get from *The Searching Satyrs*, and the character of Heracles, feasting in ribaldry while the household mourns the death of Alcestis, has something of the same quality as the gluttonous and lecherous satyrs. Perhaps we should consider the *Alcestis* with the other one and one-half plays that we possess of the genre.

Apollo speaks the prologue. He had been forced to be a servant in the house of Admetus but had been so well treated that he had rewarded Admetus by giving him an escape from death. The condition, however, was that he must find someone prepared to die for him. Only his wife, Alcestis, offered herself. Death arrives to take Alcestis away. Apollo pleads, and, when his pleas are refused, threatens that Death will be stopped. But Death replies that Alcestis is coming with him.

The chorus of citizens' function is almost entirely to build up sympathy for the dying Alcestis, to tear our heartstrings with grief. The *parodos* laments and praises her (77–131). The farewell scene between Admetus and Alcestis continues the mood. We must assume that Apollo's offer carries irrevocability, so that, once Alcestis has offered to die, Admetus cannot change places with her. If this were not so, we should find the behavior of Admetus intolerable. As it is he emerges a colorless person in comparison with his strong and loving wife.

After a *stasimon* of prayer for Alcestis on her way to Hades (435–75), Heracles arrives on his way to Thrace. Admetus cannot bear to turn away a guest, and so pretends that the corpse he is mourning is not that of a close relation. Heracles must enter the guest room, and he will be entertained.

There is a scene of bitter wrangling between Admetus and his father, Pheres, (614–733), in which each accuses the other of being too frightened to die. The mood changes abruptly as, first, a servant comes out to describe Heracles' excesses at his private dinner party, and then Heracles himself staggers drunkenly out to laugh death aside, advocating a philosophy of "eat, drink, let tomorrow go hang," and apparently attempting to seduce the servant (790–91;

the whole scene, 747–836). Once Heracles learns that the dead woman is in reality Alcestis, he is horror-struck, and the play's mood changes with his own. Alone except for the chorus, he announces his intention of rescuing Alcestis (837–60). With this speech and Apollo's announcement in the prologue, we know that Alcestis will return. The funeral procession, which arrives as Heracles leaves, stirs our hearts. Nevertheless we know that it is not real. It leads naturally into the return of Heracles with a veiled and silent woman, who is eventually discovered as Alcestis. The play could rightly be described as the earliest romantic piece. Its structure is our longing that Alcestis will be brought back. The form of the play is a series of delays before the final consummation of our hopes.

As a romantic tragicomedy the play has a serious deficiency—the character of Admetus, who gives little evidence in the course of the action that he is worth dying for. Inevitably we must ask what the lives of Admetus and Alcestis will be like afterward. But this is to treat the *Alcestis* as if it were a play of plot and character, which is to apply criteria to it applicable only to a later stage of Euripides' writing. But the fact that we can begin to treat it in this kind of way suggests that it is an awkwardly transitional play. Perhaps the character of Alcestis grew without Euripides realizing it, and turned what had been meant to be merely a fairy tale with a miraculous element into what can be described as the first romantic tragedy in the modern sense of the word, though a tragedy with a happy ending.

That the satyr play was an important element in the Dionysiac festival we cannot deny. In general terms there is little difficulty in forcing ourselves to remember a picture of leaping satyrs with erect penises dancing a celebration of sensual abandonment at some point during every tragic poet's dramatic offering during every festival. But unfortunately, when we try to put together this general statement with interpretations of the two complete plays by Euripides, only one of which is unquestionably a satyr play, the half-play by Sophocles, and the various short fragments and synopses, we realize how difficult it is to form any very conclusive generalizations. It is perhaps appropriate that the satyrs, the embodiment of the primitive, indefinable energy, should be the obvious symbol of the limits to our knowledge of the fifth-century theater, serving to remind us that we shall never recreate or even fully understand that theater without an energy of our own as primitive, as indefinable, and as fertile.

Notes

1. Plutarch, *Pericles* 5. 154E.
2. See Chapter 3, "The Beginnings of Greek Drama."
3. The story of Perseus, told in *The Net-Haulers, Phorcides*, and *Polydectes*, as we saw in Chapter 3.
4. The *Women of Crete, Alcmaeon in Psophis*, and *Telephus*.
5. I did so myself. See Leo Aylen, *Greek Tragedy and the Modern World* (London: Methuen, 1964) p. 150.

6. E.g., in *The Children of Heracles* (see Chapter 3, "Drama for Carnival Week"), and in *Prometheus Bound* and *Antigone* (see Chapter 8).

7. Apollodorus *Library* 2. 1. 4.

8. I have discussed this in more detail in "The Vulgarity of Tragedy" in *Classical Drama and Its Influence*, ed. M. J. Anderson (London: Methuen, 1965), pp. 87–100. Cf. also Aylen, *Greek Tragedy and the Modern World*, pp. 51–56.

9. Lucian *On the Dance* 19.

10. E.g., in Athenaeus *Deipnosophists* 14. 629F.

11. For the story of Pandora, see Hesiod *Works and Days* 60–105; *Theogony* 570–89.

12. I have used Page's text, and therefore his numbering of the lines, based on the complete lines that we possess. See *Select Papyri*, vol. 3, *Literary Papyri, Poetry, Texts*, trans. D. L. Page (London: William Heinemann; Cambridge: Harvard University Press, 1962), pp. 26–53.

13. For an explanation of Greek meters, see Appendix 4.

14. Cf. William Arrowsmith's Introduction to his translation of the *Cyclops*, in *The Complete Greek Tragedies*, ed. David Grene and Richmond Lattimore, *Euripides* 2:2 n.1.

15. See Horace *The Art of Poetry* 225–50, for an ancient author who thought this. For other references to the way in which later antiquity thought that farce should end a program of tragedy, see W. Beare, *The Roman Stage* (London: Methuen, 1964), p. 20.

10

TRANSITION AND DECLINE

It is not the purpose of this book to attempt to define exhaustively the nature of fifth-century drama, because any such formal definition would be an impertinence. The total fifth-century theatrical experience is a mystery we are only beginning to penetrate, and a mystery not susceptible to neat definitions. Kitto, talking particularly of Sophocles, made use of an anecdote of Schumann, who played one of his compositions and was then asked the meaning of it. Schumann's reply was to play the piece again.[1] We shall define the mystery of fifth-century drama only by performing the plays in conditions approximating as nearly as possible those in which they were performed, and even then we shall never quite come to total union with their meaning for the original audience.

Any generalizations, therefore, must be taken merely as summary short-hand, and not as definition. With this important proviso we may summarize the important facets of the drama of the fifth century as follows: first, it was created for, and derived from, the unique rite of Dionysus, a personal god with peculiar and individual characteristics. Second, the nature of the festival created a particular form of performance, which I have called dance drama, and which has never been repeated at any other time in the history of the theater. Definition can be only by analogy; we can compare the form of the fugue; we can say that it is not, and how it is not, drama of plot and interaction of characters. Third, the larger form of the dance drama depends upon the fact that the dances are made up of systems, matching *strophēs* and *antistrophēs*, where identical music and dance are repeated to different words. What exactly this dependence is we cannot define. But it is as important a formal aspect of fifth-century drama as it is for fugue that the subject is a tune that can be combined in invertible counterpoint, and therefore can appear as top line, middle, or bass, while of course the subject of a sonata or symphony need not be, and very rarely is, so combined in invertible counterpoint. Fourth, the week of the City *Dionysia* was the most important week in the year for Athens, and so its drama became the major religious and educative activity for the citizens: living Bible, pulpit, and political platform in one. As a result the plays became the obvious means whereby the city could be brought to understand its present in terms of its past, in an activity that was the equivalent of studying moral and political philosophy and taking part in religious worship, all in one. Fifth, by defining the drama primarily as a rite, there is no need to define it further in terms of theatrical tone. There is no especial tone of solemnity necessary to tragedy, or riotous laughter to comedy. There are more solemn moments in tragedy, and more riotous moments in comedy. But they are not the defining qualities of tragedy or comedy. The only thing that defines them is the rite within which they occur. The religious message defines the tone of the plays, just as it does in the plays of the miracle cycle, which also employ the full range of theatrical tone from extreme seriousness to extreme farce and make use of every available theatrical effect in the service of their message.

Finally, for a reason we cannot explain, all these aspects of fifth-century drama are related. The best summary of this occurs in the third *stasimon* of the *Oedipus the King* (863–910, especially 895–910). "If the pattern of Dikē disintegrates, what is the point of my dancing?" And in this *stasimon* the symbol of the pattern's reliability is the truth of oracles. For if there is a pattern, parts of it can be foretold in the context of worship.

The interrelated culture of the fifth century collapsed quite quickly at the end of the century. If we summarize the cultural pattern of the fourth century we are presented with something very different. The important writers of the fifth century are the poets, presenting their dance dramas as public celebrations of the gods and the city. The important writers of the fourth century are philosophers writing in prose for themselves in private and for a small school of picked pupils. The important religious activity of the fourth century was meditative speculation into the nature of God, a private activity, little connected with the affairs of the city.

To describe this change in detail would take a book in itself. The following is only the baldest summary. First, the culture of Athens changed for the very simple reason that Athens was defeated and bankrupt. For a short time, Athens was even put under a Spartan garrison:[2] Athens, who had thought herself the mother of liberty. It seems that there may have never been enough money to produce genuine Old Comedy with full chorus after *The Frogs* and its successors at the *Dionysia* of 405. And, by the time that Athens' finances had recovered in the 380s, people had learnt to do without the sacred dances.

Second, the defeat brought with it a change in Athenian political philosophy. Just as Britain in the nineteenth and early twentieth century, and the United States in the mid-twentieth century, had a philosophy of themselves as the best government in the world, in order to justify being the richest nation of the world, so the Athenians had developed a philosophy of their state as providing the best possible way of life, as justification for glorifying their city with money taken from other states in exchange for Athenian protection. They were able to discuss the ideal form of government because they were confident that their city possessed the nearest to the ideal government that had ever been achieved in the history of man. They could no longer believe this after they had seen the horrors perpetrated by Athenians on Athenians in the various revolutions of the last decade of the fifth century, culminating in the killings by the Spartan-supported oligarchical tyranny of the Thirty. And even when democracy in Athens was restored, it could never exercise the hold upon men's minds that it had in the days of Aeschylus. We possess so neatly the image of this new, tarnished democracy. For it was this government that committed the political crime whose wrongheadedness has reverberated through history as few others have: the killing of Socrates. Athens's image as land of the free froze to death in Socrates' cup of hemlock, just as Britain's faded away under the cool stare of Gandhi and America's shriveled in the napalm flames that scorched Vietnamese children.

Third, there was a change in religious attitude that is easier to point to than to explain. We may distinguish broadly between two methods of attaining truth: the analogical and the analytical. Analogy is the method of all primitive religions; it is also the method involved in the "models" of modern science, especially physics and astronomy. Analysis seeks to explain the models or stories in terms of an abstract system. Cultures have changed as one or the other method is declared primary. For both cannot be equally efficient methods; one must depend on the other. The difference between the religion of Aeschylus and that of Plato is very much one between a religion of analogy and one of analysis.

I have discussed this in greater detail elsewhere.[3] Archaic Greek polytheism had no theology, only stories. Some of the stories were concerned with explaining natural phenomena. As scientific method grew, which it was doing in the latter half of the fifth century, so the traditional stories became discredited. Polytheism and the scientific method have never coincided in history. Hinduism is antiscientific; in those parts of the world where Christian Catholicism has been very near polytheism, it is antiscientific also. In a sense this incompatibility is obvious. Extreme polytheism, such as that of archaic Greece or of Hindu India, is a denial of system. Scientific method, at any rate until very recent times, has depended almost totally on system.

We might expect that these tendencies would lead to disbelief in the Olympian gods. As I have said already, the Greeks at this time did not possess the concept of "belief in God," and so we cannot say that at this time they "ceased to believe in the Olympian gods." On the whole there was an increase in what we would call semimagical superstitious practices, and a growing sense that the traditional forms of worship were irrelevant. The change is easiest to see if we read the work of Epicurus, who flourished in Athens at the same time as Menander, during the last quarter of the fourth century. For Epicurus the gods existed, but they were remote and uninterested in human affairs. Clearly, for Sophocles they were very close.

At the center of every religion is the problem of suffering. Why do some people suffer so intolerably? The tragedies of Aeschylus and Sophocles present people suffering, and sometimes intolerably. They are concerned to show how the suffering occurred, in order that we may learn about the possibility of avoiding similar disaster ourselves. Our hearts are wrung with sympathy for the sufferers. But we are never to identify too closely with them. Our point of view is always that of participants in the rite. We are asked to share the attitude of the chorus in the *Oedipus the King*, for whom it is better that one man should suffer, however horribly, than that the pattern of things should no longer hold. For if that pattern disintegrated, there would be far worse suffering.

As human beings we are very weak. Even a totally convinced atheist can be reduced to hysteria by the worst horrors of a cancer or the grotesque humiliations of a geriatric ward. Only a confident culture can look the intolerable suffering, which is the lot of human beings, fully in the face. History is full of examples of how thinkers and artists have tried to obscure the fact that each one of us alive may suddenly be struck, through no fault of our own, by some grotesquely painful and crippling deformity, and that, come what may, we shall certainly suffer the ultimate indignity of death. Sound religion, whether polytheist, monotheist, or atheist, seems to consist in reconciling this fact of intolerable suffering with acceptance of whatever theology one adheres to: with what atheists might define as a balanced life, and theists as the practice of worship. Suffering can so horrify us that we react to our theology with hysteria. The result of this can only be incoherence, from which we must retreat into escapism.

Although *The Bacchants* is a play presenting the "how" of suffering with as clear-eyed an acceptance as any play of Sophocles, there are plays of Euripides, in which we see the nearness of this hysteria: for example, the reaction of Aphrodite in the *Hippolytus*, which seems to us so excessive; or the abruptness of the way in which disaster strikes Andromache in *The Trojan Women*. A crucial play is the *Heracles*. As a result of Heracles' noble action on behalf of his father, he is struck down with terrible suffering through the direct intervention of the goddess Hera. Confronted with intolerable suffering, we may react by hatred of the powers who created it. Surprisingly, however, it is not Euripides who creates the strongest poetic statement of this reaction. Sophocles puts it into the mouth of Philoctetes:

> It would be so. Evil has never perished.
> The powers carefully look after that,
> And somehow wickedness and treachery
> They love to turn away from death, but justice
> And nobleness they always hurry down.
> Where can I set these things, where praise, if by
> Praising the gods, I find the gods are evil.
>
> (*Philoctetes*, 446–52)

But the totality of the *Philoctetes* presents a more balanced and resigned attitude. It is in plays such as the *Hecuba* and *Trojan Women* of Euripides that we find the strongest total expression of hysteria turning into rejection of the theology. The exclamation of Talthybius at Hecuba's grovelling misery is a natural reaction to the totality of the two plays:

> Oh Zeus—what shall I say?—that you do watch men?
> Or that we have acquired a useless thought,
> A lie, that there are such beings as gods,
> While all the time chance governs human life.
>
> (*Hecuba*, 488–91)

After the anguish of *The Trojan Women*, Euripides turned to the relative escapism of the *Iphigeneia in Tauris*, *Helen*, and *Ion*.

If a theology gives us too much pain, we will reject it. I said in Chapter 3 that Euripides writes within the theology of the Olympian gods. In the same way Graham Greene, James Joyce, and Samuel Beckett all write within the theology of Christian Catholicism. Graham Greene suffers as a Catholic; Joyce and Beckett rejected Catholicism. But their writing depends completely on the background, which they personally happen to reject. The tension of their writing derives from their personal pain suffered within the theology. But for Beckett, now there is nothing left of the theology but the pain. A successor to Beckett writing completely without reference to the theology could not reach Beckett's agonies, because Beckett's agonies derive from his reaction to the theology. Similarly, the successors of Euripides lost touch with his theology and so lost touch with the focus of his pain.

The agony of *The Trojan Women*, then, in some sense expresses the end of a road for tragedy as the contemplation of the intolerable suffering that is the lot of man. After it Euripides explored theatrical textures but made no more metaphysical challenges. His last play, *The Bacchants*, presents the same vision as the *Hippolytus*, though a vision purified by the suffering that he had witnessed between writing the two plays.

In Euripides we can see examples of the beginnings of disintegration in all the aspects of fifth-century drama. These have all been discussed elsewhere, and I only summarize here. Apart from the sense of theological disintegration, we can see how the form of his plays also changed. With Euripides' later work as we saw in Chapter 6, we are presented with plays of plot, depending on the interaction of characters. The structure of the drama is borne by the dialogue, not by the sequence of chorus dances. Concurrently, as we might expect, the chorus dances become more decorative adjuncts to the play than the central element, which they are in Sophocles. Within the lyric passages, the system becomes less central. The typical *stasimon* in late Euripides is a short system followed by a longer free epode. Clearly a form such as this, where musical climaxes do not have to be repeated, suits a situation where the composer is becoming more and more important in relation to the poet. Furthermore, the growing power of the actors and their demand for theatrically effective solo arias is turning tragedy already into something nearer to eighteenth- and nineteenth-century grand opera. The various elements of theatrical presentation, all of which Aeschylus performed himself, and which Sophocles kept firmly under his own control, are beginning to assert their independence. The *Gesamtkunstwerk* is ceasing to hold together. At one and the same time the Athenians were losing their sense of the rite of Dionysus as a centrally important activity, and the various elements of the drama were asserting their independence of a central control whose only justification was that all the drama must contribute to the rite. The control gone, the drama changed very rapidly.

At the risk of trying to analyze the unanalyzable, it may be worth pointing to one more example of how the end of the fifth century was truly an end for drama. The *Oedipus at Colonus* is in every sense a dance drama, a work fully in the pattern of Sophocles' earlier work. Its apparent looseness of structure, like the apparent looseness of *King Lear,* is the assured relaxation of complete formal mastery. But there is a very considerable difference between it and earlier plays such as the *Antigone* or *Oedipus the King.* In the *Antigone* the dance drama moves in such a way that the chorus gradually come to identify themselves totally with the rebound of *Dikē.* They call in the fifth *stasimon* to Dionysus, knowing that if he comes he will bring destruction on the leaders of Thebes. In the *Oedipus the King* there is the same growing identification of the chorus with the destruction. The implications of this are revolutionary. Creon of the *Antigone* is wrong, and so he must go. Oedipus of the *Oedipus the King* is polluted, and so he must go. The implication for an audience that can take political action is clear: if the state is governed wrongly, then the government must be changed.

The development of the *Oedipus at Colonus* is just as strong. From being detached spectators the chorus are drawn more and more deeply into the events taking place. Their involvement starts with the invocation to Colonus (668–719). The first system presents the countryside and the gods of the country—Dionysus, the Muses, and Aphrodite. The second system mentions in the *strophē* the olive tree, and in the *antistrophē* the horse, the animal of Poseidon, lord of the sea. There is a political point about this *stasimon.* The Spartans, laying waste the countryside, were perhaps unable to destroy all the olive trees. And when Alcibiades returned, during the year before the play was written, he may well have succeeded in protecting some of the olive harvest by means of cavalry raids. Through their cavalry and their ships the Athenians may still win.

This involvement of the chorus is continued in the battle *stasimon* (1044–95). The words are deliberately vague. We do not think so much of a battle between Theseus and the ancient Thebans. We think of a battle now between contemporary Athens and Sparta,[5] more particularly since the first system presents two routes of invasion, one referring to Eleusis and the Sacred Way, which Alcibiades had the previous year reopened for Athens, and the other referring to the first invasion route of the Spartan army.[6] The chorus of old men, unable actually to fight, are presenting a growing mental involvement in the final struggle of Athens and Sparta.

The *Oedipus at Colonus* was, however, written after Alcibiades had left Athens in anger at his dishonor. Sophocles, the ex-general, still on the supervisory council of the war, would no doubt recognize that, with the departure of Alcibiades, Athens was almost certain to be defeated. The end of the *Oedipus at Colonus* is not political at all. It is a new dimension. It is the death of Oedipus, whose burial in the soil of Athens will be a mysterious source of power to the city for ever. The development of the dance drama is a growing involvement of the chorus in that death.

To define the end of the *Oedipus at Colonus* would be as impertinent and pointless as to define Beethoven's C-sharp minor quartet, opus 131. Certain images, however, superimpose themselves in our consciousness: the reception of Oedipus—polluted Oedipus—into Athenian territory. We cannot help associating this with Alcibiades, polluted by his blasphemy in the matter of the herms. And Theseus, the priest-king of Athens, receives the polluted creature. Sophocles, the priest of Asclepius and member of the war council, wishes himself into a position actually to receive Alcibiades. But, even more strongly, Sophocles is Oedipus himself. Old age is the pollution. How strongly Sophocles, the lover and beautiful dancer, must have raged against the deterioration of his body. The death of Oedipus is the death of Sophocles. And the structure of the dance drama is a drawing of the chorus closer and closer into that death. It is as if Sophocles were saying, "Look at me, a horrible, weak, and ugly old man, me who was once so beautiful. I am dying, but as I die I am using every power in my poetry to make my death a permanent source of power for Athens." But whatever power his death may have provided, the death itself is private. The final *stasimon* is an act of meditation in a realm where we can never venture except alone.[7] It is very reasonable to say that the last few hundred lines of the *Oedipus at Colonus* present the finest achievement of all fifth-century poetry and drama. But such an achievement has the same effect as the elements of disintegration mentioned earlier. We are moving into a world where the highest level of spiritual development, and the reconciliation of light and reason with darkness and the unconscious powers, can be attained only in private meditation. Aeschylus, on the other hand, was able to call the strange, dark, indefinable powers into his state by means of a torchlit procession full of scarlet robes.

We are best able to see the result of fifth-century drama's—and indeed fifth-century culture's—disintegration through the work of Plato. He was born in 427 B.C. and so was twenty-three when Athens fell, and twenty-eight when his beloved master was put to death by the restored democracy. In the *Seventh Letter* he describes how he had wanted to go into politics, but the execution of Socrates had disgusted him so much that he spent his life trying to inspire the possibility of an ideal state founded on philosophy, and lost interest in trying to connect his ideal state with the real world. The meditation of the *Oedipus at*

Colonus hammers harder at the unknowable than the furthest explorations of Plato, and yet Sophocles was to his dying day concerned with day-to-day politics. The contrast is as strong as it could possibly be. It is more pointed by the fact that Plato wrote a tetralogy but was urged to destroy it by Socrates.[8] For Plato, prose philosophy was to be more important than dramatic poetry and abstract thought higher than practical politics. His influence has been enormous in Western thought, and, in spite of his great genius, almost wholly bad.

I and others before have compared Plato's religion with Protestantism.[9] Certainly, his apparent belief in one God, remote from the world, and to be known only by a process of abstract intellectual intuition, seems to have gone with a Puritanism similar to that which led the Protestants at the Reformation to smash the images. The way in which this attitude affected his thought about the drama can be seen very clearly in his famous attack on the poets in the second book of *The Republic*. Making use of the situation that in the Greek language of his time there was no word for "fiction," he catches the poets on a dilemma: their stories must be either true or false, and therefore, if not true, then false (2.377). He goes on to argue interestingly that the stories must be false, because they describe such horrors. There have been modern attacks on Christianity that have fallen into the same illogicality and argued the claims of Christianity to be untrue because, if true, their implications are so dreadful. The savagery of a religious belief has nothing to do with its truth. The world is a terrible place, and any religion that ignores this terror is escapism. Plato's argument is extremely silly. How dare the poets show us the horrors of the world: everything is all right really. He continues by forbidding the poets to imply that the afterlife has terrors (3.386B), to show famous men lamenting (3.387E–388), or to indulge in excessive laughter (3.389). The just man must be shown getting his deserts (3.392A–B). Furthermore, the style must be rigidly controlled. Narrative is much better than theatrical representation, and theatrical representation must be confined. No women in sickness, love, or childbirth; no inferior classes and slaves; no thunder, no noise of wheels, no barking dogs or bleating sheep (3.392C–398). And music too must be rigidly controlled. Only two modes should be allowed, the Dorian for war, and the Phrygian for seemly peace (3.398B–399). In Book 10 he returns to the attack. The artist, and especially the poet, has no real importance because he has no real knowledge of his subjects, in the Platonic sense (10.602B). Poetry appeals to the lower part of our natures, the irrational part. It can make people lose control of themselves (10.603D–606D). All poetry must be banned from the ideal state except for hymns. The whole discussion is an extreme example of philosophical silliness, and the argument is manifestly faulty. But even though few followers of Plato have really accepted his extremism, his doctrine has poisoned a great amount of Western education.

It would be unwise to say that Plato's brilliance destroyed the theater in which he had been unable to make his way. But the religious, political, and aesthetic attitudes of Plato show us with great clarity the mind of a generation that had destroyed for itself the importance of poetry, and that was no longer able to use the theater as a way of coming to grips with the fundamental problems of what it means to be a human being. Plato, at any rate, had his wish granted. Subservient poets created after his death a drama to suit his requirements almost exactly. New Comedy presents an artificial world where the good get their deserts, and where neither laughter nor tears are excessive. It is a drama of poets in the state on sufferance, who realize that as soon as they begin to change people's lives or affect the structure of society, they will be expelled.

We can generalize very little about the drama of the early fourth century, though we possess two comedies and probably one tragedy from the period. To me it seems most likely that the *Rhesus* dates from this time, though some say that it is by Euripides.[10] It certainly does not feel like Euripides. There is no original wrong action from which the events of the play derive, no sense of *Dikē* broken and restored, and none even of the moral preoccupations that give tension to plays like the *Helen* or *Ion*. It is a story that takes place on one level only—simple adventure. A series of incidents from the tenth book of the *Iliad* are strung together. The spy Dolon volunteers to enter the lines of the besieging Greeks. That same evening Rhesus arrives in Troy from Thrace, resplendent in golden armor and possessed of magnificent chariot horses, boasting that he will defeat the Greeks single-handed the next day. Then Odysseus and Diomedes arrive in the Trojan camp, having killed Dolon, and determined to perform some act of reprisal. Athene appears to them, telling them that they are not allowed to kill any of the main Trojan leaders. Instead they kill Rhesus and steal his horses, after Athene has pretended to be Aphrodite and stopped Paris from raising the alarm. During the Trojan recriminations over the death of their newly arrived ally, the Muse who is the mother of Rhesus appears and ties up the ends of the story.

When Euripides introduces arbitrary characters into his stories, it is because he is emphasizing an idea, as with the sudden appearance of Aegeus in the *Medea*. Above all, when he makes his gods act with apparent wanton mischief, it is because he is emphasizing with maximum passion that this is the way the world works: it does indeed trip you up maliciously. In the *Rhesus*, however, there is no idea behind the incidents, and therefore no reason for one scene to follow another except the demands of the story. A moral play on the lines of the fifth-century tragedies could have been made. But it would have had to concentrate on Rhesus: his pride; his contravention of his mother's knowledge that he must not go to Troy; his belief that his intervention in the Trojan War at that particular moment would be a turning point, with him bringing off the victory single-handed; his ignominious death when he had achieved absolutely nothing. That, we might be led to say, is life. We would be left with a sense of despair, or a sense of angry frustration, depending on how the poet had made his play. But we would also have been led to an understanding of the nature of things. For that kind of pride coming before that kind of fall is a myth, a story acting on many levels. The play we possess is only a plot.

It has been customary to refer to the two fourth-century plays of Aristophanes as Middle Comedy, a form transitional between Old and New. There are far fewer allusions to contemporary Athenian personalities than there are in the fifth-century plays. We may perhaps infer that Aristophanes realized that the complete success of a play now required that it should be relatively easy to perform in cities other than Athens, and that he adapted his style accordingly. But the chief impression I derive from them is of a lack of that abounding creative energy. Fourth-century Aristophanes is like Wordsworth in his old age, a man who has lost his fire. Neither *The Women at the Assembly* nor *Wealth* are bad plays. They are full of interesting social implications and contain some funny moments. Either of them will open our eyes to implications of our society to a far greater extent than any New Comedy. We shall also laugh louder. From any other writer than Aristophanes we could applaud them. But from his inexhaustibly inventive wit they are sad anticlimaxes.

In both plays the chorus is unimportant. There are no major lyrics in proper lyric meters. *Wealth* has only one dance, in simple trochaics, and the earlier play is hardly much more elaborate. In several places the text contains an indication that the chorus performed, but no lyrics. At these places there was either some wordless dance, or possibly some popular song of the time. There are none of the traditional parts of the Old Comedy, no *parodos* in the sense of an elaborate musical sequence, no *agōn* or *parabasis* at all. What there is for the chorus in either play could be performed by relatively unskilled performers. Nothing in either of them approaches the demand made on the chorus in the fifth-century plays. Nor is there any elaborate solo singing.

In the fifth-century plays there is a constant sense of the ordinary streets of Athens. But the scenes involve some fantastic element, some brilliant surrealism that illuminates the everyday occurrences as if by a flash of lightning in which the details of normality shine over-brightly. A number of scenes in the fourth-century plays lack this surreal illumination. We see the beginnings of the even tone of naturalism, rather than the brilliant juxtapositions of documentary and fantasy. In *The Women at the Assembly* we see the first example of the husband and wife scene with which later theater would make us so familiar (520–70). It is relatively naturalistic, less fantastical, less funny, and indeed, rather nagging. The citizen who refuses to give his property over to the commune (746–876) provides another scene that is much less funny through being more naturalistic. We see the beginnings of a comedy that is constructed on the basis of a naturalistic plot, made up of possible, connecting incidents, instead of the fifth-century comedy flowing from topsy-turviness to topsy-turviness in a rhythm of laughter. The central idea of the *Wealth* is just as fantastical as that of *The Peace:* Chremylus wants to find Plutus, the god of wealth, cure the blindness that makes him favor the wrong people, and bring him home as a houseguest. But the discovery of the god is uneventful, and the description of the curing is almost the description of an ordinary doctor performing an ordinary cure with only a touch of the miraculous (727–47). In Aristophanes' case an increase of naturalism seems to spring from a failing imagination.

It is the comparative weakness that leaves the deepest impression. The idea of *The Women at the Assembly* is a strong one: women—as being more responsible than men—take over the government and then decide that all property should be common. Some of the ramifications have excellent possibilities as surrealist humor, such as the right granted to ugly women to force handsome men to go to bed with them before they may go to bed with attractive girls. There is a macabre scene of black comedy in which a lover about to visit his girl friend is waylaid by a foul old hag and then caught by another, and then yet another, each one fouler than the last. But we cannot help feeling that the Aristophanes of twenty years earlier would have shown us the scene afterwards, surely something much funnier since we should be concentrating on the young man's discomfort after excessive sex, not the old women's ugliness. It would be impossible to suggest episodes to the Aristophanes who wrote *The Frogs.* Everything is there, wilder than our wildest dreams.

I am reluctant to argue much about the nature of Middle Comedy from these two plays of Aristophanes, because so much of the difference between them and the plays of the fifth century seems due to tiredness: tiredness of the poet and tiredness of the society for which he wrote. How could Aristophanes ever write as he had done, if he had been a friend of Socrates, and if he had heard the references made to his *Clouds* at Socrates' trial.[11] However far it was from Aristophanes' mind in 423 B.C. that an Athenian could ever be put on trial for asking questions, however much Socrates might conduct his defence in the lighthearted spirit of one who may well have been a close friend of Aristophanes, and however lightly Socrates might pass over the implications *The Clouds* might have had for his condemnation, Aristophanes must have always had a nagging doubt in his mind that his comedy had helped, however slightly, to put Socrates to death. Athens deserved to lose her unique comedy. She had herself voted its death in a cup of hemlock.

Notes

1. H. D. F. Kitto, *Greek Tragedy* (London: Methuen, 1961), p. 126 n.1.

2. 404 B.C., spring to 403 B.C., autumn.

3. Leo Aylen, *Greek Tragedy and the Modern World* (London: Methuen, 1964), pp. 25–28 and passim.

4. Translation quoted in Aylen, *Greek Tragedy and the Modern World*, pp. 78–79.

5. Important in this context is the ambiguity of the word *Spartoi*, which is applied to the Thebans in line 1534. It means "sown men" and is correctly applied to the Thebans as the descendants of the dragon's teeth sown in the ground by Cadmus. But the word could hardly fail also to apply to the Spartans, and therefore suggest their current enemy to the Athenian audience of the first production.

6. Cf. Jebb's notes; *Oedipus Coloneus*, in *Sophocles, The Plays and Fragments*, trans. R. C. Jebb (Cambridge: Cambridge University Press, 1883–96), pp. 166–67.

7. This is translated at the end of Chapter 13.

8. Aelian *History* 2. 30; Diogenes Laertius *Lives of the Philosophers* 3. 5.

9. Cf. Aylen, *Greek Tragedy and the Modern World*, pp. 25–27, with references quoted.

10. It is generally believed that the *Rhesus* is a fourth-century play. It would help our understanding of the disintegration of the fifth-century religious culture if we could be absolutely sure of this. Because we are not sure of the *Rhesus'* date, we cannot use it as part of the argument that fourth-century drama lost its moral seriousness. For this argument we must rest content with what we can learn from Plato.

Apart from the moral feeling of the play, the argument that it is not by Euripides rests on metrical grounds. The iambic lines of dialogue contain relatively few resolutions of the iambus into its equivalent rhythms, particularly tribrachs (i.e., relatively few occasions of ♪ ♪ ♪ substituted for ♪ ♩). Euripides' style shows a steady tendency to increase the number of these resolutions. On these grounds therefore it would be early Euripides. On the other hand it contains trochaic tetrameters, and the earliest use of these in Euripides is in the *Heracles,* by which time he had developed a much looser iambic line than that employed in the *Rhesus.*

In other words, the iambic line would argue that the play was an early one of his, the trochees would argue that it was a late one. Given this incompatibility it is best to assume that it was not by Euripides at all.

11. Plato *Apology* 18. d. 2.

11

FORMULA PLAYS

Great theater needs a great society. It may sound extreme to say that twelve hundred years of antiquity did not produce one play worthy of serious comparison with the plays of fifth-century Athens. But it seems to be true. By the end of the fourth century both tragedy and comedy had evolved into a form that was a formula, just as today the form of an episode in a television series is a formula. There was no more demand for the poet's vision, no more belief that poetry can change society, or that a great society depends on great poets. The writers could exercise their ingenuity in discovering new variations on a more or less standard plot, and in thinking of witty remarks for their characters to say. The thoughts of Plato had triumphed. Poetry remained in the state, but only by acknowledging its inferiority to philosophy.

As I have said before, tragedies continued to be written for at least five hundred years till the reign of the Emperor Hadrian. Of all this work almost nothing survives. All that we possess are nine adaptations by the Roman philosopher and aristocrat Seneca, who was a councillor of Nero in the middle of the first century A.D., and a play, the *Octavia*, written like a Greek tragedy but about the events of Nero's reign, by an admirer of Seneca soon after Nero's death. Of Seneca's plays, only one of the nine, the *Thyestes*, is derived from a model that we do not possess. It is now generally agreed that neither they nor the *Octavia* were intended for public performance, and that they were not performed publicly until the Renaissance.[1]

Of what is called New Comedy we have work by three writers. Of Menander we have one complete play: *The Bad-tempered Man;* three nearly complete plays, which, with a little filling out, could be performed: the *Arbitration, Girl from Samos*, and *Girl's Hair-cut;* three plays of which one-third to one-half survives: the *Shield, Hated Man*, and *Man from Sicyon;* and a number of fragments, some up to a hundred lines long.[2] Then we have twenty plays and a large fragment in Latin adaptations by Plautus, who lived about two generations after Menander's death; and six plays by Terence, who was born perhaps in the year of Plautus' death.[3] We do not know whether Menander should be described as the founder of New Comedy. But it seems certain that it was during his working life that the form became standardized, and that we may at least credit him and his contemporaries as joint founders.

Seneca's tragedies had a profound effect on the playwrights of the Renaissance, and they were probably more fertile influences for the very fact of their limitations as compared with the fifth-century models he imitated, which the Renaissance writers would not have been able to understand. Since the Renaissance, it has been the formula tragedy of Seneca that has represented Classical tragedy for the Western world. Seneca is himself perhaps unimportant. What is important is that he wrote to a formula, that his work happened to survive, and that formulas are easier to imitate than works of original genius.

With New Comedy, also, we are dealing with a form that has been developed thoroughly in the post-Renaissance Western theater. The plays of Terence were relatively well known through the Middle Ages, and by the fifteenth century Plautus also was widely known.[4] Shakespeare's *The Comedy of Errors* is a free adaptation of Plautus' *The Brothers Menaechmus,* itself of course adapted from a Greek original. Molière is New Comedy; so are the plays of the Restoration. *The Importance of Being Earnest* is New Comedy, recognizably employing the same elements of Menander's formula. The form continues to the present day.

The form of great works of art is organic and indefinable. One cannot generalize about the form of Sophocles or Aristophanes; one can only feel in each unique play how one sequence leads to the next, as one feels in a cutting room the rightness of one section of film leading to another section. About the formula writing of later antiquity we can generalize. The structure of the plays was a mold into which the material was poured. We can make generalizations safely about such a structure, particularly since our interest in the three comic writers and two tragic writers is not so much in their work in itself as in the way in which it represents a formula that has been with the Western theater ever since. A historian of the theater of antiquity must also make clear that, while the plays of the fifth century are unique, inimitable, and indeed hardly understood, the plays of the fourth century and later antiquity have been very properly understood by their many imitators, who have often improved considerably on the model. It would be a strange taste that did not find Molière and Racine an advance on Terence and Seneca.

Since we are examining a formula, it is appropriate to start neither with tragedy nor with comedy, but with criticism. Aristotle wrote the *Poetics* at about the same time as the orator Lycurgus was rebuilding the theater in Athens and revising the festival procedure. The *Poetics* is in part an answer to the attack on the poets in *The Republic,* a reasoned justification for the place of drama. But it does not contest Plato's premise that poetry is a less important activity than philosophy. Aristotle is discussing a poetry that has no real importance but is nevertheless rightly part of the graces of life. Apart from Aristotle's exercise of his desire to classify poetry as he had classified almost everything else, the *Poetics* provides some good tips for play makers working within the confines of the formula.[5]

Aristotle emphasizes the importance of the story. Greek when he wrote had no word for "plot," but the *Poetics* demonstrates the beginnings of an awareness of this concept by referring to "the putting together of the incidents" (7. 1450B. 21–22). Elsewhere in his discussion of "story" he shows awareness that what is needed for a play is not simply a story. Second, he has realized that character can be shown only in actions involving choice (6. 1450B. 9–10). He has another term, "thought content," for what is shown in conversation on topics that do not involve choice. He has therefore discovered the essence of naturalistic play construction, that dialogue is different from conversation, and that a play can develop only by characters trying to do things to each other, mostly by means of dialogue. As we have seen, this is not the structure of fifth-century drama, though it is the dynamic of some of the dialogue episodes. Without the dynamic of the fifth-century dance drama, a new form had to be developed and understood. The *Poetics* demonstrates a grasp of the new form's principles.

Aristotle discusses in detail twists in the plot, which he calls "Reversals of Fortune" and "Denouements" (11, and, in a sense, 13, 16, and 18). The only fifth-century play that he mentions with approval and that also has relevance to this kind of discussion is Euripides' *Iphigeneia in Tauris.* This play's suitability as a model for the writing that Aristotle is discussing is part of what I meant by saying in Chapter 6 that Euripides is the inventor of the plot.

Denouements and reversals of fortune, however, are more a matter for New Comedy than for the standardized tragedies of the centuries following Aristotle. We do not possess the second book of the *Poetics,* which discussed comedy. But much of what Aristotle says in the first book is more appropriate to New Comedy than to tragedy. In particular we should notice how he allows himself to agree with Plato that drama should be about characters who are *chresta* (15.1454A. 17). If we translate this as about "decent fellows," then there is no great difficulty about applying it to New Comedy. But Aristotle ties himself up in knots when discussing tragedy in these terms, since the characters of the great tragedies are so patently not "decent fellows."

We may assume that in Aristotle's day tragedy had not quite settled into its formula pattern. Some of the *Poetics* seems to reflect contemporary confusions. Already, however, there was a tendency for writers to stick to the stories already used by the fifth-century poets. If one has lost the understanding of a form, the most sensible course is to take an already created form and make variations on it. Fifth-century tragedy was created from the contemplation of an event in history; through such contemplation the poet was led to see the event as an instance of the dance of *Dikē.* The fourth-century writers had greater understanding of what was historical and very much less understanding of everything else. Aristotle does not understand the importance for tragedy of presenting events that had actually happened. For him tragedy is not history (9.1451A.36–1451B.32). But what is it that makes the events of tragedy lead into one another? At one point he conceives of it as a kind of coherence

(9.1451A.37–38). But a little later he admits that "what has happened is clearly possible: for if it was not possible it could not have happened (9.1451B.17–18). He is trying to find, as succeeding critics have tried to find, some sense of tragic inevitability. Whether this has ever been achieved by a dramatist or formulated by a critic is doubtful. But at any rate it is irrelevant to the coherence of the fifth-century tragedies.

We notice some references that suggest that writers contemporary with Aristotle had been relying on spectacle (14.1453B.1–11), and there are hints later on in the same chapter that there may have been exploitation of horror for its own sake. Aristotle certainly underrates theatricality. Aeschylus' theatricality is always part of his religious and poetic purpose. Without such a purpose, theatrical display could so easily become gratuitous and tasteless. Without a strong belief that by writing a play one was taking part in obligatory worship of an important spiritual force, the best minds of the time were no longer interested by the childish trappings of the theater. Plays started to be made for reading only.[6]

In other words, we may guess that during the fourth century various attempts were made to find a new direction for tragedy: toward the romantic, on the lines suggested by the *Iphigeneia in Tauris;* toward the sensational; into chamber drama, dialogues to be read in private rooms by a small and cultured audience, a form somewhat between a play proper and a philosophical dialogue. None of these attempts were very successful, and tragedy standardized itself into continual reworkings of a relatively few fifth-century successes, whose popularity rested on the fact that the audience came to hear such and such a well-known singer in the leading role, just as opera today owes its success to the star performers.

It would be interesting to know how much influence the work of Plato and Aristotle did have on the theater. It seems to have been enormous. New Comedy is a form that might have been devised specially to fit Plato's requirements. It is recognizably minor art. Poetry and drama have lost their place at the center of life and remain only as diversion. It is perhaps significant that at the time of Menander's first production there was a restricted franchise in Athens.[7] The world of Aristophanes is one of many characters meeting openly. The world of Menander is one where young men may not marry girls out of their class. His plots are ingenious constructions whereby all can end happily without the conventions of society being flouted.

New Comedy is not about anything. Behind every play of the fifth century there is an important question of religion, morals, or politics, or of all combined. Even the fanciful plays of Euripides contain at their heart some serious preoccupation. New Comedy is surprisingly less real than the world of Aristophanes. We are shown characters supposedly very like ourselves, caught up in amusing experiences through a series of coincidences impossible to accept if we thought about them. Aristophanes never has to make his characters silly. In *The Brothers Menaechmus,* for instance, the second Menaechmus arrives from abroad on what he says is a specific search for his twin brother (232). Almost immediately he is recognized by the first Menaechmus' cook (273ff.). The plot depends upon the second Menaechmus not considering for a moment that he might have achieved the object of his search. Such silliness is necessary for all New Comedy plots from Menander to the present day. It is a kind of silliness for grown-ups only. A child would see through it immediately, just as a child would see the reality of flying to heaven on a dung beetle.

The center of Aristophanes' drama is that it was performed as part of the worship of Dionysus at the city's festival. Although the plays of Menander were produced for the festivals, the sense of the festival has gone. Aristophanes is full of the presence of the gods and the importance of Athens. In Menander both these central elements have evaporated.

The prologue of *The Bad-Tempered Man* is spoken by the god Pan. But there is little sense of the god-power we see in the fifth-century plays. He is merely an added flavor to the story. Criticism of the gods has ceased. They are now an irrelevance. Epicurus was a contemporary of Menander. His conception of the gods—happily free from care, unaffecting and unaffected by human affairs—and his moral philosophy, based on the notion of performing actions that will make us as happy as possible on as permanent a basis as possible, is a religion and philosophy possible only for the reasonably healthy and reasonably rich. It has little to say to people or cultures roused by great hopes or great despairs. Menander's plays, with their gentle humor and gentle pursuit of happiness, provide an art form entirely suitable to Epicureanism.[8]

Aristophanes' plays start from and relate to the actual Athens of his day. The plays of New Comedy are set as the story demands, and the actual town of the setting has no special relevance.[9] There is nothing particularly Athenian about the plays. It is easy to see how they could be imitated by writers of other nationalities and easily performed in any of the Mediterranean cities.

Comedy depends upon a close relationship between performers and audience. Old Comedy's traditional forms of *parodos, agōn,* and *parabasis* provided a strong medium of audience involvement. Only traces of this remain in New Comedy. Especially in Plautus, there are direct requests to the audience to applaud and frequent asides to remind us that we are still in a theater. There are such moments as the delightful self-mocking two-line prologue to his *Pseudolus:*

> Better get up—give your cocks a stretch.
> There's a long play of Plautus coming next.

The later plays of Aristophanes explore a rich kind of theatrical reality through parody and pun, involving the audience in a kind of game to see at what level of reality the action is taking place. In New Comedy there is none of the elaborate play-within-play form such as *The Women at the Thesmophoria* demonstrates so beautifully. All that remains are small touches to jolt the audience into a laugh. In *The Ghost* of Plautus, for example, Tranio can suggest that his master, whom he has just hoodwinked, should offer his story to the comic writers Diphilus or Philemon (1149–50). In *The Rope*, the first character to enter after the prologue refers to the storm of the night before as the worst one since that in Euripides' *Alcmena* (83). One of the best examples of audience involvement through this kind of theatrical self-consciousness comes from the *Pseudolus*. Pseudolus, having promised to bring about certain events, satisfies the gentry with his confidence. He then turns to the audience and accuses them of thinking that he is making such promises only to keep the play going. He then goes on to admit that he has not the slightest idea as to how he will fulfil his promises. He just knows that he will. This is what actors are for: to bring on surprises. So now he must retire to work out what comes next, and does so (562–73).

The purpose of New Comedy is to divert the audience with a series of surprises in a plot that is plausible. In order for this kind of play to work, the characters must be lowest common denominators of humanity. In 1973 the Prime Minister of Great Britain was an ex-organ scholar devoted to ocean racing; in 1984 the President of the United States was an ex–movie actor. Ability at the organ, at the helm of a yacht, or at acting cowboys is not an appropriate characteristic of a top politician. A New Comedy about two top politicians one of whom was an organist-yachtsman and the other an ex–cowboy actor would seem far-fetched. The plot's contrivances must be applied to characters who appear to be norms. Aristotle recommends that a play's characters should be decent fellows, that they should be like people in real life, and that they should be consistent, though he qualifies this last characteristic by allowing that sometimes they can be "consistently inconsistent" (15.1454A.16–28). Documentary film has made us realize the limitations of the Aristotelian approach, which has dominated the Western theater for so much of its history. Aristotle's second requirement comes down to making characters conform to what people in the audience expect of a person in the appropriate situation. Real life is richer than that.

He would be a rash man who claimed that he could provide a description of any character in New Comedy that would apply solely to that character and to no other. Although Menander, Plautus, and Terence provide some nice touches of characterization, their people are all variations on a set of types. In the theater lexicographers, we find lists of masks appropriate to various types of characters: old man, young man, bald man, slave, courtesan, cook, and so on. Each touring company would no doubt have a stock of masks adequate for the plays in their repertoire. It is not difficult to allocate all the roles occurring in New Comedy to one or other of these stock types. It would of course be impossible so to allocate the roles of Aristophanes. Old Comedy was designed to be unique within the limits set by the festival in which it was performed, so that it would win the first prize. New Comedy was designed not to stray too far from the norm of entertainment that its audience, whether Alexandrians,

Sicilians, or Romans, were expecting. It is no coincidence that we find the same name recurring in several plays.

Perhaps the most notable thing about New Comedy is its epigrams. Philip Vellacott, in his introduction to his Menander translations for Penguin Classics,[10] draws attention to the way in which Menander is, like Shakespeare, "full of quotations." The shorter fragments, which we possess mainly because they were quoted by later writers, make memorable reading as witty sayings detached from their context. Ever afterward the ability to coin epigrams has been regarded as a major part of a dramatist's ability. In Menander we meet many quotations we have always known, without knowing who originated them:

> Whom the gods love, dies young.
>
> (Frag. 125)

> Calling a spade a spade.
>
> (Frag. 545, 7)

> Conscience makes a man most cowardly.
>
> (Frag. 632, 2)[11]

There are also a number of wry witticisms that reveal considerable understanding of human nature:

> Lucky the man with property and sense.
> He will get value for what he spends.
>
> (Frag. 114)

> This "know yourself" was not a splendid saying.
> Knowing the other guy is much more paying.
>
> (Frag. 240)

> When a woman pays you compliments
> Really be on your guard.
>
> (Frag. 745)

Other fragments are full of a gentle wisdom:

> Once you are set on marriage, accept this, girls and boys:
> By bearing with small troubles you'll gain the greatest joys.
>
> (Frag. 648)

This is the feeling of the most famous line in New Comedy, which occurs in a play by Terence, known to have been adapted from a model by Menander:

> I am a man, and so related to
> Everything that is human.
>
> (Self-Punisher, 1. 1. 25)

It is interesting to ask how much Plautus and Terence altered their Greek models. One of the more recent Menander papyrus finds is the 100-line fragment of *The Double-Deceiver*. It turns out to be the model for Plautus' *The Sisters Bacchis*. Plautus has altered three out of four of Menander's names, making them grander. The character called Mnesilochus in Plautus and Sostratos in Menander has a monologue that is twice as long in Plautus as in the original. Plautus follows Menander's plot in general, but not in all the details. Plautus' language is jokier, has more of the effect of vaudeville or stand-up comic's patter. In general, it seems that Plautus expanded certain characters, especially his scheming slaves, whom he used partly as stand-up comics, playing directly to the audience.

Four or five out of Terence's six plays are adapted from Menander.[12] Only a few of Plautus' are. Most are from the work of Menander's contemporary Philemon, who seems to have written in a more boisterous style.[13] Certainly there is a gentleness that Menander and Terence seem to possess in common; this is lacking in Plautus, who, on the other hand, is theatrically the most exciting of the three. If we regard New Comedy as primarily a fast and intricate plot, then its absurdities of coincidence are best suited to farce, as in the plays of Plautus. If we regard it as primarily an opportunity to relax and enjoy wise and witty epigrams, then the quieter tone of Terence will be more pleasing. To compare two roughly contemporary practitioners from a later age, Feydeau is the successor of Plautus, Oscar Wilde of Terence. The plots of Terence seem more intricate, more carefully worked, than those of Menander. But this may well be only the chance of the surviving plays in our possession.

There is one matter in which the three writers differ considerably: the music. All that we possess of Menander is either in dialogue verse—the standard loose iambic trimeter—or in two of the chanted meters—trochaic and iambic tetrameters catalectic. There are indications in the text for interludes by a chorus, but these may have been merely dances without song, or popular songs of the day. Plautus, by contrast, moves with great virtuosity from one meter to another and makes considerable use of lyric meters. Roughly two-thirds of every Plautus play was accompanied by the *tibia*, an instrument more or less the same as the Greek *aulos*, and therefore probably involved the actors in the entire range of declamation from something very nearly speech to full song. There are, however, no songs for a chorus, and no strophic systems.[14] Terence possesses little of Plautus' metrical vitality and variety. The plays of Terence cannot have involved very much music.

Music aside, it is the similarities rather than the differences between these three writers of New Comedy that impress us. We may regard Menander's *The Bad-tempered Man* as an early, and therefore imperfect, example of the genre. The plot is based on the determination of Sostratos, a rich young man, to marry the daughter of Knemon, a bad-tempered old farmer. Sostratos gets his girl in act 4 and the changing of Knemon occurs independently of the main action.[15] It is a commonplace with us, based on centuries of work in the genre, that the most satisfactory plot is one where the complications are maintained for as long as possible until the simplest possible denouement ties up all the ends together. *The Bad-tempered Man* is a faulty play by this standard, because it was written at a time when the form was only just beginning to be understood.

We can put this "fault" in another way. Knemon is much the most vivid character. A play that depends on the vicissitudes of plot is made much more interesting if the characters seem to grow and change with the changing situations. In proportion to the original vividness and vitality of the character, so we demand that he should change and develop more, and that his development should cohere with the development of the plot. Knemon's final change is more or less forced out of him, after the main aim of the plot has been achieved. In contrast, we should compare *The Brothers*, adapted by Terence from an original by Menander. Here a major development in the principal character produces a new turn in the plot right at the end of the play. Plot and characters cohere more, because the changes in the principal characters provide changes in the plot, and the most interesting changes in the most interesting characters come at the climactic points of the plot. That is part of what we mean when we say that *The Brothers* is a better-written play than *The Bad-tempered Man.*

It is now almost inconceivable to think of New Comedy without a love interest. In the absence of a rite of worship in which actors and audience participate, the most satisfactory way of tying up a plot is by the best possible image of human togetherness—boy gets girl. The full potential of New Comedy required the fully realized idea of romantic love as developed in the Middle Ages. *The Bad-tempered Man* shows very clearly the need for a love interest. The action of the play is Sostratos' attempt to marry the farmer's daughter. The sole confrontation between him and her is in act 1 when he offers to fill her jug at the well, and she lets him (199–201). Sostratos performs certain actions in order to win her. But we never receive any insight into her feelings at all, and the marriage is arranged as a business transaction while she is offstage. Later Menander made much more use of the marriage as a culmination of his plot. In *The Girl from Samos*, for example, a young man plans to marry the girl he has made pregnant. These plans are foiled, and things are righted only at the end of the play. But the atmosphere of arranged marriages and commercial transaction could never provide the emotional tension of romantic love, in whose atmosphere both sexes could long equally for their mates. New Comedy had to wait for its full flowering till after the Middle Ages.

Plautus probably started life as an actor. Actors in Italy enjoyed a much lower social status than they did in Greece. They were little better than slaves, and often associated with slaves. The plays of Plautus are more theatrical; faster and more vulgar, better adapted for catching and holding an inattentive audience. The best parts are always slaves, around whose antics the plot revolves, and who are responsible for most of its twists and turns.

The style is more vulgar, and the plays are nearer to farce. The posturings of the title character in *The Braggart Soldier* (for example, 1216–83 and 1311–77) would have an unpleasant feel if they were played too real. As he preens himself at the thought that he is loved beyond belief, we start to feel embarrassed, as we would be at the mocking of a maniac, unless the convention of staging and acting makes it quite obvious that we are not dealing with a real person. We need the grotesque exaggerations of extreme farce.

Plautus is the only writer of the three whose exuberance can sometimes recall Aristophanes. He achieves an almost Aristophanic topsy-turviness in the *Amphitryo*, the sole example we possess of a genre popular at all stages of Greek comedy, Old, Middle and New: mythological burlesque. Jupiter, who has disguised himself as Amphitryo in order to make love to Amphitryo's wife, excuses himself from a scene by saying that he must go and sacrifice to himself (983). There is an element of topsy-turviness throughout this play, which will work only at the level of extreme farce.

Similarly, there are occasional hints in Plautus' dialogue of Aristophanes' fantastical sense of humor. We think perhaps of the conversation about the miser in *The Crock of Gold:*

> *Strobilus.* He raises hell, if a twig is burnt
> And a whiff of smoke escapes.
> I tell you, he goes to sleep with a ballon tied over his mouth.
> *Anthrax.* Why?
> *Strobilus.* In case he loses some breath while he's asleep.
> *Anthrax.* Does he block up the hole at his other end
> In case he lets out a breath of wind?
> *Strobilus.* You swallow my gag, I swallow yours.
>
> (300–306)

But such examples are only on a very small scale compared to the inexhaustible fantasies of Aristophanes.

One of the interesting points to notice about Terence is that he was a Carthaginian slave, brought to Rome and patronized by members of the intellectual aristocracy. His Latin, which has been universally praised for its style, was an adopted language. It is perhaps appropriate that the last dramatist of antiquity actually working for the theater, whose work we possess, should have been such a rootless figure, product of a culture now international.

Although later ages respected Terence enormously, he was not very successful during his short life. *The Mother-in-Law* contains two prologues, delivered on the occasion of the second and third productions of the piece. From the one written for the second production, we learn that the first had been a failure because the audience had all been distracted by the rival attraction of a tight-rope walker. In the second production the play had been doing well until the audience heard that a gladiatorial show was about to start and rushed to see that instead. Other prologues, such as that to *The Brothers,* refer to charges that work Terence had claimed as his own had actually been written by others. Such charges may have arisen through jealousy. Terence, after all, was an outsider. Nevertheless his work is not as lively as that of Plautus; it would have been less good at competing with counterattractions such as tightrope walkers or gladiatorial shows.

The Brothers is often said to be the best written of all New Comedies. Plot interest is maintained to the end, and there is a notable intelligence about the writing; a problem is posed and intelligent reactions are offered to it. The story is much less implausible. It is in our sense of the word high comedy, not farce.

One of the two brothers, Demea, is a serious countryman working a farm just outside Athens. The other, Micio, is a man-about-town. Demea has two sons, Aeschinus and Ctesipho. Aeschinus was given to Micio to bring up, since Micio never married. Ctesipho has been brought up very sternly, while Aeschinus has been given everything he has asked for. The play is set outside the house of Micio and a neighbor. It starts with Micio worrying if he has really done right to bring up the boy as he has done. Demea enters to complain that Aeschinus is a disgrace; he has just broken into a house to carry off a girl. Micio pooh-poohs this, but in the argument that follows neither is totally confident.

Aeschinus then arrives with the girl he has carried off from the pimp Sannio's house; he maintains that she is really free born and tells the pimp he will pay the required price of two thousand drachmas for her. Syrus, Micio's head slave, offers to try and get the pimp his money from Micio.

At this moment Ctesipho arrives, and we realize that the girl has been kidnapped for him. He goes into Micio's house to begin a celebration party. A moment later we see that the next-door house is in turmoil. The widow Sostrata's daughter, Pamphila, has been seduced by Aeschinus and is now about to give birth. But it appears that Aeschinus is now going with a new girl. Sostrata's only hope for her daughter's disgrace is that Aeschinus did give her a ring.

Demea arrives, horrified to learn that Ctesipho has been involved in the kidnapping, but Syrus tells him that he had a row with his brother and has left for the farm. Syrus is trying to persuade Demea to leave, but before he can persuade him to go to the farm, a friend of Demea's, Hegio, arrives, having been summoned by Sostrata to remind Aeschinus of his obligations to Pamphila.

Ctesipho comes out of his party and drives Syrus frantic at the thought that Demea, not finding him at the farm, will return. Demea does return. Syrus, however, manages to send him off on another wild goose chase. Micio arrives back with Hegio, explaining that the girl was not for Aeschinus but for Ctesipho, and that Aeschinus is not going back on his word to Pamphila. But Aeschinus has meanwhile been thrown out of Sostrata's house for his supposedly caddish behaviour. Micio starts to tease Aeschinus with a story that Pamphila is going to be given in marriage to someone else, but when Aeschinus bursts into tears he relents and tells him that he knows the whole story. Aeschinus' fault in seducing Pamphila was a small one. What was wrong was that he did nothing about it for nine months. Micio hurries him in to Pamphila.

Demea arrives back, angry at having trudged all over the town, to abuse Micio for Aeschinus' supposed double wrongdoing. Micio replies that he is moving Pamphila into his own house as Aeschinus' wife, and keeping the kidnapped girl also. "As a mistress in the same house?" asks Demea horrified. He now suspects that Micio is after the girl himself. Micio enters Sostrata's house, and Demea is confronted first by Syrus, drunk from Ctesipho's party, and then by another slave of Micio's, who comes out unfortunately mentioning Ctesipho's name. That gives the game away. Demea bursts in, and then rushes out again to confront Micio, who is unrepentant. Let Demea work hard, and leave the boys his money, Micio says. He himself will give them some of his money now, which they were not expecting. He goes on to argue that the boys will be easily recalled to sound living. Micio persuades him to let them enjoy today; tomorrow he can take both Ctesipho and the girl back to the farm; by making her work he will make sure of keeping Ctesipho there.

After what was probably a short musical interval to represent the party continuing, Demea comes out again to address the audience. In a major volte-face he protests at the way in which he has made himself unpopular by money-grubbing and says that from now on he will be generous. He staggers the slaves by his sudden affability, and then tells Aeschinus not to bother with all the wedding preparations, but simply to dig a hole in the wall between the two houses and carry Pamphila off. Then, with Aeschinus' assistance, he persuades Micio to marry Sostrata, and he also persuades Micio to give Hegio a plot of land and to free Syrus. Syrus joins in and secures the freedom of his wife and a small pension as well. Finally Demea ends with a speech of wry wit, with tongue in cheek. We had thought Demea was due for his comeuppance, since no one likes a miser, and no one likes a worthy man, and Demea was both. But Demea surprises everyone and takes command of the play. It surprises us, and yet it is properly in keeping with what we now see the character of Demea to have been all the time. In the amusing twists of its plot and the excellent motivations of its characters, *The Brothers* is deservedly considered the best extant New Comedy.

In spite of the success of the genre, we have no original New Comedy in Latin, though, as we shall see in Chapter 12, there was a flourishing folk farce. The Greco-Roman empire was culturally dependent on the works of ancient Athens. It is surprising, but it is true, that there was virtually no original Latin drama, and no drama which derived directly from the rootless society of the imperial age as the drama of fifth-century Athens had related to its society.

Such a sweeping statement asks to be challenged but seems to resist the challenges. It is true that a form of Latin tragedy was created by writers like Naevius, Ennius, Pacuvius, and Accius, and performed throughout the last two centuries of the Roman Republic.[16] But in a large corpus only about five or six plays have subjects derived from Roman history; the rest were adaptations from the Greek, just as were the comedies. It is astonishing to contemplate the continued success of both tragedy and comedy as dead arts, out of touch with spiritual and political reality.

We have, however, one play, written in Latin, and touching on political events of its own time: the *Octavia*. It adapts the style of Seneca's own writing to a story of events in Nero's reign, and it was clearly written by an admirer of Seneca soon after Nero had been killed and therefore not long after he had forced Seneca to commit suicide. The main difference between it and the plays of Seneca concerns the meter. Seneca's plays use a number of lyric meters for the choruses, though each passage consists of a number of lines in the same meter, not in the contrasting variety of the Greek lyrics, and he makes no use of strophic systems. The *Octavia,* in addition to the usual iambic dialogue, contains only passages in anapestic dimeters, given both to the chorus and to Octavia and her nurse. Since the play was not performed and therefore the choruses were not sung, this point is only of academic interest.

The plot concerns the downfall of Octavia, Nero's innocent wife, at the hands of his villainous mistress Poppaea. After Nero has put away Octavia, he marries Poppaea in spite of opposition from Seneca. There is a scene between the two men, the center of which is the confrontation of dictator and philosopher:

Nero. A prince is protected by steel.
Seneca   But better by loyalty.
Nero. The emperor should be feared.
Seneca.   He should be loved.
(456–57)

This scene is followed by the theatrical climax of the play, when the ghost of Agrippina, Nero's murdered mother, appears to the newlywed couple on their wedding night (593–645), prophesying the death of Nero in atonement for his crimes.[17] The play ends with the threat of revolt against Nero, and with Octavia being led off to death as a concomitant of the revolt's repression.

The play cannot have enjoyed a wide circulation during the troubled period following the civil wars after Nero's death. Even during the Roman Republic, the government was sensitive of its reputation as few Greek governments were. The isolated example of the *Octavia* and its lack of public performance serve to emphasize that great drama cannot associate with dictatorship. We might fairly conclude from the end of the *Oresteia*[18] that great drama depends on a society fearing the wrath of heaven with the utmost acuteness and fearing nothing else at all.

We have, however, one example from a later age than the fifth century of what appears to be artistic courage almost equivalent to that of the great fifth-century writers, and political courage considerably greater. This is a satyr play, the *Agen* of Python, almost certainly performed in 326 B.C. before Alexander's troops on campaign.[19] As well as being a satyr play it was also a satire, attacking Harpalos, Alexander's financial administrator, and therefore perhaps the most powerful man in the Near East after Alexander himself.

Harpalos had been criticized for his excessive attentions to two courtesans. He had built monuments in both Athens and Babylon, at enormous expense, to Pythionike after her death, while he had put up no monument to the soldiers who had died in Cilicia. He had even constructed a sacred shrine and precinct and had dedicated an altar and temple to Aphrodite Pythionike. A man, so it seems, most suitable for grotesque stage presentation.

The first fragment seems to come from the prologue, and it describes the setting. On one side of the stage appears to be the temple of Aphrodite Pythionike; on the other, an entrance to the underworld, being a cave, with reeds in front of it providing a suitable screen behind which an appearance could be made. Presumably the situation is that Harpalos has lost his first mistress and is disconsolate for her, though at the same time he is preparing to bring another mistress by the name of Glykera, out from Athens. He will send grain to Athens as payment for taking Athens' most elegant whore.

Satyrs, often associated with conjuring the spirits of the dead, enter for the *parodos,* and try to conjure up the spirit of Pythionike. The second fragment is a question and answer about the people of Athens. Athens at first won food as a compensation for enduring the slavery of submission to Alexander. Now they are again in desperate straits. The questioner wonders at this. Surely Harpalos sent thousands of bushels of corn to Athens. This, we learn from the other man, was simply a payment for their great whore, Glykera.

Presumably the play continues with the arrival of Glykera. Perhaps she was greeted with the act of *proskynesis,* the act with which the Persians adored their king by falling on their faces. Apparently Alexander had attempted to make his Greek followers adopt this hated Persian custom while on campaign in Bactria in 327 B.C. The finale of the play would have introduced the title character— Agen—to send Harpalos, Glykera, and the satyrs packing. Agen was a thinly disguised representation of Alexander himself.

This has the feeling of a very exciting play. And its circumstances render it even more exciting. Scholars argue as to whether it could possibly have been produced in 326, before Harpalos was disgraced, and it has been suggested that it was produced in 324, though the only reference to it, in Athenaeus, definitely says that it was produced on campaign. I feel that it is daring anyhow because it presents Alexander onstage, and because, whenever it was performed, Alexander presumably watched the performance. If there was a *proskynesis* of Glykera, it could be taken only as a dig at Alexander's own attempt to force his free Greek soldiers to conform to the hated customs of king-worshiping eastern barbarians. Humorous the play no doubt was, perhaps farcical. But underneath we sense a passionate concern for the political liberty that Python felt was slipping out of his countrymen's hands.

Alexander's conquests spread Greek culture over the known world, and, by the production of Greek plays in out-of-the-way places, stimulated not only the dreary imitations of the Roman stage, but also the lively tradition of the Indian theater. In this mobile court of Alexander, there was at least one poet willing to take a risk for the freedom he knew to be a necessary condition if the art was to live. But elsewhere Plato's philosophy triumphed. The empires that followed were hardly his Republic, but in one aspect at least they followed his precepts. Poetry was never allowed to grow strong enough for the state to have to bother about the expulsion of its practitioners.

Notes

1. The only reason to write for the depraved Roman stage would be to earn money. Seneca was one of the richest men in Rome. See W. Beare, *The Roman Stage* (London: Methuen, 1964), pp. 233, 235.

2. The texts of Menander are papyruses. Inevitably they are damaged, in some places very badly. The text of *The Man from Sicyon* was used by mummifiers to make mummy wrappings and was discovered and extricated from more than one mummy at various times during this century. There is still a possibility that more plays will be discovered.

3. See Appendix 1 for dates and Appendix 6 for a list of plays.

4. The text of Terence was printed in 1470, and that of Plautus in 1472. Margarete Bieber, *The History of the Greek and Roman Theater* (Princeton: Princeton University Press, 1961), p. 254.

5. I have discussed briefly elsewhere the irrelevance of the *Poetics* as a critique of fifth-century drama. Leo Aylen, *Greek Tragedy and the Modern World* (London: Methuen, 1964), pp. 154–57. The most complete discussion that I know is in Jones's book: John Jones, *On Aristotle and Greek Tragedy* (London: Chatto & Windus, 1962). Kitto also has much to say that is relevant. H. D. F. Kitto, *Form and Meaning in Drama* (London: Methuen, 1956).

6. Aristotle *Rhetoric* 3. 12. 1413B, 12ff. mentions Chairemon, who did this.

7. Cf. T. B. L. Webster, *Art and Literature in Fourth Century Athens* (London: Athlone Press, 1956), p. 136.

8. In *The Arbitration*, lines 872 ff., Onesimos shows himself very much an Epicurean in his theology. "How could the gods possibly look after the affairs of so many men," he asks. "There must be roughly a thousand cities in the world, each with thirty thousand people in them."

9. The setting is almost invariably urban, though *The Bad-tempered Man* is set in the country-side.

10. Menander, *Plays and Fragments*, trans. Philip Vellacott (Harmondsworth: Penguin Books, 1967), pp. 15–16.

11. Cf. Shakespeare: "Thus conscience does make cowards of us all" (*Hamlet*, 3. 1. 83).

12. Aelius Donatus the grammarian, living in the fourth century A.D., preserves a life of Terence by Suetonius, and adds a paragraph of his own in which he says that *Phormio* and *The Mother-in-Law* are adapted from Apollodorus, the rest from Menander. But the notice attached to *The Mother-in-Law* says that it was adapted from Menander.

13. See Beare, *The Roman Stage*, pp. 63–69, where he discusses Plautus' treatment of his Greek originals. Beare believes that Plautus invented relatively little. "Scarcely one scene among several hundred can with certainty be ascribed to his independent authorship" (p. 63). But it is almost impossible to be as sure as this. We do not possess enough New Comedy in Greek.

14. See ibid., pp. 219–32, for a fuller discussion.

15. I follow the usual practice and refer to the episodes between the dance interludes as "acts."

16. All four poets lived long lives. Naevius was born about 260 B.C. Ennius was born in 239 and died in 169. Pacuvius, his nephew, was born in 220 and died in 130. Accius was born in 170.

17. This scene, containing, as it does, enough circumstantial details of Nero's death, establishes that the play must have been written soon after he died.

18. See Chapter 7.

19. This discussion derives from Bruno Snell's reconstruction of the play. See Bruno Snell, *Scenes from Greek Drama* (Berkeley and Los Angeles: University of California Press; London: Cambridge University Press, 1964), pp. 99–138. Snell has succeeded in reconstructing a very plausible form for the play from a total of eighteen lines and two references.

The *Letter of Theopompos* is summarized by Athenaeus: *Deipnosophists* 13. 586C. Athenaeus quotes five lines from the play in 586D, which he requotes later when he returns to the *Agen* in 13. 595E–596B. He talks about Harpalos (594E ff.) and quotes from Theopompos (595A–C).

12

FOLK THEATER, "MIMES" AND "PANTOMIME"

For us today the history of the theater in antiquity is effectively the history of the festivals of Dionysus at Athens, their nature, origins, climactic expression in drama, and the continued imitation of that drama for centuries after the festivals had ceased to represent real worship. But even the fifth-century Athenians were able to see other shows besides the performances at the various festivals. There were forms of dramatic entertainment in other Greek cities also, and indeed among non-Greeks too. We should not confine our consideration of "theater" to plays. Vaudeville acts are part of the theater; and vaudeville acts do not have scripts. We now can say very little about the nonverbal theater of antiquity. But we must remind ourselves that it existed, even if such a reminder serves only to emphasize our ignorance.

Folk Theater

There are various indications of some kind of crude folk theater in a number of Greek states dating from early times. It is natural to infer that there were a great many slightly different variations in what was more or less the same entertainment—a few comics on an improvised platform stage, cracking the same kind of crude slapstick jokes and singing some songs. Local traditions no doubt developed of which the locals were very proud. A visitor would be told how the show he was watching had certain peculiarities that no other show possessed. He would duly note these peculiarities in the account of his travels, and perhaps the place he had visited would be credited with its own brand of folk theater, though the entertainment there was in effect very much the same as in other places. With one exception, to which I shall return, we have no evidence to help us visualize these entertainments in any detail. We are left with scattered mentions.

Athenaeus has a confused discussion in which he mentions a number of these kinds of performance (*Deipnosophists* 14.621D–622D). There was a Spartan tradition where a man would mime a fruit stealer, and some sort of comic doctor act, though this reference in Athenaeus is obscured because he seems to muddle it with something in a later comic poet. He refers to the performers as *deikelistai* and *mimetai*. The latter word is about the most general word possible: "performers" is the best translation. The former could be translated "property men." For them to have acquired this name would certainly suggest that their show involved many more props than comparable shows in other places.

Athenaeus then compares these property men with similar performers elsewhere in Greece. The Sicyonians call them "phallus bearers," or possibly just "phallus wearers." Others call them "improvisers"; the Thebans call them "volunteers." The majority call them *sophistai*, a word almost impossible to translate right here. It could perhaps mean in this context "professionals," that is, the opposite of the "volunteers"; it could certainly mean "masters," that is, experts; it could perhaps just mean "clever fellows." The rest of Athenaeus' discussion seems more to refer to the primitive *kōmos* out of which the Athenian festival comedy grew.

There are certain references in Aristophanes that confirm that there was some sort of Dorian comedy during the fifth century. Aristophanes refers to Megarian comedy, but there may be no especial significance in this; Megara was the nearest Dorian state and was therefore the most familiar to his audience. In the prologue of the *Wasps*, Xanthias announces to the audience that there will be no Megarian jokes, no nuts scattered among the spectators, and no Heracles cheated of his supper (57–60). Aristophanes does sometimes distribute tidbits among the audience (for example, *Peace*, 962–67), and it would be natural to assume that the comic will do the opposite of what he says—scatter some nuts and crack a Megarian joke or two. But the prologue of The Wasps goes on about Euripides and so gives us little clue as to the nature of "Megarian jokes." The implication is of course that Megarian comedy is cruder. But it is a stock comic trick to pretend to be less crude than you are,[1] and it is difficult to conceive of any crudity of which Aristophanes does not make use. It is, however, possible that the crude scene of the Megarian and his two daughters in *The Acharnians* (729–817) may well have contained some take-off of the Megarian style.

The iambic scenes that occupy the latter half of an Aristophanes play are usually thought to be derived from some sort of knockabout folk entertainment. Some scholars consider that this originated in the Dorian parts of Greece. But just as the early comic poets of Athens must have developed and refined the early *kōmos* to suit the requirements of the competitive festival, so they must have refined the iambic scenes as well. The peculiar characteristics of these scenes are just as likely to have developed in the context of the comic festival as independently of it.

There is a tradition that it was in Dorian Greece that "comedy" was invented.[2] The various folk shows mentioned by Athenaeus are all the product of Dorian states. It may be that there was some kind of folk theater before the chorus *kōmos* had been turned into drama in Attica. In other words, there may

be a sense in which this primitive folk theater antedated the dancing performance out of which the festival drama grew. But there is no evidence by which
we can decide which came first. Nor is there evidence to decide how much this
folk theater was exclusively Dorian. There may well have been equivalent Attic
shows, which lost importance once there was a competition at Athens to attract
the best comic talents. We do not even know who was earlier—Chionides, the
first comic poet to win the comic competition at Athens, or Epicharmus, also
writing comedies in Dorian Sicily.[3] As I said before, we can say nothing of this
primitive folk theater in Greece except that it existed. Nor can we use the
history of the Greek theater as part of the interesting general discussion: which
comes first, "folk" or "art" theater?

Once the Athenian competitions had established "art" theater, there were
bound to be "folk" derivatives. Villages copy metropolitan traditions, distort-
ing them to suit their own needs. The only clear picture we find of folk theater
in the ancient world derives from a series of vases known as the *phlyakes* vases.
These date from the fourth century and come from southern Italy.[4] The *phlyakes* were strolling players who seem to have performed versions of plays
developed in the metropolitan tradition of the major cities of Sicily such as
Syracuse.

What is shown on the vases is obviously crude, rural theater; the stage is the
rough and ready platform we associate with strolling players through the ages.
But the themes of the plays are nearly all mythological burlesques; such theater
is hardly likely to have been created by strolling players for a tour of small
towns and villages. Syracuse and other cities of Sicily had a flourishing theater
during the fifth century, which was able to offer opportunities to Aeschylus.
There is every reason to suppose that much the same kinds of drama would
have been presented at the festivals there as at Athens. We must not assume that
the only theater in Sicily and southern Italy during the fourth century was that
depicted on the *phlyakes* vases. It may be simply that for some reason or other
there was a fashion in southern Italy during the fourth century for collecting
vases with pictures of the touring companies. It may be that the artists enjoyed
the mythological scenes more, and so painted them rather than other kinds of
play. In other words the scenes depicted on the vases may not be specially
significant as theater history.[5]

But though it would be wrong to infer from a number of vase pictures that
southern Italy had a unique theatrical tradition, and that, during the fourth
century, plays of mythological burlesque were the only kind of comedy enjoyed, we can at any rate be sure that there was in southern Italy during the
fourth century a flourishing tradition of touring theater. Plays were performed
on temporary stages, platforms with a few steps leading up to them. The actors
wore the traditional comic costume with phallus, though some of the phalluses
appear rather small and apologetic.[6] Certainly, plays of mythological burlesque
must have been popular. But there is no reason to suppose that they were the
only entertainment.

By the time that Plautus came to write, there was a flourishing tradition of native Italian folk theater. Whatever else one may adapt from other sources, humor must be local. Plautus would not have been able to make his audience laugh at Greek New Comedy unless he could relate his adaptations to humorous entertainments with which his audience would be familiar. This native Italian entertainment is referred to as Atellan farce. The name probably comes from a town in Campania. The original language was Oscan, an Italian language akin to Latin, but different. Presumably the Oscan farces became popular, were transported to Rome, and were adapted into Latin. They are the only significant native Italian drama, though of course it is possible that they also were influenced by Greek performers, whether those of a touring company or in a local folk tradition.[7]

The Atellan plays were based on the antics of a set of stock characters: Maccus, Bucco, Pappus, Dossennus, and Manducus. Maccus and Bucco were fools; Pappus was the grandfather, and Manducus had great champing jaws. In the present state of our knowledge, however, they all appear to be somewhat similar: all clowns, all greedy. They would not necessarily all appear in the same play. We do not know for certain if they were masked, but it would appear that they must have been. How else would one show their grotesque faces and Manducus' champing jaws?[8]

For a short while, at the beginning of the first century B.C. Atellan farces were composed as written plays. The titles that survive indicate that the shows remained firmly southern Italian, though the writers may have used elements from Greek New Comedy to enlarge their scope. After its brief spell of relative respectability, the Atellan farce ceased to occupy the attention of serious writers, but it continued as popular folk theater for centuries, retaining a local Italian flavor in contrast to the international Greek "mime."

The "Mime"

English histories of the ancient theater have acquired the habit of referring to a type of show as a "mime." This is a literal transcription of the Greek word *mimos*, which was a very general word meaning either "performer" or the show in which he performed. The performers who were not called *mimoi* were the actors and *choreutae* of the festivals. On the one hand, therefore, we should think of *mimoi* as being more like vaudeville performers with their various acts, which might range from juggling or acrobatics to comedy sketches. On the other hand, however, we possess some examples of sketches written to be performed in private houses, and these were also called *mimoi*. In other words, I do not think that there is any point in attempting to classify or coordinate the various shows that Greek writers call *mimoi* and English writers translate "mimes." It is worth noting the various pieces of evidence, however, especially since some of it is very vivid.

The Athenians had cabaret performers, and there is an excellent contemporary account of a cabaret in Xenophon's *Drinking Party*. After the *Panathenaea* festival in 422, Callias threw a party at which Socrates was one of the guests. There is no reason why this book should be anything other than direct reporting of this actual party.

After some chat in which we learn about Philippos the comedian, who is invited out to dinner to make jokes, and whom we may therefore assume to be a semiprofessional (1. 13–15), the professional entertainers arrive, a Syracusan with a girl *aulos*-player, a dancing girl "able to perform miracles," and a beautiful boy who plays the lyre and dances (2.1). Socrates is delighted at their arrival, but there is a digression as he discourages Callias from offering the guests perfumes. Scents, says Socrates, make everyone seem alike.

As the performers prepare for the show, Socrates puts a ban on discussion. All he wants to do is to watch the dancing girl, who is being handed her hoops. She dances, juggling with them,[9] and succeeds in making use of twelve hoops— which is clearly an exceptional performance. Next, a circular frame is brought in, full of swords, sticking, point up, in the air. The girl does a tumbling dance, into and out of the frame; the spectators are frightened for her. Presumably the tumbling would include forward and backward somersaults, and the effect depended on her accuracy, which enabled her to miss the sword points.

After the boy has done an act, Socrates, having commented on the way that no part of the boy's body remains idle, asks the Syracusan to teach him some dance steps. His announcement that he is going to learn dancing is greeted with peals of laughter. But Socrates defends himself: dancing is better exercise than running or boxing, and can even be performed by oneself in a small room.

Philippos then does a burlesque of the two dances, imitating the girl's forward and back bends, making himself, like her, into a hoop, and then calling the *aulos*-girl to play very fast while he capers madly until he is exhausted.

Drink is served, and there is general conversation. People are asked to say on what they pride themselves most, and Socrates asks the Syracusan if his pride is the boy. No, says the Syracusan, because he is frightened that members of his audience might ask to spend the night with such a beautiful person. "Don't you?" asks Socrates. "Of course," replies the Syracusan. "All night and every night." He goes on to say that what he prides himself on are the fools who watch his "marionettes" and feed him (4.55).

After a song from Socrates, a potter's wheel is brought in for the girl to "perform her wonder-act." But Socrates is bored with wonder-acts, and asks for a dance to the *aulos*, such as you might see in pictures. What about something like the dance of the Graces, Hours, and Nymphs? The Syracusan agrees, and they erect a kind of throne in an inner chamber abutting on the room where the party is taking place.

The Syracusan then enters and announces: "Gentlemen, Ariadne is entering the chamber prepared for her and Dionysus. Soon Dionysus will come from among the gods, a little drunk. He will go in to her. Then they will play with each other" (9.2).

Dressed like a bride, Ariadne enters and sits on the throne. No sign of

Dionysus, but the *aulos* plays a Bacchic tune, and the company are delighted with the dancing-master because Ariadne is showing such difficulty in keeping still from the excess of pleasure she is feeling.

At last Dionysus sees her, dances to her lightly and sits on her knees, embracing and kissing her. Bashful at first, she soon embraces him too, while the audience shouts and cheers.

Dionysus then raises her from her throne. The love talk and kissing increase until the company realize that the two dancers are obviously lovers in real life. The show ends with them retiring to bed, while the guests disperse. The unmarried men swear that they will find themselves wives, while the married men gallop home on horseback.

This vivid account is a most important picture of Athenian society at a time when three of the great poets were producing their plays. First, we notice the unashamed eroticism. Certainly, the performance of the boy and girl dancer is presented as tasteful, beautiful, and discreet. We do not feel that the Syracusan would have wished to show the boy with whom he himself made love copulating in public. But there is also no doubt that the performance was designed to stimulate the audience sexually just as intensely as any strip club act of today. It was probably the more erotic for being done more tastefully.

Second, we should also notice the way in which the numinous and the erotic are inextricably linked. The love-play presented is the love-play of a god with a mortal. Dionysus enters Ariadne as life enters the world of which humans are part. I have drawn attention in Chapter 1 to the religious rituals performed at this party. The flamboyance of both ritual and sexual excitement takes us aback. But everything we know of fifth-century Athens suggests that this party is in no way unusual.

It may be significant that the performers are Dorians, from Syracuse. What is certainly significant is that they are aliens and of inferior social status.[10] The Syracusan is afraid that a man in his audience will demand to spend the night with the boy dancer. Throughout antiquity, as indeed in almost all cultures, the cabaret performer has been treated as an inferior being, little better than a slave, someone for the audience to make use of as object of sexual enjoyment.

The details of such a performance would be impossible in a mask. The dignity of the festival actor's calling depended upon the fact that he appeared in a mask. In Theophrastus' *Characters* it is the man who is "out of his mind" who is prepared to take part in a comic chorus without a mask (6).[11] We may at any rate conclude that all performers referred to as *mimoi* were of a very different social status from the actors in the festivals. We may also be fairly certain that there was a widespread custom of cabaret performance throughout Greece by small, wandering troupes of unmasked, and therefore low-class artists, whose performances were probably always a matter more of physical movement than of dialogue.

During the fifth century Sophron of Syracuse wrote "mimes" with prose dialogue, which were classified as "male" and "female," and therefore presumably involved leading performers of the respective sexes. Titles in the first category include *Messenger, Fishermen's Look-out, Old Fishermen,* and in the second *Medicine Women* and *Off to the Isthmian Games.* His son Xenarchos also wrote "mimes," apparently some sort of political satire. Aristotle mentions these as being dramatic works in prose, like a Socratic conversation (*Poetics* 1. 1447B.10–11). We may assume that they were naturalistic sketches of everyday life performed in private houses by unmasked cabaret performers, though no doubt there may have been specialization whereby certain troupes performed only dialogue pieces, and were therefore more like what we would call actors than vaudeville artists.

Theocritus, who lived during the first half of the third century and is usually regarded as the greatest poet of the Hellenistic age, wrote semidramatic, dialogue poems in hexameters. Though no doubt they were recited in gatherings of friends, they cannot have been intended even for performance in private houses. Otherwise he would never have used the undramatic meter of dactylic hexameters, which was now an exclusively literary meter. But his *Idyll 15* has very much the flavor of a "mime." It is a conversation piece between two Alexandrian women, gossiping on their way to the Adonis festival. It has a theatrical rhythm. The dialogue conveys with great vitality a sense of the streets of Alexandria. The piece builds beautifully toward its climax: the song, which tells of the return of Adonis, his lovemaking with Aphrodite, and his disappearance again to the realm of the dead. It is the poem of a writer who could have written a great play. That Theocritus did not attempt to write either tragedy or comedy is a sure indictment of the Alexandrian theater. That he wrote only a poetic version of a "mime" may be an indication either of his fastidiousness or of the relative unimportance of the form as a medium for serious writers.

Theocritus was most likely to have been born in Syracuse, though he spent his life in many parts of the Greek Mediterranean. He is therefore almost certain to have been influenced by Sophron and Xenarchos. Another follower of theirs was Herodas, who lived about a generation after Theocritus. There is doubt as to his place of birth, and even as to whether he mainly worked and lived in Athens or in Alexandria. He is perhaps typical of the rootless culture of the third and subsequent centuries.

Seven of his "mimes" survive, and there is a large fragment of an eighth. None are more than 130 lines long. In a sense they could be described as dramatic cartoons. Scholars have on the whole denigrated Herodas' wit, because they have disapproved of his coarseness. It is very much easier to write about him in the second half of the twentieth century than it was in the first half.

His work consists of naturalistic conversation pieces from real life, and, like any "realistic" writer of today, he emphasizes the seamy side. But he wrote in verse, which is perhaps surprising, since Sophron and Xenarchos had already left a tradition of such sketches in prose. As we shall see, we cannot be sure how realistic Herodas' dialogue is. There is no conversational writing of the period with which to compare his, apart from that of Theocritus. On the whole, poetry was entering a highly artificial phase. The scholar poets of Alexandria, led by Callimachus, were reacting against what they saw as the corruption of the Greek language now that it was being spoken by so many non-Greeks. They created a school of self-consciously archaizing poetry, and developed a tradition of scholarship that approached the literature of fifth-century Athens as "classical texts."

We may presume that Herodas' sketches were performed in private houses. They never require more than a few performers and seem to have been acted with minimal setting. The first piece involves considerable business of answering a door, while a slave woman goes forward and backward between her mistress's room and the front door. To provide a naturalistic set for this would be extremely complicated, but there would be no difficulty in creating an amusing atmosphere of busyness, with the old slave miming the doors.[12] On the other hand, the sixth sketch involves Koritto fussing over the arrival of her friend Metro. All that is absolutely needed is for a slave to bring on or move a seat, though other business with easily maneuverable props suggests itself.

The first sketch, called *The Procuress or Bawd*, is about a mother visiting her daughter after a long time away. Metriche, the daughter, is now on her own. Her man has been in Egypt and has not even written for the last ten months (1.24). Gyllis, the mother, advises her to take a new lover and has an excellent person to suggest: an athlete who is madly in love with Metriche. The mother's advice could be summed up: Sin this once; you'll enjoy yourself (1.62). But Metriche resists, and the sketch ends with an offer of wine to Gyllis in an atmosphere of amused friendliness.

The second sketch is called *The Pimp*. It is simply one long speech in a court, interrupted only by a clerk's reading of the law. The pimp is alleging that one of his whores, Myrtale, has been assaulted. Why should he offer his merchandise free any more than any other merchant? The humor lies in the way he treats himself as if he were a normal, respectable citizen. The theatrical climax comes when he calls upon Myrtale to show herself to the court (2.66). "Don't be ashamed," he says. "Treat them as though they were your fathers and brothers." He is at the same time demonstrating how her skin has been plucked of hair. So she is presumably nude, and no doubt posturing with mock modesty like the expertly professional stripper-whore that she is. The mood of the sketch is that of humorous pornography.

The third sketch is called *The Schoolmaster*. Metrotime, the fussy mother, has called to see Lampriskos, the schoolmaster of her son Kottalos. Kottalos spends all his time gambling and so is still illiterate. She wants him to be beaten, and he is held up for beating by the other schoolboys. She is, however, still not satisfied that he has been beaten sufficiently.

The fourth sketch, called *Offerings and Sacrifice to Asclepius*, presents two women visiting the temple, their prayers and their act of offering, but especially their chat as they walk around looking at the various scenes depicted in the precinct. Its humor and interest lies in the contrast between the setting and the tone of conversation; we can easily imagine the modern equivalent: trivial conversation in a beautiful cathedral.

The fifth sketch is the most exciting because it presents a situation involving strong dramatic conflict. Called *Jealous,* it presents Bitinna in love with her slave Gastron, but furious with him because he has been making love to another slave, Amphitaia. She orders him to be stripped and bound for flogging (5.18). Having at first protested his innocence, he now admits his fault (5.26). Pleading for forgiveness, he promises not to go wrong again. If he does, she can brand him (5.64–65).[13] Bitinna, however, piles on orders for Gastron's punishment. He is to have "a thousand lashes back and front" (5.33–34, 48–49). After he has been taken away, she sends for him to be brought back and branded instead. Finally, after her favourite girl slave, Kydilla has pleaded for him, she does, however, relent.

The sixth sketch, called *Making Friends, or on Your Own,* presents two women in relaxed conversation. Metro, who is visiting Koritto, knows that Koritto possesses the most beautiful dildo made of the softest leather. Koritto is led to say that she got it from the little bald cobbler, Kerdon, who had two, but would only sell her one and would not say to whom he was selling the second. The scene is given humor and dramatic life by the open sexual greed of the two women, the one satisfied and the other not. Even in the highly permissive society of Hellenistic Alexandria, however, such openness would have caused a small frisson. The sketch is secretively pornographic as well as humorous.

The seventh sketch must have been designed to follow the sixth closely. It presents Kerdon in his leather shop. The main joke is that though Metro is in the shop, buying in the company of some friends, there is no mention of the dildo at all. Presumably the intention was to arouse the audience's expectation of witnessing her attempt to buy the second dildo and to make them laugh when the transaction never took place. The character of Kerdon, the bustling cobbler, provides in addition an interesting study.

The verse of Herodas is not very easily speakable.[14] The construction of his sentences does not suggest a writer who understood how the stresses of dialogue must fall, and indeed there are passages that make us feel that he had not sufficiently mastered his verse form. This is a pity, more especially because there was no need for the sketches to have been written in verse at all. Herodas is a writer more interesting in promise than in fulfillment, though he gives us some vivid pictures of Hellenistic urban life, and on occasion writes with a wry nastiness that is well in keeping with styles and attitudes of some of the writers of our own time.

A papyrus from the second century A.D. happens to have been preserved with the text of another "mime" from the third century B.C. The text is merely a synopsis, and the fact of its preservation so late in synopsis form suggests that it was continuously being performed.[15]

The mistress of the house is in love with one of her slaves, Aisopos. But he is in love with his fellow slave, Apollonia. The opening scene presents the mistress, played by the leading performer. She announces her desire for Aisopos in no uncertain terms: "He takes no notice when I call him to come and fuck me" (108). When Aisopos arrives he is abused in the same strong language:

> What's so difficult? You've been bred for women. Suppose I'd told you to dig, or plough, or hump stones? Think of all that work in the fields. Now, does a woman's empty cunt seem harder than that? (117–18b)

The scene builds as she orders her loyal slave Malakos to take charge of dragging out Aisopos and his Apollonia and tying them to trees on a cliff-top, where they will die out of sight of each other. She goes inside, behind the curtain, ordering her slaves to meet her when they have finished.

The second scene presents the mistress after receiving a report that Aisopos has escaped. She orders the performance of sacrifice to the gods, since she is still happy that her wishes will be carried out. Spinther, a slave who appears to stay loyal to the master of the house, is primarily involved. The mistress then orders a search for Aisopos inside the house, from where Apollonia is now being dragged. Apollonia is to be chained and guarded, while search is made for Aisopos: "Find him. Kill him. Drag him and throw him out. I want to see him a corpse" (143–44). With these words she goes inside accompanied by Spinther and Malakos.

As scene 3 opens, the apparently dead body of Aisopos is brought on. The first half of the scene presents the mistress lamenting over the corpse of her lover. She then turns to Spinther. Whether with him or with Malakos, she will find new satisfaction.

Scene 4 shows her plotting to poison her husband. She tells Malakos to go and fetch the parasite attached to their house.

Scene 5 shows the mistress confronted with two bodies—those of Aisopos and Apollonia. She unveils that of Apollonia to gloat over it. The parasite is meanwhile sent to fetch her husband. Malakos comes out of the house with the poisoned drink. Possibly the parasite takes the cup and is about to drink, knowing that it is not really poisonous. He then goes.

The last scene starts with the mistress in triumph over the corpses of the two slaves and her husband. Spinther and the parasite, who are both in the plot, are laughing. Malakos starts to speak a lament over the master's body. "Poor man, you never knew love." At this the master leaps up, and orders Malakos to be beaten. We also see that Aisopos and Apollonia are also alive. Presumably the show ends with the downfall of the mistress.

The text we possess is clearly an acting text. The show certainly provides a basis for a performance offering many opportunities for an actor. The short plot provides sex, violence, suspense, and a farcical end. It allows the leading lady to run through most of the possible emotions, even allowing her, villain that she is, a moment of sorrow over the death of her lover at the beginning of scene 3. We cannot pretend that the piece has merit; it is worth discussing simply because it may well be a very typical, ordinary piece, the chance notes of a small company whose work had nothing to recommend it, in a not very important Greek-Egyptian town. It is useful to remember its existence as a corrective to the masterpieces with which this book has had to deal for most of its length. It is so easy for us to think that the Greeks produced nothing that was not a masterpiece.

There are other references to performances similar to this, though there is no other text as complete. During the first century B.C. the "mime" acquired a kind of respectability, as the Atellan farce had done. Literary "mimes" were composed in Latin, first by an important Roman knight, Decimus Laberius, who was born in 106 B.C., and then by a slave from Syria, Publilius Syrus, whose successful work won him his freedom. There are a number of short fragments and about forty titles of Laberius'. The evidence suggests that his main subject was adultery. His language seems to be full of puns, and he was known to have used slang.[16]

The haphazard survival of evidence for this form suggests that what we possess is the tiniest fraction of what became a widely known form of entertainment in the Hellenistic and Roman periods.[17] It seems unlikely that it was ever mass entertainment; its style and subject matter suggest that it appealed to the well-to-do middle and upper classes in whose houses it was performed. The interests of such a class are limited; their theater is limited too, confined virtually to gossip, sex, and scandal. It is a stark reminder of the speedy degradation of the Greek theater that, less than one hundred fifty years from the death of Sophocles, the nearest that Theocritus, the greatest poet of his age, would come to writing drama would be a piece of this triviality. Great theater needs a great society; and a great society is one where all classes will rub shoulders in the theater.

The Pantomime

In strong contrast to the vaguely related performances that are categorized as "mimes" in ancient authors, the pantomime was a very clearly defined art form. It was invented by two freed slaves, Pylades of Cilicia and Bathyllus of Alexandria, in A.D. 22. Rapidly it became not only the most successful but also the highest theatrical art form of the Roman Empire. Its artists never enjoyed the priestly or ambassadorial status of the great tragic actors of the fourth century B.C., but the leading pantomime artists, though always of slightly suspect social caste, could attain great financial success. The highest point was reached in the sixth century A.D. when the pantomime artist Theodora so impressed the emperor Justinian that he married her.

The essence of the pantomime was that it was a solo performance by one masked mimetic dancer with a singing chorus providing musical interludes. Its subjects were the subjects of tragedy.[18] In the fourth century A.D. the orator Libanius said that the pantomime still educated people in the ancient myths. (*Against Aristeides* 3.391).

During the first century A.D., leading poets wrote libretti for pantomimes, and we possess an embittered attack on the state of poetry by Juvenal (*Satire* 7.79–97), in which he says that writing libretti for the pantomime artist Paris is the only way in which a poet can make money. It is all very well for Lucan in his marble gardens; he is rich. Poor Statius has to sell his *Agave*, presumably a version of *The Bacchants*, to Paris. The life of Lucan, however, says that he also wrote libretti for pantomimes. Although Juvenal's attack is partly sheer personal jealousy that he has not been given these lucrative chances, we cannot imagine that the words of the pantomime libretto can have been very important. It was the dancing that was all-important. The whole art was to convey as much as possible by gesture.

The best account of the pantomime is in Lucian's dialogue *On the Dance*, written in the second century A.D. Crato the cynic, who prefers other theater, is converted by Lycinus to the pantomime. The dialogue ends on his agreement to accompany Lycinus to a pantomime.

At the beginning of the dialogue, Crato presents the typical attitude of a culture snob. He would prefer to attend the dithyrambic performances with their *aulos*-player, or to hear solo performers on the lyre, or indeed to watch either tragedy or comedy. This gives Lycinus an opportunity to ridicule the preposterous conventions of the tragedy of his day (27) where the actor struts in high boots, high mask, and padded costume, pompous and unreal. But first he has spent some time justifying the art of dance itself, which had long disappeared from tragedy and comedy. To Lycinus the art of dance had only just begun when Socrates was taking lessons (25). Dance and words had to separate, if only because of the "panting" of the singer-dancers (30).

Though the themes of tragedy and the pantomime are the same, the latter can give them more varied treatment (31). He continues his argument with the interesting comment that pantomime is too noble for competitions (32), which perhaps indicates that at this time the tragic competitions were somewhat corrupt affairs.

A large part of the book is devoted to showing how much the dancer must know of myth, how well he must know Homer and the tragic poets (37–62). A delightful footnote is given to this discussion when he tells later on of the disastrous mistake a dancer once made (80). Presenting the birth of Zeus, he was trying to perform Kronos eating his own children, but he went into the very similar movements of Thyestes eating his children. This story demonstrates very clearly how subtle the art had become; it also indicates how each pantomime was routined, using standard patterns for particular situations. No doubt there was also a considerable repertoire of mime "language," conventional gestures almost exactly equivalent to words, with which the artist could "talk" in virtual sentences of limb and body movements, as, for example, the Kathakali dancers do to this day.

The latter part of the book contains some of the extreme achievements of the art. There was Demetrius the Cynic in the reign of Nero, who accused a dancer of meaningless gestures. In reply the dancer offered to perform without any libretto, without the normal *aulos*-player and chorus, without the "stampers" who beat time. Entirely on his own he performed the love affairs between Aphrodite and Ares, Helios gossiping about the couple, Hephaestus laying his plot to trap his wife and her lover, and the actual catching of the couple in bed. He followed this with individual portraits of each of the gods who came in to see them, with a portrayal of Aphrodite's shame, and with how Ares tried to hide and begged for mercy. Finally Demetrius, totally converted, said: "I hear what you're doing. I don't only see it. To me you seem to talk with your hands" (63).

The next chapter contains the story of how a barbarian visitor to Nero's court asked for a dancer to act as interpreter. We then learn that dancers would change their masks in the course of a performance. From the various visual representations of pantomime artists, we learn that these masks did not have the open mouths of the tragic or comic masks.[19]

Lucian also makes the point that a pantomime artist would play only the roles for which he was fitted (76). He refers to the way in which an inappropriate piece of self-casting could bring great ridicule, as when a small dancer, rashly playing Hector, was jeered at, "Hey, Astyanax! Where's Hector?"[20] He includes some other appropriate catcalls.

Finally he describes how, in the great dances, the character can take possession of the performer. There was one dancer who performed Ajax' madness after being defeated by Odysseus for the arms of Achilles. The dancer seemed actually to go insane, tore the clothes off one of the time-stampers, seized an *aulos* from the instrumentalist, struck Odysseus on the head with it, and would have killed him except that a stiff cap protected his skull. The audience was raving with him as he became more and more excited. Finally he went into the audience and sat down between two ex-consuls, who became afraid that he would "whip them like a ram" (83). He refused to perform the dance again, saying that to be mad once was enough. Crato succumbs to such a statement of the dance's power and volunteers to attend a performance. Lycinus' final summary has won him over: "Dance charms, and wakes up the eyes. It rouses the mind to each of the actions."

The pantomime was strictly a solo art. But there were similar shows that involved many performers. Apuleius in *The Golden Ass*[21] describes a show somewhat on the lines of the seventeenth-century masques, but one that demanded skilful mimetic dancing. After a warm-up in which the chorus does a Greek Pyrrhic dance with complex groupings, inner curtains are opened to show a very complicated naturalistic set: Mount Ida, made of wood, but planted with real trees, grazed by real goats, and with a real stream running down from its top. A boy in Asiatic robes with a gold tiara represents Paris and is in charge of the goats. Another boy, naked except for a cloak over his left shoulder and two gold wings in his hair, dances up. He is Mercury, and he gives Paris the golden apple, while gesturing Jupiter's orders. Three girls enter to represent the three goddesses for the judgment of Paris: Juno, with white diadem and scepter; Minerva, with an olive-wreathed helmet and spear, entering at a run, as if battle; an outstandingly beautiful girl to show Venus while still a virgin, naked except for a silk cloak that "shadowed" her private parts—her body white to show that she came from heaven, the cloak blue to show that she was born in the sea. Juno, with her two attendants, Castor and Pollux, wearing helmets like half-eggshells to show how they were born from an egg, dances to Paris accompanied by the *tibia*, an instrument like the *aulos*. With simple gestures and "honorable noddings," she mimes to Paris that he will be emperor of Asia if he chooses her. Next Minerva, her two attendants, Terror and Fear, dancing with drawn swords, sings a war song like a trumpet call to battle, a contrasting mixture of deep notes and high ones. With restless head, excited eyes, and twisted gesticulations, she mimes that Paris will be the bravest soldier ever, if he chooses her. Finally, Venus comes to the center of the stage, to a warm reception from the audience. Happy little boys surround her like cupids, with torches as if for her wedding, and then a crowd of beautiful girls as Graces and Seasons throw flowers. The music is in the Lydian mode. Venus dances slowly, with slow spine-bendings; sometimes it seems that she is dancing with her eyes alone. In front of Paris she seems to promise him by the "exertion of her arms" that she would give him a beautiful wife. Paris gives her the apple. Juno and Minerva *exeunt* in sadness and anger. Venus dances her delight with the whole chorus. Then, from the top of the mountain, saffron mixed with wine sprinkles the goats with scent and colors them yellow. As scent fills the auditorium, a kind of chasm opens into which the wooden mountain disappears.

What is described here is definitely an out-of-town show. Next on the bill was to be Lucius, as the Ass, genuinely copulating with a woman criminal. There is a sense of sleazy eroticism about parts of the judgment of Paris. And clearly the stage mechanics were as sensational as possible. But clearly also there was a need for expert mimetic dancing. This kind of performance relates to that of the great pantomimists, the only part of the theater in later antiquity that seems both to have presented serious emotions and to have involved some theatrical experiment.

Pantomime then, inherited the vast passions of fifth-century tragedy. While the theaters were used more and more for water shows, for fights with wild beasts and gladiators, for actual performances of the sex act, individual artists of enormous skill and dedication refined and developed their mimes so as to stretch totally both their imagination and their physique. We, as human beings, are lazy. We do not use our senses fully. An art form such as mime stimulates one sense by excluding the chance of taking sensual shortcuts through the other senses or the coordinating power of words. A great mime artist such as Marcel Marceau wakes up the eyes indeed. But although such art will enliven our senses and stimulate our imaginations, we need words if our moral judgments are to be strengthened and our moral universe enlarged. The overpowering dominance of one art, whether it be the dancing mime of Bathyllus or the music drama of Wagner or the electronic shudder of rock music, will never change the vision of a society. The relating of our sense experiences and our moral judgments needs words. Is it such an exaggeration to ask if the Roman Empire could have owed some of its still hardly explainable collapse to the fact that it ceased to produce poets? In the last resort is it only poets who can provide society with a great enough vision to withstand the great power of empires and absolute rulers? At any rate all performers in the theater must look back to Aeschylus. Dancer, singer, actor, composer, choreographer, and director; popular entertainer, using every sensual stimulus to wake up the eyes of the audience; it was not his achievement in any or all of these crafts that he left as final memorial; it was not even his greatest achievement, the coordinating power of his poetry, that he left to remind us of his existence. It was the fact that he had helped to stand between his city and slavery.

Notes

1. See *Clouds* 537–44, discussed in Chapter 1.
2. Aristotle *Poetics* 3. 1448A. 29ff.
3. For more detail, see Chapter 2.
4. For the largest easily accessible collection of pictures, see Margarete Bieber, *The History of the Greek and Roman Theater* (Princeton: Princeton University Press, 1961), pp. 129–46.
5. There are three writers whose names have come down to us as authors of *phlyakes*, the earliest being Rhinthon of Tarentum, who lived at the turn of the fourth and third centuries and apparently wrote parodies of Euripides in broad Doric; there are two other third-century writers who have no connection with Italy. Webster suggests that the word *phlyakes* came to be applied to plays still written in the Middle Comedy manner after Athens and the fashionable centers had developed New Comedy. See Sir Arthur Pickard-Cambridge, *Dithyramb, Tragedy and Comedy*, 2d ed. rev. by T. B. L. Webster (Oxford: Clarendon Press, 1962), p. 139.
6. See Bieber, *The History of the Greek and Roman Theater*, pp. 129–46.
7. The Romans classified various types of drama in terms of the costume and footwear worn. Plays involving Greek costume were derived from Greek models; plays involving native Italian costume were original. These *fabulae togatae* and *tabernariae* are discussed by W. Beare, *The Roman Stage* (London: Methuen, 1964) Appendix D, pp. 264–66. The names of some authors are known, but nothing about their plays.
8. Further discussion of the Atellan farce can be found in Bieber, *The History of the Greek and Roman Theater*, pp. 131, 148–49, 247–48, and in Beare, *The Roman Stage*, pp. 137–48. Bieber emphasizes that the stock characters of the Atellan farces bear strong relation to the characters in the *phlyakes* plays and therefore tends to derive the Italian plays from Greek sources. Beare is concerned to emphasize their independence.
9. Unfortunately the Greek is ambiguous. It is possible that this performance was a kind of hula-hoop act.
10. See Chapter 4, "Actors."
11. See Beare, *The Roman Stage*, pp. 150, 368 n.3. Beare gives us the necessary reminder that "*without* a mask" is actually an editors' emendation, albeit one universally accepted.

12. I use the word *mime* here in the sense in which we apply it to Marcel Marceau and in general use it in the modern theater to refer to the creation of events and objects without dialogue or props. I use "mime" as a translation of the Greek *mimos*.

13. This marking for disgrace seems to have been some kind of tattooing done with ink and needles.

14. His verse line is a variation of the iambic trimeter, known as the *scazōn* or choliambic; the limping iambic. It is exactly the same as the loose iambic of comedy, except that the line ends always with a spondee, instead of always with an iambus.

15. The text, a free translation softening some of the indelicate words, and some notes, are found in Beare, *The Roman Stage*, Appendix L, pp. 314–19.

16. Cf. Beare, *The Roman Stage*, pp. 154–58.

17. For other evidence, see Bieber, *The History of the Greek and Roman Theater*, p. 107. The most interesting piece of evidence is a terra-cotta of a "mime" troupe, figure 415. The title of the "mime" is written: *The Mother-in-Law*. Three figures are shown. The most arresting is the one in the center, a grotesque bald-headed man with enormous ears. Bieber suggests that it may have become common to make use of a misshapen dwarf as part of one's troupe to contrast well with a beautiful couple who would play young lovers.

18. Both the *Ion* and *Trojan Women* are mentioned as suitable subjects for pantomime. See *Corpus Inscriptionum Latinarum*, ed. T. Boeck (Berlin: Akademie der Wissenschaften, 1828–77), 5. 2. 5889.

19. Cf. Bieber, *The History of the Greek and Roman Theater*, p. 236 and fig. 783.

20. Astyanax was Hector's infant son.

21. Apuleius, *The Golden Ass*, more properly called *Metamorphoses* 10.29.20–32.4;10.34.1–10.

13

INTO THE ABYSS?

Die Griechen unsere und jegliche Kultur als Wagenlenker in den Händen
haben, dass aber fast immer Wagen und Pferde von zu geringem Stoffe und
der Glorie ihrer Führer unangemessen sind, die dann es für einen Scherz
erachten, ein solches Gespann in den Abgrund zu jagen: über den sie selbst,
mit dem Sprunge des Achilles, hinwegsetzen.

(Nietzsche, *Die Geburt der Tragödie*)[1]

When we attempt to understand the Greek theater, or rather the theater of
fifth-century Athens, we are not merely trying to elucidate one among many
periods of great drama. We cannot but feel that here is the source, and the
center, and the finest flowering of whatever it is that we mean when we say
"theater." Once we admit this to be our purpose, we realize that we must leave
rational analysis at some stage behind, in order to make that imaginative leap
without which we shall never be able to enter into the realm where the Athenian poets move freely, as of right.

If we talk theater for any length of time, we are bound to introduce at some
point in the conversation the phrase, "But it lacks magic," or "But it has
magic." What we mean by "great theater" is something unanalyzable and
indefinable, but instantly recognizable. Now, to a certain extent this is true of
all the arts, that greatness is indefinable but recognizable. But this, which we
refer to as "magic," has always somehow seemed more central to the theater,
more elusive, and more indefinable. For it comes from such unlikely places.
Great painters or novelists or composers, such as Rembrandt or Tolstoy or
Bach, more obviously deserve their greatness through their human compassion
or spiritual insight. It is easier to see why Bach should have been a great
composer than to see why Piaf should have been a great singer, or Grock a great
clown. Today we are nowhere nearer to defining what we mean by the "magic
of the theatre." But at least we know that it has to do with something that
happens in a gathering of people all together in one place. For everything else
that the theater can give is given better by movies. And yet we feel that there is
some justification for the theater still. We come in search of this magic,
indefinable but real.

This is all very well, it may be said, but if the most important thing about theater is this indefinable magic, how can we say anything whatsoever about the theater of so long ago? I think we can say a little, because of our rediscovery of the theatrical part of poetry. So many of the greatest of the poets of the past who did not write plays were just as much men of the theater, relying for their success on performing to an audience. Homer needed to create the "magic" among his listeners, or he would have been thrown out to beg. In the English tradition, Chaucer and Langland were performers as much as anyone in the theater of their day. Poetry as a branch of literature, divorced from performance, belongs solely to the Chinese tradition and to the last three hundred years in Western Europe. The idea of the bard is more common in most cultures than the idea of the literary poet.

Now, there is a strange difficulty about defining the poet. A person who paints pictures can be called a painter; a person who makes up tunes can be called a composer. But of so many people's work we hear the comment, "It isn't really poetry." Whatever qualities the writing may have, it does not possess magic. Bad painting is still painting, bad music is still music. But bad poetry is hardly poetry.

One may go further and say that, while painting and music are definable as arts, poetry is not. Has there ever been a satisfactory definition of poetry? And yet, without any satisfactory definition, poetry is still recognizable.

Now I am going to utter three statements of belief, without any attempt at proof. First, there is a connection between "magic" in the theater and the indefinable quality that makes us say of x, "Poetry," and of y, "Not poetry." Second, this connection is based upon the nature of the bard's job; the bard, who, standing still alone before an audience, without music, or with music very much held in the background, must create "magic" with his words alone. Theater magic turns to poetry magic by the craft of the bard, who wants the words to keep on making the magic whether he is fit or tired, with full or empty stomach, there in person or sending a substitute. Third, the magic that exists in poetry of the literary tradition exists because the poets continued to write as if they were bards. The almost universal metaphor that a poet "sings" is in truth no metaphor, but a necessary condition of the craft.

What I am discussing is *duende*. And it is significant that there is no word in modern English with which to translate it. It is also significant that it is a Spanish word, and that in the twentieth century the Spanish tradition is perhaps the most important bardic tradition. Neruda performed his poetry to audiences of ten thousand and more at a time in Chile. Lorca, perhaps the greatest poet of the twentieth century, was a bard, a performer, a man of the theater. We, from northern Europe or places colonized by northern Europe, have lost the idea of the *duende* and must relearn it from India, Africa, and Latin America.

We can also relearn it by reconsideration of our own cultural sources. We can also relearn it from Greece.

In a sense this essay could be described as an attempt to point out one manifestation of the *duende*. For while in other cultures we can recognize its appearance, even its frequency, in the theater poetry of fifth-century Athens it seems to be almost constant.

Confronted with the *duende* one can only shout "Olé." One cannot analyze or plan for it. One can only play the music again or dance in front of the picture. And yet if one directs a play in the theater, one does try and plan for the magical moment to happen; although the plan will not make it happen, the plan may create the conditions in which it can happen.

A theater director must even try and analyze the *duende*, because although it is unanalyzable, his job is to create the conditions in which the *duende* can come.

This essay has been written from the point of view of a theater director, offering some preliminary thoughts on the presentation of some very great plays. It is written from this point of view because the four great poets with whom I have been principally concerned were not only poet-performers opening themselves to the *duende*. They were also theater directors, using the medium of their theatrical tradition to arrange conditions for the occurrence of the *duende*.

The art of directing in the theater has been and always will be the art of creating conditions in which the *duende* can flourish. The art of directing, therefore, surprisingly, remains the same through the ages. By attempting to consider the staging of a Sophocles play, we are led into the planning part of Sophocles' mind, though of course not into that part where the *duende* struck him.

To the scholarly historian of the theater, talk such as this may seem mystical, arrogant, and unsubstantiated. It is, however, in keeping with areas of the rest of the book where I have claimed to know about the ancient theater, and where great scholars, with far greater wisdom and far greater knowledge of the ancient theater, have been content to say that we do not know, that we can only conjecture.

This arrogance of mine, however, is only a necessary part of the craft from whose viewpoint I have chosen to write this book. It is a scholar's craft to distinguish with the utmost precision between when he is very sure, when he is adequately sure, and when he is guessing. It is a director's craft to declare firmly whether it is x or y. A director who is unsure whether it is x or y and who rests content with being unsure will create in the theater something that is neither x nor y, but a blur in between.

In this book, then, I have attempted to ask all the questions that one should ask before attempting to stage a play or the plays of a complete school, and answer them one way or the other. For I feel that the important answers that I am attempting to give are not the answers of which one says this is right or wrong, so much as answers that are like the faint sketch of a picture to which we add more and more detail, until the picture stands out before us in vivid color.

The director's craft has to do with the relationship of language and gesture. Gesture is partly conventional, and partly belongs to the common human condition. Let us consider a crude example. A large man, equipped with a plentiful supply of murderous weapons, says to a small and unarmed man, "I'll kill you." A small weak man, lying on the ground for the very good reason that a large man is standing on his chest, says to the large man, "I'll kill you." The meaning of both these combinations of word and gesture is quite clear, and depends on the nature of human beings, not on convention. But shaking the head as a gesture meaning "no" is convention. Greeks today jerk their head upwards when they are gesturing "no."

The art of directing is also an art of rhythm. If an actor says a speech in a particular way, then he must say the next speech in a way that fits with the first one. If he had said the first speech in a different way, then he would have had to say the second in a different way, one that fitted with how he said the first speech. If there are two roles, A and B, one might cast A as a very fat man, and B as a very thin man. But one might perhaps cast A as a little weedy man, and B as a strong, splendid man. Where one says of direction that it is right or wrong is in the matter of relating one decision to another, of getting the A-B relationship right, whether it be via fatness and thinness or weediness and strength. The actual choice of actor or intonation of a line is more a matter of personal taste.

I am saying, then, that we can build up a picture of the ancient theater by playing the director. We can say with confidence, "If x, then y, and then z." We must choose whether it is to be x, y, z, or whether it is to be a, b, c. We can say with great confidence that if the *Prometheus Bound* was staged with a rock structure on an *ekkyklema*, then so was *The Women at the Thesmophoria*. We choose from our own intuition of the piece whether the *ekkyklema* was used or not.

But although I have made this distinction between the x, y, z relationship and the choice of x, the two are not absolutely separate in the task of a director. Because our choices of actual x's must also cohere. As we ask, "Did Aeschylus use the *ekkyklema* here?" we must consider all the possible occasions in extant Greek drama in which the *ekkyklema* might have been used, and relate our decision to what we would decide in the other instances.

Consideration of a question like that of the use of the *ekkyklema* illustrates exactly the method I have chosen to adopt in this enquiry. We ask whether the *ekkyklema* was used for such and such a scene. We rely on our theatrical intuition to tell us whether it was used or not. Sometimes we shall be right, and sometimes we shall be wrong. Sometimes we shall be right.

If we use our intuition we shall sometimes be right; we will be that much nearer the mind of Sophocles or Aristophanes.

If we rest content with scholarship and say the evidence does not allow us to pronounce either way, then we shall not approach close enough to touch the mind of Sophocles or Aristophanes. Then we will never be right.

To summarize the beliefs that I have been trying to state in this chapter, there is a process by which one can enter the mind of a great poet from however distant an age. It is a process of intuition and feeling the coherence of one's intuitions in a rhythm. But because it is a process by which we can be wrong, it is a process by which we can also be right. We shall not necessarily know whether we are right or wrong. But others will soon tell us.

To put this another way, I am saying that the theater can be a way to truth, as significant as any philosophical way. By asking the question, "How do we show x?" we are led to know x. It is not Platonic knowledge, it is not the knowledge of philosophers. But it is knowledge in terms of the only thing that is truly important in the theater: the *duende*, and its concomitant cry of recognition, "Olé."

Now our knowledge progresses by means of a series of cries of "Olé." We understand more and more because we have recognized that particular moments of theater poetry, with their staging implications, possess *duende*. Our understanding is not so much ability to control a technique as openness to a series of lightning flashes. We return to the difference between poetry and the other arts. One learns to compose at a school of music; one learns to paint at a school of art. Where does one learn poetry? Alone, and in darkness.

As composers we can learn much from other composers who have technique, even if their music does not fire us; as painters likewise. But not as poets; not as theatrical performers. We learn by trying to stand beside our masters and be struck with sparks that ricochet from them.

In poetry and theater magic, we cannot learn anything at all unless there is *duende*.

From the death of Aristophanes until the Middle Ages, there was one and a half millennia of theater that may have possessed *duende* but could not capture it with words of fire. The great dancers of whom Lucian writes may well have been vehicles for blazing *duende*. But that *duende* is lost.

The *duende* of Aeschylus, Sophocles, Euripides and Aristophanes still burns in their words on a written page. It can be resurrected.

In all the extant plays of later antiquity from the high dignity of Seneca to the naughty pornography of Herodas, there is not one moment of *duende*. In almost every play of the fifth century we are hardly allowed to be ignorant of the *duende*'s presence for a moment.

The rich culture of the late Middle Ages discovered "Ancient Greece" and added it as one more ingredient of their inspiration. But they confronted ancient Greece only through its second-rate imitators, knew only Terence and Seneca, not Aristophanes and Aeschylus. As an ingredient of inspiration the obvious inadequacies of the Latin writers may have been more useful to them. It is said that Bach would always start a day's composing by playing a piece of someone else's music. But he very often chose some rather bad music, second rate, inadequate.

The surprising thing is how little the Western world, which claims so much to value the heritage of Greece, has returned to the originals. The easiest demonstration of this is given by the way in which, for the most part, classically educated people have been happy to refer to Jupiter or Ulysses when they meant Zeus or Odysseus. The Latin names of the characters of Greek mythology are artificial. At no point in Roman history was Jupiter real to the Romans, as Zeus was once to the Greeks. The Western world has on the whole paid lip service to the culture of ancient Athens, without confronting its reality. British public schools in the Victorian era based their education on Greek classics, but cut out, for example, the eroticism on which so many of these classics were based. We have been fobbed off with imitations too long.

There is an image of Classicism that has inspired much of what is fine in the Western tradition: white marble, rationality, scientific method. It has little relation to the culture of ancient Athens, but that is not the point here. What is more important is that it has now failed as an inspiration for us to live by.

Confronted with the neat rationality of Hitler's Final Solution, or the triumphs of scientific method such as an intercontinental ballistic missile with multiple nuclear warhead, there is a tendency to reject all reason, to indulge in total emotionalism, to abandon all disciplines, all training, for untrammeled free expression.

This also is discussed in relation to the Greeks. It is called Dionysiac frenzy. Nietzsche himself found inspiration in what he conceived as the unbridled passion of the worship of Dionysus.

I have compared already the almost limitless surging emotions of Wagner and of modern rock. Is this Dionysiac? Is this where Western culture will find its soul?

Such an answer aside, it is not the culture of fifth-century Athens. We notice in *The Bacchants* that it is the women who refused to accept Dionysus who are driven mad and rave out of control. But not the girls who followed Dionysus from the beginning. They are very sane indeed.

Duende is precise. Precise as the tiny place for the matador's sword point.

The poet who is taken most often as the type of ancient Athens is Sophocles: dancer, general, and priest. A man who started his public career by dancing naked to celebrate a victory, and who finished it by being a member of a war cabinet at over eighty. A man who won the competition more or less every other year and never came lower than second. A man to whom, after he had died, the city sacrificed.

A poet, dare we say it, of *duende*.

Duende is as precise as the stab of the matador's sword.

Theatrical magic is so often almost indistinguishable from grotesque ham.

Almost, but not quite.

The edge of the abyss. Not over the edge. But not away from the danger of the edge either.

So far I have carefully not defined *duende*. For if anyone needs to have the word defined, then what I have written will make nonsense to him anyhow. But I have in my mind all the time the talk Lorca gave on the *duende*.[2] For Lorca there are three facets of the *duende:* it is a constant sense of the presence and power of death; it is based on the nature of dance as a religious act; it operates most especially in dance, song, and spoken poetry. By this we know that these three arts are inextricably linked.

I have searched in vain for a description of the power of Dionysus. The ancients did not need to describe the one they knew. And he seems to have eluded the moderns. But as we read the last paragraph of Lorca's lecture we chill with recognition. For while he thinks that he is describing the *duende*, he is describing Dionysus.

El duende . . . ; Donde está el duende? Por el arco vacío entra un aire mental que sopla con insistencia sobre las cabezas de los muertos, en busca de nuevos paisajes y acentos ignorados; un aire con olor de saliva de niño, de hierba machacada y velo de medusa que anuncia el constante bautizo de las cosas recién creadas.[3]

We cannot but think of Heracleitus:

One is the Lord of Death, and Dionysus of the raving maenads.

The theatrical experience is the search for *duende*. The worship of Dionysus is a means of encountering the *duende*. Fifth-century Athens stands perhaps for all time as the type of a free society. Fifth-century Athens's culture was based on the worship of Dionysus, the encounter with the *duende*.

Fifth-century Athens was a place that would, after his death, worship a poet. Not a philosopher; not a pop singer; a poet.

Was the freedom of Athens inextricably linked with its cult of poetry?

We have no means, no terms for answering these questions. I raise them now, at the end of an essay about the theater, as an acknowledgement that everything we learn in the theater is unanalyzable, unexplainable.

I have merely tried to shout, "Olé" at certain manifestations of the *duende* in the drama of fifth-century Athens.

In this activity there can be no summing up. The *duende* cannot be summarized.

But the *duende* will show us a place to end.

Sophocles, the poet of the *duende*, dancer, priest, and general, was put with a few others in charge of his beloved country's war effort. The final defeat of Athens was very near. Sophocles was ninety. He could no longer go out to fight, any more than he could dance. He could still make one last poem.

The *Oedipus at Colonus* is a struggle with death: it is the poem of the *duende*. In it Sophocles tears the form of fifth-century drama as *la Niña de los Peines* tore her voice with *cazalla,* the fire-water brandy, in order to burn the tavern at Cadiz that she had failed to conquer for all her careful effects and voice control.[4]

The *Oedipus at Colonus* is the play to consider when we want to know of what the fifth century was capable. We do not use the last quartets of Beethoven as a normal method of analysis when studying quartet form; but if we do not take account of them, the string quartet is made smaller. The *Oedipus at Colonus* is like the C sharp minor quartet. Sophocles, like *la Niña de los Peines,* has thrown away the "scaffolding of the song" in order to confront death direct.

We are more conscious of the abyss's edge, because we are aware that Athens as we knew it is dying. If the city is defeated, there will be no more dances. And the city has rejected its one general capable of saving it. The city will be defeated, and there will be no more dances next year. What can Sophocles do?

Sophocles makes use of his own incapacity. He is old, and therefore weak. So he creates dances of old men, acknowledging their weakness. He creates a battle dance with the trembling limbs of old men who can no longer wield a spear. By making the battle take place through these incongruous, grotesque, incompetent actions, Sophocles can be there himself.

Sophocles is old, and therefore ugly. For to all who have been beautiful or athletic when young, old age, however distinguished, must be ugly. Old age is the worst insult to humanity imaginable. To die old, weak, and ugly is in many ways worse than to die in full possession of mental and physical strength. So Sophocles takes Oedipus, the type of the horribly ugly, polluted old man, blind and weak, and therefore somewhat grotesque. Sophocles creates Theseus, the priest-king, the type of the noblest ruler, and Theseus accepts the polluted old Oedipus into the state of Athens.

Sophocles is himself Theseus, the priest-king. He is also Oedipus, old, weak, and horrible. He, in his capacity as priest-king, accepts this example of horrible old age into the state of Athens.

Theseus accepts Oedipus. Sophocles accepts his own old age and imminent death.

But the death of Oedipus will be a source of power. His body buried in the ground will bring victory to Athens. Sophocles offers his own death as a source of power to his beloved city.

Sophocles could not have written the *Oedipus at Colonus* unless he had been at the point of death himself. May we not say that, at the point of death, he knew. Knew that Athens was defeated, and that there would be no more dances as he had led them. Knew that he himself would be among the immortals, and that while lying in the ground he would be a perpetual source of power to an Athens of the mind. Knew that it was with this poem, written on the very edge of death, and performed when he was already buried, that the reign of this *duende* would be closed, since it is inconceivable for anyone to follow the *Oedipus at Colonus* with another Greek tragedy that would not be an absurd anticlimax. Knew therefore that he had come so close to this *duende,* this Dionysus, that not only must he die for having seen so much, but also the *duende,* the Dionysus, would be frightened and flee away, lest men should know too much and walk easily on that edge where it is only right to step delicately and in great fear.

Somewhere here lies the secret: that it is right to celebrate death, that this hateful, ugly distortion of a human being into twisted rubbish is an empty arch through which blows baptism of new creation. It offends our sense of logic to the utmost. But how much can we achieve in the theater by logic? How much in life? Other ages have found means of expressing this contradiction in terms that did not drive them mad. We are aware only of the madness, the contradiction. We rage at the empty arch.

Our space is empty. We rage at the empty arch.

The statement with which I began this enquiry contradicts the statement with which I end it. That also is part of the secret, for which we have no name.

Sophocles, however, did have a name. He called it Dionysus, lord of death and lord of life. He ended his greatest play, his most open confrontation with the *duende,* with the celebration of a death. The earth swallows an ugly old man. Not even his daughters may be with the old man when he goes. No one must know the place of his death except the priest-king. The secret of the *duende* is vanishing back into the earth as Sophocles himself is dying. It vanishes; the poet dies. But something was left in that soil to fertilize our minds forever. The last dance of the *Oedipus at Colonus* is a prayer for Oedipus' death. The last line therefore of the last extant dance of the fifth century, the century of the *duende,* is an invocation to the lord of unending sleep. But what has survived to tease our minds two and a half millennia later with its still unending strength is more than sleep.

And somewhere there, perhaps, lies the secret.

As Wittgenstein said at the end of the *Tractatus:*

> Wovon mann nicht wissen kann, darüber muss mann schweigen.
> Where one cannot know, there one must be silent.

> Dare it be right for me, goddess unnameable,
> Dare it be right t'adore thee,
> Lord of the drowned in night,
> Aidoneus Underworld.
> Take all pain from his passing,
> Pain of the horror screaming.
> Let him gently achieve
> The way where all must disappear
> In the river of Hell and the valley of bones.
> Look, look, the marked face, the crass
> Permeation of his pain.
> Is there a power, below, to aid him?

Goddess and queen of dark where the untameable
Beast of your secret threshold
Trodden by all mankind
Must sleep, sleep, sleep, growl, growl
Through deep caves, never muzzled
Sentry for everlasting
As the stories have told.
Oh Lord, earth's child and child of Hell,
Oh Lord I pray that a peace may fall,
Lord guide this man through the waste,
Through the black expanse of bones.
On Thee I call Lord, the sleep unending.[5]

Notes

1. Friedrich Nietzsche, *The Birth of Tragedy,* trans. W. A. Haussmann (Edinburgh and London: J. N. Foulis, 1909), p. 114:

"The Greeks, as charioteers, hold in their hands the reins of our own and every culture, but almost always chariot and horses are of too poor material and incommensurate with the glory of their guides, who then will deem it sport to run such a team into an abyss: which they themselves clear with the leap of Achilles."

2. Federico Garcia Lorca, "Teoria y Juego del Duende," a lecture given in Havana and Buenos Aires, published in Federico Garcia Lorca, *Obras Completas* (Madrid: Aguilar, 1968), pp. 109–21. An English translation is printed in the Penguin edition of Lorca's poetry. *Lorca,* selected and trans. J. L. Gili (Harmondsworth: Penguin Books, 1960), pp. 127–39.

3. In Gili's translation:

"The *duende*—where is the *duende?* Through the empty arch comes an air of the mind that blows insistently over the heads of the dead, in search of new landscapes and unsuspected accents; an air smelling of a child's saliva, of pounded grass, and medusal veil announcing the constant baptism of newly created things."

4. Lorca, *Obras Completas,* p. 112; in Gili's translation, p. 131.

5. *Oedipus at Colonus* 1556–78. This translation published in Leo Aylen, *I, Odysseus* (London: Sidgwick & Jackson, 1971), p. 58.

Appendix 1
Chronological Summary

The Greek year changed in March. For convenience however I ignore this and take the year as starting in January. Strictly speaking, we should for instance refer to *The Frogs* as being produced at the *Lenaia* of 406–5, since the *Lenaia* was in January.

An asterisk indicates a probable but not certain date. An asterisk plus a dagger indicate a date that is conjecture. Naturally, I have had to allocate somewhat arbitrarily.

Tragedies should be assumed to have been produced at the City *Dionysia* unless indicated.

Titles in parentheses indicate a nonextant play.

DATE B.C.	PUBLIC EVENTS WITH SOME RELE- VANCE TO THE THEATER	EVENTS IN THEATER HISTORY	FIRST PRODUC- TIONS OF PLAYS
c. 650		Archilochus flourishes.	
c. 600		Arion flourishes.	
		Stesichoros flourishes.	
c. 590	Cleisthenes, tyrant of Sicyon, flourishes.		
560	Pisistratus first seizes power in Athens.	Thespis flourishes.	
534	Pisistratus founds the City *Dionysia.*	Thespis wins the first competition for tragedy.	
527	Pisistratus dies. His sons, Hippias and Hip- parchus, continue his rule.		
525		Aeschylus born.	
514	Hipparchus assas- sinated. Hippias reacts by ruling much more savagely.		

DATE B.C.	PUBLIC EVENTS WITH SOME RELE-VANCE TO THE THEATER	EVENTS IN THEATER HISTORY (continued)	FIRST PRODUC-TIONS OF PLAYS
510	Hippias is expelled from Athens.		
509		Pratinas introduces the satyr play into the tragic competition.	
495		Sophocles born.	
492			Phrynichus, (Capture of Miletus)
490	Battle of Marathon. Persian invasion de-feated by Athenian in-fantry, amongst whom was Aeschylus.		
486		First comic competi-tion. Chionides wins.	
480s		Epicharmus flourishes.	
		Seats in the theater col-lapse and are rebuilt.	
484		Aeschylus' first victory.	
480	Battle of Salamis. Per-sian invasion defeated at sea by Athenian general Themistocles. Aeschy-lus fights with infantry.	Euripides born. Sophocles dances the naked boy dance to celebrate victory.	
476			Phrynichus, (Phoeni-cian Women)
472			Aeschylus, Persians
470	Themistocles exiled from Athens.		
468		Sophocles' first victory.	
467			Aeschylus Seven against Thebes
463			Aeschylus, Suppliants tetralogy
462	Pericles and Ephialtes reform the Athenian constitution, depriving the Areopagus of all powers except that of		

DATE B.C.	PUBLIC EVENTS WITH SOME RELEVANCE TO THE THEATER	EVENTS IN THEATER HISTORY *(continued)*	FIRST PRODUCTIONS OF PLAYS
	being the supreme court.		
458			Aeschylus, *Oresteia* (1st prize)
457			Aeschylus, *Prometheus Bound** in Sicily, probably Gela
456		Aeschylus dies in Sicily.	
455		Euripides' first competition.	
449		First competition for tragic actors at City *Dionysia*.	
446		Aristophanes born.	Sophocles, *Ajax*
late 440s		Pericles rebuilds the theater, builds the Odeion, where the *proagōn* can take place.	
441		Euripides' first victory.	
440			Sophocles, *Antigone* (1st prize)
	Samian War. Sophocles a general with Pericles.		
438			Euripides, *Alcestis*
432	Peloponnesian War starts.		
430			Euripides, *Children of Heracles*
early 420s			Sophocles, *Women of Trachis**
428			Euripides, *Hippolytus*
427		Aristophanes' first production.	
		Plato born.	
426	Aristophanes prosecuted by Cleon after producing the *Babylonians*.		Euripides, *Andromache** not produced at Athens

DATE B.C.	PUBLIC EVENTS WITH SOME RELEVANCE TO THE THEATER	EVENTS IN THEATER HISTORY (continued)	FIRST PRODUCTIONS OF PLAYS
mid 420s			Sophocles, *Oedipus the King** (2d prize)
425			Aristophanes, *Acharnians* (1st prize at *Lenaia*)
			Euripides, *Hecuba, Cyclops**†
424			Aristophanes, *Knights* (1st prize at *Lenaia*)
late 420s	Sophocles becomes priest of the sacred snake of Asclepius.		Euripides, *Heracles, Suppliant Women*
423			Aristophanes, *Clouds* (3d prize at *Dionysia*)
422			Aristophanes, *Wasps* (1st or 2d prize)
421			Aristophanes, *Peace* (2d prize at *Dionysia*)
	Peace of Nikias signed with Sparta.		
417	Athens allies with Argos, enemy of Sparta.	Agathon's victory as described in Plato, *Drinking Party* or *Symposium*	Sophocles, *Electra**
416	The island of Melos surrenders. All males are massacred.		
415			Euripides, *Trojan Women* (2d prize)
	Sicilian expedition sails. Mutilation of the herms.		
414			Aristophanes, *Birds* (2d prize at *Dionysia*)
			Euripides, *Iphigeneia in Tauris**
413	Total defeat of Athenians in Sicily.		Euripides, *Electra**
	Probouloi appointed, Sophocles among them.		

DATE B.C.	PUBLIC EVENTS WITH SOME RELEVANCE TO THE THEATER	EVENTS IN THEATER HISTORY (continued)	FIRST PRODUCTIONS OF PLAYS
412			Euripides, *Helen, Ion*
411	The coup d'état of the Four Hundred oligarchs, who are then replaced by the Five Thousand.		Aristophanes, *Lysistrata*
410	Restoration of democracy at Athens.		Aristophanes, *Women at the Thesmophoria*
409	Alcibiades returns to Athens, in power.		Sophocles, *Philoctetes*
408			Euripides, *Orestes*
407	Alcibiades leaves Athens.	Euripides dies in Macedonia.	
406			Euripides, *Bacchants* and *Iphigeneia at Aulis* (1st prize)
405	Battle of Arginusae. Athens beats Sparta at sea, but puts six generals to death for negligence.	Sophocles dies.	Aristophanes, *Frogs* (1st prize at *Lenaia*)
404	Athens finally defeated by Spartan general Lysander at Aegospotami. Lysander occupies Athens, imposes oligarchic government, the Thirty.		
403	Democracy restored at Athens.		
401			Sophocles, *Oedipus at Colonus*
399	Death of Socrates.		
393			Aristophanes, *Women at the Assembly*
388			Aristophanes, *Wealth*
386		Aristophanes dies.	

DATE B.C.	PUBLIC EVENTS WITH SOME RELEVANCE TO THE THEATER	EVENTS IN THEATER HISTORY (continued)	FIRST PRODUCTIONS OF PLAYS
late 380s		Plato, *Republic.**	*Rhesus**†
343		Menander born.	
338	Athens and Thebes defeated by Philip of Macedon at Chaeronea.		
336	Philip killed. Alexander succeeds.		
330		Lycurgus rebuilds the theater at Athens.	
		Aristotle, *Poetics.*	
326			Python, *Agen*, produced on Alexander's campaign
323		Menander's first production.	
322	Alexander dies. The empire parted between his five generals.		
320s	Epicurus flourishes at Athens.		
317			Menander, *Bad-tempered Man*
316		Menander's first victory.	
293 or 290		Menander dies.	
300– 270		Theocritus flourishes.	
270s– 250		Herodas flourishes.	
254		Plautus born.	
			(Few of Plautus' plays can be dated exactly)
205			Plautus, *Braggart Soldier*
before 201			Plautus, *Cistellaria*

DATE B.C.	PUBLIC EVENTS WITH SOME RELE-VANCE TO THE THEATER	EVENTS IN THEATER HISTORY (continued)	FIRST PRODUC-TIONS OF PLAYS
200			Plautus, *Stichus*
191			Plautus, *Pseudolus*
185		Plautus dies. Terence born.	
166			Terence, *Woman of Andros* (at *Ludi Megalenses*)
165			Terence, *Mother-in-Law* (fails)
163			Terence's *Self-Tormentor* (at *Ludi Megalenses*)
161			Terence, *Eunuch* (at *Ludi Megalenses*)
			Terence, *Phormio* (at *Ludi Romani*)
160			Terence, *Brothers* and 2d production of *Mother-in-Law* (at funeral games for Scipio's father)
			Terence, 3d production of *Mother-in-Law*
A.D. 22		Bathyllus and Pylades found the pantomime.	
54	Nero accedes as emperor.		
50s		Seneca writes his plays.	
68	Nero assassinated.		
early 70s			Seneca, *Octavia**

Appendix 2
Principles of Translation

All translation is to a certain extent interpretation. We can never reproduce the whole of great poetry in another language. Any translator must start with this acknowledgment.

As a general principle I believe that the rhythm of poetry is almost as important as its sense. I therefore believe that a translation should try as much as possible to preserve the rhythms of the original.

I have therefore translated all strophic lyrics isometrically; my English versions reproduce the line patterns of the Greek exactly, granted the fact that English is a stressed language, and therefore that the note values of the verse line in English will be somewhat arbitrary. These English versions could at any rate be set to the same tune as the Greek. I have also endeavored to place the words demanding emphasis at the same point in the line as they occupy in the Greek. Especially in Sophocles, this placing of words in relation to a rhythmic climax is so important that we ignore it at our peril.

In order to do this I have not hesitated to change grammatical structure or to repeat words. English is much more monosyllabic than Greek, and usually a sentence of Greek poetry can be translated into English using fewer syllables.

In astrophic lyrics, or the epodes attached to *stasima*, I have not been so strict with myself, since the original does not require two stanzas in the same meter. I have followed the Greek lyric more or less exactly, but allowed the natural tendency of English to shorten and compress, and have also made use of rhyme to tighten the lyric as English tends to require.

There is really no exact equivalent in modern English verse for the anapest passages in Greek drama. I have translated anapests into a stressed verse with lines of varying length, often using rhyme, and sometimes allowing the English to be slightly shorter than the Greek.

I am now convinced that the best line with which to represent in today's English the iambic trimeter of tragedy is the four-stress ballad line, as used by T. S. Eliot in *Murder in the Cathedral*. For short quotations, however, I have sometimes used the traditional blank verse line, either because the translations had been done before I had decided on the principle, as in the case of those passages reproduced from *Greek Tragedy and the Modern World*, or because, for a line or two, blank verse simply seemed to work better.

I do not now consider that there is one verse form that will represent the iambic trimeter of Aristophanes. Any very loose verse form in modern English is pointless, because it simply sounds like mannered prose. I therefore mainly translate Aristophanes' dialogue into prose, going into different varieties of verse as the mood of the scene requires.

With the exception of Aristophanes' character-names, I have tried to translate all the theatrical effects in the verse of the original. When there is a pun, I have tried to present a pun, and so on. We cannot always reproduce the exact pun or wordplay. But it seems right to reproduce something as near as possible to the original. To leave out such verbal effects altogether is to fail to translate part of the original.

As I said in the Preface, I have avoided genuine translation of the names of Aristophanes' characters, and merely rendered them into a colorless English, lacking theatrical tone. As can be seen from the discussion in Chapter 7, "*The Peace*, Presentation of Theoria to the Council," a name can be a complex of pun, allusion, and cultural reference, which is not easy for us to unravel in its entirety. Each translation of a proper name involves so much discussion of the tone of the play that it would take up too much space in such a book as this. A few notes must suffice here.

First, Aristophanes' names are all convincing as names. So we must make them sound like names in English. British English possesses—as perhaps American English does not—a rich store of genuine British surnames full of suggestiveness: Plank, Slaughter, Lovett, Sidebottom. Ben Jonson makes abundant use of this. His names in *Bartholomew Fair* range from Leatherhead, which does exist as a surname, though used here for its meaning; to Littlewit, Wasp, and Cutting, which three may or may not be actual surnames, though they sound as if they were; to Overdo and Purecraft, which though I am sure they are not surnames, yet do not sound so different from Leatherhead. The names of Aristophanes' characters are perhaps best rendered into English in terms of such surnames.

Second, we must note how subtle Aristophanes is in the amount of equivocation that he puts into his names. "Disband-the-Army" is an exact rendering of Lysistrata. Its inadequacy as translation is simply that it does not sound like a name. We might call her Miss Warsend, Miss Warsender, or Miss Troopshome. The same is true of Dikaiopolis ("Just-City") who could perhaps be called Mr. Justville or of Euelpides ("Optimist") who could be called Mr. Hopewell, or—incorrect grammar conveying a less classy character—Mr. Hopegood. Strepsiades, which I have rendered "Twister," and Pheidippides, which I have rendered "Horsey," are more equivocal. The *-des* ending means "son of," and the *Pheid-* in Pheidippides has the sense of "spare." Pheidippides means "Son-of-Spare-the-Horses"; he spends all his time and money on horses, and there is a joke about his name of which we do not have all the parts (*Clouds* 60–65). The name Strepsiades is not meant immediately to imply a twister, and although the *Streps-* can imply a meaning of deceit, the connotation might be more "twirling" than "twisting." As we examine the total effect of *The Clouds*, how much do we consider Strepsiades a rogue, and how much a fool? Our answer will determine our choice of name: Mr. Twistison? Mr. Wrigley? Mr. Wriglison? Mr. Turner? Mr. Wheeler? Mr. Twiddle? Mr. Twiddlison?

This also brings out the third consideration: the need to decide on the degree of irony that we put into our version of a name. Perhaps the most complex name to work on is Pisthetairos, which I discussed very briefly in Chapter 7, "*The Birds*, Finale," is obviously relevant. Pisthetairos could be translated literally "trusty comrade," though there is an ambivalence in the Greek as to the relationship of the trust- part to the comrade part of the word. For the BBC I called him "Mr. Trustworth," and left the irony to the context. Since he is a confidence trickster, should we call him Mr. Confriend? Or on the lines of the more extravagant Ben Jonson names, Mr. Utrustmeebuddy? Or would it even be fair to take advantage of the English sound equivalence of trust = trussed, and equivocate totally with Mr. Budditrust?

On the subject of Aristophanes' bawdry there is not much that needs to be said beyond what was said in the Preface. If Aristophanes could create scenes of such flagrant sexiness as that of the Megarian's daughters (*Acharnians* 729–835), or the presentation of Theoria (*Peace* 856–921), it is hardly surprising that he should use sexual language of utter bluntness. Those who still hesitate about the propriety of using our crudest "four-letter words" in the translation of Aristophanes should refer to Dover's *Aristophanic Comedy*, in which every one of the "four-letter words" can be found as translation or paraphrase of Aristophanes. They should also read Dover's discussion on p. 38, in which he distinguishes four "strata" (Dover's own word) in Greek sexual language: the equivalent of our "four-letter words"; slang words with sexual connotation (Dover instancing "strike," though I should have thought "make" or "come" more frequent); words used by "proper" people, such as "private parts"; and finally, coy euphemisms. Dover says very firmly that the last two strata have no place in the language of Old Comedy, which only makes use of the first two. See Sir Kenneth Dover, *Aristophanic Comedy* (London: Batsford, 1972), p. 38 and passim. We find some of the same sexual forthrightness in later writing, such as the "mimes" of Herodas, or the anonymous "mime" discovered as a papyrus. See Chapter 12, "The Mime."

Appendix 3
Glossary of Terms Used

acatalectic; catalectic
There are two versions of the long chanted lines in comedy, the iambic and trochaic tetrameters. The acatalectic version is exactly four metra. In the catalectic version the last metron is syncopated: if iambic, |♪♩♩ ♩ |; if trochaic, |♩ ♪♩ ♩ | Possibly these final syllables are one of the few examples of the double long in Greek meter, so that it is strictly: if iambic, |♪♩ ♩. |; if trochaic, |♩ ♪♩. |.

agōn
Means "contest." As used technically, it is one of the three parts of the traditional form of Old Comedy. A contest between two actors, or between the leading actor and the chorus, it can have a strict form of lyric *strophē*, epirrhema, lyric *antistrophē*, antepirrhema. But Aristophanes uses the form freely.

anapest
|♪♪♩ |. An anapest metron is |♪♪♩ ♪♪♩ |. Spondees |♩ ♩ | and dactyls |♩ ♪♪ | can be substituted for anapests. Anapests are for the most part chanted, not sung. Anapest dimeters are used for the entry march of the tragic chorus, for linking passages between sung lyrics and episodes, or on their own within episodes. Anapest tetrameters are the most dignified of the three chanted meters in comedy.

antepirrhema
See *epirrhema*.

antistrophē
See *strophē*.

archon
When Athens abolished its hereditary kingship, the leading officers were annually elected *archons*. By the fifth century they retained only ceremonial functions. The King Archon performed priestly duties; the year was still named from the name of the Eponymous Archon.

astrophic
An astrophic lyric is one not composed in systems of matching *strophē* and *antistrophē*.

Atē
The destruction that comes upon those who interfere with the workings of *Dikē*, a destruction that also brings delusion upon its victims.

Attic
Attica was the entire district of which Athens was the capital, and so Attic becomes almost synonymous with "Athenian."

aulos
A reed instrument like a primitive oboe. The player would have two in his mouth at once, and with the two together he could obtain about fifteen or sixteen notes. It was the main accompanying instrument for both tragedy and the dithyramb. It is very often translated "flute," which it was not.

catalectic
See *acatalectic.*

choregos, **pl.** *choregoi*
In effect the producer. A rich citizen was liable to be nominated to perform *choregia* as a state service. The *choregos* paid for virtually the whole production except the actors' salaries.

choreutes, **pl.** *choreutai*
A member of a chorus.

coryphaeus
The leader of the chorus. He spoke the lines of dialogue marked "chorus," as well as leading the singing and dancing.

dactyl
♩ ♩ ♪ ♪ |. A metron is one dactyl. The dactylic hexameter is the meter of the Homeric epic, and also of oracles. Dactyls were chanted, and did not have accompanying movement.

Dikē
The word "justice" and sometimes can be so translated. But it is much wider in scope. It is the order of nature of which moral order is a special instance. *Dikē* involves the fact that water flows downhill. The concept nearest to it that we possess is that of Natural Law.

dimeter
A line of two metra.

dithyramb
As it were, a tragedy without any dialogue episodes, merely lyrics sung and danced. During the fifth century the dithyramb seems to have become rather stately, almost an oratorio. The dithyrambic chorus had fifty members. The competition was tribal: each tribe entered a boys' chorus and a men's chorus, though in a given year only one of the two would perform.

epirrhema; antepirrhema
The *parabasis* of Old Comedy is symmetrical. It consists of an introductory passage, usually in chanted anapest tetrameters, a lyric *strophē*, epirrhema, lyric *antistrophē*, antepirrhema. Epirrhema and antepirrhema are the same length; they are chanted "speeches" by the chorus leader in iambic or trochaic tetrameters to which the chorus dance; hence the symmetry. Aristophanes sometimes uses this symmetry in the *agōn* as well, though he is usually only approximately symmetrical there.

episode
A portion of a play between lyrics; a dialogue scene.

epode
A part of a lyric that does not have a stanza to match it. Strictly speaking, if an unmatched stanza occurs in the middle of a lyric it is called a mesode, and called an epode only if it occurs at the end, as most do.

exodos
The final song of the chorus, sometimes a dance in systems, sometimes a march out to anapest chant.

hoplite
A heavy infantryman. A soldier provided his own armor. Those who were able to provide themselves with heavy armor needed to be moderately wealthy. The hoplites therefore are the middle class. The upper class served in the cavalry, and the lowest class rowed in the fleet, or sometimes, served as light-armed soldiers.

kommos
A lament. A lyric sequence for one or two soloists and chorus.

kōmos
The revel out of which comedy grew. An informal carnival-type procession in which abuse was hurled at prominent citizens. The City *Dionysia* included a *kōmos*, either at the end, or at the end of the first day.

kothornos
The socklike boot worn by most actors and *choreutai*. Because the word was especially used for stage footwear, it came to be applied to the boots with blocked soles used on the later high stage from the third century B.C. onwards.

libation
A ceremonial action of pouring out a little wine for the gods to drink, before drinking oneself. It was customary to pour libations at drinking parties. It was also the standard practice when signing a peace treaty. So the word for a peace treaty is simply *spondai*—libations.

maenads
Girls who worship Dionysus and are ecstatically possessed by him. The fluid movements of the maenads' dance are a favourite subject for the vase painters.

mēchanē
A crane by which an actor could be swung into the air, either to appear like a

god, above the top of the *skēnē*, or else to be lowered in front of the *skēnē*. If the actor had to step out of the *mēchanē*, he would normally travel in or on some vehicle from which he could dismount more easily than out of the no doubt cumbersome harness.

mesode
See *epode*.

metron
The unit of metrical measurement. Unfortunately it is not the same as the Latin "foot." An iambic, trochaic, or an anapest metron is two iambs, trochees, or anapests. Hence the six-foot dialogue iambic line is called a trimeter—three metra. On the other hand, a dactylic metron is only one dactylic foot.

"mime"
The translation of the very general Greek word *mimos*, which refers to a sketch with or without dialogue, and also to the performer of such work.

When I use mime without quotation marks, I intend the usual modern sense of acting without dialogue and props.

monody
A solo lyric in free, i.e., astrophic, meter, found in the later tragedy of Euripides especially.

numinous
Some power other than myself. The Latin derivation implies a lack of specification as to the nature of the power. Use of this concept leaves open the question as to whether the power is supernatural or psychological—whether, in theological terms, it is transcendent or immanent. The God of Judaism or Islam is transcendent, apart from His creation. The Greek gods were conceived as immanent, part of creation. It is wrong to use the term *supernatural* with reference to Dionysus or the other Olympians. When talking of the ancient Greeks' apprehension of their gods we must not specify further than is implied by the use of the term *numinous.*

onkos
The distorted high forehead of the tragic mask in the third century and afterward, devised to balance the effect of the blocked-up shoes.

orchestra
The circular space in front of the *skēnē* in which the chorus danced. During the fifth century it was roughly sixty feet in diameter.

parabasis
Part of the traditional form of Old Comedy, in which the chorus address the audience direct, with no actors on stage. It usually consists of an introduction in chanted anapest tetrameters, then a lyric *strophē*, epirrhema, lyric *antistrophē* and antepirrhema.

parodos, pl. parodoi
The two *parodoi* were approach paths set between the ends of the auditorium's horseshoe and the *skēnē*. They afforded the main entrances into the *orchestra.*

Because this was the normal way in which the chorus would enter the *orchestra,* the word *parodos* came to be used of the opening song-dance of the chorus, whether preceded by an anapest march, chanted as they marched up the *parodos,* or merely sung systems danced in the *orchestra* itself.

periaktoi
A device whereby part of the *skēnē* wall could be revolved to show different, stylized, settings.

pnigos
Literally, a choke. To be performed in one breath. The climax of a chanted epirrhema, in dimeters instead of tetrameters.

proagōn
A ceremony preliminary to the dramatic competition. It took place in the Odeion, built by Pericles. The competing poets appeared with their *choregoi* and the actors wearing robes and wreaths but no masks. The poets outlined their plays.

prologue
I use this word in its technical Greek sense for all the scenes in iambic dialogue that precede the entry of the chorus. In Euripides this is often merely a prologue in the modern sense, spoken by a god.

scholion, pl. *scholia; scholiast*
During the third century B.C. a tradition of scholarship developed in Alexandria that studied earlier Greek writing as classical texts. The scholars wrote notes—*scholia*—in the manuscripts, and these were copied and added to in Byzantine times. They often provide useful information about the fifth-century plays. But of course we cannot be sure of the date of a particular comment. The word *scholiast* refers to a writer of such notes.

skēnē
The stage building, whose facade, built like a temple, formed the "set" for the plays.

stasimon, pl. *stasima*
A lyric sung and danced by the chorus. The word most probably came into use as referring to what is sung by the chorus when they have reached "their position in the *orchestra,*" i.e., as opposed to the *parodos,* when they are still reaching their position. Because the *parodos* is not a *stasimon*—although it is equally a dance in systems, sometimes preceded by an anapest march, but sometimes starting immediately with a system, just like a *stasimon*—*stasimon* 1 in a play will be the second lyric sequence. Unfortunately, there is no generic Greek word for the chorus song-dances in systems applicable to *parodos, stasima,* and *exodos.*

stichomythia
An interchange between speakers where each has one-line speeches.

strophē, antistrophē, system
A system consists of a *strophē* and *antistrophē,* two metrically identical stanzas

sung to the same tune. In the *antistrophē* identical dance movement is performed to that in the *strophē*, though in the opposite direction. No two systems are alike in extant drama.

tetralogy
Group of four plays linked into one complete work. Aeschylus particularly liked to compose in this way. The word *tetralogy* is not found in the fifth century.

tetrameter
Line of four metra. The characteristic lines of comedy are the chanted tetrameters: anapest, iambic, or trochaic.

theos
Has to be translated "god," though it sometimes seems right to translate it more vaguely as "power." The Greeks before Plato did not really possess the idea of gods apart from nature. The early Greek gods were immanent, not transcendent; part of nature, not its creators.

thyrsus
The wand brandished by bacchants, a sacred object.

trilogy
A group of three plays linked into one unity, in other words a tetralogy without the satyr play. The word is not found until long after the fifth century.

trimeter
A line of three metra. The most common is the iambic trimeter, the line of spoken dialogue in both tragedy and comedy.

Appendix 4
Notes on Some Greek Meters

Spoken

Iambic trimeter

The meter used for the spoken dialogue in both tragedy and comedy. ♪♩ ♪♩ | ♪'♩ ♪'♩ | ♪♩ ♪♩ . It behaves roughly like English blank verse. In various parts of the line other metrical forms can be substituted for an iambic. Not only ♪♪♪ , but also ♩ ♩ , ♪♪♩ , even ♩ ♪♪ . Generally speaking the line becomes looser as time goes on. Euripides allows more resolutions than Aeschylus. As we might expect, comedy allows a looser line than tragedy. The line is transferred into Latin more or less exactly to be the dialogue line in Latin tragedy and comedy.

Chanted

Dactylic hexameter

The line of the Homeric epics and oracles: ♩ ♪♪ | ♩ ♪♪ | ♩ ' ♪♪ | ♩ ' ♪♪ | ♩ ♪♪ | ♩ ♩ Spondees (♩ ♩) are allowed for dactyls in most parts of the line, but anapests are not. It has therefore been suggested that a dactyl was slightly different from other meters; its ♩ did not exactly equal ♪ ♪ ; but the metron was almost like the slightly uneven three-four time of a quick waltz: $\frac{3}{4}$ ♩ ♩ ♩ |

357

Tetrameter; anapest, iambic, and trochaic

anapest acatalectic: ♫♩ ♫♩ | ♫♩ ♫♩ | ♫♩ ♫♩ | ♫♩ ♫♩

anapest catalectic: ♫♩ ♫♩ | ♫♩ ♫♩ | ♫♩ ♫♩ | ♩ |

iambic acatalectic: ♪♩ ♪♩ | ♪♩ ♪♩ | ♪♩ ♪♩ | ♪♩ ♪♩ |

iambic catalectic: ♪♩ ♪♩ | ♪♩ ♪♩ | ♪♩ ♪♩ | ♪♩ ♩. |

trochaic acatalectic: ♩ ♪♩ ♪| ♩ ♪♩ ♪| ♩ ♪♩ ♪| ♩ ♪♩ ♪|

trochaic catalectic: ♩ ♪♩ ♪| ♩ ♪♩ ♪| ♩ ♪♩ ♪| ♩ ♪♩. |

Dimeters are half the length.
Anapest dimeters are the standard chanting meter of tragedy; trochaic tetrameters are found in early and late fifth-century tragedy, but not in the middle period. Comedy employs all these meters, especially in its traditional parts of *parodos, agōn,* and *parabasis.* Acatalectic versions are very rare in comparison with catalectic.

Sung

Full discussion of the lyric meters is enormously complex. I attempt only the barest summary of those that carry obvious musical implications. Learning Greek lyric meter is a little like learning orchestration; it is relatively easy to describe the purpose and use of trumpets, or dochmiacs; hard to describe the use of violins, or lyric iambics. For proper discussion, see A. M. Dale, *The Lyric Metres of Greek Drama* (London: Cambridge University Press, 1968). In this brief summary I make no distinction between meters that form a complete line, and meters that are combined in various ways to form different kinds of line.

anacreontic

| ♫♩ ♪♩ ♪♩ ♪|, a particular version derived from varying the basic ionic line (q.v.).

The meter of drinking songs, called after its creator, Anacreon, who wrote mainly drinking songs.

cretic

| ♩ ♪♩ |, often used in association with dochmiacs.

dactylo-epitrite

A combination of dactyls │ ♩ ♪♪│ and epitrites │ ♩ ♪♩ ♪│. There is virtually no limit to the possible combinations. A rhythm we find in Pindar, and used first by Sophocles in tragedy, it has a stately feel.

dochmiac

│ ♪♩ ♩ ♪♩ │. The wildest rhythm, used for extremes of sorrow, joy, or fear. Often used astrophically in short sequences of pure dochmiacs. Often also combined with other lyric meters in a system. For all possible variations see Chapter 5, "The Variety of Greek Dance."

ionic

Slow three time, associated with undulating movements. Ionic a majore is │ ♩ ♩ ♪♪│, ionic a minore │ ♪♪♩ ♩ │. But there are a great many variations and combinations.

spondee

│ ♩ ♩ │. Naturally, spondaic rhythm is the most solemn rhythm available.

syncopation

Almost unlimited variations in almost all the common meters can be obtained by syncopation. Lyric iambic metra for instance turn from │ ♪♩ ♪♩ │ to │ ♪♩ ♩ │ or │ ♩ ♪♩ │. This latter demonstrates that the cretic is syncopated iambic, which has, as it were, acquired independent status. The dochmiac, too, probably derives from syncopated iambic.

Appendix 5
The *Orestes* Fragment of Music

A fragment of a musical setting to six lines from Euripides' *Orestes* has been discovered in papyrus. Even this is not complete, and furthermore it has been suggested that this music does not date back to the time of Euripides, though, on balance, most scholars think that it does. Even though we can learn almost nothing from it, I myself find its fragmentary nature enormously exciting. This may be a tune Euripides wrote and sang himself.

It is part of the first *stasimon,* sung by the chorus.

For full discussion, see J. F. Mountford, "Greek Music in the Papyri and Inscriptions," *New Chapters in Greek Literature* 2 (1929): 146–83.

This interpretation is Mountford's. The piece seems to be in the Phrygian mode (enharmonic genus). From Aristotle *Problems* 19. 20 we learn that all good melodies return to the *mese* (mid-note), which all the Dorian fragments seem to do, their *mese* being the fifth note in the descending scale. Unfortunately we do not know the *mese* for the Phrygian mode.

The Phrygian mode is the only one on which Plato and Aristotle disagree. The former makes it a stately mode, the latter an exciting and emotional one. See Aristotle *Politics* 8.5. 1340B. 7; 8.5. 1342B. Aristoxenus (*Harmonics,* 23) says that the enharmonic genus of the Phrygian mode is the noblest mode of all.

signifies the note raised by a quarter-tone.

*There are some notes here, possibly from the accompaniment. If so, we do not know their relationship to the melody.

Appendix 6

The Surviving Plays

At some time in later antiquity a selection of plays by the four great poets was made for study: seven plays by Aeschylus, seven by Sophocles, nine by Euripides, and eleven by Aristophanes. This selection provides all the plays that we possess of Aeschylus and Aristophanes, and almost all of Sophocles. Ten other plays of Euripides, however, also survive, more or less by chance. They do not possess *scholia* and so were not specially studied in later antiquity.

The Searching Satyrs of Sophocles is a chance find, as all papyrus finds are.

All Menander that we possess is due to chance papyrus finds.

Terence's oeuvre is probably complete; Plautus' more or less so. Most probably also we have all of Seneca's plays.

The majority of short fragments survive as quotations in later authors.

Aeschylus: Seven Selected Plays
  Persians; Seven against Thebes, 3d play in a tetralogy; *Suppliants*, 1st play in a tetralogy; *Agamemnon, Libation-Bearers*, and *Eumenides*, 1st three plays in the *Oresteia* tetralogy; *Prometheus Bound*
Of these at one point a further selection was made, as we can tell from the greater quantity of *scholia*:
  Persians, Seven against Thebes, Prometheus Bound

Sophocles: Seven Selected Plays
  Ajax, Antigone, Women of Trachis, Oedipus the King, Electra, Philoctetes, Oedipus at Colonus
Of these three were specially selected:
  Ajax, Oedipus the King, Electra
Of Sophocles we also possess the major part of *The Searching Satyrs* from a papyrus.

Euripides: Nine Selected Plays
  Alcestis, Medea, Hippolytus, Andromache, Hecuba, Trojan Women, Phoenician Women, Orestes, and the almost certainly spurious *Rhesus*
Ten other plays preserved by chance:
  Children of Heracles, Heracles, Cyclops, Suppliant Women, Electra, Iphigeneia in Tauris, Helen, Ion, Iphigeneia at Aulis, Bacchants

Aristophanes: Eleven Selected Plays
  Acharnians, Knights, Clouds, Wasps, Peace, Birds, Lysistrata, Women at the
  Thesmophoria, Frogs, Women at the Assembly, Wealth

Menander: Chance Papyrus Survivals
  Bad-tempered Man, complete
  Arbitration, Girl's Hair-cut, Girl from Samos, almost complete
  About half of the Shield, Hated Man, Man from Sicyon

Plautus: Twenty Plays
  Amphitryo, Donkey-driving, Crock of Gold, Sisters Bacchis, Captives,
  Casina, Box, Worm, Epidicus, Brothers Menaechmus, Merchant, Braggart
  Soldier, Ghost, Persian, Young Carthaginian, Pseudolus, Rope, Stichus,
  Threepenny Play, Truculentus

Terence: Six Plays
  Andria, Self-Tormentor, Eunuch, Phormio, Mother-in-Law, Brothers

Seneca: Nine Plays
  Hercules Mad, Trojan Women, Phoenician Women, Medea, Phaedra,
  Oedipus, Agamemnon, Thyestes, Hercules on Oeta

Pseudo-Seneca: One Play
  Octavia

Appendix 7

Women in the Audience during the Fifth Century

There is some argument as to whether women were allowed to attend the performances in the theater during the fifth century. On balance the evidence is in favor, but a number of scholars have come to the opposite conclusion.

There does not seem much doubt that they attended performances during the fourth century. In two passages in Plato's *Laws* there is definite reference to women watching tragedy (7. 817C, and 2. 658A–D). It is very difficult to see why they should be allowed in during the fourth century, and not during the fifth.

The doubt has mainly arisen from a passage in Aristophanes' *Peace:* "I'll tell my story to the kiddies, to the growing lads, to the men. I'll tell it to the super-he-men most of all" (50–53). But not too much can be put on such a joke as that.

The evidence that points most firmly against there being women is in two lines from Menander's *Bad-tempered Man,* when he invites applause from "kiddies, boys and men" (965–67). But even this is not conclusive evidence. Anyhow, we know that in Menander's day there must have been women present, or Plato would not have written what he did in the *Laws.*

In favor of the presence of women during the fifth century is a passage in the *Peace* (962–67). The actors are throwing barleycorns at the audience. Vintage's slave says that now everyone has one. Vintage answers, "The women didn't take them." The slave replies that they'll get some from their men in the evening. The point is in a pun: the word for barleycorn also means "penis." There is no point in the joke if there are no women in the audience.

Later tradition certainly supports the presence of women in the fifth-century audience. The *Life of Aeschylus,* 9, recounts how at the first performance of the *Oresteia* women in the audience had miscarriages at the sight of the chorus of Furies. Athenaeus tells the story of how Alcibiades entered the theater as *choregos* in a purple robe and was admired not only by the men but also by the women (*Deipnosophists* 12.534C). Even if these stories are unreliable gossip, it is difficult to see why they should be invented if women had not been present. For myself, I find the evidence conclusive that women did watch the plays of the fifth century.

SELECT BIBLIOGRAPHY

For those reading this book with no background of Classical study, it may be useful to refer to *The Oxford Classical Dictionary*, 2d ed., ed. N. G. L. Hammond and H. H. Scullard (Oxford: Oxford University Press, 1970). It will provide notes on mythology and historical references. To fill out the history of the period further, it may be useful to consult a history of Greece. Probably the best and most easily available is: J. B. Bury, *A History of Greece*, 3d ed., rev. Russell Meiggs (London: Macmillan, 1956). It has very adequate maps.

Any discussion of the theater of Dionysus, setting, costumes, and so on, depends upon the work of three English scholars so enormously that they must be singled out: A. E. Haigh, Sir Arthur Pickard-Cambridge, and T. B. L. Webster. Pickard-Cambridge revised the third edition of Haigh's book, *The Attic Theatre*, and Webster revised Pickard-Cambridge's *Dithyramb, Tragedy and Comedy*. The three Pickard-Cambridge books, in their updated, revised versions, contain, in effect, all the source-material on the ancient theater, and are well supplied with illustrations.

The best collection of pictures from vases, reliefs, terra-cottas, and so on, is found in Bieber's book. Margarete Bieber, *The History of the Greek and Roman Theater* (Princeton: Princeton University Press; London: Oxford University Press, 1961). This, with the three Pickard-Cambridge books, and two books by Webster, provide sufficient coverage of the pictorial evidence. See T. B. L. Webster, *Greek Theatre Production* (London: Methuen, 1970), and T. B. L. Webster with A. D. Trendall, *Illustrations of Greek Drama* (London: Phaidon, 1971).

Beare's book on the Roman stage provides a comprehensive study of the Latin theater, and is written very much in terms of performance.

The following books constitute an essential, minimal bibliography:

Beare, W. *The Roman Stage*. London: Methuen, 1964.

Bieber, Margarete. *The History of the Greek and Roman Theater*. Princeton: Princeton University Press; London: Oxford University Press, 1961.

Haigh, A. E. *The Attic Theatre*. 3d ed., rev. Sir Arthur Pickard-Cambridge. Oxford: Clarendon Press, 1907.

————. *The Tragic Drama of the Greeks*. Oxford: Clarendon Press, 1896.

Pickard-Cambridge, Sir Arthur. *Dithyramb, Tragedy and Comedy*. 2d ed., rev., T. B. L. Webster. Oxford: Clarendon Press, 1962.

————. *The Dramatic Festivals of Athens*. 2d ed., rev., John Gould and D. M. Lewis. Oxford: Clarendon Press, 1968.

————. *The Theatre of Dionysus in Athens.* Oxford: Clarendon Press, 1946.

Webster, T. B. L. *Greek Theatre Production.* London: Methuen, 1970.

————, with A. D. Trendall, *Illustrations of Greek Drama.* London: Phaidon, 1971.

Oxford University Press has been in the process for most of this century of bringing out a series of all the fifth-century plays, one play to a volume, using the Greek text of the Oxford Classical Text for the play in question, but with introduction and extensive commentary. It now seems unlikely that the series will ever be finished, but several of the volumes are exempla of scholarship, and all are to be deferred to in matters of text and construe. Though some passages are translated, the books are intended for the reader who is fluent in Greek. I have found a number of them useful, and list them simply in alphabetical order of play (using the title used in this book, rather than the Greek original. They are to be found in catalogs under the name of the Greek author. Their press mark is Oxford: Clarendon Press.

Agamemnon. Edited by D. L. Page with J. D. Denniston. 1957.

Alcestis. Edited by A. M. Dale. 1954.

The Bacchants. Edited by E. R. Dodds. 1960.

The Clouds. Edited by Sir Kenneth Dover. 1968.

Helen. Edited by A. M. Dale. 1960.

Heracles. Edited by O. R. A. Byrde. 1914.

Ion. Edited by A. S. Owen. 1939.

Iphigeneia in Tauris. Edited by M. Platnauer. 1938.

Medea. Edited by D. L. Page. 1938.

In addition, and worthy of special mention as a climax of detailed scholarship is another edited text from the Clarendon Press, though not part of the above-mentioned series:

Aeschylus. *Agamemnon.* Edited by Eduard Fraenkel. 3 vols. Oxford: Clarendon Press, 1950.

There is also:

Sophocles. *The Plays and Fragments.* Edited and translated by R. C. Jebb. Cambridge: Cambridge University Press, 1883–1907.

For the remainder of this bibliography, I have not found it practicable to separate into sections, since so many books would overlap sections and cause messy cross-referencing. Authors accordingly are listed in alphabetical order. With a few exceptions, I have, in the case of more than one edition, listed only the most recent one.

Adams, Sinclair MacLardy. *Sophocles the Playwright.* Toronto: University of Toronto Press, 1957.

Adkins, Arthur W. H. *Merit and Responsibility: A Study in Greek Values.* Oxford: Clarendon Press, 1960.

Anti, Carlo. *Teatri Greci arcaici da Minosse a Pericle.* Monografie di archeologia, no. 1, Padova, 1947.

Arnott, Peter. *Greek Scenic Conventions in the Fifth Century B.C.* Oxford: Clarendon Press, 1962.

————. *An Introduction to the Greek Theatre.* London: Macmillan, 1959.

Arnott, W. Geoffrey. *Menander, Plautus, Terence.* Oxford: Clarendon Press, 1975.

Bates, W. N. *Sophocles, Poet and Dramatist.* Philadelphia: University of Pennsylvania Press, 1940.

Blaiklock, E. M. *The Male Characters of Euripides.* Wellington: New Zealand University Press, 1952.

Bowra, Sir Maurice. *Sophoclean Tragedy.* Oxford: Clarendon Press, 1944.

Brooke, Iris. *Costume in Greek Classic Drama.* London: Methuen, 1962.

Burnett, A. P. *Catastrophe Survived: Euripides' Plays of Mixed Reversal.* Oxford: Clarendon Press, 1971.

Burton, R. W. B. *The Chorus in Sophocles' Tragedies.* Oxford: Clarendon Press, 1980.

Cataudella, Quintino. *La Poesia di Aristofane.* Bari: Gius, Laterza & Figli, 1934.

Coppola, Goffredo. *Il Teatro di Aristofane.* Bologna: Nicola Zanichelli, 1936.

Croiset, Maurice. *Aristophane et les partis à Athènes.* Paris: Albert Fontemoing, 1906.

Dale, A. M. *The Lyric Metres of Greek Drama.* London: Cambridge University Press, 1968.

————. *Words, Music, Dance.* London: Birkbeck College, 1960.

Dawe, R. D., J. Diggle, and P. E. Easterling, eds. *Dionysiaca: Nine Studies in Greek Poetry (essays presented to Sir Denys Page).* Cambridge: The editors, 1978.

Dearden, C. W. *The Stage of Aristophanes.* London: Athlone Press, 1976.

Desportes, Marcel. *Sophocle: Antigone (a translation of the play with an essay on Greek tragedy and the life and work of Sophocles).* Paris: Bordas, 1965.

Diller, Hans, ed. *Sophocles (a collection of essays by English and German contributors).* Darmstadt: Wissenschaftliche Buchgesellschaft, 1967.

Dodds, E. R. *The Greeks and the Irrational.* Berkeley and Los Angeles: University of California Press, 1951.

Dover, Sir Kenneth. *Aristophanic Comedy.* London: Batsford, 1972.

Duckworth, G. E. *The Nature of Roman Comedy.* Princeton: Princeton University Press, 1952.

Earp, F. R. *The Style of Aeschylus.* Cambridge: Cambridge University Press, 1948.

————. *The Style of Sophocles.* Cambridge: Cambridge University Press, 1944.

Ehrenberg, Victor. *The People of Aristophanes.* Oxford: Basil Blackwell, 1951.

————. *Sophocles and Pericles.* Oxford: Basil Blackwell, 1954.

Else, Gerald F. *The Origin and Early Form of Greek Tragedy*. Cambridge: Harvard University Press; London: Oxford University Press, 1965.

Emmanuel, Maurice. *The Antique Greek Dance*. Translated by Harriet Jean Beauley. London: John Lane, 1927.

Finley, John H., Jr. *Pindar and Aeschylus*. Cambridge: Harvard University Press, 1955.

Flickinger, R. C. *The Greek Theater and Its Drama*. Chicago: University of Chicago Press, 1936.

Freedley, George, and John A. Reeves. *A History of the Theatre*. New York: Crown Publishers, 1941.

Gagarin, Michael. *Aeschylaean Drama*. Berkeley and Los Angeles: University of California Press, 1976.

Garvie, A. F. *Aeschylus' Supplices Play and Trilogy*. London: Cambridge University Press, 1969.

Gascoigne, Bamber. *World Theatre, an Illustrated History*. London: Ebury Press, 1968.

Gaster, Theodore H. *Thespis: Ritual, Myth and Drama in the Ancient Near East*. New York: Henry Schuman, 1950.

Gerlach, Franz D. *Aristophanes und Socrates, ein Vortrag*. Basel: Commissionsverlag der Chr. Meyrischen Buchhandlung (N. Meck jr.), 1876.

Germain, Gabriel. *Sophocle*. Paris: Éditions du Seuil, 1969.

Goldberg, Sander M. *The Making of Menander's Comedy*. London: Athlone Press, 1980.

Gomme, A. W. *Essays in Greek History and Literature*. Oxford: Basil Blackwell, 1937.

———. *More Essays in Greek History and Literature*. Oxford: Basil Blackwell, 1962.

Gomme, A. W., and F. H. Sandbach. *Menander: A Commentary*. Oxford: Oxford University Press, 1973.

Greenwood, L. H. G. *Aspects of Euripidean Tragedy*. Cambridge: Cambridge University Press, 1953.

Grene, David. *Reality and the Heroic Pattern*. Chicago: University of Chicago Press, 1967.

Griffith, Mark. *The Authenticity of* Prometheus Bound. Cambridge: Cambridge University Press, 1977.

Grube, G. M. A. *The Drama of Euripides*. London: Methuen, 1941.

Havemeyer, Loomis. *The Drama of Savage Peoples*. New Haven: Yale University Press; London: Humphrey Milford, 1916.

Hourmouziades [also spelled Chourmouziades], Nicolaos C. *Production and Imagination in Euripides*. Athens: Greek Society for Humanistic Studies, 1965.

Hunningher, B. *The Origin of the Theater.* The Hague: Martinus Nijhoff; Amsterdam: E. M. Querido, 1955.

Jones, John [also known as Henry J. Jones]. *On Aristotle and Greek Tragedy.* London: Chatto & Windus, 1962.

Kirkwood, G. M. *A Study of Sophoclean Drama.* Ithaca: Cornell University Press, 1958.

Kitto, H. D. F. *Form and Meaning in Drama.* London: Methuen, 1956.

———. *Greek Tragedy.* London: Methuen, 1961.

———. *Sophocles, Dramatist and Philosopher.* London: Oxford University Press, 1958.

Knox, Bernard. *The Heroic Temper: Studies in Sophoclean Tragedy.* Berkeley and Los Angeles: University of California Press; London: Cambridge University Press, 1964.

———. *Oedipus at Thebes.* New Haven: Yale University Press; London: Oxford University Press, 1957.

Kranz, Walther. *Stasimon.* Berlin: Weidmannsche Buchhandlung, 1933.

Lattimore, Richmond. *The Poetry of Greek Tragedy.* Baltimore: Johns Hopkins University Press, 1958.

———. *Story Patterns in Greek Tragedy.* London: Athlone Press, 1964.

Lawler, Lillian B. *The Dance in Ancient Greece.* London: Adam & Charles Black, 1964.

Lesky, Albin. *Greek Tragedy.* Translated by H. A. Frankfort. London: Ernest Benn; New York: Barnes & Noble, 1965.

Letters, F. J. H. *The Life and Work of Sophocles.* London and New York: Sheed & Ward, 1953.

Lloyd-Jones, Hugh. *Aeschylus: Oresteia (translated with introduction).* London: Duckworth, 1979.

———. *The Justice of Zeus.* Berkeley and London: University of California Press, 1971.

Lord, Louis E. *Aristophanes: His Plays and His Influence.* London: G. G. Harrap, 1925.

Lucas, D. W. *The Greek Tragic Poets.* London: Cohen & West, 1959.

McLeish, Kenneth. *The Theatre of Aristophanes.* London: Thames & Hudson, 1980.

Mantzius, Karl. *A History of Theatrical Art.* Translated by Louise von Cossel. London: Duckworth, 1903–21.

Méautis, Georges. *Sophocle: Essai sur le héros tragique.* Paris: Albin Michel, 1957.

Murray, Augustus T. *On Parody and Paratragoedia in Aristophanes.* Berlin: Mayer & Müller, 1891.

Murray, Gilbert. *Aeschylus, the Creator of Tragedy.* Oxford: Clarendon Press, 1940.

————. *Aristophanes and the War Party.* London: George Allen & Unwin, 1919.

————. *Aristophanes: A Study.* Oxford: Clarendon Press, 1933.

————. *Euripides and His Age.* London: Oxford University Press, 1946.

Nicoll, Allardyce. *The Development of the Theatre.* London: G. G. Harrap, 1958.

————. *Masks, Mimes and Miracles.* London: G. G. Harrap, 1931.

————. *World Drama from Aeschylus to Anouilh.* London: G. G. Harrap, 1949.

Nietzsche, *Die Geburt der Tragödie.* Leipzig: Alfred Kröner Verlag, 1872.

————. *The Birth of Tragedy.* translated by W. A. Haussmann. Edinburgh and London: J. N. Foulis, 1909.

Norwood, Gilbert. *The Art of Terence.* Oxford: Basil Blackwell, 1923.

————. *Greek Comedy.* London: Methuen, 1931.

————. *Greek Tragedy.* London: Methuen, 1948.

Owen, E. T. *The Harmony of Aeschylus.* Toronto: Irwin, 1952.

Page, D. L. [also referred to as Sir Denys]. *Actors' Interpolations in Greek Tragedy.* Oxford: Clarendon Press, 1934.

————. *A New Chapter in the History of Greek Tragedy.* London: Cambridge University Press, 1951.

Perrotta, Gennaro. *I tragici Greci.* Firenze: Casa Editrice G. D'Anna, 1931.

Podlecki, Anthony J. *The Political Background of Aeschylean Tragedy.* Ann Arbor: University of Michigan Press, 1966.

Prentice, William Kelly. *Those Ancient Dramas Called Tragedies.* Princeton: Princeton University Press, 1942.

Reich, H. *Der Mimus.* Berlin: Weidmannsche Buchhandlung, 1903.

Reinhardt, Karl. *Sophocles.* Translated by Hazel Harvey and David Harvey, with Introduction by Hugh Lloyd-Jones. Oxford: Basil Blackwell, 1979.

Ridgeway, William. *The Origin of Tragedy.* Cambridge: Cambridge University Press, 1910.

Ronnet, Gilberte. *Sophocle, poète tragique.* Paris: Éditions E. de Boccard, 1969.

Schlesinger, A. C. *Boundaries of Dionysus: Athenian Foundations for the Theory of Tragedy.* Cambridge: Harvard University Press, 1963.

Sheppard, Sir John. *Aeschylus and Sophocles, their Work and Influence.* London: G. G. Harrap, 1927.

————. *Aeschylus, the Prophet of Greek Freedom, an essay on the Oresteian Trilogy.* London: T. Murby, 1943.

Steiner, George. *Antigones.* Exeter: University of Exeter Press, 1979.

————. *The Death of Tragedy.* London: Faber & Faber, 1961.

Strauss, Leo. *Socrates and Aristophanes*. New York and London: Basic Books, 1966.

Taillardat, Jean. *Les Images d'Aristophane*. Paris: Société d'Édition "Les Belles Lettres," 1965.

Taplin, Oliver. *Greek Tragedy in Action*. London: Methuen, 1977.

———. *The Stagecraft of Aeschylus*. Oxford: Clarendon Press, 1977.

Ussher, R. G. *Aristophanes*. Oxford: Clarendon Press, 1979.

Vickers, Brian. *Towards Greek Tragedy: Drama, Myth, Society*. London: Longman, 1973.

Walcot, Peter. *Greek Drama in Its Theatrical and Social Context*. Cardiff: University of Wales Press, 1976.

Waldock, A. J. A. *Sophocles the Dramatist*. Cambridge: Cambridge University Press, 1951.

Webster, T. B. L. *Art and Literature in Fourth Century Athens*. London: Athlone Press, 1956.

———. *The Birth of Modern Comedy of Manners*. Canberra: Australian Humanities Research Council, 1959.

———. *Greek Art and Literature, 700–530 B.C.* Melbourne: University of Otago Press; London: Methuen, 1959.

———. *Greek Art and Literature, 530–400 B.C.* Oxford: Clarendon Press, 1939.

———. *The Greek Chorus*. London: Methuen, 1970.

———. *Greek Tragedy*. Oxford: Clarendon Press, 1971.

———. *Hellenistic Poetry and Art*. London: Methuen, 1964.

———. *The Interplay of Greek Art and Literature*. London: H. K. Lewis, 1949.

———. *An Introduction to Menander*. Manchester: Manchester University Press, 1974.

———. *An Introduction to Sophocles*. London: Methuen, 1969.

———. *Menander: Production and Imagination*. Manchester: John Rylands Library, 1962.

———. *Monuments Illustrating New Comedy*. London: University of London Institute of Classical Studies, 1961.

———. *Monuments Illustrating Old and Middle Comedy*. London: University of London Institute of Classical Studies, 1960.

———. *Monuments Illustrating Tragedy and Satyr Play*. London: University of London Institute of Classical Studies, 1962.

———. *Studies in Menander*. Manchester: Manchester University Press, 1960.

———. *The Tragedies of Euripides*. London: Methuen, 1967.

Whitman, Cedric H. *Aristophanes and the Comic Hero*. Cambridge: Harvard University Press, 1964.

———. *Sophocles: A Study of Heroic Humanism.* Cambridge: Harvard University Press, 1951.

Winnington-Ingram, R. P. *Euripides and Dionysus.* Cambridge: Cambridge University Press, 1948.

Woodard, Thomas, ed. *Sophocles: A Collection of Critical Essays.* Englewood Cliffs, N.J.: Prentice-Hall, 1966.

Zuntz, G. *The Political Plays of Euripides.* Manchester: Manchester University Press, 1955.

This bibliography makes no claims to being exhaustive. For full bibliographies consult those in the three books by Pickard-Cambridge. There are useful bibliographies on production in Webster's *Greek Theatre Production* and Arnott's *Greek Scenic Conventions.* Sir Kenneth Dover has published an exhaustive bibliography with comments on recent Aristophanes studies, "Aristophanes 1938–1955," in *Lustrum 2* (1957).

For complete coverage with comments on the work referred to, see Maurice Platnauer, ed., *Fifty Years (and Twelve) of Classical Scholarship* (Oxford: Basil Blackwell, 1968). This useful conspectus was first published in 1954. It gave a summary of all work done in Classical studies during the first half of the century; it was then brought up to date in 1968. The relevant chapters are: "Greek Tragedy," by T. B. L. Webster, "Greek Comedy," by K. J. Dover, and "Roman Drama," by W. A. Laidlaw.

T. B. L. Webster's *Monuments Illustrating Tragedy and Satyr Play,* and his two companion booklets on comedy, provide a complete list of all the available illustrations relating to Greek drama and say where the particular monuments can be found. Actual illustrations, unfortunately, are not included.

Proper coverage of the work done in this field in periodicals would take a long time. I append here a list of a few articles and essays in collections that I have consulted.

Allen, James Turney. "Greek Acting in the Fifth Century." *University of California Publications in Classical Philology* 2, no. 15: 279–89.

Dodds, E. R. "Morals and Politics in the *Oresteia.*" *Proceedings of the Cambridge Philological Society* (1960).

Dover, K. J. "The Political Aspect of Aeschylus' *Eumenides.*" *Journal of Hellenic Studies* 77, pt. 2 (1957).

Kitto, H. D. F. "The Dance in Greek Tragedy." *Journal of Hellenic Studies* 75 (1955).

———. "The Idea of God in Aeschylus and Sophocles." *La Notion du Divin depuis Homère jusqu'à Platon* (Geneva). Fondation Hardt pour l'étude de l'Antiquité Classique (1954).

———. "The Prometheus Trilogy." *Journal of Hellenic Studies* 54 (1934).

———. "The Vitality of Sophocles." In *From Sophocles to Picasso,* edited by Whitney J. Oates. Bloomington, 1962.

Lloyd-Jones, Hugh. "Zeus in Aeschylus." *Journal of Hellenic Studies* 76 (1956).

Méautis, Georges. "L'Authenticité et la date du 'Promethée enchainée' d'Eschyle." *Université de Neuchâtel, recueil de travaux publié par la Faculté des lettres* (Geneva) 29 (1960).

Mountford, J. F. "Greek Music in the Papyri and Inscriptions." *New Chapters in Greek Literature* 2 (1929): 146–83.

Turner, E. G. "The Lost Beginning of Menander *Misoumenos.*" *Proceedings of the British Academy* 63 (1977).

Winnington-Ingram, R. P. "A Religious Function of Greek Tragedy." *Journal of Hellenic Studies* 74 (1954).

I have also made use of Egon Wellesz, ed., *Ancient and Oriental Music*, vol. 1 of the *New Oxford History of Music* (London: Oxford University Press, 1957). Chapter 9, "Greek Music" by Isobel Henderson is useful, and Chapter 4, "Indian Music" affords interesting parallels and comparisons.

The article on music in *The Oxford Classical Dictionary* serves as an introduction to this difficult subject. See *The Oxford Classical Dictionary*, 2d ed., N. G. L. Hammond and H. H. Scullard, eds. (Oxford: Oxford University Press, 1970) under the heading "Music."

INDEX